PREFACE

Complete Preface In Volume I

The complete preface to the two volume *Canadian Tax Principles* text can be found in Volume I of this set.

Available Study Tools And Resources

The inner front cover of Volume I describes the abundant study tools, resources and software that are available to users of *Canadian Tax Principles*.

ProFile Tax Preparation Software

For users of *Canadian Tax Principles*, we provide access to Intuit's professional tax preparation software, ProFile. This includes tax return preparation capabilities for:

- Individuals
- Corporations
- Trusts

Instructions on how to access this software are available on the inner back cover of Volume I.

Web Site

Please check the web site for additions or corrections to the textbook and Study Guide before using this book. The web site for *Canadian Tax Principles* can be found at:

www.pearsoncanada.ca/byrdchen/ctp2014

Here you will find:

- Updates and corrections to the textbook and Study Guide (please check periodically)
- Glossary Flashcards and Key Terms Self-Tests
- In January, 2014, shortly after the first 2013 filing version of the ProFile tax program is available, updated sample tax returns and Tax Software Problems.

It's Our Fault

Any errors are solely the responsibility of the authors and we apologize for any confusion that they may cause you. We welcome any corrections or suggestions for additions or improvements. These can be sent to us at:

byrdinc@sympatico.ca

July, 2013

Clarence Byrd, Athabasca University
Ida Chen, Clarence Byrd Inc.

2013 Rates And Other Data (Including Web Sites)

> Note that for your convenience, this information is also available on the **Student CD-ROM** as a .PDF file.

Information Applicable To Individuals

Federal Tax Rates For Individuals

Taxable Income In Excess Of	Federal Tax	Marginal Rate On Excess
$ -0-	$ -0-	15%
43,561	6,534	22%
87,123	16,118	26%
135,054	28,580	29%

Federal Tax Credits For Individuals

Personal Credits [ITA 118]

Single Persons   This basic personal credit is equal to 15% of $11,038 ($1,656).

Married Persons This basic personal credit is equal to 15% of $11,038 ($1,656).

Family Caregiver Amount (FCA)   The relevant credits below include the $2,040 FCA.

Spousal The spousal credit is equal to 15% of $11,038 ($1,656), less 15% of the spouse's Net Income For Tax Purposes. This amount is increased by $2,040 (to $13,078) if the spouse qualifies for the FCA. Not available when the spouse's income is more than $11,038 (or $13,078).

Eligible Dependant This credit is the same as the one that is available for a spouse. This amount is also increased by $2,040 if the eligible dependant qualifies for the FCA, provided the child amount has not been claimed for this dependant.

Child 15% of $2,234 ($335) for each child who is under the age of 18 years at the end of the year. This amount is increased by $2,040 (to $4,274) if the child qualifies for the FCA.

Caregiver 15% of $4,490 ($674), less 15% of the dependant's Net Income in excess of $15,334. This amount is increased by $2,040 (to $6,530) if the related adult qualifies for the FCA.

Infirm Dependants Over 17 15% of $6,530 ($980), less 15% of the dependant's Net Income in excess of $6,548. This amount always includes the extra $2,040 for the FCA. Not available when the dependant's income is more than $13,078.

Age 15% of $6,854 ($1,028). The base for this credit is reduced by the lesser of $6,854 and 15% of the individual's net income in excess of $34,562. Not available when income is more than $80,256. If the individual cannot use this credit, it can be transferred to a spouse or common-law partner.

Pension 15% of the first $2,000 of eligible pension income. This produces a maximum credit of $300 [(15%)($2,000)]. If the individual cannot use the credit, it can be transferred to a spouse or common-law partner.

Canada Employment Credit 15% of $1,117. This produces a maximum credit of $168.

Other Credits (Various ITA)

Adoption Expenses 15% of eligible expenses, up to a maximum of $1,750 [(15%)($11,669)]. The eligible amount is reduced by reimbursements.

Public Transit Passes Credit 15% of the cost of monthly or longer transit passes.

Child Fitness Credit A maximum of 15% of $500 ($75) per year for eligible fees paid for each child who is under 16 (under 18 if the child qualifies for the disability tax credit). An additional credit, based on a maximum of $500 in fees, is available for children who qualify for the disability tax credit.

Children's Arts Credit   A maximum of 15% of $500 ($75) per year for eligible fees paid for each child under 16 (under 18 if the child qualifies for the disability tax credit). An additional credit, based on a maximum of $500 in fees, is available for children who qualify for the disability tax credit.

First Time Home Buyer's Tax Credit   15% of the first $5,000 ($750) of the cost of an eligible home.

Volunteer Firefighter Credit   15% of $3,000 ($450) for volunteer firefighters who perform at least 200 hours of volunteer firefighting services during a taxation year.

Charitable Donations The general limit on amounts for this credit is 75% of Net Income. There is an addition to this general limit equal to 25% of any taxable capital gains and 25% of any recapture of CCA resulting from a gift of capital property. In addition, the income inclusion on capital gains arising from a gift of some publicly traded shares is reduced from one-half to nil. For individuals, the credit is 15% of the first $200 and 29% of the remainder. For corporations, charitable donations are a deduction from Net Income.

Medical Expenses The medical expense tax credit is determined by the following formula:

$$[15\%] \; [(B - C) + D], \text{ where:}$$

B is the total of an individual's medical expenses for himself, his spouse or common-law partner, and any of his children who have not reached 18 years of age at the end of the year.

C is the lesser of 3% of the individual's Net Income For Tax Purposes and $2,152 (2013 figure).

D is the total of all amounts each of which is, in respect of a dependant of the individual (other than a child of the individual who has not attained the age of 18 years before the end of the taxation year), an amount determined by the formula:

$$E - F, \text{ where:}$$

E is the total of the dependant's medical expenses

F is the lesser of 3% of the dependant's Net Income For Tax Purposes and $2,152 (2013 figure).

Refundable Medical Expense Supplement   The individual claiming this amount must be over 17 and have earned income of at least $3,333. The amount is equal to the lesser of $1,142 and 25/15 of the medical expense tax credit (25% of allowable medical expenses). The refundable amount is then reduced by 5% of family Net Income in excess of $25,278. Not available when family income is more than $48,118.

Disability - All Ages 15% of $7,697 ($1,155). If not used by the disabled individual, it can be transferred to a person claiming that individual as a dependant.

Disability Supplement - Under 18 And Qualifies For The Disability Tax Credit   15% of $4,490 ($674), reduced by the total of amounts paid for attendant care or supervision in excess of $2,630 that are deducted as child care costs, deducted as a disability support amount, or claimed as a medical expense in calculating the medical expense tax credit.

Tuition Fees Which Includes Examination And Ancillary Fees
- 15% of qualifying tuition fees
- 15% of examination fees for both post-secondary examinations and examinations required in a professional program
- 15% of ancillary fees that are imposed by a post-secondary educational institution on all of their full or part-time students. Up to $250 in such ancillary fees can be claimed even if not required of all students.

Education   15% of $400 ($60) per month of full time attendance. 15% of $120 ($18) per month of part time attendance.

Textbook   15% of $65 ($10) per month of full time attendance. 15% of $20 ($3) per month of part time attendance.

Interest On Student Loans   15% of interest paid on qualifying student loans.

Transfer Of Tuition, Education, And Textbook   If the individual cannot use these credits, is not claimed as a dependant by his spouse, and does not transfer the unused credits to a spouse, then a parent or grandparent of the individual can claim up to $750 [(15%)($5,000)] of any unused tuition, education, or textbook credits. The amount that can be transferred is reduced by any amounts of these credits claimed by the student for the year.

Employment Insurance   15% of amounts paid by employees up to the maximum Employment Insurance premium of $891 (1.88% of $47,400). This produces a maximum tax credit of $134 [(15%)($891)].

Canada Pension Plan   15% of amounts paid by employees up to the maximum Canada Pension Plan contribution of $2,356 [4.95% of ($51,100 less $3,500)]. This produces a maximum tax credit of $353 [(15%)($2,356)]. For self-employed individuals the maximum payment is $4,712.

Political Donations   Three-quarters of the first $400, one-half of the next $350, one-third of the next $525, to a maximum credit of $650.

Dividend Tax Credit
- **Eligible Dividends** are grossed up by 38%. The federal dividend tax credit is equal to 6/11 of the gross up. The credit can also be calculated as 15.02% of the grossed up dividends, or 20.7272% of the actual dividends received.
- **Non-Eligible Dividends (for 2013)** are grossed up by 25%. The federal dividend tax credit is equal to 2/3 of the gross up. The credit can also be calculated as 13-1/3% of the grossed up dividends, or 16-2/3% of the actual dividends received.

Investment Tax Credits   Credits based on various rates for making certain types of qualifying expenditures.

Other Data For Individuals

Dividend Gross Up

Eligible Dividends the gross up is 38% of dividends received.

Non-Eligible Dividends (for 2013) the gross up is 25% of dividends received.

RRSP Deduction Room   For 2013, the addition to RRSP deduction room is equal to the lesser of $23,820 and 18% of 2012 Earned Income, reduced by the 2012 Pension Adjustment and the 2013 Past Service Pension Adjustment, and increased by the 2013 Pension Adjustment Reversal.

Clawback (OAS and EI) Limits   The tax (clawback) on Old Age Security (OAS) benefits is based on the lesser of 100% of such benefits and 15% of the amount of the 2013 "threshold income" in excess of $70,954. For this purpose, "threshold income" is equal to Net Income For Tax Purposes, calculated without the ITA 60(w) deduction for the tax on OAS benefits.

Under the *Employment Insurance Act*, there is a similar clawback requirement with respect to Employment Insurance (EI) benefits. In this case, EI benefits must be repaid to the extent of the lesser of 30% of the EI benefits received, and 30% of the amount by which "threshold income" exceeds $59,250 (this amount is 1.25 times the maximum insurable earnings for EI purposes). For this purpose, "threshold income" is defined as Net Income For Tax Purposes, calculated without the deduction for either the ITA 60(w) deduction for tax paid on OAS benefits or the ITA 60(v.1) deduction for repayment of EI benefits received.

Capital Gain Inclusion Rates

Period	Inclusion Rate
1972 through 1987	1/2
1988 and 1989 and February 28, 2000 through October 17, 2000	2/3
1990 through February 27, 2000	3/4
October 18, 2000 to present	1/2

Provincial Tax Rates And Provincial Credits For Individuals   Provincial taxes are based on Taxable Income, with most provinces adopting multiple rates. The number of brackets range from three (e.g., Manitoba uses 10.80%, 12.75%, and 17.40%) to five (e.g., British Columbia uses 5.06%, 7.70%, 10.50%, 12.29%, and 14.70%). The exception to this is Alberta, which uses a single flat rate of 10% on all Taxable Income. Provincial tax credits are generally based on the minimum provincial rate applied to a credit base that is similar to that used for federal credits. In addition to regular rates, several provinces use surtaxes.

Information Applicable To Individuals And Corporations

Prescribed Rate (ITR 4301)   The following figures show the base rate that would be used in calculations such as imputed interest on loans. It also shows the rates applicable on amounts owing to and from the CRA. For recent quarters, the interest rates were as follows:

Year	Quarter	Base Rate	Owing From*	Owing To
2012	All Four Quarters	1%	3%	5%
2013	**First**	1%	3%	5%
2013	Second	1%	3%	5%

*The rate on refunds to corporations is limited to the regular prescribed rate, without the additional 2%, i.e., the base rate.

Automobile Deduction Limits

- CCA is limited to the first $30,000 of the automobiles cost, plus applicable GST/HST/PST (not including amounts that will be refunded through input tax credits).

- Interest on financing of automobiles is limited to $10 per day.

- Deductible leasing costs are limited to $800 per month (other constraints apply).

- Operating Cost Benefit = $0.27 per kilometer.

- Deductible Rates = $0.54 for first 5,000 kilometers, $0.48 for additional kilometers.

CCA Rates   See Appendix to Chapter 5

Quick Method Rates (GST Only)

	Percentage On GST Included Sales	
	First $30,000	On Excess
Retailers And Wholesalers	0.8%	1.8%
Service Providers And Manufacturers	2.6%	3.6%

Note that different rates are applicable in the provinces that have adopted an HST system.

Information Applicable To Corporations

Corporate Tax Rates   The federal corporate tax rates are as follows (federal tax abatement removed):

General Business (Before General Rate Reduction)	28%
General Business (After General Rate Reduction Of 13%)	15%
Income Eligible For M&P Deduction	15%
Income Eligible For Small Business Deduction	11%
Part IV Refundable Tax	33-1/3%
Part I Refundable Tax On Investment Income Of CCPC (ART)	6-2/3%

Provincial tax rates on corporations vary from a low of nil on amounts eligible for the small business deduction in Manitoba, to a high of 16% on general corporate income in Nova Scotia and Prince Edward Island.

Small Business Deduction Formula   The small business deduction is equal to 17% of the lesser of:

A. Net Canadian active business income.

B. Taxable Income, less:

1. 100/28 times the ITA 126(1) credit for taxes paid on foreign non-business income, calculated without consideration of the additional refundable tax under ITA 123.3 or the general rate reduction under ITA 123.4; and

2. 4 times the ITA 126(2) credit for taxes paid on foreign business income, calculated without consideration of the general rate reduction under ITA 123.4.

C. The annual business limit of $500,000, less any portion allocated to associated corporations, less the reduction for large corporations.

Manufacturing And Processing Deduction Formula   The Manufacturing And Processing Deduction is equal to 13% of the lesser of:

A. Manufacturing and processing profits, less amounts eligible for the small business deduction; and

B. Taxable Income, less the sum of:

1. the amount eligible for the small business deduction;

2. 4 times the foreign tax credit for business income calculated without consideration of the ITA 123.4 general rate reduction; and

3. where the corporation is a Canadian controlled private corporation throughout the year, aggregate investment income as defined in ITA 129(4).

Foreign Tax Credits For Corporations The Foreign Non-Business Income Tax Credit is the lesser of:

- The tax paid to the foreign government (for corporations, there is no 15% limit on the foreign non-business taxes paid); and

- An amount determined by the following formula:

$$\left[\frac{\text{Foreign Non}-\text{Business Income}}{\text{Adjusted Division B Income}}\right][\text{Tax Otherwise Payable}]$$

The Foreign Business Income Tax Credit is equal to the least of:

- The tax paid to the foreign government;

- An amount determined by the following formula:

$$\left[\frac{\text{Foreign Business Income}}{\text{Adjusted Division B Income}}\right][\text{Tax Otherwise Payable}]; \quad \text{and}$$

- Tax Otherwise Payable for the year, less any foreign tax credit taken on non-business income under ITA 126(1).

Aggregate Investment Income Aggregate Investment Income is defined in ITA 129(4) as the sum of:

- net taxable capital gains for the year, reduced by any net capital loss carry overs deducted during the year; and

- income from property including interest, rents, and royalties, but excluding dividends that are deductible in computing Taxable Income. Since foreign dividends are generally not deductible, they would be included in aggregate investment income.

Additional Refundable Tax On Investment Income (ART) ART is equal to 6-2/3% of the lesser of:

- the corporation's "aggregate investment income" for the year [as defined in ITA 129(4)]; and

- the amount, if any, by which the corporation's Taxable Income for the year exceeds the amount that is eligible for the small business deduction.

Refundable Portion Of Part I Tax Payable The Refundable Portion Of Part I Tax Payable is defined as the least of three items:

Item 1 the amount determined by the formula

A - B, where

A is 26-2/3% of the corporation's aggregate investment income for the year, and

B is the amount, if any, by which the foreign non-business income tax credit exceeds 9-1/3% of its foreign investment income for the year.

Item 2 26-2/3% of the amount, if any, by which the corporation's taxable income for the year exceeds the total of:

- the amount eligible for the small business deduction;
- 100/35 of the tax credit for foreign non-business income; and
- 4 times the tax credit for foreign business income.

Item 3 the corporation's tax for the year payable under Part I.

Part IV Tax   Part IV tax is assessed at a rate of 33-1/3% of portfolio dividends, plus dividends received from a connected company that gave rise to a dividend refund for the connected company as a result of the payment.

Refundable Dividend Tax On Hand (RDTOH)   The RDTOH is defined in ITA 129(3) as:

- The Refundable Portion Of Part I tax for the year; plus
- The total of the taxes under Part IV for the year; plus
- The corporation's RDTOH at the end of the preceding year; less
- The corporation's dividend refund for its preceding taxation year.

General Rate Income Pool   A CCPC's General Rate Income Pool (GRIP) is defined as follows:

- The GRIP balance at the end of the preceding year; plus
- 72% of the CCPC's Taxable Income after it has been reduced by amounts eligible for the small business deduction and aggregate investment income; plus
- eligible dividends received during the year; plus
- adjustments related to amalgamations and wind-ups; less
- eligible dividends paid during the preceding year.

Low Rate Income Pool   A non-CCPC's Low Rate Income Pool (LRIP) is defined as follows:

- The LRIP balance at the end of the preceding year; plus
- non-eligible dividends received during the year; plus
- adjustments for reorganizations; plus
- adjustments for non-CCPCs that were a CCPC, a credit union, or an investment company, in a previous year; less
- non-eligible dividends paid during the year; less
- any Excessive Eligible Dividend Designations during the year.

Tax Related Web Sites

GOVERNMENT

Canada Revenue Agency   www.cra.gc.ca
Department of Finance Canada   www.fin.gc.ca

CHARTERED ACCOUNTING FIRMS

BDO   www.bdo.ca/library/publications/tax/index.cfm

Ernst & Young   www.ey.com/CA/en/Services/Tax

KPMG   www.kpmg.com/ca/en/services/tax

PricewaterhouseCoopers   www.pwc.com/ca/en/tax/publications.jhtml

OTHER

CPA Canada (formerly Canadian Institute of Chartered Accountants)   www.CPAcanada.ca

Certified General Accountants Association Of Canada   www.cga-canada.org

Canadian Tax Foundation   www.ctf.ca

ProFile Tax Suite   www.profile.intuit.ca/professional-tax-software

CONTENTS

The textbook is published in two Volumes:	**Volume I** = Chapters 1 to 10 **Volume II** = Chapters 11 to 21

Detailed contents of Volume II, Chapters 11 to 21 follows.

CHAPTER 13

Taxation Of
Corporate Investment Income

CHAPTER 14

Other Issues In
Corporate Taxation

CHAPTER 15

Corporate Taxation And Management Decisions

CHAPTER 16

Rollovers Under Section 85

CHAPTER 17

Other Rollovers And Sale Of An Incorporated Business

CHAPTER 18

Partnerships

CHAPTER 19
Trusts And Estate Planning

CHAPTER 20
International Issues In Taxation

CHAPTER 21
GST/HST

(continued)

CHAPTER 21, continued

Glossary

The Glossary can be found:

- at the back of the separate paper Study Guide, and

- on the Student CD-ROM within the FITAC version of *Canadian Tax Principles*.

Supplementary Readings

The Supplementary Readings can be found on the Student CD-ROM.

No. 1 - Application Of The Median Rule

No. 2 - Stock Option Shares Deemed
           Not Identical Property

No. 3 - Determining M&P Profits

No. 4 - SR & ED Expenditures

No. 5 - Final Returns For Deceased Taxpayers

No. 6 - Business Valuations

No. 7 - Tax Shelters

No. 8 - Transfer Pricing

CHAPTER 11

Taxable Income And Tax Payable For Individuals Revisited

Introduction

The Problem

11-1.   The subjects of Taxable Income for individuals and Tax Payable for individuals were introduced in Chapter 4. This earlier Chapter provided a general overview of how we arrive at the Taxable Income figure and, in addition, covered in detail the majority of credits that can be applied in the determination of Tax Payable. We chose to cover this material in Chapter 4 in order to enhance your understanding of some of the material dealing with specific types of income in Chapters 5 through 9.

11-2.   The problem with this early coverage of these subjects is that there are some concepts and procedures involved in determining Taxable Income and Tax Payable for individuals that cannot be explained without some understanding of the additional components of Net Income For Tax Purposes that are covered in subsequent chapters.

11-3.   For example, it is not possible to meaningfully discuss the deduction of loss carry overs in calculating Taxable Income without knowledge of the difference between capital and non-capital losses, a subject that is not covered until Chapter 8. A similar problem arises in dealing with the transfer of dividend tax credits to a spouse. This idea is not comprehensible to an individual who does not have an understanding of the dividend gross up and tax credit procedures which are not introduced until Chapter 7.

Our Solution

11-4.   Our solution to this problem is this second chapter on Taxable Income and Tax Payable for individuals. At this point, we have provided comprehensive coverage of all of the components of Net Income For Tax Purposes. Chapter 3, dealt with employment income, Chapters 5 and 6 dealt with CCA and business income, Chapter 7 provided coverage of property income, and Chapter 8 dealt with taxable capital gains and allowable capital losses. This coverage of income components concluded with Chapter 9's coverage of miscellaneous sources of, and deductions from, Net Income For Tax Purposes.

11-5.   With this additional background, we can now finish our coverage of Taxable Income and Tax Payable for individuals. With respect to Taxable Income, we will provide complete coverage of both loss carry overs and the lifetime capital gains deduction. In addition, we will be able to deal with the additional credits required in the determination of Tax Payable, as well as the procedures associated with the determination of alternative minimum tax.

Taxable Income Overview

11-6.   As was discussed in Chapter 4, Taxable Income is calculated by deducting certain specified items from Net Income For Tax Purposes. These deductions, which are found in Division C of the *Income Tax Act*, are as follows:

ITA 110(1)(d), (d.01), and (d.1) - Employee Stock Options   Our basic coverage of stock options and stock option deductions was included in Chapter 3. However, additional coverage of a technical issue is found in Supplementary Reading No. 2, which deals with dispositions of shares acquired through stock options. These Supplementary Readings can be found on the Student CD-ROM which accompanies this text. In this Chapter 11, we cover some special rules that are associated with gifts of shares that have been acquired through the exercise of stock options.

ITA 110(1)(f) - Deductions For Payments   This deduction is designed to ensure that certain amounts are not subject to tax. Included here are such amounts as social assistance received, workers' compensation received (covered in Chapter 4), and amounts exempted from Canadian tax by tax treaty (covered in Chapter 20). Also included here are deductions for employment income received from certain prescribed international organizations and employment income earned by a member of the Canadian forces serving in certain prescribed missions.

ITA 110(1)(j) - Home Relocation Loan   This deduction, which is available to employees who receive a loan from their employer to assist with moving, was covered in Chapter 4.

ITA 110.2 - Lump-Sum Payments   This Section provides a deduction for certain lump-sum payments (e.g., an amount received as a court-ordered termination benefit and included in employment income). It provides the basis for taxing this amount as though it was received over several periods (i.e., income averaging). Limited coverage of this provision can be found in the next section of this Chapter.

ITA 110.6 - Lifetime Capital Gains Deduction   The provisions related to this deduction are very complex and require a fairly complete understanding of capital gains. As a consequence, it was not covered in Chapter 4 and will be given coverage in this Chapter.

ITA 110.7 - Residing In Prescribed Zone (Northern Residents Deductions)   These deductions, which are limited to individuals living in prescribed regions of northern Canada, were covered in Chapter 4.

ITA 111 - Losses Deductible   This is a group of deductions that is available for carrying over various types of losses from preceding or subsequent taxation years. The application of these provisions can be complex and requires a fairly complete understanding of business income, property income, and capital gains. As a consequence, this group of deductions was not covered in Chapter 4 and will be covered in detail in this Chapter.

11-7.   As noted in the preceding list, the material in this Chapter will complete our coverage of Taxable Income for individuals. Of the Taxable Income deductions available to individuals, only amounts exempted by treaty under ITA 110(1)(f) and loss carry overs under ITA 111 are available to corporations. There are, however, additional deductions available to corporate taxpayers for charitable contributions and dividends received from other taxable Canadian corporations. These additional deductions are covered in Chapter 12.

Lump-Sum Payments

The Problem

11-8.   Individuals sometimes receive lump-sum payments that relate to services provided in one or more previous years. An example of this would be an employment termination payment that included amounts that related to service provided in previous years.

11-9.   There is an advantage in such situations in that there has been some deferral of the tax on these amounts. However, because of the presence of progressive rates in the Canadian tax system, the tax liability on such lump-sum payments may be higher than would have been the case had the payments been received and taxed in different years. This would be a particularly severe problem in situations where a very large taxable amount is involved. Because of this problem, there is tax relief available for certain lump-sum payments.

Qualifying Amounts

11-10.   The relief can be applied to payments that are referred to as "qualifying amounts". These are given a technical definition in ITA 110.2(1). In the Explanatory Notes that accompany the legislation, the following more general description is found:

> A **qualifying amount** is the principal portion of certain amounts included in income. Those amounts are: spousal or child support amounts, superannuation or pension benefits otherwise payable on a periodic basis, employment insurance benefits and benefits paid under wage loss replacement plans. Also included is the income received from an office or employment (or because of a termination of an office or employment) under the terms of a court order or judgment, an arbitration award or in settlement of a lawsuit.

Relief Mechanism

11-11.   ITA 110.2(2) provides a deduction for the "specified portion" of a "qualifying amount" that was received by an individual during a particular taxation year. The "specified portion" is the fraction of the qualifying amount that relates to an "eligible taxation year". An "eligible taxation year" is any prior year after 1977 in which the individual was a resident of Canada throughout the year and during which the individual did not become bankrupt. No deduction is available if the qualifying amount is less than $3,000. In somewhat simplified terms, this means that an individual can remove the types of payments described as qualifying amounts from the current year's income, to the extent that they relate to prior years.

11-12.   ITA 120.31 describes an alternative tax that will be payable on the amounts that are deducted under ITA 110.2(2). This tax is the total of the additional taxes that would have been triggered for each relevant preceding year, if the portion of the qualifying amount that relates to that preceding year was added to the individual's Taxable Income for that year. In addition to the tax for those years, a notional amount of interest is added to reflect the fact that the tax was not paid in the relevant years. This interest is accrued from May 1 of the year following the relevant preceding year, through the end of the year prior to the receipt of the lump-sum payment.

11-13.   The goal of these procedures is to spread the lump-sum payment over earlier years, thereby eliminating the influence of progressive rates on the total tax bill. For example, if a 2013 court settlement reflected a wage adjustment for the years 2008 through 2012, the recipient would pay the amount of taxes that would have been due if he had received the amounts in those earlier years. In many cases this will provide significant tax relief. However, if the individual is in the maximum tax bracket for all years under consideration, using this approach could result in higher taxes because of the addition of the notional amount of interest. In such cases, the taxpayer would not make the deduction under ITA 110.2(2).

Treatment Of Losses

Carry Over Provisions

General Rules

11-14.   In earlier Chapters there have been references to a taxpayer's ability to carry back or carry forward losses. Before covering the carry over rules related to specific types of losses, we will consider the general procedures associated with these carry overs.

11-15.   If a taxpayer experiences a loss in the current year with respect to a particular type of income, it must be used, to the extent possible, to offset other types of income in the current year. The taxpayer does not have any real discretion in this matter. If he is in a position to apply a loss to other types of income that are available in the loss year and he chooses not to do so, the loss cannot be carried over to either earlier or later years.

11-16.   However, there are situations in which one or more losses cannot be used during the current year. There are two basic reasons why this may be the case:

- The taxpayer may not have sufficient other sources of income to absorb the loss (e.g., a business loss that is greater than all other sources of income).

- The taxpayer may not have sufficient income of the right type to absorb the loss (e.g., an allowable capital loss that is greater than taxable capital gains).

11-17.   If either of these situations arises in the current year, the taxpayer can either carry the loss back to apply against Taxable Income in previous years or, alternatively, carry the loss forward to apply against Taxable Income in future years. Unlike the situation with current year losses, provided that the use is within the specified carry back and carry forward periods, the decision as to when a loss carry over should be used is at the discretion of the taxpayer.

Carry Backs

11-18.   With one exception, all types of current year losses can be applied against income in the three preceding taxation years. The one exception is limited partnership losses which cannot be carried back (see Chapter 18). When the loss is applied, the carry back will result in a refund of some or all of the taxes that were paid in the carry back year.

11-19.   Note that, with several types of losses, the carry back amount can only be applied against income of the same type. More specifically:

- Net capital losses can only be applied against net taxable capital gains realized in the carry back year.

- Net listed personal property losses can only be applied against listed personal property gains realized in the carry back year.

- Restricted farm losses (see Chapter 6) can only be applied against farm income realized in the carry back year.

Carry Forwards

11-20.   Because a refund is available, most taxpayers will first carry back losses to the extent possible. However, if there is not sufficient income of the appropriate type in any of the three preceding years, any unused portion of the loss becomes part of a loss carry forward balance.

11-21.   Unlike the situation with carry backs, there is some variation in the carry forward period for different types of losses. The current rules are as follows:

- **Non-Capital Losses And Farm Losses** For non-capital and farm losses, the carry forward period is 20 years. Non-capital and regular farm losses can be applied against any type of income in the carry forward year. If the farm loss is restricted, it can only be applied against farm income in the carry forward year.

Net Capital Losses Net capital losses can be carried forward indefinitely, limited only by the life of the taxpayer. However, they can only be applied against taxable capital gains that arise in the carry forward year. As will be discussed later in this Chapter, there is an exception for deceased taxpayers who can generally deduct any unused net capital losses against any type of income in the year immediately preceding death and in the year of death. Note that, as this term is used in the *Income Tax Act*, net capital loss refers to the allowable (one-half) portion of a capital loss.

Net Listed Personal Property Losses Listed personal property losses can be carried forward for 7 years. As noted previously, they can only be deducted against listed personal property gains that arise in the carry forward year.

Segregation By Type

11-22. We have noted that, with both loss carry back and loss carry forwards, some types of losses can only be applied against income of the same type. Because of this requirement, loss carry forward balances must be segregated by type. More specifically, the separate balances that must be tracked are:

- Non-Capital Losses [employment losses, business losses, property losses, and business investment losses (defined in Paragraph 11-55)]
- Net Capital Losses
- Regular Farm Losses
- Restricted Farm Losses

Applying The Deduction

11-23. With the exception of listed personal property losses (see coverage beginning in Paragraph 11-31), loss carry overs are deducted from Net Income For Tax Purposes in the determination of Taxable Income.

11-24. In the case of a carry back, there is a reduction of both Taxable Income and Tax Payable in the carry back year. Provided the taxes for that year have been paid, the result will be a refund. As you would expect, the refund will be based on the tax rates applicable to the carry back year.

11-25. With respect to carry forwards, they serve to reduce Taxable Income and Tax Payable in the carry forward year. As was the case with carry backs, the loss carry forward benefit will accrue at the tax rates applicable to the carry forward year.

Loss Carry Overs And Tax Credits

11-26. You will recall from Chapter 4 that most of the credits against Tax Payable that are available to individuals are not refundable. Further, most of them cannot be carried over to be used in subsequent taxation years. This means that, in the absence of sufficient Tax Payable to absorb these credits, they will be permanently lost.

11-27. These facts relate to loss carry overs in that, given that many tax credits have no value in the absence of a Tax Payable amount, it is generally not advisable to use loss carry overs to reduce Taxable Income to nil in the carry over year.

Example In 2012, Jan Teason's only income was a net rental loss of $30,000. She had no reported income in the three preceding years. However, in 2013, she has net rental income of $25,000. Ms. Teason's only tax credit is the basic personal credit of $1,656 [(15%)($11,038)].

Analysis If she wished to do so, Ms. Teason could reduce her 2013 Taxable Income to nil by applying $25,000 of the 2012 non-capital loss carry forward. However, if she limits her carry forward deduction to $13,962 ($25,000 - $11,038), her Taxable Income will be reduced to $11,038. The tax on this would be $1,656 [(15%)($11,038)], an amount that would be eliminated by her basic personal credit. This approach leaves an additional $11,038 in the carry forward balance, an amount that can be used in future years.

11-28. What this example illustrates is that, in practical situations, loss carry overs should not be used to reduce Taxable Income to nil. In the real world, tax preparation software should automatically limit loss carry overs to prevent this from happening. However, trying to build this consideration into the examples and problems included in this text can have the effect of significantly complicating material that is already very difficult to understand. As a result, in some problems we ask that you ignore this issue.

11-29. While this approach is not consistent with real world tax planning considerations, we feel that it can be justified in terms of aiding your understanding of this difficult material on loss carry overs.

Personal Use Property Losses

11-30. You will recall that personal use property is defined as "property owned by the taxpayer that is used primarily for the personal use or enjoyment of the taxpayer, or for the personal use or enjoyment of one or more individuals related to the taxpayer". As covered in Chapter 8, taxable capital gains on personal use property, determined on the assumption that both the proceeds of disposition and the adjusted cost base are at least $1,000, are included in the calculation of Net Income For Tax Purposes. However, unless the personal use property qualifies as "listed personal property" as described in the following material, losses on personal use property are never deductible.

Listed Personal Property Losses

General Rules

11-31. Listed personal property is a designation that has been given to 5 specific categories of personal use property. As listed in ITA 54, these categories are:

- a print, etching, drawing, painting, sculpture, or other similar work of art;
- jewelry;
- a rare folio, rare manuscript, or rare book;
- a stamp; or
- a coin.

11-32. As was the case with personal use property, taxable capital gains on listed personal property are included in Net Income For Tax Purposes, and are also calculated on the assumption that both the proceeds of disposition and the adjusted cost base are at least $1,000 (as noted in Chapter 8, this rule may not be applicable when a charitable donation is involved).

11-33. The difference here is that allowable capital losses on listed personal property can be deducted. However, they can only be deducted against taxable capital gains on listed personal property. They cannot be used to reduce taxes on any other type of income, including taxable capital gains on other types of property.

Carry Over Provisions

11-34. If a loss on listed personal property cannot be used in the current year, it can be carried back three years or forward for seven years. In the carry over year, the loss can only be used to the extent that there are gains on listed personal property in that year.

11-35. Unlike other loss carry overs, listed personal property losses are not deducted from Net Income For Tax Purposes in the calculation of Taxable Income. Under ITA 41(2), the net gain on listed personal property is defined as the gains for the current year, reduced by the carry over amounts from the seven preceding years, or the three subsequent years. If this amount is positive, it is added in the calculation of Net Income For Tax Purposes under ITA 3(b). While the process is somewhat different, the final result is the same reduction in Taxable Income that would result from the carry over of some other type of loss.

Exercise Eleven - 1

Subject: Listed Personal Property Losses

During 2012, Mr. Ronald Smothers was unemployed and had no income of any kind. In order to survive, he sold a painting on December 1, 2012 for $89,000. This painting had been left to Mr. Smothers by his mother and, at the time of her death, it had a fair market value of $100,000. During 2013, Mr. Smothers finds a job and has employment income of $62,000. In addition, during June he sells a second painting for $5,000. He had purchased this painting several years ago for $1,000. Determine Mr. Smothers' minimum Net Income For Tax Purposes and Taxable Income for 2013. Indicate the amount and type of any losses available for carry forward at the end of the year. Assume the December 1, 2012 sale had been of publicly traded shares instead of a painting. How would this change your solution?

End of Exercise.   Solution available in Study Guide.

Non-Capital Losses

General Rules

11-36.   In terms of a simple dictionary meaning, the term non-capital would mean any loss other than a loss on the disposition of a capital asset. In fact, in many situations, this non-technical approach would provide the correct result. However, ITA 111(8) contains a very technical definition that must be used in more complex situations in order to ensure that we arrive at the appropriate answer. In simplified form, this definition is as follows:

ITA 111(8) The non-capital loss of a taxpayer for a taxation year means the amount determined by the formula:

$$A - D, \text{ where}$$

A   is the amount determined by the formula:

$$E - F, \text{ where}$$

E   is the total of all amounts each of which is the taxpayer's loss for the year from an office, employment, business or property, the taxpayer's allowable business investment loss for the year, and net capital loss carry overs deducted in the calculation of Taxable Income for the year (this amount cannot exceed the taxable capital gains for the year).

F   is the amount of income determined under ITA 3(c). [Sum of ITA 3(a) non-capital positive sources and ITA 3(b) net taxable capital gains, less Division B, Subdivision e deductions.]

D   is the taxpayer's farm loss for the year.

11-37.   Note that this definition excludes both current year capital losses and farm losses. These two types of losses are subject to different rules and, as a consequence, their balances must be tracked separately. The inclusion of net capital losses in this definition will be explained in our later discussion of net capital losses.

11-38.   As can be seen in the definition, non-capital losses can result from the calculation of income from employment, income from a business, or income from property. However, given the limited number of deductions from employment income, it is very unlikely that an individual will experience an employment loss. Normally, non-capital losses would result from the operation of a business or the ownership of property. For example, a non-capital loss on a rental property could occur when expenses associated with the property exceed the rental revenues.

Exercise Eleven - 2

Subject: Non-Capital Losses

During 2013, Janice McMann has net employment income of $35,000, as well as a taxable capital gain of $13,000. In addition, she has a business loss of $58,000 and a farm loss of $2,200. Determine her 2013 non-capital loss.

End of Exercise. Solution available in Study Guide.

Carry Over Provisions

11-39.   Non-capital losses are defined in ITA 111(8) in such a fashion that a carry over is only available after the current year's income is reduced to nil. Stated alternatively, a carry over is only possible after all current year losses, other than current year capital losses, have been deducted. If losses remain and are available for carry over, they can be applied, at the taxpayer's discretion, to any of the eligible carry over years. However, ITA 111(3) indicates that a non-capital loss carry over for a particular year cannot be used until the available non-capital loss carry overs from all preceding years have been exhausted.

11-40.   As we have noted, such losses may be carried back three years and applied against any type of income in those years. If there is not sufficient income in those years to absorb the full amount of these non-capital losses, any remaining balance can be carried forward for a period of 20 years. Whether the amounts are carried back or forward, they will be deducted under ITA 111(1)(a) in the computation of Taxable Income.

Net Capital Losses

General Rules

11-41.   The term "net capital loss" is defined in ITA 111(8) as the excess of allowable capital losses over taxable capital gains for the current taxation year. Note carefully that, as the term is used in the *Act*, "net capital loss" refers to the deductible portion of capital losses, not to the 100 percent amounts. When these annual amounts are carried forward, the resulting balance is normally referred to as the "net capital loss balance".

Carry Over Provisions

11-42.   While a net capital loss for the current year cannot be deducted in the calculation of the current year's Net Income For Tax Purposes, this amount is available for carry over to other years. Such losses may be carried back three years and forward to any subsequent year.

11-43.   When they are carried forward or back, they will be deducted under ITA 111(1)(b) in the calculation of Taxable Income. However, ITA 111(1.1) restricts the deduction of such carry over amounts to the amount included in Net Income For Tax Purposes under ITA 3(b) (net taxable capital gains). Expressed in less technical terms, you can only deduct a net capital loss carry over to the extent that you have net taxable capital gains in the carry over year.

11-44.   You will recall from Chapter 8 that the inclusion rate for capital gains has varied over the years. Further, the relevant legislation is such that, when net capital losses are carried over they must be deducted at the rate that is applicable to the carry over year. However, the inclusion rate for capital gains has remained stable at one-half since 2000. Given this, our only coverage of situations involving different inclusion rates for capital gains will be in our discussion of net capital losses that are present when a taxpayer dies.

Conversion Of A Net Capital Loss Carry Over
To A Non-Capital Loss Carry Over

11-45.   A problem can arise when a taxpayer has a net capital loss carry over, taxable capital gains in the current year, and a current year non-capital loss that is large enough to reduce his Net Income For Tax Purposes to nil. As a net capital loss carry over can only be deducted to the extent of current year net taxable capital gains, the taxpayer usually prefers to use such carry overs whenever current year taxable capital gains are available. A simple example will illustrate this problem.

Example For 2013, Mr. Waring has property income of $25,000, taxable capital gains of $45,000 [(1/2)($90,000)], and a business loss of $150,000. He also has a net capital loss carry forward from 2012 of $60,000 [(1/2)($120,000)]. He does not anticipate having any further taxable capital gains in the foreseeable future.

11-46. The usual ITA 3 calculation of Net Income For Tax Purposes would be as follows:

ITA 3(a) Non-Capital Positive Sources	$ 25,000
ITA 3(b) Net Taxable Capital Gains	45,000
ITA 3(c) Sum Of ITA 3(a) And 3(b)	$ 70,000
ITA 3(d) Business Loss	(150,000)
Net Income For Tax Purposes	Nil

11-47. The business loss reduced Net Income For Tax Purposes to nil and this is a problem for Mr. Waring in that he does not anticipate having further taxable capital gains in the near future. Given this, it would appear that he has lost the ability to use this year's net taxable capital gains to absorb the net capital loss carry forward.

11-48. Fortunately, this is not the case. You will recall that, in the definition of non-capital loss in Paragraph 11-36, the taxpayer can add to the E component of the definition, any net capital loss carry overs deducted in the current year. This means that, if we assume that Mr. Waring chooses to deduct the maximum amount of his net capital loss carry forward in 2013, the non-capital loss carry over for 2013 would be as follows:

Business Loss For Year	$150,000
Net Capital Loss Carry Forward Deducted (Limited To Taxable Capital Gains)	45,000
Total For Amount E	$195,000
Amount F = Income Under ITA 3(c) ($25,000 + $45,000)	(70,000)
Non-Capital Loss Available For Carry Over	$125,000

11-49. There are two points that should be made with respect to this analysis:

- The amount of the net capital loss carry forward deducted is limited to the $45,000 in net taxable capital gains that were realized during the year. As a result, he has utilized $45,000 of the $60,000 net capital loss carry forward from 2012.

- The deduction of the net capital loss carry over is discretionary. That is, the taxpayer can deduct any amount between nil and the maximum value of $45,000. In the solution presented, he has deducted the maximum amount, which results in a non-capital loss carry over of $125,000 and leaves a net capital loss carry forward of $15,000 ($60,000 - $45,000). An alternative would have been to deduct none of the net capital loss carry forward, leaving a net capital loss carry forward of $60,000. Under this scenario, the non-capital loss for the year would be calculated as follows:

Business Loss For Year (Amount E)	$150,000
Amount F = Income Under ITA 3(c) ($25,000 + $45,000)	(70,000)
Non-Capital Loss Available For Carry Over	$ 80,000

As this calculation illustrates, the combined non-capital and net capital loss total will be the same in these situations, without regard to what amount of the net capital loss is used. If $45,000 of the net capital loss is used, the total loss remaining is $140,000 ($15,000 + $125,000). If none is used, the total is still $140,000 ($60,000 +

$80,000). In simple economic terms, this procedure allows the taxpayer to convert a net capital loss balance with restricted deductibility, into a non-capital loss balance that can be deducted against any type of income.

Exercise Eleven - 3

Subject: Net Capital Loss Carry Overs

During 2012, Ms. Laura Macky had an allowable capital loss of $15,000. Prior to 2013, she had no taxable capital gains and, as a consequence, she has not been able to deduct this loss. In 2013, her income consists of a taxable capital gain of $40,000 [(1/2)($80,000)] and a net rental loss of $30,000. She does not anticipate any future capital gains. Determine Ms. Macky's minimum 2013 Net Income For Tax Purposes and minimum 2013 Taxable Income, as well as the amount and type of any losses available for carry over at the end of the year. Ignore the effects of her tax credits.

End of Exercise. Solution available in Study Guide.

Net Capital Losses At Death

11-50. One of the difficulties with net capital loss carry overs is that they can normally only be deducted against taxable capital gains. As there is no time limit on the carry forward of such undeducted losses, an individual can die with a substantial balance of these amounts on hand. Capital losses may also arise in the year of death, either through a disposition prior to death or through a deemed disposition at death.

11-51. ITA 111(2) contains a special provision with respect to both net capital losses from years prior to death and to allowable capital losses arising in the year of death. Essentially, this provision allows these accumulated losses to be applied against any type of income in the year of death, or the immediately preceding year.

11-52. Three points should be noted with respect to the application of this provision:

- If there are taxable capital gains in the year of death, the net capital loss must first be applied at the inclusion rate for the current year to the extent of those gains. If a net capital loss balance remains, ITA 111(2) allows it to be applied against other types of income, using the inclusion rate that prevailed in the year in which the net capital loss was realized. As a reminder, the inclusion rate has been at one-half since 2000.

- The ability to use this provision is reduced by the previous deduction of amounts under the lifetime capital gains provision (see discussion later in this Chapter). This reduction reflects the actual amount of the lifetime capital gains deduction made, without regard to the capital gains inclusion rate that was applicable at the time.

- Unlike the usual procedure with capital loss carry overs, this carry over deduction is applied at the capital gain/loss inclusion rate that prevailed in the year in which the capital loss was realized.

11-53. An example will illustrate these provisions:

Example Ms. Vincent has a net capital loss of $22,500 [(3/4)($30,000)], which has been carried forward from 1990. She dies in December, 2013 and, as the result of a disposition in June of that year, has a taxable capital gain of $4,500 [(1/2)($9,000)].

Analysis The amount of the 1990 carry forward, adjusted to the 1/2 inclusion rate, is $15,000 [(1/2)($30,000)]. Of this amount, $4,500 will be deducted against the 2013 taxable capital gain. This will leave a balance of $10,500 [(1/2)($30,000 - $9,000)] which, in order to use the ITA 111(2) provision, must be adjusted back to the 3/4 inclusion rate for 1990. This will leave $15,750 [(3/2)($10,500)]. This can be verified using the 100 percent figures, which give the same $15,750 [(3/4)($30,000 -

$9,000)] amount. This $15,750 can be applied against any type of income in 2013. If there is not enough income to fully utilize the loss, it can be carried back to 2012 in an amended return.

11-54. Capital losses realized by the estate on dispositions of an individual's property in the first taxation year after his death can be carried back and applied against any type of income in the final return of the deceased. Note, however, that these losses cannot be carried back to the tax return for the year preceding death.

Exercise Eleven - 4

Subject: Net Capital Losses At Death

Mr. Derek Barnes has an undeducted net capital loss from 1990 of $7,500 [(3/4)($10,000)]. He dies during June, 2013 and, as the result of a deemed disposition on death, has a taxable capital gain on public company shares of $2,000. Mr. Barnes has made no previous use of the lifetime capital gains deduction. Describe the tax treatment of these two items in his final tax return.

End of Exercise. Solution available in Study Guide.

Allowable Business Investment Losses
Defined
11-55. A Business Investment Loss (BIL), as defined in ITA 39(1)(c), is a special type of capital loss resulting from the disposition of shares or debt of a "small business corporation". In addition to losses on arm's length sales, business investment losses can be incurred when there is a deemed disposition for nil proceeds. This could occur for shares of a small business corporation due to bankruptcy or insolvency, or if the debt is considered uncollectible.

11-56. A small business corporation is defined in ITA 248(1) as a Canadian controlled private corporation (CCPC) of which "all or substantially all", of the fair market value of its assets are used in an active business carried on "primarily" in Canada. In tax work, the term "substantially all" generally means 90 percent or more, while "primarily" is generally interpreted to mean more than 50 percent.

11-57. In making this determination, shares or debt of a connected small business corporation would count towards the required 90 percent. A corporation is connected if the potential small business corporation either controls it, or owns more than 10 percent of its voting shares and shares that represent more than 10 percent of the fair market value of all of the corporation's outstanding shares. As you would expect, an Allowable Business Investment Loss (ABIL) is the deductible one-half of a BIL.

Special Treatment
11-58. In general, allowable capital losses can only be deducted against taxable capital gains. However, ABILs are given special treatment in that the taxpayer is permitted to deduct these amounts from any source of income.

> **Example** An individual with net employment income of $50,000 has an ABIL of $10,500 [(1/2)($21,000)].

> **Analysis** This individual would be able to deduct the $10,500 ABIL against the employment income, resulting in a Net Income For Tax Purposes of $39,500. If this had been an ordinary allowable capital loss, the taxpayer's Net Income For Tax Purposes would be $50,000 and the unapplied allowable capital loss would become a net capital loss for the year which would be available for carry over to other years.

11-59. If there is sufficient income, the ABIL must be deducted in the year in which it is realized. However, if other sources of income are not sufficient for deducting all or part of an ABIL under ITA 3(d) in the current year, it becomes a part of the non-capital loss carry over balance. This permits this special type of allowable capital loss to be deducted against any type of income when they are carried back or carried forward.

11-60.   If the ABIL has not been applied during the 10 years subsequent to its occurrence, it reverts to its original status as an allowable capital loss and becomes a component of the net capital loss carry forward balance. While this restricts the types of income that the loss can be applied against, it gives the loss an unlimited carry forward period.

Effect Of The ITA 110.6 Lifetime Capital Gains Deduction

11-61.   As we shall see in our discussion of the ITA 110.6 lifetime capital gains deduction, beginning in Paragraph 11-67, the realization of a Business Investment Loss reduces the taxpayer's ability to take advantage of this deduction. Of note here, however, is the fact that under ITA 39(9), Business Investment Losses are disallowed by the use of the ITA 110.6 life-time capital gains deduction. What this means is, to the extent that the individual has made a deduction under ITA 110.6, an equivalent portion of the Business Investment Loss will be disallowed (i.e., converted to an ordinary capital loss).

Example   Mr. Mercer had a taxable capital gain in 2006 of $8,000 [(1/2)($16,000)] and deducted this amount under the provisions of the ITA 110.6 lifetime capital gains deduction. In July, 2013, he has a $60,000 loss on the sale of shares of a small business corporation. Mr. Mercer has no capital gains or losses in any other year.

Analysis   If Mr. Mercer had made no use of ITA 110.6, he would have an allowable business investment loss of $30,000 [(1/2)($60,000)] in 2013. However, since he has made a deduction under ITA 110.6, the business investment loss would be reduced as follows:

Actual Loss On Disposition	$60,000
Disallowed By Lifetime Capital Gains Deduction Use	(16,000)
Business Investment Loss	$44,000
Inclusion Rate	1/2
Allowable Business Investment Loss (ABIL)	$22,000

11-62.   As we have noted, the disallowed $16,000 does not disappear. It becomes an ordinary capital loss, subject to the usual restriction that it can only be deducted against capital gains. The remaining $22,000 ABIL can be deducted in 2013 against any source of income. If it is not deducted in that year or carried back, it becomes part of the non-capital loss carry forward for 10 (not 20) years. If it is still not used after 10 years, it becomes part of the net capital loss carry forward.

Exercise Eleven - 5

Subject: Business Investment Losses

During 2011, Mr. Lawrence Latvik used his lifetime capital gains deduction to eliminate a taxable capital gain of $13,000 [(1/2)($26,000)]. During 2013, he has capital gains on publicly traded securities of $18,000, and a loss of $50,000 on the disposition of shares of a small business corporation. His employment income for 2013 is over $200,000. Determine the amount of the Allowable Business Investment Loss that can be deducted in 2013, as well as the amount and type of any losses available for carry over at the end of the year.

End of Exercise. Solution available in Study Guide.

We suggest you work Self Study Problem Eleven-1 at this point.

Farm Losses

Regular Farm Losses

11-63.   For full time farmers, farm losses are not restricted. They are treated in the same manner as non-capital losses in that they can be carried back three years and forward for 20 years. Unlike restricted farm losses (see the following Paragraph), when they are deducted on a carry over basis, regular farm losses can be applied against any type of income.

Restricted Farm Losses

11-64.   As stated in ITA 31 (as revised by the 2013 federal budget), restricted farm losses arise if:

> ... a farmer's chief source of income for a taxation year is neither farming nor a combination of farming and some other source of income that **is a subordinate source of income** for the taxpayer ...

11-65.   In effect, if farming is only a secondary source of income, farm losses will be restricted, even if the farming operation has a reasonable expectation of a profit. The restriction, as it applies after the 2013 budget, limits losses that can be deducted against other sources of income to the first $2,500 of such losses, plus one-half of the next $30,000, for a maximum deduction of $17,500 [$2,500 + (1/2) ($32,500 maximum - $2,500)] on farm losses of $32,500 or greater. Any amount of the farm loss that is not deductible in the current year is commonly referred to as a "restricted farm loss".

11-66.   Restricted farm losses can be carried over to other years. Such losses can be carried back 3 years and forward for a maximum of 20 years. In carry over periods, restricted farm losses can only be deducted to the extent that income from farming has been included in Net Income For Tax Purposes. For example, if a restricted farm loss carry forward of $15,000 was available at the beginning of 2013 and 2013 farming income totaled $12,000, only $12,000 of the carry forward could be deducted in calculating 2013 Taxable Income. The remaining $3,000 of the restricted loss could not be deducted, even if the taxpayer had large amounts of other types of income available.

11-67.   If land used in a farming business is disposed of before the taxpayer has an opportunity to fully utilize restricted farm losses carried forward, a part of the undeducted losses can be used to increase the adjusted cost base of the property. This would have the effect of reducing any capital gains arising on the disposition of the property. This treatment is only possible to the extent that the loss was created by property taxes or interest payments on the farm property.

Exercise Eleven - 6

Subject: Farm Losses

Ms. Elena Bodkin has a full time appointment as a professor at a Canadian university. As she has considerable free time, she is developing an organic vegetable farm. In 2013, the first year of operation, she had a loss of $36,000 and deducted the maximum allowable amount. In 2014, in addition to her employment income of $85,000, her farming operation showed a profit of $3,500.

Determine Ms. Bodkin's minimum 2014 Net Income For Tax Purposes and Taxable Income, as well as the amount and type of any losses available for carry forward at the end of the year.

End of Exercise. Solution available in Study Guide.

We suggest you work Self Study Problem Eleven-2 at this point.

Lifetime Capital Gains Deduction

Background

The Original Legislation

11-68.   The lifetime capital gains legislation was first introduced in 1985 and, in its original form, it allowed every individual resident in Canada to enjoy up to $100,000 in tax free capital gains during the course of their lifetime. This privilege was available without regard to the type of property on which the gain accrued. A resident Canadian could acquire a major tax benefit through the process of owning and disposing of a Florida condominium. This original legislation was modified in 1988, providing an enhanced $500,000 deduction for qualified small business corporations and qualified farm properties.

Limiting Its Scope

11-69.   Because of the magnitude of the possible benefits and the potential for abuse, the relevant legislation was extremely complex. Further, this new tax privilege created serious distortions in the allocation of economic resources. The provision appeared to have little economic justification other than providing a near outright gift to wealthy Canadians. Given this effect, it is not surprising that actions were taken to limit the scope of this very generous tax provision.

11-70.   The limiting process took place in two steps:

- In 1992, the deduction was eliminated for gains resulting from the disposition of most real property (a.k.a., non-qualifying real estate).
- In 1994, the deduction was eliminated with respect to all dispositions other than those involving qualified farm property and shares of qualified small business corporations.

11-71.   The 1994 change was accompanied by an election that allowed holders of capital assets with accrued gains to have a deemed disposition in order to make use of any remaining general lifetime capital gains deduction that was available to them. The election created a new adjusted cost base that would be used to calculate the capital gain or loss on the future disposition of the asset.

11-72.   These changes left a very complex legacy with respect to the determination of the adjusted cost base of either non-qualifying real estate held at the time of the 1992 change, or other assets on which the 1994 election was made. While tax practitioners will have to deal with this problem for many years to come, the complex rules related to these adjusted cost base determinations go beyond the scope of this text.

Current And Future Limits

11-73.   After 1994, the $500,000 deduction was only available against gains resulting from the disposition of qualified small business corporation shares or qualified farm properties. Subsequent changes expanded the coverage of the deduction to dispositions of qualified fishing properties and increased the deduction limit from $500,000 to $750,000 for all types of qualified property.

11-74.   While it does not affect any of the examples or problems in this text, the 2013 federal budget proposes that the limit be increased from $750,000 to $800,000 for gains realized in the 2014 taxation year. Subsequent to 2014, the limit will be indexed for inflation. The budget notes that this limit will apply for all individuals, even those who have made use of the provision in previous years.

Qualified Property

Types Of Property

11-75.   The ITA 110.6 lifetime capital gains deduction is available on a disposition of shares of a qualified small business corporation, and interests in qualified farm and fishing properties. Note that the limit ($750,000 for 2013) is not available on each type of asset. Rather, it is a total amount that must be shared on dispositions of all three types of property.

11-76. As it is the most common application of this provision, we will focus our attention on shares of qualified small business corporations. With respect to the other two types of qualified property, they can be generally described as follows:

> **Qualified Farm or Fishing Property** Qualified farm property and qualified fishing property are defined in ITA 110.6(1). They include real property and eligible capital property used in Canada for farming or fishing by a taxpayer, the taxpayer's spouse, or their children. The definition also includes a share of a family farm or fishing corporation and an interest in a family farm or fishing partnership. To qualify for this deduction, the property must not be owned by a different taxpayer for at least 24 months prior to its disposition.

Small Business Corporations

11-77. As noted in our discussion of Business Investment Losses in Paragraph 11-55, ITA 248(1) defines a small business corporation as a Canadian controlled private corporation (CCPC) of which all, or substantially all (90 percent or more), of the fair market value of its assets are used in an active business carried on primarily (more than 50 percent) in Canada. In order to be a qualified small business corporation for the purposes of the lifetime capital gains deduction, the corporation is only required to satisfy this definition of a small business corporation at the point in time at which the shares are sold.

11-78. In many cases this is not a difficult criterion to satisfy. If, at a particular point in time, less than 90 percent of the fair market value of the corporation's assets are involved in producing active business income, it is often a simple matter to sell some of the non-qualifying assets and distribute the proceeds to the shareholders. This process, commonly referred to as "the purification of a small business corporation", can normally be carried out in a short period of time, thereby satisfying the small business corporation criteria prior to the disposition of the shares.

Qualified Small Business Corporations

11-79. Not all small business corporations are qualified small business corporations. To achieve this stature, ITA 110.6(1) requires that two other conditions be met. In somewhat simplified terms, they are:

- the shares must not be owned by anyone other than the taxpayer or a related person for at least 24 months preceding the disposition; and
- throughout this 24 month period, more than 50 percent of the fair market value of the corporation's assets must be used in an active business carried on primarily in Canada.

11-80. There are additional rules that are applicable when intercorporate investments are involved in the preceding determinations. More specifically, additional requirements apply when the condition that 50 percent of the assets must be used in active business for a 24 month period can only be met by adding in the shares of another small business corporation. These special rules go beyond the scope of this text and, as a result, will not be covered here.

11-81. As compared to meeting the small business corporation criteria, a failure to meet these additional qualifying criteria is more difficult to correct. As they involve measurements made over a period of time, a failure to satisfy them can only be corrected by the passage of time.

Determining The Deductible Amount

General Rules

11-82. The determination of the amount of the lifetime capital gains deduction that can be deducted in a year involves calculations that can be complex. In general terms, the available deduction is the least of the following three items:

Lifetime Capital Gains Deduction

- Capital Gains Deduction Available
- Annual Gains Limit
- Cumulative Gains Limit

11-83.   These items will be explained in detail in the following material.

Capital Gains Deduction Available

11-84.   The "capital gains deduction available" is the lifetime maximum for the capital gains deduction, less any amounts that have been used up in preceding years. The lifetime maximum is $375,000 [(1/2)($750,000)]. As noted, this is a cumulative total for all types of qualifying assets.

11-85.   A problem arises in determining the amounts used up in previous years. Clearly, it would not be appropriate to subtract a $12,000 deduction made in 1990 when it represented the taxable three-quarters portion of a $16,000 capital gain, from the 2013 limit of $375,000, which is based on one-half of the gain. However, as we noted in Paragraph 11-44, the inclusion rate has been at one-half since 2000. Given this, we will not complicate our lifetime capital gains deduction examples or problems with this issue as it is now much less common.

Annual Gains Limit

11-86.   The annual gains limit is defined in ITA 110.6(1) as follows:

Annual Gains Limit of an individual for a taxation year means the amount determined by the formula

$$A - B, \text{ where}$$

A is equal to the lesser of:

- net taxable capital gains for the current year on all capital asset dispositions [ITA 3(b)]; and

- net taxable capital gains for the current year on dispositions of qualified farm property, qualified fishing property, and qualified small business corporation shares.

B is equal to the total of:

- The amount, if any, by which net capital loss carry overs deducted for the year under ITA 111(1)(b), exceeds the excess of net taxable capital gains for the year [ITA 3(b)] over the amount determined in Part A of this formula; and

- Allowable Business Investment Losses realized during the current year.

11-87.   The annual gains limit formula is made complex by the possibility of having a capital gains on an asset that is not eligible for the deduction in the same year that there is a capital gain on a qualified property. In a year in which there is a capital gain on a qualified property and no other capital gains, the formula can be stated more simply as follows:

Annual Gains Limit is equal to the taxable capital gains on qualified property, less:

- Allowable capital losses realized.

- Net capital loss carry overs deducted.

- Allowable Business Investment Losses realized.

11-88.   We will make use of this abbreviated formula when the only capital gains during the year are those on qualified property.

11-89.   Additional points here are as follows:

- With respect to the Allowable Business Investment Losses realized, the full amount is subtracted in the preceding formula, without regard to whether they have been deducted in the calculation of Net Income For Tax Purposes. Also keep in mind that the amount of Allowable Business Investment Losses realized is based only on those amounts that have not been disallowed by the previous use of the lifetime capital gains deduction.

- As a further point here, the deduction of net capital loss carry forwards is discretionary. This means that, in cases where there is the possibility of using either the lifetime capital gains deduction or a net capital loss carry forward, the individual must choose between the two alternatives. This is inherent in the annual gains limit formula which, in most situations, will reduce the limit on a dollar for dollar basis for net capital loss carry overs deducted.

While this choice between the two alternatives may have no influence on the current year's Taxable Income, we would suggest a preference for making maximum use of the lifetime capital gains deduction. There is no time limit on using the net capital loss carry forward and, more importantly, it can be used when any type of taxable capital gain is realized. In contrast, the lifetime capital gains deduction can only be used for particular types of capital gains.

Exercise Eleven - 7

Subject: Annual Gains Limit

On January 1, 2013, your client, Miss Jana Slovena, has a net capital loss carry forward from 2011 of $45,000. During 2013, Miss Slovena has the following:

- taxable capital gains on sales of real estate in the amount of $114,000
- allowable capital losses of $82,000
- a taxable capital gain of $42,000 on sales of shares in a qualified small business corporation
- an Allowable Business Investment Loss of $3,000 on sales of shares of a small business corporation that does not qualify for the lifetime capital gains deduction

As she does not expect to have additional capital gains in the near future, Miss Slovena has asked you to deduct the full $45,000 of the 2011 net capital loss during 2013. Determine her annual gains limit for 2013 using this approach. What advice would you give Ms. Slovena regarding her net capital loss?

End of Exercise. Solution available in Study Guide.

Cumulative Net Investment Loss (CNIL)

11-90.   It was the belief of the government that it was inequitable for individuals to simultaneously deduct investment losses while sheltering capital gains through the use of the lifetime capital gains deduction. As a result, the legislation restricts the use of the lifetime capital gains deduction by an individual's Cumulative Net Investment Losses (CNIL).

11-91.   CNIL is defined as the amount by which the aggregate of investment expenses for the current year and prior years ending after 1987, exceeds the aggregate of investment income for that period. That is, the CNIL consists of post-1987 investment expenses minus investment income. You should note that, in this context, both investment income and investment expense are defined in the *Income Tax Act*. As a consequence, they have a meaning that can be different than the meaning associated with the everyday use of these terms.

11-92.   As will be explained in the following material, individuals who have a CNIL will have their ability to use the lifetime capital gains deduction reduced. As a result, if qualified capital gains are anticipated, it is advantageous to minimize any CNIL. Some examples of ways in which the impact of the CNIL can be reduced are as follows:

- Realizing capital gains on qualified assets early, if Cumulative Net Investment Losses are anticipated in future years.

- Delaying the disposition of qualified assets with accrued capital gains until the CNIL has been eliminated or reduced as much as possible.

- For owner/managers, having the business pay dividends, or interest on shareholder loan accounts, rather than salaries, to increase investment income.

Cumulative Gains Limit

11-93.   In somewhat simplified form, the cumulative gains limit can be defined as follows:

The sum of all annual gains limits for the current and previous years, unadjusted for changes in the capital gains inclusion rate. This total is reduced by:

- The sum of all amounts deducted under the lifetime capital gains deduction provision in computing the individual's taxable incomes for preceding taxation years (unadjusted for changes in the capital gains inclusion rate); and

- the individual's CNIL at the end of the year.

11-94.   In the absence of a CNIL balance, this formula would simply be the sum of all annual gains limits, reduced by all of the lifetime capital gains deductions made in previous years. As individuals will normally deduct the full amount of their annual gains limit, this balance will usually be equal to the annual gains limit for the current year. This result can be altered by an individual's failure to deduct the full amount of the annual gains limit in some previous year, either as a tax planning choice or as the result of a CNIL balance.

11-95.   The following is a simple example of cumulative gains limit calculations.

Example   In 2013, Ms. Nolan has $5,600 of deductible interest on loans for investment purposes and $2,600 of net rental income. She has had no investment income or investment expenses in years prior to 2013, so her Cumulative Net Investment Loss (CNIL) is $3,000 ($5,600 - $2,600). During August, 2013, she has a $60,000 taxable capital gain on the sale of qualified small business shares. Ms. Nolan has no other capital gains or losses in 2013.

Analysis   As she has made no previous use of her lifetime capital gains deduction, her unused lifetime limit is $375,000. While her annual gains limit would be $60,000, the amount of the taxable capital gain, her ability to use the lifetime capital gains deduction would be limited by her CNIL to her cumulative gains limit of $57,000 ($60,000 - $3,000).

Comprehensive Example

11-96.   The example that follows illustrates the basic rules involved in the application of the lifetime capital gains deduction.

Example   Dwight Treadway's 2013 Net Income For Tax Purposes is as follows:

Employment Income	$ 60,000
Taxable Capital Gain On Sale Of Qualified Farm Property	200,000
Net Income For Tax Purposes	$260,000

In 2007, Mr. Treadway realized a $20,000 taxable capital gain [(1/2)($40,000)] from the sale of shares in a qualified small business corporation and used his lifetime capital gains deduction to claim a deduction for this amount. In 2006, Mr. Treadway realized an allowable capital loss of $9,000 [(1/2)($18,000)]. He was not able to use the loss in that year, or any other year, and he intends to deduct it as a net capital loss carry forward in 2013. Other than the 2007 taxable capital gain of $20,000 and the 2006 allowable capital loss of $9,000, Mr. Treadway had no capital gains, capital losses, loss carry overs, or Business Investment Losses from 2006 through 2012. He has no CNIL balance in 2013.

Analysis For 2013, the maximum deduction under ITA 110.6 would be the least of the following amounts:

- **Capital Gains Deduction Available = $355,000** ($375,000 - $20,000).

- **Annual Gains Limit = $191,000** As Mr. Treadway has had no capital gains on non-qualified property in 2013, we can use the simplified version of this calculation. (See Paragraph 11-87.) This would result in an annual gains limit of $191,000, the $200,000 taxable capital gain for the year, less the $9,000 [(1/2)($18,000)] net capital loss carry forward deducted under ITA 111(1)(b).

- **Cumulative Gains Limit = $191,000** As the annual gains limit for 2007 would be equal to the $20,000 taxable capital gain on qualifying property, the sum of the annual gains limits would be $211,000 ($20,000 + $191,000). Subtracting from this the $20,000 lifetime capital gains deduction for 2007 leaves the cumulative gains limit of $191,000.

11-97. Given these calculations, the maximum deduction for 2013 would be $191,000, the amount of both the annual gains limit and the cumulative gains limit. The full $200,000 gain on the farm could have been deducted if Mr. Treadway had not chosen to deduct the net capital loss carry forward. The deduction of this amount reduced both the annual gains limit and the cumulative gains limit by $9,000.

Exercise Eleven - 8

Subject: Lifetime Capital Gains Deduction

Mr. Edwin Loussier had a 2006 taxable capital gain on qualifying property of $5,000 [(1/2)($10,000)] and a 2008 taxable capital gain on qualifying property of $13,000 [(1/2)($26,000)]. He used his lifetime capital gains deduction to eliminate both of these gains. He has no other capital gains, capital losses, or Business Investment Losses in the period 2006 through 2011. In December, 2012, he has a $63,000 capital loss which, because he has no capital gains in that year, he cannot deduct. In 2013, he has a $510,000 capital gain on the sale of a qualified farm property. In addition, he deducts the $63,000 capital loss from 2012. Mr. Loussier does not have a CNIL balance. Determine Mr. Loussier's maximum lifetime capital gains deduction for 2013. Provide all of the calculations required to determine the maximum ITA 110.6 deduction.

End of Exercise. Solution available in Study Guide.

We suggest you work Self Study Problem Eleven-3 at this point.

Ordering Of Deductions And Losses

Significance Of Ordering

11-98. If an individual has sufficient income to absorb all of the losses and deductions that are available in the calculation of Taxable Income, the question of ordering is not important. The real significance of provisions covering the ordering of losses and other deductions is in the determination of the amounts and types of items that can be carried over to previous or subsequent years.

11-99. For example, assume that a taxpayer has taxable capital gains of $25,000, a business loss of $25,000, and allowable capital losses of $25,000. No matter how these items are ordered, the Net Income For Tax Purposes will be nil. However, it does make a difference whether the loss carry over is for the business loss, or for the net capital losses. A net capital loss carry forward can only be deducted to the extent of taxable capital gains in the carry forward period. On the other hand, the non-capital losses can only be used for a limited period of time (20 years) while, by contrast, the net capital losses can be carried forward indefinitely. Note, however, with the extension of the carry forward period from 7 years to 20 years, this time limit is no longer likely to be a significant factor in most situations.

Ordering In Computing Net Income For Tax Purposes

11-100.   The basic rules for the computation of Net Income For Tax Purposes under Division B are found in ITA 3. In computing Net Income For Tax Purposes, ITA 3 indicates that we begin by adding together positive amounts of income from non-capital sources, plus net taxable capital gains. Net taxable capital gains are defined as the amount, if any, by which the current year's taxable capital gains exceed the current year's allowable capital losses. This, in effect, requires that capital losses, to the extent there are capital gains during the year, be deducted prior to the deduction of non-capital losses.

11-101.   The various deductions available under Subdivision e (RRSP deductions, spousal support paid, child care costs, moving expenses, etc.) are subtracted from this total. If a positive balance remains, the final step in computing Net Income For Tax Purposes is to subtract any employment, business, or property losses, as well as Allowable Business Investment Losses.

Ordering In Computing Taxable Income

11-102.   With respect to the computation of Taxable Income for individuals, the *Act* is much more specific. Under ITA 111.1, the order in which individuals must deduct Division C items is as follows:

- Various deductions provided by ITA 110 (stock options, home relocation loans)
- Retroactive lump-sum payments under ITA 110.2
- Loss carry overs under ITA 111 (non-capital, net capital, and farm)
- Lifetime capital gains deduction under ITA 110.6
- Northern residents deductions under ITA 110.7

11-103.   Within ITA 111, available loss carry overs can be deducted in any order the taxpayer wishes. The only constraint is the ITA 111(3) requirement that, within a particular type of loss (e.g., non-capital losses), the oldest losses have to be deducted first.

11-104.   When several different types of loss carry overs are available, decisions in this area can be difficult. On the one hand, certain types of carry overs have a limited period of availability (i.e., non-capital losses and farm losses can be carried forward for 20 years). In contrast, net capital losses have no time limit, but can only be deducted to the extent of taxable capital gains that have been realized in the year. Restricted farm loss carry overs and carry overs of losses on listed personal property have more onerous limitations. These losses are restricted with respect to both time and type of income (e.g., restricted farm loss carry forwards are available for 20 years and can only be deducted to the extent of farm income earned in the year).

11-105.   Decisions in this area will involve a careful weighing of which type of loss carry over is most likely to have continued usefulness in future years. For example, if a non-capital loss carry forward is 19 years old and the business is expecting no Taxable Income in the following year, then use of this carry forward would appear to be a prudent course of action. An additional constraint is that the deduction of loss carry overs should leave sufficient Taxable Income that Tax Payable does not become less than the amount of available tax credits. As discussed in Paragraph 11-26 through 11-29, tax credits that are not used during the current taxation year are, in general, permanently lost.

Example

11-106.   The following is an example of the ordering rules used in computing Taxable Income for individuals:

Example At the beginning of 2013, Miss Farnum had the following loss carry forwards available:

Non-Capital Losses	$40,000
Net Capital Losses [(1/2)($20,000)]	10,000
Restricted Farm Losses	5,000

For 2013, she can claim only the basic personal amount of $11,038. Also during 2013, she has no available subdivision e deductions. For this year, she had the following income amounts as calculated under Division B rules:

Employment Income	$15,000
Property Income (Interest)	4,000
Farm Income	2,000
Income From Sole Proprietorship	15,000
Capital Gains	12,000

Analysis Miss Farnum's 2013 Net Income For Tax Purposes would be calculated as follows:

Income Under ITA 3(a):		
Employment Income	$15,000	
Property Income	4,000	
Farming Income	2,000	
Business Income (Proprietorship)	15,000	$36,000
Income Under ITA 3(b):		
Taxable Capital Gains [(1/2)($12,000)]		6,000
Net Income For Tax Purposes		$42,000

Miss Farnum's Taxable Income would be calculated as follows:

Net Income For Tax Purposes	$42,000
Restricted Farm Loss Carry Forward (Limited to farming income)	(2,000)
Net Capital Loss Carry Forward (Limited to taxable capital gains)	(6,000)
Subtotal	$34,000
Non-Capital Loss Carry Forward ($34,000 - $11,038)	(22,962)
Taxable Income	$11,038

Loss Carry Forwards

• Restricted farm loss carry forward ($5,000 - $2,000)	$ 3,000
• Net capital loss carry forward [(1/2)($20,000 - $12,000)]	4,000
• Non-capital loss carry forward ($40,000 - $22,962)	17,038

11-107.   Note that, in this example, the amount of net capital and restricted farm losses deducted was limited by the amount of the taxable capital gains and farm income. The non-capital loss deducted was limited to the amount that would reduce her Taxable Income to her basic personal amount of $11,038. Since her Tax Payable will be nil at this point, there is no reason to deduct any further amount of the non-capital loss available.

Exercise Eleven - 9

Subject: Ordering Of Losses

At the beginning of 2013, Alan Barter had the following loss carry forwards available:

Restricted Farm Losses	$ 8,000
Non-Capital Losses	36,000
Net Capital Losses [(1/2)($40,000)]	20,000

During 2013, he had the following amounts of income:

Taxable Capital Gains	$ 9,000
Business Income	12,000
Employment Income	56,000
Farm Income	3,500

Determine Alan's Net Income For Tax Purposes, as well as his minimum Taxable Income for 2013. Indicate the amount and type of any losses available for carry forward at the end of the year.

End of Exercise. Solution available in Study Guide.

Tax Payable Overview

General

11-108.   Chapter 4 provided detailed coverage of the application of federal tax rates to Taxable Income in order to provide an initial figure for an individual's Tax Payable. In addition, coverage of most of the tax credits available to individuals was also provided. The coverage of tax credits was extended in Chapter 7 with coverage of the dividend tax credit, as well as the credit for taxes withheld on foreign source income.

11-109.   None of this material will be repeated in this Chapter. However, as many of the Self Study and Assignment Problems that accompany this Chapter are comprehensive in nature and will require you to apply tax calculations and credits, you will probably wish to review the material in Chapters 4 and 7 before attempting to deal with the problems in this Chapter.

11-110.   As was the case with the material on Taxable Income, there are issues involved with the determination of individual Tax Payable that, because of the need for additional understanding of the income concepts presented in subsequent chapters, could not be dealt with in Chapter 4. Because of this, additional coverage of Tax Payable is included in this Chapter. Specifically, the following concepts and procedures are discussed in this material:

Tax On Split Income   This special tax was designed to limit the use of income splitting with minor children. It can be better understood now that we have covered the material on income attribution in Chapter 9.

Transfer Of Dividends To A Spouse Or Common-Law Partner   The calculations related to this tax credit require an understanding of the dividend gross up and tax credit procedures which were not introduced until Chapter 7.

Charitable Donations   The basic calculation of this tax credit was presented in Chapter 4. However, it was not possible to deal with gifts of capital property until the material in Chapters 5 through 8 on business income, property income and capital gains had been covered.

Foreign Tax Credits   These credits were introduced in Chapter 7. However, the full determination of the eligible amounts requires the additional material on Taxable Income that is included in this Chapter.

11-111. Now that we have covered the material in Chapters 5 to 10, we are in a position to complete our coverage of the determination of Tax Payable for individuals.

Basic Federal Tax Payable

11-112. Basic federal Tax Payable is a figure from which some, but not all tax credits have been deducted. At one time, this was an important figure in that it was the base that the provinces and territories used in calculating their respective provincial Tax Payable. Since the provinces now base provincial taxes on Taxable Income, the basic federal tax figure is no longer of general importance.

11-113. This concept does, however, have some limited use in specialized situations and, because of this, you will see references to this figure in the T1 tax return. The most important of these is that it is used to calculate the additional federal Tax Payable that must be paid by individuals who are deemed Canadian residents but do not reside in a province (e.g., members of the Canadian Armed Forces stationed outside of Canada). However, other than indicating that this concept exists, we will give basic federal tax no further consideration.

Tax On Split Income

The Problem

11-114. In the past, a number of arrangements have been used to channel property income into the hands of related individuals with little or no income. If, for example, the owner of a corporation can arrange his affairs so that corporate income is paid out as non-eligible dividends to his children, each child can receive over $43,000 per year of such income on a tax free basis.

11-115. This amount would be even larger if they are eligible dividends subject to the enhanced gross up. However, as discussed in our chapters on corporate taxation, most dividends paid by private operating companies are paid out of income that has benefitted from the small business deduction. Such dividends are non-eligible and, as a consequence, the gross up is limited to 25 percent.

The Solution - The "Kiddie Tax"

Tax On Split Income

11-116. The federal government had little success in attacking these income splitting arrangements through the courts and decided to solve the problem through legislation. ITA 120.4(2) imposes a tax on the "split income" of specified individuals (referred to by many writers as the "kiddie tax").

11-117. This tax is assessed at the maximum federal rate of 29 percent. It is applied to all such income, beginning with the first dollar received, with only limited tax credits available.

11-118. For the purposes of this Section, a specified individual is anyone who has not attained the age of 17 years before the year (i.e., it is applicable to a child who turns 17 in the year), is a resident of Canada throughout the year, and has a parent who is a resident of Canada at any time in the year.

11-119. The "split income" that is defined in ITA 120.4(1) includes the following:

(a) taxable dividends from private companies received directly, or through a trust or partnership;

(b) shareholder benefits or loans received from a private corporation; and

(c) income from a partnership or trust if the income is derived from the provision of property or services to a business:
   - carried on by a person related to the individual,
   - carried on by a corporation of which a person related to the individual is a specified shareholder (i.e., owns 10 percent or more of the shares), or

Tax On Split Income

- carried on by a professional corporation of which a person related to the individual is a shareholder.

11-120.   Split income also includes capital gains resulting from a sale of shares by a specified individual to a non-arm's length person, provided any taxable dividends on those particular shares would have been subject to the tax on split income. Note that such gains are not included in the definition of split income. Rather ITA 120.4(4) indicates that such capital gains will be deemed to be non-eligible dividends. In effect, this brings these gains into the definition of split income more indirectly.

Calculation Of The Tax

11-121.   When split income is present, the recipient's Tax Payable is made up of two components. The first component is based on a calculation that, under ITA 20(1)(ww), removes the specified individual's split income from the total. In this calculation, all the usual tax credits, including any related to non-split income sources, are available. The second component is based on split income amounts. In this case, the only tax credits that can be used in determining Tax Payable are the dividend tax credits or foreign non-business income tax credits that relate to the split income. The following example will illustrate these procedures:

Example   Helen, who is 15 years old, receives non-eligible dividends of $20,000 from a private company controlled by her father. In addition, she has interest income of $5,500 from a savings account funded by her earnings from part-time jobs. Her only tax credits are the basic personal credit and the dividend tax credit.

Analysis   The initial calculation involves determining the tax on total income, reduced under ITA 20(1)(ww) by amounts that fall within the definition of split income (the non-eligible dividends). All of the usual tax credits can be claimed in this calculation.

Taxable Non-Eligible Dividends [(125%)($20,000)]	$25,000
Interest	5,500
Deduction For Split Income - Non-Eligible Dividends	(25,000)
Net Income For Tax Purposes = Taxable Income	$ 5,500
Tax Rate	15%
Tax Payable Before Credits	$ 825
Basic Personal Credit [(15%)($11,038)]	(1,656)
Federal Tax Payable On Regular Income	Nil

The Tax Payable on the split income would be calculated as follows:

Split Income - Taxable Non-Eligible Dividends	$25,000
Tax Rate	29%
Tax Payable Before Dividend Tax Credit	$7,250
Dividend Tax Credit [(2/3)(25%)($20,000)]	(3,333)
Tax Payable On Split Income	$3,917

With the regular component being nil, the total Tax Payable will be $3,917, the amount based on split income sources.

11-122.   To ensure that this tax is paid, the parents of the specified individual are held jointly and severally liable for its remittance.

Exceptions

11-123.   The tax on split income rules are not applicable to:

- dividends from public companies;
- reasonable remuneration paid to a minor;
- amounts paid to a minor with no parent who is resident in Canada;

- income from property inherited by a child from a parent; or
- income from property inherited from individuals other than a parent, if the child is either in full time attendance at a post-secondary educational institution, or eligible for the disability tax credit.

Evaluation

11-124.   While this legislation was met with howls of outrage from many in the tax community, in our view it was an appropriate modification of the existing system. There had been widespread use of vehicles such as family trusts to shelter income from taxes. In effect, it was possible to pay for a large portion of the expenses of raising children on a tax advantaged basis. This type of benefit is clearly not available to the majority of Canadians and it would be difficult to describe our tax system as fair if such arrangements were allowed to continue.

Exercise Eleven - 10

Subject: Tax On Split Income

During 2013, Norton James, who is 16 years old, receives non-eligible dividends of $15,000 from a private corporation controlled by his mother. He also has income of $12,200 from contracts to create computer games. As he has used the income that he has earned from these contracts in previous years to invest in the stock market, he has eligible dividends from publicly traded companies of $5,600. Assume his only tax credits are his basic personal credit and dividend tax credits on the shares that he owns. Determine Norton's federal Tax Payable for 2013.

End of Exercise. Solution available in Study Guide.

Tax Credits Revisited

Transfer Of Dividends To A Spouse Or Common-Law Partner

11-125.   There may be situations in which a taxpayer's spousal credit has been reduced or eliminated by dividends received by that spouse. The ITA 82(3) election permits a transfer of all of the dividends from the spouse or common-law partner's income to that of the taxpayer, if it creates or increases the spousal credit. Consider the following example:

Example   Mrs. Albert's total income consisted of $12,000 in eligible dividends received from taxable Canadian corporations. Mrs. Albert's basic personal tax credit, along with part of the dividend tax credit, eliminate all taxation on the grossed up amount of $16,560 [(138%)($12,000)]. However, because she has this income receipt, Mr. Albert is not able to claim a spousal tax credit.

Analysis   In this situation, the transfer of dividends under ITA 82(3) would eliminate all of Mrs. Albert's income, and Mr. Albert would be able to claim the full spousal credit of $1,656. Mr. Albert would then be taxed on the $16,560 of grossed up dividends. He would, however, be eligible for the dividend tax credit associated with these dividends. Whether this is a good alternative or not depends on Mr. Albert's marginal tax rate, as can be seen in the following calculations:

Mr. Albert's Tax Bracket	15%	29%
Increase In Taxable Income	$16,560	$16,560
Tax On $16,560	$ 2,484	$ 4,802
Increase In Spousal Credit	(1,656)	(1,656)
Dividend Tax Credit [(6/11)(38%)($12,000)]	(2,487)	(2,487)
Increase (Decrease) In Tax Payable	($ 1,659)	$ 659

As can be seen in the table, if Mr. Albert is in the 15 percent tax bracket, his federal tax would be decreased by $1,659. Alternatively, if he is in the 29 percent bracket, the transfer would not be desirable as his federal tax would be increased by $659.

Exercise Eleven - 11

Subject: Transfer Of Dividends To A Spouse

Mr. Albert Ho is 38 years old and has over $200,000 in 2013 Taxable Income. His wife's only 2013 source of income is $8,500 in eligible dividends received from taxable Canadian corporations. In terms of federal Tax Payable, would Mr. Ho benefit from the use of the ITA 82(3) election to include the eligible dividends received by his spouse in his Net Income For Tax Purposes? Justify your conclusion.

End of Exercise. Solution available in Study Guide.

We suggest you work Self Study Problems Eleven-4 and 5 at this point.

Charitable Donations Credit Revisited

Introduction

11-126.   A basic treatment of this credit was provided in Chapter 4. In that Chapter, we noted that, for individuals, the credit was calculated as 15 percent of the first $200 of donations, plus 29 percent of any additional amounts. In general, the base for calculating this credit was limited to 75 percent of the taxpayer's Net Income For Tax Purposes.

11-127.   In Chapter 4, we dealt only with simple situations involving gifts of cash. Attention was also given in Chapter 4 to the first-time donor's super credit. Coverage of more complex issues involving gifts of various types of capital property was deferred and is included in this Chapter 11.

11-128.   As many of you are aware, in recent years, a number of gift giving programs have been developed that appear to provide the taxpayer with benefits that exceed his cost and, in some cases, the value of the gift to the recipient charity.

11-129.   A classic example of this was the so-called art flips. Such arrangements might involve a taxpayer buying a large block of paintings directly from the inventories of the artist. The cost of the block was essentially a wholesale value and was significantly lower than the sum of the retail prices of the individual paintings. The paintings would then be appraised on the basis of individual retail values, followed by a gift of the art works to a registered charity. The taxpayer would then claim a tax credit based on the significantly higher appraised value, often resulting in a tax credit that was worth more than the original cost of the paintings.

11-130.   At this point in time (May, 2013) there are legislative proposals which would restrict the ability of taxpayers to use such schemes. Coverage of these provisions, located in proposed ITA 248(30) through ITA 248(41), will be found in the material which follows.

Donations Classified

11-131.   ITA 118.1 defines four types of charitable donations:

1. **Total Charitable Gifts** is defined to include all eligible amounts donated by an individual to a registered charity, a registered Canadian amateur athletic association, a Canadian municipality, the United Nations or an agency thereof, a university outside of Canada which normally enrolls Canadian students, and a charitable organization outside of Canada to which Her Majesty in right of Canada has made a gift in the year or in the immediately preceding year.

2. **Total Crown Gifts** is defined as the aggregate of eligible amounts donated to Her Majesty in right of Canada or a province.

3. **Total Cultural Gifts** is defined as the aggregate of all eligible gifts of objects that the Canadian Cultural Property Export Review Board has determined meet the criteria of the *Cultural Property And Import Act*.

4. **Total Ecological Gifts** is defined as all eligible gifts of land certified by the Minister of the Environment to be ecologically sensitive land, the conservation and protection of which is important to the preservation of Canada's environmental heritage. The beneficiary of the gift must be a Canadian municipality or a registered charity, the primary purpose of which is the conservation and protection of Canada's environmental heritage.

11-132. In addition to the items specified in the *Act*, under the U.S./Canada tax treaty, Canadians can claim gifts to any qualifying U.S. charity in amounts up to 75 percent of their net U.S. income (75 percent of their net world income if the Canadian resident lives near the U.S. border and commutes to a U.S. place of business or employment).

Eligible Amounts

11-133 In the preceding material on the classification of donations, each of the definitions contains the term "eligible amounts". The use of this term reflects the proposed anti-avoidance legislation. These proposals define this term as follows:

> **Proposed ITA 248(31)** The eligible amount of a gift or monetary contribution is the amount by which the fair market value of the property that is the subject of the gift exceeds the amount of the advantage, if any, in respect of the gift.

11-134. The proposed ITA 248(32) defines "advantage" very broadly to include a benefit to the taxpayer that is in any way related to the gift, including benefits that are contingent on future events.

> **Example** The example provided for this proposal is the gift of real property with a fair market value of $300,000, with the registered charity assuming the $100,000 mortgage on the property. In this case, the eligible amount of the donation is $200,000 ($300,000 - $100,000).

11-135. In addition to this eligibility requirement, a proposed ITA 248(30) introduces the concept of "intention to give". The basic idea here is that, if the advantage to the taxpayer resulting from making the gift exceeds 80 percent of the value of the gift, the gift will be disallowed unless the taxpayer can convince the Minister that the transfer was made with the intention to make a gift.

Deemed Fair Market Value

11-136. In order to eliminate arrangements such as the art flip that was described in Paragraph 11-129, ITA 248(35) introduces the concept of "deemed fair market value". This proposed Subsection indicates that, if a taxpayer acquires a property less than three years prior to its donation as a gift or, if a taxpayer acquires a property less than 10 years before the gift is made and it is reasonable to conclude that the taxpayer acquired the property with an intent to make a gift, the value of the gift will be based on the lesser of the cost to the taxpayer and the actual fair market value at the time of the gift. There is an exception to this rule for gifts made as a consequence of a taxpayer's death.

Gifts Of Capital Property - Transfer At Elected Value

11-137. When an individual makes a charitable, Crown, or ecological (but not cultural) gift of capital property, an election is available under ITA 118.1(6). On such properties, there will usually be a difference between the tax cost of the property (i.e., adjusted cost base for non-depreciable properties or UCC for depreciable properties) and its fair market value. If the fair market value is the higher value, the taxpayer can elect to transfer the property at any value between the tax cost of the property and its fair market value. There are special rules applicable to gifts of publicly traded securities and ecologically sensitive land that will be covered in Paragraph 11-143.

Tax Credits Revisited

11-138.   In the case of non-depreciable assets, if the fair market value exceeds the adjusted cost base of the asset, it is advisable to elect the fair market value. Any amount of elected value in excess of $200 will be eligible for a tax credit at the maximum federal tax rate of 29 percent. In contrast, only one-half of any capital gain that results from the disposition will be subject to tax.

Example Mr. Vignesh Menan has a piece of land with an adjusted cost base of $100,000 and a fair market value of $150,000. During 2013, he intends to gift this land to a registered Canadian charity and would like to know whether he should elect to make the donation at $100,000 or alternatively, at $150,000. He has other income that puts him in the 29 percent federal tax bracket, without including any gain resulting from this disposition.

Analysis The tax consequences of the two alternatives are as follows:

Elected Value	$100,000	$150,000
Tax Credit [(15%)($200) + (29%)($99,800)]	$ 28,972	
Tax Credit [(15%)($200) + (29%)($149,800)]		$ 43,472
Tax On Gain	N/A	
Tax On Gain [(1/2)($150,000 - $100,000)(29%)]		(7,250)
Credit Net Of Tax	$ 28,972	$ 36,222

11-139.   It should be noted that a proposed ITA 118.1(6) places a floor on this election. This amendment indicates that the election cannot be below the amount of any advantage received by the taxpayer as a consequence of the gift.

Example Extended Mr. Vignesh Menan has a piece of land with an adjusted cost base of $100,000 and a fair market value of $150,000. In return for making this gift, he receives a cash payment from the registered charity of $110,000.

Analysis Mr. Menan cannot elect a value below $110,000. Assuming he elects to transfer the asset at the maximum value of $150,000, the eligible amount of his gift will be $40,000 ($150,000 - $110,000).

Gifts Of Capital Property - Income Limits
11-140.   In most cases, an individual's eligible donations are restricted to 75 percent of Net Income For Tax Purposes for the year (see Chapter 4). A potential problem with electing a value that creates income is that making a gift and electing to use the fair market value may result in income that cannot be eliminated with the related tax credit. In other words, making a gift could result in the payment of taxes. To avoid this problem, two other components are added to the Net Income base for charitable donations, resulting in a total base equal to:

- 75 percent of Net Income For Tax Purposes for the year; plus
- 25 percent of any taxable capital gain resulting from a gift; plus
- 25 percent of any recaptured CCA resulting from a gift.

11-141.   An example will illustrate the importance of these additions to the overall limit:

Example In July, 2013, Jonas Anderson gifts a customized bus that was used in his proprietorship to a registered Canadian charity. The bus has a fair market value of $130,000, a capital cost of $100,000, and a UCC of $65,000. He elects to make the gift at the fair market value of $130,000. He has no other source of income, other than amounts arising as a result of the gift.

Analysis The election to make the gift at the fair market value of $130,000 will result in a total increase in Net Income For Tax Purposes of $50,000. This is comprised of a taxable capital gain of $15,000 [(1/2)($130,000 - $100,000)] and recaptured CCA of $35,000 ($100,000 - $65,000).

As Mr. Anderson has no other source of income, his basic limit for charitable donations would be $37,500 [(75%)($50,000)]. If his limit was $37,500, he would be faced with paying tax on $12,500 ($50,000 - $37,500) less his personal tax credits, as a result of his generosity in making the gift. However, with the additions to the limit, his charitable donations credit base limit is as follows:

75 Percent Of Net Income For Tax Purposes [(75%)($50,000)]	$37,500
25 Percent Of Taxable Capital Gain [(25%)($15,000)]	3,750
25 Percent Of Recaptured CCA [(25%)($35,000)]	8,750
Total Limit (Equals Income From Donation)	$50,000

11-142.   As you can see, the additions to the limit serve the purpose of creating a base for charitable donations that includes 100 percent of any income resulting from gifts of capital property. Note, however, Mr. Anderson will not want to use the full $50,000 in 2013. As amounts over $200 will generate a credit at a rate of 29 percent and all of Mr. Anderson's income will be taxed at a lower rate, use of the full $50,000 would produce a credit that is larger than his Tax Payable. In addition, he will want to make use of any non-refundable tax credits that are available for 2013. The following Exercise illustrates the determination of the amount of an available tax credit that should be taken in order to reduce Tax Payable to nil.

Exercise Eleven - 12

Subject: Donation Of Depreciable Property

Ms. Sally Felder donates some food preparation equipment to the local food bank, a registered Canadian charity. The assets have a fair market value of $85,000, a capital cost of $62,000, and a UCC of $28,000. She elects to make the donation at the fair market value of $85,000. She has no other source of income during the year and her only tax credit other than the charitable donations tax credit is her basic personal credit of $1,656. Determine her maximum charitable donations tax credit for 2013. In addition, determine the amount of the donation she should claim in 2013 in order to reduce her federal Tax Payable to nil. Calculate any carry forward of unused amounts that will be available in future years.

End of Exercise. Solution available in Study Guide.

Gifts Of Publicly Traded Securities And Ecologically Sensitive Land
11-143.   Gifts of publicly traded securities and ecologically sensitive land benefit from special rules that make gifting these assets particularly attractive. While a donor can receive a donations tax credit based on the full fair market value of such assets, ITA 38(a.1) deems the capital gain on gifts of publicly traded securities to be zero. Using the same approach, ITA 38(a.2) deems the capital gain on gifts of ecologically sensitive land to be zero.

Gifts Of Publicly Traded Securities Acquired Through Stock Options
11-144.   Without special rules, there is a potential problem for donations of publicly traded shares purchased through stock options. You will recall from Chapter 3 that, in the case of these shares, any accrued gain that is present at the time the options are exercised is treated as an employment income inclusion. In order to give such gains effective capital gains treatment, a deduction of one-half is provided in the determination of Taxable Income.

Example Roberto Cerutti is provided with options to buy 1,000 of his employer's shares at an option price of $20 per share, the fair market value of the shares at the time the options are granted. Roberto exercises these options when the shares are trading at $32 per share. He gifts the shares immediately to a registered charity.

Analysis Roberto will have an increase in Taxable Income calculated as follows:

Employment Income [(1,000)($32 - $20)]	$12,000
Deduction Under ITA 110(1)(d) [(1/2)($12,000)]	(6,000)
Increase In Taxable Income	$ 6,000

11-145.   As this increase in Taxable Income is not a capital gain, it will not be deemed to be zero by ITA 38(a.1). In the absence of a further special provision, this $6,000 would be subject to tax. Fortunately, ITA 110(1)(d.01) contains a provision which acts to eliminate this tax. This paragraph provides an additional deduction equal to one-half of the Employment Income inclusion. Using this additional provision, the results would be as follows:

Employment Income [(1,000)($32 - $20)]	$12,000
Deduction Under ITA 110(1)(d) [(1/2)($12,000)]	(6,000)
Deduction Under ITA 110(1)(d.01) [(1/2)($12,000)]	(6,000)
Increase In Taxable Income	Nil

Exercise Eleven - 13

Subject: Donation Of Listed Shares

Mr. Saheed Radeem has employment income of $90,000. He owns shares that are listed on the Toronto Stock Exchange. These shares have a fair market value of $110,000 and an adjusted cost base of $30,000. During 2013, these shares are given to a registered Canadian charity. He has no deductions in the calculation of Taxable Income (i.e., his Taxable Income is equal to his Net Income For Tax Purposes). His tax credits, other than the charitable donations credit, total $4,000. Determine Mr. Radeem's maximum charitable donations tax credit for 2013 and the amount of the donation he should claim in 2013 in order to reduce his federal Tax Payable to nil. Calculate any carry forward of unused amounts that will be available in future years.

End of Exercise.   Solution available in Study Guide.

Canadian Cultural Property

11-146.   We have noted that, when an individual makes a charitable, Crown or ecological gift of capital property, they can elect to have the proceeds of disposition be any value between the tax cost of the property and the fair market value. In the case of cultural gifts of capital property, ITA 118.1(10.1) deems the proceeds of disposition to be the fair market value of the property in all cases. Note, however, that this same Subsection indicates that the value established by the Canadian Cultural Property Export Review Board or the Minister of the Environment is deemed to be the fair market value of the donated asset.

11-147.   This fair market value rule must be considered in conjunction with the fact that a provision in ITA 39(1)(a)(i.1) indicates that, with respect to gifts of Canadian cultural property, the difference between the fair market value and the adjusted cost base of the asset does not fall within the meaning of capital gain. As a consequence, any gain on a gift of Canadian cultural property is not subject to tax. Losses, however, would be treated as normal capital losses. Given this, it is not unreasonable to require that the proceeds of disposition on cultural gifts of capital property be equal to the fair market value of the property.

Limits On Amount Claimed And Carry Forward Provisions

11-148.   As noted in Chapter 4, it is the policy of the government to limit charitable donations that are eligible for the tax credit to a portion of a taxpayer's Net Income For Tax Purposes. Note that, while corporations deduct their donations as opposed to receiving a credit against Tax Payable, the limits on the amount of eligible donations are the same for corporations as they are for individuals.

11-149.   The limit on eligible amounts of charitable gifts is 75 percent of Net Income For Tax Purposes, but there are exceptions to this general limit. For individuals, this limit is increased to 100 percent of Net Income For Tax Purposes in the year of death and the preceding year. In those situations where a gift of capital property resulted in a capital gain and/or recaptured CCA, the overall limit is increased by 25 percent of the taxable capital gain and 25 percent of any recaptured CCA resulting from such a gift. There is no income limit on the amount of Crown gifts, cultural gifts, or ecological gifts. Credits can be claimed for these gifts up to their eligible amounts.

11-150.   The *Income Tax Act* does not require that charitable donations be claimed in the year that they are made. Unused charitable donations can be carried forward and claimed in the subsequent five year period. In the carry forward period, the same income based limits will apply in determining eligible amounts.

Foreign Tax Credits Revisited

Rules For Corporations

11-151.   Corporations are allowed to use foreign non-business income and foreign business income tax paid as a basis for a credit against Canadian Tax Payable. The rules for corporations are somewhat different from those for individuals and, in addition, require an understanding of some concepts that have not been introduced at this stage in the material. As a result, the foreign tax credit rules applicable to corporations are discussed in Chapter 12.

Foreign Non-Business (Property) Income Tax Credit For Individuals

11-152.   ITA 126(1) provides for a tax credit in situations where a Canadian resident has paid foreign taxes on non-business income. We introduced coverage of foreign tax credits in Chapter 7, but could not fully discuss the calculations as we had not yet covered loss carry overs and the lifetime capital gains deduction.

11-153.   As was noted in Chapter 7, the full amount of foreign non-business income earned, including amounts withheld for taxes in the foreign jurisdiction, must be added to the taxpayer's Net Income For Tax Purposes. This 100 percent amount is then subject to Canadian taxes, with the amount withheld in the foreign jurisdiction being allowed as a credit against Canadian Tax Payable. The objective of this procedure is to tax non-business income earned in a foreign jurisdiction at the same overall rate as would apply to non-business income earned in Canada.

11-154.   There are a number of complications with this procedure. The first of these is that, for individuals, amounts withheld that exceed 15 percent of the total foreign non-business income must be deducted under ITA 20(11). If, for example, an individual earned $1,000 in a jurisdiction that withheld $200, $150 of this amount would serve as a credit against Tax Payable, with the remaining $50 being deducted under ITA 20(11).

11-155.   A further problem is that the federal government wants to ensure that taxpayers do not receive a credit that is greater than the Canadian taxes that would have been paid on the foreign non-business income. This is accomplished by limiting the foreign non-business tax credit to the lesser of the amount withheld, and the amount determined by multiplying the ratio of foreign non-business income to total income by Canadian Tax Payable. This approach is reflected in the following formula:

The **Foreign Non-Business Income Tax Credit** is the lesser of:

- The tax paid to the foreign government. For individuals, this is limited to 15 percent of foreign non-business income, and

- An amount determined by the following formula:

$$\left[\frac{\text{Foreign Non} - \text{Business Income}}{\text{Adjusted Division B Income}} \right] [\text{Tax Otherwise Payable}]$$

11-156.   The "Adjusted Division B Income" in this formula is defined as follows:

> Division B Income (i.e., Net Income For Tax Purposes), less:
> - net capital loss carry overs deducted under ITA 111(1)(b);
> - any lifetime capital gains deduction taken;
> - any amounts deductible for stock options under ITA 110(1)(d) and (d.1);
> - any amounts deductible under ITA 110(1)(f) for workers' compensation, social assistance or exempt foreign income; and
> - any amounts deductible under ITA 110(1)(j) for a home relocation loan.

11-157.   "Tax Otherwise Payable" in this calculation consists of:

> Part I Tax Payable before the deduction of:
> - dividend tax credits;
> - employment outside of Canada tax credits;
> - political contributions tax credits;
> - investment tax credits; and
> - labour sponsored funds tax credits.

11-158.   You should note that the preceding definition of Adjusted Division B Income is unique to the calculation of foreign tax credits. It starts with Net Income For Tax Purposes (Division B Income), and proceeds to deduct some, but not all, of an individual's available Division C deductions. For example, if the individual has non-capital loss carry overs, they are not deducted in this calculation. As a result, "Adjusted Division B Income" is a figure that is neither Net Income For Tax Purposes nor Taxable Income.

11-159.   The preceding rules would have to be applied on a country by country basis if non-business income was received from more than one foreign source. If the amount of foreign non-business taxes withheld exceeds the amount determined by the formula, there is no carry over of the unused amount as a tax credit. However, ITA 20(12) allows a taxpayer to deduct such amounts in the determination of Net Income For Tax Purposes.

Foreign Business Income Tax Credit For Individuals

11-160.   If a Canadian resident has income from an unincorporated business in a foreign country, ITA 126(2) provides for a credit for foreign taxes paid that is similar to that for non-business income. As is the case with foreign non-business income tax credits, individuals must include 100 percent of the foreign business income in their Net Income For Tax Purposes, with foreign taxes withheld being allowed as a credit against Tax Payable.

11-161.   While the amount of the credit that can be used does not have the 15 percent limit that is applicable to foreign non-business income tax credits, it is limited by a formula that is similar to the formula applicable to the foreign non-business income tax credit. One of the main differences between these two formulas is that, with respect to the foreign business income tax credit, there is an additional limit based on the tax otherwise payable for the year, reduced by any foreign non-business income tax credit deducted. The calculation of the foreign business income tax credit is as follows:

The **Foreign Business Income Tax Credit** is the least of:

- The tax paid to the foreign government (no 15 percent limit).

- An amount determined by the following formula:

$$\left[\frac{\text{Foreign Business Income}}{\text{Adjusted Division B Income}}\right][\text{Tax Otherwise Payable}]$$

- Tax Otherwise Payable for the year, less any foreign tax credit taken on non-business income under ITA 126(1).

11-162.   A further important difference between the two foreign tax credits is that, when foreign business income taxes paid exceed the amount that can be used as a credit during the current year, there is a three year carry back and ten year carry forward available. That is, if a taxpayer does not have sufficient Tax Payable to use all of the foreign business income tax credit during the current year, the excess can be claimed against Tax Payable in any of the 3 preceding years, or in any of the 10 subsequent years. Note, however, that it can only be used in those years within the constraints provided by the formula in Paragraph 11-161.

Exercise Eleven - 14

Subject: Foreign Tax Credits

During 2013, Sarah Cheung has net rental income of $44,000, net taxable capital gains of $2,500 and foreign non-business income of $3,500. The foreign jurisdiction withheld 11 percent of this amount, resulting in a net receipt of $3,115. In calculating Taxable Income, she deducts a $4,000 non-capital loss carry forward and a $2,500 net capital loss carry forward. Her only tax credits are the basic personal credit and the credit for foreign tax paid. Calculate her federal Tax Payable for 2013. Include a detailed calculation of her foreign non-business income tax credit.

End of Exercise. Solution available in Study Guide.

Alternative Minimum Tax

General Concept

11-163.   There is a strong public feeling that allowing wealthy individuals with high levels of income to pay little or no tax is not an equitable situation. While such cases usually involve no more than taking full advantage of the various provisions in the *Act* that allow individuals to reduce their Tax Payable, the government felt that it was necessary to have legislation in place to deal with this potential problem. As a result, an alternative minimum tax (AMT) was introduced.

11-164   This tax is directed at individuals who take advantage of tax shelters and other "tax preference" items. The basic idea is that individuals who have certain types of income, deductions, or credits, must calculate an adjusted taxable income by adding back all of the "tax preferences" that have been used in the calculation of regular taxable income.

11-165.   After deducting a basic $40,000 exemption, a flat rate of 15 percent is applied to the remaining net adjusted taxable income. The resulting Tax Payable is reduced by some, but not all, of the individual's regular tax credits to arrive at a minimum tax. The taxpayer must pay the greater of the regular Tax Payable and the minimum tax.

Minimum Tax Calculation

Definition

11-166.   The minimum tax is specified in ITA 127.51 as follows:

An individual's minimum amount for a taxation year is the amount determined by the formula

$$A (B - C) - D, \text{ where}$$

A   is the appropriate percentage for the year (15 percent for 2013);
B   is his adjusted taxable income for the year determined under section 127.52;
C   is his basic exemption for the year determined under section 127.53 (currently $40,000); and
D   is his basic minimum tax credit for the year determined under section 127.531.

Adjusted Taxable Income

11-167.   The calculation of adjusted taxable income that is described in ITA 127.52 is illustrated in a somewhat more comprehensible fashion in Form T691. The basic idea behind this adjusted taxable income is to put back into regular taxable income those items that are felt to be "tax preferences". Examples of such preference items would be losses on tax shelters and the non-taxable portion of capital gains.

11-168.   The calculation of adjusted taxable income described in ITA 127.52 is as follows:

Regular Taxable Income

Plus Additions:
- 30 percent of the excess of capital gains over capital losses (see Paragraph 11-169).
- 3/5 of the employee stock option deductions under ITA 110(1)(d) and (d.1).
- The home relocation loan deduction.
- Losses arising through the deduction of CCA on Certified Canadian Films.
- The excess of CCA and interest charges claimed on rental and leasing property, over the net income reported for such property.
- Losses arising as a result of Canadian Exploration Expense (CEE), Canadian Development Expense (CDE), or depletion, net of certain resource related income.
- Losses deducted by limited partners, and members of a partnership who have been specified members at all times since becoming partners, in respect of their partnership interests, net of certain gains allocated from the same partnership.
- Losses deducted in respect of investments identified or required to be identified under the tax shelter identification rules.

Less Deductions:
- The gross up of Canadian dividends.
- 60 percent of ABILs deducted (see Paragraph 11-170).

Equals: Adjusted Taxable Income For Minimum Tax Purposes

11-169.   Rather than require that all of the non-taxable component of capital gains be added back, which could result in an excessive number of taxpayers being exposed to alternative minimum tax, only 30 percent of the total capital gain is added in the Adjusted Taxable Income calculation. This brings the total inclusion of the excess of capital gains over capital losses to 80 percent (50 percent is already included in regular income, plus the additional 30 percent).

11-170.   The government also decided that this 80 percent treatment was appropriate for ABILs. The Adjusted Taxable Income calculation requires an additional deduction of 60 percent of any ABILs deducted in the year. Since 60 percent of an ABIL is equal to 30 percent of the total Business Investment Loss and 50 percent is already deducted from regular income, this effectively provides for a total deduction equal to 80 percent of the Business Investment Loss.

Tax Payable Before Credits
11-171.   A basic exemption is subtracted from the adjusted taxable income figure. This basic exemption is specified in ITA 127.53. Since the introduction of the AMT, this amount has been $40,000.

11-172.   After subtraction of the basic exemption, a flat rate is applied to the resulting balance. This rate is referred to in the ITA 127.51 formula as the "appropriate percentage". Appropriate percentage is defined in ITA 248 as the lowest percentage applicable in calculating federal Tax Payable. For 2013, this rate is 15 percent. The resulting figure could be described as the alternative minimum tax before the deduction of tax credits.

Tax Credits For AMT
11-173.   ITA 127.531 specifies the tax credits, as calculated for the determination of regular Tax Payable, which can be applied against the alternative minimum tax. The credits specified are as follows:

- Personal credits under ITA 118(1)
- Age credit under ITA 118(2), but not the transfer from a spouse
- Canada employment credit under ITA 118(10)
- Adoption expenses credit under ITA 118.01
- Transit pass credit under ITA 118.02
- Child fitness credit under ITA 118.03
- Children's arts credit under ITA 118.031
- Volunteer firefighter's credit under ITA 118.06
- Charitable donations credit under ITA 118.1
- Medical expense credit under ITA 118.2
- Disability credit under ITA 118.3, but not the transfer from a spouse or other dependant
- Education, textbook, tuition, and interest on student loans credits under ITA 118.5, 118.6 and 118.62, but not the transfer from a spouse or other dependant
- CPP and EI credits under ITA 118.7

11-174.   The deduction of these credits will produce the alternative minimum tax payable. If this amount exceeds the regular taxes that are payable on the regular taxable income, the amount of alternative tax must be paid.

AMT Carry Forward - ITA 120.2

11-175.   There will be individuals who become subject to this alternative minimum tax in only some taxation years. The most common example of this situation is the realization of a large capital gain that can be eliminated by the use of the lifetime capital gains deduction.

11-176.   To provide for this, an excess of alternative minimum tax over regular Tax Payable can be carried forward for up to seven years to be applied against any future excess of regular Tax Payable over the alternative minimum tax.

Exercise Eleven - 15

Subject: Alternative Minimum Tax

Mr. Norton Blouson has Taxable Income for 2013 of $85,000. This includes taxable capital gains of $22,500 and taxable eligible dividends of $27,600 [(138%)($20,000)]. In addition, he received a $50,000 retiring allowance that was contributed to his RRSP. The full contribution was deductible. His only tax credits are the basic personal credit and the dividend tax credit. Determine whether Mr. Blouson would have a liability for alternative minimum tax and, if so, the total amount of such tax.

End of Exercise. Solution available in Study Guide.

We suggest you work Self Study Problems Eleven-6 through Eleven-11.

Sample Comprehensive Personal Tax Return

11-177.   In the separate paper Study Guide, there is a comprehensive example containing a completed personal tax return, as well as a Tax Software Self Study Problem, included in the material for Chapter 11. The sample return illustrates the tax savings possible through pension income splitting.

Key Terms Used In This Chapter

11-178.   The following is a list of the key terms used in this Chapter. These terms, and their meanings, are compiled in the Glossary Of Key Terms located at the back of the separate paper Study Guide.

Active Business	Loss Carry Back
Active Business Income	Loss Carry Forward
Adjusted Taxable Income	Lump-Sum Payments
Allowable Business Investment Loss	Net Capital Loss
Alternative Minimum Tax (AMT)	Net Income For Tax Purposes
Annual Gains Limit	Non-Capital Loss
Business Investment Loss	Ordering Rule
Carry Over	Personal Use Property
Charitable Donations Tax Credit	Purification Of A
Charitable Gifts	Small Business Corporation
Crown Gifts	Qualified Farm Property
Cultural Gifts	Qualified Fishing Property
Cumulative Gains Limit	Qualified Small Business Corporation
Cumulative Net Investment Loss	Restricted Farm Loss
Ecological Gifts	Small Business Corporation
Farm Property	Specified Individual
Fishing Property	Split Income
Foreign Taxes Paid Credit	Stock Option
Lifetime Capital Gains Deduction	Taxable Income
Listed Personal Property	

References

11-179.   For more detailed study of the material in this Chapter, we would refer you to the following:

ITA 82(3)	Dividends Received By Spouse Of Common-Law Partner
ITA 110	Deductions Permitted
ITA 110.6	Lifetime Capital Gains Deduction
ITA 111	Losses Deductible
ITA 111.1	Order Of Applying Provisions
ITA 118.1	Charitable Gifts
ITA 120.2	Minimum Tax Carry Over
ITA 127.5 To 127.55	Obligation To Pay Minimum Tax
IC 75-23	Tuition Fees And Charitable Donations Paid To Privately Supported Secular and Religious Schools
IC 84-3R6	Gifts To Certain Organizations Outside Canada
S5-F2-C1	Foreign Tax Credit
IT-110R3	Gifts And Official Donation Receipts
IT-113R4	Benefits To Employees — Stock Options
IT-226R	Gift To A Charity Of A Residual Interest In Real Property Or An Equitable Interest In A Trust
IT-232R3	Losses - Their Deductibility In The Loss Years Or In Other Years
IT-244R3	Gifts By Individuals Of Life Insurance Policies As Charitable Donations
IT-288R2	Gifts Of Capital Properties To A Charity And Others
IT-295R4	Taxable Dividends Received After 1987 By A Spouse
IT-322R	Farm Losses
IT-520	Unused Foreign Tax Credits - Carry Forward And Carry Back
IT-523	Order Of Provisions Applicable In Computing An Individual's Taxable Income And Tax Payable

Sample Tax Return For Chapter 11

The Chapter 11 Sample Tax Return can be found in the Study Guide beginning on page S-228.

Problems For Self Study

(The solutions for these problems can be found in the separate Study Guide.)

NOTE   The **Tax Software Self Study Problem** for Chapter 11 is available in the separate Study Guide on page S-236.

Self Study Problem Eleven - 1 (Allowable Business Investment Losses)

During 2009, Miss Lynn Atwater invested $170,000 to acquire 100 percent of the common shares of a corporation specializing in pet food products. The company was a Canadian controlled private corporation with a fiscal year ending on January 31. All of its assets were used to produce active business income in Canada.

In 2010 and 2011, the company operated successfully, but did not pay any dividends. In 2012, it began to experience serious financial difficulties. On July 15, 2013, the company was forced into bankruptcy by its creditors and it is clear to Miss Atwater that, after the claims of the creditors have been dealt with, her investment will be worthless.

Other financial data for Miss Atwater for the years ending December 31, 2012 and December 31, 2013, is as follows:

	2012	2013
Net rental income	$34,200	$35,200
Interest income	4,000	4,200
Basic personal tax credit amount	10,822	11,038

The only tax credit available to Miss Atwater in either year is the basic personal credit. Miss Atwater had no income for 2010 and 2011. At the beginning of 2011, she did not have any loss carry forwards from previous years.

Required: Determine Miss Atwater's optimum Taxable Income for the years ending December 31, 2012 and December 31, 2013. In your solution, consider the effect of the basic personal credit. Indicate any loss carry over that is present at the end of either year, and the rules applicable to claiming the loss carry over.

Self Study Problem Eleven - 2 (Loss Carry Overs - Individuals)

Over a four year period ending on December 31, 2013, Mr. Edward Fox experienced the following income and losses:

	2010	2011	2012	2013
Employment Income	$18,000	$16,000	$19,000	$12,000
Business Income (Loss)	14,500	(39,000)	34,000	(52,000)
Farming Income (Loss)	(6,000)	Nil	8,000	(2,000)
Taxable (Grossed Up) Dividends	6,250	8,156	10,000	12,656
Capital Gains	Nil	7,400	6,300	Nil
Capital Losses	(3,600)	Nil	Nil	(6,000)

Both the business operation and the farming operation began in 2010. With respect to the farming operation, Mr. Fox expects to make some profit on this operation even though it is not a full time occupation for him. The dividend income is from taxable Canadian corporations and the amount includes the gross up.

When he has a choice, he would like to deduct the maximum amount of his net capital loss carry overs and carry back any losses to the earliest possible year. None of Mr. Fox's losses can be carried back to years prior to 2010.

Assume that Mr. Fox requires $15,000 in Taxable Income in each year to fully utilize his tax credits.

Required: For each of the four years, calculate the minimum Net Income For Tax Purposes and Taxable Income for Mr. Fox. In applying carry over amounts, do not reduce Mr. Fox's Taxable Income below the amount required to fully utilize his tax credits. Indicate the amended figures for any years to which losses are carried back. Also indicate the amount and types of loss carry overs that would be available to Mr. Fox at the end of each year.

Self Study Problem Eleven - 3 (Lifetime Capital Gains Deduction)

At the beginning of 2013, Harold Cox had an $8,900 [(1/2)($17,800)] net capital loss carry forward from 2012. His 2013 net employment income amounted to $76,000.

During the year 2013 Mr. Cox had the following:

- a capital gain of $75,000 on the sale of shares of a qualified small business corporation.
- a $32,000 capital loss on the sale of a tract of land.

Mr. Cox paid interest of $17,000 in 2013 on a loan for the investment in the shares of a Canadian controlled private corporation. These shares paid no dividends in 2013. His investment expenses and investment income prior to 2013 were nil.

In 2011, Mr. Cox had a capital gain of $5,000 which was eliminated through the use of the lifetime capital gains deduction. He has made no other use of the ITA 110.6 tax provisions.

Mr. Cox would prefer to make maximum use of his lifetime capital gains deduction prior to applying any net capital loss carry forwards.

Required: Calculate Mr. Cox's minimum Net Income For Tax Purposes and Taxable Income for 2013. Provide all of the calculations required to determine the maximum ITA 110.6 deduction. In addition, briefly explain why Mr. Cox would prefer using his lifetime capital gains deduction rather than his net capital loss carry forward.

Self Study Problem Eleven - 4
(Transfer Of Credits And Pension Income Splitting)

Mr. and Mrs. Bahry have been retired for several years. They are both in their early seventies, residents of Canada, and rely on pension income to provide for most of their needs. More specifically, the components of their income for the year ending December 31, 2013 are as follows:

	Mr. Bahry	Mrs. Bahry
Old Age Security Benefits	$ 6,550	$6,550
Receipts From Registered Pension Plan	12,340	820
Receipts From Registered Retirement Income Fund	N/A	1,000
Canada Pension Plan Receipts	3,690	830
Eligible Dividends Received From Canadian Public Corporations (100%)	1,600	336
Interest On Savings Accounts	1,239	2,500
Charitable Donations*	1,210	300
Capital Gain On Sale Of Painting	N/A	500
Capital Loss On Sale Of Public Company Shares	3,975	820

*Because they have made regular contributions to registered charities in previous years, the Bahry's are not eligible for the first-time donor's super credit.

Required:

A. Assume that Mr. and Mrs. Bahry do not elect to use the pension income splitting provisions. Determine the Taxable Income for both Mr. and Mrs. Bahry and the maximum federal tax credits that will be available to Mr. Bahry for the 2013 taxation year. Also indicate the amount and types of any loss carry overs that would be available to Mr. and Mrs. Bahry at the end of 2013.

B. If Mr. and Mrs. Bahry jointly elect to split the pension income, what objectives should they try to accomplish with the pension income split? (No calculations are required.)

Self Study Problem Eleven - 5
(Comprehensive Tax Credits With Dividend Transfer)

Mr. and Mrs. Dalton have been retired for several years. They are both in their early seventies, residents of Canada, and rely on pension income to provide for most of their needs. Mr. Dalton is sufficiently disabled that he qualifies for the disability tax credit (he has the required signed Form T2201).

The components of their income for the year ending December 31, 2013 are as follows:

	Mr. Dalton	Mrs. Dalton
Old Age Security Benefits	$ 6,550	$6,550
Receipts From Registered Pension Plan	Nil	62,000
RRIF Receipts	1,640	12,420
Interest On Government Bonds	1,420	2,580
Non-Eligible Dividends Received From		
A CCPC (100 Percent Amount)	3,420	460
Charitable Donations*	350	960

*As they have made regular contributions to charities in past years, the Daltons are not eligible for the first-time donor's super credit.

Assume that Mr. and Mrs. Dalton do not elect to use the pension income splitting provisions.

Required:

A. Calculate Mr. and Mrs. Dalton's 2013 minimum federal Tax Payable and any social benefits repayment assuming that no transfer of dividends is made under ITA 82(3).

B. Determine whether a transfer of dividends under ITA 82(3) would be permitted.

C. Calculate Mr. and Mrs. Dalton's 2013 minimum federal Tax Payable and any social benefits repayment assuming that all of Mr. Dalton's dividends are transferred to Mrs. Dalton under ITA 82(3). Comment on whether the dividend transfer should be done.

Self Study Problem Eleven - 6
(Alternative Minimum Tax And RRSP Calculations)

Cheryl Delancey, a tax consultant, has provided tax assistance on a regular basis to her two aunts, Alma and Irene Delancey. For the 2013 taxation year, Cheryl and her aunts are concerned about the impact of the alternative minimum tax on the amount of tax they will have to pay. In order to estimate the tax that will be payable, they each have estimated the amounts and types of income they expect to earn, and deductions to claim, for 2013. These estimates are as follows:

	Cheryl	Alma	Irene
Employment And Business Income	$60,800	$42,000	$ 22,900
Non-Eligible Dividends Received			
From Canadian Corporations	26,300	Nil	29,400
Taxable Capital Gains	9,100	Nil	450,000
Lifetime Capital Gains Deduction Claimed	9,100	Nil	375,000
Retiring Allowance	Nil	58,000	Nil
RRSP Contributions	3,500	58,000	Nil

On Cheryl's 2012 T4, a Pension Adjustment of $8,600 was reported. Assume that her 2012 Earned Income equals her 2013 Earned Income. She has no Unused RRSP Deduction Room or undeducted RRSP contributions at the end of 2012.

As Alma had worked for her present employer for over 46 years, she is eligible for a tax free rollover of the entire retiring allowance to an RRSP.

All taxable capital gains relate to the sale of shares of qualified small business corporations.

Assume the only tax credits available to the Delancey women are their basic personal tax credits and dividend tax credits related to dividends received.

Required: Calculate the minimum regular 2013 federal Tax Payable for each of the three women, as well as the alternative minimum tax amount.

Self Study Problem Eleven - 7 (Comprehensive Personal Tax Payable)

Ms. Linda Worthmore is employed by Intra Graphics Inc. and, for the year ending December 31, 2013, she has a gross salary of $73,532. The following amounts were withheld by her employer during the year:

Canada Pension Plan Contributions	$2,356
Employment Insurance Premiums	891
Registered Pension Plan Contributions	1,233
Donations To Registered Charities	342

During 2013, Intra Graphics Inc. paid the following amounts on behalf of Ms. Worthmore:

Premium For Private Drug Plan	$ 415
Premium For Private Extended Health Care	235

Ms. Worthmore is married and lives with her husband, Mr. John Dalton. During 2013, Mr. Dalton received $750 in interest on a five year term deposit and had earnings from part time employment of $2,475. No CPP or EI payments were deducted from this income.

Mr. Dalton was a full time student at a designated educational institution during four months of the year. His tuition fees, which were paid by Ms. Worthmore, were $2,300. His fees for dental work totalled $1,056 for 2013 and were paid by Ms. Worthmore.

Ms. Worthmore and her husband have three children, all of whom live at home. Relevant information on these children is as follows:

Joyce   Joyce is 7 years of age and has no income of her own. During 2013, Ms. Worthmore was required to pay $2,200 in medical expenses for Joyce.

Jayne   Jayne is 14 years of age and had earnings from part time employment of $1,225. On March 15, 2013, Ms. Worthmore gave her daughter 27 shares of a publicly traded Canadian company. The shares had cost Ms. Worthmore $18 per share and, at the time of the gift, they were trading at $27 per share. The shares paid no dividends during 2013 and are still held by Jayne on December 31, 2013.

June   June is 17 years of age and, during 2013, had income of $5,000. In July, 2013, June was involved in a serious accident. As a result of the accident, Ms. Worthmore was required to pay $9,850 of medical expenses on June's behalf.

Other Information:

1. In 2012, Ms. Worthmore gave her husband 52 shares of a publicly traded Canadian company. Ms. Worthmore had acquired the shares at $12 per share and, at the time of the gift, the shares were trading at $32 per share. She did not elect out of ITA 73(1). On June 15, 2013, the shares paid an eligible dividend of $3.50 per share. On August 31, 2013, Mr. Dalton sold these shares for $56 per share.

2. Ms. Worthmore is the sole shareholder of Lindworth Inc. This Canadian controlled private corporation has a December 31 year end and, during 2013, paid non-eligible dividends in the total amount of $4,325 to Ms. Worthmore. As an employee of this Company, she received a salary of $2,500 for the year. No CPP or EI payments were deducted from the salary.

3. Under the provisions of a court decree, Ms. Worthmore pays spousal support to her former husband in the amount of $225 per month.

4. During 2013, Ms. Worthmore made contributions to a Registered Retirement Savings Plan in the amount of $7,500. A Pension Adjustment of $6,351 was reported on her 2012 T4. Assume that her 2012 Earned Income equals her 2013 Earned Income. At the end of 2012, she has no Unused RRSP Deduction Room or undeducted RRSP contributions.

5. During 2013, Ms. Worthmore sold 122 shares of Lackmere Ltd. at a price of $86 per share. Ms. Worthmore owned a total of 300 shares of this Company, having acquired 122 at a price of $92, and the other 178 at a price of $71 per share. Lackmere is not a qualified small business corporation.

6. During 2013, Ms. Worthmore sold land to her older brother for $10,000. The land had a fair market value of $28,000 and had been acquired by Ms. Worthmore for $10,000 four years ago. The land had been rented out to local farmers for agricultural use. The land is not a qualified farm property.

7. During 2013, Ms. Worthmore makes contributions to the federal Liberal party in the amount of $100.

8. Because Ms. Worthmore makes regular contributions to registered charities, she is not eligible for the first-time donor's super credit.

Required:

A. Calculate Ms. Worthmore's minimum Net Income For Tax Purposes for the year ending December 31, 2013. Provide separate totals for employment income, property income, taxable capital gains, and other income and deductions.

B. Calculate Ms. Worthmore's minimum Taxable Income for the year ending December 31, 2013.

C. Calculate Ms. Worthmore's minimum federal Tax Payable for the year ending December 31, 2013. Ignore GST and PST considerations, as well as income tax payments that were made by Ms. Worthmore through instalments or withholding.

Self Study Problem Eleven - 8 *(Comprehensive Personal Tax Payable)*

The following information relates to Michael Slater for the year ending December 31, 2013:

Receipts

Gross Salary From Slater Inc.	$ 35,000
Revenue From Farming	36,000
Drawings From Proprietorship	9,000
Interest On Savings Account	4,450
Winnings From Gambling	1,600
Canada Pension Plan Benefits	5,100

Problems For Self Study

Receipts, continued

Loans To Friends:		
Interest Received	$12,000	
Principal Repaid	21,000	33,000
Cash Inheritance From Deceased Aunt		25,000
Eligible Dividends From Canadian Public Corporations (100%)		44,000
Dividends From U.S. Corporations -		
Net Of 15 Percent Withholding (Canadian Dollars)		8,500
Proceeds From Sale Of Land		111,500
Total Receipts		**$313,150**

Disbursements

Farm Expenses	$ 45,000
Personal Funds Invested In Proprietorship	42,000
Interest Paid On Bank Loan	2,300
Funds Spent Gambling	1,000
Life Insurance Premiums	11,000
Mortgage Payments On Personal Residence	15,000
Charitable Donations	2,700
Contributions To Federal Conservative Party	500
Total Disbursements	**$119,500**

Other Information:

1. Mr. Slater is 71 years old. His wife is 61 and has been blind for several years. She is in ill health and has no income of her own.

2. Mr. Slater owns 45 percent of the shares of Slater Inc., the corporation that employs him. As a result, no EI premiums were withheld. Since Mr. Slater is over 70 years old, he does not have deductions from salary for CPP or owe them on his proprietorship income.

3. Mr. Slater's organic farming operation is a sideline that he started a year ago, believing organic produce would improve his wife's health. With his vast business experience, he is confident he can make the operation profitable within another year.

4. The proprietorship began operations on May 1, 2013 and has a fiscal year end of December 31. The proprietorship had net business income, determined in accordance with the *Income Tax Act*, of $28,300 for the period May 1 to December 31, 2013. The bank loan on which interest was paid was used to finance Mr. Slater's investment in the proprietorship. The interest was not deducted in the calculation of net business income.

5. The land that was sold during 2013 was purchased at a cost of $23,000 three years ago. Mr. Slater had intended to build a cottage on it.

6. For the last several years, Mr. Slater has had consistently high levels of income and, as a consequence, the full $6,550 of Old Age Security benefits has been withheld. However, as he did apply for and receive OAS benefits in a previous year, the government continues to issue an information slip, a T4A(OAS), which shows both the taxable OAS paid and the OAS withheld as $6,550.

7. Because he makes regular contributions to registered charities, Mr. Slater is not eligible for the first-time donor's super credit.

Required: Calculate Mr. Slater's minimum federal Amount Owing (including any social benefits repayment) for the year ending December 31, 2013. Ignore GST and PST considerations, as well as any income tax payments that were made by Mr. Slater through instalments or employment income withholding. Include in your solution any carry overs that are available at the end of 2013.

Self Study Problem Eleven - 9 (Death Of A Taxpayer)

On June 3, 2013, Andrea Steele unexpectedly died of complications associated with minor surgery. Her husband, a man with little experience in financial matters, has asked you to assist him with the administration of Mrs. Steele's estate. After working with her records for several days, you have accumulated the following information:

1. Mrs. Steele has a net capital loss carry forward from 2008 of $76,500.

2. During 2013, but prior to the date of her death, Mrs. Steele's investments paid eligible dividends of $1,090. In addition, she had Canadian source interest income of $2,025 during this period.

3. Mrs. Steele was the proprietor of a successful boutique that had been in operation for eight years. The fiscal year of this unincorporated business ends on December 31. From January 1, 2013, until the date of Mrs. Steele's death, this business had net business income for tax purposes of $55,200. The fair market value of the assets of the boutique at the time of Mrs. Steele's death was $4,800 greater than their UCC. None of the individual assets had a fair market value that exceeded its capital cost.

4. In connection with the boutique, Mrs. Steele paid Mr. Steele wages of $425 during the period January 1, 2013 through June 3, 2013. This money was paid for assistance in handling the inventories of the operation. Mr. Steele's only other income for the year was $2,100 in interest on a group of mortgages, which had been given to him as a gift by Mrs. Steele three years ago.

5. Mrs. Steele had a rental property that she had owned for a number of years. Rents received in 2013, prior to her death, amounted to $41,200, while cash expenses totalled $24,650. The UCC of the building was $144,800 on January 1, 2013. The building had been purchased for $183,000. At the time of her death, an appraisal indicated that the fair market value of the building was $235,000. The land on which the building is situated has a cost of $92,000, and a fair market value at the time of her death that is estimated to be $164,000.

6. Other assets that were owned by Mrs. Steele at the time of her death are as follows:

    Shares In AGF Industries   AGF Industries is a Canadian public company and Mrs. Steele purchased common shares at a cost of $10,600. Their value at the time of Mrs. Steele's death was $7,900.

    Shares In Rolston Inc.   Rolston Inc. is also a Canadian public company and Mrs. Steele purchased shares at a cost of $36,800. Their value at the time of Mrs. Steele's death was $169,400.

    Painting   A painting Mrs. Steele had purchased for $8,000 had a fair market value of $37,000 at the time of her death.

    Residence   Mrs. Steele owned the family home. It had been purchased at a cost of $209,400. At the time of her death, the appraised value of the property was $344,000.

7. The terms of Mrs. Steele's will provide that the shares in AGF Industries and Rolston Inc., the painting, and the assets of the boutique be left to Mr. Steele. The family home and the rental property are to be left to Mrs. Steele's 27 year old daughter.

Required: Calculate Mrs. Steele's minimum Net Income For Tax Purposes for the 2013 taxation year, her minimum Taxable income for that year, and her 2013 federal Tax Payable.

Self Study Problem Eleven - 10 (Comprehensive Personal Tax Payable)

This is an extension of the Tax Software Self Study Problem for Chapter 11 that is available in the Study Guide on page S-236. It has been updated for 2013 rates. This Problem is also a continuation of Self Study Problem Four-5.

Problems For Self Study

Ms. Eleanor Victoria's husband died two years ago. After her husband died, she moved from her house in Prince George, B.C., to a rented house in Victoria, B.C.

Ms. Victoria's widowed mother, Marjorie Toshiro, lives with Ms. Victoria and takes care of the house, Ms. Victoria's younger daughter, Amy, and all of the household cooking. In addition to OAS benefits, Marjorie has a small income from her deceased husband's life insurance policy. She has never filed a tax return.

Diane Victoria, Eleanor's older daughter, is studying psychology at McGill University in Montreal. Her field is addiction research with a special emphasis on gambling. She does volunteer work at a gambling addiction treatment centre in Montreal in the summers. As Eleanor has paid for her tuition and living costs, Diane has agreed that any credits available should be transferred to her mother.

Diane has decided not to file a tax return this year as she is too busy with her studies and volunteer work. Her income was earned driving for a client of the addiction treatment centre who had lost his licence after being charged with impaired driving.

Late in December, 2013, Eleanor was notified that she had inherited $500,000 from an aunt. Eleanor loves her work and though she plans to travel more, she has no plans to retire.

Other information concerning Eleanor for 2013 is as follows:

1. Eleanor was born on May 15, 1965.

2. The birth dates and Net Income For Tax Purposes of her dependants are as follows:

	Birth Date (Y/M/D)	Net Income
Diane	1993-05-14	$2,300
Amy	2001-10-11	Nil
Marjorie	1932-05-21	$8,000

3. Eleanor's T4 for 2013 showed the following:

Salary	$60,202
Employee's EI Premiums	891
Employee's CPP Contributions	2,356
RPP Contributions	2,406
Pension Adjustment	7,829
Income Tax Deducted	11,408
Union Dues	749
Charitable Donations	175

4. Eleanor paid for the following medical expenses for 2013 :

Patient	Medical Expenses	Description	Amount
Eleanor	Grace Hospital	Ambulance Charge	$ 392
Eleanor	Paramed Home Health	Nursing Care	1,350
Marjorie	Dr. Zhang (Optometrist)	Contact Lenses	110
Marjorie	Pharmacy	Prescription	75
Diane	Dr. Glassman	Physiotherapist	100
Amy	Walk Right Foot Clinic	Orthotics	450
Amy	Dr. Tamo	Dental Fees	1,120
Total			$3,597

5. In addition to the $175 in charitable contributions withheld by Eleanor's employer, Eleanor and Diane had the following charitable donations for 2013:

Donor	Charitable Donation Receipts	Amount
Eleanor	Heart And Stroke	$ 375
Eleanor	Terry Fox Foundation	50
Diane	Addiction Research Council Of Canada	100

Because of donations in previous years, neither Diane nor Eleanor qualify for the first-time donor's super credit.

6. During 2013, Diane was in university full time for 8 months and part time for an additional 2 months. Her tuition fees for the year were $7,000.

7. Eleanor's T3 showed capital gains of $982 and foreign interest (non-business) income of $311. No foreign taxes were withheld.

8. The pension from Eleanor's previous employer totalled $22,249. Income tax deducted from the pension payments totalled $3,511.

9. Eleanor's CPP survivor benefits totaled $4,823. These benefits are fully taxable.

10. Eleanor received two T5s. The Scotia Bank T5 had interest from Canadian sources of $509. The Bank of Montreal T5 had a taxable amount of eligible dividends of $2,212 (dividends received of $1,603, plus a gross up of $609).

11. Eleanor made an RRSP contribution of $2,620 on February 10, 2014. Her Earned Income for 2012 was $38,873 and her Pension Adjustment for 2012 was $4,376. She had unused deduction room of $1,665 from 2012 and no undeducted contributions.

12. Eleanor sent Amy to the Croft Computer Camp for 2 weeks (14 days overnight). The cost was $1,000. In addition, Amy attended the Y Day Camp for 3 weeks during July, 2013. The cost was $400. Neither of the camps would issue a receipt that qualified for either the child fitness credit or the children's arts credit.

13. Eleanor did not sell her house in Prince George when she moved to Victoria as it was her intention to move back into it within three years. It has been rented on a month-to-month lease since November, 2012. She claimed a rental loss of $4,250 in 2012. The revenues, costs, and expenditures related to her Prince George rented house for 2013 are as follows:

Gross Rents	$15,600
Property Taxes	2,190
Insurance	1,093
Interest On Mortgage	5,378
Payment On Principal	3,689
Plumbing Repairs	291
Snow Plow Annual Contract	300
Lawyer's Fees For New Lease	173
Hydro (During Vacancy)	288
Cost Of Building And UCC - Beginning Of Year	168,900
UCC Of Appliances - Beginning Of Year	921
Purchase Of Stove And Refrigerator During Year	
(Old Appliances Were Traded-In)	1,500

14. Assume that Eleanor's provincial tax payable is $4,500 for 2013.

Required:

A. Calculate Eleanor's minimum combined federal/provincial Tax Payable (Refund) for 2013. List any assumptions you have made, and any notes and tax planning issues you feel should be discussed with Eleanor.

B. Calculate the maximum deductible contribution Eleanor can make to her RRSP for the 2014 taxation year. What advice would you give Eleanor concerning the various deferred savings plans available to her given the funds from her inheritance?

Self Study Problem Eleven - 11
(Comprehensive Personal Tax Payable Including Death)

At the beginning of 2013, Ms. Katherine O'Hara is 46 years old and married to Mick O'Hara. She dies in an automobile accident on December 31, 2013. Mick is the executor of her estate. He is a stockbroker and, during 2013, his Net Income For Tax Purposes is $153,000.

Problems For Self Study

Katherine and Mick had two children. Their son Sean is 15 years old and their daughter Sylvia is 20 years old. While Sylvia lives at home throughout 2013, she attends a local university on a full time basis for 11 months during 2013. Her tuition fees for the year total $8,150 and were paid for by her mother.

Medical expenses for Katherine and her family during 2013 were as follows:

Katherine	$3,700
Mick	2,420
Sean	300
Sylvia	2,360
Total	$8,780

Mick's medical plan reimburses him for 50 percent of his medical expenses, as well as those of Katherine and Sean.

Ms. O'Hara was employed by a large publicly traded company. Her salary for 2013 was $85,000. Her only employment benefit is a $150,000 interest free loan that was provided by her employer in 2012. The loan was granted to assist Katherine with the purchase of a larger home (it does not qualify as a home relocation loan). Assume that, at the time the loan was granted, the prescribed rate was 1 percent. The loan must be repaid on January 1, 2014.

Her employer withheld the following amounts from her income during 2013:

RPP Contributions	$2,875
EI Premiums	891
CPP Contributions	2,356

Katherine's employer makes a matching contribution of $2,875 to her RPP account.

On January 1, 2013, Katherine owned two Class 1 residential rental properties. Information on these properties is as follows:

	Property A	**Property B**
Capital Cost - Building	$326,000	$347,000
UCC	297,000	311,000
Adjusted Cost Base - Land	50,000	60,000
December 31, 2013 Fair Market Value:		
Building	395,000	495,000
Land	75,000	60,000
2013 Rents	26,400	28,800
2013 Expenses Other Than CCA	23,500	23,100

The family's principal residence was also owned by Katherine. It was acquired in 2012 for $472,000. There is no other property that can be designated as a principal residence in either 2012 or 2013.

On January 1, 2013, Katherine owned the following securities:

	Original Cost	**Adjusted Cost Base**
10,000 Shares Of Darcy Inc.		
(A Canadian Public Company)	$120,000	$120,000
12,000 Units Of Barton Income Trust	201,000	180,000
8,000 Units of Fidel Mutual Fund	60,000	72,000

Other information related to these investments is as follows:

1. On January 2, 2013, when the Darcy Inc. shares were trading at $14 per share, Katherine gifted 2,500 shares of Darcy Inc. to each of her two children. An additional 2,500 shares were sold to her daughter Sylvia at their market value of $14 per share. Sylvia finances the

acquisition with funds that she acquired with a winning lottery ticket. The remaining 2,500 shares are gifted to her husband Mick. None of these shares are resold during the year.

2. During July 2013, the Darcy Inc. shares pay eligible dividends of $0.90 per share.

3. The Barton Income Trust's annual distribution for 2013 is $1.50 per share. Of this amount, $0.50 is designated a return of capital.

4. During April, 2013, the Fidel Mutual Fund has a 2013 distribution of interest income of $1.00 per unit. This amount is reinvested in additional units at $10.00, the net asset value per unit on that date.

On January 1, 2013, Katherine had a net capital loss from 2008 of $10,000 [(1/2)($20,000)].

At the beginning of the year, neither child owns any investments. The only income either child has during 2013 is any income from the Darcy Inc. shares.

Katherine's will contains the following provisions:

- Her son Sean will receive the family's principal residence. At December 31, 2013, it is estimated that the fair market value of this property is $510,000. In addition, Sean will receive one-half of the Barton Income Trust units. On December 31, 2013, these units are trading at $17.50 per unit.

- Her daughter Sylvia will receive rental property B. In addition, Sylvia will receive the remaining one-half of the Barton Income Trust units.

- Her husband Mick will receive rental property A. Mick will also receive the Fidel Mutual Fund units. On December 31, 2013, these units have a net asset value of $8.30 per unit.

In discussions with the family accountant in early 2014, Mick agrees that the 2013 family medical expenses and any credits or transfers related to either child will be claimed on Katherine's return.

In order to pay for the accountant's fees, Mick sells both the rental property A and all of the Fidel Mutual Fund units in January, 2014 for their December 31, 2013 fair market values.

Assume the prescribed rate for the first quarter of 2013 is 1 percent, increasing to 2 percent in the second and subsequent quarters of the year.

Required:

A. Calculate Katherine O'Hara's minimum 2013 Net Income For Tax Purposes, her 2013 minimum Taxable Income, and her minimum 2013 federal Tax Payable without consideration of any income tax withholdings her employer may have made.

B. Calculate the Net Income For Tax Purposes that will result from Mick O'Hara's sale of the rental property and fund units.

Ignore GST and PST considerations.

Assignment Problems

(The solutions for these problems are only available in the solutions manual that has been provided to your instructor.)

Assignment Problem Eleven - 1 (Loss Carry Overs - Individual)

Over a four year period ending on December 31, 2013, Mr. Bob Barkin had the following financial data:

Assignment Problems

	2010	2011	2012	2013
Property Income (Loss)	$27,600	($22,250)	$44,100	($30,800)
Farming Income (Loss)	(12,200)	2,320	3,840	(2,400)
Non-Eligible Dividends Received	3,120	4,120	5,980	8,720
Gross Up Of Non-Eligible Dividends	780	1,030	1,495	2,180
Capital Gains	1,800	3,000	6,000	6,700
Capital Losses	(9,200)	Nil	Nil	(21,300)

Because of the nature of his farming activities, Mr. Barkin's farm losses are restricted.

When he has a choice, he would like to deduct the maximum amount of his net capital loss carry overs and carry back any losses to the earliest possible year. None of Mr. Barkin's losses can be carried back before 2010 as he has had no income in the previous three years.

Assume that Mr. Barkin requires $18,500 in Taxable Income in each year to fully utilize his tax credits. As a result, Mr. Barkin's Taxable Income should not be reduced below $18,500 when applying loss carry over amounts.

Required: Calculate Mr. Barkin's minimum Net Income For Tax Purposes and Taxable Income for each of the four years. Indicate the amended figures for any years to which losses are carried back. Also indicate the amount and types of loss carry overs that would be available at the end of each year.

Assignment Problem Eleven - 2 (Allowable Business Investment Losses)

In 2011, Ms. Dotty Parker inherited a substantial fortune. Having been a penniless performance artist prior to this, she had never had funds to invest before this time. On the advice of a friend, she invested a small portion of her inheritance in rental real estate and the shares of various growth companies.

As the result of a disposition in December, 2011, Dotty had a taxable capital gain of $25,000, all of which was eliminated through the use of the lifetime capital gains deduction.

Dotty also invested $425,000 in the shares of Spec Inc., a qualified small business corporation. While it made a small amount of money in its first year of operations in 2011, it had serious losses in 2012. The shares paid no dividends in either 2011 or 2012.

During 2013, the directors of Spec Inc. concluded that there was no hope of recovery for the business, resulting in a decision to liquidate the Company. After the claims of the creditors were settled, Dotty's shares were canceled and she received a final payment of $125,000.

During 2012 and 2013, Dotty had the following amounts of income:

	2012	2013
Taxable Capital Gains	$ 5,000	$ 6,000
Net Rental Income	16,000	14,000
Interest Income	36,000	24,000

The only tax credit available to Dotty in either year is the basic personal credit ($10,822 in 2012 and $11,038 in 2013). Dotty had no income in 2010 and Taxable Income of $8,000 in 2011. At the beginning of 2012, she did not have any loss carry forwards from previous years.

Required: Determine Dotty's optimum Taxable Income for the years ending December 31, 2012 and December 31, 2013. In your solution, consider the effect of the basic personal credit. Indicate any loss carry over that is present at the end of either year, and the rules applicable to claiming the loss carry over.

Assignment Problem Eleven - 3 (ABILs and Lifetime Capital Gains Deduction)

At the beginning of 2013, Mr. Andy Barkin had a net capital loss from 2009 of $13,700 [(1/2)($27,400)]. During 2013, Mr. Barkin had net employment income of $115,000. Additional information for the year 2013 is as follows:

- Mr. Barkin sold shares of a qualified small business corporation for proceeds of $328,000. The adjusted cost base of these shares was $153,000. Selling costs were $2,000.
- At the end of the year, Mr. Barkin had a Cumulative Net Investment Loss balance of $4,800.
- Mr. Barkin sold shares of a small business corporation that was not qualified for $55,000. These shares had cost $228,000 in 2003. Selling costs were $1,000.

In 2003, Mr. Barkin had a capital gain of $38,000. A further capital gain of $21,000 was realized in 2005. As both of these gains involved dispositions of qualified property, he deducted each amount in full under the provisions of ITA 110.6, the lifetime capital gains deduction provision. Mr. Barkin has not deducted any other amounts under ITA 110.6 in the years prior to 2013.

Mr. Barkin would prefer to make maximum use of his lifetime capital gains deduction prior to deducting any net capital loss carry forwards.

Required: Calculate Mr. Barkin's minimum Net Income For Tax Purposes and Taxable Income for 2013. Provide all of the calculations required to determine the maximum ITA 110.6 deduction.

Assignment Problem Eleven - 4   (Tax Credits With Dividend Transfer)

Both Mr. Baxter and his spouse are in their early seventies and have been retired for several years. While they sometimes go south for a few weeks in winter, they are Canadian residents.

They rely largely on pension income. This is made up of OAS payments, RRIF withdrawals, and monthly payments from an RPP sponsored by Mr. Baxter's former employer. Mrs. Baxter is sufficiently disabled she qualifies for the disability tax credit (a medical practitioner has signed the required form).

The components of their income for the year ending December 31, 2013 are as follows:

	Mrs. Baxter	Mr. Baxter
Receipts From Registered Pension Plan	Nil	$48,000
RRIF Withdrawals	Nil	28,000
Interest On Government Bonds	$1,100	3,400
Non-Eligible Dividends Received From		
A CCPC (100 Percent Amount)	3,000	Nil
Charitable Donations*	560	450
Old Age Security Benefits	6,550	6,550

*As the Baxters make regular contributions to registered charities, they are not eligible for the first-time donor's super credit.

Assume that Mr. and Mrs. Baxter do not elect to use the pension income splitting provisions.

Required:

A. Calculate Mr. and Mrs. Baxter's 2013 minimum federal Tax Payable and any social benefits repayment assuming that no transfer of dividends is made under ITA 82(3).

B. Determine whether a transfer of dividends under ITA 82(3) would be permitted.

C. Calculate Mr. and Mrs. Baxter's 2013 minimum federal Tax Payable and any social benefits repayment assuming that all of Mrs. Baxter's dividends are transferred to Mr. Baxter under ITA 82(3). Comment on whether the dividend transfer should be done.

Assignment Problem Eleven - 5 (Alternative Minimum Tax)

The following two independent cases involve taxpayers who might be subject to the alternative minimum tax in the 2013 taxation year.

Case One   Serge Lawson has made the following estimates of the various types of income and deductions that he anticipates for the year ending December 31, 2013.

Net Rental Income	$73,100
Eligible Dividends Received	14,000
RRSP Contributions	22,000

Prior to 2013, Serge has never managed to have enough funds to make any RRSP contributions, leaving him with nearly $100,000 in unused deduction room. However, in 2013, his gambling habit finally pays off, providing sufficient winnings to make a $22,000 contribution. He plans to deduct the full amount in 2013.

Case Two   Sarah Bonito has made the following estimates of the various types of income and deductions that she anticipates for the year ending December 31, 2013.

Eligible Dividends Received	$ 26,000
Net Taxable Capital Gains	263,000
Lifetime Capital Gains Deduction Claimed	260,000

In both Cases, assume the only tax credits available are the basic personal tax credit and the dividend tax credit related to any dividends received.

Required: Calculate the minimum regular 2013 federal Tax Payable in both Cases, as well as the alternative minimum tax amount.

Assignment Problem Eleven - 6 (Comprehensive Personal Tax Payable)

On January 10, 2013, Ms. Marcia Klaus formally separated from her husband and retained custody of her 15 year old son, Martin. Martin has no income during 2013. Ms. Klaus is also responsible for her 20 year old daughter, Louise, who has a severe and prolonged disability (a medical doctor has certified her disability on Form T2201). Louise has 2013 income of $6,000, resulting from income on investments that were left to her by her grandmother.

In order to get a fresh start in life, Ms. Klaus found a new job. She resigned from her position in Ottawa and moved to a similar position in Toronto. The move took place on October 31, 2013. She has asked for your assistance in preparing an estimate of her 2013 personal tax liability and, in order to assist you with your calculations, she has prepared the following list of transactions that occurred during 2013:

1. Her gross salary from her Ottawa employer, a large public company, for the first 10 months of the year was $62,000. Her employer withheld from this amount CPP contributions of $2,356, EI premiums of $891, and RPP contributions of $2,500. The employer also contributed $2,500 to the company's RPP on her behalf. She joined the company in 1976 and was a member of her employer's money purchase RPP during all of her years of employment.

    In appreciation of her many years of excellent service, the Ottawa employer paid her a retiring allowance of $30,000.

    Before leaving her Ottawa employer, she exercised stock options to acquire 2,000 of the company's shares at a price of $15 per share. The options were issued in 2011, when the market price of the shares was $12 per share. On August 12, 2013, the day that she exercised the options, the shares were trading at $20 per share. Ms. Klaus sells the shares as soon as she acquires them. Brokerage fees totalled $350 on the sale.

2. During November and December, her gross wages with her Toronto employer amounted

to $13,000. Her new employer withheld CPP contributions of $500, EI premiums of $390, and $650 in RPP contributions. Her Toronto employer also contributed $650 to the company's money purchase RPP on her behalf.

Ms. Klaus found a new home in Toronto during her September house hunting trip there. The legal arrangements for the house purchase were finalized on October 10. In Ottawa, she and her husband had lived for 10 years in a home that they rented. Her agreement with her new employer requires that they pay her moving costs. In order to simplify the record keeping, the employer paid her an allowance of $7,500 and did not require a detailed accounting of expenses. Her actual expenses were as follows:

Moving company charges	$3,800
Airfare for September Toronto trip to acquire new home	350
Meals and lodging on September Toronto trip	275
Gas for October 31 move to Toronto	65
Lodging in Ottawa on October 30	110
Meals on October 30 and October 31	250
Charges for cancellation of lease on Ottawa home	935
Legal and other fees on acquisition of Toronto home	1,500
Total	$7,285

3. In 2010, Ms. Klaus' mother died, leaving her 5,000 shares of Lintz Industries, a private company. These shares had cost her mother $50,000, and had a fair market value at the time of her death of $95,000. Ms. Klaus received non-eligible dividends of $7,500 on these shares in May and, in December, she sells the shares for $105,000. Selling costs were $1,050.

4. Ms. Klaus made $1,500 in donations to a registered Canadian charity and $900 in contributions to the Libcon Rebloc Party, a registered federal political party. Because she makes charitable contributions on a regular basis, Ms. Klaus is not eligible for the first-time donor's super credit.

5. Ms. Klaus incurred the following child care costs:

Payments To Individuals For Martin And Louise	$7,160
Fees For Martin To Attend Camp (4 Weeks At $200 Per Week)	800
Food And Clothing For The Children	6,400
Total	$14,360

6. Ms. Klaus paid the following medical expenses:

For Herself	$ 9,700
Martin	900
Louise	7,250
Total	$17,850

7. In previous years, Ms. Klaus' husband took care of her financial affairs. She has no understanding of either RPPs or RRSPs, but will make the maximum deductible RRSP contribution for 2013 as soon as you have calculated it. Her RRSP Deduction Limit Statement from the CRA states that her 2012 Earned Income was $61,100 and that, at the end of 2012, she had no Unused RRSP Deduction Room. Her 2012 T4 from her employer indicates a Pension Adjustment of $4,500. There are no undeducted contributions in her RRSP.

8. During the year, Ms. Klaus paid legal fees of $2,500 in connection with her separation agreement. This settlement requires her husband to make a lump sum payment of $25,000 on March 1, 2013, as well as child support payments of $4,000 at the end of each month beginning on January 31, 2013. All required payments were received for the year.

9. In addition to her employment income, Ms. Klaus operates an unincorporated mail order business with a December 31 year end.   Her net business income for 2013 totaled $22,500. Included in this amount is a deduction of $950 for interest that she paid on a demand loan taken out to finance inventory purchases. During the year ending December 31, 2013, Ms. Klaus withdraws $27,000 from the bank account maintained by the business.

10. Assume that she does not use the simplified method to calculate moving expenses.

Required:

A. Determine Ms. Klaus' minimum Net Income For Tax Purposes and her minimum Taxable Income for 2013. Ignore any HST considerations. In the Net Income For Tax Purposes calculation, provide separate disclosure of:

   • Net Employment Income,
   • Net Business And Property Income,
   • Net Taxable Capital Gains,
   • Other Sources Of Income, And
   • Other Deductions From Income.

B. Based on your answer to Part A, calculate Ms. Klaus' minimum federal Tax Payable and any other amounts owing to (refundable from) the CRA for 2013. Ignore any income tax withholdings that her employers would have made.   Explain why you omitted any amounts from your calculations.

Assignment Problem Eleven - 7 (Comprehensive Personal Tax Payable)

   Note   This is an extension of Tax Software Assignment Problem Eleven-2. It has been updated for 2013 rates.

George Pharmacy is a pharmaceutical salesman who has been very successful at his job in the last few years. Unfortunately, his family life has not been very happy. Three years ago, his only child, Anna, was driving a car that was hit by a drunk driver. She and her husband were killed and their 13 year old son, Kevin, was blinded in the accident. He also suffered extensive injuries to his jaw that have required major and prolonged dental work.

George and his wife, Valerie, adopted Kevin. Valerie quit her part-time job to care for him. She also cares for her mother, Joan Drugstore who lives with them.   Joan suffers from dementia, Parkinson's and severe depression. The family doctor has signed a letter stating that she is dependent on George and Valerie because of her impairments. Joan does not meet the residency requirements necessary to qualify for Canadian Old Age Security payments.

Valerie's parents separated two years ago in Scotland after her father, David Drugstore, suffered enormous losses in the stock market. They were forced to sell their home and David moved to Chile. David phones periodically to request that money be deposited in his on-line bank account.

George's brother, Martin, completed an alcohol rehabilitation program after being fired for drinking on the job. He is also living with George and Valerie while he is enrolled as a full time student at Western University. George is paying his tuition and Martin has agreed to transfer any available education related amounts to George. Although Martin plans to file his 2013 tax return, he has not done so yet.

In addition to George's salary, he also earns commissions. His employer requires him to have an office in his home and has signed the form T2200 each year to this effect.

Other information concerning George for 2013 is as follows:

1. George was born on July 2, 1949 and lives in London, Ontario.

2. The birthdates and income for the year of his family members are as follows:

	Birth Date (Y/M/D)	Annual Income
Valerie (income from CPP)	1948-12-30	$5,800
Kevin	1997-10-17	Nil
Joan Drugstore	1928-02-24	500
David Drugstore	1929-01-12	Nil
Martin	1966-06-02	8,300

3. George's T4 showed employment income of $378,000, which includes commissions of $82,000. From his gross salary, his employer withheld CPP contributions of $2,356, EI premiums of $891, income tax of $114,000, and charitable donations of $400.

4. During 2013, Mega reimbursed George $3,788 for meals and entertainment with clients, $2,268 for hotels and $4,925 for airline tickets.

5. Martin's T2202A showed tuition fees of $6,000 and full-time attendance for 8 months.

6. During the year, Valerie donated $1,000 to Mothers Against Drunk Drivers (MADD). George donated $3,000 to the Canadian National Institute For The Blind (CNIB). As George makes regular charitable contributions, he is not eligible for the first-time donor's super credit.

7. George and his family had the following medical expenses for 2013:

Patient	Medical Expenses	Description	Amount
George	Johnson Inc.	Out Of Canada Insurance	$ 731
George	Dr. Smith	Dental Fees	155
George	Optician	Prescription Glasses	109
Valerie	Pharmacy	Prescription	67
Joan	Dr. Wong	Psychiatric Counseling	2,050
David	Tropical Disease Centre	Prescription	390
Martin	Dr. Walker	Group Therapy	6,000
Kevin	Dr. Takarabe	Orthodontics and Dental	30,000
Total			$39,502

8. George paid $800 for the care and feeding of Kevin's seeing eye dog, Isis, during 2013.

9. George's home has a total area of 5,000 square feet. The area of the home used as a home office is 650 square feet. Other costs for the home are as follows:

Telephone Line (including high speed internet connection)	$ 620
Hydro	3,200
Insurance - House	4,000
Maintenance And Repairs	3,800
Mortgage Interest	6,200
Mortgage Life Insurance Premiums	400
Property Taxes	6,700
Total	$24,920

10. George purchased a new computer and software that will be used solely in his home office for employment related uses. The computer cost $3,600 and the various software programs cost $1,250.

11. For 2013, George received two child fitness tax receipts, one from a swim club for $300 and one from a summer day camp for $400. He also received a children's arts tax receipt of $250 for a course at a local theatre school.

12. During September, David was arrested in Chile. Valerie had to spend three weeks in Chile and $2,000 in bribes before she could get him released from jail. George had to pay

Nannies On Call $3,500 for in-home help to take care of Kevin while she was gone.

13. At the beginning of 2013, George had a net capital loss carry forward of $10,500 from the sale of shares in 2012. He had not disposed of any capital assets prior to 2012. During 2013, he had the following dispositions:

	Asset 1	Asset 2	Asset 3
Description	Molson Inc. Shares	Imperial Oil Shares	Sailboat
Proceeds of disposition	$37,000	$ 9,600	$74,000
Adjusted cost base	27,600	12,100	72,000
Outlays and expenses	35	29	N/A

	Asset 4	Asset 5	Asset 6
Description	Motorcycle	Painting	Coin Collection
Proceeds of disposition	$14,000	$1,100	$ 700
Adjusted cost base	21,000	450	1,800
Outlays and expenses	N/A	N/A	N/A

12. George owns a commercial property in Toronto that he purchased on August 28, 2009. The building and fixtures were being used as a drugstore and George intends to continue to operate it as such. Information related to the property is as follows:

Gross rents	$ 16,000
Property taxes	5,128
Insurance	1,890
Interest on mortgage	3,175
Payment on principal	2,200
Furnace repairs	550
Maintenance contract	3,469
UCC of building - beginning of year	107,441
UCC of fixtures - beginning of year	4,651

13. Assume that George's provincial tax payable is $52,000 for 2013.

Required: Calculate George Pharmacy's minimum combined federal/provincial Tax Payable (Refund) for 2013. List any assumptions you have made, as well as any notes and tax planning issues you feel should be placed in the file. Include the amount and type of any loss carry forwards available at the end of the year. Ignore all GST considerations.

Assignment Problem Eleven - 8 (Comprehensive Personal Tax Payable)

Jimin Son, age 44 is a single parent of one child, 8 year old Jihoon. Jihoon lives full time with Jimin as his father returned to South Korea after the couple divorced. Jimin owned all the shares in Musical Notes Inc., a CCPC, until August 31, 2013, when she sold them for $575,000. Jimin had operated the company for 20 years, but, it has been her lifelong dream to form a jazz quartet and go on tour. She found the right people to work with 5 years ago, and in September of 2013, the quartet released their first album and has spent the fall writing music and arranging performance dates for 2014.

Jimin has provided you with the following information about her income and expenses for 2013:

1. The sale of shares in Musical Notes Inc. occurred on August 31, 2013. Jimin incorporated the company in 1991, and at that time, she invested $100 in the shares she acquired. No one else has ever owned any of the shares in the company. Over the years, the company, which began with one small store selling musical instruments and other music related items, was very successful, and by the time the company shares were sold, there were two stores, both with an excellent reputation.

The company operated entirely in Canada, and has never had any income that wasn't active business income. Jimin has used $100,000 [(1/2)($200,000)] of her lifetime capital gains deduction in the past when she realized a capital gain on qualifying shares. You have correctly calculated Jimin's CNIL balance at the end of the year to be $20,000.

2. Jimin has a notice of assessment for 2012 which indicates the following carry forward balances:

Net Capital Loss [(1/2)($4,000)]	$2,000
Listed Personal Property Loss (100%)	500

3. Jimin's royalties received to date from the company that produced and marketed the quartet's album totalled $40,000. All expenses of the quartet are paid for by the producer.

4. Jihoon is enrolled in a before and after school care program operating at his school. The cost of his care for 2013 was $3,500.

5. Jihoon is enrolled in music lessons and plays soccer in the summer. The annual cost of his music lessons was $2,500, while soccer registration fees were $200. Jimin also purchased equipment to allow Jihoon to participate in soccer (shoes, shorts, t-shirts, soccer ball) for a cost of $250.

6. Medical expenses for the family were very high this year, as Jihoon required oral surgery, followed by extensive dental work. The total cost, paid entirely by Jimin was $20,000. No other medical costs were incurred.

7. In 2012, when Jimin first made the decision to sell her shares in her company, she realized that she would no longer need the vacant land near her downtown store that she owned personally. She had been renting the land to a parking lot operator and had made a minimal profit each year. The land had originally cost her $25,000 in 2002. As the area was undergoing some significant developments, Jimin sold the lot for $175,000 in early January, 2013. The property taxes that she had paid on the land during the period she owned it totalled $12,650.

8. While cleaning out her stores prior to giving the keys to the new owners, Jimin found a painting that she had purchased in 2007, and put away in a store room. The painting cost her $200, and was purchased from a struggling musician who was also a watercolor painter. Since she had purchased this piece, the artist had become extremely well known internationally, and when Jimin had the work appraised, it turned out it was worth $50,000. Since Jimin was not going to be home much to enjoy the painting, she decided to sell it at auction, and it sold for its appraised value.

9. Prior to selling her shares in the business, Jimin received a salary of $150,000 from which CPP of $2,356 was deducted. As Jimin was the sole shareholder in the company, her earnings are not insurable for EI purposes.

10. Jimin continues to own 15% of the shares in Son Enterprises Limited, a family corporation started by her parents. This company is a CCPC, and Jimin received a non-eligible dividend from it in 2013 of $60,000. When Jihoon was born, he was given shares that were owned by his grandmother. As a result, he owns 5% of the shares in this corporation. He received non-eligible dividends of $20,000. Jihoon has no other income.

11. Jimin receives child support of $1,000 per month from her ex-husband. She is saving this money to use to pay for university tuition costs for Jihoon in the future. All of the money received has been placed directly in a South Korean bank account in her name. In 2013, this account earned the Canadian dollar equivalent of $500 in interest. A total of $50 was withheld by the South Korean government, so that the net amount received was $450.

12. Jimin took several trips out of the country in 2013 and purchased the local foreign currency before leaving Canada. As a result, for 2013, she had $700 in gains on foreign currencies and $100 in losses when she converted the foreign currencies back into

Assignment Problems

Canadian dollars. She had no capital transactions that involved foreign currency.

13. Over the years, Jimin had personally collected vinyl records, vintage sheet music and a great deal of music memorabilia. She had kept meticulous records and found that she had spent $36,500 purchasing these items. Jimin had them appraised and was disappointed to learn that her collection was worth only $17,500. She donated everything to the music school at the local university in 2013 receiving nothing in return except a donation receipt for the maximum amount possible.

Jimin is interested in your advice with respect to her RRSP and TFSA. She has $340,000 in her RRSP as of December 31, 2012. During 2013 she made a fully deductible contribution of $9,500. She also has $42,500 in her TFSA.

Because of the sale of Musical Notes Inc., Jimin currently has large cash resources. However, she anticipates that it may take several years for her activities as a musician to prove as financially rewarding as her former business activities.

For the last 5 years, she has been a tenant in a modest townhouse. Within six months she is planning to buy a condo large enough to accommodate her grand piano. Since she does not want to live with any debt (such as a mortgage), this raises the possibility of a need for additional cash. If this is the case, she would like your advice on whether the required funds should be withdrawn from her RRSP or from her TFSA.

Required: In determining the following amounts, ignore GST, PST and HST considerations and show all your calculations.

A. For the 2013 taxation year, calculate Jihoon Son's minimum:

1. Net Income For Tax Purposes,
2. Taxable Income,
3. federal Tax Payable.

B. For the 2013 taxation year, calculate Jimin Son's minimum:

1. Net Income For Tax Purposes,
2. Taxable Income,
3. federal Tax Payable, including Alternative Minimum Tax if applicable.

C. What advice would you give Jimin regarding her concerns with respect to her potential need for additional cash in the next few years?

Assignment Problem Eleven - 9 (Comprehensive Personal Tax Payable Including Death And Pension Income Splitting)

Mr. Wally Bronson is 67 years old and has been retired for several years. His spouse, Melissa, is 62 and has been blind for the last ten years. Mr. Bronson receives pension income of $83,000 in 2013 from his employer's registered pension plan. Due to his high income in the last few years, Mr. Bronson has not applied for OAS benefits. However, he has applied for Canada Pension Plan payments and received $10,680 in CPP benefits in 2013.

Melissa has no income and none of the family's investments are in her name.

Wally and Melissa have two children. Their son, Jerome, is 42 years old and their daughter, Jerri, is 38 years old. Neither child is dependent on Mr. Bronson. While Jerome has no children, Jerri has a 12 year old daughter, Brenda.

In December, 2012, Mr. Bronson is diagnosed with terminal cancer, with the doctor indicating that he probably has about 12 months to live. To this point, Mr. Bronson had not dealt with the prospect of death and, beyond the preparation of a fairly simple will which left all of his assets to Melissa, had done little in the way of estate planning. Given his current state of health, he has decided to undertake a number of transactions in order to minimize the tax consequences of his death.

He is particularly concerned with the fact that, in the province in which he lives, probate fees equal 1.5 percent of the fair market value of all of the assets that are transferred in his will. Given this, he intends to transfer a significant amount of his assets into the hands of others prior to his death. At this time he also revises his will, leaving some property to his two children with the remainder going to his wife.

Mr. Bronson owns two tracts of vacant land. Plot A has a cost of $125,000 and a fair market value of $150,000. Plot B has a cost of $175,000 and a fair market value of $210,000. While he had intended to develop rental properties on these sites, he has decided that this is no longer feasible and the properties should be sold. Because his younger brother, Phil, is in a low tax bracket, during 2013, he sells Plot A to him, with the only consideration being a note for $50,000 which is paid on December 1, 2013. In contrast, his older brother, Gary, is very wealthy and is in the highest tax bracket. Given Gary's substantial bank balances, during 2013, Mr. Bronson sells Plot B to him for $250,000 in cash.

On January 1, 2013, Mr. Bronson acquires units in the YP Real Estate Income Trust at a cost of $300,000. These units distribute $800 per month on the 25th of each month. This distribution represents only rental income and does not include dividends, capital gains, or a return of capital. On February 1, 2013, after receiving the January payment of $800, Mr. Bronson gifts all of these units to his granddaughter, Brenda. At this time, the units have a fair market value of $310,000.

Mr. Bronson owns a large block of Baron Inc. shares. He acquired 4,000 shares of this widely held public company in 2011 at $50 per share. In 2012, he acquired an additional 8,000 shares at $65 per share. On March 1, 2013, he gifts 1,500 shares to each of his children and an additional 1,500 shares to his wife. At this time, the shares are trading at $68 per share. On July 1, 2013, Baron Inc. pays an eligible dividend of $1.50 per share.

Mr. Bronson owns three identical units in a condominium building. Each unit cost $300,000 nine years ago and, on January 1, 2013, each had a separate class UCC of $205,000. The value of the land on which the condominiums are situated was $100,000 at the time they were acquired and has not changed since that time. During 2013, these units produced net rental income, before consideration of CCA, of $93,750.

On December 31, 2013, Mr. Bronson dies peacefully in his home. On this date he has the following assets:

Baron Inc. Shares The 7,500 shares that remain in Mr. Baron's name on this date are trading at $70 per share. Mr. Bronson's will leaves all of these shares to his spouse, Melissa.

Condominium Units In his will, Mr. Baron has left one of these units to each of his two children, with the remaining unit going to his spouse. On the date of Mr. Bronson's death, each of these units has a fair market value of $420,000.

Principal Residence Mr. Bronson and his wife have lived in the same home since 1972. The house is owned by Mr. Bronson. It cost $145,000 and has a current market value of $562,000. Mr. Bronson's will leaves this property to his spouse.

During 2013, medical expenses for Mr. Bronson totaled $45,000, while those of his spouse totaled $12,000.

In 1989, Mr. Bronson had a net capital loss of $40,000 [(2/3)($60,000)]. He has not been able to use this loss in any previous or subsequent year. He has never claimed the lifetime capital gains deduction.

Required: Ignore GST and PST considerations.

A. Assume Mr. Bronson's accountant does not split his pension income with his spouse. Calculate Mr. Bronson's minimum 2013 Net Income For Tax Purposes, his 2013 minimum Taxable Income, and his minimum 2013 federal Tax Payable without consideration of any instalment payments he may have made.

B.   Assume Mr. Bronson's accountant splits his pension income with his spouse and allocates $41,500 in pension income to her. Calculate the overall federal tax savings due to the pension splitting.

Tax Software Assignment Problems

Tax Software Assignment Problem Eleven - 1

This problem is a continuation of the Chapter 4 problem.

DISCLAIMER: All characters appearing in this problem are fictitious. Any resemblance to real persons, living or dead, is purely coincidental.

Mr. Buddy Musician (SIN 527-000-061) was born in Vancouver on August 28, 1945. He has spent most of his working life as a pianist and song writer. He and his family live at 111 WWW Street, Vancouver, B.C. V4H 3W4, phone (604) 111-1111.

Mr. Musician's wife, Natasha (SIN 527-000-129), was born on June 6, 1987. She and Mr. Musician have four children. Each child was born on April 1 of the following years, Linda; 2007, Larry; 2008, Donna; 2009, and Donald; 2010. Natasha's only income during 2012 is $4,800 [(4)($100)(12)] in universal child care benefits.

Buddy and Natasha Musician have two adopted children. Richard (SIN 527-000-285) was born on March 15, 1995 and has income of $2,800 for the year. Due to his accelerated schooling, he started full time attendance at university in September of 2012 at the age of 17. His first semester tuition fee is $3,000 and he requires books with a total cost of $375. These amounts are paid by Mr. Musician.

The other adopted child, Sarah, was born on September 2, 1992, and is in full time attendance at university for all of 2012 (including a four month summer session). Her tuition is $9,600 and she requires textbooks which cost $750. These amounts are also paid by Mr. Musician. Sarah has no income during the year.

Neither Richard nor Sarah will have any income in the next three years. Any unused credits of either child are available to be transferred to their father.

Mr. Musician's mother, Eunice, was born on April 10, 1925 and his father, Earl, was born on November 16, 1923. They both live with Mr. Musician and his wife. While his father is still physically active, his mother is blind. Eunice Musician had income of $9,500 for the year, while Earl Musician had income of $7,500.

Other information concerning Mr. Musician and his family for 2012 is as follows:

1.   Mr. Musician earned $16,500 for work as the house pianist at the Loose Moose Pub. His T4 showed that his employer withheld $500 for income taxes and $301.95 for EI. No CPP was withheld as he has filed an election stop contributing to the CPP.

2.   During the year, Mr. Musician made $3,000 in donations to Planned Parenthood Of Canada, a registered Canadian charity.

3.   Mr. Musician has been married before to Lori Musician (SIN 527-000-319). Lori is 52 years old and lives in Fort Erie, Ontario.

4.   Mr. Musician has two additional children who live with their mother, Ms. Dolly Nurse (SIN 527-000-582), in Burnaby, British Columbia. The children are Megan Nurse, aged 12 and Andrew Nurse, aged 14. Neither child has any income during 2012. While Ms. Nurse and Mr. Musician were never married, Mr. Musician acknowledges that he is the father of both children. Although Buddy has provided limited financial aid, the children are not dependent on Buddy for support.

5. Mr. Musician wishes to claim all his medical expenses on a calendar year basis. On December 2, 2012, Mr. Musician paid dental expenses to Canada Wide Dental Clinics for the following individuals:

Himself	$1,200
Natasha (wife)	700
Richard (adopted son)	800
Sarah (adopted daughter)	300
Linda (daughter)	100
Earl (father)	1,050
Lori (ex-wife)	300
Dolly Nurse (mother of two of his children)	675
Megan Nurse (daughter of Dolly Nurse)	550
Total	$5,675

6. Mr. Musician paid four quarterly instalments of $1,000 each (total of $4,000) for 2012, as requested on his Instalment Reminders from the CRA. He paid each instalment on the due date.

7. Mr. Musician receives $6,510.60 in Old Age Security payments and $5,500 in Canada Pension Plan "retirement benefit" payments over 12 months. There was no tax shown as withheld on his T4A(OAS) or his T4A(P).

8. Mr. Musician builds a state-of-the-art home theatre in a new extension of his home. In order to finance it, he sells stock in his RRSP and withdraws the funds from his RRSP. His T4RSP showed $52,000 in withdrawals (Box 22) and total tax of $15,600 deducted from these payments.

9. Several of Mr. Musician's songs, including his outstanding hit, "Drop Kick Me Jesus Through The Goal Posts Of Life", have provided him with substantial royalty payments over the years. In 2012, the Never Say Die Record Company paid him $78,000 in royalty payments. No T5 was issued by the Company.

10. In order to ensure the financial security of his family, Mr. Musician decided to return to songwriting in earnest. On November 1, 2012, he rented a small, quiet studio for $700 a month and purchased a Roland electric piano for $7,750 that was delivered there. He does not plan to use the space or piano for personal enjoyment, only for composing.

11. Mr. Musician elects not to make any further CPP contributions on his self-employed income.

12. Mr. Musician is required by a court order to pay spousal support of $400 per month to his former spouse, Lori Musician. Mr. Musician made spousal support payments of $4,800 during 2012.

13. Mr. Musician is required by a 2005 court order to make child support payments of $350 per month for his two children, Megan and Andrew Nurse. A total of $4,200 was paid during the year.

14. Mr. Musician made contributions to the Federal Liberal Party in the amount of $610 during the year.

15. Mr. Musician made a $5,000 contribution to his TFSA during the year. Thanks to the excellent investing advice of his gardener, the balance in his TFSA account has grown to more than $105,007 by the end of the year.

Required: Prepare Mr. Musician's 2012 income tax return using the ProFile tax software program. List any assumptions you have made, and any notes and tax planning issues you feel should be placed in the file. Ignore GST/HST implications in your solution.

Tax Software Assignment Problem Eleven - 2

This problem is a continuation of the Chapter 4 Tax Software problem.

A version of this problem, which does not require tax software, has been updated for 2013 rates and credits and is available as Assignment Problem Eleven-7.

DISCLAIMER: All characters appearing in this problem are fictitious. Any resemblance to real persons, living or dead, is purely coincidental.

George Pharmacy is a pharmaceutical salesman who has been very successful at his job in the last few years. Unfortunately, his family life has not been very happy.

Three years ago, his only child, Anna, was driving a car that was hit by a drunk driver. She and her husband were killed and their 13 year old son, Kevin, was blinded in the accident. He also suffered extensive injuries to his jaw that have required major and prolonged dental work.

George and his wife, Valerie, adopted Kevin. Valerie quit her part-time job to care for him. She also cares for her mother, Joan Drugstore who lives with them. Joan suffers from dementia, Parkinson's and severe depression.

The family doctor has signed a letter stating that she is dependent on George and Valerie because of her impairments. Joan does not meet the residency requirements necessary to qualify for Canadian Old Age Security payments.

Valerie's parents separated two years ago in Scotland after her father, David Drugstore, suffered enormous losses in the stock market. They were forced to sell their home and David moved to Chile. David phones periodically to request that money be deposited in his on-line bank account.

George's brother, Martin, completed an alcohol rehabilitation program after being fired for drinking on the job. He is also living with George and Valerie while he is enrolled as a full time student at Western University.

George is paying his tuition and Martin has agreed to transfer any available education related amounts to George. Although Martin plans to file his 2012 tax return, he has not done so yet.

In addition to George's salary, he also earns commissions. His employer requires him to have an office in his home and has signed the form T2200 each year to this effect.

Other information concerning George for 2012 is given on the following pages.

Required: Prepare the 2012 income tax return of George Pharmacy using the ProFile tax software program. List any assumptions you have made, and any notes and tax planning issues you feel should be placed in the file. Ignore HST implications in your solutions.

Personal Information	Taxpayer
Title	Mr.
First Name	George
Last Name	Pharmacy
SIN	527-000-509
Date of birth (Y/M/D)	1948-07-02
Marital Status	Married
Canadian citizen?	Yes
Provide information to Elections Canada?	Yes
Own foreign property of more than $100,000 Canadian?	No

Taxpayer's Address	
123 ZZZ Street, London, Ontario N0Z 0Z0	
Phone number (519) 111-1111	

Family Members	Spouse	Child	Mother-In-Law
First Name	Valerie	Kevin	Joan
Last Name	Pharmacy	Pharmacy	Drugstore
SIN	527-000-483	527-000-517	None
Date of birth (Y/M/D)	1947-12-30	1996-10-17	1927-02-24
Net income	$5,800 in CPP	Nil	$500

Family Members	Father-In-Law	Brother
First Name	David	Martin
Last Name	Drugstore	Pharmacy
SIN	None	527-000-533
Date of birth (Y/M/D)	1928-01-12	1965-06-02
Net income	Nil	$8,300

For 2012, George received two child fitness tax receipts, one from a swim club for $300 and one from a summer day camp for $400. He also received a children's arts tax receipt of $250 for a course at a local theatre school.

During September, David was arrested in Chile. Valerie had to spend three weeks in Chile and $2,000 in bribes before she could get him released from jail. George had to pay Nannies On Call $3,500 for in-home help to take care of Kevin while she was gone.

T2202A - (Martin)	Box	Amount
Tuition fees - for Martin Pharmacy (brother)	A	6,000
Number of months in school - part-time	B	0
Number of months in school - full-time	C	8

T4	Box	Amount
Issuer - Mega Pharma Inc.		
Employment income	14	378,000.00
Employee's CPP contributions	16	2,306.70
Employee's EI premiums	18	839.92
Income tax deducted	22	114,000.00
Employment commissions	42	82,000.00
Charitable donations	46	400.00

During 2012, Mega reimbursed George $3,788 for meals and entertainment with clients, $2,268 for hotels and $4,925 for airline tickets.

Tax Software Assignment Problems

Donor	Charitable Donation Receipts	Am't
Valerie	Mothers Against Drunk Drivers (MADD)	1,000
George	Canadian Institute For The Blind (CNIB)	3,000

(Y/M/D)	Patient	Medical Expenses	Description	Am't
2012-12-31	George	Johnson Inc.	Out of Canada insurance	731.30
2012-08-31	George	Dr. Smith	Dental fees	155.40
2012-09-19	George	Optician	Prescription glasses	109.00
2012-11-07	Valerie	Pharmacy	Prescription	66.84
2012-06-07	Joan	Dr. Wong	Psychiatric counseling	2,050.00
2012-03-22	David	Tropical Disease Centre	Prescription	390.00
2012-12-20	Martin	Dr. Walker	Group therapy	6,000.00
2012-10-01	Kevin	Dr. Takarabe	Orthodontics and Dental	30,000.00

George paid $800 for the care and feeding of Kevin's seeing eye dog, Isis, during 2012.

House Costs	
Area of home used for home office (square feet)	650
Total area of home (square feet)	5,000
Telephone line including high speed internet connection	620
Hydro	3,200
Insurance - House	4,000
Maintenance and repairs	3,800
Mortgage interest	6,200
Mortgage life insurance premiums	400
Property taxes	6,700

During 2012, George purchased a new computer and software that will be used solely in his home office for employment related uses. The computer cost $3,600 and the various software programs cost $1,250.

At the beginning of 2012, George had a net capital loss carry forward of $10,500 from the sale of shares in 2011. He had not disposed of any capital assets prior to 2011.

Asset Dispositions	Asset 1	Asset 2	Asset 3
Description	Molson Inc. shares	Imperial Oil shares	Sailboat
Number of units	150	387	N/A
Year of acquisition	2009	2010	2010
Date of disposition	February 14	June 6	October 1
Proceeds of disposition	37,000	9,600	74,000
Adjusted cost base	27,600	12,100	72,000
Outlays and expenses	35	29	N/A

Asset Dispositions	Asset 4	Asset 5	Asset 6
Description	Motorcycle	Painting	Coin collection
Year of acquisition	2012	2006	2009
Date of disposition	November 17	August 28	March 24
Proceeds of disposition	14,000	1,100	700
Adjusted cost base	21,000	450	1,800
Outlays and expenses	N/A	N/A	N/A

Real Estate Rental - Commercial Property	Amount
Address - 888 YYZ Drive, Toronto, Ontario M0M 0M0	
Year of purchase	2008
Gross rents	16,000
Property taxes	5,128
Insurance	1,890
Interest on mortgage	3,175
Payment on principal	2,200
Furnace repairs	550
Maintenance contract	3,469
Building purchased for $120,100 - UCC beginning of year	107,441
Fixtures purchased for $8,500 - UCC beginning of year	4,651

The building and fixtures were purchased on August 28, 2008. At the time the building and fixtures were being used as a drugstore and Mr. Pharmacy has retained the same tenant.

Tax Software Assignment Problem Eleven - 3

This Tax Software Assignment Problem was introduced in Chapter 4 and is continued in Chapters 6 through 11. Each Tax Software Assignment Problem must be completed in sequence. While it is not repeated in this problem, all of the information in each of the previous problems (e.g., Mary's T4 content) is applicable to this problem.

If you have not prepared a tax file incorporating the Tax Software Assignment Problem information for the previous Chapters, please do so before continuing with this problem.

On February 14, 2013, you receive a call from Mary Career. She has just received an amended T4. The original T4 had not included information on the stock options in her employer, MoreCorp (a public company), that she had exercised.

Mary had options to purchase 500 shares of MoreCorp at $42 per share. When she received the options, the shares were trading at $40 per share. On December 20, 2012, when the shares were trading at $125 per share, she exercised her options for 200 shares. She left verbal instructions for MoreCorp to immediately donate all of the shares to Tax Behind Bars, a Canadian registered charity whose volunteers provide extensive tax education to inmates in prisons across Canada.

Unfortunately for Mary, the donation was not done and she did not receive a 2012 charitable donation receipt.

Tax Software Assignment Problems

Amended T4 - Mary	Box	Original Am't	Amended Am't
Issuer - MoreCorp			
Employment income	14	152,866.08	169,466.08
Employee's CPP contributions	16	2,306.70	2,306.70
Employee's EI premiums	18	839.97	839.97
RPP contributions	20	Nil	Nil
Income tax deducted	22	48,665.11	48,665.11
Stock option deduction 110(1)(d)	39	Nil	8,300.00
Charitable donations	46	1,000.00	1,000.00

Mary informs you that she received more than $1 million in life insurance benefits and has made all of the RRSP contributions for 2012 and 2013 that you advised (see Chapter 10 version), but has not yet received the receipt from TD Asset Management.

In checking Seymour's file, you find he has a net capital loss carry forward of $17,500 [(1/2)($35,000)] from the sale of his XXX Art Films Ltd shares in 2011.

Required:

A. If the shares from her stock options had been donated immediately:
    i.   what effect would this have had on her Taxable Income?
    ii. how much would it have reduced her federal Tax Payable?

B. Open the file that you created for the Chapter 10 version of this Software Problem and save a copy under a different name. This will enable you to check the changes between different versions of this Software Problem.

C. Revise Mary's tax return for the amended T4 and new RRSP contributions.

D. With the objective of minimizing the tax liability for the family, prepare Mary's 2012 income tax return and make any revisions necessary to Seymour's final 2012 return. Print both returns. List any assumptions you have made and provide any explanatory notes and tax planning issues you feel should be placed in the files.

E. Access and print Mary's summary (Summary on the Form Explorer, not the T1Summary). This form is a two column summary of the couple's tax information. By opening this form from Mary's return, the order of the columns is the same as the one in the previous chapter. For both returns, list the changes on this Summary form from the previous version of this Software Problem. Exclude totals calculated by the program, but include the final Balance Owing (Refund) amount.

CHAPTER 12

Taxable Income And Tax Payable For Corporations

Computation Of Net Income

12-1. The day-to-day records of most corporations are kept in terms of accounting procedures and policies that are normally referred to as Generally Accepted Accounting Principles (GAAP). As noted in Chapter 6, Business Income, many of the rules for computing business income under the *Income Tax Act* are identical to those used under GAAP. However, there are a number of differences that are specifically provided for and, as a result, the first step in the computation of Taxable Income for a corporation is to convert accounting Net Income as determined under GAAP into Net Income For Tax Purposes. Only then can we move from Division B's Net Income For Tax Purposes to Division C's Taxable Income.

12-2. In making this conversion, there are many adjustments that could be required in particular circumstances. Some adjustments are necessary because of different allocation patterns that result in timing differences between accounting and tax income. Examples of this would be differences between accounting amortization and CCA, as well as alternative approaches to the determination of pension cost deductions. Other adjustments involve permanent differences between accounting and tax amounts. An example of this type of difference would be the non-taxable one-half of capital gains. While accounting records include 100 percent of such gains, one-half of such gains will never be included in Net Income For Tax Purposes.

12-3. As is noted in Chapter 6, a reconciliation between accounting Net Income and Net Income For Tax Purposes is a required part of the corporate tax return. The form that the CRA provides for this reconciliation is designated Schedule 1. The most common adjustments from this Schedule are listed in Figure 6-1 in Chapter 6 and that list has been duplicated as Figure 12-1 (following page) for your convenience.

12-4. Chapter 6 on business income provided a detailed discussion of the conversion of Net Income for accounting purposes into Net Income For Tax Purposes. As that discussion is equally applicable to corporations and unincorporated businesses, it will not be repeated here. However, if you are not familiar with the material in Chapter 6, we suggest that you review it before proceeding with these Chapters on corporate taxation.

Figure 12 - 1
Conversion Of Accounting Net Income To Net Income For Tax Purposes

Additions To Accounting Income:
- Income tax expense
- Amortization, depreciation, and depletion of tangible and intangible assets (accounting amounts)
- Recapture of CCA
- Tax reserves deducted in the prior year
- Losses on the disposition of capital assets (accounting amounts)
- Pension expense (accounting amounts)
- Scientific research expenditures (Accounting amounts)
- Warranty expense (accounting amounts)
- Amortization of discount on long-term debt issued (see discussion in Chapter 7)
- Foreign tax paid (accounting amounts)
- Excess of taxable capital gains over allowable capital losses
- Interest and penalties on income tax assessments
- Non-deductible automobile costs
- 50 percent of business meals and entertainment expenses
- Club dues and cost of recreational facilities
- Non-deductible reserves (accounting amounts)
- Charitable donations
- Asset write-downs including impairment losses on intangibles
- Fines, penalties, and illegal payments

Deductions From Accounting Income:
- Capital cost allowances (CCA)
- Amortization of cumulative eligible capital (CEC)
- Terminal losses
- Tax reserves claimed for the current year
- Gains on the disposition of capital assets (accounting amounts)
- Pension funding contributions
- Deductible scientific research expenditures
- Deductible warranty expenditures
- Amortization of premium on long-term debt issued
- Foreign non-business tax deduction [ITA 20 (12)]
- Allowable business investment losses
- Landscaping costs

Exercise Twelve - 1

Subject: Schedule 1 Reconciliation

Available information for the S1 Company for the year includes the following:

1. A capital asset was sold for $48,300. It had a cost of $120,700 and a net book value of $53,900. It was the last asset in its CCA class and the UCC balance in this class was $34,600 before the disposition. There were no other additions or dispositions during the year.
2. During the year, the Company acquired goodwill at a cost of $180,000. Since there was no impairment of the goodwill during the year, no write-down was required for accounting purposes.
3. During the year, the Company expensed charitable donations of $15,000.
4. Premium amortization on the Company's bonds payable was $4,500 for the year.

You have been asked to prepare a Schedule 1 reconciliation of accounting Net Income and Net Income For Tax Purposes. Determine the addition and/or deduction that would be made in Schedule 1 for each of the preceding items.

End of Exercise. Solution available in Study Guide.

We suggest you work Self Study Problem Twelve-1 at this point.

Computation Of Taxable Income

Deductions Available To Corporations

12-5.   The reconciliation schedule illustrated in Figure 12-1 is used to establish a corporation's Net Income For Tax Purposes. When this task is completed, certain specified items are deducted from the resulting Net Income For Tax Purposes figure in order to arrive at Taxable Income. These deductions are specified in Division C of the *Income Tax Act* and the relevant items for individuals were given detailed coverage in Chapters 4 and 11. However, there are significant differences in the Division C deductions available to individuals and those available to corporations.

12-6.   With respect to the Division C items that are available to individuals, the following are not available to corporations:

- employee stock option deduction
- deduction for payments (social assistance and workers' compensation benefits)
- home relocation loan deduction
- lump-sum payments
- lifetime capital gains deduction
- northern residents deductions

12-7.   A further significant difference relates to two items that, with respect to individuals, serve as a base for credits against Tax Payable. While these items are not available as a base for credits against corporate Tax Payable, they are available as deductions in the calculation of corporate Taxable Income. These items are:

Charitable Donations   Unlike the situation for individuals where charitable donations are the basis for a tax credit, corporations deduct charitable donations from Net Income For Tax Purposes in the determination of Taxable Income. While corporations have a deduction rather than a tax credit, the rules for determining which donations can be deducted by a corporation are essentially the same as the rules for determining which donations qualify for the tax credit for individuals. Further, corporations are subject to the same limits that apply to individuals, with respect to the amount that can be deducted in the current taxation year. The five year carry forward provision is also applicable to corporations. These matters are given detailed consideration in Chapters 4 and 11 and will not be repeated here.

Dividends   As noted in previous Chapters, individuals must gross up dividends received from taxable Canadian corporations by 25 percent for non-eligible dividends or 38 percent for eligible dividends. This is accompanied by a federal dividend tax credit equal to either two-thirds of the gross up or 6/11 of the gross up. There is no corresponding gross up or tax credit with respect to dividends received by a corporation. However, a corporation is permitted to deduct the full amount of such dividends in the calculation of Taxable Income. Note that, while this deduction removes dividends from Taxable Income and the Tax Payable calculation, they must be included in determining Net Income For Tax Purposes.

12-8.   In addition to the two preceding deductions, corporations are allowed to deduct loss carry overs from previous or subsequent years in the calculation of Taxable Income. Other than in situations where a corporation has been the subject of an acquisition of control (see Chapter 14), the rules related to the deduction loss carry overs by corporation are basically the same as those applicable to individuals. These general rules are covered in Chapter 11 and will not be repeated here.

12-9.   The calculation of corporate Taxable Income is outlined in Figure 12-2 (following page).

Figure 12 - 2

Conversion Of Corporate Net Income For Tax Purposes To Taxable Income

Net Income (Loss) For Tax Purposes

Less:
- Charitable donations (Limited to 75 percent of Net Income For Tax Purposes with a five year carry forward of unused amounts)
- Dividends received from taxable Canadian corporations
- Loss carry overs from subsequent or prior taxation years

Equals Taxable Income (Loss)

Dividends From Other Corporations

Deduction From Taxable Income

12-10.   In the calculation of Taxable Income, ITA 112(1) permits a corporation to deduct dividends that are received from taxable Canadian corporations in the determination of Taxable Income.

12-11.   The reason for this deduction is fairly obvious. If taxes were levied on transfers of dividends between companies, it could result in taxes being repeatedly assessed on the same diminishing stream of income. That is, the paying corporation would be taxed on the income that provided the dividend and if, in addition, the receiving corporation had to include the amount received in its Taxable Income, double taxation of the same income would result. In more complex, multi-level corporate structures, this could extend to triple, quadruple, or even greater applications of tax to a single stream of income.

Example   Mr. X owns 100 percent of the common shares of Company X, and Company X owns 100 percent of the common shares of Company Y. Both Companies pay out all of their after tax income as dividends. Company Y has income of $1,000 for the year and Company X has no income other than dividends from Company Y. Assume both Company X and Company Y are subject to a combined federal/provincial tax rate of 30 percent and Mr. X is subject to a combined federal/provincial tax rate on non-eligible dividends received of 33 percent.

Analysis   A comparison of the after tax flow through, with and without the intercompany dividend deduction, would be as follows:

	No Deduction	Deduction
Company Y Income	$1,000	$1,000
Corporate Taxes At 30 Percent	(300)	(300)
Dividends To Company X	$ 700	$ 700
Corporate Taxes At 30 Percent	(210)	Nil
Dividends To Mr. X	$ 490	$ 700
Personal Taxes At 33 Percent	(162)	(231)
After Tax Retention	$ 328	$ 469

12-12.   Without the deduction, the after tax retention is only $328. This means that the total tax rate on the $1,000 of income earned by Company Y is an almost confiscatory 67.2 percent. While the application of the dividend deduction provides a more reasonable level of taxation, you should note that the combined corporate and personal tax on the $1,000 income stream is $531 ($300 + $231). This heavy level of taxation reflects the fact that, with a corporate tax rate of 30 percent, flowing income through a corporation can result in the payment of higher taxes than would be the case with the direct receipt of income. This point is discussed more fully in Chapter 13, which provides coverage of the concept of integration.

Exercise Twelve - 2

Subject: Corporate Taxable Income

The Chapman Company had Net Income For Tax Purposes for the year ending December 31, 2013 of $263,000. This amount included $14,250 in taxable capital gains, as well as $14,200 in dividends received from taxable Canadian corporations. Also during 2013, the Company made donations to registered charities of $8,600. At the beginning of the year, the Company had a non-capital loss carry forward from 2009 of $82,000, as well as a net capital loss carry forward from 2010 of $18,000 [(1/2)($36,000)]. Determine the Company's minimum Taxable Income for the year ending December 31, 2013 and the amount and type of any carry forwards available at the end of the year.

End of Exercise. Solution available in Study Guide.

Dividends From Untaxed Income

12-13. While the preceding justifications for not taxing intercorporate dividends make sense in the majority of situations, problems can arise. One problem involves situations in which the corporation paying the dividend was not taxed on the funds prior to their distribution. Given the fact that, for most companies, accounting income is higher than Taxable Income, it would not be surprising to find cases where there is sufficient accounting income to warrant a dividend payment, combined with a tax loss for the period.

12-14. In this case, there will be no taxation of the original income at the corporate level. This means that only personal taxes will be paid on the income stream and, as a consequence, the use of a corporation will result in a significantly lower level of taxation than would be the case if the income was received directly by the individual. In addition, because no tax will be assessed until the income is paid out in dividends, this situation may result in a significant deferral of the taxation that is applicable to the income stream.

Term And Other Preferred Shares

12-15. A further problem arises when corporations attempt to achieve what is sometimes referred to as "after tax financing". Because of the favourable tax treatment given to both individual and corporate recipients of dividend income, rates that corporations will have to pay on preferred shares will sometimes be lower than rates paid on debt securities.

12-16. For most corporations, debt securities will continue to remain attractive because the tax deductibility of interest payments provides a lower after tax cost of funds than would be the case with the use of preferred shares. However, this is not the case when the corporation is in a loss position and, as a consequence, such companies have often issued preferred shares.

12-17. To make these preferred shares more attractive to investors, issuers add features such as redemption provisions. These features produce a preferred share that has most of the characteristics of debt. In fact, IAS 32, *Financial Instruments: Presentation*, may require that such preferred shares be treated as debt for accounting purposes.

12-18. Despite many debt-like features, the payments made on such preferred shares are, for tax purposes, dividend income. As previously discussed, this type of income is taxed very favourably in the hands of individual investors and is not taxed at all in the hands of corporate investors.

12-19. The loss of tax revenues on this type of security could be very high. To prevent this loss, the ITA either imposes special taxes under Part IV.1 and Part VI.1, or denies the dividend deduction to alter the treatment of dividends on these preferred shares. However, these provisions go beyond the scope of this material.

Computation Of Taxable Income

Dividends On Shares Sold For Loss (Stop Loss Rules)

12-20.   As the declaration and payment of dividends by a corporation reduces the corporation's net assets, it would be expected that the value of the shares would fall by approximately the amount of any dividend declared and paid. Given this, it would be possible for one corporation to acquire shares in another corporation at a time when it was anticipated that a dividend would be paid on the acquired shares. The dividends on these shares could be received tax free and, if the value of the shares declined when they went ex-dividend, they could be sold to create a capital loss. The following example illustrates the problem that is created by this situation:

> **Example**   On June 30, 2013, Brian Company acquires 1,000 shares of Leader Company, a public company, at a cost of $20 per share. On July 1, 2013, the Leader Company declares and pays its regular $3 per share dividend. Because this dividend had been anticipated by the market, the price of the Leader Company stock falls $3 per share to $17 per share. On July 15, 2013, Brian Company sells all of its Leader Company shares at a price of $17 per share.

> **Analysis**   In the absence of a special rule, the preceding situation would provide very favourable results for Brian Company. They would have received $3,000 in dividends which, because of the deduction for intercorporate dividends, would not be included in their Taxable Income. In addition, they would have a potentially deductible capital loss of $3,000 on the disposition of the shares.

12-21.   To prevent this from happening, ITA 112(3) and (3.01) contain "stop loss" rules applicable to shares held as capital property, and ITA 112(4) and (4.01) contain similar rules for shares held as inventory. Under these rules, any loss resulting from a disposition of shares by a corporation must be reduced by the amount of dividends received that are eligible for deduction under ITA 112(1). These rules apply if:

- the shares are held for less than one year; or
- the corporation holding the shares, along with other non-arm's length persons, owns more than 5 percent of the class of shares on which the dividend was received.

12-22.   In the preceding example, since the Brian Company held the shares for less than one year, the $3,000 capital loss would be eliminated by the $3,000 dividend received. The second condition, whether the Brian Company owns more than 5 percent of the class of shares, is not relevant given the length of time the shares were owned.

Exercise Twelve - 3

Subject: Stop Loss Rules

On June 16, 2012, Loren Ltd. acquires 1,000 of the 10,000 shares of Manon Inc. at a cost of $25.30 per share. On July 1, 2013, these shares pay a dividend of $2.16 per share. These are the only dividends that were received on these shares. Loren sells the shares on July 29, 2013 for $21.15 per share. Loren Ltd. has taxable capital gains of $50,000 in the year. What is the amount of the allowable capital loss that Loren Ltd. will include in its tax return for the taxation year ending December 31, 2013?

End of Exercise. Solution available in Study Guide.

Foreign Source Dividends Received

12-23.   The situation for dividends received from non-resident corporations is more complex. The general rules are discussed in Chapter 7, which notes that foreign source dividends are included in income on a gross basis, before the deduction of any foreign taxes withheld. However, in Chapter 11 we introduced the foreign non-business tax credit provisions. These credits against federal Canadian Tax Payable are designed to compensate the recipient of foreign source non-business income for foreign taxes withheld at source, provided the income has been subject to a reasonable amount of Canadian taxation. You will recall that, in many situations, the credit against Canadian Tax Payable will be equal to the amount of foreign taxes withheld at source. Note that foreign source dividends are not deducted in the determination of Taxable Income.

We suggest you work Self Study Problem Twelve-2 at this point.

Non-Capital Loss Carry Over For A Corporation

Additional Issues

12-24.   As the general rules for loss carry overs are the same for all taxpayers, most of the relevant material on this subject is dealt with in Chapter 11 where we discuss the determination of Taxable Income for individuals. There is, however, an additional problem in calculating the amount of the current year non-capital loss carry over for a corporation. This problem relates to the fact that dividends received from taxable Canadian corporations can be deducted by a corporation in the determination of its Taxable Income. To illustrate this problem, consider the following:

> **Example** During 2013, Marco Inc. has net taxable capital gains of $30,000 [(1/2)($60,000)], dividends of $25,000 received from taxable Canadian corporations, and an operating loss of $60,000. The Company also has a net capital loss carry forward from 2011 of $50,000 [(1/2)($100,000)].
>
> **Analysis** Using the ITA 3 rules for calculating Net Income For Tax Purposes, the result would be as follows:

ITA 3(a)	Dividends Received	$25,000
ITA 3(b)	Net Taxable Capital Gains	30,000
ITA 3(c)	Subtotal	$55,000
ITA 3(d)	Operating Loss	(60,000)
Net Income For Tax Purposes And Taxable Income		Nil

12-25.   From an intuitive point of view, it would appear that the non-capital loss for the year is $5,000, the ITA 3(c) subtotal less the operating loss. Further, as Net Income is nil, it appears that none of the net capital loss carry forward can be deducted, despite the $30,000 taxable capital gain. In addition, it does not appear that the Company will get any benefit from the potential deduction of the $25,000 in dividends that were received during the year. Fortunately, the ITA 111(8) definition of non-capital loss solves both of these problems.

An Expanded Definition

12-26.   You may recall that the ITA 111(8) definition was discussed previously in Chapter 11 (see the material starting at Paragraph 11-36). In that material, we explained how the definition permits a net capital loss carry over to be deducted even in cases where current year losses result in a nil Net Income For Tax Purposes. In effect, the definition allows a net capital loss carry over to be converted to a non-capital loss carry over.

12-27.   In the Chapter 11 discussion, we were dealing only with the Taxable Income of individuals. Given this, we did not consider the additional problem that arises with the fact that dividends received by a corporation can be deducted in the calculation of corporate Taxable Income. While this was not apparent from the simplified version of the non-capital loss definition that was presented in Chapter 11, a more complete version of the ITA 111(8) definition deals with this problem. The expanded definition is as follows:

ITA 111(8) The non-capital loss of a taxpayer for a taxation year means the amount determined by the formula:

$$A - D, \text{ where}$$

A   is the amount determined by the formula:

$$E - F, \text{ where}$$

E   is the total of all amounts each of which is the taxpayer's loss for the year from an office, employment, business or property, the taxpayer's allowable business investment loss for the year, net capital loss carry overs deducted in the calculation of Taxable Income for the year (this amount cannot exceed the taxable capital gains for the year), and **dividends received from taxable Canadian corporations and deducted in computing Taxable Income**.

F   is the amount of income determined under ITA 3(c). [Sum of ITA 3(a) non-capital positive sources and ITA 3(b) net taxable capital gains, less Division B, Subdivision e deductions.]

D   is the taxpayer's farm loss for the year.

12-28.   The only difference in this definition from the one that was presented in Paragraph 11-36 is the addition of "dividends received from taxable Canadian corporations and deducted in computing Taxable Income" in the E component. However, it is an important change in that it allows dividends that cannot be deducted because of insufficient Net Income For Tax Purposes to be added to the non-capital loss carry over balance.

Example

12-29.   All of these points can be illustrated by returning to the example presented in Paragraph 12-24. If we assume that Marco Inc. wishes to deduct the maximum amount of the 2011 net capital loss carry forward in 2013, the non-capital loss for the year would be calculated as follows:

Amount E ($60,000 + $30,000* + $25,000)	$115,000
Amount F - ITA 3(c) Balance ($25,000 + $30,000)	(55,000)
Non-Capital Loss For The Year	$ 60,000

*The net capital loss carry forward deduction is limited to $30,000, the amount of taxable capital gains realized during the year. This leaves a net capital loss carry forward of $20,000 ($50,000 - $30,000).

12-30.   Note the results of applying the non-capital loss definition. In effect, if there is not sufficient Net Income to allow their deduction in the calculation of Taxable Income, both dividends and net capital loss amounts deducted can be added to the non-capital loss carry over balance. Although subject to a 3 year carry back, 20 year carry forward limit, the loss carry over can be deducted against any type of income.

Exercise Twelve - 4

Subject: Non-Capital Loss With ABIL

For the taxation year ending December 31, 2013, Hacker Inc. has business and property income of $63,500. Also during this year, capital asset dispositions result in capital gains of $23,100 and capital losses of $38,400. The Company experiences a further loss on the arm's length sale of shares of a small business corporation in the amount of $151,500. Determine Hacker Inc.'s Net Income For Tax Purposes for 2013. Indicate the amount and type of any loss carry overs available at the end of the year.

End of Exercise. Solution available in Study Guide.

Exercise Twelve - 5

Subject: Non-Capital Loss Carry Forward

The following information is for Loser Ltd., a Canadian public company, for the taxation year ending December 31, 2013:

Capital Gains On Capital Asset Sales	$111,000
Capital Losses On Public Company Stock Sales	84,000
Allowable Business Investment Loss	5,250
Dividends Received From Taxable Canadian Corporations	48,000
Canadian Source Interest Income	27,200
Business Loss	273,000

The Company has a net capital loss carry forward of $19,000. It would like to deduct this loss during 2013. Determine the non-capital loss balance [ITA 111(8)] and net capital loss carry forward for Loser Ltd. at the end of the 2013 taxation year.

End of Exercise. Solution available in Study Guide.

Ordering Of Taxable Income Deductions

12-31.   Chapter 11 covered the specific ordering rules in ITA 111.1 for claiming deductions in the calculation of Taxable Income. However, these rules are directed at individuals and do not apply to corporations. The *Act* does not contain an equivalent provision for corporations and, as a consequence, there is a question as to how deductions should be ordered for a corporation.

12-32.   Charitable donations in excess of 75 percent of Net Income For Tax Purposes are not deductible in the current year, but can be carried forward for five years, subject to the same 75 percent limitation in those years. As this is shorter than the carry forward period for any other type of loss, this would suggest using these amounts prior to claiming loss carry forwards. However, in reaching this conclusion, it should be noted that these donations can be deducted against any type of income.

12-33.   Turning to the deduction of loss carry overs, ITA 111(3) requires that losses within any single category must be deducted in chronological order. That is, if a corporation chooses to deduct a portion of its non-capital loss balance during the current year, the oldest losses of this type must be deducted first. However, there are no rules with respect to the order in which the individual types of loss carry forwards must be deducted.

12-34.   Farm loss carry forwards and non-capital loss carry forwards have restrictions on the time for which they are available. This would suggest that they be deducted first. However, while there is no restriction on the period of availability for capital loss carry forwards, these amounts can only be used to the extent that there are net taxable capital gains during the period.

12-35.   For a corporation that experiences only limited capital gains, these restrictions may be a more important consideration than the period of time during which the loss will be available. With the carry forward period for non-capital losses lasting 20 years, this would appear to leave plenty of time to recover this type of loss.

12-36.   An additional factor in making decisions on whether to deduct non-capital or farm losses is the period left to their expiry. Clearly, items that expire in the current year should be deducted immediately, with additional consideration given to items near the end of their carry forward period.

We suggest you work Self Study Problems Twelve-3 and 4 at this point.

Geographical Allocation Of Income

Permanent Establishments

12-37.　After Taxable Income is calculated, in order to determine the amount of provincial taxes that are payable and the province(s) to which they are due, it is necessary to allocate the income of the corporation to the various provinces. Given the variations in provincial tax rates on corporations, this can be a matter of considerable significance.

12-38.　The key concept here is the idea of a "permanent establishment". This concept is defined as follows:

> **ITR 400(2)**　Permanent establishment means a fixed place of business of the corporation, including an office, a branch, a mine, an oil well, a farm, a timberland, a factory, a workshop or a warehouse.

12-39.　This meaning has been extended to include having an agent or employee in a province, if that agent or employee has the general authority to contract for a corporation, or carries a stock of merchandise from which orders are regularly filled. The mere presence of a commission salesperson or an independent agent is not considered evidence of a permanent establishment. In addition, the presence of a controlled subsidiary in a province is not necessarily indicative of a permanent establishment.

12-40.　However, ITR 400(2)(d) indicates that where a corporation that has a permanent establishment anywhere in Canada owns land in a province, such land will be deemed to be a permanent establishment. In addition, ITR 400(2)(e) indicates that where a corporation uses substantial machinery or equipment in a particular place, that corporation shall be deemed to have a permanent establishment in that place.

Activity At Permanent Establishments

12-41.　Once the location of permanent establishments has been determined, income will be allocated on the basis of two variables. These are gross revenues from the permanent establishment, and salaries and wages paid by the establishment.

12-42.　Once these values are established, ITR 402(3) provides a formula for using these variables to allocate Taxable Income to provinces. It requires calculating, for each province, that province's gross revenues as a percentage of total corporate gross revenues, and that province's salaries and wages as a percentage of total corporate salaries and wages. A simple average of these two percentages, without regard to the relative dollar values associated with the corporate totals, is then applied to corporate Taxable Income to determine the amount of Taxable Income that will be allocated to that province.

12-43.　Note that, if the corporation has permanent establishments outside of Canada, not all of its Taxable Income will be allocated to a province. The presence of these foreign permanent establishments will be reflected in the calculation of the federal tax abatement (see Paragraph 12-46).

Example - Permanent Establishments

12-44.　The following example illustrates the process of allocating Taxable Income on a geographic basis:

> **Example**　The Linford Company has permanent establishments in Alberta, Manitoba, and Ontario. The Company's Taxable Income for the current year totaled $100,000, with gross revenues of $1,000,000 and salaries and wages of $500,000.
>
> The following allocation of the gross revenues and the salaries and wages among the provinces occurred during the current year:

| Province | Gross Revenues | | Salaries And Wages | |
	Amount	Percent	Amount	Percent
Alberta	$ 250,000	25.0	$100,000	20.0
Manitoba	400,000	40.0	200,000	40.0
Ontario	350,000	35.0	200,000	40.0
Totals	$1,000,000	100.0	$500,000	100.0

Analysis   Using the average of the two percentages for each province, the Linford Company's Taxable Income would be allocated to the three provinces as follows:

Province	Average Percent	Taxable Income	Amount Allocated
Alberta	22.5	$100,000	$ 22,500
Manitoba	40.0	100,000	40,000
Ontario	37.5	100,000	37,500
Totals	100.0	N/A	$100,000

We suggest you work Self Study Problem Twelve-5 at this point.

Federal Tax Payable

Basic Rate

12-45.   All corporations are initially subject to the same basic tax rate. This rate is specified in ITA 123 and, for many years, has been set at 38 percent.

Federal Tax Abatement

12-46.   ITA 124(1) provides a reduction of 10 percentage points in the federal tax rate. This is normally referred to as the federal tax abatement and it is designed to leave room for the provinces to apply their respective tax rates. When deducted from the basic rate of 38 percent, this leaves a net rate of 28 percent.

12-47.   Note that this 10 percentage point reduction in the federal tax rate is only applicable to income earned in a Canadian jurisdiction. When a corporation has foreign operations in permanent establishments outside of Canada, less than 100 percent of its income will be allocated to the various provinces. When this is the case, the amount of abatement to be deducted is reduced by multiplying the 10 percent abatement by the total percentage of Taxable Income that was allocated to the provinces. For example, if only 80 percent of a corporation's Taxable Income was allocated to one or more provinces, the abatement would effectively be reduced to 8 percent [(10%)(80%)].

General Rate Reduction

General Rate Reduction Percentage

12-48.   It has been the policy of recent governments to reduce the tax rates applicable to Canadian corporations. In order to provide flexibility with respect to managing these changes, they have chosen to do this in a less than straightforward manner. Rather than simply reducing the rate specified in ITA 123, they introduced ITA 123.4(2) that provides for a deduction based on multiplying the corporation's "general rate reduction percentage" by its "full rate taxable income" for the year.

12-49.   This general rate reduction percentage was introduced in 2007 at 7 percent. The amount of the reduction was increased in each subsequent year until 2012. Beginning in 2012, the reduction is 13 percent and is not scheduled to change.

12-50.   In those situations where all of a corporation's income is allocated to a province and eligible for the general rate reduction, the corporate rate at the federal level is 15 percent:

Basic Corporate Rate	38%
Less: Federal Tax Abatement	(10%)
Balance	28%
Less: General Rate Reduction	(13%)
General Federal Corporate Rate	15%

Full Rate Taxable Income

12-51.   As noted, the "general rate reduction percentage" must be applied to "full rate taxable income". In fairly simple terms, full rate taxable income is income that does not benefit from certain other tax privileges. The most common of these privileges are the small business deduction, the manufacturing and processing profits deduction (M&P deduction), and the refundability of certain types of taxes on the investment income of private companies.

12-52.   Both the small business deduction and the M&P deduction are discussed later in this Chapter. Full Rate Taxable Income will also be considered in this Chapter, with detailed coverage beginning at Paragraph 12-142. The coverage of refundable taxes on the investment income of private companies will not be dealt with until Chapter 13.

Exercise Twelve - 6

Subject: Geographical Allocation And Federal Tax Payable

Sundown Ltd., a Canadian public company, has Taxable Income for the taxation year ending December 31, 2013 in the amount of $226,000. It has Canadian permanent establishments in Ontario and Manitoba. The Company's gross revenues for the 2013 taxation year are $2,923,000, with $1,303,000 of this accruing at the permanent establishment in Ontario, and $896,000 accruing at the permanent establishment in Manitoba. Wages and salaries total $165,000 for the year. Of this total, $52,000 is at the permanent establishment in Ontario and $94,000 is at the permanent establishment in Manitoba.   Sundown has sales to the U.S. through a U.S. permanent establishment. Calculate federal Tax Payable for the taxation year ending December 31, 2013. Ignore any foreign tax implications.

End of Exercise. Solution available in Study Guide.

Provincial Tax Payable

General Rules

12-53.   In calculating Tax Payable for individuals, a graduated rate structure is involved at both the federal and provincial levels. While limits on the brackets may differ from those used at the federal level, all of the provinces except Alberta assess taxes on individuals using graduated rates applied to Taxable Income.

12-54.   In contrast, provincial corporate taxes are based on a flat rate applied to a Taxable Income figure. With the exception of Alberta and Quebec, the federal Taxable Income figure is used. While these two provinces collect their own corporate taxes, the Taxable Income figure that they use is normally similar to that used at the federal level.

Figure 12 - 3
Combined Federal/Provincial Corporate Rates - January 1, 2013

	General Rate	M&P Rate	Small Business Rate
Federal Tax Only	15.0%	15.0%	11.0%
Combined Federal/Provincial			
Alberta	25.0%	25.0%	14.0%
British Columbia	25.0%	25.0%	13.5%
Manitoba	27.0%	27.0%	11.0%
New Brunswick	25.0%	25.0%	15.5%
Newfoundland	29.0%	20.0%	15.0%
Nova Scotia	31.0%	31.0%	14.5%
Ontario	26.5%	25.0%	15.5%
Prince Edward Island	31.0%	31.0%	12.0%
Quebec	26.9%	26.9%	19.0%
Saskatchewan	27.0%	25.0%	13.0%

General Rate

12-55.   As calculated in Paragraph 12-50, the general federal corporate rate is 15 percent. When the varying provincial rates are added to this percentage, Figure 12-3 shows that the general corporate tax rate ranges from a low of 25 percent in Alberta, British Columbia, and New Brunswick, to a high of 31 percent in Nova Scotia and Prince Edward Island.

Manufacturing And Processing Rate

12-56.   At one point in time, manufacturing and processing income (M&P) benefitted from a special deduction at the federal level. As will be discussed later in this Chapter, the deduction is still in place. However, as the deduction is now set equal to the general rate reduction percentage for the year, it is no longer of any benefit to corporations in terms of federal taxes payable. As shown in Figure 12-3, the federal M&P rate is identical to the federal general rate.

12-57.   This is also the situation with a majority of the provinces. However, Newfoundland, Ontario, and Saskatchewan apply reduced rates to this type of income. Because of this, it is still relevant to provide coverage of this subject. This coverage is included in this Chapter.

Small Business Rate

12-58.   The lowest rates in Figure 12-3 are referred to as the small business rates. As will be discussed later in this Chapter, Canadian controlled private corporations (CCPCs) are eligible for a small business deduction that lowers the federal rate to 11 percent on a limited amount of income. In general, the availability of this reduced rate is limited to the first $500,000 of active business income earned in a year.

12-59.   In general, the provinces provide reduced rates on the same $500,000 amount of active business income. However, for 2013, the limit in Manitoba and Nova Scotia is $400,000.

12-60.   When the reduced federal and provincial rates are combined, the resulting rates range from a low of 11 percent in Manitoba, to a high of 19 percent in Quebec.

Investment Income Rates

12-61.   While this is not illustrated in Figure 12-3, different rates are applicable to certain types of investment income. We will provide coverage of these rates in Chapter 13.

Other Provincial Taxes

12-62. In addition to their basic corporate income tax, most provinces also levy capital and payroll taxes on corporations. Unlike provincial income tax on corporations, these taxes are treated as deductions in the calculation of Taxable Income, a situation that lowers the amount of federal tax that can be collected on that corporation's income. This, in effect, reduces the cost of these capital and payroll taxes to the paying corporation.

12-63. However, the use of such taxes at the provincial level also reduces federal tax revenues and, as a consequence, the federal government has threatened for a long time to eliminate the deductibility of capital and payroll taxes. At present, there is an interim measure that has denied deductibility to any increases in these taxes after March, 1993. This "interim" measure is still in place at the time of writing (June, 2013).

Other Goals Of The Corporate Tax System

12-64. If raising revenues was the only goal of the corporate taxation system, there would be nothing much to discuss with respect to this matter, and there would be little need for the Chapters on corporate taxation that follow. However, in addition to raising revenues, the Canadian corporate taxation system has been structured to accomplish a number of other objectives. These include:

- **Incentives For Small Business**   While there are several features of the tax system directed at encouraging small businesses, the major tax incentive for these organizations is the small business deduction.

- **Incentives For Certain Business Activities**   The Canadian tax system encourages scientific research through a generous system of tax credits and a liberal policy towards deductible amounts. Tax credits are available to encourage business activities such as the employment of apprentices and the creation of child care spaces. Support is also provided to the natural resource industries through a variety of programs.

- **Incentives For Certain Regions**   Certain regions of Canada are given assistance through investment tax credits and other programs.

- **Integration**   One of the goals of the Canadian tax system is to keep the level of taxes paid on a given stream of income the same, regardless of whether or not a corporation is placed between the original source of the income and the ultimate recipient.

12-65. The small business deduction and the manufacturing and processing profits deduction will be examined in this Chapter. Integration will be dealt with in detail in Chapter 13. Our material on scientific research and experimental development expenditures and investment tax credits can be found in Chapter 14.

Small Business Deduction

Introduction

12-66. It has been a longstanding goal of the Canadian taxation system to provide incentives to small business. The underlying assumption is that, particularly during their formative years, these businesses need some degree of tax relief in order to allow them to accumulate the capital required for expansion. In order to provide this relief, the small business deduction was introduced in 1972. In somewhat simplified terms, it provides a deduction against the Tax Payable of a Canadian controlled private corporation.

12-67. The federal deduction is equal to 17 percent of the first $500,000 of active business income. While most provinces have this same limit for their small business rate, in Nova Scotia and Manitoba, the provincial small business rate is restricted to the first $400,000 of active business income.

Example A Canadian controlled private corporation has Taxable Income of $100,000 for the year ending December 31, 2013. All of this income is earned in Canada and eligible for the small business deduction. The provincial tax rate applicable to income eligible for the small business deduction is 3 percent.

Analysis The corporation's Tax Payable would be calculated as follows:

Base Amount Of Part I Tax [(38%)($100,000)]	$38,000
Federal Tax Abatement [(10%)($100,000)]	(10,000)
Small Business Deduction [(17%)($100,000)]	(17,000)
General Rate Reduction (Note)	Nil
Federal Tax Payable	$11,000
Provincial Tax Payable [(3%)($100,000)]	3,000
Total Tax Payable	$14,000

Note As explained later in this Chapter, the general rate reduction is not available on income that is eligible for the small business deduction.

12-68. As can be seen in the example, when the small business deduction is available, it reduces the federal rate to 11 percent ($11,000 ÷ $100,000). We have also applied a provincial rate of 3 percent (roughly the average provincial rate). This produces a combined federal/provincial rate of 14 percent ($14,000 ÷ $100,000).

12-69. The small business deduction provides a significant incentive to businesses that qualify. Only certain types of corporations qualify for this deduction and it is only available on certain amounts and types of income. The criteria for qualification can be described in non-technical terms as follows:

Type Of Corporation The availability of the small business deduction is restricted to Canadian controlled private corporations (CCPCs).

Type Of Income The deduction is only available on income earned in Canada that qualifies as "active business income". This would include the income of professional corporations and management companies, provided they are private and Canadian controlled. However, the income of specified investment businesses and personal services corporations (see definitions later in this Chapter) does not qualify.

Limit On Amount The deduction is available on the first $500,000 of active business income earned in a year (in Manitoba and Nova Scotia the limit is $400,000). This amount is referred to as the annual business limit and, in some circumstances, it is subject to a reduction formula.

Associated Corporations The $500,000 annual business limit must be shared among associated corporations.

12-70. The issues associated with these criteria are discussed in the material that follows.

Canadian Controlled Private Corporation (CCPC)

12-71. CCPCs are defined in ITA 125(7) as private corporations that are not controlled, directly or indirectly, by one or more non-resident persons, by one or more public corporations, or a combination of non-resident persons and public corporations. In addition, corporations that have shares listed on a designated stock exchange, in or outside of Canada, do not qualify as CCPCs. As an additional point here, in order to qualify for the small business deduction, the corporation must be a CCPC throughout the taxation year.

Active Business Income

The General Idea

12-72. ITA 125(7) contains the following definition of "active business":

Active business carried on by a corporation means any business carried on by the corporation other than a specified investment business or a personal services business and includes an adventure or concern in the nature of trade.

12-73.   While the preceding defines active business, a further definition in ITA 125(7) defines income from an active business as follows:

Income of the corporation for the year from an active business means ... the income of the corporation for the year from an active business carried on by it, including any income for the year pertaining to or incident to that business, other than income for the year from a source in Canada that is a property ... [The definition goes on to cover an amount under ITA 12 (10.2) that is of no interest to users of this material.]

12-74.   While this definition is not a model of clarity, it expresses the basic idea that active business income involves "doing something" to produce income. The concept excludes what is usually referred to as property income. Property income is distinguished by the fact that it generally becomes available with little or no effort on the part of the recipient (e.g., interest earned on long-term bonds).

The Problem With Defining Property Income

12-75.   As noted, the preceding definitions of active business and active business income are largely directed towards excluding property income such as interest, dividends, and rents from eligibility for the small business deduction. The federal government does not wish to allow individuals to have access to the small business deduction by simply placing their passive investments in the shelter of a Canadian controlled private corporation. However, a blanket exclusion of property income is inappropriate since there are corporations that are "actively" involved in earning such income.

12-76.   The difficulty is in finding a way to distinguish between corporations that are simply being used as tax shelters for property or passive income, and corporations that engage in active property management. For example, if a corporation has a single residential rental property, the rents from this property would undoubtedly be viewed as passive income.

12-77.   Alternatively, a corporation that owns a chain of hotels with more than 10,000 rooms would certainly be entitled to view the rentals of these properties as an active business. The question is, at what point does the corporation cross the line between earning passive income and active business income?

12-78.   Similar, but less obvious problems arise with interest income. If a corporation has no activity other than collecting interest on term deposits, the amounts that it earns would almost certainly be viewed as passive income. Alternatively, interest earned by a company actively involved in providing mortgage financing to corporate clients could be viewed as business income. Again, a problem exists in finding the point at which a crossover is made between the two situations.

The Solution - Specified Investment Business

12-79.   The concept of a "specified investment business" provides a somewhat arbitrary solution to this problem. The term is defined in ITA 125(7) as follows:

Specified Investment Business carried on by a corporation in a taxation year, means a business (other than a business carried on by a credit union or a business of leasing property other than real or immovable property) the principal purpose of which is to derive income (including interest, dividends, rents and royalties) from property but, except where the corporation was a prescribed labour-sponsored venture capital corporation at any time in the year, does not include a business carried on by the corporation in the year where

(i)   the corporation employs in the business throughout the year more than 5 full-time employees, or

(ii) any other corporation associated with the corporation provides, in the course of carrying on an active business, managerial, administrative, financial, maintenance or other similar services to the corporation in the year and the corporation could reasonably be expected to require more than 5 full-time employees if those services had not been provided.

12-80.   As the activities of these specified investment businesses are excluded from the definition of active business, it means that income from property generated by such businesses is not eligible for the small business deduction. Stated alternatively, for corporations that are primarily engaged in earning income from property, the *Act* specifies that only those with more than five full time employees involved in earning such income are considered to be earning active business income and eligible for the small business deduction.

12-81.   While this is an arbitrary solution to the problem of distinguishing between active and passive income from a business, it does serve to resolve most of the uncertainty in this area. With respect to interpreting this rule, IT-73R6 states that "more than five full-time employees" means that at least six employees are working full business days on each working day of the year. However, this interpretation has been overturned in a Tax Court of Canada Decision (489599 B.C. Ltd. vs. The Queen).

12-82.   In this decision, the court indicated that a combination of five full time employees and one part time employee would constitute "more than five full time employees". While IT-73R6 has not been revised to reflect the results in this case, the CRA has indicated that they accept this decision and will rule accordingly in future applications of the specified investment business definition.

Incidental Property Income
12-83.   The definition of active business income includes incidental property income that is earned by a corporation engaged in an active business. In this regard, many corporations experience temporary excess cash balances, and these balances will usually be invested in interest bearing assets. Within reasonable limits, such interest can be included as a component of active business income. In similar fashion, revenues resulting from temporary rentals of excess space may be included in active business income.

Property Income Received From An Associated Corporation
12-84.   Property income, income from a specified investment business, and non-incidental property income earned by an active business do not qualify for the small business deduction. However, when a corporation derives income from holding property, and the income is received from an associated company that deducted the amounts in computing active business income, ITA 129(6)(b) deems the income to be active business income to the recipient.

12-85.   The logic behind this is that, while the amounts received by one of the associated companies must be considered property income, because of its legal form, the deduction by the payer corporation reduces the total active business income within the associated group.

> **Example** Lardin Inc. is associated with Dwarm Ltd. Lardin lends $100,000 to Dwarm to use in active business activities. During the current year, Dwarm pays $6,000 of interest to Lardin.

> **Analysis** Normally, Lardin could not classify the interest received as active business income. However, if Dwarm is earning active business income, the payment to Lardin reduced the amount of this income, as well as the total active business income of the associated group. In order to prevent this reduction, the recipient corporation is allowed to treat such interest as active business income.

Annual Business Limit
12-86.   The federal limit on the amount of active business income that is eligible for the small business deduction is $500,000 per taxation year. As discussed in the paragraph which follows, this annual limit must be shared by associated corporations.

Allocation Among Associated Companies

12-87.   In the absence of special rules, it would be very easy to avoid the annual limit that applies to the small business deduction. This could be accomplished by dividing a single corporation's activities between two separate corporations, thereby doubling up on the annual business limit of $500,000. However, the *Act* prevents this by requiring that associated companies share their annual business limit.

12-88.   In some cases, association is fairly obvious. If, for example, a single individual owned all of the shares to two separate corporations, these corporations are clearly associated. However, a complete coverage of this subject becomes very complex. Because of this, we have allocated our detailed coverage of this subject to Chapter 14, Other Issues In Corporate Taxation.

12-89.   While we are deferring our detailed coverage of this subject, we would note here that a group of associated companies can allocate the $500,000 limit in any manner that they wish. It can be divided equally among the group, allocated 100 percent to a single member of the group, or split in any proportions that the group chooses to use.

Calculating The Small Business Deduction

The General Formula

12-90.   After noting that to qualify for this deduction, a corporation must be a CCPC throughout the year, ITA 125(1) specifies that the deduction from federal Tax Payable is equal to 17 percent of the least of three figures (note that for ease of reference, this formula is included at the front of this book under "Rates and Other Data"):

(a) Net Canadian active business income.

(b) Taxable Income, less:

   (i) 100/28 times [See **Note**] the ITA 126(1) credit for taxes paid on foreign non-business income, calculated without consideration of the additional refundable tax under ITA 123.3 (see Chapter 13) or the general rate reduction under ITA 123.4; and

   (ii) 4 times [See **Note**] the ITA 126(2) credit for taxes paid on foreign business income, calculated without consideration of the general rate reduction under ITA 123.4.

(c) The annual business limit of $500,000, less any portion allocated to associated corporations, less the reduction for large corporations.

Note   The numbers in (b)(i) and (b)(ii) are not the ones in current legislation. However, they reflect draft legislation that is being enforced for years after 2011. We feel the details and history of these changes will not be of interest to our users.

Constraints - Type Of Income And Annual Business Limit

12-91.   We have already noted that the deduction is only available on active business income earned in Canada, the item A constraint. We have also noted that the annual business limit of $500,000, the item C constraint, must be shared by associated companies.

Constraints - Taxable Income

12-92.   With respect to the limit which uses Taxable Income, we would note that active business income earned during the taxation year is included in Net Income For Tax Purposes. In many cases, this amount will also be included in full in Taxable Income. However, it is possible that large Division C deductions could eliminate all or part of this income from the Taxable Income total. Examples of such Division C deductions would be as follows:

• charitable donations
• non-capital loss carry overs
• farm loss carry overs

12-93.   You will notice that neither dividends nor net capital losses are included in this list. This reflects the fact that these amounts can only be deducted to the extent that either dividends or taxable capital gains are included in Net Income. Given this, they cannot serve to offset amounts of active business income that are included in Net Income For Tax Purposes.

12-94.   A simple example will illustrate the need for this Taxable Income constraint on the small business deduction:

Example   During the current year, Allard Ltd. has active business income of $123,000, taxable capital gains of $15,000, and dividends received from taxable Canadian corporations of $50,000. At the beginning of the year, Allard Ltd. has a net capital loss carry forward of $35,000 and a non-capital loss carry forward of $105,000. The Company will use the loss carry forwards to the extent possible during the current year. The calculation of Allard's Net Income For Tax Purposes and Taxable Income would be as follows:

Net Income For Tax Purposes	
($123,000 + $15,000 + $50,000)	$188,000
Dividends Received	(50,000)
Net Capital Loss Carry Forward	
(Restricted To Taxable Capital Gains)	(15,000)
Subtotal (Equal To Active Business Income)	$123,000
Non-Capital Loss Carry Forward	(105,000)
Taxable Income	$ 18,000

12-95.   Note that if only the net capital loss carry forward and dividends were deducted, Taxable Income would have been equal to the $123,000 in active business income. The problem is the non-capital loss carry forward. It has further reduced Taxable Income to $18,000, an amount well below the active business income.

12-96.   If, in this case, the small business deduction was based on active business income, the amount would be $20,910 [(17%)($123,000)]. As this deduction is far in excess of the Tax Payable on $18,000 of Taxable Income, this is not a reasonable outcome. The example clearly illustrates the need for the Taxable Income constraint on the small business deduction.

Constraints - Foreign Tax Credits

12-97.   Another concern of the federal government is to ensure that the small business deduction is not provided on income that has not been taxed in Canada. To prevent this from happening, the B component of the ITA 125(1) formula reduces Taxable Income by:

- 100/28 times the ITA 126(1) credit for taxes paid on foreign non-business income, calculated without consideration of the additional refundable tax under ITA 123.3 (see Chapter 13) or the general rate reduction under ITA 123.4; and

- 4 times the ITA 126(2) credit for taxes paid on foreign business income, calculated without consideration of the general rate reduction under ITA 123.4.

12-98.   The 100/28 figure is based on the notional assumption that foreign non-business income will be subject to a federal tax rate of 28 percent (i.e., if the credit is equal to the taxes paid at 28 percent, 100/28 times the credit will equal the notional amount of income received).

12-99.   In similar fashion, the 4 times figure that is applicable to foreign business income is based on the notional assumption that this income will be subject to a federal tax rate of 25 (1 ÷ 4) percent.

12-100.   Based on the preceding analysis, subtracting these amounts from Taxable Income has the effect of removing from this figure the amounts of foreign income on which the foreign tax credit has eliminated the Canadian taxation at the assumed rates of 28 and 25 percent. A simple example can be used to clarify this point:

Example A corporation earns $100,000 in foreign non-business income, with $18,000 being withheld by the foreign government.

If this income had been earned in Canada, it is assumed that the tax would be $28,000 (using the notional rate on this type of income of 28 percent). Being received from a foreign source, the $28,000 in Canadian Tax Payable will be offset by the $18,000 foreign tax credit. This will leave a net Canadian Tax Payable of $10,000.

Using the foreign tax credit of $18,000 and an assumed tax rate of 28 percent, the formula removes $64,286 [(100/28)($18,000)] from Taxable Income, leaving $35,714 ($100,000 - $64,286). This demonstrates how the formula ensures that the small business deduction is not available on Taxable Income on which foreign tax credits have eliminated Canadian taxation.

If the foreign tax withheld and the foreign tax credit had been $28,000 [(28%)($100,000)], the formula would have removed $100,000 [(100/28)($28,000)], or all of the foreign source income.

Exercise Twelve - 7

Subject: Amount Eligible For The Small Business Deduction

Kartoom Ltd. is a CCPC throughout the year and is not associated with any other corporation. For the year ending December 31, 2013, Kartoom has Net Income For Tax Purposes of $570,000. This amount is made up of dividends from taxable Canadian corporations of $85,000, active business income of $425,000, and foreign non-business income of $60,000. The foreign income was subject to withholding in the foreign jurisdiction at a rate of 15 percent. Kartoom receives a foreign tax credit against federal Tax Payable that is equal to the amount withheld. Kartoom has a non-capital loss carry forward of $160,000 which it intends to deduct during 2013. Determine the amount eligible for the small business deduction for the year ending December 31, 2013.

End of Exercise. Solution available in Study Guide.

Elimination Of Small Business Deduction For Large CCPCs

The Problem

12-101. As the name implies, the small business deduction was designed to provide assistance to small corporations. For a variety of reasons, including the belief that such corporations have a positive impact on employment growth, and the fact that small corporations often experience financing difficulties in their formative years, the generous tax advantages provided by this deduction were thought to be appropriate.

12-102. However, in designing the small business deduction provisions, eligibility was based on the type of income earned (active business income) and the type of corporation (CCPCs). No consideration was given to the size of the corporation's income or assets. As a consequence, under its usual provisions, some very large private corporations received the benefit of the small business deduction on amounts of active business income that were below the annual business limit. This was clearly not in keeping with the intent of this legislation.

The Solution

12-103. To deal with this problem, the government introduced a formula that reduces the annual business limit on the basis of the size of the CCPC's Taxable Capital Employed In Canada. As found in ITA 125(5.1), the formula is as follows:

Annual Business Limit Reduction $= A \times \dfrac{B}{\$11{,}250}$ where,

A   is the amount of the corporation's annual business limit for the year ($500,000 or less if shared with associated corporations).

B   is 0.225 percent (.00225) of the excess of, the previous year's total Taxable Capital Employed In Canada by the corporation and its associated companies, over $10 million.

12-104.   "Taxable capital employed in Canada" is defined in ITA 181.2.   In somewhat simplified terms, it has the following meaning:

Taxable Capital Employed In Canada (TCEC)   GAAP determined debt and equity capital of the corporation, less debt and equity investments in other corporations. When not all of the corporation's Taxable Income is allocated to a province, the resulting amount is multiplied by the same percentage that is applied to the abatement in order to determine the portion of the total capital that is employed in Canada.

12-105.   The mechanics of this formula are easily understood.   Note that this formula calculates the **reduction** in the annual business limit, **not** the limit after the reduction.   If a corporation has $10 million or less TCEC, B will equal nil ($10 million or less, minus the $10 million specified deduction).   This means the formula amount will be nil and there will be no reduction in the corporation's annual business limit.

12-106.   When the amount of TCEC reaches $15 million, B in the formula will be equal to $11,250 [(.00225)($15,000,000 - $10,000,000)].   The annual business limit will then be multiplied by one ($11,250 ÷ $11,250) and the reduction in the annual business limit will be 100 percent of the available amount.

12-107.   Not surprisingly, a CCPC that is associated with one or more other corporations in a taxation year ending in a given calendar year will be required to take into account the TCEC of all of these firms.

Example

12-108.   The following example illustrates the reduction of the small business deduction for a large CCPC:

Example   Largess Inc. is a CCPC with a December 31 year end.   All of its income is earned in Canada, and it is not associated with any other corporation.   On December 31, 2013, the following information is available:

2013 Active Business Income	$ 523,000
2013 Taxable Income	550,000
Taxable Capital Employed In Canada During 2012	13,700,000

12-109.   For the preceding year, 2012, B in the reduction formula would be equal to $8,325 [(.00225)($13,700,000 - $10,000,000)].   Using this in the ITA 125(5.1) formula would produce the following reduction in the 2013 annual business limit:

$$\$500{,}000 \times \frac{\$8{,}325}{\$11{,}250} = \$370{,}000 \text{ \bf Reduction}$$

12-110.   Given this, the reduced annual business limit would be $130,000 ($500,000 - $370,000) and the small business deduction for 2013 would be 17 percent of the least of:

Active Business Income	$523,000
Taxable Income	550,000
Reduced Annual Business Limit ($500,000 - $370,000)	130,000

12-111.   The reduced annual business limit is the least of the three figures and the 2013 small business deduction would be $22,100 [(17%)($130,000)], a significant reduction from the $85,000 [(17%)($500,000)] that would have been available in the absence of the ITA 125(5.1) requirement for reducing the annual business limit for large CCPCs.

Exercise Twelve - 8

Subject: Small Business Deduction Reduction

Largely Small Inc. is a Canadian controlled private corporation. For the year ending December 31, 2013, its Net Income For Tax Purposes is $1,233,000, all of which is active business income, except for $36,000 in foreign source non-business income. Fifteen percent of this amount was withheld in the foreign jurisdiction and the corporation receives a foreign tax credit against federal Tax Payable that is equal to the amount withheld. The corporation's only deduction in the calculation of Taxable Income is for a non-capital loss carry forward of $914,000. The corporation had Taxable Capital Employed In Canada of $11,300,000 for the year ending December 31, 2012, and $11,600,000 for the year ending December 31, 2013. It is not associated with any other corporation. Determine the amount of Largely Small Inc.'s small business deduction for the year ending December 31, 2013.

End of Exercise. Solution available in Study Guide.

Personal Services Corporations

12-112.   The small business deduction represents a very significant reduction in corporate taxes and, as a consequence, taxpayers have a strong incentive to channel income into a corporation qualifying for this benefit.

12-113.   At one point in time, this could be accomplished by having an executive of a corporation resign, establish a company, and immediately have his company sign a contract with his former employer to provide the same services as the individual was previously performing as an employee. Since this new corporation could then qualify for the small business deduction, the use of such personal services corporations provided significant tax deferral and, in some cases, significant tax avoidance, for individuals such as executives, professional athletes, and entertainers.

12-114.   Under the current rules, such blatant tax avoidance schemes are no longer possible. To begin, ITA 125(7) defines a "personal services business" as follows:

... a business of providing services where

(a) an individual who performs services on behalf of the corporation (referred to as an incorporated employee), or
(b) any person related to the incorporated employee

is a specified shareholder of the corporation and the incorporated employee would reasonably be regarded as an officer or employee of the person or partnership to whom or to which the services were provided but for the existence of the corporation, unless

(c) the corporation employs in the business throughout the year more than five full time employees, or
(d) the amount paid or payable to the corporation in the year for the services is received or receivable by it from a corporation with which it was associated in the year.

12-115.   In somewhat less technical language, a business will be classified as a personal services business of a corporation when a "specified" shareholder of the corporation is providing services to another business and the individual who is performing the services can reasonably be regarded as an officer or employee of the entity for which the services are performed. As the term is used in this definition, "specified shareholder" refers to an individual who owns, directly or indirectly, not less than a 10 percent interest in the company under consideration.

12-116.   Being classified as a personal services corporation is costly in terms of tax. Such a corporation is not eligible for the small business deduction, so any of its income from the personal services business is subject to tax at full corporate rates. In addition, a personal services corporation is not eligible for the general rate reduction (see Paragraph 12-140). A further restriction is that no deduction is permitted to the corporation for any expenses other than:

- salaries, wages, other remuneration, and benefits paid in the year to the individual who performed the services on behalf of the corporation; and

- other expenses that would normally be deductible against employment income, for example, travel expenses incurred to earn employment income.

12-117.   These rules are designed to remove the availability of the small business deduction and the general rate reduction in certain situations where a corporation is being used as a device to channel an individual's income from performing services into a more favourably taxed classification.

12-118.   With respect to personal services corporations established to replace an executive's personal employment arrangements, these rules have served to eliminate most of the tax incentives for such arrangements. However, athletes, entertainers and consultants may still find it attractive to incorporate. In many cases, they will qualify for the small business deduction either because they have sufficient diversity of income, or more than five full time employees.

Professional Corporations And Management Companies

12-119.   In general terms, these two types of corporations can be described as follows:

Professional Corporations   This term is used where a corporation is established to carry on the practice of a specified profession. These situations include the professional practice of an accountant, dentist, lawyer, medical doctor, veterinarian, or chiropractor. At one time, very few provinces permitted the incorporation of a professional practice. However, this is changing, as several provinces, including Alberta and Ontario, now permit this practice.

Management Companies   This is a term that refers to corporations established to provide various management services, primarily to an unincorporated business. The unincorporated business is usually a professional practice, such as that of a doctor or dentist, which is not permitted to incorporate because of provincial legislation.

The services provided by this type of company include various personnel functions, such as payroll and accounting services, purchasing all supplies and equipment necessary to carry on the business, and providing the necessary office space required by the professional practice.

The unincorporated business pays fees to the company to cover the cost of providing management services and to provide for some income. A 15 percent markup for profit is usually allowed. The fees paid are deductible from the revenues of the professional practice. These companies are often used to transfer a portion of a professional's income to a lower income spouse or other related parties.

12-120.   Both types of companies are eligible for the small business deduction. However, the fact that medical services are exempt goods under the GST/HST legislation has made management companies unattractive for doctors and dentists. While GST/HST must be paid on services billed by the management company, these amounts cannot be recovered by medical professionals because their services are GST/HST exempt. (For coverage of GST/HST exempt services, see Chapter 21, GST/HST.) Given this situation, and the fact that professionals can incorporate in some provinces, management companies for medical professionals delivering GST/HST exempt services are not as common as they once were.

Manufacturing And Processing Profits Deduction

Introduction

12-121. Given the importance of such activity to the Canadian economy, it is not surprising that the federal government has provided tax assistance to enterprises that are involved in manufacturing and processing (M&P). As an example of this, in Chapter 5, Capital Cost Allowances And Cumulative Eligible Capital, we noted that the government is providing significantly enhanced CCA rates on both buildings used for M&P and for M&P machinery and equipment.

12-122. A more general incentive is the M&P deduction available to some corporations for their M&P profits. However, as was explained previously, the rate for this deduction is now set at the same percentage as the general rate reduction. As the general rate reduction does not apply to income that is eligible for the M&P deduction, the use of the M&P deduction does not provide any direct tax benefits at the federal level.

12-123. Given this situation, it would seem logical for the government to eliminate the legislation related to the M&P deduction. However, this does not appear to be happening. The probable explanation for this is that some provinces (Newfoundland, Ontario, and Saskatchewan) still provide special treatment for income that qualifies for the federal M&P deduction. Because of this, and the special CCA rates for M&P assets, we will continue to provide some coverage of the M&P rules.

Calculating The Deduction

General Formula

12-124. ITA 125.1 provides for a deduction from Tax Payable equal to the general rate reduction of 13 percent, times the company's M&P profits. Given that this amount is deducted from Tax Payable, it would be more consistent to refer to this "deduction" as a tax credit. However, ITA 125.1 uses the term deduction and, as a consequence, we will also use this terminology.

12-125. While the basic idea is that the deduction is equal to the general rate reduction percentage applied to M&P profits, there are a number of other constraints on the amount that is eligible for this deduction. ITA 125.1(1) specifies that the deduction will be equal to the corporation's general rate reduction percentage multiplied by the lesser of:

    A. Manufacturing and processing profits, less amounts eligible for the small business deduction; and

    B. Taxable income, less the sum of:

        1. the amount eligible for the small business deduction;

        2. 4 times the foreign tax credit for business income calculated without consideration of the general rate reduction under ITA 123.4; and

        3. where the corporation is a Canadian controlled private corporation throughout the year, aggregate investment income as defined in ITA 129(4).

12-126. Part A of this formula provides the basic limit based on the amount of M&P profits earned during the year. As will be noted subsequently, M&P profits is a technical term and must be calculated by a formula established in ITR 5200. In many cases, particularly for large public companies, this will be the factor that limits the amount of the M&P deduction.

12-127. Like the small business deduction formula, for ease of reference, this M&P deduction formula is included at the front of this book under "Rates and Other Data".

Constraints - Small Business Deduction

12-128. As was previously discussed, the small business deduction provides certain corporations with a deduction equal to 17 percent of the first $500,000 of their active business income. It appears that the government believes that granting both the 13 percent M&P

deduction, and the 17 percent small business deduction on the same income stream would be too generous. As a consequence, any amounts of income that are eligible for the small business deduction are not eligible for the M&P deduction. In the preceding ITA 125.1(1) formula, this is accomplished by removing amounts eligible for the small business deduction from both the A and B components. Note that it is the "amount eligible" for the small business deduction that is removed, not the deduction itself.

Constraints - Taxable Income

12-129.   As was explained in our discussion of constraints on the availability of the small business deduction, the government wants to ensure that credits are not given on amounts that are not included in Taxable Income. As was the case with the active business income that is eligible for the small business deduction, M&P profits that are included in Net Income For Tax Purposes may not find their way into Taxable Income.

12-130.   This can occur when the corporation has deductions for such items as charitable donations, non-capital loss carry overs, or farm loss carry overs. For reasons that were discussed and illustrated in the discussion of the small business deduction, amounts eligible for the M&P deduction are limited by the amount of Taxable Income for the year.

Constraints - Foreign Tax Credits

12-131.   As was the case with the Taxable Income constraint, the nature of the constraint created by deducting a multiple of foreign tax credits was explained in our discussion of the small business deduction. There is, however, one significant difference.

12-132.   In the ITA 125.1(1) formula for the M&P deduction, Taxable Income is reduced by a multiple of the foreign business income credit only. It is not adjusted for the foreign non-business income credit as was the case with the ITA 125(1) formula for the small business deduction. This probably reflects the fact that the M&P formula contains an extra deduction from Taxable Income for aggregate investment income, an amount that includes foreign non-business income.

Constraints - Aggregate Investment Income

12-133.   This constraint is more difficult to explain at this stage. It is based on the fact that a part of federal tax paid on the "aggregate investment income" of a Canadian controlled private corporation can be refunded to the corporation. (This procedure is discussed in detail in Chapter 13.) As it would not appear to be appropriate to provide a tax credit against taxes that may eventually be refunded, these amounts are removed from the Taxable Income that is eligible for the M&P deduction.

12-134.   Note the reference to "aggregate investment income as defined in ITA 129(4)" in the formula in Paragraph 12-125. This somewhat unusual concept of investment income includes net taxable capital gains, interest, rents, and royalties, but does not include dividends that a corporation can deduct in the calculation of Taxable Income. It includes both foreign and Canadian amounts for these items, and the balance is reduced by net capital loss carry overs deducted during the year under ITA 111(1)(b). For ease of reference, this aggregate investment income definition is included at the front of this book under "Rates and Other Data".

Eligibility

12-135.   On the surface, eligibility for the M&P deduction appears to be easily determinable. Any corporation that derives 10 percent or more of its Canadian active business gross revenues from Canadian manufacturing or processing is eligible. The problem with this rule is the determination of what constitutes M&P activity.

12-136.   The *Income Tax Act* does not define the terms manufacturing or processing. However, ITA 125.1(3) specifically excludes several types of activity from the designation of manufacturing or processing. These include logging, farming and fishing, construction, producing industrial minerals, and processing mineral resources.

12-137.   More guidance on the nature of manufacturing and processing is available in IT-145R. This IT Bulletin notes that manufacturing generally involves the creation of something or the shaping, stamping, or forming of an object from something. Correspondingly, processing is described as techniques of preparation, handling, or other activity designed to effect a physical or chemical change in an article or substance.

12-138.   Needless to say, these descriptions have not settled the issue and, as a consequence, the distinction between qualified and non-qualified activity has been the subject of numerous court cases. In fact, there is often a very fine line between qualified and non-qualified activities. For example, for the owner of a pub, IT-145R advises:

> The mixing of a number of ingredients of a drink is considered processing but the mere pouring of liquor or beer into a glass and the dispensing of draft beer are not considered processing.

M&P Profits Defined

12-139.   We have noted that the M&P deduction is calculated by multiplying the general rate reduction percentage by "M&P profits". The determination of M&P profits is based on a fairly complex calculation that is found in ITR 5200. Given that this is largely a mechanical process and the fact that the M&P deduction no longer has an effect on the amount of federal Tax Payable, we are not providing coverage of this calculation in our basic text. However, if you have further interest in this calculation, coverage is provided in Supplementary Reading No. 3, *Determining M&P Profits*. Supplementary Readings can be found on the Student CD-ROM which accompanies this text.

Exercise Twelve - 9

Subject: Amounts Eligible For Small Business and M&P Deductions

Marion Manufacturing is a Canadian controlled private corporation throughout 2013 and is not associated with any other company. It has Net Income For Tax Purposes of $462,000, a figure that includes $411,000 in manufacturing and processing profits (as per ITR 5200). The $462,000 also includes foreign source business income of $21,000 and taxable capital gains of $30,000. Because of withholding on the foreign source business income, the Company is entitled to a foreign tax credit of $3,150 [(15%)($21,000)].   The Company's only deduction in the calculation of Taxable Income is donations to registered Canadian charities in the amount of $310,000. Marion anticipates large increases in Taxable Income in the next few years. Determine the amount of Marion's small business deduction and M&P deduction for the year ending December 31, 2013, assuming that the Company deducts all of the $310,000 of charitable donations. Do you believe that deducting all of the donations is the best alternative for Marion? Explain your conclusion.

End of Exercise. Solution available in Study Guide.

General Rate Reduction - ITA 123.4(2)

Approach To Rate Reductions

12-140.   In our discussion of the basic federal tax rate for corporations, we noted that, in implementing reductions in corporate tax rates, the government has left the basic rate of 38 percent unchanged (see Paragraph 12-45). Instead of reducing the basic rate, they have created a deduction from this rate. This deduction is referred to as the "general rate reduction" percentage and, for 2013, the rate is 13 percent.

12-141.   While the government wished to reduce corporate tax rates through the use of this general rate reduction, they did not want it to be available on income that was already benefitting from some other tax privilege (e.g., the small business deduction). To deal with this potential problem, the government introduced the concept of Full Rate Taxable Income.

Full Rate Taxable Income

12-142.   In defining Full Rate Taxable Income, the goal was to develop a measure of income that did not benefit in a significant way from other types of benefits. In particular, the government did not want the general rate reduction to be applied to income that was eligible for:

• The small business deduction. This deduction is only available to CCPCs.

• The M&P deduction. This deduction is available to CCPCs, public companies, and private companies that are not Canadian controlled.

• Refundable Taxes. Refundable taxes are applicable to the investment income of CCPCs and, in some applications to the investment income of private companies that are not Canadian controlled. They are not applicable to public companies. While we need to consider the impact of refundable taxes on Full Rate Taxable Income at this point, the detailed procedures related to refundable taxes are discussed in Chapter 13.

12-143.   Since the availability of the relevant benefits depends on the type of company, we will have to give separate attention to the calculation of the Full Rate Taxable Income of CCPCs, and to the Full Rate Taxable Income of companies that are not CCPCs (public companies and private companies that are not Canadian controlled).

Application To Companies Other Than CCPCs

12-144.   For these companies, the only adjustment to Taxable Income that is required to determine Full Rate Taxable Income is the removal of income eligible for the M&P deduction. Given this, for companies other than CCPCs, Full Rate Taxable Income is defined as follows:

Regular Taxable Income	$x,xxx
Income Eligible For The M&P Deduction	(xxx)
Full Rate Taxable Income	$x,xxx

12-145.   A simple example will serve to illustrate the relevant calculations:

Example   For the year ending December 31, 2013, Daren Ltd., a Canadian public company, has Taxable Income equal to $100,000, with $40,000 of this amount eligible for the M&P deduction.

Analysis   Full Rate Taxable Income is equal to $60,000 ($100,000 - $40,000). Given this, total federal Tax Payable for Daren Ltd. would be calculated as follows:

Base Amount Of Part I Tax [(38%)($100,000)]	$38,000
Federal Tax Abatement [(10%)($100,000)]	(10,000)
M&P Deduction [(13%)($40,000)]	(5,200)
General Rate Reduction [(13%)($100,000 - $40,000)]	(7,800)
Federal Tax Payable	$15,000

12-146.   For a corporation with income consisting entirely of M&P profits, there is no general rate reduction as there is no Full Rate Taxable Income. This is illustrated by revising the example in Paragraph 12-145:

Revised Example   Assume that the $100,000 in Taxable Income of Daren Ltd. was generated solely by M&P activities.

Analysis   Total federal Tax Payable for Daren Ltd. would be calculated as follows:

Base Amount Of Part I Tax [(38%)($100,000)]	$38,000
Federal Tax Abatement [(10%)($100,000)]	(10,000)
M&P Deduction [(13%)($100,000)]	(13,000)
General Rate Reduction [(13%)($100,000 - $100,000)]	Nil
Federal Tax Payable	$15,000

12-147.   This calculation illustrates the fact that the overall federal rate on income that is eligible for the M&P deduction is 15 percent. This is, of course, identical to the overall rate on income that is eligible for the general rate reduction, illustrating the fact that the M&P deduction is no longer advantageous at the federal level.

Exercise Twelve - 10

Subject: Federal Tax Payable For A Public Company

For the year ending December 31, 2013, Marchand Inc., a Canadian public company, has Taxable Income of $320,000. Of this total, $180,000 qualifies for the M&P deduction. Calculate Marchand's federal Tax Payable for the year ending December 31, 2013. Include in your solution any M&P deduction available.

End of Exercise. Solution available in Study Guide.

Application To CCPCs

12-148.   Not surprisingly, the calculation of Full Rate Taxable Income for a CCPC is somewhat more complex than it is for a public company. As we have noted, in addition to the M&P deduction, these companies may benefit from the small business deduction and the refundable tax provisions on investment income.

12-149.   Given the potential presence of these additional tax privileges, Full Rate Taxable Income for a CCPC is defined as follows:

Taxable Income, reduced by:

1. Income eligible for the small business deduction.

2. Income eligible for the M&P deduction.

3. The corporation's aggregate investment income for the year as defined in ITA 129(4). [This is to remove income that will benefit from refundable taxes when it is distributed by the corporation. These taxes are explained in Chapter 13.]

12-150.   The definition of aggregate investment income in ITA 129(4) was discussed in the coverage of the M&P deduction (see Paragraph 12-134). It includes both foreign and Canadian amounts of net taxable capital gains, interest, rents, and royalties, but not dividends that are deductible in computing Taxable Income. The balance is reduced by net capital loss carry overs deducted during the year.

12-151.   As is covered in Chapter 13, a portion of the Part I tax paid by CCPCs on their aggregate investment income is refunded when dividends are paid. Since this type of income is already taxed advantageously when it is flowed through a CCPC, it does not receive the benefit of the general rate reduction.

12-152.   The following example illustrates the application of the general rate reduction rules to a CCPC with no investment income.

Example For the year ending December 31, 2013, Zaptek Ltd., a CCPC, has $200,000 in Taxable Income. This amount is made up entirely of active business income earned in Canada, none of which relates to M&P activity. Zaptek is associated with another company and, as per the agreement with that company, Zaptek is entitled to $100,000 of the annual business limit.

Analysis The federal Tax Payable for Zaptek Ltd. would be calculated as follows:

Base Amount Of Part I Tax [(38%)($200,000)]	$76,000
Federal Tax Abatement [(10%)($200,000)]	(20,000)
Small Business Deduction [(17%)($100,000)]	(17,000)
General Rate Reduction [(13%)($200,000 - $100,000)]	(13,000)
Federal Tax Payable	$26,000

12-153.   The overall rate of federal tax in this example is 13 percent ($26,000 ÷ $200,000). This reflects a combination of a rate of 11% (38% - 10% - 17%) on the $100,000 of income that was eligible for the small business deduction, and a rate of 15% (38% - 10% - 13%)] on income that is not eligible for this deduction.

Exercise Twelve - 11

Subject: Federal Tax Payable For A CCPC

Redux Ltd. is a Canadian controlled private corporation. For the year ending December 31, 2013, the Company has Taxable Income of $200,000, all of which is active business income. Of this amount, $145,000 results from M&P activity. As it is associated with two other corporations, its share of the annual business limit is $140,000. Determine the Company's federal Tax Payable for the year ending December 31, 2013. Include in your solution any M&P deduction available.

End of Exercise. Solution available in Study Guide.

We suggest you work Self Study Problems Twelve-6, 7, 8, and 9 at this point.

Foreign Tax Credits For Corporations

Introduction
12-154.   The foreign tax credits that are available to individuals earning foreign business or non-business income are discussed in detail in Chapter 11. Under rules that are very similar to those applicable to individuals, corporations are also allowed to use foreign taxes paid on business and non-business income as credits against Canadian Tax Payable. While the rules are similar to those for individuals, there are differences that will be discussed here.

Calculation Of Foreign Tax Credits
Foreign Non-Business (Property) And Business Tax Credits
12-155.   The formula that limits the Canadian tax credit for foreign taxes paid on foreign source non-business income is as follows:

The **Foreign Non-Business Income Tax Credit** is the lesser of:

- The tax paid to the foreign government (for corporations, there is no 15 percent limit on the foreign non-business taxes paid); and

- An amount determined by the following formula:

$$\left[\frac{\text{Foreign Non} - \text{Business Income}}{\text{Adjusted Division B Income}} \right] [\text{Tax Otherwise Payable}]$$

12-156.   The meaning of "Adjusted Division B Income" and "Tax Otherwise Payable" are explained beginning at Paragraph 12-159. Both of the foreign tax credit formulae are included at the front of this book under "Rates and Other Data".

12-157.   The formula that limits the amount of foreign business income taxes paid that can be used as a foreign tax credit is as follows:

The **Foreign Business Income Tax Credit** is the least of:

- The tax paid to the foreign government

- An amount determined by the following formula:

$$\left[\frac{\text{Foreign Business Income}}{\text{Adjusted Division B Income}} \right] [\text{Tax Otherwise Payable}]$$

- Tax Otherwise Payable for the year, less any foreign tax credit taken on non-business income under ITA 126(1).

12-158.   As was the case with individuals, there is an additional factor to consider in the case of foreign business income tax credits. This is the "Tax Otherwise Payable", reduced by any foreign non-business income tax credit deducted under ITA 126(1).

Adjusted Division B Income

12-159.   While the general descriptions in the formulae (e.g., Adjusted Division B Income and Tax Otherwise Payable) are the same as those applicable to individuals, their meaning is somewhat different. More specifically, for a corporation, "Adjusted Division B Income" is determined as follows:

Division B Income (Net Income For Tax Purposes)	$x,xxx
Net Capital Loss Carry Overs Deducted Under ITA 111(1)(b)	(xxx)
Taxable Dividends Deducted Under ITA 112	(xxx)
Dividends From A Foreign Affiliate Deductible Under ITA 113	(xxx)
Adjusted Division B Income	$x,xxx

Tax Otherwise Payable

12-160.   The following table compares the components included in the calculation of Tax Otherwise Payable for foreign non-business tax credits with those used to calculate foreign business tax credits.

Tax Otherwise Payable Components	Non-Business	Business
Base Amount Of Part I Tax (38%)	Yes	Yes
Plus: Additional Refundable Tax (ART) On		
Investment Income Of CCPC (See Chapter 13)	Yes	No
Minus: Federal Tax Abatement	Yes	No
Minus: General Rate Reduction	Yes	Yes

12-161.   "Tax Otherwise Payable" is a particularly confusing term as its calculation is different for individuals and corporations. As shown in the table, adding to the confusion is the fact that its components differ depending on whether it is being used to calculate foreign non-business tax credits or foreign business tax credits for corporations.

12-161.   You will recall that the purpose of the 10 percent federal tax abatement is to leave room for the provinces to tax corporations. It is deducted in the formula for determining foreign non-business tax credits because non-business income will, in general, be taxed in a province. As a consequence, it is appropriate to deduct this abatement in determining the limit on the foreign non-business tax credit.

12-162.   In contrast, in the calculation of the foreign business income tax credit, "Tax Otherwise Payable" is not reduced by the 10 percent federal tax abatement, reflecting the fact that foreign business income will not be taxed in a province. Also different is the fact that this calculation of "Tax Otherwise Payable" does not include the additional refundable tax on investment income under ITA 123.3. (See Chapter 13.)

12-163.   You may recall that the foreign tax credit constraint in the small business deduction calculation uses foreign tax credit amounts that do not consider the general rate reduction (see Paragraph 12-97). The reason for this is a potentially circular calculation. Since the general rate reduction amount uses the amount eligible for the small business deduction and the small business deduction calculation uses the foreign tax credits, these amounts cannot all be calculated at the same time. As a result, the foreign tax credits used in calculating the small business deduction may not be equal to the actual foreign tax credits.

Foreign Tax Credit Carry Overs

12-164.   Unlike the situation with individuals, where the amount of foreign taxes that can be used as a credit is limited to 15 percent of the foreign source non-business income, the only limit for a corporation is the limit that is found in the second component of the formula. If the actual amount of foreign taxes paid is greater than this limit, there is no carry over of the excess as a tax credit. However, as was noted in Chapter 11, unclaimed amounts can be deducted under ITA 20(12) in the determination of Net Income For Tax Purposes.

12-165.   Unlike the case with foreign non-business income taxes paid in excess of amounts used as tax credits, unused foreign business taxes paid can be carried over as a tax credit to the 3 preceding taxation years or the 10 subsequent taxation years. In calculating the allowable tax credit for such carry overs, these unused amounts will be added to the foreign tax paid factor in the calculation of the foreign business income tax credit.

Exercise Twelve - 12

Subject: Foreign Tax Credits

Internat Inc. is a Canadian public company. For the year ending December 31, 2013, it has Net Income For Tax Purposes of $146,000, including foreign business income of $20,000. The foreign government withheld $3,000 in taxes on this income, resulting in a net remittance of $17,000. None of the Company's income involves manufacturing and processing and, based on the ITR 402(3) formula, 88 percent of the Company's income was allocated to a province. In calculating Taxable Income, the Company deducts $30,000 in dividends received from taxable Canadian companies, a non-capital loss carry forward of $75,000, and a net capital loss carry forward of $25,000. Determine the Company's Part I Tax Payable for the year ending December 31, 2013. Include in your answer any carry overs available at the end of the year.

End of Exercise. Solution available in Study Guide.

We suggest you work Self Study Problem Twelve-10 at this point.

Key Terms Used In This Chapter

12-166.   The following is a list of the key terms used in this Chapter. These terms, and their meanings, are compiled in the Glossary located at the back of the separate paper Study Guide.

Active Business	General Rate Reduction
Active Business Income	Loss Carry Back
Adjusted Active Business Income	Loss Carry Forward
Allowable Business Investment Loss	Manufacturing And Processing Profits
Allowable Capital Loss	Deduction (M&P Deduction)
Annual Business Limit	Net Business Income
Associated Corporations	Net Capital Loss
Business Income	Non-Capital Loss
Business Investment Loss	Ordering Rule
Canadian Controlled Private Corporation	Permanent Establishment
Carry Over	Personal Services Business
CCPC	Preferred Shares
Common Shares	Private Corporation
Corporation	Property Income
Designated Stock Exchange	Public Corporation
Disposition	Small Business Deduction
Federal Tax Abatement	Specified Investment Business
Foreign Taxes Paid Credit	Stop Loss Rules
Full Rate Taxable Income	Taxable Capital Employed In Canada
GAAP	Term Preferred Shares

References

12-166.   For more detailed study of the material in this Chapter, we refer you to the following:

ITA 89(1)	Definitions (Private Corporation And Public Corporation)
ITA 110	Deductions Permitted
ITA 111	Losses Deductible
ITA 112	Deduction Of Taxable Dividends Received By Corporations Resident In Canada
ITA 113	Deduction In Respect Of Dividend Received From Foreign Affiliate
ITA 123	Basic Part I Rate For Corporations
ITA 123.3	Additional Refundable Tax On CCPC's Investment Income
ITA 123.4(2)	General Deduction From Tax
ITA 124	Federal Abatement
ITA 125	Small Business Deduction
ITA 125.1(1)	Manufacturing And Processing Profits Deductions
S5-F2-C1	Foreign Tax Credit
IT-67R3	Taxable Dividends From Corporations Resident In Canada
IT-73R6	The Small Business Deduction
IT-145R	Canadian Manufacturing And Processing Profits — Reduced Rate Of Corporate Tax (Consolidated)
IT-177R2	Permanent Establishment Of A Corporation In A Province And Of A Foreign Enterprise In Canada (Consolidated)
IT-189R2	Corporations Used By Practising Members Of Professions
IT-206R	Separate Businesses
IT-232R3	Losses — Their Deductibility In The Loss Year Or In Other Years
IT-391R	Status Of Corporations
IT-458R2	Canadian Controlled Private Corporation

Problems For Self Study

(The solutions for these problems can be found in the separate Study Guide.)

Self Study Problem Twelve - 1 (Corporate Net Income)

One of your assistants has been calculating Net Income For Tax Purposes for the Sanklee Company. For both accounting and tax purposes, the Company uses a December 31 year end. Your assistant has been able to complete most of the required Schedule 1. However, there are a number of items that he would like you to review. The items are as follows:

1. The Company has recorded amortization expense in its accounting records of $254,000. The maximum deductible CCA for the taxation year is $223,000.

2. The Company has recorded interest expense of $57,000. The accounting Balance Sheet indicates that the bonds payable premium account declined by $2,000 during the year.

3. On August 12 of the current year, the Company sold an asset with an original cost of $80,000 for $120,000. In the accounting records, the asset had a net book value of $53,000. It was a Class 43 asset and, at the end of the year, there is a positive balance in this class. The Company still owns other Class 43 assets. Only $72,000 of the $120,000 sales price is received in cash, with the remainder to be paid at the end of the following taxation year.

4. During the year, the Company paid $8,000 for two memberships in the Ottawa Ritz Golf And Country Club. The two Company executives that hold the memberships billed the Company $12,000 for entertainment of clients at this Club. Both of these amounts were deducted in the Company's accounting records.

5. During the year, the Company made charitable donations of $11,000. This amount was deducted in their accounting records.

6. During the year, the Company sold a Class 10 asset for $23,000. The original cost of the asset was $50,000 and its net book value at the time of sale was $39,000. This was the last asset in Class 10 and, at the beginning of the year, the balance in Class 10 was nil. No Class 10 assets were acquired during the current year.

Required: For each of the items listed, indicate the addition to and/or deduction from accounting Net Income that would be required in the calculation of the minimum Net Income For Tax Purposes.

Self Study Problem Twelve - 2 (Corporate Taxable Income)

The following information relates to Margo Ltd. for the year ending December 31, 2013.

1. The calculation of Cost Of Goods Sold was based on an opening inventory of $225,000 and a closing inventory of $198,600. In addition, the closing inventory was reduced by $15,000 for a reserve for future declines in value. This is the first year the Company has used an inventory reserve.

2. Property Taxes include $1,200 for tax paid on vacant land. The company has held this land for 5 years, in anticipation of relocating its head office.

3. As the result of a business combination on January 15, 2013, Margo Ltd. recorded $34,000 in goodwill. As of December 31, 2013, this goodwill was found to be impaired and a goodwill impairment loss of $1,700 was recorded. The goodwill qualifies as an eligible capital expenditure for tax purposes. At the beginning of the year, there is no balance in the cumulative eligible capital account.

4. The legal fees are made up of $1,200 paid to appeal an income tax assessment and $1,020 paid for general corporate matters.

5. The gain on the sale of investments involved marketable securities with a cost of $21,000. The securities were sold for $30,500.

6. The gross foreign interest income of $1,800 was received net of $270 in foreign tax withholdings.

7. The maximum CCA for the current year is $78,000.

The Income Statement that has been prepared by Margo Ltd.'s accountant for the year ending December 31, 2013, is as follows:

Sales Revenue		$925,000
Cost Of Goods Sold (Note 1)		(717,000)
Gross Profit		$208,000
Operating Expenses:		
Salaries And Wages	($40,200)	
Rents	(22,200)	
Property Taxes (Note 2)	(8,800)	
Amortization Expense	(35,600)	
Write-Down Of Goodwill (Note 3)	(1,700)	
Charitable Donations	(19,800)	
Legal Fees (Note 4)	(2,220)	
Bad Debt Expense	(7,100)	
Warranty Provision	(5,500)	
Social Club Membership Fees	(7,210)	
Other Operating Expenses	(39,870)	(190,200)
Operating Income		$ 17,800
Other Revenues (Expenses):		
Gain On Sale Of Investments (Note 5)	$9,500	
Interest Revenue	2,110	
Interest On Late Income Tax Instalments	(1,020)	
Investment Counsellor Fees	(500)	
Foreign Interest Income (Note 6)	1,530	
Dividends From Taxable Canadian Corporations	3,000	
Premium On Redemption Of Preferred Shares	(480)	14,140
Income Before Taxes		$ 31,940

Required: Determine the minimum Net Income For Tax Purposes and Taxable Income of Margo Ltd., for the year ending December 31, 2013.

Self Study Problem Twelve - 3 (Corporate Loss Carry Forwards)

The following information relates to the operations of Notem Inc. for the taxation year ended December 31, 2013 (all amounts are based on the relevant tax rules):

Net Business Loss	$141,800
Dividends From Taxable Canadian Corporations	33,500
Taxable Capital Gains	9,600
Allowable Capital Losses	4,425
Charitable Donations	5,400

At the beginning of the taxation year, the Company had a carry forward of unused charitable donations of $1,350 from the previous year, and a net capital loss carry forward of $10,500 [(1/2)($21,000)].

It is the policy of the Company to minimize net capital loss balances prior to using any other type of carry over balance.

Required: Calculate the corporation's minimum Net Income For Tax Purposes and Taxable Income for its 2013 taxation year. Indicate any balances available for carry forward to subsequent years.

Self Study Problem Twelve - 4 (Corporate Loss Carry Forwards - 4 Years)

Linden Industries Inc. began operations in 2010 and has a December 31 fiscal year end. While it was fairly successful in its first year of operation, excessive production of an unmarketable product resulted in a large operating loss for 2011. Profits have come back in 2012 and 2013.

The relevant Division B income and loss figures, along with charitable donations made during the years under consideration are as follows:

	2010	2011	2012	2013
Business Income (Loss)	$95,000	($205,000)	$69,500	$90,000
Capital Gains (Losses)	(10,000)	(14,000)	9,000	10,000
Dividends Received	12,000	42,000	28,000	32,000
Charitable Donations	21,400	4,600	8,000	22,000

All of the dividends have been received from taxable Canadian corporations. It is the policy of the Company to minimize its net capital loss carry forward balance.

Required: For each of the four years 2010 through 2013, provide the following information:

- The minimum Net Income For Tax Purposes and Taxable Income that would be reported for Linden Industries. Indicate the amount and type of any current year losses that are available for carry back or carry forward.
- The amended figures for any years to which losses are carried back.
- An analysis of the amount and type of carry forwards that would be available at the end of the year.

Self Study Problem Twelve - 5 (Geographical Allocation Of Income)

The Sundean Company has its national headquarters in Toronto, and all of its senior management people have their offices at this location. The Company also has operations in Vancouver, Calgary, Saskatoon, and Halifax. In each of these cities, warehouse space is maintained and orders are filled. In addition, a sales staff operates out of office space in each warehouse, taking orders throughout the province in which the warehouse is located.

For the current taxation year, the Company's Taxable Income totalled $1,546,000, on gross revenues of $10,483,000. Also during the current year, the Company had salaries and wages totalling $1,247,000. These gross revenues and expenses were distributed among the provinces where the Company has operations in the following manner:

	Gross Revenues	Wages And Salaries Accrued
Alberta	$ 1,886,940	$ 261,870
British Columbia	2,306,260	274,340
Nova Scotia	1,362,790	174,580
Saskatchewan	1,257,960	99,760
Ontario	3,669,050	436,450
Total	$10,483,000	$1,247,000

Required: Calculate the amount of the Sundean Company's Taxable Income for the current year that would be allocated to each of the five provinces. Any percentages used in your calculations should be rounded to one decimal place.

Self Study Problem Twelve - 6 (Part I Tax With Reduced SBD)

Kannon Inc. is a Canadian controlled private corporation that retails photographic equipment. During its taxation year ending December 31, 2013, its Taxable Income was correctly determined to be $473,000, including $440,000 in Canadian active business income. The remainder of this income was foreign business income and, because of favourable treaty provisions, no foreign taxes were withheld on this income. The revenues were earned and the wages paid in a country where Kalec has a permanent establishment.

The provincial and international distribution of its gross revenue and wages and salaries is as follows:

	Wages And Salaries	Gross Revenues
Saskatchewan	$ 560,000	$1,200,000
Manitoba	642,000	1,232,000
Foreign	96,000	447,000
Total	$1,298,000	$2,879,000

Kannon had Taxable Capital Employed In Canada of $12,488,890 for the year ending December 31, 2012, and $11,200,000 for the year ending December 31, 2013. It is not associated with any other corporation.

Required: Calculate Kannon's federal Part I Tax Payable for the year ending December 31, 2013.

Self Study Problem Twelve - 7 (Corporate Tax Payable - Simple)

The Serendipity Shop Corp. sells art works on consignment in Winnipeg. The shares of Serendipity Shop Corp. are all owned by Elizabeth Montgomery, a Canadian, resident in Winnipeg.

The Serendipity Shop Corp. has Net Income For Tax Purposes of $240,000 for the year ending December 31, 2013. The Net Income For Tax Purposes is comprised of $220,000 from business activity and $20,000 in dividends from various investments in Canadian public companies. None of the Company's income qualifies for the M&P deduction.

In May, 2013, the Serendipity Shop Corp. donated $48,000 to the Canadian Indigenous Art Foundation, a registered Canadian charity. There are no carry forwards of donations or losses, and the corporation paid no dividends in the year.

Because Serendipity is associated with another corporation, its 2013 annual business limit is reduced to $135,000.

Required: Determine Taxable Income and Part I federal Tax Payable for the Serendipity Shop Corp. for the year ending December 31, 2013.

Self Study Problem Twelve - 8 (Net And Taxable Income, Tax Payable)

Borscan Inc.'s shares are publicly traded. None of its income is from manufacturing or processing. During the taxation year ending December 31, 2013, the condensed Income Statement of Borscan Inc. was prepared in accordance with generally accepted accounting principles. In condensed form it is as follows:

Borscan Inc.
Condensed Income Statement (Pre-Tax Amounts)
Year Ending December 31, 2013

Revenues	$2,800,000
Expenses (Excluding Taxes)	(1,550,000)
Income Before Results Of Discontinued Operations	$1,250,000
Results Of Discontinued Operations	25,000
Accounting Income Before Taxes	$1,275,000

Other Information:

1. The results of discontinued operations reflect the expropriation of a building and the land it is situated on for total proceeds of $625,000. The building had a capital cost of $500,000. The land on which the building is situated cost $100,000. Since this was also the fair market value of the land at the time of the expropriation, $100,000 of the proceeds is allocated to the land. As the Company leases all of its other assets, the building was the only asset in Class 1. The UCC balance of this class, prior to the disposition of the building was $350,000.

2. Amortization included in the accounting expenses amounts to $255,000. Maximum available deductions for CCA amount to $287,000, without consideration of the building that was expropriated.

3. Expenses include interest and penalties of $500 resulting from a failure to file the previous year's tax return on time.

4. Revenues include dividends from taxable Canadian corporations in the amount of $25,000.

5. Expenses include a deduction for charitable donations in the amount of $13,500.

6. Prior to the deduction of any 2013 amortization, the December 31 balance in the Company's cumulative eligible capital account is $85,000. The items reflected in this balance have been charged to expense in previous years for accounting purposes.

7. The Company has available non-capital loss carry forwards from previous years that total $35,000 and a net capital loss carry forward of $30,000 [(1/2)($60,000)].

Required:

A. Calculate the minimum Net Income For Tax Purposes for Borscan Inc. for 2013.

B. Calculate the minimum Taxable Income for Borscan Inc. for 2013. Indicate the amount, and type, of any carry overs that are available at the end of the year.

C. Calculate the minimum federal Part I Tax Payable for Borscan Inc. for 2013.

Self Study Problem Twelve - 9 (Net And Taxable Income, Tax Payable)

During its taxation year ending December 31, 2013, the condensed Income Statement of Industrial Tools Ltd. was prepared in accordance with generally accepted accounting principles. In condensed form it is as follows:

Industrial Tools Ltd.
Condensed Income Statement (Pre-Tax Amounts)
For The Year Ending December 31, 2013

Revenues	$6,585,000
Expenses (Excluding Taxes)	(4,280,000)
Net Income Before Taxes	$2,305,000

Other Information:

1. The Company's shares are publicly traded and none of its income is from manufacturing or processing.

2. The January 1, 2013 balance in the Company's cumulative eligible capital account is $115,000.

3. Revenues include an accounting gain of $225,000, resulting from the sale of a building for $1,150,000 in cash. The property had cost $1,075,000. This was made up of $200,000 for the land and $875,000 for the building. It is the only asset in Class 1, and the UCC balance in this class prior to the sale was $625,000. At the time of the sale, the value of the land was unchanged at $200,000.

4. There is a net capital loss carry forward available of $90,000 [(1/2)($180,000)].

5. Expenses included a deduction for charitable donations in the amount of $28,000.

6. The Expenses include interest and penalties of $2,500, resulting from a failure to file last year's tax return within the prescribed time period.

7. Expenses include a warranty reserve of $20,000. This is the first year that the Company has deducted such a reserve.

8. Revenues include dividends from taxable Canadian corporations of $42,000.

9. Amortization included in the accounting Expenses amounts to $478,000. Maximum available deductions for CCA amount to $523,000.

Required:

A. Calculate the minimum Net Income For Tax Purposes for Industrial Tools Ltd. for the year ending December 31, 2013.

B. Calculate the minimum Taxable Income for Industrial Tools Ltd. for the year ending December 31, 2013. Indicate the amount and type of any loss carry overs that are still available for use in subsequent years.

C. Calculate the minimum federal Part I Tax Payable for Industrial Tools Ltd. for the year ending December 31, 2013. As the corporation operates in a province that has a reduced tax rate for M&P activity, a separate calculation of the federal M&P deduction is required.

Show all calculations, whether or not they are necessary to the final solution.

Self Study Problem Twelve - 10 (Net And Taxable Income, Tax Payable, FTC)

The Mercury Company is a private corporation with two shareholders. Jennifer Mercury owns 47 percent of the voting shares and lives in Hamilton, Ontario. She is in charge of the Canadian operations, which are located in Hamilton. John Mason owns 53 percent of the voting shares and lives in Rochester, New York. He is in charge of the U.S. operations, which are located in Rochester. The Company's fiscal year ends on December 31.

All money amounts are expressed in Canadian dollars.

For the year ending December 31, 2013, the Company had accounting income, before any provision for income taxes, of $530,400. This amount included the following (all amounts are in Canadian dollars):

Dividends From Taxable Canadian Corporations	$ 9,400
Gain On Sale Of A Long-Term Investment In Shares	22,900
Interest Income From Canadian Sources	7,800
Donations To Registered Canadian Charity	18,700
Dividends From U.S. Portfolio Investments	
(Before $4,845 Of Taxes Withheld In U.S.)	32,300
U.S. Business Income (Before $20,700 Of Taxes Withheld In U.S.)	64,200

The Company has available a non-capital loss carry forward of $21,950 and a net capital loss carry forward of $13,500 [(1/2)($27,000)].

The Company's Canadian sales occur in Ontario and Manitoba. U.S. sales are all in the state of New York. Its head office and manufacturing operations are in Ontario. However, the Company has warehouses and sales people in Ontario and New York. Manitoba customers are serviced through Ontario warehouses and sales people. Sales, salaries and wages for these locations are as follows:

	Ontario	Manitoba	New York	Total
Sales	$3,850,000	$1,875,000	$565,000	$6,290,000
Salaries And Wages	$3,540,000	Nil	$438,000	$3,978,000

Using ITR 5200, the Company has determined that their M&P profits are $410,000.

Required:

A. Calculate the minimum Net Income For Tax Purposes for Mercury Company for 2013.

B. Calculate the minimum Taxable Income for Mercury Company for 2013. Indicate the amount, and type, of any carry overs that are available at the end of the year.

C. Assume the foreign business and non-business tax credits are equal to the amounts withheld. Calculate the minimum federal Part I Tax Payable for Mercury Company for 2013. As the corporation operates in a province that has a reduced tax rate for M&P activity, a separate calculation of the federal M&P deduction is required.

D. Using the amounts determined in Part C, calculate the actual foreign tax credits that will be deducted (they may be equal to the amount withheld).

Show all calculations, whether or not they are necessary to the final solution.

Assignment Problems

(The solutions for these problems are only available in
the solutions manual that has been provided to your instructor.)

Assignment Problem Twelve - 1 (Schedule 1 Adjustments)

Hartman Ltd. has a December 31 year end. It has been determined that, for the 2013 taxation year, the Company's accounting Net Income, determined in accordance with generally accepted accounting principles, is $362,450. Additional information was available for preparing the corporation's Schedule 1.

1. During 2013, the Company deducted a $45,000 charitable donation. The donation was a depreciable asset with a UCC of $36,500 and a capital cost of $42,000. The net book value of the asset in the accounting records was $38,000.

2. Amortization expense for the year was $32,450. The Company intends to deduct the maximum CCA for the year of $27,650.

3. At the beginning of 2013, the Company had a liability for estimated warranties of $8,460. During the year, warranty costs were incurred in the amount of $9,420 and, at the end of the year, the remaining warranty liability was estimated to be $10,470.

4. During 2013, the Company sold temporary investments for $12,320. The adjusted cost base of the investments was $12,870.

5. During 2013, the Company paid bond interest of $27,400. The discount on the bond issue declined by $2,600.

6. During the year, the Company sold depreciable assets with a capital cost of $189,000 and a net book value of $107,000 for cash proceeds of $92,190. These assets were the last assets in their CCA class, and there were no additions to the class during the year. At the beginning of the current year, the UCC balance in the CCA class was $101,770.

Required: For each of the preceding pieces of information, indicate the adjustment(s) that would be required to convert the Company's $362,450 accounting Net Income to minimum Net Income For Tax Purposes. Explanations for the adjustments are not required and no calculation of the total Net Income For Tax Purposes is required.

Assignment Problem Twelve - 2 *(Corporate Taxable Income)*

The following information on Dunway Ltd., a Canadian public company, is applicable to the year ending June 30, 2013:

Sales Of Merchandise	725,000
Operating Expenses	533,000
Dividends From Controlled Subsidiary	37,500
Dividends From Non-Controlled Public Companies	15,000
Capital Gain On Investment Sale	222,000
Dividends Paid	182,000
Donation To Canadian Government	26,000
Donations To Registered Canadian Charities	141,000

At the beginning of this fiscal year, the Company has available a net capital loss carry forward of $180,000 [(1/2)($360,000)] and a non-capital loss carry forward of $137,000. Dunway Ltd. does not anticipate having any capital gains in the foreseeable future.

Required: Calculate the minimum Net Income For Tax Purposes and Taxable Income for Dunway Ltd. for the year ending June 30, 2013. Indicate the amount and type of any carry forwards that will be available for use in future years.

Assignment Problem Twelve - 3 *(Corporate Net And Taxable Income)*

When it was incorporated, Sedux Inc. chose to have a December 31 year end. However, the nature of their business is such that winter is a peak period and having a September 30 year end would coincide with their slack period. For 2013, it has received permission from the CRA to change its year end to September 30.

Its Income Statement for the period January 1, 2013 through September 30, 2013, prepared in accordance with GAAP, is as follows:

Sedux Inc.
Income Statement
9 Month Period Ending September 30, 2013

Sales (All Within Canada)		$763,000
Cost Of Sales		(402,000)
Gross Margin		$361,000
Other Expenses (Excluding Taxes):		
Wages And Salaries	($126,000)	
Amortization	(46,000)	
Rent	(72,000)	
Interest Expense	(4,600)	
Foreign Exchange Loss	(3,400)	
Travel And Promotion	(28,000)	
Bad Debt Expense	(4,900)	
Warranty Reserve	(4,700)	
Charitable Donations	(2,400)	
Other Operating Expenses	(17,000)	(309,000)
Operating Income		$ 52,000
Gain On Sale Of Investments		3,000
Income Before Taxes		$ 55,000

Other Information:

1. During the period January 1, 2013 through September 30, 2013, the Company declared and paid dividends of $23,000.

2. On January 1, 2013, the Company has a $16,000 non-capital loss carry forward and a $5,000 [(1/2)($10,000)] net capital loss carry forward.

3. In determining the Cost Of Sales, the Company deducted a $15,000 reserve for inventory obsolescence.

4. Wages and salaries includes a $10,000 bonus to Sedux Inc.'s CEO. Because he anticipates retiring at the end of 2014, this bonus will not be paid until January, 2015.

5. Amortization is on the furniture and fixtures and delivery vehicles. The capital cost of the furniture and fixtures is $125,000 and, at January 1, 2013, the Class 8 UCC balance is $68,000. During 2013, new furniture was acquired at a cost of $18,000. Old furniture with a capital cost of $12,000 was sold for $8,000.

   On January 1, 2013, the Class 10 UCC balance was $85,000. There were no additions or disposals in this Class during the 9 month period ending September 30, 2013.

6. The interest expense relates to a line of credit that was used to finance seasonal fluctuations in inventory.

7. The foreign exchange loss resulted from the financing of merchandise purchases in Italy.

8. The travel and promotion expense consisted of the following items:

Business Meals And Entertainment	$10,000
Hotels And Airfare	14,000
Golf Club Memberships	4,000
Total Travel And Promotion Expense	$28,000

9. This is the first year that the Company has deducted a warranty reserve.

Required: Calculate the minimum Net Income For Tax Purposes and Taxable Income for Sedux Inc., for the 9 month period ending September 30, 2013. Indicate the amount and type of any carry forwards that will be available for use in future years.

Assignment Problem Twelve - 4 *(Corporate Loss Carry Forwards)*

At the beginning of 2013, Lyric Ltd. has a net capital loss balance of $78,250, a non-capital loss carry forward of $61,400, undeducted charitable contributions of $6,400. It is the policy of the Company to minimize any net capital loss balance, prior to using either non-capital loss or charitable contribution carry overs.

During 2013, the Company's overall operations were unsuccessful, resulting in a business loss of $225,000. Offsetting this were $51,500 in dividends from taxable Canadian corporations and capital gains of $41,500. However, the capital gains were offset by capital losses of $7,300.

Despite the business loss, the Company continued its charitable giving program, making 2013 donations of $6,300.

Required: Calculate the corporation's minimum Net Income For Tax Purposes and Taxable Income for its 2013 taxation year. Indicate any balances available for carry forward to subsequent years.

Assignment Problem Twelve - 5 *(Corporate Loss Carry Forwards - 4 Years)*

Rodem Inc. is a Canadian controlled private corporation. The Company began operations on January 1, 2010, and uses a taxation year that ends on December 31. Its income (loss) before taxes, calculated using generally accepted accounting principles, and amounts included in the GAAP income figures, for the four years 2010 through 2013 are as follows:

	2010	2011	2012	2013
Income (Loss) Before Taxes (GAAP)	$110,000	($180,000)	$85,000	($42,000)
Charitable Donations	3,200	5,800	4,100	2,900
Accounting Gains (Losses) On Land*	18,000	(9,000)	12,000	2,000
Dividends From Taxable				
Canadian Corporations	11,000	19,000	18,000	12,000

*The accounting gains and losses on the disposition of land are equal to the capital gains and losses for tax purposes. Also note that GAAP requires that charitable donations be deducted in the determination of accounting income.

It is the policy of the Company to deduct charitable donations prior to any loss carry overs. They also have a policy of minimizing non-capital loss carry overs, as opposed to net capital loss carry overs.

Required: For each of the four years 2010 through 2013, provide the following information:

• The minimum Net Income For Tax Purposes and Taxable Income that would be reported for Rodem Inc. Indicate the amount and type of any current year losses that are available for carry back or carry forward.

• The amended figures for any years to which losses are carried back.

• An analysis of the amount and type of carry forwards that would be available at the end of the year.

Assignment Problem Twelve - 6 (Corporate Loss Carry Forwards - 4 Years)

Brockton Ltd. has a December 31 fiscal year end. It began operations on January 1, 2010. During the 4 years 2010 through 2013, the components of its income were as follows:

	2010	2011	2012	2013
Net Business Income (Loss)	$123,000	$18,000	($85,000)	$32,000
Capital Gains (Losses)	(12,000)	32,000	(25,000)	16,000
Dividends Received	6,000	7,000	6,000	9,000
Charitable Donations	1,500	8,500	4,200	1,800

The Company uses tax rules to determine its Net Business Income (Loss). All of the dividends have been received from taxable Canadian corporations.

It is the policy of the Company to minimize its net capital loss carry forward balance, prior to minimizing other types of carry forwards.

Required: For each of the four years 2010 through 2013, provide the following information:

• The minimum Net Income For Tax Purposes and Taxable Income that would be reported for Brockton Ltd. Indicate the amount and type of any current year losses that are available for carry back or carry forward.

• The amended figures for any years to which losses are carried back.

• An analysis of the amount and type of carry forwards that would be available at the end of the year.

Assignment Problem Twelve - 7 (Geographical Allocation Of Income)

Brawn Inc. has permanent establishments in Manitoba, Ontario, Quebec, and the United States. During the current year, the company had total wages and salaries of $2,465,000 and gross revenues of $6,260,000. These were distributed among the provinces where the Company has operations in the following manner:

Province	Wages And Salaries Accrued	Gross Revenues
Manitoba	$ 369,750	$1,252,000
Ontario	616,250	1,565,000
Quebec	986,000	2,191,000
United States	493,000	1,252,000
Total	$2,465,000	$6,260,000

For the current taxation year, the Company's Taxable Income totaled $1,467,000.

Required: Calculate the amount of the Brawn Inc.'s Taxable Income for the current year that would be allocated to each province. Any percentages used in your calculations should be rounded to one decimal place. Ignore any foreign tax implications.

Assignment Problem Twelve - 8 (Part I Tax With Reduced SBD)

Kalec Inc. has a December 31 year end for both tax and accounting purposes. It is a Canadian controlled private company (CCPC) and, for the taxation year ending December 31, 2013, it had a Taxable Capital Employed In Canada of $11,556,000. The corresponding figure for the year ending December 31, 2012 was $12,235,000.

Taxable Income for the 2013 taxation year was $879,000. This was made up of Canadian active business income of $762,000, along with foreign business income of $117,000. The foreign jurisdiction withheld $17,550 in taxes, remitting the balance of $99,450 to Kalec.

The Company's 2013 gross revenues totalled $2,550,000, with 22 percent of this total being generated outside of Canada. Of their total 2013 wages of $895,000, 17 percent were paid outside of Canada. The revenues were earned and the wages paid in a country where Kalec has a permanent establishment.

Kalec Inc. is required to share its small business deduction with three other associated companies. They have agreed that Kalec would be allocated 40 percent of the total amount available.

Assume that Kalec's foreign tax credit will be equal to the amount of foreign taxes paid.

Required: Calculate Kalec's minimum federal Part I Tax Payable for the year ending December 31, 2013.

Assignment Problem Twelve - 9 (Corporate Tax Payable)

For the taxation year ending December 31, 2013, Lorne Inc., a Canadian controlled private company, has Net Income For Tax Purposes of $410,500. This is made up of $312,400 of active business income and $98,100 of dividends from various Canadian public companies. It has been determined that $211,300 of the active business income qualifies as manufacturing and processing profits.

During 2013, the Company makes donations to registered charities totaling $31,400.

At the beginning of 2013, the Company has a non-capital loss carry forward of $29,300. It intends to deduct all of this carry forward during 2013.

Lorne Inc. is associated with three other CCPCs. The companies have agreed that each company will claim one-quarter of the annual business limit.

Required: Determine the minimum Taxable Income and Part I federal Tax Payable for Lorne Inc. for the year ending December 31, 2013. Show all calculations, whether or not they are necessary to the final solution. As the corporation operates in a province that has a reduced tax rate for M&P activity, a separate calculation of the federal M&P deduction is required.

Assignment Problem Twelve - 10 (Corporate Tax Payable)

For the year ending December 31, 2013, the Income Statement of Morland Industries Ltd. (MIL), a Canadian controlled private corporation, prepared in accordance with generally accepted accounting principles, is as follows:

Revenues		$1,734,000
Expenses:		
Cost Of Goods Sold	($456,000)	
Selling And Administrative Costs	(270,000)	
Amortization Expense	(285,000)	
Other Expenses	(246,000)	(1,257,000)
Operating Income		$ 477,000
Other Income And Losses		
Foreign Business Income		
(Net Of $2,400 Withholding)	$ 9,400	
Dividends From Taxable Canadian Corporations	37,000	
Gain On Sale Of Building	75,000	
Gain On Sale Of Vacant Land	51,000	
Loss On Sale Of Vehicles	(40,000)	132,400
Accounting Income Before Taxes		**$609,400**

Other Information:

1.   On January 1, 2013, MIL had the following UCC balances:

Class 1	$819,354
Class 8	985,261
Class 10	96,417
Class 13	187,000

The Class 1 balance relates to a single building acquired at a cost of $1,145,000. It is estimated that the land that is included in this amount is $200,000. On February 1, 2013, this building is sold for $1,185,000, including an estimated value for the land of $225,000. In the accounting records, this real property was carried at $1,110,000, a net book value of $910,000 for the building and $200,000 for the land.

The old building is replaced on February 15, 2013 with a new building acquired at a cost of $1,425,000, of which $260,000 is allocated to land. The building is used 95 percent for manufacturing and processing activity and it is allocated to a separate Class 1.

There are no dispositions of Class 8 assets during the year. However, there are acquisitions in the total amount of $98,000.

As the Company has decided to lease all of its vehicles in the future, all of the assets in Class 10 are sold during the year. The capital cost of these assets was $193,000 and the proceeds of disposition amounted to $77,000. The net book value of these assets was $117,000.

The Class 13 balance relates to a single lease that commenced on January 1, 2011. The lease has an initial term of 7 years, with two successive options to renew, each for 3 years. Expenditures on this leasehold were $180,000 in 2011 and $36,000 in 2012. There were no further expenditures in 2013. The write-off of these expenditures for accounting purposes is included in Amortization Expense.

It is the policy of MIL to deduct maximum CCA in each year.

2.   Some years ago, MIL acquired a tract of land for $572,000. Until recently, they had intended to construct a new building for their operations on this site. However, with the 2013 purchase of a new building, their plans changed and they sold the tract for $623,000. The buyer provided a $50,000 cash payment, with MIL taking back a mortgage

for the balance. The balance will be paid in 10 equal instalments in the years 2014 through 2023.

3. Selling And Administrative Costs include $32,000 in business meals and entertainment. This balance also includes membership fees of $14,600 that were paid for several employees in a local golf and country club. This club is used for entertaining business clients.

4. As the Company expects to issue more shares during 2014, it made a number of amendments to its articles of incorporation and included the legal costs in Other Expenses. These costs totaled $13,500.

5. Other Expenses also includes the following:

Bond discount amortization	$3,500
Donations to registered charities	3,400
Interest on late income tax instalments	900
Interest on late municipal tax payments	475

6. The Company spent $15,000 during the year on landscaping for its new building. For accounting purposes this was treated as an asset. MIL will not amortize this balance as it believes the work has an unlimited life.

7. During 2012, MIL acquired a competing business at a price that included goodwill of $85,000. For accounting purposes, there has been no impairment or write-down of the goodwill purchased since its acquisition. MIL had not acquired any eligible capital expenditures prior to 2012.

9. At the beginning of 2013, MIL had a net capital loss carry forward of $128,000, as well as a non-capital loss carry forward of $60,300.

10. For 2013, MIL has active business income in Canada of $320,000, all of which results from M&P activity.

11. MIL is associated with several other CCPCs. MIL's share of the group's annual business limit for 2013 is $150,000.

12. Using the formula found in the *Income Tax Regulations*, 93 percent of MIL's income has been allocated to provinces. Assume that the tax credit for the foreign taxes on the foreign business income is equal to the amount withheld.

Required:

A. Calculate the minimum Net Income For Tax Purposes for Morland Industries Ltd. for 2013. In addition, calculate the UCC for each class of assets and the cumulative eligible capital balance on January 1, 2014.

B. Calculate the minimum Taxable Income for Morland Industries Ltd. for 2013. Indicate the amount, and type, of any carry overs that are available at the end of the year.

C. Calculate the minimum federal Part I Tax Payable for Morland Industries Ltd. for 2013. As the corporation operates in provinces that have a reduced tax rate for M&P activity, a separate calculation of the federal M&P deduction is required.

CHAPTER 13

Taxation Of Corporate Investment Income

Integration

The Basic Concept

13-1.   In designing a system for assessing taxes on business income, there are two theories or perspectives as to the appropriate treatment of corporations. These two perspectives are referred to as the entity view and the integration view. They can be described as follows:

Entity View   The entity view holds that corporations have a perpetual life of their own, that they are independent of their shareholders, and that they are legal entities. As such, they should pay tax separately on their earnings.

Integration View   Under the integration approach to the taxation of business income, corporations are viewed as simply the legal form through which one or more individuals (shareholders) carry on business. Therefore, business income that flows through a corporation to an individual should not be taxed differently, in total, from business income earned directly by that individual as a proprietor or partner.

13-2.   In practice, we find a variety of relationships between corporations and their share-holders. Given this situation, it would not be reasonable to apply either of these views to all Canadian corporations. For large corporations, where the shares are widely held and publicly traded, the entity view seems appropriate:

• Management of the corporation is separate from its ownership, with income allocation and distribution decisions being made without directly consulting the shareholders.

• Not all corporate profits are paid out to the shareholders.

• Some of the amounts distributed are paid to foreign shareholders, subject only to the non-resident withholding tax.

13-3.   In this type of situation, the entity view's treatment of the corporation as a separate taxable unit appears to be an equitable way to tax business income.

13-4.   This would not be the case for small corporations where the shares are privately held, either by a single individual or a small group of related individuals. With these owner managed businesses, the affairs of the shareholders and the business are closely related. Tax planning decisions involving salaries, dividends, or capital gains affect both personal and corporate taxes and the line between the corporation and its owners is often faint. This would lead to the conclusion that the taxation of business income in these situations should not be influenced by the presence of the corporation. This conclusion is consistent with the integration view of business income taxation.

13-5.   In a strict legal sense, the *Income Tax Act* reflects the entity view in that corporations are considered to be taxable units that are separate from their owners. Both the corporation and the owners are subject to taxation and this, in effect, involves double taxation of the income earned initially by the corporation. In the absence of special provisions, there would be a significantly higher level of taxation on income earned by a corporation and paid out as dividends, than there would be on income earned directly, either through a proprietorship or partnership.

13-6.   Fortunately, there are special provisions that mitigate the effects of both the corporation and its shareholders being treated as taxable entities. The most important of these provisions is the dividend tax credit that is available to individuals who have received dividends from taxable Canadian corporations.

AN IMPORTANT NOTE   An understanding of dividend gross up and tax credit procedures is essential to the material which follows in this Chapter and Chapters 14, 15, and 16. If you do not fully understand these procedures, you should review Paragraphs **7-70** through **7-103** in Chapter 7 of this text. You will also find it useful to review the brief description of Capital Dividends that is found in Paragraphs **7-138** and **7-139**.

Dividend Gross Up And Tax Credit Procedures
Eligible Dividends
13-7.   You may recall from Chapter 7 that ITA 89(1) defines eligible dividends as any taxable dividend that is designated as such by the company paying the dividend. Dividends that are designated as eligible qualify for the enhanced gross up and tax credit procedures.

13-8.   With the exception of capital dividends, all types of dividends may be designated as eligible dividends. This includes the cash and stock dividends that were discussed in Chapter 7, as well as the various types of deemed dividends that will be introduced in Chapter 14 (e.g., ITA 84(3) dividend on redemption of shares).

Non-Eligible Dividends
13-9.   We will refer to dividends that have not been designated as eligible as non-eligible dividends. These non-eligible distributions will be dealt with by continuing to apply the 25 percent gross up that has been in effect for many years. Recipients of these dividends will benefit from a federal dividend tax credit equal to two-thirds of the 25 percent gross up.

13-10.   Any dividend that has not been designated as eligible will be considered to be non-eligible. This includes cash dividends, stock dividends, dividends in kind, and the various types of deemed dividends that are discussed in Chapter 14. Note, however, as capital dividends are not taxable dividends, they do not qualify for either dividend gross up and tax credit procedure.

Who Can Declare Eligible Dividends?
13-11.   Again referring to the discussion of dividends in Chapter 7, the reason for introducing the enhanced dividend gross up and tax credit procedures for eligible dividends was to provide better integration for corporate income that was subject to the general corporate tax rate. As demonstrated in that Chapter, the combined federal/provincial tax on income flowing through a large public company was far greater than the taxes that would be paid had

the shareholders received the income directly. Given this, we will find that most of the dividends paid by large public companies can be designated as eligible.

13-12.   In contrast, the income of a CCPC may benefit from the small business deduction that was discussed in Chapter 12, or refundable taxes that will be discussed at a later point in this Chapter. Until recently, the government believed that the 25 percent dividend gross up and tax credit procedures provided a reasonable level of integration. However, the Department of Finance appears to have changed its assessment of this situation. As introduced in the 2013 Budget, as of January 1, 2014, the 25 percent gross up is reduced to 18 percent, and the related tax credit is based on 13/18 of the gross up, thereby increasing effective tax rates on non-eligible dividends for individuals. Note, however, this change will not be reflected in the calculations for this year's edition of *Canadian Tax Principles* which focuses on the 2013 year.

13-13.   It would be very convenient to have a rule that says that taxable dividends paid by non-CCPCs are eligible dividends, while dividends paid by CCPCs are non-eligible. Unfortunately, this simple dichotomy does not work because:

- some CCPCs may have a portion of their income taxed at full rates (e.g., active business income in excess of the annual business limit of $500,000), and

- some non-CCPCs may have a portion of their income taxed at favourable rates (e.g., a CCPC that goes public with a retained earnings balance that contains amounts that benefited from the small business deduction).

13-14.   Because of these complications, legislation specifies the conditions necessary for a corporation to designate a dividend payment as being eligible for the enhanced gross up and tax credit procedure. While we could discuss this legislation at this point, it will be much easier to understand after you have covered this Chapter's material on the taxation of corporate investment income. Given this, we will defer our coverage of this material until the end of this Chapter.

Integration And Business Income
Required Rates And Credits
13-15.   In Chapter 7 we noted that the goal of integration is to ensure that, if an individual chooses to channel an income stream through a corporation, he will retain the same after tax amount of funds that he would have retained if he had received the income directly. Stated alternatively, integration procedures are directed at equating the amount of taxes paid by an individual on the direct receipt of income, with the combined corporate/individual taxes that would be paid if that same stream of income was channeled through a corporation.

13-16.   In Chapter 7, we also demonstrated that, for integration to work, certain assumptions were required with respect to both the combined federal/provincial tax rate on corporations and the combined federal/provincial dividend tax credit. As noted in that chapter, those assumptions are as follows:

Federal/Provincial Tax Rate On Corporations The combined 2013 corporate tax rate that will make integration effective depends on the type of dividends:

- For eligible dividends (38 percent gross up), the required rate is 27.54 percent.

- For non-eligible dividends (25 percent gross up), the required rate is 20 percent.

If the applicable rate exceeds these benchmarks, the use of a corporation will result in additional taxation.

Federal/Provincial Dividend Tax Credit For integration to be effective, the combined federal/provincial dividend tax credit must be equal to the gross up. The required 2013 provincial dividend tax credit that will produce the combined credit depends on the type of dividends:

- For eligible dividends (38 percent gross up), the federal dividend tax credit is equal to 6/11 of the gross up. This means that, for the combined credit to equal

Integration

the gross up, the provincial credit must be equal to 5/11 (≈ 45.5 percent) of the gross up.

- For non-eligible dividends (25 percent gross up), the federal dividend tax credit is equal to 2/3 of the gross up. This means that, for the combined credit to equal the gross up, the provincial credit must be equal to 1/3 of the gross up.

If the combined federal/provincial dividend tax credit is less than one, the use of a corporation will result in additional taxation.

Actual Corporate Tax Rates

13-17.   With respect to eligible dividends, integration requires a 2013 federal/provincial tax on corporations of 27.54 percent. Actual rates for the public companies that pay such dividends are generally fairly close to this level. For 2013, the rates range from a low of 25 percent in Alberta, British Columbia, and New Brunswick, to 31 percent in Nova Scotia and Prince Edward Island (see Chapter 12, Paragraph 12-54). It appears that, for public companies, integration is working reasonably well, with modest amounts of over or under integration in individual provinces.

13-18.   The situation is even better for CCPCs earning income eligible for the small business deduction. As dividends that are paid out of income that has benefited from the small business deduction will be non-eligible, the required rate for integration to work is 20 percent. For 2013, the combined federal/provincial rates on income that is eligible for the small business deduction range from a low of 11 percent in Manitoba, to a high of 19 percent in Quebec (see Chapter 12, Paragraph 12-54). As all of the combined federal/provincial rates are below the required 20 percent, it appears that channeling income eligible for the small business deduction through a CCPC can result in a lower level of taxation. Note, however, that these low rates on income that benefits from the small business deduction are likely the reason that the dividend gross up and credit procedures for non-eligible dividends are being made less favourable in years subsequent to 2013 (see Paragraph 13-12).

13-19.   As we shall see later in this Chapter, the situation is worse for CCPCs that are earning investment income. Such income is not eligible for either the general rate reduction or the small business deduction. This means that the basic federal rate is 28 percent (38% - 10%). In addition, there is a further federal tax on such income at a rate of 6-2/3 percent. When this federal rate of 34-2/3 percent is combined with provincial rates ranging from 10 percent to 16 percent, overall rates on this income range from just under 45 percent to just over 50 percent.

13-20.   While integration would clearly not work with overall corporate rates at this level, we will find that the effect of these rates is mitigated by the fact that a substantial portion of these taxes are refunded to the corporation when the investment income is paid out to shareholders as dividends.

Actual Dividend Tax Credits

13-21.   We have noted that, for integration to work with respect to eligible dividends, the 2013 provincial dividend tax credit has to be equal to 5/11 (45.5%) of the gross up. For 2013, actual rates on eligible dividends ranged from a low of 23 percent of the gross up, to a high of 44 percent of the gross up (see Paragraph 7-93). All of these rates are below the required 45.5 percent and this means that integration is not fully effective with respect to eligible dividends

13-22.   For non-eligible dividends the required provincial credit is equal to one-third (33.3%) of the gross up. For 2013, the range of actual provincial credits was from 5 percent to 40 percent of the gross up (see Paragraph 7-83). Clearly, with respect to this factor, the effectiveness of integration depends heavily on the province in which the recipient of the dividend resides. As we have pointed out, if the provincial dividend tax credit is less than one-third of the gross up, the use of a corporation will tend to result in increased taxes. In contrast, if it exceeds one-third, channeling this income through a corporation can result in a lower level of taxation.

Alternative Calculations

13-23.   We would also note that, while federal legislation calculates the dividend tax credit as a fraction of the gross up, other jurisdictions may base this credit on a percentage of dividends received, or on the grossed up amount of the dividends.

13-24.   Because our focus is largely on federal legislation, we will generally present dividend tax credits as a fraction of the gross up. There is, however, no problem in converting different approaches to a uniform base. For example, if a non-eligible dividend of $100 is paid, the federal dividend tax credit of $16.67 can be calculated as:

- two-thirds of the $25 [(25%)($100)] gross up. (Which is our standard approach.)
- 16-2/3 percent of the $100 in dividends received, or
- 13-2/3 percent of the $125 of grossed up dividends.

Exercise Thirteen - 1

Subject: Integration (Non-Eligible Dividends)

Jan Teason has a business that she estimates will produce income of $100,000 per year. If she incorporates this business, all of the income would be eligible for the small business deduction and any dividends paid will be non-eligible. In the province where she lives, such corporate income is taxed at a combined federal/provincial rate of 15 percent. Ms. Teason has other income sources that place her in a combined federal/provincial tax bracket of 45 percent. In her province, the provincial dividend tax credit on non-eligible dividends is equal to 30 percent of the gross up. Would Ms. Teason save taxes if she was to channel this source of income through a corporation? Explain your result.

Exercise Thirteen - 2

Subject: Integration (Eligible Dividends)

John Horst has a business that he estimates will produce income of $100,000 per year. Because he controls another corporation that fully utilizes $500,000 of its small business deduction, if he incorporates this business, none of this income will be eligible for the small business deduction and any dividends paid would be designated eligible. In the province where he lives, such corporate income is taxed at a combined federal/provincial rate of 30 percent. Mr. Horst has other income sources that place him in a combined federal/provincial tax bracket of 42 percent. In his province, the provincial dividend tax credit on eligible dividends is equal to 28 percent of the gross up. Would Mr. Horst save taxes if he was to channel this source of income through a corporation? Explain your result.

End of Exercises. Solutions available in Study Guide.

We suggest you work Self Study Problem Thirteen-1 at this point.

Refundable Taxes On Investment Income

Meaning Of Aggregate Investment Income

13-25.   In the following material on refundable taxes, we will be using the term "investment income". For purposes of determining the amount of refundable taxes available, this term has a very specific meaning. Further, it is not the usual meaning that we associate with this term. Under ITA 129(4), the relevant "aggregate investment income" is defined as follows (for your convenience, this definition is included at the front of this book in "Rates And Other Data"):

Refundable Taxes On Investment Income

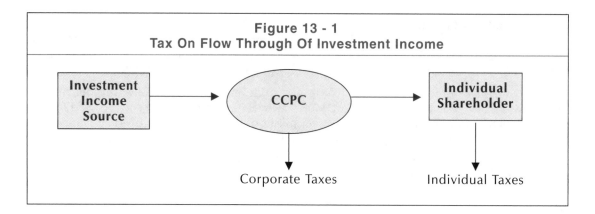

- Net taxable capital gains for the year, reduced by any net capital loss carry overs deducted during the year.

- Income from property including interest, rents, and royalties, but excluding dividends that are deductible in computing Taxable Income. Since foreign dividends are generally not deductible, they would be included in aggregate investment income. These amounts would be reduced by property losses.

13-26. Note carefully the differences between this "aggregate investment income" and what we normally think of as property or investment income. Unlike the normal definition of property or investment income, this concept includes net taxable capital gains for the current year, reduced by net capital loss carry overs deducted during the year.

13-27. The other difference between aggregate investment income and the usual definition of investment income is that it excludes most dividends from other Canadian corporations. This reflects the fact that dividends from Canadian corporations generally flow through a corporation without being subject to corporate taxes. You should also note that aggregate investment income includes income from both Canadian and foreign sources.

Basic Concepts

The Problem

13-28. As shown in Figure 13-1, when income is flowed through a corporation, it is subject to two levels of taxation. It is taxed first at the corporate level and, if the after tax corporate amount is distributed to the individual shareholder, it will be taxed again in the hands of that individual. If we assume that the corporate tax rate on the investment income of a CCPC is 45 percent and that the individual shareholder is taxed at a rate of 30 percent on non-eligible dividends received, the overall rate of taxation on investment income flowed through a corporation would be 61.5 percent [45% + (1 - 45%)(30%)].

13-29. If the same individual had received the investment income directly, without it having been flowed through a corporation, the individual's tax rate on investment income would have been about 45 percent. This difference is clearly not consistent with the concept of integration. Integration attempts to neutralize the influence of using a corporation on the after tax amount of income received by an individual.

The Solution

13-30. The most obvious solution to this problem would be to lower the rate of corporate taxation on the investment income of a CCPC. For example, if the corporate rate was lowered to 21 percent, the overall rate on the flow through of income would be taxed at 44.7 percent [21% + (1 - 21%)(30%)]. This is within the range of rates that are applied to high net worth individuals who receive business or property income directly.

13-31. The problem with this solution is that it would provide for a significant deferral of taxes on investment income. If an individual received the investment income directly, the full amount of taxes must be paid when the income is earned. In contrast, when a corporation is used, only the first, or corporate level, of taxation is assessed when the income is earned. If the after tax amount is left in the corporation, the assessment of the individual level of tax can be deferred indefinitely.

13-32.   For higher income individuals who do not require their investment income for current expenditures, this would present an outstanding opportunity for tax deferral. This would be the case whenever the corporate tax rate on investment income was below the rate applicable to the individual on the direct receipt of income.

13-33.   Given the opportunity for tax deferral that would result from the use of lower corporate tax rates, it is not surprising that a different solution to the problem of excessive tax rates on the flow through of a CCPC's investment income has been adopted. This solution involves leaving the corporate tax rate at a high level, but having a portion of the tax being designated as refundable. The refund of this portion of the corporate tax occurs when the income is distributed in the form of dividends that will be subject to the second level of taxation in the hands of the shareholders.

13-34.   We would remind you that, consistent with this concept of keeping the basic rate high on the aggregate investment income of a CCPC, this type of income is excluded from the definition of Full Rate Taxable Income and, as a consequence, is not eligible for the general rate reduction.

Refundable Tax Procedures

13-35.   While the detailed procedures related to these refundable taxes are complex, the basic concept is not. A portion of the tax paid on investment income at the corporate level is refunded when the income is distributed to investors in the form of dividends. This keeps the combined corporate and personal tax rate in line with the rate that would be applicable to an individual on the direct receipt of income. The high rate of corporate tax discourages tax deferral, while at the same time, the refund procedures avoid the excessive rate of taxation that would occur if this high corporate tax rate was combined with individual taxes on the same income stream.

13-36.   Stated simply, the use of a refundable tax allows the government to charge a corporate tax rate that is high enough to remove much of the incentive for accumulating investment income in a corporation and, at the same time, provides a reasonable overall rate of taxation when the income is flowed through the corporation and taxed in the hands of the individual shareholder.

13-37.   In implementing this refundable tax approach, the *Income Tax Act* designates three different components of total taxes paid that can be refunded on the payment of dividends. They can be described as follows:

Ordinary Part I Tax   At this point, you should be familiar with the calculation of the regular Part I tax that is assessed on the Taxable Income of a corporation. A portion of this tax, basically a portion of the Part I tax that is applicable to investment income, will be designated as refundable on the payment of dividends. Note the fact that a portion of the Part I tax being designated as refundable does not change, in any way, the manner in which the Part I tax is calculated.

Additional Refundable Tax On Investment Income (ART)   In the early 1990s, the provincial tax rates applicable to individuals had increased to the point where leaving investment income in a corporation was attractive, despite the fairly high combined rate of federal/provincial taxes on this type of income earned by a corporation. In order to discourage the use of corporations to defer tax on investment income, it was felt that a higher rate of corporate taxation was required. To implement this view, an additional Part I tax was added under ITA 123.3, applicable only to the aggregate investment income of CCPCs.

This additional refundable tax, often referred to by the acronym ART, is assessed at a rate of 6-2/3 percent on the investment income of CCPCs, and is refundable when the corporation pays dividends. This tax will be given detailed consideration in this Chapter. It might be noted that this tax has been left in place, despite the fact that, in more recent years, provincial tax rates on individuals have fallen in some provinces.

Part IV Tax   Even with the Part I refundable tax and ART in place, there is still the possibility of using a related group of corporations to defer taxation on investment income. The Part IV refundable tax is a 33-1/3 percent tax on certain intercorporate dividends that is designed to prevent this from happening. This Part IV tax will also be given detailed consideration in this Chapter.

13-38.   In dealing with this material, we will first consider the issues involved with a single corporation. In these single corporation situations, only the refundable Part I tax and the additional refundable tax on investment income will be considered.

Refundable Part I Tax On Investment Income

Additional Refundable Tax On Investment Income (ART)
Basic Calculations
13-39.   As was noted previously, tax legislation contains a refundable tax on the investment income of a Canadian controlled private corporation (CCPC). This additional refundable tax (ART) is assessed under ITA 123.3 (the definition is available at the front of this book under "Rates and Other Data"). The amount payable is equal to 6-2/3 percent of the lesser of:

* the corporation's "aggregate investment income" for the year [as defined in ITA 129(4)]; and

* the amount, if any, by which the corporation's Taxable Income for the year exceeds the amount that is eligible for the small business deduction.

13-40.   The basic objective of this tax is to make it less attractive to shelter investment income within a corporate structure in order to defer full taxation of the amounts earned. When this additional 6-2/3 percent is added to the usual rates applicable to a CCPC's investment income, the combined rate is in the 44-2/3 to 50-2/3 percent range. This is made up of 34-2/3 percent at the federal level (38% - 10% + 6-2/3%), plus 10 percent to 16 percent at the provincial level. As noted in Chapter 4, the combined federal/provincial maximum rates on individuals range from 39 to 50 percent (see Paragraph 4-23).

13-41.   This means that, with the addition of the ART, rates on the investment income of a CCPC will generally be higher than the rates applicable to an individual receiving the same income. Given this, there is little or no incentive to use a corporation to defer taxation on this type of income.

13-42.   As described in Paragraph 13-39, the ART is based on the lesser of aggregate investment income and the amount of Taxable Income that is not eligible for the small business deduction. The reason for the latter limit is to ensure that such deductions as charitable donations or non-capital loss carry overs have not totally or partially eliminated the investment income from the amount flowing through to Taxable Income. The goal is to prevent the ART from being inappropriately applied to active business income.

Exercise Thirteen - 3

Subject: Additional Refundable Tax On Investment Income

Zircon Inc. is a CCPC with a December 31 year end. Zircon is not associated with any other company. For the 2013 taxation year, its Net Income For Tax Purposes is equal to $281,000. This is made up of active business income of $198,000, dividends from taxable Canadian corporations of $22,000, taxable capital gains of $46,000 and interest income on long-term investments of $15,000. The Company also has a net capital loss carry forward from 2011 of $26,000 and a non-capital loss carry forward of $23,000. The Company intends to deduct both of these carry forwards in the 2013 taxation year. Determine Zircon's Taxable Income and its additional refundable tax on investment income for the 2013 taxation year.

End of Exercise. Solution available in Study Guide.

ART And Foreign Tax Credit Calculations

13-43.   As discussed in Chapter 12, the use of foreign taxes paid as credits against Canadian Tax Payable is limited by a formula that includes the "tax otherwise payable". In the case of foreign taxes paid on non-business income, the "tax otherwise payable" in the formula adds the ART that is assessed under ITA 123.3.

13-44.   This creates a potential problem in that the calculation of the ART includes the amount eligible for the small business deduction. Since one of the factors limiting the small business deduction [ITA 125(1)(b)] is Taxable Income reduced by 100/28 of the foreign non-business income tax credit and 4 times the foreign business income tax credit, this could have created an insolvable circular calculation.

13-45.   As is explained in Chapter 12, there is a similar circularity issue involving the general rate reduction under ITA 123.4.   The calculation of this amount also requires knowing the amount of income that is eligible for the small business deduction.

13-46.   To avoid both of these problems, for the purposes of calculating the small business deduction, ITA 125(1)(b)(i) permits the foreign tax credit for taxes paid on foreign non-business income to be calculated using a "tax otherwise payable" figure that does not include the ART under ITA 123.3 or the general rate reduction. ITA 125(1)(b)(ii) permits the foreign tax credit for taxes paid on foreign business income to be calculated using a "tax otherwise payable" figure that does not include the general rate reduction.

13-47. This means that in situations where the small business deduction, foreign tax credits, and the ART are involved, the following procedures should be used:

1. Calculate the foreign non-business tax credit using a "tax otherwise payable" figure that excludes both ITA 123.3 (ART) and ITA 123.4 (general rate reduction). This initial version of the foreign non-business tax credit will be used only for the purpose of determining the small business deduction, with the actual credit available calculated after the ITA 123.3 and 123.4 amounts have been determined.

2. Calculate the foreign business tax credit using a "tax otherwise payable" figure that excludes ITA 123.4 (as business income is involved, ITA 123.3 is excluded by definition). However, this credit is limited by the amount of tax otherwise payable, reduced by the foreign non-business tax credit. As a consequence, it will be necessary to calculate an initial version of this foreign business tax credit, using the initial version of the foreign non-business tax credit. This initial version will be used only for the purpose of determining the small business deduction and the M&P deduction.

3. Calculate the amount eligible for the small business deduction and M&P deduction using the numbers determined in steps 1 and 2.

4. Using the amount eligible for the small business deduction and the M&P deduction determined in step 3, calculate the ART and the general rate reduction.

5. Calculate the actual foreign non-business tax credit using a "tax otherwise payable" figure that includes the ART and the general rate reduction determined in step 4.

6. Calculate the actual foreign business tax credit using the actual foreign non-business tax credit determined in step 5 and the general rate reduction from step 4.

Problem One: Excessive Tax Rates On The Flow Through Of A CCPC's Investment Income

13-48.   With the addition of the 6-2/3 percent ART on the investment income of a Canadian controlled private corporation, this investment income is taxed at a combined federal/provincial rate ranging from 44-2/3 percent to 50-2/3 percent (see Paragraph 13-40).

13-49.   All of these combined rates are more than double the 20 percent rate required for perfect integration (the 20 percent rate is used as the investment income of a CCPC cannot be used as a basis for paying eligible dividends). In the absence of some type of relieving mechanism, the objective of integrating corporate and individual tax rates would not be met.

13-50.   The problem of excessive rates of tax on investment income flowed through a corporation was discussed previously in Paragraph 13-28. A more complete example will be presented here.

Example   Mr. Monroe has investments that generate interest income of $100,000 per year. He is personally subject to a combined federal/provincial tax rate of 43.5 percent. The dividend tax credit in his province of residence is equal to one-third of the gross up. Calculate the amount of cash Mr. Monroe will retain from this investment income under the following alternative assumptions:

Case A   He receives the $100,000 in interest income directly.

Case B   Mr. Monroe is the sole shareholder of a Canadian controlled private corporation that earns the $100,000 of investment income. The corporation is subject to a combined federal/provincial tax rate, including the ITA 123.3 tax on investment income, of 50 percent. The corporation pays out all of its after tax earnings as non-eligible dividends, resulting in a dividend to Mr. Monroe of $50,000. Ignore any refund of Part I tax paid.

13-51.   The calculations comparing the investment income if it was received directly (Case A) and if it was earned through a corporation (Case B), are as follows:

Case A - Investment Income Received Directly

Investment Income - Direct Receipt	$100,000
Personal Tax At 43.5 Percent	(43,500)
After Tax Cash Retained Without Corporation	$ 56,500

Case B - Investment Income Flowed Through Corporation
Assume No Refundable Part I Tax

Corporate Investment Income	$100,000
Corporate Tax At 50 Percent (Includes The ART)	(50,000)
Non-Eligible Dividends Paid To Mr. Monroe	$ 50,000

Non-Eligible Dividends Received	$ 50,000
Gross Up Of 25 Percent	12,500
Personal Taxable Income	$ 62,500
Personal Tax Rate	43.5%
Tax Payable Before Dividend Tax Credit	$ 27,188
Dividend Tax Credit [(2/3 + 1/3)(Gross Up)]	(12,500)
Personal Tax Payable With Corporation	$ 14,688

Non-Eligible Dividends Received	$ 50,000
Personal Tax Payable	(14,688)
After Tax Cash Retained With Corporation	$ 35,312

Savings - Direct Receipt

Income Received Directly	$ 56,500
Income Flowed Through Corporation	35,312
Net Savings On Direct Receipt	$ 21,188

13-52.   The results show that, in the absence of the refundable component of Part I tax, interest income flowed through a corporation is subject to an effective tax rate of nearly 65 percent [($100,000 - $35,312) ÷ $100,000]. This is significantly higher than the 43.5 percent rate that is applicable to the direct receipt of the investment income, an outcome that would represent a major failure in the government's attempt to achieve integration.

13-53.   Before leaving this example you should note that, with the inclusion of the ART on investment income, there is no deferral advantage associated with using a corporation. Prior to the introduction of this tax, in some situations, the amount of tax paid at the corporate level on investment income was less than the amount that would be paid by an individual receiving the income directly. This is no longer the case. In our example, corporate taxes alone are $50,000, well in excess of the $43,500 that would be paid if Mr. Monroe had received the income directly.

13-54.   Even if we use the highest provincial rates on individuals in effect in Canada (50% combined rate), there is no deferral associated with using a corporation. In most provinces, where the maximum individual rate is lower than 50 percent, using a corporation results in an effective prepayment of tax.

Solution To Problem One: Refundable Portion Of Part I Tax
Basic Concepts
13-55.   The preceding example makes it clear that taxes on investment income earned by a CCPC and flowed through to its shareholders are potentially much higher than would be the case if the shareholders received the income directly. This major imperfection in the system of integration results from a federal/provincial tax rate on the investment income of CCPCs that is between 44-2/3 and 50-2/3 percent.

13-56.   In those cases where the income is retained in the corporation, this is an equitable arrangement in that this high rate discourages the use of a CCPC to temporarily shelter passive income from a portion of the taxes that would be assessed on the direct receipt of the income by the individual. However, when the investment income is flowed through a CCPC and paid as dividends, the result is not consistent with the government's desire to tax CCPCs under the integration view of corporate taxation.

13-57.   As noted previously, the government could have dealt with this problem by reducing the corporate tax rate on the investment income of CCPCs. However, this would have allowed the owners of CCPCs to defer personal taxes on this income by leaving the investment income in the corporation. To avoid this, the refundable tax approach is used.

13-58.   Under this approach, the investment income of Canadian controlled private corporations is taxed at the usual high rates, including the ART on investment income. However, when the corporation distributes its after tax income in the form of dividends, a part of this tax is refunded. The refund is based on the amount of dividends paid by the corporation, with the refund being equal to $1 for each $3 of dividends paid.

Concepts Illustrated
13-59.   In order to give you a better understanding of how the concepts associated with the refund of Part I tax work, we will use an example based on the corporate tax rates that are inherent in the integration procedures contained in the *Income Tax Act*. You will recall that, for non-eligible dividends, the dividend gross up and tax credit procedures are based on an assumed rate of corporate tax of 20 percent. In our example, we will assume that this is the combined federal/provincial rate applicable to income eligible for the small business deduction.

Refundable Part I Tax On Investment Income

13-60.   For income that is not eligible for the small business deduction, we will assume a combined federal/provincial rate of 40 percent (38% basic federal, less 10% abatement, plus 12% provincial rate). This is before the addition of the ART and without the benefit of the general rate reduction (not available on the aggregate investment income of a CCPC). While individual provincial rates will be either higher or lower, the use of this notional rate of 12 percent will permit us to illustrate how integration is supposed to work in this situation. We will subsequently present a second example that uses more realistic rates.

13-61.   The basic idea here is that the investment income of a Canadian controlled private corporation will be taxed at a rate of 46-2/3 percent (the 40 percent described in the preceding Paragraph, plus the ART of 6-2/3 percent). When the residual after tax income is paid out in dividends, a refund of the tax in excess of 20 percent will be provided. This can be accomplished by providing a dividend refund equal to $1 for each $3 of dividends paid.

13-62.   These ideas can be illustrated with the following example:

Example   Ms. Banardi has investments that generate interest income of $100,000 per year. You have been asked to advise her as to whether there would be any benefits associated with transferring these investments to her wholly owned Canadian controlled private corporation. Ms. Banardi is personally subject to a combined federal/provincial tax rate of 43.5 percent. The dividend tax credit in her province of residence is equal to one-third of the gross up. Her corporation would be taxed on this income at a combined federal/provincial rate of 46-2/3 percent, including the ART on investment income.

13-63.   The calculations comparing the after tax investment income if it was earned in a corporation and if it was received directly, are as follows:

After Tax Retention - Use Of A Corporation

Corporate Investment Income	$100,000
Corporate Tax At 46-2/3 Percent (Includes The ART)	(46,667)
After Tax Income	$ 53,333
Dividend Refund (See Note)	26,667
Non-Eligible Dividends Paid To Ms. Banardi	$ 80,000
Non-Eligible Dividends Received	$ 80,000
Gross Up Of 25 Percent	20,000
Personal Taxable Income	$100,000
Personal Tax Rate	43.5%
Tax Payable Before Dividend Tax Credit	$ 43,500
Dividend Tax Credit [(2/3 + 1/3)(Gross Up)]	(20,000)
Personal Tax Payable With Corporation	$ 23,500
Non-Eligible Dividends Received	$ 80,000
Personal Tax Payable	(23,500)
After Tax Cash Retained With Corporation	$ 56,500

After Tax Retention - Direct Receipt

Investment Income - Direct Receipt	$100,000
Personal Tax At 43.5 Percent	(43,500)
After Tax Cash Retained Without Corporation	$ 56,500

Note In these somewhat academic examples of the dividend refund mechanism, it is assumed that all of the after tax income of the corporation will be paid out as dividends. As this will trigger a $1 for $3 refund ($26,667 ÷ $80,000), the after tax balance represents two-thirds of the dividend ($53,333 ÷ $80,000). This means that the amount of the refund will be calculated as one-half (1/3 ÷ 2/3) of the after tax balance of corporate income. This approach is not consistent with the real world approach in which the amount of the dividend is determined by a variety of factors (e.g., availability of cash or alternative investment opportunities) and the refund is calculated as one-third of the amount paid.

13-64.   The same amount of after tax cash is retained under both scenarios, demonstrating that this refundable tax restores integration to the system with respect to total taxes paid. Also of importance is the fact that the use of a corporation has not provided any tax deferral. Corporate taxes prior to the refund total $46,667, an amount that is in excess of the $43,500 in taxes that would be paid by Ms. Banardi on direct receipt of the income.

Use Of Other Rates In Refundable Part I Tax Example

13-65.   The preceding example is useful in that it illustrates how perfectly integration can work if the appropriate rates are used. As has been discussed in Chapters 4 and 12, there is considerable variance in provincial rates for both corporations and individuals. Not surprisingly, these variations will influence how well the integration measures succeed. In order to illustrate this effect, we will present the following second example using different rates.

Example Mr. Leoni has investments that generate interest income of $100,000 per year. He has over $200,000 in other income and is subject to a combined federal/provincial tax rate of 47 percent. The provincial dividend tax credit is equal to 25 percent of the gross up. Mr. Leoni is the sole shareholder of a Canadian controlled private corporation and is considering the transfer of these investments to his corporation. His corporation would be taxed on this income at a combined federal/provincial rate of 50.7 percent, including the ART on investment income (38% - 10% + 6-2/3% + 16%).

13-66.   The calculations comparing the after tax investment income if it was earned through a corporation and if it was received directly, are as follows:

After Tax Retention - Use Of A Corporation

Corporate Investment Income	$100,000
Corporate Tax At 50.7 Percent (Includes The ART)	(50,700)
After Tax Income	$ 49,300
Dividend Refund ($1 For Each $3 Of Dividends Paid)	24,650
Non-Eligible Dividends Paid To Mr. Leoni	$ 73,950
Non-Eligible Dividends Received	$ 73,950
Gross Up Of 25 Percent	18,488
Personal Taxable Income	$ 92,438
Personal Tax Rate	47%
Tax Payable Before Dividend Tax Credit	$ 43,446
Dividend Tax Credit [(2/3 + 25%)($18,488)]	(16,947)
Personal Tax Payable With Corporation	$ 26,499
Non-Eligible Dividends Received	$ 73,950
Personal Tax Payable	(26,499)
After Tax Cash Retained With Corporation	$ 47,451

After Tax Retention - Direct Receipt

Investment Income - Direct Receipt	$100,000
Personal Tax At 47 Percent	(47,000)
After Tax Cash Retained Without Corporation	$ 53,000

13-67.   While the numbers are quite different, the conclusion on deferral is the same as the one for the example presented in Paragraph 13-62. Corporate taxes before the refund are $50,700, significantly higher than the $47,000 that would have been paid if Mr. Leoni had received the income directly. As was the case in the previous example, the use of a corporation does not provide tax deferral. In fact, the opposite is true in that, when a corporation is used, there is actually a prepayment of a larger amount of tax.

13-68.   With respect to the after tax flow through of income, in our previous example the use of a corporation was neutral. After tax income was the same, without regard to whether a corporation was used. This is not the case here. After the income is flowed through the corporation, Mr. Leoni retains only $47,451, significantly less than the $53,000 he would have retained on the direct receipt of income. With the use of these fairly realistic numbers, there is clearly a tax disadvantage in flowing investment income through a CCPC. In this example, both the high provincial tax rate on the corporation and the low provincial dividend tax credit rate are unfavourable to the use of a corporation.

Exercise Thirteen - 4

Subject: Flow Through Of Investment Income

Ms. Shelly Nicastro has investments that generate interest income of $100,000 per year. Due to her employment income, she is in the top tax bracket, with a combined federal/provincial rate of 46 percent. She is considering the transfer of these investments to her CCPC which would be subject to a tax rate on investment income of 48 percent (including the ART). The dividend tax credit in her province is equal to 37 percent of the gross up. Any dividends paid by the CCPC out of investment income will be non-eligible. Advise her as to whether there would be any tax benefits associated with this transfer.

End of Exercise. Solution available in Study Guide.

Refundable Part IV Tax On Dividends Received

Problem Two: Use Of Multi-Level Affiliations To Defer Taxes On Investment Income

13-69.   In the preceding section, we demonstrated how refund procedures applicable to Part I tax payable are used to lower the overall rate of taxation on the investment income of a CCPC, while at the same time preventing the use of a corporation to defer a portion of the overall taxation on such income. While varying provincial tax rates on corporations and individuals prevent these procedures from providing perfect results, they appear to produce results that come close to achieving the goal of integration of personal and corporate taxes.

13-70.   The situation becomes more complex when a group of related companies is involved. The refundable tax procedures that were previously described are not effective in preventing tax deferral in this case. As a result, there is a need for additional procedures.

Example   Eastern Inc. has a 100 percent owned subsidiary, Western Ltd. Both Companies are Canadian controlled private corporations and have a December 31 year end. During the year ending December 31, 2013, Western has income of $100,000, made up entirely of interest and taxable capital gains. Assume that the

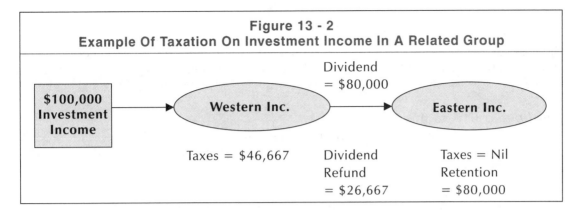

Figure 13 - 2
Example Of Taxation On Investment Income In A Related Group

combined federal/provincial tax rate for both Companies is 46-2/3 percent, including the ART. Western pays out all of its after tax income in dividends to Eastern Inc. This situation is illustrated in Figure 13-2.

Analysis   On receipt of the $100,000 of investment income, Western would pay taxes of $46,667 [($100,000)(46-2/3%)]. However, when the remaining $53,333 is paid out in dividends, a refund of $26,667 (one-third of the $80,000 total dividend) becomes available, resulting in a total dividend of $80,000 as shown in the following calculation:

Investment Income Of Western	$100,000
Corporate Tax At 46-2/3 Percent (Includes The ART)	(46,667)
Income Before Dividends	$ 53,333
Dividend Refund ($1 For Each $3 Of Dividends Paid)	26,667
Dividends Paid To Eastern	$ 80,000

As the dividends from Western will be received tax free by Eastern, they will have after tax retention of $80,000. Unless Eastern pays out taxable dividends to its shareholders, no additional Part I tax will be assessed. This means that, in the absence of additional procedures, there could be a significant deferral of taxes on investment income resulting from the use of two related corporations.

Solution To Problem Two: Refundable Part IV Tax
Corporations Subject To Part IV Tax
13-71.   To eliminate this potential flaw in integration, a Part IV tax is assessed on dividends received by a private corporation from certain other types of corporations. Note that this tax is assessed without regard to whether or not the private corporation is Canadian controlled.

13-72.   In general, only private corporations are liable for Part IV tax. However, there remains the possibility that a company that is controlled largely for the benefit of an individual, or a related group of individuals, might use a small issue of shares to the public in order to avoid this tax. Such corporations are referred to as "subject corporations" and they are defined in ITA 186(3) as follows:

> **Subject Corporation** means a corporation (other than a private corporation) resident in Canada and controlled, whether because of a beneficial interest in one or more trusts or otherwise, by or for the benefit of an individual (other than a trust) or a related group of individuals (other than trusts).

13-73.   ITA 186(1) indicates that, for purposes of Part IV tax, subject corporations will be treated as private corporations. This means that both private corporations, as well as those public corporations that fall within the definition of subject corporations, will be liable for the payment of Part IV tax. In this Chapter, any subsequent references to private corporations should be considered to include subject corporations.

Rates

13-74.   The Part IV tax is assessed at a rate of 33-1/3 percent. It is applicable to portfolio dividends as well as some dividends from connected corporations (both of these terms will be subsequently explained). The rate at which this tax is refunded is the same as the rate for refunds of Part I tax. Refunds of Part IV tax are equal to $1 for each $3 of dividends paid.

Applicable Dividends

13-75.   The Part IV tax is not applicable to all of the dividends received by a private corporation. Specifically, Part IV tax is payable on dividends received by private corporations in the following circumstances:

- A dividend is received from an unconnected company that is deductible in the calculation of the recipient's Taxable Income. While the *Income Tax Act* refers to such dividends as "assessable dividends", it is a common practice to refer to such dividends as "portfolio dividends", a practice we will follow in the remainder of this text.

- The dividend is received from a connected company, and the company paying the dividend received a refund as a consequence of making the dividend payment.

13-76.   Each of these types of dividends will be given attention in the material which follows.

Part IV Tax On Portfolio Dividends Received

Portfolio Dividends And Connected Corporations Defined

13-77.   A portfolio dividend is defined as a dividend received by a private corporation from a corporation to which it is not connected, and that is deductible in the determination of the private corporation's Taxable Income. As with many *Income Tax Act* terms, the definition of a portfolio dividend includes another term which requires definition. This term is "connected corporation" and the definition is found in ITA 186(4). Under this definition, a connected corporation is either:

- a controlled corporation, where control represents ownership of more than 50 percent of the voting shares by any combination of the other corporation and persons with whom it does not deal at arm's length, or

- a corporation in which the other corporation owns more than 10 percent of the voting shares, and more than 10 percent of the fair market value of all of the issued shares of the corporation.

13-78.   Given the definition of connected corporation, a 10 percent shareholding test is generally used to determine whether the dividends received are portfolio dividends or dividends from a connected corporation.

Example   A dividend is received on an investment made by a private company in 500 shares of a large publicly traded company that has 15 million shares outstanding.

Analysis   The 500 shares would be significantly less than 10 percent of the total shares outstanding and would not constitute control of the company. As a consequence, the dividends would be considered portfolio dividends and the Part IV tax would be applicable.

Portfolio Dividends And Integration

13-79.   The tax policy issue with respect to portfolio dividends relates to integration. If such dividends are received by an individual, they are normally subject to taxation. For example, assume that an individual receives $100,000 in dividends. This individual is subject to a combined federal/provincial marginal rate of 45 percent and lives in a province with a dividend tax credit equal to 5/11 of the eligible dividend gross up and 1/3 of the non-eligible dividend gross up. The resulting Tax Payable would be calculated as follows:

	Eligible Dividends	Non-Eligible Dividends
Dividends Received	$100,000	$100,000
Gross Up Of 38 or 25 Percent	38,000	25,000
Taxable Income	$138,000	$125,000
Personal Tax Rate	45%	45%
Tax Payable Before Dividend Tax Credit	$ 62,100	$ 56,250
Dividend Tax Credit:		
[(6/11 + 5/11)(Gross Up)]	(38,000)	
[(2/3 + 1/3)(Gross Up)]		(25,000)
Personal Tax Payable	$ 24,100	$ 31,250

13-80.   As an alternative, consider what would happen if the same $100,000 in dividends had been received by a corporation. Under the general rules for intercorporate dividends, the $100,000 would be deductible in the calculation of the corporation's Taxable Income, resulting in no Part I tax at the corporate level. While tax will ultimately be paid when the corporation distributes this income to its shareholders, there is a potential for significant deferral of taxes until such time as this corporation distributes the income as dividends.

13-81.   In order to correct this flaw in the corporate tax integration system, Part IV tax is applied as follows:

Part IV Tax - Portfolio Dividends   When a private corporation receives a dividend on shares that are being held as a portfolio investment, the recipient company is liable for a Part IV tax of 33-1/3 percent of the dividends received. This Part IV tax is refundable, on the basis of $1 for each $3 of dividends paid, when such dividends are passed on to the shareholders of the recipient corporation.

13-82.   We can see the reasoning behind the rate of this tax by referring back to the preceding example in Paragraph 13-79. You will notice that the effective tax rate on the eligible dividends received by the individual is 24.1 percent ($24,100 ÷ $100,000). By charging a Part IV tax of 33-1/3 percent at the corporate level, the tax paid by the corporation is in excess of the 24.1 percent effective tax rate that would apply to eligible dividends received by an individual with a tax rate of 45 percent. This makes it unattractive to use a private corporation as a shelter to defer the payment of taxes on dividend income. Again, however, by making the tax refundable, it allows the dividends to flow through the recipient corporation without a permanent increase in taxes.

13-83.   The Part IV rate of 33-1/3 percent was established prior to the enhanced dividend gross up and tax credit procedures for eligible dividends. At that time, individual tax rates on all dividends were in the 30 percent range. See, for example, the second column of the example in Paragraph 13-79 where the rate is 31.25 percent. In order to prevent a corporation being used to defer taxation on dividend income, the rate had to be over 30 percent.

13-84.   With the introduction of the enhanced gross up and tax credit procedures, the Part IV tax rate could have been reduced. For example, reducing the rate from 33-1/3 percent to perhaps 25 percent could have been effective in preventing deferral at the corporate level when the maximum rate on eligible dividends is 24.1 percent. The probable reason for not reducing the Part IV tax likely reflects the fact that some of the dividends that will generate a Part IV refund will be non-eligible dividends as they are paid out of a connected corporation's investment income. (See following text.)

Dividends From A Connected Corporation
The Investment Income Problem
13-85.   It is the intent of the government to allow a Canadian controlled private corporation to be used to defer taxes on active business income. Earning such income entitles the

corporation to the use of the small business deduction and this, in most situations, provides a rate of corporate taxation that will effectively defer taxes on income left in the corporation. To the extent that a connected corporation is paying dividends out of such income, there will be no dividend refund and no Part IV tax to be paid by the recipient corporation. This maintains the tax deferral on active business income as it moves between corporations.

13-86. However, when the connected corporation is a private company (whether or not it is Canadian controlled) and the dividends are paid out of investment income, a problem arises. This problem was illustrated by the example presented in Paragraph 13-70.

13-87. In that example, Western paid an $80,000 dividend to Eastern, a payment that included a $26,667 refund of taxes previously paid by Western. Under the general rules for dividends, the $80,000 dividend paid by Western would be included in the calculation of Eastern's Net Income For Tax Purposes and deducted in the determination of its Taxable Income, with the net result that no Part I taxes would be paid on the $80,000. This would, in effect, allow retention of 80 percent of the investment income within the corporate group, a result that is contrary to the general concept of integration.

The Solution

13-88. In order to correct this situation, a second application of Part IV tax is as follows:

Part IV Tax - Connected Companies When a private corporation receives dividends from a connected private corporation that has received a dividend refund under ITA 129(1) as a result of paying the dividends, the recipient company is liable for a Part IV tax equal to its share of the refund received by the paying corporation. If the dividend paid is eligible for a full $1 refund on each $3 paid, the Part IV tax can also be expressed as 33-1/3 percent of the dividends received.

However, the payor corporation may be earning both active business income and investment income. In such situations, if dividends reflect a distribution of both types of income, the dividend refund will not be at the full $1 for $3 rate. (See the Paragraph 13-96 example.) This is why the Part IV tax on dividends received from a connected corporation is expressed in terms of the recipient's share of the refund received by the paying corporation, not in terms of a specific rate.

As was the case with the Part IV tax on portfolio dividends, this Part IV tax is refundable on the basis of $1 for each $3 of dividends paid by the assessed corporation.

Example Of Connected Corporation Dividends

13-89. Returning to the example presented in Paragraph 13-70, you will recall that Western has $100,000 in investment income and pays maximum dividends of $80,000 to Eastern. When the Part IV tax is taken into consideration, the tax consequences for the two companies are as follows:

Investment Income Received By Western		$100,000
Basic Corporate Tax At 40 Percent	($40,000)	
ART At 6-2/3 Percent	(6,667)	(46,667)
Income Before Dividends		$ 53,333
Dividend Refund ($1 For Each $3 Of Dividends Paid)		**26,667**
Dividends Paid To Eastern		$ 80,000
Investment Income (Dividends Received From Western)		$80,000
Part IV Tax Payable (100% Of Western's Refund*)		**(26,667)**
Income Retained By Eastern		$53,333

*Because all of Western's income was from investments, Western's dividend refund is the full $1 for each $3 of dividends. This means that Eastern's Part IV tax can also be calculated as 33-1/3% of the $80,000 in dividends received from Western.

13-90.   As this simple example shows, after the application of the Part IV tax, the amount retained in Eastern is the same $53,333 that was retained in Western. This retention reflects a tax rate on the amount retained within the corporate group of 46.7 percent [($100,000 - $53,333) ÷ $100,000], about the same rate that would be paid by an individual taxpayer in the maximum federal/provincial tax bracket on the direct receipt of the $100,000 in investment income. Clearly, the application of Part IV tax has served to maintain integration in situations involving connected companies.

13-91.   If Eastern decides to distribute the retained income to its shareholders, the results would be as follows:

Income Retained By Eastern	$53,333
Dividend Refund ($1 For Each $3 Of Dividends Paid)	**26,667**
Non-Eligible Dividend To Shareholders	$80,000

13-92.   In effect, the $100,000 of investment income has passed through two corporations and into the hands of individual shareholders, subject to corporate taxes of only 20 percent. This has been accomplished, despite the fact that the initial level of corporate taxation was sufficiently high to discourage allocating investment income to a multi-level corporate structure.

13-93.   Note, however, the effective corporate tax rate is only 20 percent. It is for this reason that the aggregate investment income of a CCPC is subtracted in the determination of Full Rate Taxable Income. This, in turn, means that the dividends paid out by Eastern will not be eligible dividends. The applicable gross up will only be 25 percent and the federal dividend tax credit will be two-thirds of the gross up.

Applicability
13-94.   We would remind you again that the Part IV tax on dividends from a connected company is only applicable when the paying corporation has received a dividend refund. This means that dividends paid out of a corporation's aggregate investment income or paid out of portfolio dividends received will be subject to Part IV tax. If the paying corporation was earning only active business income, no refund would be available when this after tax income was paid out as dividends. As a consequence, no Part IV tax would be assessed on the corporation receiving the dividend.

13-95.   This result is consistent with the goals of integration in that, when a corporation is earning active business income that is taxed at the low small business rate, tax deferral is permitted on income that is retained in the corporation, and not paid out as dividends.

Dividends Paid Out Of Mixed Income
Of A Connected Corporation
13-96.   In many cases, a corporation will be earning both investment income and active business income. This will result in a situation, unlike the example previously presented, where some part of the dividends paid by the corporation will be eligible for a refund, and the remainder will not. In this type of situation, the Part IV tax will not be equal to 33-1/3 percent of the dividends received. An example will make this point clear:

Example   On December 1, 2013, Lower Ltd. declares and pays a dividend of $45,000. As a result of paying this dividend, the Company receives a dividend refund of $8,000. Upper Inc. owns 60 percent of the outstanding shares of Lower Ltd. and receives dividends of $27,000.

Analysis   In this case, the dividend refund is clearly less than one-third of the dividends paid, indicating that Lower's income is made up of a combination of investment income and other income. In this more realistic situation, the Part IV Tax Payable by Upper will be based on Upper's 60 percent share of the $8,000 dividend refund of Lower that resulted from paying the dividend. Upper's Part IV tax would be $4,800 [(60%)($8,000)].

Exercise Thirteen - 5

Subject: Part IV Tax

Opal Ltd., a Canadian controlled private corporation, received the following amounts of dividends during the current year:

Dividends On Various Portfolio Investments	$14,000
Dividends From Emerald Inc. [(100%)($41,500)]	41,500
Dividends From Ruby Inc. [(30%)($60,000)]	18,000

Opal Ltd. owns 100 percent of the voting shares of Emerald Inc. and 30 percent of the voting shares of Ruby Inc. The fair market value of the Ruby Inc. shares is equal to 30 percent of the fair market value of all Ruby Inc. shares. As a result of paying the $60,000 dividend, Ruby Inc. received a dividend refund of $15,000. Emerald Inc. received no dividend refund for its dividend payment.

Determine the amount of Part IV Tax Payable by Opal Ltd. as a result of receiving these dividends.

End of Exercise. Solution available in Study Guide.

Other Part IV Tax Considerations

13-97.   The preceding material has dealt with the basic features of the Part IV tax on dividends received by private corporations. There are a few additional points to be made. First, you should note what kinds of dividends are not subject to Part IV tax. For a private company, or a subject company, the only dividends that will not be subject to Part IV tax are those received from a connected corporation that does not get a dividend refund as a result of paying the dividend.

13-98.   A second point is that ITA 186(1)(b) allows a corporation to use unabsorbed non-capital losses to reduce any Part IV tax. One-third of any non-capital or farm losses claimed for this purpose is deducted from the Part IV tax otherwise payable. However, if this option is chosen, the corporation has effectively used a possible permanent reduction in future taxes to acquire a reduction of Tax Payable that could otherwise ultimately be refunded. This would only make sense in situations where the non-capital loss carry forward was about to expire, or where the company did not expect to have Taxable Income in the carry forward period. With the non-capital loss carry forward period set at 20 years, this is unlikely to be a very useful strategy.

Refundable Dividend Tax On Hand (RDTOH)

Basic Concepts

A Tracking Mechanism

13-99.   In the simple examples we used to illustrate refundable taxes, it was easy to see the direct connection between the amounts of investment income and the amount of the refund that could be made on the payment of dividends. In the real world, such direct relationships do not exist.

13-100.   Corporations usually earn a combination of investment and business income, they seldom pay out all of their earnings in the form of dividends, and there are usually lags between the period in which income is earned and the period in which dividends are paid. As a consequence, some mechanism is needed to keep track of amounts of taxes that have been paid that are eligible for the refund treatment. This mechanism is the Refundable Dividend Tax On Hand account (RDTOH).

General Overview

13-101.   The RDTOH will normally start with an opening balance, reflecting amounts carried over from the previous year. One common point of confusion is that the RDTOH balance at the end of the taxation year is calculated without deducting the dividend refund for that year. As a result, any dividend refund for the preceding year must be deducted from the RDTOH carried forward from the preceding year in order to calculate the opening RDTOH.

13-102.   This balance will be increased by the payment of the various types of refundable taxes. In somewhat simplified terms (which will be explained in the following material), these additions will be:

- The refundable portion of Part I tax paid, calculated as 26-2/3 percent of aggregate investment income (there are a number of technical complications here).

- Part IV tax on dividends received, calculated at a rate of 33-1/3 percent of portfolio dividends, plus an amount equal to the recipient's share of the dividend refund received by a connected corporation paying dividends.

13-103.   The dividend refund for the current year will be limited by the balance in this account. That is, the dividend refund for the current year will be equal to the lesser of the balance in the RDTOH at the end of the year, and one-third of the dividends paid for the year. These concepts will be presented in a more technical form in the following material.

RDTOH - General Definition

13-104.   ITA 129(3) defines the RDTOH at the end of a taxation year as the aggregate of four items. The first three are additions and can be described as follows:

ITA 129(3)(a)   Refundable Part I tax for the year.

ITA 129(3)(b)   The total of the taxes under Part IV for the year.

ITA 129(3)(c)   The corporation's RDTOH at the end of the preceding year.

13-105.   The fourth item, the corporation's dividend refund for its preceding taxation year, is subtracted under **ITA 129(3)(d)**. This definition is available at the front of this book under "Rates and Other Data".

13-106.   The only one of these four items that requires further elaboration is ITA 129(3)(a), the refundable portion of Part I tax for the year.

Refundable Portion Of Part I Tax Payable

The Problem

13-107.   The situation here is made complex by the fact that in calculating a corporation's Part I tax payable, there is no segregation of taxes on investment income from taxes on other types of income. This means that there is no direct measure of what portion of the regular Part I tax payable should be refunded. To deal with this situation, the RDTOH definition limits this addition to the refundable balance as the least of three amounts. These are specified under ITA 129(3)(a)(i), (ii), and (iii).

Investment Income Constraint

13-108.   The basic amount of Part I tax that should be considered refundable is based on the amount of investment income for the year:

ITA 129(3)(a)(i)   the amount determined by the formula

$$A - B, \text{ where}$$

A   is 26-2/3 percent of the corporation's aggregate investment income for the year, and

B   is the amount, if any, by which the foreign non-business income tax credit exceeds 9-1/3 percent of its foreign investment income for the year.

Refundable Dividend Tax On Hand (RDTOH)

13-109.   Aggregate investment income is as defined in ITA 129(4). As indicated previously, the components of aggregate investment income are:

• Net taxable capital gains for the year, reduced by any net capital loss carry overs deducted during the year.

• Net Income from property, excluding dividends that are deductible in computing the corporation's Taxable Income, reduced by any property losses.

13-110.   These amounts do not include interest or rents that are incidental to the corporation's efforts to produce active business income. As noted in Chapter 12, these amounts would be considered active business income. Note, however, the definition does include both Canadian and foreign sources of the types of income listed.

13-111.   If the corporation has no foreign source investment income, the ITA 129(3)(a)(i) amount is simply 26-2/3 percent of aggregate investment income. From a conceptual point of view, this 26-2/3 percent is the difference between a notional 46-2/3 percent combined federal/provincial rate on investment income, and the 20 percent rate that is assumed in the integration procedures. The idea here is, that if 26-2/3 percent of the Part I tax paid is refunded, it will restore the overall corporate rate to the 20 percent that is assumed in the dividend gross up and tax credit procedures that are applicable to non-eligible dividends.

13-112.   With respect to foreign non-business income, the RDTOH legislation is based on the assumption that the Canadian tax rate on this foreign income is 36 percent (note that this is different from the 28 percent rate that is assumed in the small business deduction calculations). Reflecting this assumption, the B component in the ITA 129(3)(a)(i) formula subtracts any amount of foreign tax credit that is in excess of 9-1/3 percent of foreign investment income for the year.

13-113.   The basic idea here is that a foreign tax credit of 9-1/3 percent will reduce the Canadian taxes paid to 26-2/3 percent (36 percent, less 9-1/3 percent, equals 26-2/3 percent, the rate applicable to the refund). If the foreign tax credit exceeds 9-1/3 percent of the foreign investment income, the Canadian taxes paid would be less than the potential refund of 26-2/3 percent. In other words, without the 9-1/3 percent subtraction, the Canadian government would be providing a refund that is larger than the amount of Canadian tax paid on the foreign investment income.

Example   A CCPC earns $50,000 in foreign investment income. The government in the foreign jurisdiction withholds 15 percent of this amount and, as a consequence, the company receives a foreign non-business tax credit of $7,500.

Analysis   At the assumed rate of 36 percent, Canadian tax on this income would be $10,500 [(36%)($50,000) - $7,500]. This results in a Canadian tax rate on this income of only 21 percent ($10,500 ÷ $50,000). In the absence of some type of adjustment, the refundable taxes on this $50,000 of income would be at a rate of 26-2/3% and would be equal to $13,333 [(26-2/3%)($50,000)], $2,833 in excess of the $10,500 in Canadian taxes that would be paid. This is clearly not an appropriate result.

To correct this situation, the excess of the foreign non-business income tax credit over 9-1/3 percent of the foreign investment income is subtracted from the 26-2/3 percent refund on the foreign investment income. The 9-1/3 percent reflects the difference between the notional rate of 36 percent and the refund rate of 26-2/3 percent.

In our example, the calculations would be as follows:

26-2/3 Percent Of Foreign Investment Income		$13,333
Deduct Excess Of:		
Foreign Non-Business Tax Credit	($7,500)	
Over 9-1/3 Foreign Investment Income	4,667	(2,833)
ITA 129(3)(a)(i)		**$10,500**

This procedure has, in effect, reduced the amount of the refund to $10,500. As calculated at the beginning of this analysis, this is equal to the notional amount of Canadian taxes paid on the foreign investment income.

Taxable Income Constraint

13-114.   A further problem with respect to determining the refundable portion of Part I tax payable is that the corporation's Taxable Income may include amounts that are not taxed at full corporate rates (e.g., amounts eligible for the small business deduction). Further, Taxable Income may be reduced by such items as non-capital loss carry overs to a level that is less than the amount of investment income on which ITA 129(3)(a)(i) would provide a refund. To deal with this, the refundable portion of the Part I tax is limited as follows:

ITA 129(3)(a)(ii)   26-2/3 percent of the amount, if any, by which the corporation's taxable income for the year exceeds the total of:

A   the amount eligible for the small business deduction;
B   100/35 [see **Note**] of the tax credit for foreign non-business income; and
C   4 times [see **Note**] the tax credit for foreign business income .

Note   The 100/35 factor and 4 multiplier are not the ones in current legislation. However, they reflect draft legislation that is being enforced for years after 2011. We feel the details and history of these changes will not be of interest to our users.

13-115.   Component B is designed to remove foreign investment income that is not taxed because of the foreign non-business tax credit. The elimination is based on the assumption that it is taxed at a notional rate of 35 percent (35/100). In similar fashion, Component C is designed to remove foreign business income that is not taxed because of the foreign business income tax credit. The elimination here is based on the assumption that this type of income is taxed at a notional rate of 25 percent (1 ÷ 4).

Tax Payable Constraint

13-116.   A final problem here relates to the fact that the dividend refund could exceed the corporation's actual Tax Payable for the year. This could happen if, for example, the company had large amounts of tax credits for scientific research and experimental development. To deal with this problem, the refundable portion of Part I tax paid is limited as follows:

ITA 129(3)(a)(iii)   the corporation's tax for the year payable under this Part [Part I].

Formula For Part I Tax Addition To RDTOH

13-117.   The following formula is available in the front of this book under "Rates And Other Data". For 2013, the addition to the RDTOH for Part I tax is the least of:

ITA 129(3)(a)(i)   26-2/3 percent of aggregate investment income, reduced by the excess of foreign non-business income tax credits over 9-1/3 percent of foreign investment income.

ITA 129(3)(a)(ii)   26-2/3 percent of the amount, if any, by which Taxable Income exceeds the sum of:

- the amount eligible for the small business deduction,
- 100/35 of the foreign non-business tax credit, and
- 4 times the foreign business tax credit.

ITA 129(3)(a)(iii)   Part I tax payable.

The Dividend Refund

13-118.   While in theory, dividend refunds should only be available when dividends are paid out of investment income, corporate tax legislation does not provide a basis for tracking the income source of a particular dividend payment. As a consequence, a dividend refund is available on any taxable dividend that is paid by the corporation as long as there is a balance in the RDTOH. Given this, the dividend refund will be equal to the lesser of:

- the balance in the RDTOH account at the end of the year; and
- 1/3 of all taxable dividends paid during the year.

Example Of RDTOH Calculations

13-119.   The following simplified example illustrates the refundable tax calculations.   In the Chapter 13 material in the separate paper Study Guide which accompanies this text, there is an example containing a completed corporate tax return. The tax return example includes an additional illustration of this material on the RDTOH account.

Example   Fortune Ltd. is a Canadian controlled private corporation. Based on the formula in ITR 402(3), 90 percent of the Company's income is earned in a province. The following information is available for the year ending December 31, 2013:

Canadian Source Investment Income	
(Includes $25,000 In Taxable Capital Gains)	$100,000
Gross Foreign Non-Business Income (15 Percent Withheld)	20,000
Gross Foreign Business Income (15 Percent Withheld)	10,000
Active Business Income (No Associated Companies)	150,000
Portfolio Dividends Received	30,000
Net Income For Tax Purposes	$310,000
Portfolio Dividends	(30,000)
Net Capital Loss Carry Forward Deducted	(15,000)
Taxable Income	$265,000

RDTOH - December 31, 2012	$110,000
Dividend Refund For 2012	20,000
Taxable Dividends Paid During 2013	40,000

Analysis   The Part I Tax Payable would be calculated as follows:

Base Amount Of Part I Tax [(38%)($265,000)]	$100,700
Federal Tax Abatement [(10%)(90%)($265,000)]	(23,850)
Small Business Deduction (Note 1)	(25,500)
ART (Note 2)	7,000
General Rate Reduction (Note 3)	(1,300)
Foreign Non-Business Tax Credit (Note 1)	(3,000)
Foreign Business Tax Credit (Note 1)	(1,500)
Part I Tax Payable	$ 52,550

Note 1   In order to simplify the calculation of the small business deduction, the foreign tax credits are assumed to be equal to the amounts withheld (15 percent). Additional calculations would be required to support this conclusion.

The small business deduction would be equal to 17 percent of the least of:

1.	Active Business Income	$150,000
2.	Taxable Income	$265,000
	Deduct:	
	[(100/28)($3,000 Foreign Non-Business Tax Credit)]	(10,714)
	[(4)($1,500 Foreign Business Tax Credit)]	(6,000)
	Adjusted Taxable Income	$248,286
3.	Annual Business Limit	$500,000

The small business deduction is $25,500 [(17%)($150,000)].

Note 2   Aggregate Investment Income is equal to $105,000 ($100,000 + $20,000 - $15,000). The $7,000 Additional Refundable Tax (ART) is equal to the lesser of:

- [(6-2/3%)($105,000)] $7,000
- [(6-2/3%)($265,000 - $150,000 SBD)] $7,667

Note 3   The general rate reduction would be calculated as follows:

Taxable Income	$265,000
Amount Eligible For Small Business Deduction (Note 1)	(150,000)
Aggregate Investment Income	(105,000)
Full Rate Taxable Income (= Foreign Business Income)	$ 10,000
Rate	13%
General Rate Reduction	$ 1,300

13-120.   Based on the preceding information, the refundable portion of Part I tax would be the least of the following three amounts:

26-2/3% Of Aggregate Investment Income		
[(26-2/3%)($105,000)]		$ 28,000
Deduct Excess Of:		
Foreign Non-Business Tax Credit	($3,000)	
Over 9-1/3% Of Foreign Investment		
Income [(9-1/3%)($20,000)]	1,867	(1,133)
Amount Under ITA 129(3)(a)(i)		**$ 26,867**

Taxable Income		$265,000
Deduct:		
Amount Eligible For Small Business Deduction	($150,000)	
[(100/35)($3,000 Foreign Non-Business Tax Credit)]	(8,571)	
[(4)($1,500 Foreign Business Tax Credit)]	(6,000)	(164,571)
Total		$100,429
Rate		26-2/3%
Amount Under ITA 129(3)(a)(ii)		**$ 26,781**

Amount Under ITA 129(3)(a)(iii) = Part I Tax Payable (Given)	**$ 52,550**

The refundable portion of Part I tax is equal to $26,781, which is the least of the preceding three amounts.

13-121.   The Part IV tax would be $10,000, one-third of the $30,000 in portfolio dividends received. Given this, the balance in the RDTOH account at the end of the year is as follows:

RDTOH - End Of Preceding Year	$110,000	
Less: Dividend Refund For Preceding Year (Given)	(20,000)	$ 90,000
Refundable Portion Of Part I Tax	$ 26,781	
Part IV Tax Payable [(33-1/3%)($30,000)]	10,000	36,781
RDTOH - December 31, 2013		$126,781

13-122.   The dividend refund for the year would be $13,333, the lesser of:

- One-Third Of Taxable Dividends Paid ($40,000 ÷ 3) = $13,333
- RDTOH Balance - December 31, 2013 = $126,781

13-123.   Using the preceding information, the total federal Tax Payable for Fortune Ltd. is calculated as follows:

Part I Tax Payable	$52,550
Part IV Tax Payable	10,000
Dividend Refund	(13,333)
Federal Tax Payable	$49,217

Exercise Thirteen - 6

Subject: Refundable Part I Tax

Debut Inc. is a Canadian controlled private corporation. During the taxation year ending December 31, 2013, Debut Inc. has the following amounts of property income:

Dividends From Portfolio Investments	$22,000
Foreign Non-Business Income (Net Of 5 Percent Withholding)	14,250
Capital Gains	38,250
Net Rental Income	6,500
Interest Income On Ten Year Bond	9,200

The Company's Net Income For Tax Purposes is $121,825. The only deductions in the calculation of Taxable Income are the dividends on portfolio investments and a net capital loss carry forward of $9,000 [(1/2)($18,000)]. An $8,500 small business deduction and a foreign tax credit of $750 served to reduce Tax Payable. Assume that the Company's Part I Tax Payable has been correctly determined to be $18,903. Determine the refundable amount of Part I tax for the current year.

Exercise Thirteen - 7

Subject: Dividend Refund

Quan Imports Ltd. is a Canadian controlled private corporation. At the end of the previous year, it had an RDTOH balance of $12,500. It paid taxable dividends during that year of $6,000. During the current year, Quan Import's only income is $24,000 in taxable capital gains and $6,000 in dividends received from an investment in Royal Bank shares. During the year, the Company declares and pays a $15,000 dividend on its common shares. Determine the Company's dividend refund for the year.

End of Exercises. Solutions available in Study Guide.

Working Through Large Corporate Tax Problems

13-124.   At this point we have completed our general coverage of Taxable Income and Tax Payable for corporations. As we are sure you are aware, there are a great many concepts and procedures involved in this process. While we have illustrated the concepts and procedures in individual examples and Exercises, we have not provided a comprehensive example that encompasses all of these items.

13-125.   You will find, however, that several of the Self Study and Assignment Problems involve fairly comprehensive calculations of corporate Taxable Income and Tax Payable. Given the complexity of these problems, it is useful to have a systematic approach to dealing with this type of problem. To fill that need, we would suggest you approach the required calculations in the following order (we are assuming that only federal taxes are being calculated as this is generally the case with the problem material in this text):

- Net Income For Tax Purposes. Depending on the problem, this may require converting an accounting Net Income figure into the required tax figure.

- Taxable Income. This would include making deductions for charitable donations, dividends from taxable Canadian corporations, and loss carry overs.

- Basic federal Part I Tax Payable at the 38 percent rate.

- Federal tax abatement. If there is foreign income, this may require a calculation of the amounts that are to be allocated to Canadian provinces.

- Small business deduction for CCPCs (without consideration of the general rate reduction or the ART in the foreign income tax credit constraints).

- Aggregate investment income for CCPCs.

- Additional refundable tax on investment income (ART) for CCPCs. Note that this is an addition to Part I Tax Payable, not a deduction.

- Manufacturing and processing profits deduction (without consideration of the general rate reduction in the foreign income tax credit constraints).

- General rate reduction.

- Foreign non-business income tax credit.

- Foreign business income tax credit.

- Part IV tax payable for CCPCs and other private corporations.

- Refundable portion of Part I tax for CCPCs.

- Balance in the refundable dividend tax on hand account (RDTOH) for CCPCs.

- Dividend refund for CCPCs.

We suggest you work Self Study Problems Thirteen-2 and 3 at this point.

Designation Of Eligible Dividends

Basic Concepts

The Problem

13-126.   Prior to 2006, the dividend gross up and tax credit procedures were based on the assumption that the combined federal/provincial tax rate was 20 percent for all corporations. Although this rate was fairly realistic for the income of a CCPC benefitting from the small business deduction, it was well below the rates applicable to other types of Taxable Income. As a result, income flowed through a corporation could be taxed at rates in excess of 60 percent. As this was well above any combined federal/provincial rate applicable to income received directly by an individual, there was clearly a defect in the integration system.

The Solution

13-127.   The government's solution to this problem was to change the gross up and tax credit procedures on dividends that are paid out of income that has been taxed at full corporate rates. While the numbers were changed as lower tax rates on public corporations were phased in, for 2012 and subsequent years the gross up percentage is 38 percent and the federal dividend tax credit is equal to 6/11 of the gross up. These rates are based on a notional corporate tax rate of 27.54 percent and, as this rate is consistent with actual real world rates on corporate Taxable Income, the integration of the Canadian tax system has been improved.

13-128.   Currently (in 2013), with these gross up and credit numbers applied to eligible dividends, the tax rates on eligible dividends are very close to those on non-eligible dividends. This spread will increase in 2014 when the gross up and credit procedures for non-eligible dividends will be changed and will increase their effective tax rate. The following table compares 2013 effective tax rates on different types of investment income for an individual with sufficient other income to place him in the 29 percent federal bracket and 14 percent provincial bracket for any additional income. We have assumed a provincial dividend tax credit of:

- one-third of the gross up for non-eligible dividends
- 30 percent of the gross up for eligible dividends

	Interest Income	Capital Gains	Non-Eligible Dividends	Eligible Dividends
Tax Rate (In Maximum Bracket)	43.0%	21.5%	28.8%	27.2%

13-129. While the use of different provincial rates and credits will produce variations in these results, interest income will always be subject to the highest rates, while eligible dividends will always have a lower rate than non-eligible dividends. We would call your attention to the fact that capital gains continue to be subject to lower rates than either eligible or non-eligible dividends. Note that in 2013, the spread between the two types of dividends is only 1.6 percent (28.8% - 27.2%). As previously mentioned, this spread will increase beginning in 2014.

Implementing The Solution

13-130. The eligible dividend rules were introduced to deal with maintaining integration in situations where a corporation is taxed at rates that do not benefit from the small business deduction or refundable taxes on dividend distributions. In order to keep the combined corporate and individual tax rate on income that is flowed through a corporation at roughly the same level that would be paid by an individual on direct receipt of income, these procedures serve to reduce the individual tax rate applicable to eligible dividends. This difference in rates for eligible vs. non-eligible dividends creates a problem in that we need a procedure for distinguishing between the two types of dividends.

13-131. A possible solution to this problem would be to simply state that dividends paid by public corporations would be eligible dividends (these corporations are generally subject to full corporate rates) and dividends paid by CCPCs would be non-eligible dividends (these corporations usually get either the small business deduction or a partial refund of taxes paid). However, public corporations may have income that has been taxed at low rates and, somewhat more commonly, CCPCs may have income that has been taxed at full corporate rates.

13-132. Given this situation, a system has been developed that has different procedures for CCPCs and non-CCPCs:

CCPCs It will be assumed that, in general, dividends paid by CCPCs are non-eligible. However, to track components of their income that have been taxed at full corporate rates, CCPCs will have a notional account referred to as a General Rate Income Pool (GRIP). The balance in this account will be available to pay eligible dividends.

Non-CCPCs In general, non-CCPCs are comprised of public companies and private companies that are not Canadian controlled. For these companies, it will be assumed that, in general, dividends paid are eligible. However, to track components of their income that have been taxed at low rates, they will have to use a notional account referred to as a Low Rate Income Pool (LRIP). The balance in this account must be reduced to nil by the payment of non-eligible dividends prior to the payment of eligible dividends.

13-133. We will provide a separate discussion of the procedures applicable to both CCPCs and non-CCPCs.

CCPCs And Their GRIP
Default Treatment
13-134. Provided no associated corporations are involved, a CCPC qualifies for a small business deduction equal to 17 percent of up to $500,000 per year of active business income. This currently has the effect of reducing the federal rate on this income to 11 percent and the combined federal/provincial rate to an average of 14.3 percent (the range is from 11 percent to 19 percent).

13-135. In addition, the investment income of these corporations has an available refund of tax that, in a manner similar to the small business deduction, reduces the effective federal/provincial tax rate on such income to a rate that is generally below 20 percent, provided the after tax amounts have been distributed to shareholders.

13-136. For many, perhaps the majority of CCPCs, all of their income benefits from one of these two provisions. With a corporate tax rate that is generally below 20 percent, the enhanced dividend gross up and tax credit procedures for eligible dividends are not required to achieve the objectives of integration. Given this situation, the government has concluded that dividends paid by CCPCs will, in general, be non-eligible dividends.

General Rate Income Pool (GRIP)
13-137. The legislation recognizes, however, that some types of CCPC income should provide a basis for designating eligible dividends. In order to provide for this, ITA 89(1) defines a notional account to track the amounts that qualify. This account is referred to as the General Rate Income Pool (GRIP) and, to the extent there is a balance in this account, dividends declared by a CCPC can be designated as eligible.

13-138. In ITA 89(1), the definition is based on an amount A, reduced by an amount B, with this latter amount defined in a way that adjusts for future events such as non-capital loss carry backs. (The following definition is available at the front of this book in "Rates and Other Data".) As dealing with the B component goes beyond the scope of this text, we will focus on the content of A. For 2013 the component A is defined as follows:

$$A = C + [(72\%)(D - E - F)] + G + H - I, \text{ where}$$

C is the CCPC's GRIP at the end of the preceding taxation year.
D is the CCPC's taxable income for the year.
E is the amount eligible for the small business deduction for the year.
F is the lesser of the CCPC's aggregate investment income for the year and its Taxable Income.
G is the amount of eligible dividends received by the CCPC during the year.
H involves a group of technical additions related to becoming a CCPC, amalgamations, and wind-ups.
I is the amount of eligible dividends paid during the **preceding** year, less the amount of any Excessive Eligible Dividend Designation (EEDD) made during the preceding year (see Paragraph 13-145).

13-139. Several comments on this formula are relevant at this point:

- The (D - E - F) component calculates a Taxable Income that is adjusted to eliminate the types of income for which CCPCs receive favourable tax treatment. As dividends are paid out of after tax funds, the residual income is multiplied by 72 percent, reflecting a 2013 notional federal/provincial tax rate of 28 percent.

- If a CCPC receives eligible dividends that qualify for the enhanced dividend gross up and tax credit, the addition in G allows these dividends to retain that status on their flow through to the shareholders of the CCPC.

- Note that the balance is reduced, not by eligible dividends paid in the current year, but by eligible dividends paid in the preceding year.

13-140. A simple example will illustrate these provisions:

Example Norgrave Ltd., a CCPC, had no GRIP balance at the end of 2011. During 2012, the Company received eligible dividends of $106,600 and designated $25,000 of its dividends paid as eligible. At the end of 2012, Norgrave has a GRIP of $106,600. For 2013, Norgrave has Taxable Income of $225,000. This amount includes aggregate investment income of $55,000. In addition, the Company receives eligible dividends during the year of $50,000.

In determining 2013 Tax Payable, the Company has a small business deduction of $25,500 [(17%)($150,000)]. During 2013, Norgrave pays dividends of $40,000, with $20,000 of this amount being designated as eligible.

Analysis The 2013 ending balance in GRIP will be calculated as follows:

C - GRIP Balance At End Of 2012		$106,600
D - Taxable Income	$225,000	
E - Income Eligible For SBD	(150,000)	
F - Aggregate Investment Income		
(Less Than Taxable Income)	(55,000)	
Adjusted Taxable Income	$ 20,000	
Rate	72%	14,400
G - Eligible Dividends Received		50,000
I - Eligible Dividends Designated in 2012		(25,000)
GRIP At End Of 2013		$146,000

The eligible dividends paid during 2013 will be deducted from the GRIP in 2014.

Exercise Thirteen - 8

Subject: GRIP Balance

Lanson Inc., a CCPC, had no GRIP balance at its year end on December 31, 2011. During 2012, the Company received eligible dividends of $365,000 and designated $140,000 of its $165,000 in dividends paid as eligible. At the end of 2012, Lanson has a GRIP of $365,000.

For 2013, Lanson has Taxable Income of $960,000. This amount includes net taxable capital gains of $65,000, mortgage interest received of $23,000, and a net capital loss carry forward deduction of $14,000. In addition, the Company receives eligible dividends during the year of $85,000. In determining 2013 Tax Payable, the Company has a small business deduction of $38,250. During 2013, Lanson pays dividends of $78,000, with $42,000 of this amount being designated as eligible. Determine the Company's GRIP balance at the end of 2013.

End of Exercise. Solution available in Study Guide.

Non-CCPCs And Their LRIP
Low Rate Income Pool (LRIP)
13-141. For non-CCPCs, their income will generally be taxed at full corporate rates. This means that, in general, their dividends can be designated as eligible. However, in some situations, a non-CCPC may have balances that have not been taxed at full corporate rates. This could include amounts of income retained by a CCPC before it became a public company, as well as non-eligible dividends received from a CCPC.

13-142. Such balances will be allocated to a notional account referred to as a Low Rate Income Pool (LRIP). This account, defined in ITA 89(1), is similar to the GRIP account in that it is used to track certain types of income. However, the two accounts serve very different purposes:

- The GRIP account is used to track balances that can be used by a CCPC as the basis for designating eligible dividends. To the extent that a GRIP balance is present, CCPC dividends can be designated as eligible until such time as the balance is exhausted. Note, however, the presence of a GRIP balance does not require that dividends be designated as eligible. Designation as eligible is at the discretion of the corporation.

- The LRIP account is used to track balances that have not been subject to full corporate tax rates. When an LRIP balance is present, any dividends paid by the corporation will be considered non-eligible. Stated alternatively, a corporation with a positive LRIP balance cannot designate any of its dividends as eligible until the LRIP balance is exhausted. In this situation, the corporation has no discretion.

13-143.   The definition of the LRIP balance, as found in ITA 89(1) (and also available at the front of this book in "Rates and Other Data"), is as follows:

$$(A + B + C + D + E + F) - (G + H), \text{ where}$$

A   is the non-CCPCs LRIP at the end of the preceding year.
B   is the amount of non-eligible dividends received by the non-CCPC from a CCPC.
C   is a group of technical additions related to corporate reorganizations.
D   is an adjustment for a non-CCPC that was a CCPC in some preceding year.
E   is an adjustment for a non-CCPC that was a credit union in some preceding year.
F   is an adjustment for a non-CCPC that was an investment company in some preceding year.
G   is the amount of taxable dividends, other than eligible dividends, paid by the non-CCPC during the year.
H   is the amount of any EEDD made by the non-CCPC during the year.

13-144.   A simple example will serve to illustrate this definition.

Example   At the end of 2012, Ovamp Ltd. has an LRIP balance of $450,000. During 2013, the Company receives non-eligible dividends from a CCPC in the amount of $225,000. During 2013, the Company pays dividends of $360,000.

Analysis   Given the presence of a positive LRIP balance in excess of the total dividends paid, none of the Ovamp dividends could be designated eligible.

Part III.1 Tax On Excessive Eligible Dividend Designations
Calculation
13-145.   The enhanced dividend gross up and tax credit is available on any dividend that the paying corporation has designated as eligible. This raises the possibility that a corporation might designate a dividend as eligible under circumstances where such a designation is not appropriate (e.g., a CCPC designating a dividend as eligible when it has no balance in its GRIP at the end of the year). To discourage this, the government has introduced a Part III.1 tax on what is referred to as an Excessive Eligible Dividend Designation (EEDD).

13-146.   If the EEDD is inadvertent, the Part III.1 tax is equal to 20 percent of the excess amount. In these circumstances, Part III.1 provides for an election that will allow the taxpayer to effectively undo the designation.

13-147.   If the CRA concludes that the EEDD reflects an attempt to artificially manipulate either a GRIP or an LRIP, the Part III.1 tax rate goes to 30 percent. In addition, there are two other consequences:

- The tax applies to the entire dividend, not just the EEDD.
- No election is available to undo the excessive election.

Designation Of Eligible Dividends

13-148.   In order to appropriately track all dividend payments, any resident Canadian corporation that pays a taxable dividend is required to file a return for the year under Part III.1.

13-149.   ITA 89(1) defines EEDD differently for CCPCs and non-CCPCs. These definitions will be considered separately in the following material.

EEDD For A CCPC

13-150.   If a CCPC designates an amount of eligible dividends that is in excess of its GRIP at the end of the year, it will be considered an EEDD and be subject to Part III.1 tax.

> **Example**   At its December 31, 2012 year end, Sandem Inc., a CCPC, has a GRIP of $45,000. It paid no dividends in 2012. During 2013, the Company pays dividends of $100,000, of which $60,000 are designated as eligible. There are no additions to the Company's GRIP during 2013.
>
> **Analysis**   The Company has an EEDD of $15,000 ($60,000 - $45,000). Provided the CRA believes that this was an inadvertent result, this amount will be subject to a Part III.1 tax of 20 percent on the excess of $15,000. There is also the possibility of electing to have the EEDD treated as a non-eligible dividend.
>
> If the CRA concludes that the EEDD was a deliberate attempt to manipulate the Company's GRIP, an additional 10 percent is added to the Part III.1 tax. In addition, the applicable 30 percent tax is assessed on the entire eligible amount of $60,000, not just the $15,000 EEDD amount and no election is available to undo the excessive election.

EEDD For A Non-CCPC

13-151.   In somewhat simplified terms, an EEDD for a non-CCPC is equal to the lesser of its eligible dividends paid and its LRIP at the time the dividend is paid. For example, if a non-CCPC paid an eligible dividend of $50,000 at a point in time that its LRIP was equal to $40,000, the EEDD would be $40,000. Note that, unlike the situation with EEDDs for CCPCs, where the amount is based on the end of year balance of the GRIP, the EEDD for a non-CCPC is based on the balance of the LRIP at the point in time when the eligible dividend becomes payable.

13-152.   A simple example will illustrate these provisions:

> **Example**   Victor Ltd., a Canadian public company, receives $42,000 in non-eligible dividends from a CCPC on June 15, 2013. Its LRIP has a balance of nil prior to this. On September 23, 2013, Victor pays dividends of $100,000, with $30,000 of this amount being designated as eligible.
>
> **Analysis**   At September 23, 2012, the balance in the LRIP would be $42,000. The lesser of this amount and the eligible dividend would be $30,000 and this would be the amount of the EEDD.
>
> This result seems somewhat counter-intuitive in that a non-eligible dividend was paid in an amount sufficient to eliminate the LRIP. However, the legislation is clear that the LRIP is measured at a particular point in time and, if an eligible dividend is paid when there is a positive balance in this account, it creates an EEDD. We would note that this situation could have been avoided had the non-eligible dividend been paid before, even by one day, the payment of the eligible dividend.
>
> Provided there were no further dividend transactions, the LRIP balance at the end of the year would be nil as the payment of $70,000 in non-eligible dividends would have eliminated the $42,000 balance created by the non-eligible dividends received.
>
> With respect to the Part III.1 tax, a tax of 20 percent would normally be assessed on the EEDD of $30,000. However, if the CRA concludes that a deliberate attempt to manipulate the LRIP was involved, the tax rate will be increased to 30 percent.

A Final Word On Eligible Dividends

13-153.   You should be aware that the preceding is a fairly simplified version of the provisions related to eligible dividends and their designation. The complete legislation is far more complex, dealing with a number of transitional situations, changes in a corporation's classification, as well as problems associated with corporate reorganizations. However, we feel that this version of the material is appropriate for an introductory text in taxation.

We suggest you work Self Study Problems Thirteen-4, 5, 6, and 7 at this point.

Key Terms Used In This Chapter

13-154.   The following is a list of the key terms used in this Chapter. These terms, and their meanings, are compiled in the Glossary Of Key Terms located at the back of the separate paper Study Guide.

Additional Refundable Tax On Investment Income (ART)	General Rate Income Pool (GRIP)
	Integration
Aggregate Investment Income	Low Rate Income Pool (LRIP)
ART	Part IV Tax
Canadian Controlled Private Corporation	Portfolio Dividend
CCPC	Private Corporation
Connected Corporation	Public Corporation
Dividend Gross Up	RDTOH
Dividend Tax Credit	Refundable Dividend Tax On Hand
Dividends	Refundable Part I Tax
Eligible Dividends	Subject Corporation
Excessive Eligible Dividend Designation (EEDD)	

References

13-155.   For more detailed study of the material in this Chapter, we refer you to the following:

ITA 82(1)	Taxable Dividends Received
ITA 89(1)	Definitions (Canadian Corporations, GRIP, LRIP, and EEDD)
ITA 123.3	Refundable Tax On CCPC's Investment Income
ITA 123.4	General Rate Reduction
ITA 129(1)	Dividend Refund To Private Corporation
ITA 129(3)	Definition Of Refundable Dividend Tax On Hand
ITA 129(4)	Aggregate Investment Income
ITA 186	Part IV Tax
IT-67R3	Taxable Dividends From Corporations Resident In Canada
IT-243R4	Dividend Refund To Private Corporations
IT-269R4	Part IV Tax On Taxable Dividends Received By a Private Corporation Or A Subject Corporation
IT-391R	Status Of Corporations
IT-458R2	Canadian Controlled Private Corporation

Sample Corporate Tax Return For Chapter 13

The Sample Tax Return for this Chapter can be found in the Study Guide beginning on page S-292.

Problems For Self Study

(The solutions for these problems can be found in the separate Study Guide.)

Self Study Problem Thirteen - 1 (Integration Example)

For the taxation year 2013, assume the following with respect to an individual who owns 100 percent of the shares of a Canadian public company.

- The combined federal and provincial corporate tax rate on his corporation is 27 percent.
- The corporation's Net Income For Tax Purposes for 2013 is $500,000.
- Any dividends paid by the corporation are designated eligible dividends.
- The individual's marginal federal tax rate is 29 percent and his marginal provincial tax rate is 16 percent.
- The provincial dividend tax credit for 2013 on eligible dividends is equal to 4/11 of the gross up.

Required: Indicate, using these assumptions, whether integration is working perfectly. If your answer is no, briefly explain why this is the case.

Self Study Problem Thirteen - 2 (Refundable Dividend Tax On Hand)

Mr. Stevens, a Canadian resident, owns 100 percent of the shares of Stevens Holdings Inc. (SHI), which owns 100 percent of Fancy Operating Ltd. (FOL). Both SHI and FOL have a December 31 year end. Neither Company paid any dividends in 2012.

The following information pertains to the year ending December 31, 2013:

Fancy Operating Ltd.

- The balance in the Refundable Dividend Tax On Hand account at December 31, 2012 was $2,000.
- The Company earned active business income of $80,000 and Canadian interest income of $7,000.
- The Company paid taxable dividends to SHI of $75,000.

Stevens Holdings Inc.

- The balance in the Refundable Dividend Tax On Hand account at December 31, 2012 was $10,000.
- The Company received a taxable dividend from FOL of $75,000.
- The Company received a taxable dividend on BCE common shares of $8,000.
- The Company earned Canadian interest income of $12,000.
- The Company realized a capital gain of $47,250.
- The Company paid a taxable dividend of $50,000 to Mr. Stevens.

Assume that, for each Company, the refundable portion of Part I tax is equal to 26-2/3 percent of aggregate investment income.

Required:

A. Calculate the dividend refund for FOL for 2013.

B. Calculate the Part IV Tax Payable for SHI for 2013.

C. Calculate the dividend refund for SHI for 2013.

Self Study Problem Thirteen - 3 (Part I and Part IV Refundable Taxes)

Burton Investments Ltd. is a Canadian controlled private corporation that sells office supplies. It owns 52 percent of the outstanding shares of Puligny Inc. On December 15, 2013, Puligny Inc. declared and paid a dividend of $122,000, of which Burton Investments Ltd. received $63,440 (52 percent). As a result of paying the $122,000 dividend, Puligny Inc. received a dividend refund in the amount of $12,500.

Other 2013 income that was reported by Burton Investments consisted of the following amounts:

Capital Gain	$18,000
Dividends From Bank Of Montreal Common Shares	13,480
Interest	1,150

The capital gain was on the sale of land that had been used as an auxiliary parking lot, but was no longer needed.

Burton's office supply business is seasonal and, as a consequence, temporary cash balances must be set aside for the purchase of inventories during the busy parts of the year. All of the $1,150 in interest was earned on such temporary cash balances.

At the end of 2012, the Company's Refundable Dividend Tax On Hand balance was $22,346. The 2012 dividend refund was $7,920.

The Company's Taxable Income for the year ending December 31, 2013 was $62,800. No foreign income was included in this total. Assume the Part I Tax Payable for the year ending December 31, 2013 was correctly calculated as $12,560. Because of its association with Puligny Inc., its share of the annual business limit on income eligible for the small business deduction is $40,000. Burton's active business income is equal to its share of the annual business limit.

Burton Investments paid taxable dividends of $22,500 in 2013.

Required: For the taxation year ending December 31, 2013, determine the Part IV and refundable Part I taxes that will be payable by Burton Investments Ltd. In addition, determine the balance in the Refundable Dividend Tax On Hand account at December 31, 2013, and any dividend refund available.

Self Study Problem Thirteen - 4 (Part I And Part IV Refundable Taxes, GRIP)

Vader Ltd. is a Canadian controlled private corporation involved in the distribution of domestically produced laser products. For the taxation year ending December 31, 2013, its Net Income For Tax Purposes was made up of the following components:

Active Business Income	$216,300
Dividends From Canadian Corporations:	
Wholly-Owned Subsidiary (All Non-Eligible)	108,000
Portfolio Investments (All Eligible)	56,000
Interest On Government Bonds	36,300
Taxable Capital Gains [(1/2)($114,600)]	57,300
Net Income For Tax Purposes	$473,900

On December 31, 2012, Vader Ltd., has a GRIP balance of $59,000 and a nil balance in its Refundable Dividend Tax On Hand account. During 2012, Vader Ltd. paid no dividends.

The dividends paid to Vader Ltd. by the wholly-owned subsidiary in 2013 did not entitle the subsidiary to any dividend refund. The wholly-owned subsidiary is allocated $200,000 of the annual small business deduction. The remainder is allocated to Vader Ltd.

On October 1, 2013, Vader Ltd. paid taxable dividends to its shareholders in the amount of $32,400. Of this total, $15,000 was designated eligible.

Required: Show all of the calculations used to provide the following required information, including those for which the result is nil.

For Vader Ltd.'s 2013 taxation year, calculate the following items:

A. Federal Part I Tax Payable.
B. Part IV Tax Payable.
C. The balance in the Refundable Dividend Tax On Hand account on December 31, 2013.
D. The balance in the GRIP account on December 31, 2013.
E. The dividend refund, if any.
F. Federal Tax Payable (net of any dividend refund).

Self Study Problem Thirteen - 5 (Tax Payable With SBD, ART, FTC, And GRR)

Sinzer Ltd. is a Canadian controlled private corporation. Its business operations consist of sales and consulting with respect to interior design and decoration, and its head office is in Windsor, Ontario. For the taxation year ending December 31, 2013, Taxable Income for Sinzer Ltd. was calculated as follows:

Income From Design Consulting	$103,000
Income From Sales	386,000
Interest Income From Canadian Sources (Note 1)	48,300
Dividends From Taxable Canadian Corporations (Note 2)	88,100
Foreign Investment Income (Note 3)	55,000
Taxable Capital Gains On Sale Of Shares	24,500
Net Income For Tax Purposes	**$704,900**
Dividends From Taxable Canadian Corporations	(88,100)
Donations To A Registered Charity	(24,600)
Non-Capital Loss Carry Forward Deducted	(76,400)
Net Capital Loss Carry Forward Deducted	(12,300)
Taxable Income	**$503,500**

Note 1   The Canadian interest is from the following sources:

Interest On Loan To A Majority Owned Subsidiary (The Subsidiary Has No Active Business Income)	$43,250
Term Deposit And Bank Interest Arising From Seasonal Investment Of Excess Cash From Operations	5,050
Total	$48,300

Note 2   The dividends from taxable Canadian corporations consisted of the following:

Portfolio Dividends From Non-Connected Corporations	$19,600
Dividends From 75 Percent Owned Subsidiary (Total Dividend Refund Of $12,750 To The Subsidiary)	68,500
Total	$88,100

Note 3   The $55,000 is before withholding of $8,250 in foreign taxes. Assume that the foreign non-business income tax credit in the calculation of Part I Tax Payable is equal to $8,250.

Other Information:

1. Sinzer was allocated $200,000 of the annual business limit. Assume that this is the amount that is eligible for the small business deduction.

2. During 2013, Sinzer declared four quarterly taxable dividends in the amount of $28,000 each. The first of these dividends was paid in March, 2013, the second in June, 2013, the third in October, 2013, and the fourth was paid in January, 2014. A $25,000 taxable dividend declared in December, 2012, was paid in January, 2013.

3. The balance in the Refundable Dividend Tax On Hand account on December 31, 2012 was $23,500, and the dividend refund for 2012 was $9,600.

4. Using the formula found in the *Income Tax Regulations*, it has been determined that 72.95 percent of Sinzer's Taxable Income has been earned in a province. A total of $34,300 was paid in U.S. taxes on the foreign business income earned in the U.S. Assume that the foreign business income tax credit in the calculation of Part I Tax Payable is equal to $34,300.

Required: Show all of the calculations used to provide the following required information, including those for which the result is nil.

A. Calculate Sinzer's Part I Tax Payable for the 2013 taxation year.

B. Calculate Sinzer's Part IV Tax Payable for the 2013 taxation year.

C. Determine the December 31, 2013 balance in Sinzer's Refundable Dividend Tax On Hand account.

D. Determine the amount of Sinzer's dividend refund for 2013.

Self Study Problem Thirteen - 6 (Tax Payable With SBD, ART, And GRR)

Acme Imports Ltd. is a Canadian controlled private corporation. Its basic business activity is importing a variety of consumer products for distribution to wholesalers in Canada. The before income taxes Balance Sheet and Income Statement of Acme Imports Ltd. for the year ending December 31, 2013 are as follows:

Acme Imports Ltd.
Balance Sheet Before Income Taxes
As At December 31, 2013

Assets

Accounts Receivable		$1,080,000
Inventories		1,065,000
Investment In Sarco Ltd.		695,000
Land		385,000
Equipment - Cost	$840,000	
Accumulated Amortization	(414,000)	426,000
Intangible Assets		183,000
Total Assets		$3,834,000

Equities

Bank Overdraft		$ 87,000
Note Payable To Bank		306,000
Accounts Payable		682,000
Mortgage On Land		244,000
Future Income Tax Liability		53,000
Common Stock - No Par		32,000
Retained Earnings		2,430,000
Total Equities		$3,834,000

Acme Imports Ltd.
Income Statement Before Income Taxes
Year Ending December 31, 2013

Sales	$7,387,700
Dividend Income	24,000
Interest Revenue	10,000
Gain On Sale Of Equipment	57,000
Total Revenues	$7,478,700
Cost Of Goods Sold	$6,071,400
Rent	118,000
Selling Expenses	283,000
Wages And Salaries	276,000
Employee Benefits	32,000
Office Expenses	158,000
Fees For Professional Services	43,000
Interest	47,000
Promotional Expenses	99,000
Amortization Expense	20,000
Charitable Donations	25,000
Vehicle Costs	74,000
Total Expenses Not Including Income Taxes	$7,246,400
Income Before Taxes	$ 232,300

Other Information: The following additional information is available with respect to the 2013 operations of Acme Imports Ltd.:

1.   The Intangible Assets consist of an amount paid for a list of potential customers. This list was acquired during December, 2013 from a competitor who had ceased doing business. The intangible asset has been tested for impairment, but none was found. As a consequence, no write-down is included in Total Expenses.

2.   On January 1, 2013, the Equipment, which is all in Class 8, had a UCC of $256,000.

3.   The gain on the sale of Equipment resulted from selling display fixtures and equipment with an original cost of $62,000 and a net book value of $27,500, for cash proceeds of $84,500.

4.   A small group of new shares were issued during the year. The cost of printing these shares was $950 and was included in Office Expenses. In addition, $7,000 of the professional fees paid were for legal and other costs associated with obtaining the supplementary letters patent required to issue these shares.

5.   The interest income came from corporate bonds that had been held for four years and sold during the year. The bonds were purchased and sold at their maturity value.

6.   Included in Promotional Expenses is a $2,800 membership fee to a local golf and country club. In addition, there were charges at this club for business meals and entertainment totalling $6,720.

7.   The Company provides cars for the principal shareholder and the manager of the Company. Both of these individuals are considered to be employees of the Company. Included in vehicle costs are lease payments of $500 per month, for 12 months, for each car, and a total of $11,000 in operating costs associated with providing these cars. While these individuals use the cars for some business purposes, it is estimated that over 80 percent of their usage is personal.

8.   Acme Imports Ltd. did not declare or pay any dividends during the year. On December 31, 2012, Acme Imports Ltd. had a nil balance in its Refundable Dividend Tax On Hand

account.

9. The dividend income of $24,000 was Acme's share of a dividend declared by Sarco Ltd., a 60 percent owned subsidiary company. As a result of declaring the dividend, Sarco received a total dividend refund of $5,000. None of the annual limit for the small business deduction was allocated to Sarco.

10. During the year, the Company decided that it had grown to the point where additional space was needed and, rather than continue to rent space, it has decided to acquire its own premises. It paid a fee of $3,500 (included in Fees For Professional Services) to a site consultant and, on the basis of his recommendation, acquired land at a cost of $385,000. The site was purchased on April 1, 2013, and construction of the new facility is to begin early in 2013. The Company's Other Expenses included $12,300 in interest on the mortgage used to finance this land.

Required: Show all of the calculations used to provide the following required information, including those for which the result is nil.

A. Determine Acme Imports Ltd.'s minimum Net Income For Tax Purposes and Taxable Income for the year ending December 31, 2013.

B. Determine Acme Imports Ltd.'s active business income for the year ending December 31, 2013.

C. Determine Acme Imports Ltd.'s minimum federal Tax Payable for the year ending December 31, 2013. This should include both Part I and Part IV Tax Payable, net of any dividend refund.

D. Determine the December 31, 2013 balance in Acme Imports Ltd.'s Refundable Dividend Tax On Hand account.

Self Study Problem Thirteen - 7
(Tax Payable With SBD, ART, FTC, GRR, And GRIP)

Brasco Distributors is a Canadian controlled private corporation. Its primary business is the distribution of a variety of consumer products to retailers throughout Canada. Its fiscal year ends on December 31.

While its current operations are providing a reasonable rate of return on invested capital, losses have been experienced in previous years. As a result, at the beginning of the year ending December 31, 2013, it has available a non-capital loss carry forward of $25,800 and a net capital loss carry forward of $64,500 [(1/2)($129,000)].

Other Information:

1. During the year ending December 31, 2013, the Company made donations of $11,900 to registered Canadian charities.

2. Its net taxable capital gains for 2013 amounted to $36,000 [(1/2)($72,000)].

3. The Company's 2013 active business income, computed in accordance with the requirements of the *Income Tax Act*, amounted to $171,000.

4. On December 31, 2012, the balance in the Company's Refundable Dividend Tax On Hand account was $7,000. Brasco paid no dividends in 2012.

5. On December 31, 2012, Brasco had a GRIP balance of $126,000.

6. During 2013, the total taxable dividends declared and paid to shareholders of the Company amounted to $39,000. Brasco designated all of these dividends as eligible.

7. During 2013, the Company received $2,200 in interest from long-term Canadian bonds. In addition, on common shares that represent portfolio investments in taxable Canadian companies, the Company received eligible dividends of $15,800. The Company received

foreign source investment income of $3,825. This was the net amount, after the withholding of $675 in taxes by the taxation authorities in the foreign jurisdiction.

8. Brasco owns 60 percent of the outstanding voting shares of Masco, a Canadian subsidiary. During the year, Brasco received $37,800 in non-eligible dividends from Masco. The total 2013 dividends paid by the subsidiary amounted to $63,000 and, as a result of paying these dividends, Masco claimed a dividend refund of $21,000. Because it is an associated Company, Brasco must share the annual limit on its small business deduction with Masco. Brasco has been allocated $125,000 of the annual business limit.

Required: Show all of the calculations used to provide the following required information, including those for which the result is nil.

A. Calculate Brasco's minimum Net Income For Tax Purposes and Taxable Income for the year ending December 31, 2013.

B. Calculate Brasco's minimum federal Tax Payable for the year ending December 31, 2013. This should include both Part I and Part IV Tax Payable, net of any dividend refund. For purposes of this calculation, assume that the foreign non-business income tax credit is equal to the amount withheld.

C. Determine Brasco's GRIP balance at December 31, 2013.

D. Do the complete calculation required to determine the foreign non-business income tax credit that will be used in determining the small business deduction, as well as the complete calculation that will be used to determine the foreign non-business income tax credit that will be deducted.

Assignment Problems

Assignment Problem Thirteen - 1 (Integration Example)

For the taxation year 2013, assume the following with respect to the shareholder of a CCPC who is an individual.

- The corporation's business income for the year is $80,000.
- Any dividends paid are designated non-eligible dividends.
- The individual's marginal federal tax rate is 26 percent and his marginal provincial tax rate is 8 percent.
- The provincial dividend tax credit on non-eligible dividends is equal to 13 percent of the gross up.
- The combined federal and provincial corporate tax rate on business income is 13 percent.

Required: Indicate, using these assumptions, whether integration is working perfectly. If your answer is no, briefly explain why this is the case.

Assignment Problem Thirteen - 2 (Part I And Part IV Refundable Taxes)

Insal Ltd. is a Canadian controlled private corporation. It has a December 31 year end. The following information relates to its 2013 taxation year.

1. Insal Ltd. paid taxable dividends of $18,250 during the year.

2. During 2013, Insal Ltd. has Taxable Income of $123,400. Tax Payable for the year was correctly calculated to be $23,960. These totals do not include any foreign source income and no net capital losses were deducted during the year.

3. Insal Ltd. owns 45 percent of the voting shares of Dorne Inc., another CCPC with a December 31 year end. During 2013, Dorne Inc. paid taxable dividends of $25,200. As a consequence of paying these dividends, Dorne Inc. received a dividend refund of $8,400.

4. At the end of 2012, the Company's Refundable Dividend Tax On Hand balance was $6,450. The 2012 dividend refund was $2,300.

5. Other income that was reported by Insal Ltd. consisted of the following amounts:

Capital Gain On Sale Of Land	$24,600
Dividends From Enbridge Preferred Shares	6,200
Net Rental Income From Residential Properties	4,200

6. Insal Ltd. is associated with several other corporations. Insal has been allocated $45,000 of the associated group's annual business limit. This amount is significantly less than the Company's active business income for 2013.

Required: For the taxation year ending December 31, 2013, determine the Part IV and refundable Part I taxes that will be payable by Insal Ltd. In addition, determine the balance in the Refundable Dividend Tax On Hand account at December 31, 2013, and any dividend refund available. Show all of the calculations used to provide the required information, including those for which the result is nil.

Assignment Problem Thirteen - 3 *(Part I And Part IV Refundable Taxes, GRIP)*

Fracto Inc. is a Canadian controlled private corporation with a December 31 year end. For the taxation year ending December 31, 2013, its Net Income For Tax Purposes was made up of the following components:

Active Business Income (Note 1)	$ 514,400
Dividends From Canadian Corporations:	
Wholly-Owned Subsidiary (Note 2)	297,400
Portfolio Investments (All Eligible Dividends)	89,600
Canadian Source Interest	44,300
Taxable Capital Gains	93,100
Net Income For Tax Purposes	$1,038,800

Note 1   As determined under ITR 5200, $326,000 of this total qualified as M&P profits. As these amounts are allocated to a province which has a special rate for M&P profits, the company calculates the federal M&P deduction.

Note 2   As a result of paying these dividends, the subsidiary received a dividend refund of $52,800. None of these dividends were designated as eligible.

Other Information:

1. Fracto Inc. is part of a group of several associated companies. It has been agreed that Fracto Inc. will be allocated $100,000 of the group's annual business limit for purposes of determining the small business deduction.

2. At December 31, 2012, Fracto Inc. had a Refundable Dividend Tax On Hand balance of $12,000. During 2012, Fracto Inc. paid no dividends.

3. At December 31, 2012, Fracto Inc. had a GRIP balance of $26,700.

4. On July 1, 2013, Fracto Inc. paid taxable dividends to its shareholders in the amount of $132,400. Of this total, $42,600 was designated as eligible.

5. The Company has available a net capital loss carry forward of $12,000 [(1/2)($24,000)] and a non-capital loss carry forward of $163,400. It plans to deduct both of these items to the extent possible during 2013.

Required: Show all of the calculations used to provide the following required information, including those for which the result is nil.

For Fracto Inc.'s 2013 taxation year, calculate the following items:

A.   Federal Part I Tax Payable.
B.   Part IV Tax Payable.
C.   The balance in the Refundable Dividend Tax On Hand account on December 31, 2013.
D.   The balance in the GRIP account on December 31, 2013.
E.   The dividend refund, if any.
F.   Federal Tax Payable (net of any dividend refund).

Assignment Problem Thirteen - 4 (Comprehensive Corporate Tax Payable)

Gardner Distributing Company, a Canadian controlled private corporation, was established ten years ago by Mr. Hugh Gardner. Its only business activity is the distribution of specialty gardening products to retailers across Canada. Mr. Gardner is a Canadian resident and is the sole shareholder of the Company. The Company has a fiscal year ending on December 31, and, for 2013, the Company's accountant produced the following Income Statement:

Sales Revenue		$1,900,000
Cost Of Goods Sold		(940,000)
Gross Profit		$ 960,000
Operating Expenses:		
Selling And Administration	($315,000)	
Amortization Expense	(47,000)	
Charitable Donations	(15,000)	(377,000)
Operating Income		$ 583,000
Other Income And Losses:		
Eligible Dividends Received	$ 27,000	
Loss On Sale Of Truck	(19,000)	
Gain On Sale Of Investments	7,000	15,000
Pre-Tax Accounting Income		$ 598,000

Other information:

1.   The Company had depreciable assets with the following undepreciated capital cost (UCC) balances at the beginning of its 2013 taxation year:

	UCC
Class 3 (5%)	$726,000
Class 8 (20%)	472,000
Class 10 (30%)	22,000

The balance in Class 10 reflects a single truck that was used for deliveries. It had an original cost of $38,000 and a net book value for accounting purposes of $29,000. It was sold in 2013 for $10,000, and replaced with a leased truck.

The only other transaction involving depreciable assets during the year was the acquisition of $82,000 in Class 8 assets.

2.   On December 31, 2012, the Company had a balance in its Refundable Dividend Tax On Hand account of $19,000. The Company claimed a dividend refund of $5,000 in its 2012 corporate tax return.

3.   At the end of 2012, Gardner has a GRIP balance of $32,500. During 2012, the Company designated $9,600 of its dividends as eligible.

4.   During 2013, the Gardner Distributing Company paid $17,000 in dividends to Mr. Gardner. All of these dividends were designated as eligible.

5. The investments that were sold during the year had been purchased for $93,000. They were sold for $100,000.

Required: Show all of the calculations used to provide the following required information, including those for which the result is nil.

A. Determine Gardner Distributing Company's minimum Net Income For Tax Purposes and Taxable Income for the year ending December 31, 2013.

B. Determine Gardner Distributing Company's Part I federal Tax Payable for the year ending December 31, 2013.

C. Determine the December 31, 2013 balance in the Gardner Distributing Company's Refundable Dividend Tax On Hand account.

D. Determine Gardner Distributing Company's minimum federal Tax Payable for the year ending December 31, 2013. This should include both Part I and Part IV Tax Payable, net of any dividend refund.

E. Determine the December 31, 2013 balance in Gardner Distributing Company's GRIP.

Assignment Problem Thirteen - 5 *(Comprehensive Corporate Tax Payable)*

B & C Limited is a Canadian controlled private corporation throughout its taxation year ending December 31, 2013. For that year, its Net Income For Tax Purposes and Taxable Income can be calculated as follows:

Canadian Manufacturing And Processing Profits As Per ITR 5200 Formula	$123,000
Other Canadian Active Business Income	78,000
Canadian Source Interest Income	10,000
Canadian Source Taxable Capital Gains	24,000
Foreign Non-Business Income (Before $3,000 Withholding)	20,000
Foreign Business Income (Before $6,000 Withholding)	40,000
Eligible Portfolio Dividends	26,000
Net Income For Tax Purposes	**$321,000**
Eligible Portfolio Dividends	(26,000)
Charitable Donations	(32,000)
Net Capital Loss Carry Forward	(18,000)
Taxable Income	**$245,000**

Other Information:

1. B & C Limited declared and paid taxable dividends of $124,000 during 2013. Of this total, $66,000 was designated as eligible.

2. It has been determined that 91 percent of B & C Limited's Taxable Income can be allocated to a Canadian province.

3. The December 31, 2012 balance in the Refundable Dividend Tax On Hand account was $132,000. The dividend refund for the year ending December 31, 2012 was $28,000.

4. At the end of 2012, B & C Ltd. has a GRIP of $114,000. During 2012, the company designated $72,000 of its dividends paid as eligible.

5. B & C Limited is associated with another Canadian controlled private corporation. B & C Limited has been allocated $100,000 of the annual business limit.

6. Assume that the foreign tax credits for the foreign business and non-business income are equal to the amounts withheld.

Required: Show all of the calculations used to provide the following required information, including those for which the result is nil.

A. Determine B & C Limited's minimum federal Part I Tax Payable for the year ending December 31, 2013.

B. Determine the December 31, 2013 balance in the Refundable Dividend Tax On Hand account.

C. Determine the dividend refund for the year ending December 31, 2013.

D. Determine B & C Limited's minimum federal Tax Payable for the year ending December 31, 2013. This should include both Part I and Part IV Tax Payable, net of any dividend refund. As the corporation operates in a province that has a reduced tax rate for M&P activity, a separate calculation of the federal M&P deduction is required.

E. Determine the December 31, 2013 balance in B & C's GRIP.

Assignment Problem Thirteen - 6 *(Comprehensive Corporate Tax Payable)*

Expro Ltd. is a Canadian controlled private corporation that was established in Saskatchewan several years ago. It has a December 31 year end and, for the year ending December 31, 2013, the components of its Net Income For Tax Purposes and Taxable Income are as follows:

Active Business Income (Note 1)	$273,000
Gross Foreign Business Income (Note 2)	34,000
Gross Foreign Non-Business Income (Note 2)	26,000
Interest On Long-Term Investments	43,000
Taxable Capital Gains [(1/2)($28,000)]	14,000
Eligible Dividends Received On Portfolio Investment	17,000
Net Income For Tax Purposes	**$407,000**
Eligible Dividends Received	(17,000)
Charitable Contributions	(72,000)
Net Capital Loss Deducted	(12,000)
Non-Capital Loss Deducted	(232,000)
Taxable Income	**$ 74,000**

Note 1   As determined by the *Income Tax Regulations*, $126,000 of this active business income was manufacturing and processing profits. As the corporation operates in a province that has a reduced rate for M&P activity, a separate calculation of the federal M&P deduction is required.

Note 2   Foreign jurisdictions withheld $5,100 from the foreign business income and $6,500 from the foreign non-business income.

Other Information:

1. As determined by the *Income Tax Regulations*, 90 percent of Expro's Taxable Income can be allocated to a Canadian province.

2. As of December 31, 2012, the balance in Expro's RDTOH account was $23,000. A dividend refund of $11,000 was claimed in the 2012 corporate tax return.

3. As of December 31, 2012, Expro Ltd. has a GRIP of $41,600. During 2012, the Company designated $16,000 of its dividends paid as eligible.

4. During the year ending December 31, 2013, the Company used its existing cash resources to pay taxable dividends of $186,000. Of this total, $40,500 were designated as eligible.

Required: Show all of the calculations used to provide the following required information, including those for which the result is nil.

A. Calculate Expro's Part IV federal Tax Payable for the year ending December 31, 2013.

B. Assume that the foreign business and non-business tax credits are equal to the foreign taxes withheld. Calculate Expro's minimum Part I federal Tax Payable for the year ending December 31, 2013.

C. Assume the foreign business and non-business tax credits are equal to the foreign taxes withheld. Calculate Expro's dividend refund for the year ending December 31, 2013.

D. Determine the December 31, 2013 balance in Expro's GRIP account.

Assignment Problem Thirteen - 7 *(Comprehensive Corporate Tax Payable)*

Startop Ltd. is a Canadian controlled private corporation that operates in Saskatchewan. For the year ending December 31, 2013, its accounting Net Income Before Taxes, as determined under generally accepted accounting principles, was $462,000. Other information for the 2013 fiscal year follows.

Other Information:

1. Startop sold depreciable assets for $450,000. These assets had an original cost of $390,000 and a net book value of $330,000. They were Class 8 assets and, at the beginning of 2013, the UCC balance in this class was $350,000. The Company has other assets left in this class at the end of the year.

2. The Company's amortization expense was $546,000. Maximum deductible CCA for the year was $730,000.

3. The Company spent $50,000 on business meals and entertainment.

4. During the year, the Company begins selling a product on which they provide a five year warranty. At the end of the year, they established a warranty reserve of $20,000 to reflect the expected costs of providing warranty services. No costs were incurred in 2013.

5. It has been determined that Startop has active business income of $190,000 for the year. Included in this amount were manufacturing and processing profits, as determined by the *Income Tax Regulations*, of $150,000.

6. The Company's revenues included foreign source non-business income of $17,000 (Canadian dollars). This was the amount that was received after the withholding of $3,000 (15 percent of the gross amount) by the foreign tax authorities.

7. During the year, the Company had the following amounts of Canadian source investment income:

Interest On Long-Term Investments	$25,000
Taxable Capital Gains On Sale Of Depreciable Assets	30,000
Eligible Dividends On Bank of Nova Scotia Shares	11,000

8. The Company has available a non-capital loss carry forward of $205,000 and a net capital loss carry forward of $19,000 [(1/2)($38,000)]. Management has indicated that they would like to deduct as much of these amounts as possible in the 2013 tax return.

9. As of December 31, 2012, the balance in Startop's RDTOH account was $17,000. A dividend refund of $2,000 was claimed in the 2012 corporate tax return.

10. As of December 31, 2012, Startop Ltd. has a GRIP of $13,400. During 2012, the Company designated all of the $6,000 in taxable dividends paid as eligible.

11. During the year ending December 31, 2013, the Company used its existing cash resources to pay taxable dividends of $210,000. Of this total, $16,000 were designated as eligible.

Required: Show all of the calculations used to provide the following required information, including those for which the result is nil.

A. Calculate Startop's minimum Net Income For Tax Purposes and Taxable Income for the year ending December 31, 2013.

B. Calculate Startop's Part IV Tax Payable for the year ending December 31, 2013.

C. Assume the foreign non-business tax credit is equal to the foreign tax withheld. Calculate Startop's Part I federal Tax Payable for the year ending December 31, 2013. As the corporation operates in a province that has a reduced rate for M&P activity, a separate calculation of the federal M&P deduction is required.

D. Assume the foreign non-business tax credit is equal to the foreign tax withheld. Calculate Startop's dividend refund for the year ending December 31, 2013.

E. Determine the December 31, 2013 balance in Startop's GRIP account.

F. Do not assume the foreign non-business tax credit is equal to the foreign tax withheld, but assume that any excess of foreign tax withheld over the federal foreign tax credit will be applied against the provincial tax liability. Using the amounts calculated in Part C, compare your results under this new scenario with the Part C calculation of Part I Tax Payable. As part of your solution, provide a detailed calculation of the small business deduction, the ITA 123.3 refundable tax (ART) and the foreign tax credit available to Startop for the year ending December 31, 2013.

G. Assume that any excess of foreign tax withheld over the federal foreign tax credit cannot be applied against the provincial tax liability. Comment on any tax planning issues that should be reviewed because of this change in assumption.

Assignment Problem Thirteen - 8 *(Comprehensive Corporate Tax Payable)*

Angie's Amazing Getups Incorporated is a Canadian controlled private corporation with a head office in London, Ontario. The company is a manufacturer of high end custom costumes and makeup used in movie and theatre productions with sales in Canada and the U.S.

The company started in business in 2010 when the sole shareholder, Angela Q. Snodgrass, was photographed by the paparazzi after a particularly enthusiastic night of partying. When Angela saw herself on the front page of every tabloid newspaper the next day, she knew that fame was not for her. Since Angela was a highly trained clothing designer and makeup artist, she felt she would be able to use those skills to start her own business and keep out of the limelight.

In November, 2013, after discovering that her bookkeeper, Ponzi Madoff, had been defrauding her, Angela fired him and took over the bookkeeping responsibilities herself, despite having a limited knowledge of accounting. She has produced the following Income Statement and miscellaneous financial information for the year ended December 31, 2013 and needs your help.

Angie's Amazing Getups Incorporated
Income Statement
Year Ending December 31, 2013

Sales		$7,578,903
Cost Of Goods Sold		(5,468,752)
Gross profit		$2,110,151
Expenses:		
General And Administrative Expenses	($852,000)	
Amortization Expense	(550,000)	
Interest	(8,500)	(1,410,500)
Operating Income		$ 699,651
Other Income:		
Gain On Disposal Of Intangible Assets		98,000
Interest Income		110,532
Income Before Income Taxes		$ 908,183
Income Taxes		
Current	($182,000)	
Future	(35,000)	(217,000)
Net Income		$ 691,183

During your review of Angela's work and last year's tax return for the corporation, you have made the following notes.

1. In the accounting records, the Allowance For Doubtful Accounts was $25,000 at December 31, 2013, and $20,000 at December 31, 2012. During 2013, the company had actual write-offs of $11,750. As a result, the accounting Bad Debt Expense was $16,750. This amount is included in General and Administrative Expenses on the Income Statement.

   A review of the listing of receivables (for tax purposes), indicates that the actual items that may be uncollectible total $15,000 at December 31, 2013. In 2012, the company deducted a reserve for bad debts of $13,000 for tax purposes.

2. General And Administrative Expenses include:

Donations To Registered Charities	$ 27,000
Accrued Bonuses - Accrued September 1, 2013, Paid June 15, 2014	78,000
Meals And Entertainment Costs:	
$1,000 Per Month For Premium Membership At Golf Club For Angie	12,000
$200 Per Month For Memberships At Golf Club For Salespeople	2,400
$32,000 For Meals While Entertaining Clients	32,000
$5,000 In Food Costs For Angie's Personal Chef For Her Meals At Home	5,000
$6,000 For Annual Summer BBQ For All Staff	6,000
Sponsorship Of Various Theatre Productions That Use Angie's Costumes	100,000
Advertising In A U.S. Theatre Magazine Directed At U.S. Clients	15,000
New Software Purchased October 1, 2013 ($13,000 For Applications And $25,000 For Systems)	38,000
Accounting And Legal Fees For Amended Articles Of Incorporation	6,000
Costs To Attend Annual Convention Of Costume Designers Held In Thailand	17,000

Assignment Problems

3. Interest Expense consists of the following:

Interest Expense - Operations	$5,000
Penalty And Interest For Late And Insufficient Instalment Payments	2,000
Interest On Late Payment Of Municipal Property Taxes	1,500

4. Travel costs (included in General and Administrative costs) include both air travel and travel reimbursement to employees for business travel. The company policy is to reimburse employees $0.58 per kilometre for the business use of their automobiles. During the year, seven employees each drove 4,000 kilometres on employment related activities and one employee drove 7,500 kilometres. None of the kilometre based allowances are required to be included in the income of the employees.

5. Maximum CCA has always been taken on all assets. The undepreciated capital cost balances at January 1, 2013 were as follows:

Class 1 (4%)	$650,000
Class 8	95,000
Class 10.1	17,850
Class 14	68,000
Class 29	135,000
Class 44	65,000

    In 2010, used manufacturing and processing equipment was purchased for $4,750,000 from another clothing manufacturer who had gone bankrupt. All of the other manufacturing and processing equipment was purchased in 2012 for $180,000.

6. The gain on disposal of intangible assets consists of two amounts, which have been netted together.

    a. There was a loss on disposal of a limited life licence to produce costumes for productions based on a popular theme park. This licence originally cost the company $95,000, and it was sold for $63,000 in 2013. The book value of the license at the time of sale was $80,000. When the license was sold, it was the only asset in its CCA class.

    b. The second property that was sold in 2013 was a customer list of her private clients who were willing to pay a very high premium for exclusive custom designed creations. Since Angela wanted to focus her efforts on expanding into the U.S. entertainment world, she sold this client list to a custom clothing designer for $115,000. As the list was developed internally, its adjusted cost base was nil.

7. The cumulative eligible capital balance at January 1, 2013 was $18,098. Three-quarters of the $30,000 cost of incorporating the business was put in the CEC account in 2010. No other items were included in this account prior to the current year. Maximum CEC deductions have been taken in each year.

8. Purchases and sales of equipment and other capital assets made during 2013 were as follows (note: some items are discussed in other sections of this problem). All amounts were capitalized for accounting purposes:

    a. The company purchased land and constructed a new building on it during the year. The building will be used 95% for manufacturing and processing. The cost of the land was $350,000, and the building cost $475,000 to construct.

    b. The company purchased a new set of furniture for the reception area for $1,200.

    c. Some outdated desks used by the finance department with a cost of $5,000 were sold for proceeds of $3,500.

    d. Landscaping of the grounds around the new building cost $35,000. This amount was capitalized for accounting purposes.

    e. A company car for use by the president of the company was purchased for $90,000. This car replaced the only other existing company car, which was purchased in 2011 for $95,000. The old car was sold for $60,000.

    f. A fence around the new building, high enough to prevent the paparazzi from taking pictures of Angela while she was at the office cost $52,000.

9. The company sold some shares that had been purchased several years ago. The capital gain on these shares was $152,708. Angela didn't know how to account for this, so she credited the entire amount to retained earnings.

10. Included in the financial statement income is income earned in the United States. The amounts reported in the financial statements are net of the tax paid, because Angela was unsure of the appropriate accounting treatment. All amounts are reported in Canadian dollars. The foreign income consisted of:

    a. Foreign business income of $70,000. US tax returns have been filed, and the US taxes paid on this amount totals $6,000.

    b. Foreign portfolio dividend income of $15,000. Foreign taxes of $2,000 have been paid on this dividend income.

11. The Investment Income account balance on the Income Statement consists of the foreign dividend income (point 10) and the following Canadian source investment income:

Interest on long term investments	$ 56,532
Eligible dividends on bank shares	$ 16,000
Non-eligible dividend from Snodgrass Ltd.	$ 25,000

Angie's Amazing Getups Incorporated owns 8 percent of the shares of Snodgrass Ltd., a very profitable CCPC owned by Angela's mother. Snodgrass Ltd. received no dividend refund from the payment of dividends in 2013.

12. Except for the investment income noted in points 10 and 11, and any additional investment income you may calculate, all income is Canadian Active Business Income.

13. Included in the income of the company are manufacturing and processing profits. It has been determined that manufacturing and processing profits as determined under the Income Tax Regulations are $65,000.

14. The corporation has permanent establishments in Ontario and the United States. Its gross revenue and salary and wages information is as follows:

	Gross Revenue	Salary and Wages
Ontario	73.8%	89.1%
United States	26.2%	10.9%

15. As Angela did not know how to deal with the dividends paid to her personally by Angie's Amazing Getups Incorporated, she included them in General And Administrative Expenses. A total of $60,000 in non-eligible dividends were paid to her during 2013.

16. The balances in the tax accounts on December 31, 2012 were as follows:

Charitable donation carry forward	$ 3,500
Non-capital loss carry forward	52,500
Net capital loss carry forward [(1/2)($17,666)]	8,833
Refundable dividend tax on hand	40,500
Dividend refund for 2012	9,500
GRIP	76,500

None of the dividends paid in 2012 were designated eligible.

Required: Show all of the calculations used to provide the following required information, including those for which the result is nil. Ignore GST/HST/PST implications.

Determine Angie's Amazing Getups Incorporated's:

A.   Minimum Net Income For Tax Purposes and Taxable Income for the year ending December 31, 2013.

B.   Part I Tax Payable for the year ending December 31, 2013. Any percentages used in your calculations should be rounded to one decimal point. For the purposes of dealing with any foreign tax credits that the company is eligible for, assume that the foreign tax credit is equal to the foreign tax paid when determining the amount of the small business deduction and the manufacturing and processing profits deduction.

C.   December 31, 2013 balance in the Refundable Dividend Tax On Hand account.

D.   Minimum federal Tax Payable for the year ending December 31, 2013. This should include both Part I and Part IV Tax Payable, net of any dividend refund. Actual foreign tax credits should be calculated in order to determine the final balance of taxes owing by the company.

E.   December 31, 2013 balance in the GRIP account.

CHAPTER 14

Other Issues In Corporate Taxation

Introduction

14-1. Chapters 12 and 13 dealt with basic issues associated with the determination of Taxable Income and Tax Payable for a corporation. Specifically, Chapter 12 described the basic adjustments associated with converting Net Income For Tax Purposes to corporate Taxable Income. This was followed by consideration of how this Taxable Income is allocated to individual provinces for the determination of provincial Tax Payable. With respect to Tax Payable, Chapter 12 dealt with the rates applicable to corporations, the small business deduction, the M&P deduction, foreign tax credits, and the general rate reduction.

14-2. After a fairly detailed discussion of the concept of integration, Chapter 13 focused on taxation of investment income earned by Canadian controlled and other private corporations. This Chapter concluded with coverage of the designation of eligible dividends for both public companies and Canadian controlled private corporations.

14-3. In presenting the material in Chapters 12 and 13, we focused on what we view as basic issues, skipping over some of the more technical considerations related to the determination of corporate Taxable Income and corporate Tax Payable. This was done in the belief that avoiding the more technical considerations would enhance your understanding of the basic procedures associated with these determinations.

14-4. In this Chapter 14, we are turning our attention to these technical issues. In this Chapter we will provide coverage of:

- the acquisition of control rules;
- the associated company rules;
- investment tax credits;
- tax basis shareholders' equity; and
- distributions of corporate surplus, including capital dividends and deemed dividends.

Acquisition Of Control Rules

Economic Background

14-5. Over a period of years, some corporations may experience sufficiently large losses that they have no hope of recovering their economic health. While they may have accumulated large amounts of net capital or non-capital loss carry forwards, they have no real prospect of being able to use these amounts. Such companies can become attractive takeover targets for profitable corporations that can structure their business to make use of the tax benefits associated with these losses. For example, if a profitable company can acquire a company for $100,000 that has $1,000,000 in loss carry forwards that can be utilized in the future, it is clearly a bargain for the purchaser. Further, if the acquiree cannot make use of the losses, receiving the $100,000 may be a better alternative than declaring bankruptcy.

14-6.   This situation is of concern to the government in that there are billions of dollars of such benefits available in the economy at any point in time. If access to these benefits was relatively trouble-free, the cost to the government could be enormous. As a consequence, the government has enacted legislation which significantly restricts the use of loss carry forwards in situations where there has been an acquisition of control.

Acquisition Of Control Legislation

14-7.   ITA 111(4) through 111(5.5) contain rules that are applicable when there has been an acquisition of control by a person or group of persons. IT-302R3, which deals with the losses of a corporation, indicates that control requires ownership of shares that carry with them the right to elect a majority of the board of directors.

14-8.   An acquisition of control most commonly occurs when a majority shareholder sells his shares to an arm's length person. However, it can also occur through the redemption of shares. For example, if Ms. A owns 75 percent of AB Ltd. and Ms. B, an unrelated person, owns the other 25 percent, there would be an acquisition of control by Ms. B if AB Ltd. was to redeem all of Ms. A's shares.

Deemed Year End

14-9.   To prevent losses from being used prior to the end of the taxation year in which the acquisition of control took place, ITA 249(4) requires that the corporation have a deemed year end on the day preceding an acquisition of control.

14-10.   If the acquisition of control occurs prior to the corporation's normal year end, a short fiscal period will be created. For example, if the corporation's normal year end was December 31, and the acquisition of control took place on February 1, 2013, the deemed year end would create a fiscal year with only one month (January 1, 2013 through January 31, 2013). Further, if the corporation retains its old year end after the acquisition of control, there will be a second short fiscal year that runs from February 1, 2013 through December 31, 2013.

14-11.   Note, however, ITA 249(4) allows the corporation to change its year end when there is an acquisition of control. This means that the corporation could have avoided a second short fiscal period by establishing January 31 as the new year end. This means that the first fiscal year after the acquisition of control will end on January 31, 2014.

14-12.   The extra year end is of importance in that the non-capital losses that may be available after the acquisition of control are time limited. In our example, the deemed year end creates, in effect, an extra year end that shortens the period during which time-limited losses can be used. However, with a 20 year carry forward period for non-capital losses, this is unlikely to be an important consideration.

14-13.   Other implications of such short fiscal periods include the need to base CCA calculations on a fraction of the year, the need to prorate the annual business limit for the small business deduction, as well as the usual year end procedures such as inclusions of reserves.

Restrictions On The Use Of Charitable Donations

14-14.   ITA 110.1(1.2) places two restrictions on the deduction of charitable donations:

- Undeducted amounts that are present at the time of the acquisition of control cannot be carried forward to taxation years subsequent to that date.

- No deduction is available on a gift made subsequent to the acquisition of control if the gifted property was acquired prior to the acquisition date in anticipation of the acquisition of control.

14-15. An example of the latter restriction would be a situation where an individual, who does not have sufficient tax payable to use a credit on the donation of a particular property, transfers that property to a corporation he controls, with the expectation that he will sell the shares in the corporation and the corporation will make the donation and take the deduction.

Restrictions On The Use Of Losses
General Rules
14-16. The acquisition of control rules apply to any losses that have not been deducted at the deemed year end. This would include losses that have been carried forward from prior years, as well as any additional losses that accrue in the taxation year which is created by the deemed year end.

14-17. As will be explained later, the losses in this deemed taxation year may be increased by provisions that require the recognition of unrealized losses on capital assets. They can also be reduced by gains resulting from an election to have one or more deemed dispositions.

Capital Losses
14-18. The acquisition of control rules are particularly harsh in their treatment of net capital losses. ITA 111(4)(a) indicates that any net capital losses that are present at the deemed year end are simply lost. They cannot be carried forward to future years and, as a consequence, they will be of no benefit to the corporation subsequent to the acquisition of control. Note that this would include any unused Allowable Business Investment Losses that are present at the deemed year end.

14-19. In addition, if there are capital gains in the three years before the deemed year end, ITA 111(4)(b) prevents net capital losses from years subsequent to the deemed year end from being carried back to those years.

Non-Capital Losses
14-20. While non-capital losses can be carried forward, they too are subject to restrictions. These restrictions, found in ITA 111(5), are that:

- after the acquisition of control has taken place, the corporation must continue to carry on the business in which the loss occurred;
- there must be a reasonable expectation of profit in that business; and
- the losses can only be applied against future income generated by the same, or a similar business.

14-21. A brief example can be used to illustrate these provisions:

Example Bostox Ltd. operates two separate lines of business, manufacturing cameras and the sale of specialty food products. During the year ending December 31, 2012, the camera business experienced a loss for tax purposes of $5 million, while the food specialty products operation had business income for tax purposes of nil. The $5 million loss could not be carried back and, as a result, it became a loss carry forward. On January 1, 2013, Bostox Ltd. is acquired by another company. During the year ending December 31, 2013, the camera business lost an additional $1 million, while the food products business earned $7 million.

Analysis If there was no acquisition of control, both the current 2013 loss of $1 million and the $5 million loss carry forward resulting from the camera business could be deducted against the income of the specialty food products business. This would have resulted in a 2013 Taxable Income of $1 million ($7 million profit on food products, offset by a current loss of $1 million on cameras and a non-capital loss carry forward of $5 million).

However, with the acquisition of control at the beginning of 2013, the loss carry forward can only be used against profits produced by the camera business. This means that none of the loss carry forward can be deducted in 2013, but the $1 million 2013 camera business loss can be netted against the $7 million food products income, resulting in a 2013 Taxable Income of $6 million. The $5 million loss carry forward will still be available, but can only be applied against future camera business income.

Exercise Fourteen - 1

Subject: Acquisition Of Control

India Inc. operates two separate lines of business, one of which sells fountain pens, while the other provides professional accounting services. In its first year of operations ending on December 31, 2012, the pen business had a loss of $192,000, and the accounting business had income of $57,000, resulting in a Net Income For Tax Purposes and Taxable Income of nil. This leaves a non-capital loss carry forward of $135,000. For the taxation year ending December 31, 2013, the pen business had income of $42,000, and the accounting business had income of $247,000, resulting in a Net Income For Tax Purposes of $289,000.

Determine the minimum Taxable Income for 2013 assuming (1) that there was no acquisition of control in either year and (2) that there was an acquisition of control on January 1, 2013. The Company has no deductions from Net Income For Tax Purposes other than possible loss carry forwards from 2012.

End of Exercise. Solution available in Study Guide.

Unrecognized Losses At Deemed Year End
The Problem
14-22.   As previously indicated, the acquisition of control restrictions apply to losses that accrue in the taxation year that has been created by the deemed year end. As there has been a deemed year end, there may be a loss from normal operations for the fiscal period that has ended. In addition, there may be losses resulting from actual dispositions of capital assets during the period.

14-23.   However, the acquisition of control rules are also concerned with accrued losses that have not been recognized at the deemed year end. The problem is that, if such accrued losses are realized after that time, they will not be subject to the acquisition of control restrictions.

> **Example** A corporation owned a parcel of land with an adjusted cost base of $200,000 and a fair market value of $150,000. If the land was to be disposed of subsequent to the acquisition of control, the result would be a deductible capital loss. This could be viewed as a way of avoiding the restrictions imposed by the acquisition of control rules.

Special Rules
14-24.   In recognition of this problem, the acquisition of control rules require a number of special procedures at the deemed year end. They are as follows:

> **Non-Depreciable Capital Property**   ITA 111(4)(c) requires that non-depreciable capital property be written down to its fair market value, if that value is below its adjusted cost base. ITA 111(4)(d) requires that the amount of the write-down be treated as a capital loss. The new lower value becomes the adjusted cost base of the property. The resulting allowable capital loss can be applied against available taxable capital gains, or carried back. However, if it is not used at the deemed year end, it is lost forever.

Depreciable Capital Property   ITA 111(5.1) requires that depreciable capital property be written down to its fair market value, if that value is below the UCC. The write-down amount is treated as CCA to be deducted in the deemed taxation year. This will reduce the income for that period and, in some cases, create or increase the loss for that year. For capital gains purposes, the property will retain the original capital cost.

Eligible Capital Property   ITA 111(5.2) requires that eligible capital property be written down to three-quarters of its fair market value, if that value is below the Cumulative Eligible Capital balance. The write-down is a deduction under ITA 20(1)(b) and, as was the case with the write-down of depreciable capital property, this deduction can reduce income, increase a loss, or create a loss in the deemed taxation year.

Accounts Receivable   ITA 111(5.3) does not permit the deduction of a reserve for doubtful accounts under ITA 20(1)(l). Rather, amounts must be written off as specific bad debts on the basis of the largest possible amount. If a doubtful account is not written off at the time an acquisition of control occurs, no deduction is available if the account subsequently becomes uncollectible. This procedure will generally result in a larger deduction and will reduce income, increase a loss, or create a loss in the deemed taxation year.

Exercise Fourteen - 2

Subject: Write-Downs At Deemed Year End

On November 15 of the current year, Parkat Ltd. acquires control of Sparkat Ltd. On November 14, Sparkat Ltd. has the following assets:

- Land with an adjusted cost base of $293,000 and a fair market value of $215,000.

- Class 8 depreciable assets with a capital cost of $416,000, a UCC balance of $276,000 and a fair market value of $184,000.

- A cumulative eligible capital balance of $216,000. The fair market value of these assets is $225,000.

Indicate the tax consequences of the procedures that will be applied to these assets in the deemed year end that results from the acquisition of control.

End of Exercise. Solution available in Study Guide.

Deemed Disposition Election
The Problem
14-25.   The requirement that non-depreciable capital property be written down to fair market value at the deemed year end is particularly onerous in that the resulting capital losses may simply disappear. To offset the harshness of this requirement, ITA 111(4)(e) allows the corporation to elect, at the time of the deemed year end, to have a deemed disposition/reacquisition of any depreciable or non-depreciable capital property on which there is an accrued gain or recapture of CCA. This election can be used to trigger capital gains that will offset either unused losses of the current period or unused loss carry forwards from earlier periods.

14-26.   The election can also be used to trigger recapture which can absorb non-capital losses from the current or previous years. This is a less important application in most situations as non-capital losses do not disappear at the deemed year end. However, as noted in Paragraph 14-20, there are restrictions on the use of such losses after the deemed year end. Given this, it may be desirable to minimize non-capital loss carry forwards when an acquisition of control occurs.

Procedures

14-27.   The elected value, which will serve as the deemed proceeds of disposition, cannot exceed the fair market value of the asset at the time of the deemed disposition. The minimum value for the election is the adjusted cost base or capital cost of the property. The elected value can be any amount between this minimum and maximum. This means that, in the case of property on which CCA has been taken, any election that will create a capital gain will also create recapture of CCA.

14-28.   If the corporation has net capital losses and there are non-depreciable properties with accrued gains, this election is clearly desirable in that it will generate capital gains, which can be used to offset the net capital losses that would disappear as a result of the acquisition of control.

14-29.   The situation is less clear cut when the gains are on depreciable capital property. While the deemed disposition will create the needed capital gains, it will generally result in recapture of CCA. This may or may not be a desirable situation.

Example

14-30.   The following example will illustrate the procedures associated with the ITA 111(4)(e) deemed disposition election:

Example Burkey Ltd. has a December 31 year end. On June 1, 2013, a new investor acquires control of the Company. While its basic operations have been profitable for many years, it has a net capital loss carry forward of $200,000 [(1/2)($400,000)]. On May 31, 2013, the Company has non-depreciable capital assets with a fair market value of $800,000 and an adjusted cost base of $500,000. Its depreciable capital assets have a fair market value of $1,200,000, a capital cost of $1,100,000, and a UCC of $600,000.

Analysis The ITA 111(4)(e) election is clearly desirable with respect to the non-depreciable capital property. It generates a taxable capital gain of $150,000 [(1/2)($800,000 - $500,000)]. Deducting a $150,000 carry forward against this 2013 gain will use up $150,000 of the net capital loss. This will leave an unused amount of $50,000 ($200,000 - $150,000).

Using the ITA 111(4)(e) election on the depreciable capital property will create a $50,000 [(1/2)($1,200,000 - $1,100,000)] taxable capital gain. Deducting a $50,000 loss carry forward against this amount will use up the remaining $50,000 of the net capital loss balance. However, the election will also create recaptured CCA of $500,000 ($1,100,000 - $600,000), an amount on which it appears that tax would have to be currently paid. Given that, in the absence of this election, taxation on the recapture could be deferred indefinitely, the election may not be desirable with respect to the depreciable capital property. One other factor that should be considered is that the election would result in increased CCA in the future.

Adjusted Cost Base After Election

14-31.   In addition to serving as the deemed proceeds of disposition, the elected value also becomes the adjusted cost base or capital cost of the asset on which the election was made. If the elections were made at fair market value on both properties in the preceding example, the new adjusted cost base of the non-depreciable assets would be $800,000, while the capital cost of the depreciable assets would be $1,200,000.

14-32.   However, if the $1,200,000 value was allowed to be used for CCA purposes, the Company would be able to deduct 100 percent of the $100,000 difference between the $1,200,000 elected value and the old capital cost of $1,100,000, despite the fact that they have, in effect, paid tax on only one-half of this amount.

14-33.   To prevent this from happening, ITA 13(7)(f) specifies that, when an election is made under ITA 111(4)(e), the new capital cost of the property for CCA purposes only, is equal to the original capital cost of the asset, plus one-half of the excess of the elected value over the asset's original capital cost. In the example in Paragraph 14-30, this value would be $1,150,000 [$1,100,000 + (1/2)($1,200,000 - $1,100,000)]. You might recall that other paragraphs in ITA 13(7) contain the same rule for both non-arm's length transfers of depreciable property and for some changes in use.

14-34. Future CCA would be based on this $1,150,000 figure and, in addition, if the assets were sold for more than $1,150,000, the new capital cost of $1,150,000 would be subtracted from the UCC to determine any recapture. However, any future capital gain would be based on the new adjusted cost base of $1,200,000.

Exercise Fourteen - 3

Subject: Election On Acquisition Of Control

Means Ltd. has a December 31 year end. On May 1, 2013, all of the Company's shares are acquired by a new owner. For the period January 1, 2013 through April 30, 2013, the Company has an operating loss of $45,000. On April 30, 2013, the Company has available a net capital loss carry forward of $110,000 [(1/2)($220,000)]. Also at that time, the Company has the following assets:

Asset Type	Adjusted Cost Base Or Capital Cost	UCC	Fair Market Value
Non-Depreciable	$350,000	N/A	$500,000
Depreciable	400,000	350,000	500,000

Advise the Company with respect to the most appropriate elections to be made prior to the acquisition of control and explain your results.

End of Exercise. Solution available in Study Guide.

We suggest you work Self Study Problems Fourteen-1 and 2 at this point.

Associated Companies

The Problem

14-35. In the absence of special rules, it would be very easy to avoid the annual limit that applies to the small business deduction. This could be accomplished by dividing a single corporation's activities between two separate corporations, thereby doubling up on the annual business limit of $500,000. However, as was noted in Chapter 12, the *Act* makes this more difficult by requiring that associated companies share their annual business limit.

14-36. For example, assume that Mr. Robards owns all of the outstanding voting shares of both the Mark Company and the Grand Company. These two Companies would be considered to be associated and, as a consequence, would have to share the $500,000 annual business limit. As was indicated in Chapter 12, they can elect to allocate the annual limit in any proportion they wish, provided the total does not exceed $500,000. If the Mark Company has active business income and the Grand Company does not, it would be most advantageous to allocate the entire annual limit to the Mark Company, so that it could claim the maximum small business deduction.

14-37. The preceding example is very clear cut and results in an allocation of the small business deduction that reflects the goals of the relevant legislation. However, with a deduction that can be worth $85,000 [(17%)($500,000)] per year in federal tax alone, there is a significant incentive to develop arrangements that will avoid the intent of the legislation. Correspondingly, there is a need to have legislation that is sophisticated enough to frustrate these arrangements. As a consequence, the identification of associated companies can be very complex.

Definitions

14-38.   Association between corporations is defined in ITA 256(1). However, there are a number of definitions and rules that are used in the provisions related to identifying associated corporations. The most important of these are as follows:

ITA 251(2)(a) - Related Persons   With respect to individuals, Paragraph (a) notes that individuals are related if they are connected by blood relationship, marriage, common-law partnership, or adoption. Various other Subsections in ITA 251 and 252 elaborate on this statement to point out that all of the following individuals would be "related" to the taxpayer:

- Parents and grandparents, as well as parents and grandparents of the taxpayer's spouse or common-law partner.
- The taxpayer's spouse or common-law partner, as well as the spouse or common-law partner's siblings and their spouses and common-law partners.
- Siblings of the taxpayer, as well as spouses or common-law partners of the taxpayer's siblings.
- Children, including those that are adopted, or born outside of marriage. Also included here would be spouses and common-law partners of children and children of the taxpayer's spouse or common-law partner.

ITA 251(2)(b) indicates that a corporation is related to:
- a person who controls it, if it is controlled by one person;
- a person who is a member of a related group that controls it; or
- any person related to a person who controls it or who is related to a member of a related group that controls it.

ITA 251(2)(c) indicates that two corporations are related if:
- they are controlled by the same person or group of persons;
- each of the corporations is controlled by one person and the person who controls one of the corporations is related to the person who controls the other corporation;
- one of the corporations is controlled by one person and that person is related to any member of a related group that controls the other corporation;
- one of the corporations is controlled by one person and that person is related to each member of an unrelated group that controls the other corporation;
- any member of a related group that controls one of the corporations is related to each member of an unrelated group that controls the other corporation; or
- each member of an unrelated group that controls one of the corporations is related to at least one member of an unrelated group that controls the other corporation.

ITA 256(1.1) - Specified Class, Shares Of   In simplified terms, this definition refers to non-voting shares that have a fixed dividend rate and redemption amount. Such shares are normally referred to as preferred shares.

ITA 256(1.2)(a) - Definition Of Group   For purposes of defining associated companies, a group is two or more persons, each of whom owns shares in the corporation in question. A related group involves a group of persons, each member of which is related to every other member. An unrelated group is any group, other than a related group.

ITA 256(1.2)(c) - Control   The definition of associated corporations also involves the concept of control. For purposes of determining association, a corporation is deemed to be controlled by another corporation, a person, or a group of persons, if the corporation, person, or group of persons owns either:

- shares (common and/or preferred) of capital stock with a fair market value of more than 50 percent of all issued and outstanding shares of capital stock; or

- common shares with a fair market value of more than 50 percent of all issued and outstanding common shares.

Deeming Rules The most relevant deeming rules can be described as follows:

- **ITA 256(1.2)(d) - Holding Companies** This provision indicates that where shares of a corporation are held by another corporation, a shareholder of the holding corporation is deemed to own the shares of the held corporation in proportion to his interest in the holding corporation. Similar provisions apply to shares held by partnerships and trusts. Note, however, if a holding corporation holds a controlling interest in an investee, the holding corporation is considered to control all of the shares held by that investee.

- **ITA 256(1.3) - Children Under 18** This provision requires that shares of a corporation owned by a child under the age of 18 be deemed to be owned by a parent of the child for the purpose of determining whether the corporation is associated with any other corporation that is controlled by that parent or a group that includes that parent.

- **ITA 256(1.4) - Rights And Options** This provision requires that rights to acquire shares be treated as though they were exercised for purposes of determining associated companies. This Subsection also indicates that, where a person has a right to require a shareholder to redeem, cancel, or acquire its own shares, for purposes of determining association, the corporation is deemed to have carried out the redemption, cancellation, or acquisition.

- **ITA 256(1.5) - Person Related To Himself, Herself, Or Itself** This provision indicates that, where a person owns shares in two or more corporations, the person shall as shareholder of one of the corporations be deemed to be related to himself, herself or itself as shareholder of each of the other corporations.

ITA 256(2) - Association Through A Third Corporation This provision indicates that two corporations, both of which are associated with a third corporation, are deemed to be associated with each other. This Subsection also includes an election that can mitigate this rule. The third corporation can elect to not be associated with the other two corporations. A consequence of this is that the third corporation's annual business limit will be set at nil. However, the election will allow the other two corporations to be exempt from the association rules under ITA 256(2).

14-39. Given these definitions and rules, we are now in a position to look at the definition of associated companies as it is found in ITA 256(1).

Examples - Associated Corporation Rules

14-40. The preceding definitions are essential to the understanding of the associated corporation rules found in ITA 256(1). This Subsection contains five Paragraphs designated (a) through (e), with each Paragraph describing a relationship involving association. These five Paragraphs will be given individual attention in the material that follows.

14-41. The first of these paragraphs indicates that one corporation is associated with another in a taxation year if, at any time in the year;

ITA 256(1)(a) one of the corporations controlled, directly or indirectly in any manner whatever, the other.

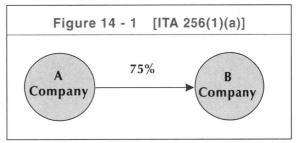

Figure 14 - 1 [ITA 256(1)(a)]

14-42. This type of association can be illustrated by the situation shown in Figure 14-1 in which A Company owns 75 percent of the outstanding voting shares of B Company. In this situation, Company A and Company B are associated by virtue of ITA 256(1)(a).

14-43. The second Paragraph in ITA 256(1) indicates that one corporation is associated with another in a taxation year if, at any time in the year;

ITA 256(1)(b) both of the corporations were controlled, directly or indirectly in any manner whatever, by the same person or group of persons.

14-44. This type of association can be illustrated by the situation shown in Figure 14-2. In this situation, Mr. A owns 75 percent of the voting shares of both A Company and B Company. As a consequence, these two Companies are associated by virtue of ITA 256(1)(b), in that they are both controlled by the same person.

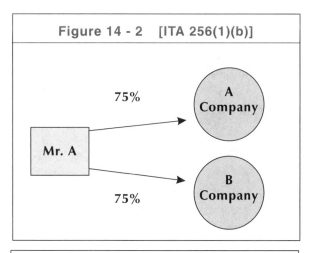

14-45. The third Paragraph in ITA 256(1) indicates that one corporation is associated with another in a taxation year if, at any time in the year;

ITA 256(1)(c) each of the corporations was controlled, directly or indirectly in any manner whatever, by a person and the person who so controlled one of the corporations was related to the person who so controlled the other and either of those persons owned, in respect of each corporation, not less than 25 percent of the issued shares of any class, other than a specified class, of the capital stock thereof.

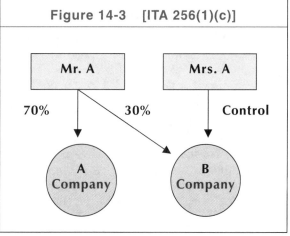

14-46. This type of association can be illustrated by the situation shown in Figure 14-3. In this situation, Mr. A owns 70 percent of the voting shares of A Company and his spouse, Mrs. A, owns 70 percent of the voting shares of B Company. In addition, Mr. A owns not less than 25 percent of the shares of B Company. Provided that the B Company shares owned by Mr. A are not of a specified class, Companies A and B are associated under ITA 256(1)(c). As the required cross ownership can be in either direction, the two Companies would also be associated if the cross ownership was by Mrs. A in A Company.

14-47. The fourth Paragraph in ITA 256(1) indicates that one corporation is associated with another in a taxation year if, at any time in the year;

ITA 256(1)(d) One of the corporations was controlled, directly or indirectly in any manner whatever, by a person and that person was related to each member of a group of persons that so controlled the other corporation, and that person owned, in respect of the other corporation, not less than 25 percent of the issued shares of any class, other than a specified class, of the capital stock thereof.

14-48. This type of association can be illustrated by the situation in Figure 14-4. In this situation, Mr. A owns 80 percent of the voting shares of A Company, while Mrs. A and Mr. A's brother each own 35 percent (70 percent in total) of the voting shares of B Company. This means that Mr. A is related to each member of a group that controls B Company. Mr. A also has the required cross ownership, in that he owns 30 percent of the shares of B Company. Provided that the shares of B Company owned by Mr. A are not of a specified class, A Company and B Company are associated by virtue of ITA 256(1)(d). Note that, under ITA 256(1)(d), the cross ownership has to be by Mr. A in B Company. If the cross ownership was in the other direction (e.g., Mrs. A owns 30 percent of A Company), the two Companies would not be associated under ITA 256(1)(d).

14-49.   The final Paragraph in ITA 256(1) indicates that one corporation is associated with another in a taxation year if, at any time in the year;

> **ITA 256(1)(e)**   Each of the corporations was controlled, directly or indirectly in any manner whatever, by a related group and each of the members of one of the related groups was related to all of the members of the other related group, and one or more persons who were members of both related groups, either alone or together, owned, in respect of each corporation, not less than 25 percent of the issued shares of any class, other than a specified class, of the capital stock thereof.

14-50.   This type of association can be illustrated by the situation in Figure 14-5. Mr. and Mrs. A are a related group that control A Company, and Mr. and Mrs. B are a related group that control B Company. If we assume that Mrs. B is Mr. A's sister, then each member of one related group is related to all of the members of the other related group. Mr. and Mrs. A each own 50 percent of the voting shares of A Company, Mr. and Mrs. B each own 30 percent of the voting shares of B Company. Mr. A owns the remaining 40 percent of the voting shares of B Company. In this situation, A Company and B Company are associated under ITA 256(1)(e). Once again, Mr. A's cross ownership has to be shares other than those of a specified class. However, if A Company shares were available, the cross ownership could be in the other direction (e.g., Mrs. B owns not less than 25 percent of A Company).

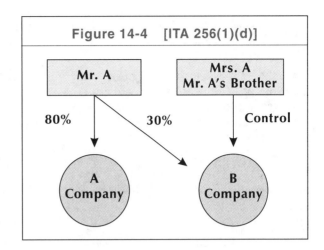

Figure 14-4   [ITA 256(1)(d)]

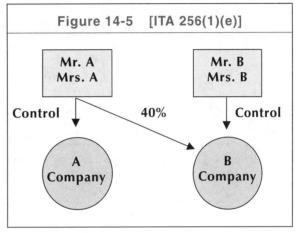

Figure 14-5   [ITA 256(1)(e)]

Exercise Fourteen - 4

Subject: Associated Companies

The Top Company owns 65 percent of the shares of Middle Company, as well as 10 percent of the shares of Bottom Company. Middle Company owns 35 percent of the shares of Bottom Company. Mr. Top, who owns all of the shares of Top Company, also owns 5 percent of the shares of Bottom Company and has options to acquire another 10 percent of the Bottom Company's shares. Mr. Top's 12 year old son owns 15 percent of the Bottom Company shares. Indicate which of these Companies are associated, citing the relevant provisions of the *Income Tax Act*.

End of Exercise. Solution available in Study Guide.

We suggest your work Self Study Problems Fourteen-3 and 4 at this point.

Investment Tax Credits

Background

14-51.   In terms of directing economic incentives to specific regions or types of activities, investment tax credits are a very effective tax policy tool. They can be used to provide tax reductions that are very specifically targeted (e.g., scientific research expenditures). In addition, by making some of them refundable, they can even provide benefits for enterprises with no Tax Payable.

14-52.   Despite their advantages in terms of targeting benefits, the use of investment tax credits has declined over the last 10 to 20 years. At the present time, their use is limited to some very targeted areas that will be described in this part of the Chapter.

Procedures

14-53.   Investment tax credits are tax incentives that are available to Canadian taxpayers who are earning business income or undertaking scientific research and experimental development. With some exceptions, they are available on the same terms for corporations as they are for individuals.

14-54.   In general terms, the procedures for investment tax credits, which are contained in ITA 127(5) through ITA 127.1(4), allow the taxpayer to deduct a specified percentage of the cost of certain types of current and capital expenditures from federal Tax Payable. The credits provide for a direct reduction in the amount of tax that is payable.

14-55.   When capital expenditures are involved, the amount of the investment tax credit must be removed from the capital cost of the asset, so that only the net capital cost is deductible through capital cost allowances (CCA). The legislation is such that the deduction from capital cost occurs in the taxation year following the year in which credit is claimed.

14-56.   The capital cost must also be reduced by any government or non-government assistance received or receivable for the property, such as grants or subsidies. However, the reduction for these other types of assistance is made in the year in which the assistance is received or receivable.

14-57.   When the investment tax credits are earned by making deductible current expenditures, this amount will be added to income in the following year.

14-58.   In effect, the tax mechanism that is involved with investment tax credits is that the enterprise gives up $1 of current or future tax deductions, in return for a $1 reduction in the amount of Tax Payable. This is clearly beneficial in that the cost of losing a $1 deduction is only $1 multiplied by the company's tax rate, a figure that could be below $0.20. By contrast, $1 of reduced tax payable is a cash flow savings of $1.

Eligible Expenditures

14-59.   To provide a general picture of the applicability of investment tax credits, brief descriptions are provided of expenditures that qualify for these credits:

Salaries And Wages Of An Eligible Apprentice   An eligible apprentice is defined in ITA 127(9) and can be described as follows:

Eligible apprentice means an individual who is employed in Canada in a prescribed trade (a trade currently listed as a "Red Seal Trade") in the first two years of their apprenticeship contract. This contract must be registered with a federal, provincial or territorial government under an apprenticeship program designed to certify or license individuals in the trade.

Eligible Child Care Space Expenditures   An eligible child care space expenditure is also defined in ITA 127(9). It indicates that such expenditures must be for the sole purpose of creating one or more child care spaces in a licensed child care facility that will be used by the children of the taxpayer's employees. Costs include both expenditures for depreciable property, as well as various start up costs.

Qualified Property is defined in ITA 127(9) with further elaboration provided in ITR 4600 and 4601. As presented in this material, qualified property must be newly acquired primarily for use in Canada, and it must be available for use in specified activities. These activities include manufacturing and processing, logging, farming or fishing, and storing grain.

Qualified Scientific Research And Experimental Development (SR&ED) Expenditures include amounts spent for basic or applied research, and for the development of new products and processes. For 2013, qualifying expenditures may be current or capital. The formal definitions related to SR&ED are very technical. For those of you with an interest in this subject, additional information is found in Supplementary Reading No. 4, SR & ED Expenditures.

Note On 2014 Changes   Beginning in 2014, capital expenditures will no longer qualify for SR&ED investment tax credits.

Rates
General
14-60.   Current rates for the investment tax credits that we have described are as follows:

Type Of Expenditure	Rate
Salaries And Wages Of Eligible Apprentices	
(Limited To The First $20,000 Of Salaries And Wages For Each Apprentice)	10%
Eligible Child Care Space Expenditures	
(Limited To The First $10,000 Of Such Expenditures For Each Space)	25%
Qualified Property	
In Atlantic Provinces And Gaspe Peninsula	10%
Prescribed Offshore Regions (East Coast)	10%
Rest Of Canada	Nil
Scientific Research And Experimental Development	
Incurred By Any Taxpayer - 2013	20%
Incurred By Any Taxpayer - Beginning 2014 (Current Expenditures Only)	15%
Incurred By CCPCs (See Paragraph 14-61)	35%

Exercise Fourteen - 5

Subject: Investment Tax Credit Procedures

During 2013, Colus Inc. pays salaries to five eligible apprentices totalling $125,000 ($25,000 per apprentice). In addition, it acquires $3,000,000 in Class 29 assets on which a 10 percent investment tax credit is available. Describe the 2013 and 2014 tax consequences associated with making these expenditures and claiming the related investment tax credits. Include in your solution the CCA for 2013 and 2014.

End of Exercise. Solution available in Study Guide.

Special Rate On SR&ED Expenditures By CCPCs
14-61.   With respect to the 35 percent rate for SR&ED expenditures, this overall rate results from providing an additional 15 percent for some expenditures made by a corporation that is a CCPC throughout a taxation year under ITA 127(10.1).

Note On 2014 Changes   When the regular SR&ED rate goes from 20 percent to 15 percent in 2014, this addition for CCPCs will increase from 15 percent to 20 percent, thereby maintaining the overall rate of 35 percent.

14-62.   Assuming that the corporation is not associated with any other corporations, the amount on which this 35 percent rate is applicable is limited by ITA 127(10.2) as follows:

Annual Expenditure Limit = ($8 million – 10A) x [($40 million – B) ÷ $40 million]

Where

A   is the greater of $500,000 and the corporation's Taxable Income for the preceding taxation year.

B   is nil if the corporation's Taxable Capital Employed In Canada for the preceding taxation year is $10 million or less. If it exceeds $10 million, B is equal to the lesser of $40 million and the amount by which the Taxable Capital Employed In Canada exceeds $10 million.

14-63.   If a CCPC has previous year Taxable Income that is less than $500,000 and previous year Taxable Capital Employed In Canada of less than $10 million, the limit on which the 35 percent investment tax credit will be applicable is $3 million. However, the formula contains two factors which will serve to limit this amount:

- If the CCPC's Taxable Income for the preceding year exceeds $500,000, the limit will be reduced by $10 for every $1 of the excess. The limit will be completely eliminated when the Taxable Income for the previous year reaches $800,000 [$8,000,000 - (10)($800,000) = Nil].

- If the CCPC's Taxable Capital Employed In Canada for the preceding year exceeds $10 million, the limit will be reduced by $3 for every $40 of the excess. It will be completely eliminated when the Taxable Capital Employed In Canada for the preceding year reaches $50 million as shown in the following calculation:

$$[\$3 \text{ Million}]\left[\frac{\$40 \text{ Million} - (\$50 \text{ Million} - \$10 \text{ Million})}{\$40 \text{ Million}}\right] = \text{Nil}$$

Exercise Fourteen - 6

Subject: SR&ED Credits For CCPCs

Anfax is a CCPC throughout its taxation year ending December 31, 2013. During the 2012 taxation year, it had Taxable Income of $560,000. Also for that year, its Taxable Capital Employed In Canada equaled $12,500,000. Determine its annual SR & ED expenditure limit for the 2013 taxation year.

End of Exercise. Solution available in Study Guide.

Refundable Investment Tax Credits
General Rules - 40 Percent Refund
14-64.   A problem with tax credits is that, in general, they have value only when the taxpayer has a tax liability. To deal with this problem, some tax credits are "refundable". What this means is that, when a taxpayer has earned a tax credit and does not have sufficient Tax Payable to use it in full, the government will pay ("refund") all or part of the unused amount to the taxpayer. We have encountered this type of situation previously for individuals with respect to the refundable medical expense supplement tax credit (see Chapter 4).

14-65.   A refund can be made for up to 40 percent of the investment tax credits earned by a taxpayer, provided the taxpayer is:

- an individual;
- a "qualifying corporation", which is a Canadian controlled private corporation throughout the year with Taxable Income in the previous year, less an adjustment for Taxable Capital Employed In Canada the adjustment is the same as the one illustrated in Paragraph 14-63), that is $500,000 or less before loss carry backs; or

- a trust where each beneficiary is an individual or a qualifying corporation.

14-66. This means that if an individual had $1,000,000 in SR&ED current expenditures, he would be eligible for a $200,000 [(20%)($1,000,000)] investment tax credit. If the individual did not have sufficient Tax Payable in the current year or the three previous years to use this credit, there would be a refund (payment) of up to $80,000 [(40%)($200,000)].

Additional Refund - 100 Percent Refund

14-67. In the case of a qualifying corporation, additional amounts are refundable. To the extent that current SR&ED expenditures are eligible for the 35 percent investment tax credit, the resulting credit is eligible for a 100 percent refund. This means that a qualifying corporation that spends $3,000,000 on current SR&ED expenditures is eligible for a refund payment of up to $1,050,000 [(35%)($3,000,000)] from the government (qualifying corporations are described in Paragraph 14-65).

14-68. The 100 percent refund is only available on the first $3,000,000 of current expenditures that qualify for the 35 percent investment tax credit. Capital expenditures (prior to 2014) that qualify for this enhanced credit are refundable at a lower rate of 40 percent. An example will clarify this point:

> **Example** In 2013, Research Inc., a Canadian controlled private corporation, has current SR&ED expenditures of $750,000 and capital SR&ED expenditures of $600,000. The Company has no Taxable Income in the current or the three preceding years.

> **Analysis** The Company's total investment tax credit will be $472,500 [(35%)($750,000 + $600,000)]. The refundable portion will be $346,500 [(100%)(35%)($750,000) + (40%)(35%)($600,000)].

> **Note On 2014 Changes** We would remind you that, as of 2014, capital expenditures no longer qualify for SR&ED tax credits. This means that refunds will only be available on credits related to current SR&ED expenditures.

Carry Overs Of Investment Tax Credits

14-69. Under the definition of investment tax credit in ITA 127(9), unused investment tax credits may be carried back for up to 3 years and forward for 20 years. A taxpayer is required to claim all other available tax credits before calculating and claiming the investment tax credit for the year. Also, a taxpayer must reduce, to the fullest extent possible, federal Tax Payable for the current year before using investment tax credits to reduce previous years' federal Tax Payable.

Exercise Fourteen - 7

Subject: Refundable Investment Tax Credits

Sci-Tech Inc. has made a number of expenditures that qualify for investment tax credits. They have invested $123,000 in Qualified Property in Nova Scotia. In addition, they have $1,200,000 in current expenditures for scientific research and experimental development, as well as $2,500,000 in capital expenditures for scientific research and experimental development. The Company is a Canadian controlled private corporation and, for the previous taxation year, has Taxable Income of $176,000 and Taxable Capital Employed In Canada of $6,000,000. The Company has no Tax Payable for the current year or the three previous years.

Determine the amount of the refund that Sci-Tech will receive as a result of earning these investment tax credits and any available carry forwards. Include in your answer any other tax consequences of these investment tax credits.

End of Exercise. Solution available in Study Guide.

We suggest you work Self Study Problem Fourteen-5 at this point.

Effect Of Acquisition Of Control On Investment Tax Credits

14-70.   As was the case with companies having accumulated loss carry forwards, the government is concerned about the large amount of unused investment tax credits that are being carried forward in the tax records of Canadian corporations. The carry forwards reflect the fact that these corporations have experienced losses and, as a consequence, have not had a tax liability to which the credits could be applied.

14-71.   While the government does not object to these credits being used against Tax Payable resulting from improved profitability for the corporations that have experienced losses, there is concern that these loss corporations will be acquired by profitable corporations in order to make use of these credits. As a consequence, there are acquisition of control rules that apply to the carry forward of investment tax credits in a manner similar to the acquisition of control rules that apply to the carry forward of non-capital losses.

14-72.   These rules are found in ITA 127(9.1) and (9.2). Their effect is described in IT-151R5 (Consolidated) as follows:

> **Paragraph 84**   If control of a corporation has been acquired by a person or group of persons, subsections 127(9.1) and (9.2) and paragraphs (j) and (k) of the definition of "investment tax credit" in subsection 127(9) may apply to restrict the availability of the corporation's investment tax credits. In general, these provisions limit the application of investment tax credits to the tax on the income from a particular business carried on by the corporation before the acquisition of control or any other business substantially all the income of which is from the sale, leasing, rental, or development of properties or the rendering of services similar to those of the particular business carried on by the corporation before the acquisition of control.

14-73.   The effect of these provisions is to treat investment tax credits in a manner similar to the treatment of non-capital loss carry forwards when there is an acquisition of control.

Tax Basis Shareholders' Equity

Shareholders' Equity Under GAAP

14-74.   In this Chapter, we will be considering various distributions to shareholders. In order to comprehend this material, some understanding of the tax basis components of shareholders' equity is required.

14-75.   You are all familiar with the components of Shareholders' Equity as they appear in a Balance Sheet prepared using generally accepted accounting principles (GAAP). The two basic components of the total balance disclosed are:

> **Contributed Capital**   This is the amount that has been paid by investors in return for shares issued. In jurisdictions where par value shares can still be used, this balance may be divided into par value amounts and an excess over par amount, commonly designated contributed surplus.

> **Earned Capital (Retained Earnings)**   This component reflects amounts that have been earned by the corporation and retained in the business. While this balance is sometimes referred to as earned surplus, the more common designation is retained earnings. In some situations, part of this balance may be segregated as reserves.

14-76.   This segregation is based on the general legal requirement that dividends cannot be paid out of contributed capital. By using this disclosure, investors are informed as to the legal basis for payment of dividends by the corporation. However, this legal basis may not be supported by the cash resources that would be needed to, in fact, pay cash dividends.

Paid Up Capital (Tax Basis Contributed Capital)

14-77.   ITA 89(1) defines paid up capital, normally referred to as "PUC". This Subsection indicates that the amount should be calculated without reference to the *Income Tax Act*, telling us that PUC should be based on legal stated capital as determined under the legislation governing the particular corporation (*Canada Business Corporations Act* or relevant provincial legislation). As contributed capital under GAAP is also based on legal stated capital, the initial PUC for shares issued will be equal to contributed capital under GAAP. However, as will be discussed in this and subsequent Chapters, there will be adjustments to PUC that have no equivalent adjustment under GAAP.

14-78.   PUC is applied on an average per share basis to each class of shares. This means, for example, that if a corporation issues 100,000 shares to one individual at $10 per share and, at a later point in time, issues an additional 100,000 shares of the same class to a different individual at $15 per share, the per share PUC will be $12.50 for all of the shares of that class. Stated alternatively, all shares of a particular class will have the same per share PUC value.

14-79.   Note the difference between the PUC value per share and the adjusted cost base (ACB) of a share. The ACB of a share is the average cost of the shares held by a particular shareholder. In the example in Paragraph 14-78, the taxpayer acquiring the first issue has an adjusted cost base of $10 per share, while the purchaser of the second issue has an adjusted cost base of $15 per share.

14-80.   The importance of PUC lies in the fact that it is a capital contribution and does not reflect accumulated earnings of the corporation. Because of this, it can be distributed to shareholders as a return of capital (subject to any restrictions imposed by corporate law), without tax consequences for either the corporation, or the shareholder. This may not be the case, however, when capital distributions are made to shareholders of public corporations.

Exercise Fourteen - 8

Subject: Determination Of PUC And Adjusted Cost Base

Halide Ltd. has one class of shares. The Company issued its first 100,000 shares at a price of $1.10 each. Two years later, an additional 50,000 shares were issued for $1.35 per share. During the current year, a further 30,000 shares were issued for $1.82 per share. One of the investors in the Company acquired 2,400 shares of the first group of shares issued, and an additional 3,850 shares from the most recent issue. Determine the adjusted cost base per share, as well as the total PUC of this investor's shares.

End of Exercise. Solution available in Study Guide.

Tax Basis Retained Earnings

Amount

14-81.   The situation with respect to Retained Earnings is much more complex. To begin, we will be dealing with a different total for tax purposes. As you are aware, there are significant differences between accounting Net Income and Net Income For Tax Purposes.

14-82.   While the accounting literature defines accounting/tax differences as temporary differences with reference to Balance Sheet accounts (e.g., the difference between the Net Book Value and the UCC of a depreciable asset), most of these Balance Sheet differences are created by Income Statement differences (e.g., the difference between Amortization Expense and CCA). As a result, total Retained Earnings as determined under GAAP will, in most cases, be a significantly different number than the corresponding tax figure.

14-83.   A further point here relates to terminology. In general, the term Retained Earnings has replaced Earned Surplus in accounting literature and in published financial statements.

However, the term surplus is still alive and well in tax work. As evidence, we would note that the *Income Tax Act* contains only 13 references to Retained Earnings, in contrast to 178 references to Surplus.

Basic Components

14-84.   Moving beyond the differences in the total amount, we encounter further problems in relating tax and GAAP figures. Under GAAP, Retained Earnings is often a single homogeneous balance. While some companies still segregate parts of this balance into reserves, such components have no formal meaning beyond assisting with disclosure.

14-85.   In contrast, the corresponding tax balance has four components, each with a well defined role in tax work. The four components are as follows:

- Capital Dividend Account (private companies only)
- Post-1971 Undistributed Surplus
- Pre-1972 Undistributed Surplus (no longer covered in this text)
- Pre-1972 Capital Surplus On Hand (no longer covered in this text)

14-86.   The Capital Dividend Account is available to all private companies. It is discussed in detail in this Chapter beginning at Paragraph 14-90.

14-87.   "Post-1971 Undistributed Surplus" tracks the earnings retained after 1971 that do not have any special tax status.

14-88.   In Chapter 8 we noted that, prior to 1972, capital gains were not subject to tax in Canada. The 1972 introduction of capital gains taxation resulted in the need to have a complex set of transitional rules to avoid taxation of gains accrued prior to that date. Although at one time these rules were very important, with the passage of time this is no longer the case.

14-89.   "Pre-1972 Undistributed Surplus" is simply earnings that accrued prior to 1972 that are retained in the corporation. The "Pre-1972 Capital Surplus On Hand" tracks capital gains and losses that accrued prior to 1972, but were realized after 1971. Such transactions are no longer of sufficient importance to warrant coverage in a general text such as this. If this area is of interest, the median rule (a rule that deals with dispositions of assets acquired before 1972) is covered in Supplementary Reading No. 1 that is included on the Student CD-ROM which accompanies this text.

Capital Dividend Account

Objective

14-90.   The objective of the capital dividend account is to track items that can be distributed on a tax free basis to the shareholders of the corporation. While a number of different items can be included in this account, the reason for its use can best be understood in the context of capital gains.

> **Example**   During 2008, Uval Ltd. acquires land at a cost of $150,000. During 2013, the land is sold for $190,000, resulting in a capital gain of $40,000 ($190,000 - $150,000).
>
> **Analysis**   It is the intent of tax legislation to assess tax on only one-half of capital gains. This means that Uval will have a taxable capital gain of $20,000 [(1/2)($40,000)]. However, the remaining $20,000 is still being held by the corporation. While the goal of tax legislation is not to have taxes assessed on this balance, in the absence of some special provision, its distribution would be subject to tax in the hands of the recipient shareholders.

14-91.   The capital dividend account provides the required relief in this situation. The untaxed balance of $20,000 will be added to the capital dividend account. This balance can then be used to pay a capital dividend, a special type of dividend that can be distributed tax free to the shareholders of the corporation. Such dividends will be discussed in more detail at a later point in this chapter.

14-92.   While this analysis would appear to be relevant to all types of corporation, only private corporations can have a capital dividend account. Note, however, the use of this account is available to all private corporations, without regard to whether they are Canadian controlled.

Procedures
14-93.   As indicated in the preceding section, there are a number of different items that can be allocated to the capital dividend account. The complete definition of these items is found in ITA 89(1) and is very complex. Without becoming involved in some of the more complex issues found in that Subsection, the basic items that can be included in the Capital Dividend Account are as follows:

1. The non-taxable portion of net capital gains realized during the year is added to the account (the non-taxable portion of capital gains, less the non-deductible portion of capital losses and Business Investment Losses). This would include 100 percent of the gain on publicly traded shares that have been gifted to a registered Canadian charity.

2. Capital dividends received from other corporations are added. This preserves the tax free status of non-taxable amounts that pass through more than one corporation.

3. The non-taxable portion of gains on the sale of eligible capital property is added to the account.

   Note   You will not be able to understand this example unless you are familiar with the cumulative eligible capital procedures that were presented in Chapter 5. If you have not covered this material recently, we suggest that you review it prior to dealing with this example.

   Example   A corporation acquires goodwill for $100,000 during 2011. Three-quarters of this amount, or $75,000, is added to the cumulative eligible capital (CEC) balance. This would be amortized at a 7 percent rate for two years, leaving a balance of $64,868 [($75,000)(93%)(93%)]. The goodwill is sold during 2013 for $150,000.

   Analysis   The relevant calculations here are as follows:

2011 Addition To CEC	$ 75,000
2011 And 2012 Amortization ($75,000 - $64,868)	(10,132)
Balance - January 1, 2013	$ 64,868
Proceeds Deducted [(75%)($150,000)]	(112,500)
Subtotal	($ 47,632)
Income Inclusion For Amortization Taken	10,132
Remaining Negative Balance	($ 37,500)
Conversion Factor (3/4 Inclusion To 1/2)	2/3
Additional Income Inclusion	$ 25,000

   In economic terms, there has been a gain on the disposition of $50,000 ($150,000 - $100,000). As discussed in Chapter 5, CCA and Cumulative Eligible Capital, ITA 14(1) acts to treat this gain in the same manner as a capital gain. That is, only one-half of the total is subject to tax. That one-half is the $25,000 that has been calculated in the preceding table (it was converted from a three-quarters inclusion rate to a one-half inclusion rate because the CEC rules were not changed in 2000 when the capital gains inclusion rate went from three-quarters to one-half). An equivalent amount of $25,000 will be added to the capital dividend account.

4. Life insurance proceeds received by the corporation are added to the account, net of the adjusted cost base of the policy. This can be an important addition

when the company insures the life of one or more of its shareholders. This is a common procedure in owner-managed businesses, where life insurance proceeds are sometimes used to finance the buyout of the shares from the estate of a deceased shareholder.

5. The account is reduced by capital dividends paid. As will be discussed in Paragraph 14-109, an ITA 83(2) election is required.

Exercise Fourteen - 9

Subject: Capital Dividend Account

The following transactions involve the Knerd Corporation's capital dividend account:

- In 2009, they sold a capital asset with an adjusted cost base of $86,000, for cash of $108,000.

- During the year ending December 31, 2012, the Company received a capital dividend of $8,200.

- On July 1, 2013, they sold goodwill for proceeds of $42,000. They had paid $37,000 for this goodwill in the previous year. It is the Company's policy to make maximum CCA and CEC deductions.

- On October 31, 2013, the Company paid an ITA 83(2) capital dividend of $16,000. The appropriate election was made.

Determine the balance in the capital dividend account at December 31, 2013.

End of Exercise. Solution available in Study Guide.

We suggest you work Self Study Problems Fourteen-6 and 7 at this point.

Distributions Of Corporate Surplus

Introduction

14-94.   Corporate surplus, generally referred to by accountants as Retained Earnings, is periodically distributed to shareholders of the corporation. This happens most commonly through the cash dividends that are paid by most Canadian companies. Less commonly, we encounter stock dividends and dividends in kind (distributions of corporate assets other than cash).

14-95.   These fairly routine types of dividends were given coverage in Chapter 7 in our material on property income. However, they will be reviewed at this point as an introduction to the various types of deemed dividends that are under consideration here. We will also give further attention to ITA 83(2) capital dividends.

14-96.   The types of deemed dividends that will be covered in this section are as follows:

- ITA 84(1) Deemed Dividend on Increase of PUC
- ITA 84(2) Deemed Dividend on Winding Up or Reorganization of a Business
- ITA 84(3) Deemed Dividend on Redemption, Acquisition, or Cancellation of Shares
- ITA 84(4) and (4.1) Deemed Dividend on Reduction of PUC

14-97.   With the exception of capital dividends, all of the dividends considered here are subject to taxes when they are received by an individual. This means they will generally be subject to the dividend gross up and tax credit procedures. Provided they are designated as such by the payor, they will be treated as eligible dividends.

14-98.   As you will recall from Chapter 12, when dividends are received by a corporation, they are usually included in Net Income For Tax Purposes and deducted in the calculation of Taxable Income.

Regular Cash Dividends

14-99.   Regular cash dividends are paid out of a corporation's unrestricted surplus balances. The payment of cash dividends serves to reduce these balances. Unlike the payment of interest on debt, the payment of cash dividends does not create a tax deduction for the corporation.

14-100.   If cash dividends are received by an individual or a trust, they are subject to the usual gross up and tax credit procedures. In contrast, if they are paid to another corporation, they are generally received on a tax free basis.

14-101.   A further point here relates to the accounting treatment of dividends on certain types of preferred shares. IAS 32, *Financial Instruments - Presentation*, recommends that shares which require mandatory redemption by the issuer be classified as liabilities. Consistent with this, the dividend payments on these shares must be disclosed as interest, resulting in the amount of the distribution being deducted in the determination of accounting net income.

14-102.   To date, this treatment has not been recognized by the CRA. From a tax point of view, the dividends paid on preferred shares with mandatory redemption provisions will be given the same treatment as any other dividend. This means that, even if the GAAP based financial statements of the enterprise present preferred dividends as interest expense, they will not be deductible to the paying corporation.

Stock Dividends

14-103.   From an accounting perspective, a stock dividend is a pro rata distribution of new shares to the existing shareholder group of the corporation, normally accompanied by a capitalization of Retained Earnings equal to the fair market value of the shares issued.

Example   Jessica Rabin owns 100 shares of Fergis Ltd. She acquired these shares several years ago for $2,500 ($25 per share). On January 1, 2013, the Shareholders' Equity of Fergis Ltd. is as follows:

No Par Common Stock (1,000,000 Shares)	$ 7,500,000
Retained Earnings	12,500,000
Total Shareholders' Equity	$20,000,000

On December 31, 2013, the publicly traded shares of Fergis have a fair market value of $30 per share. On this date, the Company declares a 10 percent stock dividend. This dividend is not designated as eligible.

Analysis - Fergis Ltd.   At the time of the stock dividend, Fergis would transfer an amount equal to the $3,000,000 [($30)(10%)(1,000,000)] market value of these shares from Retained Earnings to the contributed capital account. Subsequent to this transfer, the Shareholders' Equity of Fergis would be as follows:

No Par Common Stock (1,100,000 Shares)	$10,500,000
Retained Earnings ($12,500,000 - $3,000,000)	9,500,000
Total Shareholders' Equity	$20,000,000

From a tax point of view, the $3,000,000 increase in contributed capital would generally be an increase in PUC, reflecting an increase in the amount that could be distributed to the shareholders of the company on a tax free basis.

Analysis - Jessica Rabin   As a result of the stock dividend, she will receive 10 shares [(10%)(100)] of stock worth $300 [(10)($30)]. This dividend will be taxable to the extent that it reflects an increase in PUC. Provided the increase in the Fergis Ltd. PUC is equal to the $3,000,000 increase in Contributed Capital (the usual case), Jessica will have a dividend of $300 [($3,000,000)(100 ÷ 1,000,000)]. This non-eligible dividend will be grossed up to a taxable amount of $375 [($300)(125%)].

With respect to the adjusted cost base of the new shares, ITA 52(3) will deem her to have acquired 10 additional shares at a cost of $300. With this addition, the average per share adjusted cost base would be $25.45 [($2,500 + $300) ÷ 110].

Note On PUC   In most accounting and tax texts, the usual procedure is to transfer an amount equal to the fair market value of the dividend shares issued to Retained Earnings. However, this may not be the case. In some provinces, the amount of legal stated capital to be assigned to the dividend shares is discretionary. If the assigned amount is a value that is lower than fair market value, the corresponding transfer to PUC will be lower. This results in a lower taxable value for the stock dividend and a smaller addition to the adjusted cost base of the shares.

14-104.   These rules create an unfortunate situation for the taxpayer. An individual receiving stock dividends will require a cash outflow (taxes on the dividend received) with no corresponding cash inflows (the dividends are not received in cash). This approach to the taxation of stock dividends serves to significantly discourage their use in Canada, particularly in the case of large publicly traded companies.

14-105.   As noted, however, it is possible for a company to issue shares with a legal stated capital and a PUC that is less than fair market value. When this is the case, the negative tax effect that was described in the preceding paragraph can be reduced.

Exercise Fourteen - 10

Subject: Stock Dividends

On June 30, 2013, the Shareholders' Equity of Sturgis Inc. is as follows:

Common Stock (23,400 Shares Outstanding)	$351,000
Retained Earnings	462,000
Total Shareholders' Equity	$813,000

On this date, the Company declares a 5 percent stock dividend. This dividend is not designated as eligible. At this time, the shares are trading at $25 per share. The Company increases its PUC by the fair market value of the new shares issued. The dividend is not designated as eligible.

Jean Tessier is holding 1,000 of the Sturgis shares which he acquired several years ago at a cost of $18 per share. Determine the effect of this transaction on Jean's 2013 Net Income For Tax Purposes and 2013 federal Tax Payable. In addition, determine the adjusted cost base per share of his Sturgis Inc. holding.

End of Exercise. Solution available in Study Guide.

Dividends In Kind

14-106.   While somewhat unusual, corporations do sometimes declare dividends that are payable in assets other than cash, or the corporation's own shares. An example of this might be a situation in which a corporation has a major holding of another corporation's shares and wishes to dispose of them. If the block is large, sale on the open market could significantly depress the proceeds received. A possible alternative is to distribute the shares on a pro rata basis to the corporation's existing shareholders.

14-107. From the point of view of the corporation, the dividend is treated as a disposition of the distributed property. Under ITA 52(2), the proceeds of disposition will be deemed to be the fair market value of the property distributed. Depending on the type of property, this could result in a capital gain, capital loss, recapture or terminal loss for the corporation.

14-108. Also under ITA 52(2), the shareholders are deemed to have acquired the assets at their fair market value. This amount is considered to be a taxable dividend subject to the usual gross up and tax credit procedures for eligible and non-eligible dividends.

Example Hold Ltd. owns shares in Bold Inc. These shares have an adjusted cost base of $800,000 and a fair market value of $3,500,000. Hold Ltd. decides to distribute the Bold Inc. shares as a dividend in kind to its shareholders, all of whom are individuals. The dividend is declared in June, 2013 and will be paid to the existing shareholders of Hold Ltd. in July, 2013.

Analysis The tax consequences of this dividend are as follows:

- Based on deemed proceeds of $3,500,000, Hold Ltd. will have a taxable capital gain of $1,350,000 [(1/2)($3,500,000 - $800,000)].

- Hold Ltd. will have declared a dividend of $3,500,000, resulting in a decrease in its undistributed surplus of this amount.

- The shareholders will have received a taxable dividend of $3,500,000, subject to either the eligible or non-eligible dividend gross up and tax credit procedures.

- The adjusted cost base of the Bold Inc. shares to the Hold Ltd. shareholders will be $3,500,000.

Exercise Fourteen - 11

Subject: Dividends In Kind

Sandrine Cloutier owns 15 percent of the 500,000 outstanding shares of Cloutier Ltd. Cloutier Ltd. owns 150,000 shares of Botan Inc. The Botan Inc. shares were acquired at a cost of $42 per share and have a current fair market value of $51 per share. On June 30, 2013, Cloutier Ltd. declares a non-eligible dividend involving the distribution of all of the Botan shares on a pro rata basis to its existing shareholders.

Determine the effect of the payment of this dividend on Cloutier Ltd.'s 2013 Net Income For Tax Purposes. In addition, determine the effect of the payment of this dividend on Sandrine Cloutier's 2013 Net Income For Tax Purposes and 2013 federal Tax Payable.

End of Exercise. Solution available in Study Guide.

Capital Dividends Under ITA 83(2)

14-109. As we have previously indicated, the balance in the capital dividend account reflects amounts that can be distributed on a tax free basis to the shareholders of the private corporation. However, this tax free status does not happen automatically. When a corporation makes a distribution, an amount not in excess of the balance in the capital dividend account can be designated as a capital dividend. This is accomplished through an election under ITA 83(2), using Form T2054. Note that, provided there is a balance in the capital dividend account, this election can be made both for regular and for deemed dividends.

14-110. Distributing a capital dividend reduces the balance in the capital dividend account. It will be received by the taxpayer, whether the taxpayer is a corporation, a trust or an individual, on a tax free basis with no reduction in the adjusted cost base of their shares. You will also recall that, if the recipient of the capital dividend is a private corporation, the amount of the dividend will be added to the recipient corporation's capital dividend account.

14-111. If an election is made to pay a capital dividend in excess of the balance in the capital dividend account, a tax equal to 60 percent of the excess will be assessed under ITA 184(2) of the *Income Tax Act*. This will not affect the tax free nature of the dividend to the recipient.

14-112. In some circumstances, an excess election can occur inadvertently. For example, the non-taxable portion of a capital gain may be added to the capital dividend account and, at a subsequent point in time, a reassessment will cause the gain to be reclassified as business, rather than capital. This in turn means that the capital dividend account will be reduced through the reassessment process. If this happens, ITA 184(3) and 184(4) contain provisions that allow for a revision of the election in order to avoid the 60 percent penalty.

14-113. As a final point, the fact that capital dividends are not taxable dividends means that they are not subject to the dividend gross up and tax credit procedures. In turn, this means that they cannot be classified as eligible dividends under any circumstances.

Deemed Dividends Under ITA 84(1) - Increase In PUC
General Rules
14-114. ITA 84(1) dividends involve a situation where there has been an increase in the corporation's PUC, accompanied by a smaller increase in the net assets of the corporation. This would include situations where the increase in PUC is accompanied by no increase in the net assets of the corporation.

14-115. The most common example of this type of deemed dividend would involve situations where a corporation issues shares to settle a debt obligation that has a carrying value that is smaller than the fair market value of the shares.

> **Example** A corporation issues shares with a PUC of $500,000 to a creditor, in settlement of debt with a carrying value of $450,000. Because of a decline in interest rates since the debt was issued, the $500,000 reflects the market value of the debt.

> **Analysis** This transaction would result in an ITA 84(1) deemed dividend of $50,000 ($500,000 - $450,000).

14-116. The reason for treating this $50,000 as a form of income to the shareholders is that it represents an increase in the amount that can be distributed to them on a tax free basis. As a group, their economic position has clearly been improved as a result of this transaction.

14-117. It is important to note that, because the extra $50,000 in PUC will be allocated to all of the shareholders of the particular class, a corresponding treatment will be given to the deemed dividend. That is, the $50,000 dividend will be allocated on a pro rata basis to all of the shareholders of the class, not just the new shareholder who acquired his shares by giving up $450,000 in debt securities.

14-118. In order to provide equity in this situation, the amount assessed as a dividend will be added to the adjusted cost base of the shares. For the new shareholder, his share of the $50,000 ITA 84(1) deemed dividend is added to the adjusted cost base of the shares that were issued to him, resulting in an adjusted cost base for these shares of $450,000 plus his share of the deemed dividend. Note that this will not be the PUC of these shares, since PUC is calculated as an average value for all of the outstanding shares on a class by class basis.

> **Example** Lantin Inc. has 250,000 shares outstanding at the beginning of the current year. These shares were sold for $12 each, resulting in a PUC of $3,000,000. Jeanne Moreau owns 25,000 of these shares which she acquired at the time of their issue for $12 each.

> During the current year, the company issues 50,000 new shares with a market value of $750,000 ($15 per share) in order to retire debt with a carrying value of $675,000.

> Shortly after the 50,000 new shares were issued, Ms. Moreau sells her 25,000 shares for $450,000 ($18 per share).

Analysis   The ITA 84(1) deemed dividend will be calculated as follows:

PUC Of New Shares [(50,000)($15)]	$750,000
Increase In Net Assets (Carrying Value Of Debt Retired)	(675,000)
ITA 84(1) Deemed Dividend	$ 75,000

This would be allocated to all of the outstanding shares in the amount of $0.25 ($75,000 ÷ 300,000) per share. This would be a taxable dividend, subject to either the eligible or non-eligible dividend gross up and tax credit procedures.

With respect to Ms. Moreau's holding, this would increase her per share adjusted cost base to $12.25 ($12.00 + $0.25). Given this, the tax consequences of her sale would be calculated as follows:

Proceeds Of Disposition [(25,000)($18)]	$450,000
Adjusted Cost Base [(25,000)($12.25)]	(306,250)
Capital Gain	$143,750
Inclusion Rate	1/2
Taxable Capital Gain	$ 71,875

Exercise Fourteen - 12

Subject: ITA 84(1) Deemed Dividends

At the beginning of the current year, Unilev Inc. has 126,000 shares of common stock outstanding. The shares were originally issued at $10.50 per share for total proceeds of $1,323,000, with this amount constituting the PUC. During the current year, a creditor holding $450,000 of the Company's debt agrees to accept 40,000 newly issued common shares of the Company in exchange for settlement of the debt obligation. At the time of this exchange, the shares are trading at $12.70 per share. Subsequent to the exchange, Mr. Uni, who had purchased 5,000 Unilev Inc. shares at the time of their original issue, sells the shares for $13.42 per share.

Describe the tax consequence(s) to all of the shareholders of Unilev Inc. as a result of the exchange of debt for common shares. In addition, describe the tax consequences to Mr. Uni resulting from the sale of his Unilev Inc. shares.

End of Exercise. Solution available in Study Guide.

Excluded Transactions

14-119.   There are a number of transactions involving increases in PUC that are specifically excluded from the ITA 84(1) deemed dividend treatment . The most important of these are:

- **Stock Dividends**   While there will be an increase in PUC in excess of the increase in net assets when a stock dividend is declared, such dividends are not considered to be an ITA 84(1) deemed dividend. Rather, they are taxed under ITA 82(1) as regular dividends. From the point of view of the recipient of the dividend, this distinction is of no consequence.

- **Shifts Between Classes**   When the PUC of one class of shares is decreased and, at the same time, the PUC of a different class is increased by a corresponding amount, there is no ITA 84(1) deemed dividend.

- **Conversion Of Contributed Surplus**   In situations where the consideration received for shares issued is in excess of the amount added to PUC, for tax purposes a contributed surplus balance is created. This contributed surplus balance can generally be converted to PUC, without the increase in PUC being treated as a deemed dividend under ITA 84(1).

Deemed Dividends Under ITA 84(2) - On Winding-Up

14-120.   When there is a winding-up of a Canadian corporation under the provisions of ITA 88(2), the corporate assets will be sold and the liabilities, including taxes on the various types of income created by the sale of the assets, will be paid. The remaining cash will then be distributed to the shareholders of the corporation. Subsequent to this distribution, the shares of the corporation will be canceled. This process is covered in detail in Chapter 17.

14-121.   In this Chapter, we would note that ITA 84(2) indicates that the excess of the fair market value of the amount distributed over the PUC of the shares that are canceled is considered to be a deemed dividend. While ITA 84(2) defines this entire amount as a deemed dividend, some components of this total are, in effect, redefined under ITA 88(2)(b). Specifically, ITA 88(2)(b) indicates that the ITA 84(2) dividend will be dealt with as follows:

Capital Dividend   To the extent that the corporation has a balance in its capital dividend account, ITA 88(2)(b) indicates that this amount of the distribution will be considered a separate dividend, which will be received on a tax free basis under ITA 83(2). As was noted in our discussion of capital dividends, this treatment will only apply if an appropriate election is made.

Taxable Dividend   Any remaining distribution will be treated as a taxable dividend under ITA 84(2), subject to either the eligible or non-eligible dividend gross up and tax credit procedures.

Distribution Of Pre-1972 Capital Surplus On Hand   As mentioned previously in this Chapter, the importance of Pre-1972 Capital Surplus On Hand has diminished greatly over time and is no longer of importance to most users of a general text such as this. However we would point out here that if the corporation has pre-1972 Capital Surplus On Hand, the distribution of this amount will be deemed not to be a dividend.

14-122.   To illustrate these provisions, consider the following:

Example   After selling its assets and paying all of its liabilities, a corporation has cash of $1,200,000 available for distribution to its only shareholder. The PUC of the company's shares is $100,000 and this is also their adjusted cost base. The balance in the capital dividend account is $175,000. The company makes the appropriate election to have the distribution of the $175,000 treated as a capital dividend under ITA 83(2).

Analysis   The analysis of the $1,200,000 distribution would be as follows:

Cash Distributed	$1,200,000
PUC Of Shares	(100,000)
ITA 84(2) Deemed Dividend	$1,100,000
ITA 83(2) Capital Dividend	(175,000)
ITA 88(2)(b) Taxable Dividend	$ 925,000

Depending on whether or not the $925,000 wind-up dividend is designated as eligible, it would be subject to either the eligible or non-eligible dividend gross up and tax credit procedures.

14-123.   From the point of view of the shareholder, there has been a disposition of his shares, an event that requires the determination of a capital gain or loss. In the absence of a mitigating provision, this capital gain or loss would be calculated using the $1,200,000 as the proceeds of disposition, an approach that would double count $1,100,000 of this amount as both a deemed dividend and a capital gain or loss.

14-124.   Fortunately, this problem is resolved by the ITA 54 definition of "proceeds of disposition". This definition indicates that, to the extent that an amount received is considered to be a deemed dividend under ITA 84(2), it is excluded from the proceeds of disposition. This means that the capital gain on the disposition of the shares in the example would be calculated as follows:

Cash Distributed	$1,200,000
Less: ITA 84(2) Deemed Dividend	(1,100,000)
ITA 54 Proceeds Of Disposition	$ 100,000
Adjusted Cost Base	(100,000)
Capital Gain	Nil

Exercise Fourteen - 13

Subject: ITA 84(2) Deemed Dividends

After selling its assets and paying all of its liabilities, a corporation has cash of $2,350,000 available for distribution to its only shareholder. The corporation was established 20 years ago with an investment of $250,000. This figure is both the PUC and the adjusted cost base of the shares. The balance in the capital dividend account is $340,000 and the company makes the appropriate election to have the distribution of this amount be treated as a capital dividend under ITA 83(2).   What are the tax consequences of distributing the $2,350,000 to the corporation's only shareholder?

End of Exercise. Solution available in Study Guide.

Deemed Dividends Under ITA 84(3) -
On Redemption, Acquisition, Or Cancellation Of Shares

14-125.   An ITA 84(3) deemed dividend occurs most commonly when a corporation redeems some of its outstanding shares. Such dividends can also occur when the corporation acquires or cancels some of its outstanding shares. To the extent that the redemption amount paid by the corporation exceeds the PUC of the shares redeemed, a deemed dividend is assessed under ITA 84(3).

14-126.   For the corporation, this is a distribution of their unrestricted surplus balance. From the point of view of the person receiving the redemption proceeds, the deemed dividend component of the proceeds will be treated as an ordinary taxable dividend, subject to either the eligible or non-eligible dividend gross up and tax credit procedures.

14-127.   However, there is a problem here. As a redemption of shares is also a disposition of the redeemed shares, the proceeds of redemption will also be used as the proceeds of disposition. As was the case with the ITA 84(2) deemed dividends on winding up, this creates the possibility that some amount of the proceeds will be double counted as both a deemed dividend and a capital gain.

14-128.   The solution to this problem is similar to the one we described in our discussion of ITA 84(2) deemed dividends. The ITA 54 definition of proceeds of disposition excludes any amounts received that are deemed to be ITA 84(3) dividends.

Example   Mr. Jonas owns all of the preferred shares of Jonas Ltd. They were issued with a PUC of $75,000. However, their adjusted cost base to Mr. Jonas is $25,000. They are redeemed by the corporation for $200,000.

Analysis   The analysis of this transaction is as follows:

Distributions Of Corporate Surplus

Cash Distributed	$200,000
PUC Of Shares Redeemed	(75,000)
ITA 84(3) Deemed Dividend	$125,000

This deemed dividend would be subject to either the eligible or non-eligible dividend gross up and tax credit procedures.

The capital gain on the disposition would be calculated as follows:

Proceeds Of Redemption	$200,000
Less: ITA 84(3) Deemed Dividend	(125,000)
ITA 54 Proceeds Of Disposition	$ 75,000
Adjusted Cost Base	(25,000)
Capital Gain (PUC - ACB)	$ 50,000
Inclusion Rate	1/2
Taxable Capital Gain	$ 25,000

We would note that, in situations where the PUC and adjusted cost base are equal, these calculations will result in no capital gain or loss. If the PUC exceeds the adjusted cost base, the result will be a capital gain. Alternatively, if the PUC is less than the adjusted cost base, a capital loss will result from the disposition. Note that, if the individual shareholder receiving redemption proceeds is affiliated with the corporation, any capital loss arising on the disposition will be disallowed.

Exercise Fourteen - 14

Subject: ITA 84(3) Deemed Dividends

When first incorporated, Tandy Ltd. issued 233,000 common shares in return for $1,922,250 in cash ($8.25 per share). All of the shares were issued to Ms. Jessy Tandy, the founder of the Company. Except for 15,000 shares, she is still holding all of the originally issued shares. The 15,000 shares were sold to Ms. Tandy's brother, Jesuiah, for $7.90 per share, the estimated market value of the shares at that time. Because of ongoing difficulties between the two siblings, Ms. Tandy has arranged for Tandy Ltd. to redeem all of her brother's shares at a price of $11.75 per share during the current year. Any dividends resulting from the redemption will be non-eligible. Determine the tax consequences of this redemption to Ms. Tandy and Jesuiah.

End of Exercise. Solution available in Study Guide.

Deemed Dividends Under ITA 84(4) And ITA 84(4.1)

14-129.   This type of dividend is not as common as the other deemed dividends we have discussed. It arises when a corporation resident in Canada distributes a part of its invested capital to its shareholders, without redeeming or canceling any of its shares. It might occur, for example, if a corporation divested itself of a major division and did not wish to reinvest the proceeds from the sale in other corporate assets. In this type of situation, the proceeds may be distributed to shareholders. Such distributions are commonly referred to as liquidating dividends.

14-130.   In order to make all, or part, of the distribution tax free, it is usually accompanied by a reduction in PUC. For a non-public company, if the reduction in PUC is equal to the amount distributed, no ITA 84(1) dividend arises. However, if the distribution exceeds the PUC reduction, an ITA 84(4) deemed dividend is created. Note that ITA 84(4.1) contains a different set of rules for public companies. Under these alternative rules, a deemed dividend can arise, even if the distribution does not exceed the PUC reduction.

Example Jong Ltd., a CCPC, has shares with a PUC of $5,000,000 and a nil balance in its capital dividend account. As it has disposed of a major division for cash, it will distribute $1,000,000 to its shareholders. In order to limit the tax effects of this distribution, the PUC of the shares will be reduced by $700,000.

Analysis Under ITA 84(4), $700,000 of the total distribution will be a tax free distribution of PUC. The remaining $300,000 is treated as a deemed dividend, subject to the usual gross up and tax credit procedures. The adjusted cost base of the shares would be reduced by $700,000, the amount of the tax free distribution to shareholders. However, there would be no reduction in the adjusted cost base for the $300,000 distribution as it would be subject to tax as a deemed dividend.

14-131.   ITA 84(4.1) provides a different rule that overrides ITA 84(4) in the case of public companies. For these companies, if a payment is made to shareholders in conjunction with a reduction of PUC that is not part of a reorganization of the corporation's business or its capital, and there is no redemption, acquisition, or cancellation of shares, the entire distribution is generally treated as a deemed dividend. Note that ITA 84(3) would be applicable if there was a redemption, acquisition, or cancellation of shares.

14-132.   With respect to our example, this means that, if Jong Ltd. is a public company, the entire $1,000,000 distribution will be considered to be a deemed dividend under ITA 84(4.1). As the $1,000,000 amount will be subject to tax, the adjusted cost base of the shares will not be reduced by this distribution.

14-133.   There is an exception to this general rule for public corporations. If the payment can reasonably be considered to be derived from a transaction that is outside the ordinary course of business for the corporation, it can be considered a tax free return of capital to the extent that it is accompanied by a PUC reduction.

14-134.   An example of this would be where the company disposes of a business unit of the corporation and does not wish to reinvest the proceeds in some other line of business activity. The distribution would have to be made within 24 months of the occurrence of the non-ordinary transaction and the exception would only apply to the first such payment made. If there is more than one payment, the second and any subsequent payments would come under the general ITA 84(4.1) deemed dividend rule.

Exercise Fourteen - 15

Subject: ITA 84(4) Deemed Dividends

Mr. Jondo owns all of the outstanding shares of Jondo Ltd., a CCPC. The shares have a PUC of $450,000 and an adjusted cost base of $625,000. Because it has recently consolidated its operations, Jondo Ltd. pays a liquidating dividend of $330,000, accompanied by a PUC reduction of $225,000. What are the tax consequences of this distribution to Mr. Jondo?

End of Exercise. Solution available in Study Guide.

We suggest you work Self Study Problem Fourteen-8 at this point.

Key Terms Used In This Chapter

14-135.   The following is a list of the key terms used in this Chapter. These terms, and their meanings, are compiled in the Glossary Of Key Terms located at the back of the separate paper Study Guide.

Acquisition Of Control
Annual Business Limit
Apprenticeship Job Creation Tax Credit
Associated Corporations
Capital Dividend
Capital Dividend Account
CCPC
Child Care Spaces Tax Credit
Common Shares
Contributed Capital
Control [ITA 256(1.2)(c)]
Corporation
Deemed Dividends
Deemed Disposition
Dividends
Dividends In Kind
Earned Capital
Earned Surplus
Group Of Persons

Investment Tax Credit
Liquidating Dividend
Paid Up Capital
Preferred Shares
PUC
Qualified Property
Qualifying Corporation
Redemption Of Shares
Refundable Investment Tax Credit
Related Persons
Retained Earnings
Scientific Research And
  Experimental Development (SR&ED)
Shareholders' Equity
Specified Class ITA 256(1.1)
Specified Shareholder ITA 248(1)
Stock Dividend
Taxable Capital Employed In Canada
Winding-Up Of A Canadian Corporation

References

14-136.   For more detailed study of the material in this Chapter, we refer you to the following:

ITA 52(2)	Cost Of Property Received As Dividend In Kind
ITA 52(3)	Cost Of Stock Dividends
ITA 82(1)	Taxable Dividends Received
ITA 83(2)	Capital Dividend
ITA 84	Deemed Dividend
ITA 88(2)	Winding Up Of A Canadian Corporation
ITA 127(5) to 127.1(4)	Investment Tax Credits
ITA 249(4)	Year End On Change In Control
ITA 251	Arm's Length
ITA 256	Associated Corporations
ITR 4600	Investment Tax Credit - Qualified Property
ITR 4601	Investment Tax Credit - Qualified Transportation Equipment
ITR 4602	Certified Property
IC 78-4R3	Investment Tax Credit Rates
IC 86-4R3	Scientific Research And Experimental Development
IT-64R4	Corporations: Association And Control (Consolidated)
IT-66R6	Capital Dividends
IT-149R4	Winding Up Dividend
IT-151R5	Scientific Research And Experimental Development Expenditures (Consolidated)
IT-302R3	Losses Of A Corporation
IT-419R2	Meaning Of Arm's Length
IT-463R2	Paid-Up Capital

Problems For Self Study

(The solutions for these problems can be found in the separate Study Guide.)

Self Study Problem Fourteen - 1 (Acquisition Of Control Rules - Losses)

Tasty Bread Inc. opened a large bakery operation on January 1, 2011. At this time, the Company's year end was established as December 31. In addition to baking bread, the Company was in charge of the wholesale distribution of its products, and operated a large retail outlet on the bakery premises.

The owners of the corporation had little experience in any aspect of baking or selling bread and, as a consequence, during the first two years they experienced the following losses:

Type Of Loss	2011	2012
Non-Capital Losses	$63,500	$78,500
Capital Losses (100%)	68,000	85,000

At the beginning of 2012, the owners did not see any real hope for improved results under their own management and they began looking for new investors with more experience in the bakery industry. Their efforts met with success when, on April 1, 2013, Dough Products Ltd. acquired 72 percent of the outstanding shares of Tasty Bread Inc. Dough Products is a large Canadian public company with a December 31 year end, and many years of successful operation in the industry. It is the intent of the new owners to inject additional capital and management expertise with a view to making Tasty's operations profitable within two years.

As this acquisition of control will result in a deemed year end, Tasty prepared an Income Statement for the period January 1, 2013 through March 31, 2013. This three month Income Statement showed an additional business loss of $23,000 for the period, but no further capital losses.

On March 31, 2013, the values of the Company's assets were as follows:

Asset	Cost	UCC	Fair Market Value
Temporary Investments	$ 53,000	N/A	$ 23,000
Accounts Receivable	45,000	N/A	33,000
Land	275,000	N/A	420,000
Building	285,000	$270,000	320,000
Fixtures And Equipment	120,000	95,000	90,000
Vehicles	110,000	80,000	87,000

Shortly after taking over Tasty Bread Inc., Dough Products Ltd. decided that some of the extra space in Tasty's facilities could be used for manufacturing illuminated glass figurines. Tasty's income (loss) from the two separate businesses for the period April 1, 2013 through December 31, 2013, was as follows:

Business	Income (Loss)
Figurines	$123,000
Bread Operations	(45,000)

For 2014, the income (loss) figures for the two separate businesses were as follows:

Business	Income (Loss)
Figurines	($ 40,000)
Bread Operations	211,000

Required:

A. If Tasty Bread Inc. makes all possible elections to minimize the net capital and non-capital loss balances, determine the amount of the non-capital loss balance that will be carried forward after the acquisition of control by Dough Products Ltd., and the amount of the net capital loss carry forward that will be lost as a result of this change in ownership.

B. Indicate the maximum amount of the non-capital loss carry forward that can be used during the period April 1 through December 31, 2013, and the amount remaining at December 31, 2013.

C. Indicate the maximum amount of the non-capital loss carry forward that can be used during 2014, and the amount remaining at December 31, 2014.

Self Study Problem Fourteen - 2 (Acquisition Of Control Rules - Losses)

On May 1, 2013, Ontario Lawn Care Ltd. (OLC), which provides gardening and lawn services for the southern Ontario market, purchased, from an arm's length party, all of the shares of Lawn Fertilizer Inc. (LF), a company in the business of manufacturing lawn fertilizers. LF has a December 31 year end.

A highly competitive fertilizer market has resulted in the following losses for LF:

Year	Non-Capital Loss	Net Capital Loss
2011	$180,000	$65,000
2012	140,000	Nil

It is estimated that business losses of $125,000 for the 2013 year will be experienced. This is made up of an actual loss of $55,000 up to April 30, 2013, and an estimated loss of $70,000 for the remainder of the year.

Relevant values for LF's assets on May 1, 2013 were as follows:

Asset	Cost	UCC	Fair Market Value
Inventory	$100,000	N/A	$105,000
Land	450,000	N/A	925,000
Class 1 - Building Purchased In 1995	675,000	$515,000	650,000
Class 8 - Furniture	25,000	10,000	15,000
Class 29 - Manufacturing Equipment	415,000	375,000	285,000

Required:

A. Describe the general tax implications resulting from the acquisition of control.

B. Indicate the elections that could be made to maximize income during the short fiscal period ending April 30, 2013.

C. Assume that LF is confident of having sufficient business income in the future to absorb any non-capital loss carry forward. Advise the Company as to any elections that should be made and determine the amount and type of any loss carry forwards that will be available in the future.

D. Assume that LF is not confident of having sufficient business income in the future and would like to minimize any non-capital loss carry forward. Advise the Company as to any elections that should be made and determine the amount and type of any loss carry forwards that will be available in the future.

Self Study Problem Fourteen - 3 (Associated Companies)

The following situations are **independent** of each other. All of the corporations involved are Canadian controlled private corporations and have only one class of shares.

A. John Fleming and Eric Flame are married to women who are sisters. John Fleming owns 100 percent of the outstanding common shares of Fleming Ltd. and 32 percent of the outstanding common shares of Lartch Inc. Eric Flame owns 100 percent of the outstanding common shares of Flame Ltd. and 28 percent of the outstanding common shares of Lartch Inc. The remaining common shares of Lartch Inc. are owned by an unrelated party.

B. Mr. Cuso owns 80 percent of the outstanding common shares of Male Ltd. The remaining 20 percent of the Male Ltd. shares are owned by his spouse, Mrs. Cuso. Mrs. Cuso owns 82 percent of the outstanding common shares of Female Inc. Her spouse owns the remaining 18 percent of the shares in this Company.

C. Ms. Jones, Mrs. Kelly, and Miss Lange are unrelated individuals. Ms. Jones owns 50 percent of the outstanding common shares of Alliance Ltd. and 25 percent of the outstanding voting shares of Breaker Inc. Mrs. Kelly does not own any of the Alliance Ltd. shares, but owns 50 percent of Breaker Inc.'s outstanding voting shares. Miss Lange owns 50 percent of the outstanding common shares of Alliance Ltd. and 25 percent of the outstanding voting shares of Breaker Inc.

D. Mr. Martin and Mr. Oakley each own 50 percent of the shares of Oakley Ltd. In addition, they each own 50 percent of the shares of Martin Inc. Mr. Martin and Mr. Oakley are not related.

E. Lily Fung owns 100 percent of the shares of 123LF Inc. Her husband, James Fung, owns 100 percent of the shares of 456JF Inc.

Required: For each of the preceding situations, indicate whether the corporations are associated and explain your conclusion with reference to the *Income Tax Act*. In order to assist you in answering this question, we have provided you with the content of ITA 256(1).

ITA 256(1) Associated corporations — For the purposes of this Act, one corporation is associated with another in a taxation year if, at any time in the year,

(a) one of the corporations controlled, directly or indirectly in any manner whatever, the other;

(b) both of the corporations were controlled, directly or indirectly in any manner whatever, by the same person or group of persons;

(c) each of the corporations was controlled, directly or indirectly in any manner whatever, by a person and the person who so controlled one of the corporations was related to the person who so controlled the other, and either of those persons owned, in respect of each corporation, not less than 25% of the issued shares of any class, other than a specified class, of the capital stock thereof;

(d) one of the corporations was controlled, directly or indirectly in any manner whatever, by a person and that person was related to each member of a group of persons that so controlled the other corporation, and that person owned, in respect of the other corporation, not less than 25% of the issued shares of any class, other than a specified class, of the capital stock thereof; or

(e) each of the corporations was controlled, directly or indirectly in any manner whatever, by a related group and each of the members of one of the related groups was related to all of the members of the other related group, and one or more persons who were members of both related groups, either alone or together, owned, in respect of each corporation, not less than 25% of the issued shares of any class, other than a specified class, of the capital stock thereof.

Problems For Self Study

Self Study Problem Fourteen - 4 (Associated Companies)

Each of the following is an **independent** Case involving the ownership of voting shares of Canadian controlled private corporations. All of the corporations have taxation years that end on December 31 and have only one class of shares.

1. Mr. Jones owns 35 percent of the shares of Jones Ltd. and 20 percent of the shares of Twitty Inc. Mr. Twitty owns 20 percent of the shares of Jones Ltd. and 40 percent of the shares of Twitty Inc. Mr. Jones and Mr. Twitty are not related.

2. Ms. Wynette owns 60 percent of the shares of Wynette Enterprises Ltd. and 30 percent of the shares of Lynn Inc. The remaining 70 percent of the shares of Lynn Inc. are held by Ms. Wynette's sister and her spouse.

3. Mr. Travis, Mr. Jennings, and Mr. Cash, three unrelated individuals, each hold one third of the shares of Cowboys Ltd. In addition, Mr. Travis and Mr. Cash each hold 50 percent of the shares of Horses Inc.

4. Mr. Nelson owns 80 percent of the shares of Willie's Hits Ltd. and 30 percent of the shares of Randy's Boots Inc. Willie's Hits Ltd. owns 20 percent of the shares of Hill Inc. Randy's Boots Inc. owns 80 percent of the shares of Hill Inc.

5. Ms. Parton owns 90 percent of the shares of Alpha Company and her spouse owns 100 percent of the shares of Centra Company. Ms. Parton and her spouse each own 40 percent of the shares of Beta Company.

6. Ms. Gale owns 90 percent of the shares of Kristal Enterprises Ltd. and 10 percent of the shares of Norton Music Inc. Her 12 year old son owns 30 percent of the shares of Norton Music Inc., and Ms. Gale holds an option to buy 20 percent of the shares of Norton Music Inc. from an unrelated shareholder.

Required: For each of the preceding Cases, determine whether the corporations are associated. Support your conclusions with references to specific provisions of ITA 256. In order to assist you in answering this question, we have provided you with the content of ITA 256(1).

ITA 256(1) Associated corporations — For the purposes of this Act, one corporation is associated with another in a taxation year if, at any time in the year,

(a) one of the corporations controlled, directly or indirectly in any manner whatever, the other;

(b) both of the corporations were controlled, directly or indirectly in any manner whatever, by the same person or group of persons;

(c) each of the corporations was controlled, directly or indirectly in any manner whatever, by a person and the person who so controlled one of the corporations was related to the person who so controlled the other, and either of those persons owned, in respect of each corporation, not less than 25% of the issued shares of any class, other than a specified class, of the capital stock thereof;

(d) one of the corporations was controlled, directly or indirectly in any manner whatever, by a person and that person was related to each member of a group of persons that so controlled the other corporation, and that person owned, in respect of the other corporation, not less than 25% of the issued shares of any class, other than a specified class, of the capital stock thereof; or

(e) each of the corporations was controlled, directly or indirectly in any manner whatever, by a related group and each of the members of one of the related groups was related to all of the members of the other related group, and one or more persons who were members of both related groups, either alone or together, owned, in respect of each corporation, not less than 25% of the issued shares of any class, other than a specified class, of the capital stock thereof.

Self Study Problem Fourteen - 5 (Investment Tax Credits)

The following three independent cases involve the tax procedures associated with various types of investment tax credits.

Case A

During 2012, Domus Inc. pays salaries to 13 eligible apprentices totalling $292,500 ($22,500 per apprentice). In addition, it acquires $1,600,000 in Class 8 assets on which a 10 percent investment tax credit is available.

Required: Describe the 2012 and 2013 tax consequences associated with making these expenditures and claiming the related investment tax credits. Include in your solution the CCA for 2012 and 2013.

Case B

Bertolli Ltd. has been a Canadian controlled private corporation since its incorporation. Its taxation year ends on December 31. It had the following Taxable Income and Taxable Capital Employed In Canada:

	2012	2013
Taxable Income	$ 672,000	$ 692,000
Taxable Capital Employed In Canada	13,420,000	12,221,000

Required: Determine its annual SR & ED expenditure limit for the 2013 taxation year.

Case C

Research At Rest (RAR) has been a Canadian controlled private corporation since its incorporation. Its taxation year ends on December 31. RAR has no Tax Payable for the 2013 taxation year or the three previous years. It had the following Taxable Income and Taxable Capital Employed In Canada:

	2012	2013
Taxable Income	$ 423,000	$ 491,000
Taxable Capital Employed In Canada	11,500,000	9,753,000

RAR has made a number of expenditures in 2013 that qualify for investment tax credits.

- They have invested $187,000 in Qualified Property In Prince Edward Island.
- They have incurred $1,560,000 in current expenditures for scientific research and experimental development.
- They have acquired $1,960,000 in capital assets to be used for scientific research and experimental development.

Required: Determine the amount of the refund that RAR will receive as a result of earning these investment tax credits and any available carry forwards. Include in your answer any other tax consequences of these investment tax credits.

Self Study Problem Fourteen - 6 (Capital Dividend Account)

During the current year, Hemingway Industries Ltd. sold a number of its capital properties. None of the properties disposed of were depreciable capital properties. The relevant facts are as follows:

Property	Proceeds Of Disposition	Adjusted Cost Base	Selling Expenses
1	$8,100	$4,200	$200
2	7,900	3,950	375
3	2,200	4,300	700
4	1,900	3,450	260

Problems For Self Study

Required: Compute the effects of the dispositions on the capital dividend account assuming Hemingway Industries is:

A. a Canadian controlled private corporation.

B. a private corporation that is not a CCPC.

Self Study Problem Fourteen - 7 (Capital Dividend Account)

Nardin Inc. was incorporated in 2000. It has always been a Canadian controlled private corporation with a December 31 year end. Between its incorporation date and December 31, 2013, the following transactions involve the Company's capital dividend account:

1. In 2002, the Company sold a capital asset with an adjusted cost base of $225,000 for $343,500.

2. In 2003, the Company received life insurance proceeds, net of the adjusted cost base of the policy, in the amount of $162,000.

3. In 2005, the Company sold a non-depreciable capital asset for $150,000. The adjusted cost base of this asset was $220,000.

4. During 2007, the Company received a capital dividend of $26,000.

5. During 2011, the company sold an unlimited life franchise for $320,000. As the Company had developed the franchise product internally, there was no balance in the cumulative eligible capital account.

6. During each of 2011, 2012 and 2013, the Company paid an ITA 83(2) capital dividend of $45,000. The appropriate election was made in each year.

Required: Determine the balance in the Company's capital dividend account as of December 31, 2013.

Self Study Problem Fourteen - 8 (Corporate Surplus Distributions)

Groman Ltd. is a Canadian controlled private corporation. On December 31 of the current year, the Company's condensed Balance Sheet is as follows:

Total Assets		$62,000
Liabilities		$22,000
Shareholders' Equity:		
500 Preferred Shares (Paid Up Capital)	$11,000	
600 Common Shares (Paid Up Capital)	15,600	
Retained Earnings	13,400	40,000
Total Equities		$62,000

Any dividends paid or deemed to be paid by Groman Ltd. would be non-eligible.

Required: Discuss the tax consequences of each of the following **independent** transactions. Tax consequences would include both the increase or decrease in the individual shareholder's Taxable Income, as well as any change in the adjusted cost base of any shares that are still in the hands of the individual shareholder after the described transaction(s).

A. (i) A long-term debtholder has agreed to convert $10,000 of his debt to 500 Preferred Shares, with a Paid Up Capital (PUC) of $11,000. This conversion does not qualify for the ITA 51 rollover that is described in Chapter 17 of the text.

   (ii) After the conversion described in A(i), a different shareholder, with 250 Preferred

Shares, sold them for $5,500 in an arm's length transaction. His shares cost $4,100 a number of years ago.

B. The Company declared and distributed a 5 percent stock dividend on the Common Shares. An addition of $780 was made to Paid Up Capital, with Retained Earnings reduced accordingly.

C. In return for assets with a fair market value of $17,500, the Company issued a demand note for $12,000 and 250 fully paid Preferred Shares having a per share Paid Up Capital equal to those currently outstanding.

D. An investor owns 100 of the Common Shares. They were purchased at a price of $15 per share. The Company redeems these shares at a price of $32 per share.

Assignment Problems

(The solutions for these problems are only available in
the solutions manual that has been provided to your instructor.)

Assignment Problem Fourteen - 1 (Acquisition Of Control Rules - Losses)

Blackburn Inc. began operations in 2011. It was in the business of providing cleaning services to residential properties. All of the shares were owned by Aaron Blackburn and, in addition, he was actively involved in managing the business. The Company adopted a taxation year that ended on December 31.

Mr. Blackburn, whose previous career was as a professor of business strategy at a major Canadian university, showed little aptitude for actually running a business. In 2011, the business showed an operating loss of $123,000. An additional operating loss of $87,000 in 2012 brings the total non-capital loss carry forward balance to $210,000 at December 31, 2012.

When the business commenced, Blackburn Inc. had acquired a parcel of land. Mr. Blackburn had intended to build there after the first location became successful. As success did not appear to be on the horizon, Blackburn Inc. sold this land in 2012. As a result of this disposition, Blackburn Inc. had a $96,000 net capital loss on December 31, 2012.

In early 2013, Mr. Blackburn had to concede that his management skills were not adequate for the operation of Blackburn Inc. and he decided to return to his position as a business strategy professor. White Enterprises, a large public company agreed to buy all of his shares and, on May 1, 2013, the shares of Blackburn were transferred to that company.

As this acquisition of control resulted in a deemed year end, Blackburn Inc. prepared an Income Statement for the period January 1, 2013 through April 30, 2013. This short fiscal period statement showed an additional business loss of $46,000 for this period. There were, however, no further capital losses.

On April 30, 2013, the values of the Company's assets were as follows:

Asset	Cost	UCC	Fair Market Value
Temporary Investments	$ 45,000	N/A	$ 12,000
Accounts Receivable	90,000	N/A	76,000
Land	180,000	N/A	262,000
Building	325,000	$300,000	380,000
Equipment	93,000	60,000	45,000
Vehicles	145,000	110,000	132,000

Shortly after taking over Blackburn Inc., White Enterprises decided that some of the extra space in Blackburn's facilities could be used for manufacturing customized small kitchen appliances. Blackburn's income (loss) from the two separate businesses for the period May 1, through December 31, 2013 and the 2013 taxation year was as follows:

Business	May 1 to Dec. 31, 2013	2014 Year
Kitchen Appliances	$146,000	($ 52,000)
Cleaning Services	(23,000)	263,000

Required:

A. If Blackburn Inc. makes all possible elections to minimize the net capital and non-capital loss balances, determine the amount of the non-capital loss balance that will be carried forward after the acquisition of control by White Enterprises, and the amount of the net capital loss carry forward that will be lost as a result of this change in ownership.

B. Indicate the maximum amount of the non-capital loss carry forward that can be used during the period April 1 through December 31, 2013, and the amount remaining at December 31, 2013.

C. Indicate the maximum amount of the non-capital loss carry forward that can be used during 2014, and the amount remaining at December 31, 2014.

Assignment Problem Fourteen - 2 (Acquisition Of Control Rules - Losses)

Nicastro Ltd. has been in business for many years and, until recently, it has been fairly profitable. All of its shares are owned by Luigi Nicastro and it qualifies as a Canadian controlled private company. It has a December 31 year end.

The Company has always manufactured and sold fresh pasta, largely to restaurants and stores in the local Italian community. All went well until the beginning of 2012 when a local Italian newspaper discovered that Mr. Nicastro's real name was Stanley Kowalski and that he had never been to Italy. Demand for his Company's products immediately fell off, resulting in a net business loss for 2012 of $189,000.

In addition during 2012, he was forced to sell some of the business assets in order to meet his cash flow needs. This resulted in an allowable capital loss of $48,000 [(1/2)($96,000)].

While $114,000 of the business loss could be carried back to previous years, all of the net capital loss had to be carried forward.

In early 2013, he began looking in the local community for a buyer for his Nicastro Ltd. shares. After considerable searching, he found a buyer and, as of June 1, 2013, all of the Nicastro Ltd. shares were sold to Stella d'Oro Inc.

For the period January 1, 2013 through May 31, 2013, Nicastro Ltd.'s accountant determined that there was a net business loss of $79,000. During this period, the Company had net rental income of $5,500 from an apartment above the store. There was also a disposition of preferred shares that resulted in an allowable capital loss of $7,200.

On May 31, 2013, Nicastro Ltd.'s assets had the following values:

Asset	Cost	UCC	Fair Market Value
Investments In TD Common Stock	$ 32,000	N/A	$ 28,000
Land	85,000	N/A	235,000
Building	427,000	$285,000	327,000
Equipment	120,000	60,000	50,000

Required:

A. Calculate Nicastro's Net Income For Tax Purposes and Taxable Income for the period ending May 31, 2013. Indicate the amount of any non-capital and net capital loss carry forwards that would remain after the May 31, 2013 acquisition of control, using the assumption that Nicastro makes all of the available elections using the maximum elected values.

B. Provide the information required in Part A assuming that Nicastro makes only those elec-
    tion(s) required to eliminate losses that might expire at the deemed year end.

C. Briefly discuss which course of action (Part A or B) would be more advantageous for Stella
    d'Oro Inc.

Assignment Problem Fourteen - 3 (Associated Companies)

Each of the following is an **independent** Case involving the ownership of voting shares of
Canadian controlled private corporations. All of the corporations have taxation years that end
on December 31 and have only one class of shares.

1. Mr. Anson, a resident of Alberta, owns 80 percent of the shares of Anson Ltd. and 15
    percent of the shares of Baron Inc. Mr. Baron, a resident of Quebec, owns 85 percent of
    the shares of Baron Inc. and 20 percent of the shares of Anson Ltd. Mr. Anson and Mr.
    Baron are not related.

2. Dunston Ltd. owns 70 percent of the shares of Edson Ltd. Edson Ltd. owns 80 percent of
    the shares of Farley Ltd.

3. Mr. Larry Grange owns 100 percent of the shares of LG Inc. His common-law partner, Mr.
    George Lawrence, owns 100 percent of the shares of GL Inc.

4. Ms. Patricia Hanson owns 80 percent of the shares of Hanson Inc. Her common-law
    partner Ms. Helen Porter owns 90 percent of the shares of Porter Inc. Ms. Hanson and Ms.
    Porter each own 30 percent of Lilith Ltd.

5. Mr. Bruce Korngold owns 80 percent of the shares of BK Ltd. and 15 percent of the shares
    of Lorey Ltd. BK Ltd. owns 30 percent of the shares of Lorey Ltd. Bruce's 10 year old son
    owns 20 percent of the shares of Lorey Ltd. There are no other shareholders who hold
    shares in both companies.

Required: For each of the preceding Cases, determine whether the corporations are associated. Support your conclusions with references to specific provisions of ITA 256. In order to
assist you in answering this question, we have provided you with the content of ITA 256(1).

> **ITA 256(1) Associated corporations** — For the purposes of this Act, one corporation is
> associated with another in a taxation year if, at any time in the year,
>
> (a) one of the corporations controlled, directly or indirectly in any manner whatever, the
>   other;
> (b) both of the corporations were controlled, directly or indirectly in any manner what-
>   ever, by the same person or group of persons;
> (c) each of the corporations was controlled, directly or indirectly in any manner what-
>   ever, by a person and the person who so controlled one of the corporations was
>   related to the person who so controlled the other, and either of those persons owned,
>   in respect of each corporation, not less than 25% of the issued shares of any class,
>   other than a specified class, of the capital stock thereof;
> (d) one of the corporations was controlled, directly or indirectly in any manner whatever,
>   by a person and that person was related to each member of a group of persons that so
>   controlled the other corporation, and that person owned, in respect of the other
>   corporation, not less than 25% of the issued shares of any class, other than a specified
>   class, of the capital stock thereof; or
> (e) each of the corporations was controlled, directly or indirectly in any manner what-
>   ever, by a related group and each of the members of one of the related groups was
>   related to all of the members of the other related group, and one or more persons who
>   were members of both related groups, either alone or together, owned, in respect of
>   each corporation, not less than 25% of the issued shares of any class, other than a
>   specified class, of the capital stock thereof.

Assignment Problem Fourteen - 4 (Associated Companies)

The following situations are **independent** of each other. All of the corporations involved are Canadian controlled private corporations and have only one class of shares.

A. Janice and Sarah Holt are sisters. Janice owns 100 percent of the shares of JH Inc. and 28 percent of Holt Ltd. Her sister Sarah owns 60 percent of the shares of SH Inc., with the remaining 40 percent of the shares held by her father. Sarah also owns 41 percent of the shares of Holt Ltd. The remaining shares of Holt Ltd. are held by an unrelated party.

B. Mr. Martin and Mr. Osbourne are not related. Mr. Martin and Mr. Osbourne each own 50 percent of the shares of Kannon Inc. Mr. Martin owns 60 percent of the shares of Press Ltd. Mr. Osbourne owns the remaining 40 percent of Press Ltd.'s shares.

C. Mr. Jared, Mr. Kapok, and Mr. Lee are three unrelated individuals.

   • Mr. Jared owns 50 percent of the shares of Arbor Inc. and 25 percent of the shares of Broton Ltd.
   • Mr. Kapok owns 50 percent of the shares of Broton Ltd.
   • Mr. Lee owns 50 percent of the shares of Arbor Inc. and 25 percent of the shares of Broton Ltd.

D. Ms. Phig owns 24 percent of Heron Inc., a company that owns 60 percent of Land Ltd. She also owns 65 percent of the shares of Nortex Inc. Nortex Inc. owns 30 percent of Land Ltd.

E. Mr. Brady owns 55 percent of Solex Inc. Solex Inc. owns 40 percent of Bolex Ltd. Mr. Brady also owns 14 percent of HC Ltd., which in turn owns 54 percent of the shares of Bolex Ltd. Mr. Brady's 15 year old son owns 6 percent of the shares of Bolex Ltd.

Required: For each of the preceding situations, indicate whether the corporations are associated and explain your conclusion with reference to the *Income Tax Act*. In order to assist you in answering this question, we have provided you with the content of ITA 256(1).

> **ITA 256(1) Associated corporations** — For the purposes of this Act, one corporation is associated with another in a taxation year if, at any time in the year,
>
> (a) one of the corporations controlled, directly or indirectly in any manner whatever, the other;
> (b) both of the corporations were controlled, directly or indirectly in any manner whatever, by the same person or group of persons;
> (c) each of the corporations was controlled, directly or indirectly in any manner whatever, by a person and the person who so controlled one of the corporations was related to the person who so controlled the other, and either of those persons owned, in respect of each corporation, not less than 25% of the issued shares of any class, other than a specified class, of the capital stock thereof;
> (d) one of the corporations was controlled, directly or indirectly in any manner whatever, by a person and that person was related to each member of a group of persons that so controlled the other corporation, and that person owned, in respect of the other corporation, not less than 25% of the issued shares of any class, other than a specified class, of the capital stock thereof; or
> (e) each of the corporations was controlled, directly or indirectly in any manner whatever, by a related group and each of the members of one of the related groups was related to all of the members of the other related group, and one or more persons who were members of both related groups, either alone or together, owned, in respect of each corporation, not less than 25% of the issued shares of any class, other than a specified class, of the capital stock thereof.

Assignment Problem Fourteen - 5 (Investment Tax Credits)

The following three independent cases involve the tax procedures associated with various types of investment tax credits.

Case A

Since its incorporation, Luxor Ltd. has been a Canadian controlled private corporation. For the taxation year ending December 31, 2012, it had Taxable Income of $756,000. The corresponding figure for 2013 is $812,000.

Its Taxable Capital Employed In Canada was $11,500,000 in 2012 and $12,200,000 in 2013.

Required: Determine Luxor's SR&ED annual expenditure limit for the 2013 taxation year.

Case B

Gargle Search Engine (GSE) has been a Canadian controlled private corporation since its incorporation. During 2012 it had Taxable Income of $12,000. The corresponding figure for 2013 is $6,000. The Company has no Tax Payable for the taxation year ending December 31, 2013, or for any of the three preceding years.

Its Taxable Capital Employed in Canada is $12,300,000 in 2012 and $14,600,000 in 2013.

During 2013, the Company has made a number of expenditures that qualify for investment tax credits:

- $86,000 for qualified expenditures in the Atlantic Provinces.
- $1,300,000 in current expenditures for SR&ED.
- $1,900,000 in capital expenditures on assets used for SR&ED.

Required: Determine the amount of the refund that GSE will receive as a result of earning these investment tax credits and any available carry forwards. Include in your answer any other tax consequences of these investment tax credits.

Case C

In 2012, Bow Inc. pays salaries to 10 eligible apprentices. The total amount is $250,000 with 5 apprentices paid $15,000 per apprentice and 5 apprentices paid $35,000 per apprentice. In addition, it acquires $800,000 in Class 10 assets on which a 20 percent investment tax credit is available.

Required: Describe the 2012 and 2013 tax consequences associated with making these expenditures and claiming the related investment tax credits. Include in your solution the CCA for 2012 and 2013.

Assignment Problem Fourteen - 6 (Capital Dividend Account With CEC)

Carson Ltd. was incorporated in 2001 and, since that time, it has been a Canadian controlled private company. Between the date of its corporation and December 13, 2013, it has had the following transactions that relate to the Company's capital dividend account.

- In 2002, the Company received life insurance proceeds, net of the adjusted cost base of the policy, in the amount of $186,000.

- In 2004, the Company received a capital dividend of $26,300.

- During 2008, the Company sold an unlimited life franchise for $250,000. This franchise was acquired in 2006 for $225,000. The Company took maximum amortization in both 2006 and 2007.

- In 2009, the Company paid a capital dividend of $45,200. The required election was made.

- In 2010, the Company sold a capital asset with an adjusted cost base of $184,300 for proceeds of $226,100.

- In 2012, the Company sold two parcels of land. The first parcel of land, which had an adjusted cost base of $48,600, was sold for $93,400. The second parcel of land, which had an adjusted cost base of $112,600, was sold for $108,300.

- In 2013, the Company paid a capital dividend of $16,400. The required election was made.

Required: Determine the balance in the Company's capital dividend account as of December 31, 2013. Provide a separate calculation of the income inclusion resulting from the sale of the franchise.

Assignment Problem Fourteen - 7 (Corporate Surplus Distributions)

Provide the information that is required in each of these **independent** cases.

Case 1

When Saber Ltd. was incorporated several years ago, 500,000 common shares were issued at a price of $23 per share, for a total value of $11,500,000. As the original owner wished to retire, all of the shares were sold to Milly Brant for $9,300,000. The following year, the Company redeemed 125,000 of the Saber Ltd. shares for $3,200,000. Determine the tax consequences of this redemption for Ms. Brant.

Case 2

After liquidating all of its assets and paying off all of its liabilities, a corporation is left with cash of $2,750,000. The shares of the corporation have a PUC of $75,000. The balance in the company's capital dividend account at this time is $243,000, with the company making the appropriate election to distribute this amount as a capital dividend. The adjusted cost base of the shares to their current owner is $463,000. What are the tax consequences of distributing the $2,750,000 to the corporation's only shareholder?

Case 3

Martha Stew owns all of the outstanding shares of Stew's Brews Ltd. (SBL). SBL is a Canadian controlled private corporation and its shares have a PUC of $427,000. Their adjusted cost base to Martha Stew is $562,000. During the current year SBL pays a liquidating dividend of $152,000. This was accompanied by a PUC reduction of $78,000. What are the tax consequences of this distribution to Ms. Stew?

Case 4

When Marley Ltd. was formed, it issued 179,000 shares for a total of $5,370,000. Robbie Marley purchased 15 percent of these shares at issuance.

A creditor of the Company has agreed to accept 21,000 new Marley Ltd. shares in settlement of debt with a face value of $700,000. At this time, the shares are valued at $35 per share. What are the tax consequences of this transaction for the shareholders of Marley Ltd.?

Shortly after this debt settlement, Robbie Marley sells his shares to an arm's length party for $37 per share. What are the tax consequences for Robbie resulting from this sale?

Assignment Problem Fourteen - 8
(Comprehensive Corporate Tax Payable, Associated Companies, and ITCs)

Meredith Markby Corporation (MMC) was incorporated on January 1, 2008 and is involved in the sale and manufacture of high tech detection equipment used by police forces across the country. Meredith Markby, the controlling shareholder, is a woman who is fascinated by detective shows on TV, but she doesn't know much about tax or accounting. She has asked you for assistance in preparing the corporate income tax return for 2013. The company is a CCPC throughout the 2013 fiscal year.

Meredith has prepared the following income statement for the company:

Meredith Markby Corporation
Income Statement
For the year ended December 31, 2013

Sales	$17,338,000
Expenses	
Salaries and wages	$5,758,000
Advertising and promotion	253,500
Amortization expense	905,875
Bad debt expense	75,700
Dividends paid to shareholders	235,000
Office expenses	418,975
Goodwill write off	540,000
Penalty and interest on income taxes	3,500
Cost of goods sold	9,000,000
Total Expenses	$17,190,550
Operating Income	$ 147,450
Other Income and Expenses:	
Investment income - Canadian source	271,650
Net foreign dividend income	25,000
Rental income from Alan Markby Limited	150,000
Tax refund from 2012	131,000
US Income tax paid	(87,000)
Sale of license	575,000
Gain on disposal of equipment	20,000
Net income	**$ 1,233,100**

Additional information follows:

1. The company declared and paid dividends of $235,000 during the year. Prior to paying the dividend, the company filed an election under ITA 83(2) to designate the balance in the capital dividend account at December 31, 2013, as a capital dividend. The remaining portion of the payment was designated as an eligible dividend for 2013.

2. The following information from the working paper file will be useful in determining the balance in the capital dividend account:

   2008 - Sold a depreciable capital asset with a capital cost of $97,000 for proceeds of $127,000.

   2009 - Capital dividend of $25,000 received from investment in Meredith's father's corporation. The Company discontinued operations shortly after his death and was wound up.

   2010 - Capital dividend of $15,000 paid to Meredith.

   2011 - Sold a non-depreciable capital asset with an ACB of $21,000 for proceeds of $15,000.

   2011 - Life insurance proceeds of $70,000 received by MMC on death of Meredith's father, a key employee of MMC. The adjusted cost base of his policy was $20,000.

3. The company has sales in the Canadian provinces of Ontario, BC, Manitoba, and Saskatchewan. They also have U.S. sales in the state of Michigan. The head office and manufacturing operations are in Ontario. There are employees in all provinces and states

where the company has sales who have general authority to contract on behalf of the employer. However, the company has warehouses in Ontario and Michigan only. All Canadian customers are serviced through the Ontario office and warehouse. Sales, salaries and wages in Canadian dollars for these five locations are:

	Salaries	Sales
Ontario	$4,724,000	$ 7,137,000
BC	615,000	3,657,000
Manitoba	177,000	2,958,000
Saskatchewan	127,000	2,546,000
Michigan	115,000	1,040,000
Total	$5,758,000	$17,338,000

4. The December 31, 2012 balance in the Refundable Dividend Tax on Hand account was $156,000. The dividend refund for 2012 was $42,000. All the dividends paid in 2012 were designated as eligible dividends. These totaled $126,000.

5. At the end of 2012, MMC has a GRIP of $165,000.

6. Meredith Markby owns 70% of the voting shares of MMC, and her husband owns 20%. Their 6 year old daughter, Suzie owns the final 10%. Meredith has indicated to you that she is concerned that the corporation may be considered to be associated with one or both of the following two corporations:

    a. Alan Markby Limited is owned 100% by Meredith's husband, and has taxable and active business income of $92,000. MMC rents Alan Markby Limited property at an annual cost equal to $150,000. This is to fair market rent for the property. Alan Markby Limited has only active business income.

    b. Jordan's Murder Mystery Shows Incorporated is owned 100% by Meredith's sister's husband. This company has taxable income of $452,000 in 2013.

    Meredith is willing to allocate up to $100,000 of the annual business limit to any associated company or companies. None of the companies (including MMC) has Taxable Capital Employed in Canada for 2012 or 2013 in excess of $10,000,000.

7. Included in the financial statement income is business income earned in the United States. This foreign income totals $538,000. US tax returns have been filed, and the US tax paid on this amount totals $87,000. All amounts are in Canadian dollars.

8. The company also has foreign portfolio dividend income of $37,000. $12,000 in foreign taxes has been paid on this dividend income. All amounts are in Canadian dollars. The amount was reported net of the tax paid as Net Foreign Dividend Income in the financial statements, because Meredith was unsure of the appropriate accounting treatment.

9. The following are the opening balances in undepreciated capital cost:

Class 8 - Equipment	$2,631,250
Class 1 - New building used 98% for manufacturing, acquired May 10, 2010	$4,897,532
Class 1 - Office building - acquired January 10, 2008	$653,246
Class 10 - Delivery Vehicles	$358,000

10. During the year, the company had the following additions and disposals of capital assets:

    a. Sold equipment for $100,000. The original cost of the equipment was $150,000. Its net book value at December 31, 2012 was $80,000.
    b. Purchased Class 8 assets costing $45,000.
    c. Added a new delivery vehicle to their fleet at a cost of $75,000.

   d. In 2012, the company spent $150,000 on adding a child care facility to the office building, which contained 5 licensed child care spots for the children of employees. The resulting investment tax credit was $12,500. This credit was fully utilized to reduce taxes owing in 2012.

11. The advertising and promotion line of the Income Statement includes the following items:

   a. $40,000 in clothing worn by Meredith and Alan on sales calls to demonstrate the ability of the product manufactured by the company to assist in crime solving efforts.

   b. $32,000 in meals for Meredith, Alan and Suzie. These meals were necessary because Meredith has no time to cook for her family since she is busy running the business.

   c. $120,000 for meals for the sales staff of the company while on sales calls outside of the town where the head office is located.

   d. $15,000 golf club membership fee, plus $5,000 for business meals at the golf club.

   e. $2,500 for sponsoring the local police hockey team in the international police hockey tournament.

   f. $7,000 donation to registered charities supported by the family.

12. Included in the income of the company are manufacturing and processing profits. It has been determined that manufacturing and processing profits as determined under the Income Tax Regulations are $535,000.

13. Canadian source investment income totals $271,650, and includes the following:

Interest on long term investments	$ 67,000
Capital gain on sale of shares	186,000
Eligible dividends on bank shares	18,000
Interest on surplus cash in checking account	650

14. The company has a net capital loss carryforward of $137,000 [(1/2)($274,000)].

15. During 2013, the company hired 5 apprentices. The amount paid to each apprentice during the year was $27,000. The apprentices began work on May 1, 2013, and worked for MMC for the remainder of the year. These apprentices work in "Red Seal Trades", and the contracts are registered with the Federal government.

16. MMC provides an allowance for doubtful accounts each year based on 1% of year end accounts receivable. The reserve for uncollectible accounts for tax purposes was $52,000 at the end of 2012, and your review of the situation for 2013 indicates that an appropriate reserve for 2013 would be $37,000. The allowance for doubtful accounts for 2012 was $25,000, and for 2013 it was $31,000.

17. The company filed its tax return late for 2011. As a result, penalties and interest were assessed, and paid of $3,500. This amount has been deducted in determining income for 2013.

18. When Meredith first started out in business, she purchased the assets of another company, and this purchase included goodwill of $540,000. This goodwill is reflected in the Cumulative Eligible Capital account for tax purposes, which had a balance of $281,754 at December 31, 2012. During 2013, the brand name of the old company was retired, and as a result, it was determined that the goodwill carried on the balance sheet was impaired. Meredith wasn't sure what to do with this, but she has written it off, and called it goodwill write off on the income statement.

19. During the current year, MMC sold an unlimited life licence to produce and sell one of their products in Europe, for $600,000. Legal fees associated with the sale of this license were $25,000. The net proceeds of $575,000 are included in the income statement as Other Income.

Required: Show all of the calculations used to provide the following required information, including those for which the result is nil.

A. Determine Meredith Markby Corporation's minimum Net Income For Tax Purposes and Taxable Income for the year ending December 31, 2013. In the determination of Net Income for Tax Purposes, explain why any amounts were irrelevant.

B. Determine Meredith Markby Corporation's Part I Tax Payable for the year ending December 31, 2013. Any percentages used in your calculations should be rounded to one decimal point. For the purposes of dealing with any Foreign Tax Credits that the company is eligible for, assume that the Foreign Tax Credit is equal to the foreign tax paid when determining the amount of the small business deduction, the manufacturing and processing profits deduction and the general rate reduction. For inclusion in total Tax Payable, complete the full foreign tax credit using the figures you determined for the small business deduction, the manufacturing and processing profits deduction and the general rate reduction.

C. Determine the December 31, 2013 balance in Meredith Markby Corporation's Capital Dividend Account prior to the payment of the capital dividend for 2013.

D. Determine the December 31, 2013 balance in the Meredith Markby Corporation's Refundable Dividend Tax On Hand account.

E. Determine Meredith Markby Corporation's minimum federal Tax Payable for the year ending December 31, 2013. This should include both Part I and Part IV Tax Payable, net of any dividend refund.

F. Determine the December 31, 2013 balance in Meredith Markby Corporation's GRIP.

Tax Software Assignment Problem

Tax Software Assignment Problem Fourteen - 1

Note   The following problem contains 2012 (not 2013) information as the current Profile software release does not support fiscal periods ending after April 30, 2013. Shortly after the first filing version of the 2013 Intuit ProFile software is available in January, 2014, the updated 2013 version of this problem will be available on the text-book web site at:

www.pearsoncanada.ca/byrdchen/ctp2014

RadionFaux Industries Ltd. (RIL) is a Canadian controlled private corporation, located at 123 ABC Street in Ottawa, Ontario   K4E 1A1. Its Ontario Corporation tax account number is 1234567. Its phone number is (613) 111-1111. It was incorporated on February 24, 1990 in Ottawa.

The government's Crown Copyright no longer permits us to use fake Business Numbers in software problems. To reduce the number of ProFile's error messages because of this, enter NR (for not registered) in the Business Number field.

The Company has 1,000 shares of common stock issued and outstanding, all of which are held by Margaret Ottawa (SIN 527-000-301).

Ms. Ottawa, the president and director of the Company, is the person who should be contacted with respect to matters concerning the Company's books and records. She is the authorized person as well as the signing officer.

RIL is a retailer of pet supplies. All of its sales occur within Canada. It has net assets of $235,000 on December 31, 2012. RIL also holds some of the investments that Ms. Ottawa inherited from a substantial estate two years earlier.

It owns all of the 500 common shares of OttawaFaux Inc., which holds most of Ms. Ottawa's inherited investments. The common shares have a book value of $1,200,000. OttawaFaux Inc. has the same location and phone number as RadionFaux Industries Ltd. OttawaFaux Inc. has a December 31 fiscal year end. Enter NR (for not registered) in the Business Number field for OttawaFaux Inc.

OttawaFaux Inc. is also involved in earning active business income through the breeding and sale of championship dogs. It has total assets of $2,000,000 and total revenues for 2012 of $200,000. Its Taxable Capital Employed In Canada as at December 31, 2011 was $350,000.

As at December 31, 2011, the following information applied to RIL:

Taxable Capital Employed In Canada	$4,620,000
RDTOH	5,200
Dividends Declared And Paid During 2011	Nil
GRIP Balance	11,750
Capital Dividend Account Balance	6,000

RIL complies with the requirements of the *CICA Handbook*, but does not use International Financial Reporting Standards (IFRS). For the taxation year ending December 31, 2012, RIL's Income Statement, before any deduction for income taxes, was as follows:

Sales Revenues	$580,000
Interest On Long-Term Debt	27,500
Interest Received On Foreign Bank Account (Note 1)	18,000
Eligible Dividends On Royal Bank Shares	17,500
Non-Eligible Dividends From OttawaFaux Inc. (Note 2)	42,000
Gain On Sale Of Shares (Note 3)	27,000
Total Revenues	$712,000
Cost Of Goods Sold	$208,000
Amortization Expense	122,000
Other Operating Expenses	147,000
Total Expenses (Excluding Taxes)	$477,000
Net Income (Before Taxes)	$235,000

Note 1 This interest is net of $2,000 in taxes withheld in Ireland.

Note 2 As a result of paying this $42,000 in dividends to RIL, OttawaFaux Inc. received a dividend refund of $14,000.

Note 3 On March 23, 2012, RIL sold 2,700 shares of Canadian Imperial Bank of Commerce. The common shares had cost $118,800 on June 6, 2009 and were sold for net proceeds of $145,800.

Other Information:

1. Expenses include a deduction for charitable donations to the Ottawa Civic Hospital in the amount of $5,000.

2. RIL's Expenses include penalties of $3,500 resulting from a judgment in the Tax Court Of Canada.

3. RIL reimbursed Ms. Ottawa $34,000 for business meals and entertainment for clients and suppliers during the year.

4. During the year, RIL incurred $20,000 in landscaping costs. For accounting purposes these are being treated as a capital asset, to be amortized using the straight-line method over 10 years. The related amortization is included in the Amortization Expense shown on the Income Statement.

Tax Software Assignment Problem

5. The opening UCC balances were $246,000 for Class 1, $135,000 for Class 8 and $90,000 for Class 10. The only fixed asset disposition during the year was the sale of a delivery truck. The truck had cost $35,000 and was sold for its net book value of $12,000. The only fixed asset acquisition was $52,000 in office furniture.

6. During 2012, RIL paid taxable dividends of $92,000. Of these dividends, $25,000 was designated as eligible. On September 1, 2012, RIL also elects to pay the maximum capital dividend allowable.

7. RIL allocates $60,000 of the annual business limit to OttawaFaux Inc. This is $5,000 more than OttawaFaux Inc. can utilize in 2012, but RIL cannot use the excess.

8. RIL paid no income tax instalments during 2012.

Required: Prepare the federal corporate tax return for RIL for the 2012 taxation year using the ProFile T2 corporate software program. On the ProFile schedule titled "Info", answer the Filing question "Complete return from GIFI?" with No. Ignore the GIFI requirements except as follows:

On GIFI Schedule 125:
- Input the total revenues on the line "Total Sales Of Goods And Services" (Code 8000).
- Choose "Amortization of tangible assets" (Code 8670) from the drop down menu under Operating Expenses and input the amortization expense.
- Choose "Other expenses" (Code 9270) from the drop down menu under Operating Expenses and input the Total Expenses less Amortization Expense.

On GIFI Schedule 100:
- Input the Net Income figure as "Cash and deposits" (Code 1000) in order to make the total assets equal to the total liabilities and equity.

Although this will not properly complete the GIFI statements, it will eliminate the warning messages that would otherwise be generated when the Net Income figure and Amortization Expense are input on Schedule 1. These GIFI entries will have no effect on the calculations in the tax return.

In addition, to prevent audit warnings, S141, "Notes Checklist", has to be completed. Assume there are no notes to the financial statements and answer "No" to any other relevant questions.

CHAPTER 15

Corporate Taxation And Management Decisions

The Decision To Incorporate

Basic Tax Considerations

Deferral And Reduction

15-1. One of the more important decisions facing the owner of a business is deciding whether or not the business should be incorporated. There are, of course, a number of non-tax considerations involved in this decision and these factors will be reviewed in this Chapter. At this point, however, we are concerned with the influence of corporate taxation on this decision.

15-2. The decision to incorporate, both from a legal and a tax point of view, has the effect of separating the business from its owners. This means that, in order for incorporated business income to be made available to the owner, it must go through two levels of taxation. First, the amount of Tax Payable applicable to the corporation will be determined. Then, when any after tax amounts are distributed to the owner, either as salary or as dividends, additional personal taxes will be payable on the amounts received.

15-3. This dual system of taxation may or may not be advantageous to the owner of the business. In terms of the types of tax advantage that can result from an individual incorporating business income, there are two possibilities:

Tax Reduction In some situations, the total taxes that would be paid at the combined corporate and personal level will be less when the business is incorporated than would be the case if the individual had earned the business income directly as an individual proprietor.

Tax Deferral As was noted in Paragraph 15-2, getting income from its source through a corporation and into the hands of a shareholder involves two levels of taxation. If the shareholder does not require all available income for his personal needs, after tax funds can be left in the corporation, resulting in a postponement of the second level of taxation. If the rate at which the corporation is taxed is lower than the rate at which the individual would be taxed on the direct receipt of the income, the use of a corporation provides tax deferral.

15-4.   As you probably discerned while proceeding through the earlier chapters on corporate taxation, whether the presence of a corporation will provide a deferral or reduction of taxes depends on both the type of corporation and the type of income that is being earned by that business entity. An additional important factor, as will be discussed in this Chapter, is the province in which the individual and the corporation pay income taxes.

15-5.   This means that there is no one answer to the question of whether incorporation will provide tax reduction and/or tax deferral. Given this, we will devote a major section of this Chapter to examining the various possible combinations of income types and corporate classifications in order to provide you with a general understanding of the availability of these two tax features. This material begins in Paragraph 15-12.

Using Imperfections In The Integration System

15-6.   We have previously noted that the integration provisions that are contained in Canadian tax legislation are based on the assumption that certain corporate and personal tax rates prevail. Even at the federal level, actual corporate tax rates vary from the notional rates required for effective integration.

15-7.   In addition, there are significant variations in the corporate tax rates used by the provinces. This means that it is unlikely that the combined federal/provincial rate in any given province will be equal to the notional combined rates assumed in the integration model. As it may be possible to use incorporation to take advantage of these imperfections in the integration system, it is important for you to understand how the imperfections can influence the decision to incorporate. We will provide a section which deals with this issue, beginning in Paragraph 15-60.

Income Splitting

15-8.   Even in situations where the use of a corporation neither reduces, nor defers significant amounts of taxes for a single individual, incorporation may be attractive to a family or other related group of individuals. In a typical family situation, it is fairly common to find some individuals earning amounts far in excess of the amount required to put them in the maximum personal tax bracket while, at the same time, other members of the group have incomes that leave them in a lower bracket or free of taxes altogether.

15-9.   As was discussed in Chapter 1, if some method can be found to redistribute the aggregate family or group income from high income to low income individuals, the tax savings can be significant. While we did not discuss this in Chapter 1, using a corporation can be one of the most effective approaches to achieving income splitting goals. Given this, we will provide a section which deals with this possibility beginning in Paragraph 15-91.

Other Advantages And Disadvantages

Advantages

15-10.   Other advantages that are normally associated with the use of a corporation are as follows:

> **Limited Liability**   Because a corporation is a separate legal entity, the shareholders' liability to creditors is limited to the amount that they have invested. That is, creditors of the corporation can look only to the assets of the corporation for satisfaction of their claims. However, for smaller corporations, obtaining significant amounts of financing will almost always require the owners to provide personal guarantees on any loans, making this advantage somewhat illusory for this type of company. Note, however, limited liability may still be important for a smaller corporation if it is exposed to significant product or environmental claims.

> **Lifetime Capital Gains Deduction**   Individuals who dispose of the shares of a qualified small business corporation are eligible to claim the $750,000 lifetime capital gains deduction. To qualify, a business must be a Canadian controlled private corporation with substantially all of the fair market value of its assets (at least 90 percent)

used in an active business carried on primarily in Canada (at least 50 percent) at the time of disposition. In addition, no one other than the seller, or related persons, can own the shares during the 24 months preceding the sale. During this 24 month period, more than 50 percent of the fair market value of the assets must have been used in active business carried on primarily in Canada. For a more complete discussion of this provision, see Chapter 11.

Flexibility On Timing, Type And Distribution Of Income   In the case of a corporation with a single shareholder, the owner can determine when his compensation will be paid and the form that it will take (e.g., salary vs. dividends). As mentioned previously, he can also use the corporate form to split income with family members.

Foreign Taxes   Foreign estate taxes can often be avoided by placing foreign property in a Canadian corporation.

Estate Planning   A corporation can be used in estate planning, particularly with respect to freezing the asset values of an estate (see Chapter 19).

Disadvantages

15-11.   Disadvantages that are normally associated with incorporation include the following:

Use Of Losses   An individual can deduct business and unrestricted farm losses against any other source of income, including employment and property income. If the business or farm is incorporated, such losses can only be deducted against past or future corporate income. The corporation's losses belong to the corporation and cannot be used to offset income earned by the individual shareholder. This is of particular importance to operations that are just getting started as they will frequently experience significant losses in their formative years.

Tax Credits   A corporation is not eligible for personal tax credits, such as the basic personal, tuition fee, education, age, pension, and disability tax credits.

Charitable Donations   Charitable donations provide the basis for a tax credit for individuals, largely at the maximum 29 percent federal rate. In contrast, they are a deduction in calculating Taxable Income for a corporation. If the corporate tax rate is low, they will be of less value to a corporation than they would be to an individual.

Additional Maintenance Costs   The legal, accounting, and other costs associated with maintaining a business operation will be significantly higher in the case of a corporation (e.g., the cost of filing a corporate tax return on an annual basis).

Winding Up Procedures   The complications associated with the termination of an incorporated business will be greater than would usually be the case with a proprietorship or partnership. In addition, there may be adverse tax effects on winding up.

We suggest you work Self Study Problem Fifteen-1 at this point.

Tax Reduction And Deferral

Approach

15-12.   As we have noted, whether the use of a corporation will result in a reduction or deferral of taxes will depend on the type of income being earned, as well as the type of corporation. In this section, we will examine this issue by using a basic example to consider this issue in the following situations:

• A public corporation.

• A CCPC earning active business income that is eligible for the small business deduction and income that is not eligible for the small business deduction.

- A CCPC earning investment income (net taxable capital gains and other property income, excluding dividends).
- A CCPC earning both eligible and non-eligible dividend income.

15-13.   These cases should serve to provide you with a good understanding of the ability of incorporation to provide either tax reductions or tax deferral for an individual taxpayer under current rates of corporation taxation. We also give some attention to how these conclusions will change as the scheduled corporate tax reductions are phased in over the next few years.

15-14.   To assist you in understanding this material (which is covered in detail in Chapter 13), we remind you that eligible dividends include:

- Designated dividends paid by non-CCPCs that do not have a positive Low Rate Income Pool (LRIP) balance at the time the dividend is paid.
- Designated dividends paid by CCPCs with a positive General Rate Income Pool (GRIP) at the end of the taxation year in which the dividend is paid.

Basic Example
Data On The Individual Taxpayer
15-15.   In order to consider the various results that can be achieved by incorporating a source of income, we will use a simple example in which an individual, Mr. Renaud, has access to $100,000 in income that he can either receive directly or channel through a corporation. We will assume that, before any consideration of this additional $100,000, Mr. Renaud has sufficient Taxable Income to place him in the maximum federal tax bracket of 29 percent ($135,055 for 2013). The Tax Payable on his other income is sufficient to absorb all of his personal and other tax credits.

15-16.   To illustrate the effects of incorporating different types of income, several cases will be presented with varying assumptions as to the source of this income and the type of corporation that will be established. However, before turning to these cases, we will give consideration to the various personal and corporate tax rates that will be used.

Personal Tax Rates And Tax Payable
15-17.   In these examples, we will assume that Mr. Renaud lives in a province where the maximum provincial tax rate on individuals is 16 percent. As all of Mr. Renaud's additional income will be subject to this maximum rate, his combined federal/provincial marginal rate will be 45 (29 + 16) percent. Referring to the listing of combined rates on ordinary income in Paragraph 4-23 of the text, the 16 percent provincial rate is roughly the average provincial rate for individuals in the top income bracket.

15-18.   This 45 percent rate is applicable to the direct receipt of income. This means that, if Mr. Renaud receives the $100,000 in income without channeling it through a corporation, taxes of $45,000 will be paid and $55,000 will be retained.

15-19.   If the income is channeled through a corporation, the situation becomes more complex. Taxes must be paid at the corporate level, leaving only part of the total income available for distribution to shareholders. When this after tax amount is distributed to the shareholders, the amount of dividends received must be grossed up, with this amount providing the basis for a credit against taxes payable. The amounts involved will depend on whether the dividends are non-eligible (e.g., paid by a CCPC out of income that has benefited from the small business deduction), or eligible (e.g. paid by a non-CCPC out of fully taxed income):

Non-Eligible Dividends These dividends are grossed up by 25 percent and benefit from a federal dividend tax credit of 2/3 of the gross up. We will assume that Mr. Renaud lives in a province where the dividend tax credit on non-eligible dividends is 22 percent of the dividend gross up (the 2013 average for the 10 provinces).

Eligible Dividends These dividends are grossed up by 38 percent and benefit from a federal dividend tax credit of 6/11 (54.5%) of the gross up. We will assume that Mr. Renaud lives in a province where the dividend tax credit on eligible dividends is 37 percent of the dividend gross up (the 2013 average for the 10 provinces).

15-20. Using these gross up and tax credit amounts, the rates applicable to Mr. Renaud on eligible and non-eligible dividends can be calculated as follows:

Personal Tax On Dividends	Non-Eligible Dividends	Eligible Dividends
Provincial Dividend Tax Credit	22.0%	37.0%
Dividends Received	100.0%	100.0%
Gross Up	25.0%	38.0%
Taxable Dividends	125.0%	138.0%
Times The Combined Federal/Provincial Tax Rate	45.0%	45.0%
Equals: Combined Federal/Provincial Tax Rate On Dividends Received	56.3%	62.1%
Less: Dividend Tax Credit [(2/3 + 22%)(25%)]	(22.2%)	
Less: Dividend Tax Credit [(6/11 + 37%)(38%)]		(34.8%)
Effective Personal Tax Rate On Dividends Received	34.1%	27.3%

15-21. For use in our examples, we will round these rates to 34 percent and 27 percent, respectively.

Corporate Tax Rates

15-22. In making the required calculations, we will use the corporate federal tax rates that apply for the 2013 calendar year. With respect to provincial rates, we will use 3 percent for income eligible for the small business deduction and 12 percent for other income. These rates are roughly the average of the rates that are used in the 10 provinces. When these provincial rates are added to the corresponding federal rates, the combined rates are 14 percent (11% + 3%) for income eligible for the small business deduction and 27 percent (15% + 12%) for other income. The following table provides the rates that will be used in our examples:

General Part I Tax Rate	38%
Federal Tax Abatement	10%
General Rate Reduction (GRR)	13%
Refundable Tax On Investment Income Of A CCPC (ART)	6-2/3%
Federal Small Business Deduction	17%
Provincial Tax Rates	
Income Eligible For Federal Small Business Deduction	3%
Income Not Eligible For Federal Small Business Deduction	12%
Refundable Portion Of Part I Tax On Investment Income	26-2/3%
Refundable Part IV Tax	33-1/3%

15-23. Note that the general rate reduction is not applicable to income that benefits from either the small business deduction or the M&P deduction. In addition, it is not applicable to aggregate investment income of a CCPC which attracts the 6-2/3 percent Additional Refundable Tax (ART).

15-24. We will apply this basic information, in a number of different situations, in order to examine the question of whether the incorporation of $100,000 in income will serve to either reduce or defer taxes for an individual taxpayer.

Public Corporation
M&P Deduction
15-25. As discussed in Chapter 12, both the M&P deduction and the GRR are at the same rate. As these two provisions cannot be used simultaneously, the effective federal tax rate will not be altered by the use of the M&P deduction. Given this, we will not give separate attention to situations where a public corporation is earning income that is eligible for the M&P deduction. Keep in mind, however, that companies will continue to make the M&P calculation in those provinces where there is a favourable provincial rate for this type of income.

General Results
15-26. With only $100,000 of income, there is no possibility that Mr. Renaud would be in a position to establish a public company. However, this case does serve to illustrate a simple calculation of corporate taxes. In addition, this same tax calculation would apply to a CCPC on amounts of active business income in excess of the CCPC's allocated annual business limit.

15-27. As discussed in Chapter 13, dividends paid by non-CCPCs, a category that includes public companies, will generally be designated as eligible. There will be situations, however, where a public corporation has an LRIP. While this raises the possibility that at least some of the dividends paid by such a company would be non-eligible, we do not feel that this situation is of sufficient importance that an illustration of the tax reduction and deferral results is warranted. It should be fairly obvious to you that for non-eligible dividends, the tax reduction results would be significantly worse than those illustrated in the following calculations.

Public Corporation

Federal Tax [(38%)($100,000)]	$38,000
Federal Tax Abatement [(10%)($100,000)]	(10,000)
General Rate Reduction [(13%)($100,000)]	(13,000)
Federal Tax Payable	$15,000
Provincial Tax Payable [(12%)($100,000)]	12,000
Corporate Tax Payable	$27,000
Corporate Business Income	$100,000
Corporate Tax Payable	(27,000)
Maximum Eligible Dividend Payable	$ 73,000
Personal Tax On Eligible Dividends [(27%)($73,000)]	(19,710)
Income Retained By The Individual	$ 53,290
After Tax Retention - With Corporation	$ 53,290
After Tax Retention - Without Corporation	(55,000)
Advantage (Disadvantage) With Corporation	($ 1,710)

Analysis
15-28. If the $100,000 had been received directly, $55,000 [($100,000)(1 - .45)] would be retained, an amount greater than the $53,290 that is retained when the $100,000 is flowed through a public corporation. In terms of total taxes, incorporation is clearly not desirable.

15-29. However, there is a deferral of tax on income that is left within the corporation. Taxes at the corporate level are $27,000, significantly less than the $45,000 that would be paid on the direct receipt of income. There is some question as to whether this amount of deferral would justify the payment of an additional $1,710 in taxes.

15-30. More to the point is that, in real world terms, deferral is not an issue for shareholders of publicly traded companies. In the case of private corporations with a single shareholder or a small shareholder group, these individuals can control the extent to which their corporation distributes resources. If they do not have an immediate need for funds, tax deferral can be achieved by leaving resources in their corporation.

15-31. This is not the case with large publicly traded companies. Their dividend decisions are based on a large number of factors, including corporate cash needs and the maximization of share values. The cash flow needs of individual shareholders would rarely be at the top of this list.

Integration And Eligible Dividends

15-32. The preceding example is based on the public corporation paying eligible dividends. The government's stated goal in bringing in the eligible dividends legislation was to improve integration by lowering the total corporate and personal taxes paid on income flowed through a public company. The calculations in Paragraph 15-27 make it clear that, at current corporate tax rates, this stated goal has not been achieved.

15-33. As discussed in Chapter 7, the gross up and tax credit procedures on eligible dividends are based on a notional corporate tax rate of 27.54 percent. As combined federal/provincial rates for 2013 average 27 percent, which is close to the required rate for integration to be effective, corporate tax rates are not the main problem.

15-34. The problem is with the dividend tax credit rates. Effective integration requires the combined federal/provincial tax credit to be equal to the gross up. This means that, given the federal rate of 6/11, the provincial dividend tax credit would have to be 5/11 or 45.5 percent. In actual fact, the average provincial dividend tax credit rate for 2013 is 37 percent, with the lowest rate at 23 percent and the highest rate at 44 percent.

Exercise Fifteen - 1

Subject: Eligible Dividends And Integration

Ms. Jennifer Ashley is the owner of a number of successful CCPCs. For 2013, she has sufficient income that any additional personal income will be taxed at a combined federal/provincial rate of 45 percent. She lives in a province where the provincial tax credit on eligible dividends is equal to 44 percent of the gross up. Ms. Ashley has made an investment in a business venture that she anticipates will generate $100,000 of active business income during the coming year. If she retains personal ownership of this investment, she will retain $55,000 [($100,000)(1 - 45%)] after taxes. If she transfers this investment to a new private corporation, it would not be allocated any amount of the small business deduction and its income would be taxed at a combined federal/provincial rate of 25 percent (15% + 10%). She has asked your advice as to whether she should retain the investment personally, or transfer it to a new corporation. Provide the information required by Ms. Ashley.

End of Exercise. Solution available in Study Guide.

CCPC - Active Business Income

General Results

15-35. A CCPC can be subject to two different tax rates on its active business income. A low rate is available on up to $500,000 of income that is eligible for the small business deduction, with a higher tax rate assessed on income that is not eligible for this valuable deduction. With respect to the provinces, there is a similar dual rate system. In addition, we will have to take into consideration the fact that dividends that have been paid out of income that has benefited from the small business deduction cannot be designated as eligible dividends.

15-36. We will continue to use the Mr. Renaud example from Paragraph 15-15 to illustrate the tax consequences of applying these two rates. While continuing to use the basic data from this example, we will consider two different cases:

Case One   In Case One, we will assume that the corporate income is eligible for the small business deduction. This means that dividends that are received by Mr. Renaud will be non-eligible and subject to tax at a rate of 34 percent (see Paragraph 15-21).

Case Two   In Case Two, we will assume that none of the corporate income is eligible for the small business deduction (the full amount has been allocated to an associated corporation). This means that the dividends that are received by Mr. Renaud can be designated as eligible and subject to tax at a rate of 27 percent. You will note that the results in this case are identical to those for a public corporation (see Paragraph 15-27).

Active Business Income Of CCPC	Case One SBD Deduction	Case Two No SBD
Federal Tax [(38%)($100,000)]	$ 38,000	$ 38,000
Federal Tax Abatement [(10%)($100,000)]	(10,000)	(10,000)
Small Business Deduction [(17%)($100,000)]	(17,000)	N/A
General Rate Reduction [(13%)($100,000)]	N/A	(13,000)
Federal Tax Payable	$ 11,000	$ 15,000
Provincial Tax Payable:		
At 3 Percent	3,000	N/A
At 12 Percent	N/A	12,000
Corporate Tax Payable	$ 14,000	$ 27,000
Corporate Business Income	$100,000	$100,000
Corporate Tax Payable	(14,000)	(27,000)
Maximum Dividend Payable	$ 86,000	$ 73,000
Personal Tax At 34 Percent	(29,240)	N/A
Personal Tax At 27 Percent	N/A	(19,710)
Income Retained By The Individual	$ 56,760	$ 53,290
After Tax Retention - With Corporation	$ 56,760	$ 53,290
After Tax Retention - Without Corporation	(55,000)	(55,000)
Advantage (Disadvantage) With Corporation	$ 1,760	($ 1,710)

Analysis

15-37.   As can be seen in the preceding table, there is a tax advantage associated with using a corporation to earn income that benefits from the small business deduction. After tax retention is $1,760 more when the $100,000 of income is flowed through a corporation.

15-38.   More importantly, in this situation the use of a corporation provides substantial tax deferral, whether or not the income benefits from the small business deduction. On income that benefits from this deduction, the tax that is assessed at the corporate level is $14,000, well below the $45,000 that would be applicable if Mr. Renaud had received the income directly. Even on the more heavily taxed ineligible income, the corporate taxes of $27,000 are still below the $45,000 that would be applicable on the direct receipt of the $100,000.

15-39.   It is unlikely that it would be worthwhile to incorporate a business purely for the small tax advantage that arises when the small business deduction is available. However, it could be very advantageous in terms of tax deferral. It is important to note, however, that this advantage is only available on income that is left in the corporation. If the individual's personal needs require all of the income that is produced by the business, the deferral advantage is lost.

15-40.   A further point related to tax deferral is sometimes overlooked. Any income that is left in the corporation should not be left idle. If it is not needed in the principal activities, it is likely that it will be invested in assets that will produce investment income. If this income is taxed as investment income, the result will be prepayment of taxes at the corporate level. This will be illustrated in a later example when we look at the taxation of investment income received by a Canadian controlled private corporation.

"Bonusing Down" Active Business Income

15-41.   A traditional tax planning technique for owners of CCPCs that have active business income in excess of their annual business limit is to "bonus down". As our example has shown, income that is eligible for the small business deduction benefits from significant tax deferral, as well as a modest tax savings. In contrast, if a CCPC's Taxable Income does not benefit from the small business deduction, the after tax retention of this excess income will be lower than that from direct receipt of the income. As shown in Paragraph 15-36, the after tax retention on $100,000 of income that is not eligible for the small business deduction is $1,710 less than if the income is received directly.

15-42.   When it is likely that a CCPC will have Taxable Income in excess of its annual business limit ($500,000 if there are no associated companies), the simple solution is for the owner of the CCPC to pay himself sufficient additional salary that the corporation's Taxable Income will be reduced to the amount of income that is eligible for the small business deduction.

> **Example**   In our example, if Mr. Renaud had a CCPC with active business income of $600,000, paying additional salary of $100,000 would result in after tax retention of $55,000 on receipt of this salary. This, of course, is $1,710 higher than the $53,290 that would be paid if the $100,000 ($600,000 - $500,000) that is not eligible for the small business deduction was taxed at the corporate level, with the residual amount being paid to Mr. Renaud as eligible dividends.

15-43.   At one point in time, there was concern as to whether such bonusing down arrangements would be attacked by the CRA using the General Anti-Avoidance legislation. Fortunately, this is not the case. In Income Tax Technical News #30 (May 21, 2004), the CRA explained their policy of not challenging the reasonableness of remuneration to a shareholder who is active in the operations of the business.

> The general purpose of the policy is to provide flexibility to a CCPC and its active shareholder/managers to take advantage of marginal tax rates by reducing the corporation's taxable income to, or below, the small business deduction limit through the payment of salaries and bonuses from income derived from normal business operations, and to provide certainty as to the taxable status of the transactions.

15-44.   Given this statement, it seems clear that bonusing down to a level that will eliminate all corporate Taxable Income that is not eligible for the small business deduction will generally not be questioned by the CRA.

15-45.   As a final point here, many owner-managers may not be convinced that bonusing down is a good idea. The problem is that bonusing down involves paying taxes out of the owner-manager's personal funds. It is not uncommon to encounter individuals who, even in situations where there is a clear cut tax advantage to using this procedure, will simply refuse to make the required salary payments. While this is usually not a rational decision, it appears to reflect a greater level of comfort for an owner-manager when he does not have to pay the taxes directly out of his personal assets.

Electing Out Of The Small Business Deduction

15-46.   ITA 89(11) allows a CCPC to make an election not to be a CCPC. The good news is that making this election will allow the corporation to designate its dividends as eligible. The bad news is that it will lose the small business deduction.

15-47.   If this election is made, the tax reduction and deferral results would be the same as those shown in Paragraph 15-36 for the no small business deduction case. While there may be some situations where this election may be useful, the fact that it appears to have a significant tax cost would suggest that its application would not be common.

Exercise Fifteen - 2

Subject: Incorporation Of Active Business Income

Keith Slater has an unincorporated business that he anticipates will have active business income of $126,000 during the coming year. He has employment income in excess of $200,000, with additional amounts subject to a provincial tax rate of 14 percent. The provincial dividend tax credit is equal to one-third of the dividend gross up for all dividends. Also in his province of residence, the corporate tax rate is 3 percent on income eligible for the small business deduction and 12 percent on other income. Mr. Slater has asked your advice as to whether he should incorporate this business. Advise him with respect to any tax deferral that could be available on income left in the corporation and on any tax savings that could be available if all of the income is paid out as dividends.

End of Exercise. Solution available in Study Guide.

CCPC - Investment Income Other Than Dividends

15-48.   As was discussed in Chapter 13, the aggregate investment income of a CCPC is taxed at full corporate rates. Neither the small business deduction nor the general rate reduction is available to offset these rates. In addition, there is an additional refundable tax under ITA 123.3 (the ART) equal to 6-2/3 percent of investment income.

15-49.   To offset this high level of taxation, a dividend refund is available on dividends paid at a rate of $1 for each $3 of dividends paid.   Note, however, investment income that is eligible for a refund does not add to the corporation's GRIP balance. This means that it does not contribute to the corporation's ability to pay dividends that are eligible for the enhanced gross up and tax credit procedures.

15-50.   Continuing our Mr. Renaud example from Paragraph 15-15, after tax retention on $100,000 of investment income received by a CCPC, compared to the direct receipt of investment income, would be as follows:

Investment Income Of CCPC

Federal Tax [(38%)($100,000)]	$ 38,000
Additional Refundable Tax [(6-2/3%)($100,000)]	6,667
Federal Tax Abatement [(10%)($100,000)]	(10,000)
Federal Tax Payable	$ 34,667
Provincial Tax Payable [(12%)($100,000)]	12,000
Corporate Tax Payable	$ 46,667
Corporate Investment Income	$100,000
Corporate Tax Payable	(46,667)
Net Corporate Income Before Dividend Refund	$ 53,333
Maximum Dividend Refund (See Note)	26,667
Maximum Dividend Payable	$ 80,000
Personal Tax On Non-Eligible Dividends At 34 Percent	(27,200)
Income Retained By The Individual	$ 52,800
After Tax Retention - With Corporation	$ 52,800
After Tax Retention - Without Corporation	(55,000)
Advantage (Disadvantage) With Corporation	($ 2,200)

Note The dividend refund is the lesser of one-third of dividends paid and the balance in the RDTOH account. One-third of the $80,000 dividend is $26,667. The RDTOH balance would also be $26,667 [(26-2/3%)($100,000)].

15-51. In terms of either tax deferral or tax savings, there does not appear to be any advantage associated with using a CCPC to receive investment income. Not only is there no deferral, there is a prepayment of taxes when a corporation is used ($46,667 vs. $45,000). In addition, the total tax bill on the flow through of the income is $2,200 higher using this approach.

Exercise Fifteen - 3

Subject: Incorporation Of Interest Income

David Slater has investments that he anticipates will earn interest income of $126,000 during the coming year. He has employment income in excess of $200,000, with additional amounts subject to a provincial tax rate of 14 percent. The provincial dividend tax credit is equal to one-third of the dividend gross up for all dividends. Also in his province of residence, the corporate tax rate is 3 percent on income eligible for the small business deduction and 12 percent on other income. Mr. Slater has asked your advice as to whether he should transfer these investments to a corporation in which he would own all of the shares. Advise him with respect to any tax deferral that could be available on income left in the corporation and on any tax savings that could be available if all of the income is paid out as dividends.

End of Exercise. Solution available in Study Guide.

We suggest you work Self Study Problem Fifteen-2 at this point.

CCPC - Dividend Income

Possible Sources Of Dividend Income

15-52. A CCPC can only designate dividends as eligible to the extent that it has a balance in its GRIP. Given this, it is important to understand the effect of various types of dividends received on this balance. Dividend receipts that increase this balance enhance the CCPC's ability to designate its dividends as eligible — dividends received that do not change this balance do not provide a basis for increased payments of eligible dividends. In somewhat simplified form, the various possibilities here are as follows:

Eligible Portfolio Dividends These dividends will be subject to Part IV tax. However, because they are eligible dividends, they will be added to the CCPC's GRIP balance.

Non-Eligible Portfolio Dividends These dividends will be subject to Part IV tax. They will not be added to the CCPC's GRIP balance.

Connected Company Dividends - Dividend Refund These dividends will be subject to Part IV tax. As these dividends were paid out of the investment income of a CCPC, they will not be added to the recipient CCPC's GRIP.

Connected Company Dividends - No Dividend Refund These dividends will not be subject to Part IV tax. The fact that there is no refund generally means that the connected company paid these amounts out of income that benefitted from the small business deduction. This means they will not be added to the recipient CCPC's GRIP balance.

Analysis

15-53.   Recalling that Mr. Renaud would pay taxes on eligible dividends received at a rate of 27 percent (see Paragraph 15-21), his after tax retention on the direct receipt of $100,000 of these dividends would be $73,000 [($100,000)(1 - .27)]. His rate on non-eligible dividends is 34 percent (see Paragraph 15-21) and this would result in after tax retention of $66,000 [($100,000)(1 - .34)]. A comparison of this retention with the after tax results from using a corporation would be as follows:

Dividend Income Of CCPC	Eligible Portfolio Dividends	Non-Eligible Portfolio Dividends	Connected With Refund	Connected No Refund
Corporate Dividend Income	$100,000	$100,000	$100,000	$100,000
Part IV Tax Payable At 33-1/3%	(33,333)	(33,333)	(33,333)	N/A
Net Corporate Income Before Dividend Refund	$ 66,667	$ 66,667	$ 66,667	$100,000
Dividend Refund ($1/$3)	33,333	33,333	33,333	N/A
Maximum Dividend Payable	$100,000	$100,000	$100,000	$100,000
Personal Tax On:				
Eligible Dividends At 27%	(27,000)			
Non-Eligible Dividends At 34%	N/A	(34,000)	(34,000)	(34,000)
Income Retained By Individual	$ 73,000	$ 66,000	$ 66,000	$ 66,000
After Tax Retention:				
With Corporation	$ 73,000	$ 66,000	$ 66,000	$ 66,000
Without Corporation	(73,000)	(66,000)	(66,000)	(66,000)
Advantage (Disadvantage)	Nil	Nil	Nil	Nil

15-54.   In all cases, the dividends that can flow through to the investor total the full $100,000 that was received by the corporation. As a result, the total Tax Payable on dividends is the same whether the investment is held personally or in a corporation.

15-55.   The Part IV tax does, however, influence the conclusions on tax deferral. If the dividends are subject to Part IV tax, this 33-1/3 percent tax is higher than the 27 percent tax rate on eligible dividends received by Mr. Renaud, and slightly less than the 34 percent tax rate applicable to non-eligible dividends. As a result, there is a prepayment of taxes on eligible dividends that are flowed through a corporation.

15-56.   The situation is different in the absence of a Part IV tax in that no taxes will be assessed on dividends received at the corporate level. This, of course, provides for a significant deferral of Tax Payable on dividends not subject to Part IV tax.

Conclusions On Tax Reductions And Deferrals

15-57.   The results that we have calculated in the preceding cases can be summarized as follows:

	Corporate Taxes Before Dividend Refund	After Tax Retention On Flow Through
Public Corporation ($100,000 Of Income) (Paragraph 15-27):	$27,000	$53,290
CCPC ($100,000 Of Active Business Income):		
Eligible For SBD (Paragraph 15-36)	$14,000	$56,760
Not Eligible For SBD (Paragraph 15-36)	27,000	53,290
CCPC ($100,000 Of Interest Income):		
Investment Income (Paragraph 15-50)	$46,667	$52,800

	Corporate Taxes Before Dividend Refund	After Tax Retention On Flow Through
CCPC ($100,000 Of Dividend Income):		
Eligible Portfolio Dividends (Paragraph 15-53)	$33,333	$73,000
Non-Eligible Portfolio Dividends (Paragraph 15-53)	33,333	66,000
Connected With Refund (Paragraph 15-53)	33,333	66,000
Connected No Refund (Paragraph 15-53)	Nil	66,000

15-58.   The conclusions reached can be summarized as follows:

Tax Reduction Available   As illustrated previously, Mr. Renaud is subject to taxes on the direct receipt of income, other than dividends, at a rate of 45 percent, while his rate on the direct receipt of dividends is 27 percent (eligible) or 34 percent (non-eligible). This means that his after tax retention resulting from the direct receipt of income would be:

- $55,000 On $100,000 Of Business Or Interest Income
- $73,000 On $100,000 Of Eligible Dividend Income
- $66,000 On $100,000 Of Non-Eligible Dividend Income

Comparing these amounts to those in the preceding table we find tax reduction only in the case of a CCPC earning income that is eligible for the small business deduction. The retention of $56,760 is $1,760 larger than the $55,000 that would be retained on direct receipt of income.

When a public company is involved, the use of a corporation results in the payment of $1,710 more taxes and correspondingly less retention ($53,290 vs. $55,000). The same $1,710 shortfall results when a CCPC is earning active business income that is not eligible for the small business deduction. The situation is even worse for investment income earned by a CCPC. The shortfall here is $2,200 ($52,800 vs. $55,000).

In the case of dividend income received by a CCPC, the after tax results are the same whether the income is received directly or flowed through a corporation.

Tax Deferral Available   Tax deferral occurs when income is not distributed to shareholders and taxes paid at the corporate level are less than those that would be paid if the income was received directly by the shareholder. On direct receipt of relevant amounts, Mr. Renaud would pay the following amounts in income tax:

- $45,000 On $100,000 Of Business Or Interest Income
- $27,000 On $100,000 Of Eligible Dividend Income
- $34,000 On $100,000 Of Non-Eligible Dividend Income

Comparing these amounts to the corporate tax amounts in the preceding table, we find that there is tax deferral in all cases except those involving interest or eligible dividends earned by a CCPC. The corporate taxes on $100,000 of interest income earned by a CCPC total $46,667, which is more than the $45,000 that would be paid on the direct receipt of the interest income. In the cases where Part IV tax is applicable, the $33,333 that would be required when that tax is assessed, is larger than the $27,000 that would be paid on the direct receipt of eligible dividends. However, it is slightly smaller than the $34,000 that would be paid on the direct receipt of non-eligible dividends.

The most significant amounts of deferral are available to a CCPC earning active business income eligible for the small business deduction, or dividend income that is not subject to Part IV tax. In the case of income eligible for the small business deduction, taxes at the corporate level are $14,000, $31,000 less than the $45,000 that would have been paid on the direct receipt of this income.

Even if a CCPC has active business income that is not eligible for the small business deduction, taxes on $100,000 of this additional income would only be $27,000, $18,000 less than the amount payable on direct receipt of this amount of income. The tax deferral is the same $18,000 in the case of public companies.

There is also deferral in the case of dividend income when it is not subject to Part IV tax. However, for dividends to not be subject to Part IV tax, they must be received from a connected corporation that did not receive a dividend refund as a result of their payment. This would generally involve payment from a CCPC earning business income. This means that deferral would have been available at the level of the paying corporation, without the use of an additional corporation to receive the dividends.

15-59.   These conclusions are based on assumed provincial personal and corporate tax rates as outlined previously. While the rates we have used are within the range of current actual rates, the use of other rates will produce different results. As these differences can be important, we will give some attention to this issue in the next section of this Chapter.

Exercise Fifteen - 4

Subject: Incorporation Of Interest And Dividend Income

One of your clients has asked your advice on whether he should transfer a group of investments to a new Canadian controlled private corporation that can be established to hold them. He anticipates that the transferred investments will have the following amounts of income during the 2013 taxation year:

Eligible Dividends On Portfolio Investments	$46,000
Non-Eligible Dividends From 100 Percent Owned Subsidiary	
(A Dividend Refund Of $29,000 Will Be Received by The Payor)	87,000
Interest Income	32,000

Although he has employment income of over $200,000, your client needs all of the income that is produced by these investments as he has newborn quintuplets. On additional amounts of income, your client is subject to a provincial tax rate of 15 percent. The provincial dividend tax credit is equal to one-third of the dividend gross up for eligible and non-eligible dividends. The corporation will be subject to a provincial tax rate of 4 percent on income eligible for the small business deduction and 12 percent on other income. The corporation will make the maximum eligible dividend designation. Provide the requested advice and explain your conclusions.

Exercise Fifteen - 5

Subject: Incorporation Of Capital Gains

One of your clients has asked your advice on whether she should transfer a group of investments to a new corporation that can be established to hold them. The corporation will be a Canadian controlled private corporation and she anticipates that, during the coming year, the market value of these investments will increase by $92,000. No other income will be generated by the investments. Your client has employment income in excess of $200,000 and will sell these investments by the end of the year to finance her trip across Canada by bicycle. The corporation will be subject to a provincial tax rate of 3 percent on income eligible for the small business deduction and 12 percent on other income. On additional personal income, your client is subject to a provincial tax rate of 16 percent. The provincial dividend tax credit is equal to one-third of the dividend gross up for all dividends. Provide the requested advice, including an explanation of your conclusions.

End of Exercises. Solutions available in Study Guide.

We suggest you work Self Study Problem Fifteen-3 at this point.

Provincial Taxes And Integration

Introduction

15-60.   We have presented a number of different cases dealing with the question of whether it is better, both in terms of tax reduction and tax deferral, for an individual to receive income directly or, alternatively, channel that income through a corporation. In doing so, we have given consideration to both the type of income being earned, and whether the corporation would be a public company or, alternatively, a CCPC.

15-61.   The conclusions that we reached were presented in Paragraph 15-58. We found that, while in many of the cases the use of a corporation provided some degree of tax deferral, there was only one scenario that provided a reduction in taxes.

15-62.   It is important to note, however, that all of our conclusions were based on calculations that used average provincial tax rates. As discussed in other Chapters of this text, there are wide variations in all of these provincial amounts. Further, these variations can provide results that are different than those summarized in Paragraphs 15-57 and 15-58. For example, if a province legislates a tax free period of time for corporations that move within its jurisdiction, this will make the use of a corporation more attractive in that province.

15-63.   This section will be concerned with how variations in provincial tax rates can influence the decision to incorporate. In doing so, we will not attempt to delineate every possible combination of rates, types of income, and corporate classification. With 10 provinces and 3 territories, several different types of income, three different rates to consider, as well as two different classifications of corporations, there are literally hundreds of possible combinations. Given this, our goal will be to help you understand how changes in each of the provincial rates will act to influence conclusions on the use of a corporation for tax deferral or tax reduction purposes.

Tax Deferral

15-64.   The analysis of using a corporation to provide tax deferral is very straightforward. If the combined federal/provincial tax rate on corporations is less than the combined federal/provincial tax rate on individuals, the use of a corporation provides for deferral. Some examples of this analysis are as follows:

> **Alberta CCPC Earning Active Business Income**   The combined federal/provincial tax rate on the corporation would be 14 percent. For an Alberta resident individual in the maximum tax bracket, the combined federal/provincial rate would be 39 percent. In this case, the use of a corporation would clearly provide deferral.

> **Manitoba CCPC Earning Investment Income**   The combined federal/provincial tax rate on the corporation would be 46.7 percent. For a Manitoba resident individual in the maximum tax bracket, the combined federal/provincial rate would be 46.4 percent. In this case, the use of a corporation would not provide deferral.

> **British Columbia Public Corporation**   The combined federal/provincial tax rate on the corporation would be 25 percent. For a British Columbia resident individual in the maximum tax bracket, the combined federal/provincial rate would be 43.7 percent. In this case, the use of a corporation would clearly provide deferral.

15-65.   We would remind you not to look at the deferral issue in isolation from other considerations. For example, in the case of the British Columbia public corporation, the available deferral is not without cost. In this case, the use of the corporation would result in significant additional taxes once the income is distributed out of the corporation. This would not be the case with the Alberta CCPC. When there is a possibility that the income will be distributed out of the corporation in the near future, both tax deferral and tax reduction must be considered.

Provincial Taxes And Integration

Tax Reduction

Introduction

15-66.   The question of whether a corporation can be used to reduce tax involves a more complex analysis. In looking at the after tax retention when income is received directly, only the combined federal/provincial tax rate on individuals is relevant. However, in looking at after tax retention of income that is flowed through a corporation, three factors must be considered:

1. The combined federal/provincial tax rate on individuals.
2. The combined federal/provincial tax rate on corporations.
3. The combined federal/provincial dividend tax credit.

15-67.   As we will demonstrate in the next section, the first of these factors is not influential in this analysis. For any given combination of corporate tax rates and dividend tax credit rates, the conclusion on whether a corporation can be used to reduce taxes will be the same, without regard to the tax rate on individuals.

15-68.   The real determinate here is the relationship between the combined corporate tax rate and the combined dividend tax credit. As our later analysis will show, if the combined dividend tax credit exceeds the combined corporate taxes paid, the use of a corporation will reduce taxes. Alternatively, if the credit is less than the corporate taxes, direct receipt of income will be preferable.

Provincial Rates On Individuals

15-69.   Maximum provincial tax rates on individuals range from a low of 39 percent in Alberta to a high of 50 percent in Nova Scotia. Note, however, variations in these rates influence both the direct receipt of income and the amounts that are flowed through a corporation. That is, a high tax rate on individuals will reduce after tax retention on both the direct receipt of income, as well as on the after tax retention of income flowed through a corporation. Correspondingly, a low tax rate on individuals will increase both types of after tax retention.

15-70.   What this means is that, for any specific combination of corporate tax rate and dividend tax credit rate, the tax rate applicable to individuals will not alter the conclusion on whether the use of a corporation will serve to reduce taxes. While the amount of the advantage or disadvantage associated with the use of a corporation will vary with the tax rate on individuals, the conclusion on the ability of a corporation to reduce taxes will not. This is illustrated by the following example.

Example   A CCPC has $100,000 of active business income that will be taxed at a combined federal/provincial rate of 15 percent. The provincial dividend tax credit on non-eligible dividends is equal to one-third of the gross up. We will consider two cases, the first based on the assumption that the shareholders are taxed at a combined federal/provincial rate of 39 percent (29% federal, plus 10% provincial), the second based on the assumption that the shareholders are taxed at a combined federal/provincial rate of 50 percent (29% federal, plus 21% provincial).

Analysis   If the individuals received the $100,000 directly, their after tax retention would be $61,000 [($100,000)(1 - .39)] and $50,000 [($100,000)(1 - .50)], respectively. The after retention if the income is flowed through a corporation would be as follows:

Comparison - Rates For Individuals	39% Rate	50% Rate
Corporate Income	$100,000	$100,000
Corporate Taxes At 15 Percent	(15,000)	(15,000)
Available For Dividends	$ 85,000	$ 85,000

	39% Rate	**50% Rate**
Non-Eligible Dividends Received	$ 85,000	$ 85,000
Gross Up (25%)	21,250	21,250
Taxable Dividends	$106,250	$106,250
Individual Tax Rate	39%	50%
Taxes Before Dividend Tax Credit	$ 41,438	$ 53,125
Dividend Tax Credit (Equal Gross Up)	(21,250)	(21,250)
Individual Taxes	$ 20,188	$ 31,875
Dividends Received	$ 85,000	$ 85,000
Individual Taxes	(20,188)	(31,875)
After Tax Retention	$ 64,812	$ 53,125
After Tax Retention With Corporation	$ 64,812	$ 53,125
Direct Receipt Retention	(61,000)	(50,000)
Advantage With Corporation	$ 3,812	$ 3,125

15-71.   This example involves a low corporate tax rate of 15 percent, a factor that favours the use of a corporation. That is why, in this example, the conclusion on the use of a corporation is the same at either the lowest maximum provincial tax rate on individuals in Canada, or the highest maximum tax rate. While the amount of the advantage varies with the provincial tax rate on individuals, the conclusion that a corporation can be used to reduce taxes does not.

Provincial Dividend Tax Credit And Provincial Corporate Tax Rates

15-72.   As can be seen in the preceding example, the major determinate of whether the use of a corporation will provide tax reduction is the relationship between the combined federal and provincial taxes paid at the corporate level, and the combined federal/provincial dividend tax credit. As the federal components of these values do not vary, the provincial rates become the determining factor.

15-73.   The rules here can be stated fairly simply:

Favourable To Incorporation   If the combined dividend tax credit exceeds the combined taxes paid at the corporate level, the use of a corporation will reduce taxes and provide a higher level of after tax retention.

Unfavourable To Incorporation   If the combined dividend tax credit is less than the combined taxes paid at the corporate level, the use of a corporation will increase taxes and reduce the amount of after tax retention.

Examples - Effects Of Provincial Rates On Integration

Data

15-74.   The range of values in the 10 provinces for provincial corporate tax rates and provincial dividend tax credit rates are as follows:

Corporate Tax Rates   The provincial rates for public companies range from 10 percent to 16 percent. When these are combined with the federal rate of 15 percent, the combined rates range from 25 percent to 31 percent.

The provincial rates for CCPCs earning income eligible for the small business deduction range from zero percent to 8 percent. When these are combined with the federal rate of 11 percent, the combined rates range from 11 percent to 19 percent.

Dividend Tax Credit Rates   The provincial rates for eligible dividends range from 23 percent of the gross up to 44 percent. When combined with the federal rate of 6/11 of the gross up, the combined rates range from 77.5 percent of the gross up to 98.5 percent of the gross up.

The provincial rates on non-eligible dividends range from 5 percent of the gross up to 40 percent. When combined with the federal rate of two-thirds of the gross up, the combined rates range from 71.7 percent to 106.7 percent of the gross up.

15-75.   The following two examples illustrate the effects of provincial corporate tax rates and provincial dividend tax credit rates on the after tax retention for individuals. They both use the following information:

Example   The company has $100,000 in business income. The shareholders will be taxed at a combined federal/provincial rate of 45 percent. If the $100,000 of income is received directly by the individuals, they will retain $55,000 [($100,000)(1 - .45)].

Public Company Paying Eligible Dividends

15-76.   Dealing first with public companies that are paying eligible dividends, we will consider the following three alternative cases:

Perfect Integration   For a public company paying eligible dividends, perfect integration occurs when the combined federal/provincial tax rate on corporations is 27.53623 percent (for this example, we have rounded this to 27.536) and the dividend tax credit is equal to one (6/11 + 5/11).

Worst Case   Here we will use a combination of the highest corporate tax rate (31%) and the lowest dividend tax credit rate (77.5%).

Best Case   Here we will use a combination of the lowest corporate tax rate (25%) and the highest dividend tax credit rate (98.5%).

Analysis   If the income is flowed through a corporation, the after tax retention under the three cases described would be as follows:

Public Company	Perfect Integration	Worst Case (31%/77.5%)	Best Case (25%/98.5%)
Corporate Income	$100,000	$100,000	$100,000
Corporate Taxes:			
At 27.536 Percent	(27,536)		
At 31 Percent		(31,000)	
At 25 Percent			(25,000)
Available For Dividends	$ 72,464	$ 69,000	$ 75,000
Eligible Dividends Received	$ 72,464	$ 69,000	$ 75,000
Gross Up (38%)	27,536	26,220	28,500
Taxable Dividends	$100,000	$ 95,220	$103,500
Individual Tax Rate	45%	45%	45%
Taxes Before Dividend Tax Credit	$ 45,000	$ 42,849	$ 46,575
Dividend Tax Credit:			
[($27,536)(1)]	(27,536)		
[($26,220)(77.5%)]		(20,321)	
[($28,500)(98.5%)]	N/A		(28,073)
Individual Taxes	$ 17,464	$ 22,528	$ 18,502
Eligible Dividends Received	$72,464	$69,000	$75,000
Individual Taxes	(17,464)	(22,528)	(18,502)
After Tax Retention With Corporation	$55,000	$46,472	$56,498

Public Company	Perfect Integration	Worst Case (31%/77.5%)	Best Case (25%/98.5%)
After Tax Retention With Corporation	$55,000	$46,472	$56,498
Direct Receipt Retention	(55,000)	(55,000)	(55,000)
Advantage (Disadvantage)	Nil	($ 8,528)	$ 1,498

Analysis Continued   This example clearly illustrates the influence of varying provincial rates for corporate taxes and dividend tax credits. After tax retention extends from a negative value of $8,528, to a positive amount of $1,498, a range of $10,026. Considering that only $100,000 of income was involved, this represents a significant difference in the results achieved through using a corporation.

CCPC Paying Non-Eligible Dividends

15-77.   This example calculates the after tax retention of non-eligible dividends paid by a CCPC. We will consider the following three alternative cases:

Perfect Integration   As you may recall from earlier examples in the text, for a CCPC paying non-eligible dividends, perfect integration occurs when the combined federal/provincial tax rate on corporations is 20 percent and the dividend tax credit is equal to one (2/3 + 1/3).

Worst Case   Here we will use a combination of the highest corporate tax rate (19%) and the lowest dividend tax credit rate (71.7%).

Best Case   Here we will use a combination of the lowest corporate tax rate (11%) and the highest dividend tax credit rate (106.7%).

CCPC - Non-Eligible Dividends	Perfect Integration	Worst Case (19%/71.7%)	Best Case (11%/106.7%)
Corporate Income	$100,000	$100,000	$100,000
Corporate Taxes:			
At 20 Percent	(20,000)		
At 19 Percent		(19,000)	
At 11 Percent			(11,000)
Available For Dividends	$ 80,000	$ 81,000	$ 89,000
Non-Eligible Dividends Received	$ 80,000	$ 81,000	$ 89,000
Gross Up (25%)	20,000	20,250	22,250
Taxable Dividends	$100,000	$101,250	$111,250
Individual Tax Rate	45%	45%	45%
Taxes Before Dividend Tax Credit	$ 45,000	$ 45,563	$ 50,063
Dividend Tax Credit:			
[($20,000)(1)]	(20,000)		
[($20,250)(71.7%)]		(14,519)	
[($22,250)(106.7%)]	N/A		(23,741)
Individual Taxes	$ 25,000	$ 31,044	$ 26,322
Non-Eligible Dividends Received	$80,000	$81,000	$89,000
Individual Taxes	(25,000)	(31,044)	(26,322)
After Tax Retention With Corporation	$55,000	$49,956	$62,678

CCPC - Non-Eligible Dividends	Perfect Integration	Worst Case (19%/71.7%)	Best Case (11%/106.7%)
After Tax Retention With Corporation	$55,000	$49,956	$62,678
Direct Receipt Retention	(55,000)	(55,000)	(55,000)
Advantage (Disadvantage)	Nil	($ 5,044)	$ 7,678

Analysis   Extending from a negative $5,044 to a positive $7,678, the range of values is $12,722, which is more than the $10,026 range of values for eligible dividends.

Summary: Tax Deferral And Tax Reduction

15-78.   The preceding examples make it clear that the province in which the corporation and the individual is taxed (which may not be the same province) is a significant factor in deciding whether the use of a corporation will be advantageous. Depending on the type of corporation and the type of income, whether tax deferral is possible depends heavily on the province in which the income is taxed. In a similar fashion, the applicable combination of corporate tax rate and dividend tax credit will determine whether the use of a corporation will serve to reduce taxes.

We suggest you work Self Study Problem Fifteen-4 at this point.

Tax Free Dividends

Tax Rates On Dividends

15-79.   In this Chapter we are concerned with owner-managed businesses and these will typically be CCPCs. In most cases, the bulk of their income will either be active business income that benefits from the small business deduction or, alternatively, investment income that qualifies the corporation for a refund of taxes paid. While such corporations may have a positive GRIP account that will allow them to pay eligible dividends, most of their dividends will be non-eligible. Given this, our analysis will focus on non-eligible dividends that are subject to the limited gross up of 25 percent.

15-80.   For an individual in the 29 percent federal tax bracket, subject to a 16 percent provincial tax rate on Taxable Income, and living in a province where the dividend tax credit is equal to one-third of the gross up on non-eligible dividends and 5/11 of the gross up on eligible dividends, the combined federal/provincial rate on non-eligible dividends received is 31.25 percent [(29% + 16%)(125%) - (2/3 + 1/3)(25%)]. This rate is well above the 22.5 percent rate [(29% + 16%)(1/2)] that is applicable to capital gains and the 24.1 percent rate that would apply to eligible dividends [(29% + 16%)(138%) - (6/11 + 5/11)(38%)]. However, it is well below the maximum 45 percent rate (29% + 16%) that would be applicable to most other types of income.

15-81.   In addition to the fact that dividends are taxed at favourable rates, the structure of the dividend tax credit system is such that a substantial amount of dividends can be received without incurring any taxation. This very desirable result will be explained and illustrated in this section on tax free dividends.

Use Of Tax Credits

Credits In General

15-82.   For 2013, every individual has a personal credit against federal Tax Payable based on $11,038 multiplied by the 15 percent rate applicable to the lowest federal tax bracket. This means that the first $11,038 of an individual's income can be received tax free.

15-83.   Extending this analysis, it can be said that, for most types of income, the amount that can be received tax free is limited to the total tax credit amounts available to the individual. That is, for every dollar of tax credit amount, one dollar of income can be received on a tax free basis. There are two exceptions to this:

Charitable Donations   The tax credit on amounts of charitable donations over $200 is based on 29 percent, rather than the 15 percent applicable to other credit amounts. This means that a dollar of charitable donations in excess of $200 will allow an individual in the lowest tax bracket to receive $1.93 in tax free income. More specifically, a $1 contribution in excess of $200 is eligible for a tax credit of $0.29. This $0.29 would eliminate $0.29 of tax payable, the amount of tax that an individual in the lowest bracket would pay on $1.93 of income [(15%)($1.93) = $0.29]. This is unlikely to be an important exception in that it would be unusual for someone in the 15 percent federal tax bracket to be making significant charitable donations.

Dividends   An individual with only the basic personal credit of $1,656 [(15%)($11,038)] can receive tax free dividends of nearly four times the $11,038 base for this credit. More specifically, such an individual can receive $43,438 in dividends without incurring any liability for federal tax. (See the calculations in Paragraph 15-88). Note that, depending on the amount of the provincial dividend tax credit, this amount may or may not be totally free of provincial tax.

Special Rules For Dividends

15-84.   How can an individual receive such a large amount of dividends without paying federal tax? The answer lies in the dividend gross up and tax credit mechanism. For an individual in the lowest tax bracket, the increase in tax associated with one dollar of non-eligible dividends received compared to one dollar of interest income can be calculated as follows:

	Dividend	Interest
Cash Received	$1.0000	$1.0000
Gross Up At 25 Percent	.2500	N/A
Taxable Income	$1.2500	$1.0000
Federal Tax Payable At 15 Percent	$0.1875	$0.1500
Federal Dividend Tax Credit [(2/3)($0.25)]	(0.1667)	N/A
Increase In Federal Tax Payable	$0.0208	$0.1500

15-85.   For each dollar of non-eligible dividends received, an individual must add a taxable dividend of $1.25 ($1 + $0.25 gross up) to Taxable Income. For individuals in the lowest federal tax bracket, the federal tax on this amount will be $0.1875 [($1.25)(15%)]. However, there will be a federal credit against this tax payable equal to two-thirds of the gross up, or $0.1667 [(2/3)($0.25)]. This means that there is only a $0.0208 increase in federal tax for each one dollar increase in non-eligible dividends. This is in contrast to an increase in federal tax of $0.1500 for each one dollar increase in non-dividend income. As these calculations demonstrate, dividend income uses up an individual's available tax credits at a much lower rate than other types of income.

15-86.   For example, one dollar of interest income will use up one dollar [($1.00)($.15 ÷ $.15)] of an individual's personal tax credit base of $11,038. In contrast, one dollar of non-eligible dividends received will use up only $0.1387 of this base [($1.00)($.0208 ÷ $.1500)]. This means that, in comparison with other types of income, a much larger amount of dividends can be received before an individual's tax credits are absorbed and taxes will have to be paid.

15-87.   The amount of dividends that can be received tax free by an individual with no other source of income is a function of the total amount of personal tax credits available and can, in fact, become a fairly large amount. You should note however, that even for an individual with no other income, the amount of tax free dividends is such that the grossed up amount is more than $43,438, the top of the lowest tax bracket. As the taxable amount of dividends goes beyond this bracket limit, the additional amount will be taxed at 22 percent and the relationship described in Paragraph 15-85 becomes less favourable.

Tax Free Amounts For 2013

15-88.   For 2013, ignoring possible tax credits other than the basic personal and spousal, the amount of non-eligible dividends that can be received free of federal tax by a single individual, and by an individual with a dependent spouse (or eligible dependant) with no other source of income, is as follows:

	Single Individual	Dependent Spouse
Non-Eligible Dividends Received	$43,438	$58,725
Gross Up Of 25 Percent	10,860	14,681
Taxable Income	$54,298	$73,406
Taxed At 15%	(43,561)	(43,561)
Taxed At 22%	$ 10,737	$29,845
Federal Tax At 15%	$6,534	$6,534
Federal Tax At 22%	2,362	6,565
Dividend Tax Credit - 2/3 Of Gross Up	(7,240)	(9,787)
Basic Personal Credit [(15%)($11,038)]	(1,656)	(1,656)
Spousal Credit [(15%)($11,038)]	N/A	(1,656)
Federal Tax Payable	Nil	Nil

Note While this is not relevant to our analysis in this section, you might wish to note that, with respect to eligible dividends, the tax free amount for a single individual would be $49,740, and $65,728 for an individual with a dependent spouse.

15-89.   There may or may not be provincial tax payable on the amounts in the preceding table. A number of provincial factors would have to be considered. These include the provincial tax rates, the provincial tax brackets, the provincial personal tax credit amounts and the provincial dividend tax credit rates.

15-90.   The alternative minimum tax is not a factor in determining the amount of non-eligible dividends that can be received on a tax free basis. As the dividend tax credit is not available in the calculation of the alternative minimum tax payable, the dividend gross up is deducted in the calculation of adjusted taxable income for alternative minimum tax purposes. Given this, the $40,000 basic exemption that is provided by the alternative minimum tax legislation, combined with the $11,038 basic personal tax credit (plus the $11,038 spousal credit in the dependent spouse example), would serve to eliminate the alternative minimum tax on the tax free non-eligible dividends calculated in Paragraph 15-88. However, alternative minimum tax may be a consideration when a large amount of eligible dividends are involved. See Chapter 11 for our coverage of alternative minimum tax.

Income Splitting

Basic Concept

15-91.   In Chapter 1 we provided a very simple example of income splitting. As illustrated in that example, if an individual can find a way to share a large block of income with related parties in lower tax brackets, the result can be a significant reduction in taxes, not just in the current year, but on an ongoing basis.

15-92.   While the examples presented earlier in this Chapter suggested that there are limits on an individual's ability to reduce or defer taxes through the use of a corporation, these examples did not take into consideration that a corporation could be used to effectively implement income splitting. This possibility is further enhanced by the fact that, as discussed in the preceding section, individuals without other sources of income can receive substantial amounts of dividends without paying any taxes at the federal level. If any family members are under 18 years of age, the tax on split income (see Chapter 11) may have to be considered.

15-93. This section will provide a fairly simple example of how a corporate structure can be used to significantly reduce taxes within a large family group.

Example

15-94. While there are a variety of ways a corporation could be used to accomplish income splitting, at this stage we will use a simple illustration involving the establishment of a holding company. The data for this example is as follows:

> **Example** Mrs. Breck has an investment portfolio with a fair market value of $1,000,000. Because of Mrs. Breck's great skill in assessing stock market trends, her annual return on this portfolio has averaged 25 percent per year before taxes. All of this return has been in the form of capital gains resulting from very active trading. In addition to her investment income, Mrs. Breck has employment income sufficient to place her in a combined federal/provincial tax bracket of 45 percent. Mrs. Breck has five children over 17 years of age, none of whom have any income of their own. Although she wishes all of her children to have an equal share of the income from her investments, Mrs. Breck wants to retain control over the management of these funds. As he is already in the maximum tax bracket, she does not wish to share any of the income with her husband.

15-95. Mrs. Breck's wishes can be accomplished through the use of an investment company, established with two classes of shares. The preferred shares will have the right to vote and 10 of these shares will be issued to Mrs. Breck at a price of $1 per share. The common shares will not have voting rights and 20 of these shares will be issued to, and will be paid for by, each of her five children at a price of $10 per share. The initial capital structure of the company would be as follows:

10 Voting Preferred Shares	$ 10
100 Non-Voting Common Shares	1,000
Total Equities	**$1,010**

15-96. At this point, Mrs. Breck's $1,000,000 in investments would be transferred to the corporation in return for long-term debt that pays interest at a rate of 1 percent. Assuming this is the prescribed rate at the time of the transfer, there will be no corporate income attributed back to Mrs. Breck. If there are accrued, but unrealized gains on any of Mrs. Breck's investments, they can be transferred to the corporation on a tax free basis using the provisions of ITA 85(1). This procedure is discussed in Chapter 16.

15-97. The resulting initial Balance Sheet of this Canadian controlled private corporation would be as follows:

Assets

Cash	$ 1,010
Investments	1,000,000
Total Assets	**$1,001,010**

Equities

Long-Term Debt	$1,000,000
Preferred Stock	10
Common Stock	1,000
Total Equities	**$1,001,010**

15-98.   All of the income of this CCPC will be investment income and, as a result, a dividend refund will be available when dividends are paid. Continuing to use the corporate rates that were presented in Paragraph 15-22, we will base our analysis of the situation on a combined federal/provincial corporate rate of 46-2/3 percent (38% - 10% + 6-2/3% + 12%). Assuming Mrs. Breck's investments earn $250,000 in capital gains (a 25 percent rate of return on the $1,000,000 of investments) during the corporation's first year, corporate taxes and the maximum dividend payable are calculated as follows:

Taxable Capital Gains [(1/2)($250,000)]	$125,000
Interest On Debt [(1%)($1,000,000)]	(10,000)
Taxable Income	$115,000
Corporate Tax Payable At 46-2/3%	(53,667)
Income Before Dividends	$ 61,333
Dividend Refund (See Note)	30,667
Maximum Non-Eligible Dividend	$ 92,000
Capital Dividend [(1/2)($250,000)]	125,000
Total Dividends	$217,000

Note   The $61,333 of income would support a dividend of $92,000 [(3/2)($61,333)], resulting in a dividend refund of $30,667 [(1/3)($92,000)]. While the refund is limited to the lesser of one-third of dividends paid and the balance in the RDTOH account, the balance in the RDTOH is also $30,667 [(26-2/3%)($115,000)].

15-99   Based on the preceding calculations, each of the five children would receive a total of $43,400, $25,000 ($125,000 ÷ 5) in the form of a tax free capital dividend and $18,400 ($92,000 ÷ 5) in the form of a taxable dividend. However, as these children have no other source of income, they could receive the $18,400 in taxable dividends without any payment of taxes.

15-100.   As a consequence, the only taxes that would be paid on the $250,000 of investment income would be at the corporate level, plus the personal taxes that Mrs. Breck would pay on the interest received from the corporation. A comparison of taxes payable with, and without, the investment company would show the following:

Tax If Income Directly Received By Mrs. Breck [(45%)(1/2)($250,000)]	$56,250
Net Taxes Paid By The Company ($53,667 - $30,667)	(23,000)
Taxes Paid By Mrs. Breck On Interest [(45%)($10,000)]	(4,500)
Federal Tax Savings	$28,750

15-101.   This example makes a basic point clear — incorporation can significantly reduce taxes payable when it is used to split income among family members in lower tax brackets, particularly when those family members have little or no other source of income and can receive dividends on a tax free basis. Of importance is the fact that the tax savings are not a one-time improvement in Mrs. Breck's tax position. These savings will continue to be available in subsequent years, as long as the conditions that produced them remain unchanged.

We suggest you work Self Study Problem Fifteen-5 at this point.

Shareholder Benefits Including Loans

The Owner-Manager Environment

15-102.   Much of the material in this Chapter deals with owner managed corporations. These are typically CCPCs with either a single shareholder or a small group of shareholders. When there is a shareholder group, the group often consists of members of a single family.

15-103.   Unlike the situation with publicly traded companies, in this environment the owner-manager is subject to few constraints on the use of the corporate assets. In effect, he is in a position to provide significant benefits to himself and other related individuals.

15-104.   This situation is complicated by the fact that some things that might be considered benefits are, in fact, necessary to the operation of the business. For example, the owner-manager may need an automobile to use in carrying out the business of the corporation. If he provides himself with a $30,000 Honda, this cost would appear to be a legitimate business expense. However, if he provides himself with a $450,000 Bentley, there is some question as to whether calling on clients really requires this type of vehicle.

15-105.   As was discussed in earlier Chapters, the CRA deals with potential abuses in the area of corporate ownership and leasing of vehicles by:

- restricting the corporation's ability to deduct the costs of owning or leasing vehicles; and
- assessing taxable benefits for personal use of corporate vehicles.

15-106.   Another problem area is travel costs. Most owner-managers have legitimate reasons to travel on matters related to corporate business. However, there is always the temptation of trying to find some business reason for spending a week in a luxury resort in Phoenix. In fact, there is a thriving industry that encourages such behaviour. It is not difficult to find a 30 minute seminar on human resource management that is conveniently conducted just before the ski lifts open at Whistler.

15-107.   Unlike the situation with automobiles, there are no provisions that deal specifically with travel costs. Such costs are only subject to the general constraint that requires a business purpose for their incurrence. In addition, they must be reasonable in the circumstances. Not surprisingly, there are frequent disputes in this area.

Shareholder Benefits Other Than Loans

15-108.   ITA 15(1) deals with situations where a corporation has provided a benefit to a shareholder that does not appear to have a business purpose. Examples of this type of situation would include:

- a corporation providing a shareholder with a jet for personal use;
- a corporation building a swimming pool at a shareholder's personal residence; or
- a corporation selling assets to a shareholder at prices that are substantially below fair market value.

15-109.   When any of these events occur, the shareholder is required to include the value of these benefits or appropriations in his income. Such amounts will not be considered dividends and, as a consequence, they will not be eligible for the dividend tax credit.

15-110.   A further point here is that, when an amount is included in a shareholder's income under ITA 15(1), IT-432R2 indicates that the corporation is not allowed to deduct the amount that has been included in the shareholder's income.

Example   A corporation provides a shareholder with a $10,000 holiday trip to Italy.

Analysis   ITA 15(1) requires the inclusion of the $10,000 cost of the trip in the shareholder's income. Despite the fact that this amount is being taxed in the hands of the shareholder, the corporation would not be able to deduct the cost of the trip.

15-111.   It would seem clear, given this non-deductibility, that corporations should avoid providing benefits that will be assessed to shareholders under ITA 15(1).

Shareholder Loans

General Rule

15-112.   ITA 15(2) is applicable when a corporation makes a loan to a shareholder or an individual connected to a shareholder. Under ITA 15(2.1), persons are connected for this purpose if they do not deal with each other at arm's length. When such loans are made, this general rule requires that the full principal amount of the loan be included in the Net Income For Tax Purposes of the recipient of the loan (the shareholder or the person connected to the shareholder) in the taxation year in which the loan is made.

15-113.   This general rule applies without regard to the amount of interest paid on the loan. Note, however, in periods subsequent to the inclusion of the principal amount of the loan in the income of the shareholder, there is no imputed interest benefit, even in cases where the loan is on an interest free basis.

15-114.   Under this general rule, the granting of the loan to a shareholder has the same tax consequences as the payment of an equivalent amount of salary to the shareholder. However, there is an important difference. Taxes paid on salary cannot normally be recovered by repaying the salary. In contrast, when all or part of a shareholder loan that has been included in the taxpayer's income under ITA 15(2) is repaid, the amount of the repayment can be deducted from Net Income For Tax Purposes under ITA 20(1)(j).

Exceptions To The General Rule

15-115.   There are three exceptions to this general rule that are available to shareholders, without regard to whether or not they are also employees of the corporation. They can be described as follows:

Non-Resident Persons   ITA 15(2.2) indicates that the general rule does not apply to indebtedness between non-resident persons. This means that, if both the corporation and the shareholder receiving the loan were non-residents, the principal amount of any loan would not have to be included in income.

Loans In Ordinary Course Of Business   ITA 15(2.3) indicates that the general rule does not apply when the loan is in the ordinary course of the corporation's business. This would cover such situations as a customer, who is also a shareholder, taking advantage of an on-going promotion by a furniture store that provides interest free loans to purchase furniture. In addition, ITA 15(2.3) notes that this would apply to loans made by a corporation that is in the business of making loans. This covers situations where, for example, an individual happens to be a shareholder of the bank that provides him with a personal loan.

Repayment Within One Year   ITA 15(2.6) indicates that the general rule does not apply when the loan is repaid within one year after the end of the taxation year of the lender or creditor in which the loan was made or the indebtedness arose. If, for example, a corporation with a June 30 year end extended a $100,000 loan to a shareholder on January 1, 2013, the $100,000 would not have to be included in income if it is repaid by June 30, 2014.

A further point with respect to this exception is that IT-119R4 indicates that this exception is not available when the repayment is part of a series of loans and repayments. The primary evidence of this type of situation would be a repayment near the end of a corporate taxation year, followed by a loan for a similar amount early in the following corporate taxation year.

15-116.   Additional exceptions to the general rule requiring the principal of shareholder loans to be included in income involve situations where the shareholder is also an employee of the corporation making the loan. These exceptions are found in ITA 15(2.4) and can be described as follows:

Not Specified Employee   ITA 15(2.4)(a) indicates that loans made to a shareholder, who is an employee, are not subject to the general rule if the shareholder is not a specified employee. A specified employee is one who, at any time of the year, owns 10 percent or more of any class of the shares of the corporation, or who does not deal at arm's length with the corporation. This exception applies without regard to the purpose of the loan.

Dwelling Loans ITA 15(2.4)(b) indicates that loans made to a shareholder, who is an employee, to acquire a dwelling to live in are not subject to the general rule. This would also apply to loans made to the spouse or common-law partner of the employee.

Stock Acquisition Loans ITA 15(2.4)(c) indicates that loans made to a shareholder, who is an employee, to acquire shares in the lending corporation or a corporation related to the lending corporation, are not subject to the general rule.

Motor Vehicle Loans ITA 15(2.4)(d) indicates that loans made to a shareholder, who is an employee, to acquire a motor vehicle to be used in employment duties, are not subject to the general rule.

15-117. In order for these exceptions to apply, the following conditions must be met:

- the loan must be made to the individual because he is an employee, not because he is a shareholder [ITA 15(2.4)(e)]; and

- at the time the loan is made, bona fide arrangements must be made to repay the loan within a reasonable period of time [ITA 15(2.4)(f)].

15-118. The first of these conditions can create significant problems for owner-managers of private corporations wishing to give themselves loans. In order to avoid having the principal amount of the loan included in Net Income For Tax Purposes, the owner-manager must demonstrate that he received the loan because of his role as an employee.

15-119. In order to do this, the owner-manager will likely have to make similar loans available to all employees with duties similar to those of the owner-manager. That is, if the company gives the owner-manager a $100,000, low interest loan to purchase a residence, such loans would have to be made available to all employees with duties similar to those of the owner-manager. If this is not the case, the CRA is likely to conclude that the owner-manager received the loan because of his role as a shareholder.

15-120. A further problem would arise if, as would not be uncommon in owner-managed situations, there are no other senior employees of the business, or no other employees at all. It is not clear in this case whether the owner-manager would be able to demonstrate that he received a loan in his capacity as an employee. However, the CRA will look at the loan practices of other similar corporations as an approach to making this determination.

Imputed Interest Benefit

15-121. It was previously noted that, if the principal amount of a shareholder loan is included in the taxpayer's income, there is no imputed interest benefit related to a low rate or interest free loan. However, if the loan is exempted from the general inclusion in income rule by one of the exceptions described in Paragraphs 15-115 and 15-116, ITA 80.4(2) is applicable and a benefit may be assessed. The analogous benefit for employees, which was discussed in Chapter 3, is assessed under ITA 80.4(1).

Example On July 1, 2013, Andros Ltd. extends a $100,000 loan to its only shareholder, George Andros. The loan is interest free and, because it will be repaid in January, 2014, the $100,000 principal amount does not have to be included in his income. Assume the prescribed rate throughout 2013 is 2 percent.

Analysis For 2013, Mr. Andros will be assessed a taxable benefit under ITA 80.4(2) equal to $1,000 [(2% - Nil)($100,000)(6/12)]. In the examples in IT-421R2, "Benefits To Individuals, Corporations, And Shareholders From Loans Or Debt", interest is calculated on the basis of the number of months the loan is outstanding. While not illustrated, calculations could also be based on the number of days the loan is outstanding. We would remind you that, if the loan proceeds are invested in income producing assets, the imputed interest that is assessed on the loan will be deductible.

15-122. In the fairly common situation where the shareholder also works as an employee of the business, the benefit may be assessed under either ITA 80.4(1) or ITA 80.4(2). If the benefit is assessed under ITA 80.4(1), it will be classified as employment income. In contrast, if it is assessed under ITA 80.4(2), it will be considered property income. There are additional differences when the loan is made to assist an employee/shareholder with the purchase of a home.

15-123.   In the case of a home purchase loan, for the first five years the loan is outstanding, the benefit assessed to an employee under ITA 80.4(1) will use a rate no higher than the prescribed rate that prevailed when the loan was made. Should the rate go down, the employee is entitled to use the lower prescribed rate for the benefit calculation. Alternatively, in the case of a home purchase loan to a shareholder, the ITA 80.4(2) benefit must be calculated using the actual quarterly prescribed rates that prevail over the term of the loan.

15-124.   A further difference between home purchase loans to employees and home purchase loans to shareholders relates to the home relocation loan deduction. As discussed in Chapters 3 and 4, if a loan qualifies as a home relocation loan, an employee may get a deduction in the calculation of Taxable Income equal to the benefit on a $25,000 interest free home purchase loan from the calculated benefit on the loan. This deduction is not available on shareholder loans where the benefit is taxed under ITA 80.4(2).

Exercise Fifteen - 6

Subject: Shareholder Loans - Car Purchase

Ms. Martha Rourke is an employee of Rourke Inc., a large private company in which her husband owns 70 percent of the outstanding shares. Ms. Rourke owns the remaining 30 percent of the shares. On July 1, 2013, she receives a $50,000 interest free loan that will be used to purchase an automobile to be used in her employment duties. The loan is to be repaid on June 30, 2017. Assume the prescribed rate for all of 2013 is 1 percent. What are the tax implications of this loan for Ms. Rourke in 2013?

Exercise Fifteen - 7

Subject: Shareholder Loans - Term Outstanding

On June 1, 2013, Generic Inc. loans $162,000 to its principal shareholder, Ms. Jan Fisk, in order to finance her gambling debts. Generic Inc. has a taxation year that ends on June 30. The loan is interest free. Assume that, during all periods, the relevant prescribed rate is 2 percent. What are the tax consequences to Ms. Fisk if the loan is repaid (1) on January 1, 2014 and (2) on December 31, 2014?

Exercise Fifteen - 8

Subject: Shareholder Loans - Home Purchase

On November, 1, 2013, Hasid Ltd. loans Mr. Aaron Hasid, the CEO and principal shareholder of the Company, $123,000 in order to assist in his purchase of a principal residence. The loan does not qualify as a home relocation loan. The Company has a taxation year that ends on December 31. The loan does not bear interest and, during all periods, assume that the relevant prescribed rate is 2 percent. The loan is to be repaid in four annual instalments, the first occurring on October 31, 2014. What are the tax consequences of this loan to Mr. Hasid? State any assumptions that you have made in providing your answer.

End of Exercises. Solutions available in Study Guide.

We suggest you work Self Study Problems Fifteen-6 and 7 at this point.

Management Compensation

General Principles

Salary As The Bench Mark

15-125.   The most obvious and straightforward way to compensate managers is to pay salaries. Provided they are reasonable, the amounts are a deductible expense to the corporation. At the same time, they are fully taxable to the recipient, rendering such payments neutral in terms of tax planning. For large publicly traded corporations, where the managers are not the principal owners of the business, salary is the usual starting point in negotiating management compensation. However, for some high income executives, stock based compensation may be of greater importance than salary.

15-126.   Even with a public corporation, however, the tax effects of various methods of compensation should not be ignored. By paying salaries, a corporation receives a deduction from Taxable Income in the year of accrual, while the recipient employee receives an equal addition to Taxable Income in the year of payment.

15-127.   Any form of compensation that creates an excess of the corporation's deductions over the employee's inclusions creates an aggregate tax savings. In addition, any form of compensation that is deductible to the corporation prior to inclusion in the income of the employee involves tax deferral. These considerations can allow for improved after tax benefits to the employee or, alternatively, a lower after tax cost to the corporation.

Tax Effective Alternatives

15-128.   Some simple examples of compensation features that can be used to defer or reduce the payment of taxes are as follows:

- **Registered Pension Plans**   Within prescribed limits, a corporation can deduct contributions to Registered Pension Plans in the year of contribution. These contributions will not become taxable to the employee until they are received as a pension benefit, resulting in an effective tax deferral arrangement.

- **Deferred Profit Sharing Plans**   In a fashion similar to Registered Pension Plans, amounts that are currently deductible to the corporation are deferred with respect to inclusion in the employee's Taxable Income.

- **Provision Of Private Health Care Plans**   The premiums paid by the corporation for such benefits as dental plans can be deducted in full by the corporation and will not be considered a taxable benefit to the employee. This can generate a significant tax savings.

- **Stock Options**   Stock options provide employees with an incentive to improve the performance of the enterprise. In addition, taxation of any benefits resulting from the options is deferred until they are exercised or sold (for a full discussion of the deferral of stock option benefits, see Chapter 3). Further, the value of the employment benefit received is enhanced by the fact that, in general, one-half of the amount can be deducted in the calculation of Taxable Income.

  From the point of view of the corporation, evaluation of stock option compensation is more complex. Discouraging the use of options is the fact that no tax deduction is available for the granting of options. However, IFRS 2, *Share-Based Payment*, requires that the estimated value of options be charged to expense for accounting purposes when they are granted, despite the fact that the cost of issuing stock options is not deductible for tax purposes.

15-129.   Changes in tax legislation over the years have served to restrict the tax benefits associated with employee compensation. Perhaps most importantly, the rules related to taxable benefits on employer provided automobiles can be quite unfavourable, in some cases resulting in a taxable benefit that exceeds the value derived from having use of the vehicle. The rules related to employee fringe benefits and employee stock options were covered in

Chapter 3. Chapter 10 contained coverage of deferred compensation plans and this Chapter 15 included coverage of shareholder loans.

Salary Vs. Dividends

15-130.   For large public corporations, there is little point in considering the tax benefits related to salary/dividend trade-offs. The dividend policy of public corporations is normally based on considerations that extend well beyond the compensation that is provided to the management group of the company.

15-131.   In situations where the manager of the business is also an owner, such an individual is in a position to receive compensation in the form of either salary or dividends. If there are no other owners involved in the decision, the choice is completely at the discretion of the owner-manager and tax factors will generally be an important consideration in making this decision. The choice between compensation in the form of salary or in the form of dividends, the salary vs. dividend decision, is the subject of the remainder of this Chapter.

Salary Vs. Dividends For The Owner - Manager

The Basic Trade-Off
Example - Data
15-132.   To illustrate the basic trade-off that is involved in salary vs. dividend decisions, assume that Ms. Olney owns all of the shares of a corporation that has $100,000 in Taxable Income, and that she has sufficient property income from other sources to place her in the 45 percent federal/provincial tax bracket (29% federal rate plus 16% provincial rate).

15-133.   If the full $100,000 of corporate income is paid to Ms. Olney in the form of salary, it can be deducted by the corporation and will reduce the corporation's Taxable Income to nil. This means that no taxes will be paid at the corporate level. However, the $100,000 will be taxed at Ms. Olney's marginal rate of 45 percent. This means that she will pay tax of $45,000 and be left with after tax funds of $55,000.

15-134.   If no salary is paid to Ms. Olney, corporate taxes will be assessed and any remaining amount, after adjustments for any refundable taxes, will be paid in dividends. This amount will be subject to personal tax and the resulting after tax cash flow to her can be determined. These amounts, which are dependent on the type of corporation and the type of income earned, were calculated earlier in this Chapter. The results of those calculations were summarized in Paragraph 15-57. You may wish to refer to this summary as you work through the remainder of this Chapter.

Analysis Of The Example
15-135.   In looking at the question of whether or not to incorporate an income source, we looked at the possibilities for both tax deferral and tax reduction through the use of a corporation. In salary vs. dividend decisions, we are not concerned with deferral. The question we need to answer here is:

"What is the most tax effective way to have a corporation provide its owner-manager with a required amount of after tax income?"

15-136.   There is, of course, no deferral available on amounts that are to be removed from the corporation.

15-137.   In comparing Ms. Olney's $55,000 retained with the various results listed in Paragraph 15-57, in most cases the use of dividends as opposed to tax deductible salary results in the same or higher levels of taxation. The exception to this is the case of a CCPC earning income that is eligible for the small business deduction. In this case, after tax retention was $56,760, which is higher than the $55,000 that would be retained if salary was paid.

15-138.   This would suggest that, in general, salary should be used. However, the preceding analysis is based on a number of assumptions with respect to provincial tax rates on personal and corporate income. In addition, other factors such as RRSP contributions, CPP contributions and payroll tax costs have been ignored. These factors will be considered in the following material.

Other Considerations

Provincial Tax Rates And Credits

15-139. The results that were presented in Paragraph 15-57 assumed a provincial tax rate on individuals of 16 percent, a provincial dividend tax credit on non-eligible dividends equal to 22 percent of the gross up, and provincial rates on corporations for income eligible for the small business deduction and other types of income of 3 and 12 percent, respectively. While these numbers are fairly representative, they are not the only possible rates.

15-140. In assessing the importance of these differences, you should recognize that the payment of salaries is analogous to the direct receipt of income. That is, if a corporation has $100,000 in income and pays this entire amount in salaries, there will be no corporate Tax Payable. Further, the taxes paid by the individual on the salary will be similar to the taxes that would be paid if the income were received directly. This means that the comparison of salary payments with dividends involves the same type of analysis as the comparison of the after tax retention from the direct receipt of income with the after tax retention resulting from channeling income through a corporation.

15-141. Given this, we can discuss the effect of varying provincial tax rates on the salary vs. dividend decision by using the conclusions reached in the comparison of the direct receipt vs. flow through decisions. Direct receipt vs. flow through decisions were considered in Paragraphs 15-60 through 15-78. Applying that analysis to salary vs. dividend decisions, the following statements can be made:

Tax Rates For Individuals In the analysis contained in Paragraphs 15-69 through 15-71, we noted that higher tax rates on individuals made the use of a corporation more attractive from the point of view of deferring taxes on income retained within the corporation. Here, however, we are concerned only with amounts that will be distributed, either in the form of dividends or in the form of salary and, as a consequence, tax deferral is not an issue. This means that the level of individual tax rates is not a major issue in this type of decision. This point is illustrated with the example found in Paragraph 15-70.

Dividend Tax Credit And Corporate Tax Rates For integration to work, the combined federal/provincial dividend tax credit must be equal to the combined corporate taxes paid.

- **Eligible Dividends** For eligible dividends subject to a 38 percent gross up, this would require a combined corporate tax rate of 27.54 percent and a dividend tax credit equal to the gross up. This in turn would require a provincial corporate tax rate of 12.54 percent (27.54 - 15) and a provincial dividend tax credit of 5/11 (1.0 - 6/11), or approximately 45.45 percent.

- **Non-Eligible Dividends** For non-eligible dividends (usually paid by a CCPC) subject to a 25 percent gross up, this would require a combined corporate tax rate of 20 percent and a dividend tax credit equal to the gross up. This in turn would require a provincial corporate tax rate of 9 percent (20 - 11) and a provincial dividend tax credit equal to one-third of the gross up (1.0 - 2/3).

The examples in Paragraphs 15-74 and 15-76 illustrate the results of applying the current range of values for corporate tax rates and dividend tax credit rates in all of the Canadian provinces. While these examples were designed to illustrate the desirability of using a corporation, they can also be used to evaluate salary vs. dividend decisions. As noted, paying salary is, from a tax point of view, the equivalent of direct receipt of income.

Analyzing these examples in the context of salary/dividend decisions, it is clear that, in situations where the dividend tax credit exceeds the corporate taxes paid, paying dividends will result in lower taxes than would be the case with paying salary. Similarly, when the dividend tax credit is less than the corporate taxes paid, the payment of salary, all other things being equal, will result in lower taxes.

Dividend Benefit - Income Splitting

15-142.   When a corporation is used for income splitting purposes, amounts may be distributed to individuals with little or no other source of income. As was noted in Paragraph 15-91, over $42,000 in non-eligible dividends can be paid to such an individual without any federal tax liability being incurred. The fact that this is a much larger amount than can be distributed tax free in any other form clearly favours the use of dividends for distributions of corporate assets in these circumstances.

15-143.   A constraint on this approach is the tax on split income, a.k.a., the kiddie tax (see Chapter 11). When a family member is 17 years old or younger, taxable dividends from private companies are subject to this tax. Given that the federal rate for the kiddie tax is the maximum rate of 29 percent, when related individuals are under the age of 18, the use of dividends for income splitting becomes less attractive.

Dividend Benefit - CNIL Reduction

15-144.   An individual's Cumulative Net Investment Loss (CNIL) is the cumulative amount by which investment expenses exceed investment income since 1987 (see Chapter 11 for an explanation of this amount, as well as the general provisions of the lifetime capital gains deduction). An individual's ability to make a deduction under the provisions of the lifetime capital gains deduction is reduced, on a dollar-for-dollar basis, by the balance in the CNIL account. This means that, if an individual contemplates selling shares of a qualified small business corporation, or an interest in a qualified farm or fishing property, sensible tax planning would suggest the elimination of any CNIL balance.

15-145.   For an individual whose income is provided by his owner-managed corporation, dividends can assist with this problem. The receipt of dividends reduces the CNIL by $1.25 for each $1.00 of non-eligible dividends received. In contrast, salary payments leave this balance unchanged. Another possibility, if the corporation has an amount owing to the shareholder, is to pay interest to the shareholder on the balance outstanding. This interest would also decrease any CNIL.

Salary Benefit - Earned Income For RRSP And CPP

15-146.   One of the most attractive features of the Canadian income tax system is the fact that individuals can make deductible contributions to RRSPs. Not only are the contributions deductible at the time that they are made, once inside the plan they enjoy the tremendous benefits associated with tax free compounding over, what may be, a period of many years. Most individuals will want to take advantage of these provisions.

15-147.   Dividends do not constitute Earned Income for the purposes of determining the maximum RRSP contributions, nor do they count as pensionable earnings on which CPP contributions can be based. As a result, if the owner-manager has no other source of Earned Income (e.g., employment income from a source other than his corporation), it will be necessary for the corporation to pay salary if the individual wishes to make RRSP and CPP contributions.

15-148.   For 2014, the maximum annual RRSP contribution is equal to the lesser of $24,270 and 18 percent of the individual's Earned Income for the previous year. This means that, if the owner-manager has no other source of Earned Income, a 2013 salary of at least $134,833 will be required to make the maximum annual RRSP contribution in 2014. The maximum for CPP pensionable earnings in a year is considerably less than this figure ($51,100 for 2013). In order to be eligible for the maximum CPP payments at retirement, salary of at least the maximum pensionable earnings for the year should be paid.

Salary Benefit - Earned Income For Child Care Costs

15-149. If an individual is in a position to deduct child care costs, they are limited to two-thirds of earned income. Salary payments would add to this limit while dividends would not. For a detailed discussion of the deductibility of child care costs, see Chapter 9.

Salary Benefit - Corporate Tax Savings Carry Over

15-150. In a particular year, an owner-manager may wish to withdraw amounts in excess of the earnings of the corporation. If this happens, there will be no current tax savings associated with the payment of salaries, a fact that would tend to make the payment of such amounts less attractive.

15-151. However, payment of salaries in this situation would serve to create a loss carry over and, if we assume that the loss carry over can be used in some past or future year, the corporate tax savings associated with the payment of salaries would not be lost. The savings, however, will be deferred in the case of a carry forward and this means that, to properly evaluate the payment of salaries in this situation, consideration would have to be given to the time value of money.

Salary Cost (Possible) - Provincial Payroll Taxes

15-152. With respect to provincial payroll taxes, four provinces and two territories assess such taxes. Rates are as follows:

Manitoba (Health And Post-Secondary Education Levy) No tax on the first $1.25 million of payroll. Excess is taxed at a rate of 2.15 or 4.3 percent.

Newfoundland/Labrador (Health And Post-Secondary Education Levy) No tax on the first $1.2 million of payroll. Excess is taxed at a rate of 2 percent.

Ontario (Employer Health Tax) This tax starts at 0.98 percent on the first $200,000 of payroll. Between $200,000 and $400,000 there is a schedule of increasing rates, reaching 1.95 percent of amounts over $400,000.

Quebec (Health Services Fund) The rate on the first $1 million of payroll is 2.7 percent. Excess is taxed at varying rates of up to 4.26 percent.

Territories (Payroll Tax) Nunavut and the Northwest territories tax all payroll at a rate of 2 percent.

Salary Costs - CPP And EI

15-153. In our example from Paragraph 15-132, we ignored the fact that salaries cannot be paid without contributions being made to the CPP. In addition, some provinces levy a payroll tax on salaries and wages. These costs can constitute a significant reduction in the after tax cash flow associated with the payment of salaries.

15-154. We have not mentioned Employment Insurance (EI) premiums in this context because, if the owner-manager owns more than 40 percent of the voting shares of the corporation, he cannot participate in this program.

15-155. With respect to CPP contributions, 2013 employee contributions are based on 4.95 percent of $51,100 (maximum pensionable earnings), less a basic exemption of $3,500. This results in a maximum employee contribution for 2013 of $2,356. The employer is required to withhold this contribution and, in addition, is required to make a further contribution in an amount that is equal to the contribution made by the employee. This brings the total CPP cost of paying salaries of $51,100 or more to $4,712.

15-156. While generally not relevant here, an employee's maximum EI premium for 2013 is 1.88 percent of $47,400 (maximum insurable earnings), with no basic exemption. This gives a maximum employee premium of $891. In addition, the employer must contribute 1.4 times the employee's premium, an amount of $1,247. This results in a total cost of $2,138 for an employee with maximum insurable earnings in excess of $47,400.

Salary Benefit - CPP And Canada Employment Tax Credits

15-157.   While CPP is an added cost of choosing the salary alternative, the payment of these costs adds a benefit in the form of future CPP benefit payments, as well as a benefit from the CPP tax credit. You will recall from Chapter 4 that this credit is equal to 15 percent of amounts paid. This provides a maximum credit of $353 on the payment of the 2013 maximum CPP of $2,356. Note that this would not be a consideration if the individual has other sources of income which required the payment of maximum CPP.

15-158.   A further benefit of paying salary is the Canada employment credit of $168 [(15%)($1,117)] for 2013. Unless the individual has other sources of employment income in excess of the base amount for this credit, the Canada Employment credit is only available on the payment of salary by the corporation.

Example Extended

15-159.   Returning to our example of Ms. Olney from Paragraph 15-132, as the owner of 100 percent of the shares of the corporation, she is not eligible to participate in the EI program. In addition, assume the province in which she lives assesses a 2.7 percent payroll tax to finance its health care program and provides a provincial credit for CPP contributions at a 6 percent rate. Her corporation is a Canadian controlled private corporation and all of its $100,000 in income is eligible for the small business deduction. Given this income and the costs associated with paying salary, the maximum salary that could be paid to Ms. Olney would be $95,077, a figure that would result in no corporate Tax Payable.

Pre-Tax Corporate Income	$100,000
Employer's CPP Contribution	(2,356)
Gross Salary [($100,000 - $2,356) ÷ 1.027]	(95,077)
Payroll Tax [(2.7%)($95,077)]	(2,567)
Corporate Taxable Income	Nil

15-160.   If $95,077 is paid to Ms. Olney as salary, her personal taxes are as follows:

Combined Tax Before Credits [(29% + 16%)($95,077)]	$42,785
Credit For Employee's CPP Contribution	
[(15% + 6%)($2,356)]*	(495)
Canada Employment Credit [(15%)($1,117)]	(168)
Personal Tax Payable	$42,122

*We have assumed that Ms. Olney has sufficient property income to place her in the maximum federal tax bracket. This income would absorb other tax credits and, as a consequence, only the CPP and Canada employment credits that result from the payment of salary are included in this analysis.

15-161.   With this amount of taxes payable, Ms. Olney's after tax retention would be calculated as follows:

Salary Received	$95,077
Employee's CPP Contribution - Maximum	(2,356)
Personal Tax Payable	(42,122)
After Tax Cash Retained	$50,599

15-162.   This more realistic result is considerably less cash than the after tax retention of salary when CPP, payroll taxes and the Canada Employment credit are ignored of $55,000 (see Paragraph 15-133). Using the numbers from the table in Paragraph 15-57, this makes payment of salary in this situation less desirable than dividends paid out of:

- income eligible for the small business deduction (retention was $56,760),
- investment income (retention was $52,800), or
- business income ineligible for the small business deduction (retention was $53,290).

Exercise Fifteen - 9

Subject: Salary And Dividend Compensation

Broadmoor Inc. is a Canadian controlled private corporation with Net Income For Tax Purposes and Taxable Income of $550,000 for the year ending December 31, 2013. All of this income is from active business activities. The cash balance of the Company, prior to any payments on the current year's taxes, is also equal to this amount. The Company makes the maximum eligible dividend designation each year. It is subject to a provincial tax rate of 4 percent on income eligible for the small business deduction and 14 percent on other income. Its only shareholder, Ms. Sarah Broad, has no income other than dividends or salary paid by the corporation and has combined federal/provincial personal tax credits of $3,800. She lives in a province that has a flat personal tax rate equal to 10 percent. The provincial dividend tax credit is equal to 30 percent of the gross up for all dividends. There is no payroll tax in this province. Determine the amount of after tax cash that Ms. Broad will retain if:

(1) the maximum salary is paid by the corporation out of the available cash of $550,000. Ignore the required CPP contributions and the Canada employment tax credit.

(2) the maximum amount of eligible and non-eligible dividends are paid.

End of Exercise. Solution available in Study Guide.

Use Of Tax Credits

15-163. Our example in this section has involved an individual with other sources of income that placed her in the maximum federal tax bracket. This amount of income would generally be sufficient to absorb any tax credits available to the individual. However, there may be situations where a salary vs. dividend decision is being made with respect to an individual with no other source of income. This would be a fairly common situation when a corporation is being used for income splitting purposes, or for a corporation with only a limited amount of income to distribute.

15-164. If the individual has no other source of income and provincial tax rates favour the use of dividends, there may be a problem with the full use of available tax credits. We noted earlier in this Chapter that dividend payments use up tax credits at a much lower rate than other types of income, such as salary. If only limited amounts of income are being distributed, the use of dividends may leave a portion of the individual's tax credits unused. When this is the case, some combination of salary and dividends may provide the optimum solution.

15-165. A further potential complication stems from the fact that provincial tax credits can only be deducted against the provincial tax liability and federal tax credits can only be deducted against the federal tax liability. In our examples and problems we have not taken this into consideration and have given a single figure for combined federal/provincial tax credits.

15-166. In the real world, it would be possible to have a situation where an individual would have to pay some federal tax in order to use up all of their provincial tax credits, or alternatively, a situation where an individual would have to pay some provincial tax in order to use up all of their federal tax credits, for example the federal Canada employment tax credit. Given this text's focus on federal income taxes, no further attention will be given to this issue.

15-167. The following example illustrates the salary vs. dividend issue when the full utilization of tax credits is a consideration.

Salary Vs. Dividends For The Owner - Manager

Example   Mr. Eric Swenson is the sole shareholder of Swenson Sweets, a Canadian controlled private corporation. The Company has a December 31 year end and, at December 31, 2013, it has Taxable Income for the year of $29,500, all of which results from active business activities. This amount is available in cash, prior to the payment of any salary or dividends. Mr. Swenson has combined federal/provincial personal tax credits of $3,920.

The corporation operates in a province with a corporate tax rate on active business income of a CCPC of 3 percent and no payroll taxes. The provincial tax rate on personal income is 10 percent of the first $43,561 of Taxable Income, with a provincial dividend tax credit on non-eligible dividends that is equal to one-third of the gross up. In solving this problem, we will ignore CPP contributions and the Canada employment tax credit.

15-168.   If the full $29,500 is paid out in salary, there would be no corporate tax and Mr. Swenson's after tax cash retention would be as follows:

Salary Received		$29,500
Taxes At 25% (15% + 10%)	$7,375	
Personal Tax Credits (Given)	(3,920)	(3,455)
After Tax Cash Retained (All Salary)		$26,045

15-169.   As dividends are not tax deductible, corporate tax must be paid prior to any dividend distribution. The combined federal/provincial tax rate would be 14 percent (38% - 10% - 17% + 3%) resulting in corporate taxes of $4,130. This means that the maximum dividend that can be paid will be $25,370 ($29,500 - $4,130). The after tax retention in this case is as follows:

Non-Eligible Dividends Received	$25,370
Gross Up Of 25%	6,343
Taxable Dividends	$31,713
Personal Tax Rate	25%
Personal Tax Payable Before Tax Credits	$7,928
Personal Tax Credits (Given)	(3,920)
Dividend Tax Credit [(2/3 + 1/3)($6,343)]	(6,343)
Tax Payable ($2,335 In Unused Credits)	Nil

Dividends Received	$25,370
Personal Tax Payable	Nil
After Tax Cash Retained (All Dividends)	$25,370

15-170.   While the low federal/provincial tax rate on corporations suggests that dividends should be the best alternative, the preceding results do not confirm this view. The problem is that dividend income absorbs available tax credits at a much lower rate than other types of income. The fact that the all dividend solution leaves $2,335 of unused tax credits suggests that a better solution might be to pay a lesser amount of dividends, plus sufficient salary to absorb these unused credits.

15-171.   To investigate this possibility, we need to determine the salary/dividend mix that will fully utilize all of Mr. Swenson's credits. To begin, consider what would happen when we add a $1,000 salary payment to the all dividends case. As the salary will be fully deductible, the after tax cost of making this payment is $860.00 [($1,000)(1 - 0.14)]. As a consequence, in this type of situation, where the goal is to distribute all of the available corporate income, dividends will only have to be reduced by this $860.00 per $1,000 of salary increase.

15-172.   The resulting decrease in taxes payable can be calculated as follows:

Salary Vs. Dividends For The Owner - Manager

Increase In Salary	$1,000.00
Decrease In Dividends	(860.00)
Decrease In Dividend Gross Up [(25%)($860)]	(215.00)
Decrease In Taxable Income	($ 75.00)
Personal Tax Rate	25%
Decrease In Tax Payable Before Dividend Tax Credit	($ 18.75)
Decrease In Dividend Tax Credit	
= Increase In Tax Payable [(2/3 + 1/3)($215.00)]	215.00
Net Increase In Personal Tax Payable	$ 196.25

15-173.   This analysis demonstrates that each $1,000 increase in salary results in an increase in personal Tax Payable of $196.25. Alternatively, this can be stated as an increase in personal Tax Payable of $0.19625 for every dollar of increase in salary. This means that to utilize Mr. Swenson's $2,335 in unused tax credits, he will have to receive salary of $11,898 ($2,335 ÷ $0.19625). This results in the following amount being available for dividends:

Corporate Taxable Income Pre-Salary	$29,500
Salary	(11,898)
Corporate Taxable Income	$17,602
Corporate Tax At 14%	(2,464)
Available For Dividends	$15,138

15-174.   When this dividend is paid out to Mr. Swenson, his after tax retention is as follows:

Non-Eligible Dividends Received	$15,138
Gross Up Of 25%	3,785
Taxable Dividends	$18,923
Salary	11,898
Taxable Income	$30,821
Personal Tax Rate	25%
Personal Tax Payable Before Tax Credits	$ 7,705
Personal Tax Credits (Given)	(3,920)
Dividend Tax Credit [(2/3 + 1/3)($3,785)]	(3,785)
Personal Tax Payable (Salary And Dividends)	Nil

Comparison	All Salary	All Dividends	Salary And Dividends
Non-Eligible Dividends Received	N/A	$25,370	$15,138
Salary Received	$29,500	N/A	11,898
Personal Tax Payable	(3,455)	Nil	Nil
After Tax Cash Retained	$26,045	$25,370	$27,036

15-175.   As shown in the preceding calculations, this mix of salary and dividends is such that it utilizes all of Mr. Swenson's tax credits and leaves Tax Payable of nil. This results in a solution that not only improves on the $25,370 that was retained in the all dividend scenario, it also improves on the $26,045 that was retained in the all salary case. It would appear to be the optimum solution for this example.

Optimizing A Limited Payment Of Cash

15-176.   A similar analysis could be done if the corporation had limited cash. Assume that, while the corporation in the example (Paragraph 15-167) had Taxable Income of $29,500, it had only $16,000 in cash. To determine the maximum salary that can be paid, it is necessary to solve the following equation for X:

$$X = \text{maximum salary} = \$16,000 - [(14\%)(\$29,500 - X)]$$

$$X - 0.14X = [\$16,000 - (14\%)(\$29,500)]$$

15-177.   Solving this equation indicates that the maximum salary that could be paid, given the available cash of $16,000, would be $13,802. Corporate taxes of $2,198 [(14%)($29,500 - $13,802)] would have to be paid. The total corporate cash outflow equals the cash available of $16,000 ($13,802 + $2,198). The basic personal taxes on the salary would be $3,451 [(25%)($13,802)]. As this amount is less than the $3,920 in personal credits, no personal taxes would be paid and the full $13,802 would be retained.

15-178.   As dividends are not deductible, in the dividend approach, corporate taxes of $4,130 [(14%)($29,500)] would have to be paid. This leaves cash available for dividends of $11,870 ($16,000 - $4,130). As no individual taxes would be payable on this amount of dividends (see Paragraph 15-88), the full $11,870 would be retained.

15-179.   It is clear that the salary approach results in a considerably larger after tax retention than the dividend approach. This result would be expected given that the corporate cash was insufficient to utilize the personal tax credits in either approach.

Exercise Fifteen - 10

Subject: Salary vs. Dividends

Mortell Inc. has Net Income For Tax Purposes and Taxable Income for the year ending December 31, 2013 of $198,000. The Company's cash balance is over $200,000. It is subject to a combined federal/provincial tax rate of 14 percent. Ms. Mortell, the Company's only shareholder, has employment income of over $150,000 and, under normal circumstances, does not make withdrawals from the corporation. However, because of an increasing fondness for certain types of mood enhancing chemicals, she needs an additional $30,000 in cash. Ms. Mortell lives in a province where the provincial tax rate in her bracket is equal to 16 percent and the provincial dividend tax credit is equal to 25 percent of the dividend gross up for all dividends. She has asked your advice as to whether the payment of salary or, alternatively, the payment of non-eligible dividends, would have the lowest tax cost. Provide the requested advice.

Exercise Fifteen - 11

Subject: Salary vs. Dividends - Limited Corporate Cash

Fargo Ltd. has Net Income For Tax Purposes and Taxable Income for the year ending December 31, 2013 of $21,500. The Company's cash balance, prior to the payment of any taxes for the year is $18,500. The Company's Taxable Income is subject to a combined federal/provincial tax rate of 15 percent. There is no payroll tax in this province. Mr. Fargo, the Company's president and sole shareholder, is 71 years of age and has no other source of income (he is not eligible for OAS). He has combined federal/provincial personal tax credits of $3,950 and lives in a province that has a personal tax rate on the first $43,561 of Taxable Income equal to 10 percent. The provincial dividend tax credit is one-third of the gross up for all dividends. Mr. Fargo would like to remove all of the cash from the corporation and has asked your advice as to whether it would be better to take it out in the form of all non-eligible dividends or all salary. As Mr. Fargo is over 70 years old, no CPP contributions are required. Ignore the Canada employment tax credit. Provide the requested advice.

End of Exercises. Solutions available in Study Guide.

Conclusion

15-180. As the preceding discussion makes clear, the salary vs. dividend decision is complex. Determination of the total tax consequences of the two alternatives does not necessarily resolve the issue. Among other factors that are specific to individual taxpayers, consideration should be given to:

• other sources of income and cash,
• the need to have Earned Income for RRSP purposes and to deduct child care costs,
• the ability to split the corporation's income among various members of a family unit,
• the personal level of expenditures desired, and
• the possible advantage resulting from reducing corporate income to the annual limit for the small business deduction.

15-181. The preceding material does not give you a comprehensive approach to solving these problems on a quantitative basis. In actual fact, there are problems here that are probably not subject to quantitative solutions. For example, whether or not an individual feels a need for retirement income involves many subjective considerations. With an issue such as this, a tax advisor can only outline the various possible outcomes.

We suggest you work Self Study Problems Fifteen-8 and 9 at this point.

Key Terms Used In This Chapter

15-182. The following is a list of the key terms used in this Chapter. These terms, and their meanings, are compiled in the Glossary Of Key Terms located at the back of the separate paper Study Guide.

Active Business Income	Limited Liability
Aggregate Investment Income	Low Rate Income Pool (LRIP)
Annual Business Limit	Manufacturing And Processing
Bonusing Down	Profits Deduction (M&P Deduction)
Canadian Controlled Private Corporation	Private Corporation
Charitable Donations Tax Credit	Public Corporation
Eligible Dividends	Specified Employee
Estate Planning	Tax Avoidance
General Rate Income Pool (GRIP)	Tax Deferral
Income Splitting	Tax Planning
Integration	Taxable Benefit
Lifetime Capital Gains Deduction	

References

15-183. For more detailed study of the material in this Chapter, we refer you to the following:

ITA 6(1)	Amounts To Be Included As Income From Office Or Employment
ITA 15(1)	Benefit Conferred On Shareholder
ITA 15(2)	Shareholder Debt
ITA 18(1)	General Limitations (On Deductions)
ITA 20(1)(j)	Repayment Of Loan By Shareholder
ITA 67	General Limitation Re Expenses
ITA 80.4	Loans - Imputed Interest
ITA 80.5	Deemed Interest

ITA 82(1)	Taxable Dividends Received
ITA 121	Deduction For Taxable Dividends
ITA 123 To 125.4	Rules Applicable To Corporations
ITA 146	Registered Retirement Savings Plans
ITA 147	Deferred Profit Sharing Plans
IT-67R3	Taxable Dividends From Corporations Resident In Canada
IT-119R4	Debts Of Shareholders And Certain Persons Connected With Shareholders
IT-124R6	Contributions To Registered Retirement Savings Plans
IT-307R4	Spouse Or Common-Law Partner Registered Retirement Savings Plans
IT-421R2	Benefits To Individuals, Corporations And Shareholders From Loans Or Debt
IT-432R2	Benefits Conferred On Shareholders
IT-470R	Employee's Fringe Benefits (Consolidated)
IT-487	General Limitation On Deduction Of Outlays Or Expenses
IT-533	Interest Deductibility And Related Issues

Problems For Self Study

(The solutions for these problems can be found in the separate Study Guide.)

Self Study Problem Fifteen - 1 (Advantages Of Incorporation)

Mr. Copley is in his late forties. He is married and has two children who are attending university. For over ten years he has worked full time on the development of an unincorporated manufacturing business. The business is currently earning about $250,000 per year and, in recent years, Mr. Copley has been using about $160,000 per year of this amount to meet his personal living costs. The remainder has been left in the business to assist in financing a continued expansion of its activities.

His wife works in the office of the business and, during the summer months, both of his children are employed by his organization.

Mr. Copley has come to you for advice related to the operations of his business. He is considering the possibility of incorporating the business and is interested in knowing whether this will be an advantageous move from a tax point of view.

Required: Give Mr. Copley a list detailing the advantages and disadvantages of incorporation.

Self Study Problem Fifteen - 2 (Flow Through Of Interest Income)

Mrs. Martin is considering investing $200,000 in interest bearing securities for one year at a rate of 7 percent per annum. The pre-tax interest income on this investment would be $14,000 and Mrs. Martin will have no other investment income in the year.

The combined federal and provincial corporate tax rate on investment income is 50 percent, including the ITA 123.3 refundable tax on the investment income of a Canadian controlled private corporation. Mrs. Martin is subject to a federal marginal tax rate of 29 percent and a provincial marginal tax rate of 17 percent. The provincial dividend tax credit is equal to 25 percent of the dividend gross up for all dividends.

Required: Prepare calculations that will compare the after tax retention of income that will accrue to Mrs. Martin if:

A. The investment in the interest bearing securities is owned by her as an individual.

B. The investment is owned by a corporation in which she is the sole shareholder, and which pays out all available income in dividends.

Self Study Problem Fifteen - 3 (Flow Through Of Dividend Income)

Mr. Martin is considering investing $200,000 in the preferred shares of a Canadian public company on January 1, 2013. These shares will pay eligible dividends at a rate of 7 percent, resulting in annual pre-tax dividend income of $14,000 for the year. Mr. Martin has no other investment income.

The combined federal and provincial corporate tax rate on investment income is 50 percent, including the ITA 123.3 refundable tax on the investment income of a Canadian controlled private corporation. Mr. Martin is subject to a federal marginal tax rate of 29 percent and a provincial marginal tax rate of 17 percent. The provincial dividend tax credit on all dividends is equal to 25 percent of the dividend gross up.

Required: Prepare calculations that will compare the after tax retention of income that will accrue to Mr. Martin in 2013 if:

A. The investment in the dividend paying securities is owned by him as an individual.

B. The investment is owned by a corporation in which he is the sole shareholder, and which pays out all available income in dividends.

Self Study Problem Fifteen - 4 (Partner As Individual Or Corporation)

Cora Yates is an architectural engineer who is joining the real estate firm Glenora Developers as a junior partner. She will join the partnership on January 1, 2013 and will receive a 10 percent share in the partnership.

She is considering three different approaches to structuring her participation in Glenora. They are as follows:

Alternative 1   Cora will join the partnership as an individual. Her share of the partnership income will be taxed as business income.

For Alternatives 2 and 3, Cora will establish a new corporation and this corporation will become a member of the partnership. Assume that the new corporation is not a personal services business. The corporation will be a CCPC eligible for the small business deduction. Its share of the small business deduction will be $50,000 [(10%)($500,000)].

Alternative 2   Her new corporation will pay corporate tax on its full share of the partnership income, with the after tax funds being paid to Cora as dividends.

Alternative 3   In this alternative, Cora will receive sufficient salary to reduce the corporation's income to its $50,000 share of the annual business limit. Corporate taxes will be paid on the remaining Taxable Income.

Cora knows that a corporation will not provide the benefit of limited liability for her professional actions, but she would like to know if it could be advantageous in maximizing her after tax income from the partnership.

Cora estimates that for the partnership's fiscal year ended December 31, 2013, her or her corporation's share of the partnership income will be $70,000 (10 percent of the $700,000 Taxable Income of the partnership), all of which will be active business income.

Assume Cora is subject to graduated provincial tax rates of 8 percent on the first $43,561 of Taxable Income and 12 percent on the next $43,561 and the combined federal/provincial dividend tax credit is equal to the gross up on both eligible and non-eligible dividends. She has combined federal/provincial personal tax credits of $3,342.

If she forms a new corporation it would be subject to combined federal/provincial taxes on income eligible for the small business deduction at a rate of 15 percent and on other active business income at a rate of 27 percent.

Cora needs all of her after tax partnership income for personal living expenses as she has no other source of income.

Problems For Self Study

Required: Calculate the after tax personal retention of Cora's share of the partnership income for each of the three approaches. Ignore CPP considerations and the Canada employment tax credit. Which approach would you recommend? Briefly explain why this alternative is the best and any other factors she should consider.

Self Study Problem Fifteen - 5 (Income Splitting With Management Company)

Dr. Ashley is a successful dentist with an established practice in a major Canadian city. On January 1, 2013, she established a new CCPC, Ashley Management Services, to manage her professional practice and to hold some of her investments. The Company's year end is December 31.

Dr. Ashley's husband became unemployed in 2012. She hired him to manage this Company and he is paid a salary of $18,400 per year. This salary is reasonable in view of the services that he performs for Ashley Management Services.

During its first year of operation, the Company had the following revenues:

Interest Income	$ 21,600
Eligible Dividends From Canadian Public Companies	13,900
Management Fees	82,900
Rental Revenues	34,600
Total Revenues	$153,000

In the process of earning these revenues, Ashley Management Services incurred the following expenses, including the salary paid to Dr. Ashley's husband:

Expenses On Rental Property (Including CCA)	$27,800
Mr. Ashley's Salary	18,400
Office Salaries	25,400
Office Rent	8,180
CCA On Office And Dental Equipment	5,700
Other Business Expenses	2,170
Total Expenses	$87,650

The corporation's active business income will be taxed at a combined federal/provincial rate of 14 percent, and its investment income will be taxed at a combined federal/provincial rate of 47 percent (including the ITA 123.3 refundable tax on the investment income of Canadian controlled private corporations). It is the intended policy of the Company to pay out all of the after tax corporate income as dividends.

Mr. Ashley owns 60 percent of the voting shares in the Company. The shares were purchased with funds that he earned in his previous job. Dr. Ashley holds the remaining 40 percent.

Dr. Ashley's professional income, without inclusion of any income from Ashley Management Services, is sufficient to give her a combined federal/provincial tax rate of 47 percent. Mr. Ashley's only income is his salary and dividends from Ashley Management Services. Assume that Mr. Ashley's combined federal/provincial rate is 30 percent. They live in a province where the dividend tax credit on both eligible and non-eligible dividends is equal to 25 percent of the gross up.

Required: (Ignore personal tax credits, the Canada employment tax credit, CPP contributions and GST in your solution.)

A. Calculate the minimum Tax Payable by Ashley Management Services and its shareholders for 2013 and the total after tax retention.

B. Assume Dr. Ashley had not established a corporation and had received all of the income personally, with no salary being paid to Mr. Ashley. Calculate the minimum Tax Payable by Dr. Ashley for 2013 and her after tax retention.

Self Study Problem Fifteen - 6 (Loans To Shareholders)

For the last 12 years, Miss Stone has been the president and only shareholder of Stone Enterprises, a Canadian controlled private corporation. She handles all marketing and oversees the day-to-day operations of the business. Her annual salary is $180,000.

The Company has a December 31 year end. During the four year period, January 1, 2010 through December 31, 2013, there were a number of transactions between Miss Stone and her Company. They can be described as follows:

2010   Stone Enterprises loaned $28,000, on an interest free basis, to Miss Stone for various personal expenditures.

2011   The Company loaned an amount of $40,000 to Miss Stone in her capacity as an employee to assist her with the acquisition of a new car. The loan calls for payments of $10,000 per year for the next four years, but does not require the payment of any interest. Payments have been made in 2012 and 2013. The car is to be used solely for Company business. Stone Enterprises makes car loans available to all employees with at least five years of service with the Company.

2012   The Company provided Miss Stone with a $90,000 loan to assist her in purchasing a new home. The loan is interest free and is to be paid off at the rate of $6,000 per year. Stone Enterprises makes housing loans available to all employees with at least five years of service with the Company.

Also in 2012, the Company accrued a bonus to Miss Stone in the amount of $32,000 to be paid in 2013.

2013   Miss Stone receives her 2012 bonus in March, 2013. The bonus is redeposited in the Company on March 31, 2013 and is used by the Company for purchasing inventories. The Company considered $28,000 of these redeposited funds a repayment of the 2010 loan to Miss Stone.

During 2013 the Company declared and paid non-eligible dividends of $22,000.

Miss Stone has only one competitor in her region and, in order to diminish the effectiveness of this company, Miss Stone purchases 40 percent of its outstanding shares for $72,000. Stone Enterprises loans her the entire $72,000 in 2013 on an interest free basis and Miss Stone anticipates that she will repay the loan in 2016.

Required: Discuss, without showing any numerical calculations, the tax effects of the transactions described in the preceding paragraphs.

Self Study Problem Fifteen - 7 (Loans To Shareholders - Tax Planning)

Mr. Arthur Blaine is president and sole shareholder of Blaine Enterprises, a Canadian controlled private corporation with 10 employees. He is also employed by the Company at a salary of $57,000 per year. Since arriving at his office this morning by bicycle, two things have come to Mr. Blaine's attention. They are as follows:

1. Mr. Blaine's accountant has submitted financial statements indicating that his Company has income before taxes of $180,000 for the current year. As the Company is eligible for the small business deduction, this income is taxed at a rate of about 15 percent, leaving an after tax profit in excess of $150,000.

2. Mr. Blaine's neighbour has just informed him he is planning to put his house on the market. Mr. Blaine has coveted that house for many years. To purchase it, Mr. Blaine would need a $125,000 mortgage immediately.

Putting these two items of information together, Mr. Blaine concludes that it would make sense for his corporation to lend him the required $125,000 on an interest free basis for a period of ten years. He believes that there should be no problem with this action in that he is the sole shareholder of the Company, and the Company has sufficient extra cash to make the loan without interfering with its basic business operations.

Required: As Mr. Blaine's personal and corporate tax advisor, give your advice on Mr. Blaine's solution to his mortgage problem.

Self Study Problem Fifteen - 8 (Salary Vs. Dividends)

Ms. Lusk is divorced and has no dependants. She is the sole shareholder and only employee of Lusk Esthetics, a Canadian controlled private company. All of the income of this Corporation is derived from active business activity. Lusk Esthetics qualifies for the small business deduction on all of its 2013 income and, as a consequence, is subject to a combined federal and provincial tax rate of 13 percent on its Taxable Income. During 2013, the Corporation has not paid any salaries or dividends to Ms. Lusk. Any dividends paid would be non-eligible.

Ms. Lusk estimates her 2013 Taxable Income will be $44,385 before consideration of any salary or dividend payments from Lusk Esthetics. This includes $52,000 of employment income from a lucrative part-time job.

The provincial tax rate applicable to Ms. Lusk's personal income is a flat rate of 10 percent. The provincial dividend tax credit is equal to one-third of the dividend gross up for both eligible and non-eligible dividends.

In reviewing her budget, it is clear to Ms. Lusk that by the end of 2013, she will need an additional $10,000 of after tax funds to meet all of her personal expenditures. She expects Lusk Esthetics to be the source of this additional amount, as her Company has had a successful year. She would like to acquire the funds in a manner that will minimize the combined tax cost to both herself and her corporation.

Required: Determine the amount that would be required in the way of salary and in the way of dividends, in order to provide Ms. Lusk with the required after tax funds of $10,000. Which alternative would have the lowest combined tax cost to Ms. Lusk and Lusk Esthetics?

Self Study Problem Fifteen - 9 (Salary Vs. Dividends - Optimum Mix)

Mr. Bedford is happily married to a very successful tax accountant and is the father of 2 year old triplets. He is the only shareholder of Bedford Inc., a Canadian controlled private corporation that was formed a year ago to provide various services to multiple birth families. The Company has a December 31 year end and, at December 31, 2013, Mr. Bedford determines that the Taxable Income of the Company for the year will be $27,500. The Company has this amount available in cash, prior to the payment of taxes, dividends, or salary. All of the Company's income qualifies as active business income.

The Company's activities are confined to a province in which the applicable corporate rate of taxation is 4 percent on income that is eligible for the small business deduction. The province does not levy a payroll tax for health care or post-secondary education. Any dividends paid by Bedford Inc. would be non-eligible.

Mr. Bedford has no other source of income. In his tax bracket, the combined federal/provincial tax rate is 25 percent. For both eligible and non-eligible dividends, the provincial dividend tax credit is equal to 30 percent of the dividend gross up. Mr. Bedford has combined federal/provincial personal tax credits for the 2013 taxation year in the amount of $3,750.

Required:

A.   Determine the after tax amount of cash that Mr. Bedford will retain if all of the Company's income is paid to him in the form of salary. Ignore CPP contributions and the Canada employment tax credit.

B.   Determine the after tax amount of cash that Mr. Bedford will retain if the Company pays the maximum possible dividend.

C. Can Mr. Bedford improve his after tax cash retention by using a combination of salary and dividends? Explain your conclusion.

D. Determine the combination of salary and dividends that will produce the maximum after tax cash balance for Mr. Bedford. Calculate the amount of this after tax cash retention.

E. Briefly describe any other factors that Mr. Bedford should consider in deciding whether to pay himself dividends or, alternatively, salary.

Assignment Problems

(The solutions for these problems are only available in
the solutions manual that has been provided to your instructor.)

Assignment Problem Fifteen - 1 (Advantages Of Incorporation)

Philip Caron is in his mid-fifties and he is married with two teen aged children. For over fifteen years, he has worked as an unincorporated welder. The business is currently netting approximately $250,000 per year. In recent years, Mr. Caron has been using about half of the business earnings for personal living expenses.

In the last five years, he has been refining a fork lift which can be attached to half-ton trucks. He has a product which is selling well with few malfunctions and he is in the process of patenting the design. As a result, his welding business is now predominantly manufacturing these fork lift units.

Some of his welding equipment is old and he is faced with the need to replace it. Also, he needs to acquire larger welders and pipe benders to mass manufacture the fork lift. The business expansion will require substantial capital investment for which external financing will be required.

Required: Briefly discuss whether Mr. Caron should incorporate his business.

Assignment Problem Fifteen - 2 (Example Of Integration)

Your client, Keith Slater, is contemplating the creation of Slater Ltd. He would be the sole shareholder and he plans to transfer his accounting business and investment portfolio to the Company. All of the after tax corporate income would be paid out to him in dividends, to finance his passion for art collecting. He has annual pension and RRIF income of over $200,000, placing him in the maximum federal tax bracket of 29 percent. This income is sufficient to absorb all of his currently available tax credits.

Having taken tax courses in the distant past, he vaguely remembers that something called integration plays a role in whether a corporation is tax advantageous or not. After some discussion and research, you compile the following estimated income amounts and tax rates:

Taxable income of accounting business (Active Business Income)	$80,000
Eligible portfolio dividends	96,000
Federal corporate tax rate after federal abatement	28%
Federal small business deduction	17%
General rate reduction	13%
Provincial corporate tax rate - CCPC rate	3%
Marginal federal personal tax rate	29%
Marginal provincial personal tax rate	13%
Provincial dividend tax credits on:	
Eligible dividends	5/11 of dividend gross up
Non-eligible dividends	1/3 of dividend gross up

Required:

A. Briefly summarize the concept of integration.

B. Assume no corporation is used and the income is received directly. Calculate Mr. Slater's personal Tax Payable, showing separately the Tax Payable on the active business income and the dividends.

C. Assume the income and dividends are received by Slater Ltd. Calculate corporate Tax Payable, after tax income available for distribution, and personal taxes that would be payable on the distribution. Your calculations should show separately the Tax Payable on the active business income and any eligible or non-eligible dividends.

D. Compare the Tax Payable with and without the use of Slater Ltd. and explain why the Tax Payable amounts are different.

Assignment Problem Fifteen - 3 (Flow Through Of Interest Income)

Ms. Martha Abdul is employed by a large public company and has an annual salary of $225,000. The following facts relate to her province of residence:

- The highest marginal tax rate on individuals is 16 percent.
- The provincial dividend tax credit on all dividends is equal to 28 percent.
- The provincial tax rate on the investment income of CCPCs is 12 percent.

Near the end of the current year, Ms. Abdul won $400,000 in the provincial lottery. As she has no current need for these funds and is not keen on investment risk, she intends to invest the full amount for one year in a debt security that pays interest at an annual rate of 3.5 percent. She will not have any other investment income during the year.

Required: Prepare calculations that will compare the after tax retention of income that will accrue to Ms. Abdul if:

A. The investment is owned by her as an individual.

B. The investment is owned by a CCPC in which she is the sole shareholder, and which pays out all available income in dividends.

Assignment Problem Fifteen - 4 (Flow Through Of Dividend Income)

Ms. Martha Abdul is employed by a large public company and has an annual salary of $225,000. The following facts relate to her province of residence:

- The highest marginal tax rate on individuals is 16 percent.
- The provincial dividend tax credit on all dividends is equal to 28 percent.
- The provincial tax rate on the investment income of CCPCs is 12 percent.

Near the end of the current year, Ms. Abdul won $400,000 in the provincial lottery. As she has no current need for these funds and is not keen on investment risk, she intends to invest the full amount for one year in preferred shares that pay eligible dividends of 5.5 percent each year. She will not have any other investment income during the year.

Required: Prepare calculations that will compare the after tax retention of income that will accrue to Ms. Abdul if:

A. The investment is owned by her as an individual.

B. The investment is owned by a CCPC in which she is the sole shareholder, and which pays out all available income in dividends.

Assignment Problem Fifteen - 5 *(Incorporation Of Investment Income)*

Ryan Taylor lives in a province with a combined federal and provincial corporate tax rate on the investment income of CCPCs of 48 percent. This rate includes the ITA 123.3 tax on the investment income. Assume that provincial tax is assessed on individuals at a flat rate of 12 percent. The provincial dividend tax credit is equal to 35 percent of the dividend gross up on all dividends.

Ryan owns the following investments, and anticipates the following Canadian source income for 2013.

	Value At 31/12/2012	Type Of Income	Expected Income For 2013
ABC Company Bonds	$100,000	Interest	$11,000
XYZ Canada Company Shares	400,000	Dividends	20,000
Ace Technology Shares	50,000	Capital Gains	10,000
Safe Bank Of Canada Shares	50,000	Dividends	4,000
		Capital Gains	3,500
Totals	$600,000	N/A	$48,500

Ryan only invests in the shares and debt of large, publicly traded companies. He does not own more than 1 percent of the shares or debt in any of these corporations. All of the dividends received will be designated as eligible by the paying corporation.

In 2013, in addition to the above investment income, Ryan expects to earn $110,000 in employment income. He has combined federal/provincial personal tax credits of $2,650. The total adjusted cost base for his investments is $450,000.

Ryan asks you whether it is financially more attractive for him to have his investments owned by a corporation or to own them directly, as he currently does. Assume that he and his investments will generate the anticipated amounts of income.

Ryan's lifestyle requires him to use all available income. As a consequence, he would like you to assume that, if the investments are transferred to his corporation, the corporation will pay out all available funds as dividends.

Required: Provide an appropriate analysis for Ryan Taylor.

Assignment Problem Fifteen - 6 *(Partner As Individual Or Corporation)*

Joan Wells is a project manager who has been very successful as an individual proprietor. However, she would like to give more attention to some of her personal interests and, to facilitate this objective, she has decided to join Project Design Associates (PDA) as a fifth partner. She will join the partnership on January 1, 2013.

She is considering three different approaches to structuring her participation in PDA. They are as follows:

Alternative 1　Joan will join the partnership as an individual. Her share of the partnership income will be taxed as business income.

For Alternatives 2 and 3, Joan will establish a new corporation and this corporation will become a member of the partnership. Assume that the new corporation is not a personal services business. The corporation will be a CCPC. Its share of the small business deduction will be $100,000 [(20%)($500,000)].

Alternative 2　Her new corporation will pay corporate tax on its full share of the partnership income, with the after tax funds being paid to Joan as dividends.

Assignment Problems

Alternative 3   In this alternative, Joan will receive sufficient salary to reduce the corporation's income to its $100,000 share of the annual business limit.   Corporate taxes will be paid on the remaining Taxable Income.

Assume that Joan lives in a province where the provincial tax rate on individuals is a flat 12 percent of all Taxable Income. In this province, the provincial dividend tax credit is equal to 28 percent of gross up on both eligible and non-eligible dividends. Joan's tax credits for 2013 total $3,920.

If she forms a new corporation it would be subject to a combined federal/provincial tax rate on income eligible for the small business deduction of 14 percent. The rate on other active business income would be 29 percent.

During the PDA's taxation year ending December 31, 2013, it is expected to have Taxable Income of $725,000. All of this income will be active business income and Joan or her corporation will be entitled to 20 percent of the total.

Because she has no other source of income, she requires all of the income that is generated by her participation in PDA.

Required: Calculate the after tax personal retention of Joan's share of the partnership income for each of the three approaches. Ignore CPP considerations and the Canada employment tax credit in your calculations. Which approach would you recommend? Briefly explain why this alternative is the best and any other factors she should consider.

Assignment Problem Fifteen - 7 (Shareholder Loans)

Marian Copps owns 100 percent of the shares of outstanding shares of Copp's Copper Ltd., a Canadian controlled private corporation that specializes in producing copper artifacts for various religious organizations. Ms. Copps is the top salesperson at Copp's Copper Ltd.

The Company has an October 31 year end. It is known for its generous treatment of its employees. This includes the extension of low-interest loans to all employees with more than 2 years of service with the Company. More specifically, the Company will:

- Provide a loan of up to $150,000 to assist an employee in acquiring a residence. When granted, such loans bear interest at 1 percent and must be repaid at the end of five years.

- Provide a loan of up to $30,000 to assist an employee in acquiring an automobile that will be used in their employment duties. As with the home purchase loans, these loans bear interest at 1 percent and must be repaid at the end of five years.

During the calendar year ending December 31, 2013, Ms. Copps received loan proceeds from her company as follows:

1. On January 31, Ms. Copps borrows $150,000 in order to purchase a new residence. The loan bears interest at an annual rate of 1 percent. The loan will be repaid in two annual instalments of $75,000, beginning on February 1, 2014. It does not qualify as a home relocation loan.

2. On March 1, Ms. Copps borrows $349,000 to acquire a new Ferrari F12. She will use it to cut down the driving time to and from her cottage. The loan bears interest at an annual rate of 1 per cent and will be repaid on March 1, 2018.

3. On June 1, Ms. Copps borrows $35,000 to cover cosmetic surgery procedures that will enhance her appearance. The loan is interest free and will be repaid on May 31, 2014.

4. On July 1, Ms. Copps borrows $100,000 in order to stock the wine cellar of her new residence. The loan is interest free and will be repaid on July 1, 2015.

5. On November 1, Ms. Copps borrows $25,000 from her company to finance a much needed week at a luxurious health spa. Since she has already borrowed a significant

amount of funds, she decides the loan will bear interest at 3 percent. It will be repaid on October 1, 2015.

All repayments are made as scheduled. In all of the years under consideration, assume the relevant prescribed rate is 2 percent.

Required:

A. Indicate the tax consequences that will accrue to Ms. Copps as a result of receiving these loans. Briefly explain your conclusions for each loan for the years it is outstanding. Base your interest calculations on the number of months the loans are outstanding.

B. Identify any tax planning issues that are associated with these loans.

Assignment Problem Fifteen - 8 (Bonusing Down)

Morcan Inc. is a Canadian controlled private corporation with a single shareholder, Mrs. Nadia Litvak. Since its inception, all of Morcan's income has been active business income.

For the taxation year ending December 31, 2013, after the deduction of a $300,000 salary to Mrs. Litvak, Morcan expects to have Taxable Income of $750,000. This is the first year during which Morcan's Taxable Income has exceeded the annual business limit for the small business deduction.

Morcan is subject to a combined federal/provincial tax rate of 27 percent on active business income in excess of $500,000. As Mrs. Litvak's tax consultant, you have advised her that she should consider taking out additional salary of $250,000 in order to reduce her Company's Taxable Income to the annual business limit of $500,000. She is resisting this suggestion because she feels her present salary is more than adequate to meet her current living needs.

In Mrs. Litvak's province of residence, the maximum combined federal and provincial tax bracket is 45 percent. The combined federal/provincial dividend tax credit is equal to the dividend gross up for all dividends.

Required: Would it be advantageous for Ms. Litvak to bonus down by paying herself a salary of $250,000? Justify your conclusion.

Assignment Problem Fifteen - 9 (Salary Vs. Dividends)

Miss Morgan established and has operated an extremely successful retail operation. The business is incorporated and Miss Morgan is the sole shareholder. All of the income of this Corporation qualifies for the small business deduction and, as a consequence, is subject to a combined federal and provincial tax rate of 15 percent on its Taxable Income.

Due to the excellent returns on her portfolio investments, Miss Morgan is in the 29 percent federal tax bracket and the 12 percent provincial tax bracket. In her province, the dividend tax credit is equal to 25 percent of the dividend gross up for all dividends.

During the 2013 fiscal year, Miss Morgan expects the business to have Net Income For Tax Purposes of about $170,000. This figure includes a deduction for the payment of her own salary of $84,000.

As Miss Morgan wishes to take an extended holiday during January and February of next year, she is in need of an extra $20,000 in cash in December of 2013. Her company has sufficient excess cash to allow her to either pay additional salary or to declare a dividend. Any dividends paid would be non-eligible.

Required: Determine the amount that would be required in the way of salary and in the way of dividends, in order to provide Miss Morgan with the required after tax funds of $20,000. Which alternative would have the lowest tax cost to Miss Morgan and her corporation?

Assignment Problem Fifteen - 10 (Salary Vs. Dividends - Optimum Mix)

Robert Lucas is the sole shareholder of Speelburg Films Ltd. The company qualifies as a CCPC and has a December 31 year end. For 2013, it has Taxable Income, before consideration of salaries or dividends, of $123,000. All of this income is active business income.

Because of large amounts of capital expenditures during the year, the total amount of cash available for corporate income taxes, dividends, or salary is only $49,000.

As the corporation is in its formative years, it requires the full time attention of Mr. Lucas. Because of this, he has no other source of income. For 2013, he has available tax credits of $3,900 (combined federal and provincial).

Relevant tax information is as follows:

- In his province of residence, the tax rate for individuals on the first $43,561 of taxable income is 6 percent.

- In his province of residence, the dividend tax credit is equal to 35 percent of the gross up on eligible dividends and 30 percent of the gross up on non-eligible dividends.

- All of the company's activities are confined to a province in which the applicable corporate rate of taxation is 3 percent on income eligible for the small business deduction. The province does not levy a payroll tax.

Required: Ignore the required CPP contributions and the Canada employment tax credit when answering Parts A to D in this problem.

A. Determine the after tax amount of cash that Mr. Lucas will retain if all of the company's cash is used to pay taxes and salary.

B. Determine the after tax amount of cash that Mr. Lucas will retain if the Company pays the maximum possible dividend.

C. Can Mr. Lucas improve his after tax cash retention by using a combination of salary and dividends? Explain your conclusion.

D. If your answer to Part C is positive, determine the combination of salary and/or dividends that will produce the maximum after tax cash retention for Mr. Lucas. Calculate the amount of this after tax cash retention.

E. Briefly describe any other factors that Mr. Lucas should consider in deciding whether to pay himself dividends or, alternatively, salary.

CHAPTER 16

Rollovers Under Section 85

Rollovers Under Section 85

Introduction

16-1.   Chapter 15 gave detailed consideration to the question of whether it would be advantageous to establish a corporation in order to reduce, defer, or redistribute the amount of Tax Payable. If the results of this analysis favour the use of a corporation, Section 85 of the *Act* provides an attractive basis for the transfer of property to the new corporation.

16-2.   The problem that is involved with such a transfer is that the assets may have been owned by the transferor for some period of time. In these circumstances, it is possible that their fair market values may be well in excess of their adjusted cost base and/or their undepreciated capital cost. As a transfer by a taxpayer to a corporation would be considered a disposition by that taxpayer, the incorporation of an existing business could result in a need to include both capital gains and recapture in the transferor's Taxable Income. In a typical situation, where the owner of an operating business decides to transfer all of its assets to a newly formed corporation, the resulting tax liability could be significant.

> **Example**   Joanne Browski has an unincorporated business that is using assets with a fair market value of $572,000. The tax values for these assets total $225,000. Ms. Browski would like to transfer these assets to a corporation and continue her operations in that legal form.

> **Analysis**   Under the usual tax rules, the transfer of these assets to a new corporation would result in capital gains and recapture of $347,000. The potential taxation of this income would be a significant deterrent to the incorporation of Ms. Browski's business.

16-3.   Section 85 of the *Income Tax Act* is designed to provide relief in this type of situation. In somewhat simplified terms, it permits Ms. Browski's property to be transferred to a corporation on either a tax free basis, or with a level of taxation that is determined at her discretion. As noted in earlier Chapters, such transactions are referred to in tax work as rollovers.

16-4.   Of the rollovers that are available, the provisions in Section 85 provide for one of the most important and widely used. In this Chapter we will provide detailed coverage of the application of this Section. Other rollovers involving corporations will be given coverage in Chapter 17.

General Rules For The Transfer

Transferor And Transferee

Transferors

16-5.   As indicated in the introduction, we are concerned here with transfers of property to a corporation at a value that can be elected by the transferor and the corporation. There are several possibilities with respect to the identity of the transferor:

- The transferor may be an **individual** who wishes to incorporate his proprietorship.
- The transferor may be a **corporation** that wishes to transfer some of its assets to a different corporation.
- The transferor may be a **trust** that wishes to transfer some of its assets to a corporation.
- The transferor may be a **partner** who wishes to incorporate his partnership interest.

16-6.   ITA 85(1) refers to taxpayers and this subsection covers the rules related to transferors who are individuals, corporations, and trusts. As partnerships are not "taxpayers" for income tax purposes, a separate ITA 85(2) provides for the transfer of partnership assets to a corporation.

Transferees

16-7.   With respect to transferees, Section 85 requires that they be taxable Canadian corporations. A "Canadian corporation" is defined in ITA 89(1) as a corporation that is currently resident in Canada and that was either incorporated in Canada, or has been a resident continuously since June 18, 1971. ITA 89(1) also defines a "taxable Canadian corporation" as a Canadian corporation that was not, by virtue of a statutory provision, exempt from taxation under Part I of the *Income Tax Act*.

Eligible Property

16-8.   Only "eligible property", the components of which are defined in ITA 85(1.1), can be transferred under Section 85. The major items listed in the Subsection include:

- both depreciable and non-depreciable capital property, generally not including real property owned by non-residents;
- eligible capital property;
- Canadian resource properties;
- foreign resource properties;
- inventories, other than inventories of real property; and
- real property owned by a non-resident person and used in the year in a business carried on by that person in Canada.

16-9.   The general exclusion of real property owned by non-residents reflects the fact that this type of property is Taxable Canadian Property and gains on its disposition are subject to Canadian taxes, without regard to the residency of the seller. The exclusion is designed to prevent a non-resident who owns Canadian real estate from being able to transfer the property on a tax free basis to a corporation, and subsequently selling the shares in the corporation on a tax free basis. As explained in Chapter 20, gains on such dispositions are typically exempted from Canadian tax by international tax treaties.

16-10.   The second exclusion from assets eligible for the Section 85 rollover would be Canadian resident owned real property that constitutes an inventory. That is, if a group of real property assets is being actively traded, rather than being held for their income producing ability, they are not eligible for a tax free rollover under ITA 85.

16-11.   This latter exclusion of inventories of real property can be a particularly troublesome provision due to the fact that, in practice, some taxpayers may not be certain as to the status of their real estate holdings. If a taxpayer was to go through the Section 85 rollover procedures and then, after the fact, find that the transferred real estate holdings were considered inventory by the CRA, the tax consequences would be very severe. In this type of situation, it would be advisable that any real properties transferred be held by the corporation for some period of time before they are sold.

Consideration To Transferor

16-12.   In return for the property transferred to the corporation, the corporation may provide various types of consideration to the transferor. The one requirement that is specified in ITA 85(1) is that some part of this consideration must consist of shares of the transferee corporation.

16-13.   The shares issued may be either preferred, common, or some combination of the two types. Further, the requirement for share consideration to be used can be satisfied by the issuance of as little as one share to the transferor. For reasons that will become evident later in this Chapter, the usual Section 85 transaction involves the use of a combination of shares and non-share consideration (e.g. cash or debt securities). In this context, the non-share consideration is usually referred to as the "boot".

16-14.   A further point here is that, without regard to the values that are elected for the exchange, the fair market value of the consideration provided to the transferor should be equal to the total fair market value of the assets transferred to the corporation. As will be discussed later in this Chapter, if these amounts are not equal, the difference may be viewed as a benefit to the transferor, or a gift to a related party.

Making The Election

16-15.   Both the transferor and the transferee corporation must elect to have the Section 85 provisions apply. This joint election is accomplished by filing Form T2057 (transfers from individuals, trusts, and corporations) or T2058 (transfers from partnerships), on or before the earliest of the dates on which the normal tax returns are due for the two taxpayers.

16-16.   A late election may be filed for up to three years after this date and, with the permission of the CRA, a late election will be accepted after the end of this three year period. Whenever there is a late election, a penalty of one-quarter of 1 percent of any deferred gain will be assessed for each month beyond the normal filing date. The maximum penalty is $100 per month to a maximum of $8,000.

16-17.   In making the election, it is crucial that the taxpayer list all of the properties that are to be covered. If a property is omitted from the forms, the normal rules associated with dispositions will apply. This could result in the need to recognize capital gains, recapture, or business income on the transfer, an outcome that might require needless payment of taxes.

Establishing The Transfer Price

Importance

16-18.   One of the most significant features of ITA 85 is that it provides for the transfer of various properties to a corporation at values that are jointly elected by the transferor and transferee. Careful consideration must be given to the election of an appropriate transfer price in that, in general, this elected value establishes three important values. These are:

Transferor   The deemed proceeds of disposition for the property given up.

Transferor   The adjusted cost base of the property received from the corporation.

Transferee   The tax cost of the property received by the corporation (adjusted cost base, UCC, or CEC).

16-19.   As will be discussed at a later point in this Chapter, the elected value is also influential in determining the PUC of the newly issued shares.

Basic Rules

16-20.   While there are a number of complications associated with establishing transfer prices, the basic rules are very straightforward. The elected values cannot exceed fair market values and cannot be less than the adjusted cost base of non-depreciable assets, or the UCC of depreciable assets. As we will see in the next section, the floor elected value is also limited by the boot, or non-share consideration, received.

> **Example** Mr. Thompson owns non-depreciable capital assets with a fair market value of $750,000 and an adjusted cost base of $500,000. On the transfer of these assets to a corporation, he will receive consideration with a fair market value of $750,000. However, under the provisions of ITA 85, the elected value can be any value between a floor of $500,000 and a ceiling of $750,000.

> **Analysis** In most situations, the transferor wishes to avoid recognizing income on the transfer and, in order to do this, the elected value will be the floor of $500,000. The election of this value will have the following tax consequences for the transferor and the transferee:

> - The $500,000 will be the proceeds of disposition to the transferor. As this is equal to his adjusted cost base for the assets, there will be no capital gain on the transfer.

> - The adjusted cost base to the corporation will be $500,000. This means that, if the corporation were to sell the assets immediately for their fair market value of $750,000, a capital gain of $250,000 ($750,000 - $500,000) would have to be recognized. This reflects the fact that the gain on the assets at the time of transfer was only deferred, not eliminated, by the use of the ITA 85 rollover.

> - While we have not specified the type of consideration that will be received by the transferor, the election of $500,000 as the transfer price means that the adjusted cost base of the consideration will be this amount. This will be less than the $750,000 fair market value of the consideration.

16-21. You should note that this scenario raises the possibility of double taxation on the $250,000 gain. The adjusted cost base of the property transferred and the consideration received by the transferor is $500,000. If the corporation sells the assets for their fair market value of $750,000, there will be a $250,000 gain at the corporate level. If the consideration received by the transferor is in the form of shares, a sale of these shares at their fair market value of $750,000 would result in the $250,000 gain being taxed a second time at the individual level. This would suggest that, if either the assets transferred, or the consideration received by the transferor are to be sold, the election should be made at the fair market value of $750,000.

Non-Share Consideration (Boot)

16-22. The term, "boot", is commonly used to refer to non-share consideration given to the transferor in an ITA 85 rollover. It would include cash paid to the transferor and new debt of the transferee corporation issued to the transferor. In those cases where an existing business is being transferred under these provisions, boot would include the assumption by the transferee corporation of any debt of the existing business that is being transferred.

16-23. Other types of non-share consideration (e.g., capital assets) could be used in an ITA 85 rollover and, if this was the case, the term boot would still be appropriate. However, in almost all situations, boot is restricted to cash, new debt issued by the transferee corporation, or existing debt of the transferor assumed by the transferee corporation.

16-24. Boot is of considerable significance in that, if the rollover is properly structured, it constitutes an amount of cash or cash equivalent that will be received by the transferor on a tax free basis. Because of this, the other basic rule on establishing a transfer price is that the elected amount cannot be less than the value of the non-share consideration provided to the transferor.

16-25. The example that was presented in Paragraph 16-20 involved non-depreciable capital assets with an adjusted cost base of $500,000 and a fair market value of $750,000. With respect to the consideration received by Mr. Thompson, assume that it is as follows:

Cash	$600,000
Shares Of Transferee Corporation	150,000
Total (Equals Fair Market Value Of Assets Transferred)	**$750,000**

16-26. Because the elected value cannot be below the value of the non-share consideration, the minimum elected value would be $600,000. If $600,000 was the elected value, it would result in the following tax consequences:

• The proceeds of disposition to the transferor would be $600,000, resulting in a taxable capital gain of $50,000 [(1/2)($600,000 - $500,000)].

• The adjusted cost base of the assets for the corporation would be the transfer price of $600,000. This means that if the corporation sells the assets for their fair market value of $750,000, the capital gain would be $150,000.

• The adjusted cost base of the consideration received by the transferor would be $600,000. As will be discussed at a later point, all of this amount must be allocated to the non-share consideration, leaving the share consideration with a nil adjusted cost base.

The Usual Scenario

16-27. As illustrated in the preceding example, if the boot exceeds the tax values (adjusted cost base or UCC) of the assets transferred, the result is income for tax purposes. As one of the usual goals in using ITA 85 is to avoid a tax liability on the transfer of assets, the normal procedure is to set the transfer price at an amount equal to the tax values of the assets and to restrict the use of boot to this value. In the example presented, this would mean using $500,000 as the elected value and paying or issuing non-share consideration in this same amount.

16-28. In addition, the fair market value of the consideration received by the transferor must be equal to the fair market value of the assets transferred to the corporation. In the example presented in Paragraph 16-20, this value is $750,000. This means that if the maximum non-share consideration of $500,000 is used, shares must be issued with a fair market value of $250,000.

16-29. If we apply this scenario to the example presented in Paragraph 16-20, the results would be as follows:

• As the proceeds of disposition would be $500,000, no capital gain would arise on the transfer to the corporation.

• The adjusted cost base to the corporation of the assets acquired will be $500,000.

• The adjusted cost base of the non-share consideration to the transferor would be $500,000. This means that the adjusted cost base of the share consideration would be nil.

16-30. There are a number of complications associated with rollovers under ITA 85 and they will be the subject of much of the remainder of this Chapter. However, the great majority of these transactions will follow the pattern illustrated in the preceding simple example.

Transfer Prices - Detailed Rules

Rules Applicable To All Assets

16-31. There are a number of rules in ITA 85 that apply to all types of property. To begin, ITA 85(1)(a) establishes that the amount elected by the taxpayer and corporation shall be deemed to be the taxpayer's proceeds of disposition, as well as the cost of the property to the corporation.

16-32. A further general rule is as follows:

ITA 85(1)(b)   ...where the amount that the taxpayer and corporation have agreed on in their election in respect of the property is less than the fair market value, at the time of the disposition, of the consideration therefor (other than any shares of the capital stock of the corporation or a right to receive any such shares) received by the taxpayer, the amount so agreed on shall, irrespective of the amount actually so agreed on by them, be deemed to be an amount equal to that fair market value;

16-33.   This establishes that the elected value cannot be less than the boot ("consideration other than shares of stock of the corporation").

16-34.   Finally, a further provision limits the elected value to the fair market value of the property transferred:

ITA 85(1)(c)   ... where the amount that the taxpayer and the corporation have agreed on in their election in respect of the property is greater than the fair market value, at the time of the disposition, of the property so disposed of, the amount so agreed on shall, irrespective of the amount actually so agreed on, be deemed to be an amount equal to that fair market value;

16-35.   These general rules apply to all assets transferred, thereby establishing a range for the election. This range can be outlined as follows:

Ceiling Value   Fair market value of the assets transferred to the corporation.

Floor Value   The floor value will be equal to the greater of:

- the fair market value of the non-share consideration (boot) given to the transferor in return for the assets transferred; and

- the tax values (adjusted cost base or UCC) of the assets transferred.

16-36.   The application of the term, "tax values", in the preceding outline of the rules will vary with the type of asset involved. Attention will be given to these differences in the material which follows.

Accounts Receivable

16-37.   As was discussed in Chapter 6, when accounts receivable are transferred in conjunction with all of the other assets of a business, under the usual rules, the disposition will be treated as a capital transaction, with any resulting loss being only one-half deductible. Further, as the transferee has not included these amounts in income, no deduction can be made for bad debts. If the transferee collects less than the transfer amount, the difference must be treated as a capital loss and again, only one-half of this loss will be deductible.

16-38.   To avoid these results, the usual procedure is to use a joint election under ITA 22. This election allows any loss to be treated as a fully deductible business loss and permits the transferee to deduct bad debts after the transfer. You may recall that this election was discussed in Chapter 6, starting at Paragraph 6-179. If you do not recall the application of ITA 22, you should review this material now as this election will be commonly used in the problem material in this Chapter.

16-39.   While accounts receivable can be transferred under ITA 85, taxpayers are not permitted to elect under both ITA 85 and ITA 22. In general, it will be to the advantage of the taxpayer to make the ITA 22 election and, as a result, accounts receivable will usually not be one of the assets listed in the ITA 85 election.

16-40.   Note, however, this does not prevent these assets from being transferred. Using the ITA 22 joint election, they can be transferred at fair market value, with any resulting loss being fully deductible to the transferor. The corporation will have to include the difference between the face value and the price paid in income, but any difference between the face value and the amounts collected will be 100 percent deductible.

Inventories And Non-Depreciable Capital Property

16-41.   Unlike the situation with accounts receivable, when inventories are disposed of in conjunction with the sale of substantially all of the assets of a business, any difference between fair market value and cost is automatically treated as business income or loss, not as a capital gain or loss. This is specifically provided for in ITA 23, with no election being required to bring this provision into effect.

16-42.   Non-depreciable capital property of a business would include land, temporary investments, and long-term investments. As capital property is involved, any gain or loss on their disposition would be treated as a capital gain or loss.

16-43.   In making the election here, the highest value will be the fair market value of the assets transferred to the corporation. The minimum election cannot be below the amount of the boot received by the transferor. However, a further floor limit is specified for the inventories and non-depreciable capital property in ITA 85(1)(c.1) to ensure that artificial losses cannot be created. This limit is the lesser of the fair market value of the property and its tax cost. For non-depreciable capital assets, the tax cost would be the adjusted cost base of the property. For inventory, tax cost would be either cost or market, depending on how the inventory balance is carried for tax purposes.

16-44.   Putting these limits together means that the minimum elected value for the floor, as specified in ITA 85(1)(e.3), will be the greater of:

A. The fair market value of the boot (the general floor for all assets); and

B. The lesser of:
   • the tax cost of the property; and
   • the fair market value of the property.

16-45.   These rules can be illustrated using the three examples that follow:

	Example One	Example Two	Example Three
Fair Market Value Of Property	$15,000	$10,000	$20,000
Adjusted Cost Base	12,000	12,000	14,000
Fair Market Value Of The Boot	5,000	5,000	17,000

16-46.   In Example One, the maximum transfer value is the fair market value of $15,000 and the minimum value is the cost of $12,000. The normal election value would be $12,000. Also note that up to $12,000 of boot could have been taken out without changing the minimum election, or creating immediate tax consequences.

16-47.   In Example Two, the $10,000 fair market value is both the floor and the ceiling. If the property is inventories, this required election will result in a fully deductible business loss of $2,000 ($12,000 - $10,000). Alternatively, if the election was made on non-depreciable capital property, the result would be an allowable capital loss of $1,000 [(1/2)($12,000 - $10,000)]. As explained beginning in Paragraph 16-50, this capital loss would be disallowed.

16-48.   In Example Three, the maximum value is again the fair market value. While the $14,000 cost is lower than the $20,000 fair market value, it is also lower than the boot. This means that, in this example, the minimum value that can be elected is the boot of $17,000. If this property is inventory, this election will result in fully taxable business income of $3,000 ($17,000 - $14,000). If the election was made on non-depreciable capital property, the result will be a taxable capital gain of $1,500 [(1/2)($17,000 - $14,000)].

16-49.   If the goal is to structure the rollover to avoid any gain on the transfer of assets, Example Three will not accomplish this objective. In order to avoid a gain, the usual procedure is to limit the non-share consideration to the minimum elected value as otherwise determined, or $14,000 in Example Three.

Exercise Sixteen - 1

Subject: Elected Value For Non-Depreciable Property

Jean Doan's unincorporated business has inventories with a fair market value of $125,000 and a tax cost of $140,000. In addition, he owns land with a fair market value of $350,000 and a tax cost of $110,000. He intends to transfer these assets to a new corporation, taking back $125,000 in cash for the inventories and $150,000 in cash for the land. If he uses ITA 85 for the transfer, what is the possible range of values that can be elected for the two properties? Assume he elects the lowest possible value in each case. What are the tax consequences for Mr. Doan?

End of Exercise. Solution available in Study Guide.

Non-Depreciable Capital Property - Disallowed Capital Losses
General Rules
16-50.   The special rules described in the following material apply only to non-depreciable capital assets. They do not apply to either inventories or depreciable capital assets as it is not possible to have capital losses on these types of assets.

16-51.   While we are discussing these rules in the material related to Section 85 rollovers, you should note that they are applicable to transfers to affiliated persons, without regard to whether Section 85 is being used. The discussion is located here because, when a non-depreciable capital asset is transferred under ITA 85, the recognition of a loss may be unavoidable because of the rules limiting the elected values. This was the case in Example Two in Paragraph 16-45.

16-52.   The basic rule applicable to these situations is found in ITA 40(2)(g), which indicates that a taxpayer's loss, to the extent that it is a "superficial loss", is deemed to be nil. As with many other concepts related to capital assets, the definition of "superficial loss" is found in ITA 54:

> **"superficial loss"** of a taxpayer means the taxpayer's loss from the disposition of a particular property where
>
> (a) during the period that begins 30 days before and ends 30 days after the disposition, the taxpayer or a person affiliated with the taxpayer acquires a property (in this definition referred to as the "substituted property") that is, or is identical to, the particular property, and
>
> (b) at the end of that period, the taxpayer or a person affiliated with the taxpayer owns or had a right to acquire the substituted property.

16-53.   Read together, these provisions deem to be nil any capital loss arising on a transfer to an affiliated person. While the allocation of the loss will depend on whether the transferor is an individual, a trust or a corporation, the denial of the loss is applicable to all taxpayers. The actual allocation of the denied loss will be dealt with after our discussion of affiliated persons.

Affiliated Persons
16-54.   The term "affiliated person" is defined in ITA 251.1(1) as follows:

A.   An individual is affiliated to another individual only if that individual is his spouse or common-law partner.

B.   A corporation is affiliated with:
1.   a person who controls the corporation;
2.   each member of an affiliated group of persons who controls the corporation; and
3.   the spouse or common-law partner of a person listed in (1) or (2).

    C. Two corporations are affiliated if:

1. each corporation is controlled by a person, and the person by whom one corporation is controlled is affiliated with the person by whom the other corporation is controlled;
2. one corporation is controlled by a person, the other corporation is controlled by a group of persons, and each member of that group is affiliated with that person; or
3. each corporation is controlled by a group of persons, and each member of each group is affiliated with at least one member of the other group.

16-55.   ITA 251.1(3) contains definitions that are required in the application of these rules. The two that are of importance here are:

> **Affiliated group of persons** means a group of persons each member of which is affiliated with every other member.

> **Controlled** means controlled, directly or indirectly, in any manner whatever. [The reference here is to de facto control, which does not necessarily require majority ownership of all shares.]

16-56.   As was previously noted, if a capital loss arises on a transfer to an affiliated person, it is deemed to be nil. This rule applies to all taxpayers, including both individuals and corporations. You should also note that, for purposes of the affiliated person rules, the term "person" includes partnerships.

Allocation Of Disallowed Capital Loss

16-57.   When the transferor is an individual, the disallowed loss is allocated to the adjusted cost base of the transferred property. This requirement is dictated by ITA 53(1)(f), which describes adjustments to the cost base of a transferred property.

> **Example**   Ms. Hannah Howard, the sole shareholder of HH Ltd., transfers land with an adjusted cost base of $50,000 and a fair market value of $40,000, to HH Ltd. The transfer is made under Section 85 at an elected value of $40,000.

> **Analysis**   The $10,000 loss ($40,000 - $50,000) on the transfer is disallowed. As the transferor is an individual, it will be allocated to the adjusted cost base of the land in the tax records of HH Ltd. This means that the adjusted cost base to HH Ltd. will be the same $50,000 ($40,000, plus the $10,000 loss) that was the adjusted cost base to Ms. Howard.

16-58.   When the transferor is a corporation, trust, or partnership, the allocation of the disallowed loss is covered under ITA 40(3.4). In effect, this provision keeps the loss in the tax records of the transferor, to be recognized when one of the following events occurs:

- the transferee disposes of the property to a non-affiliated person (includes deemed dispositions);
- if the transferor is a corporation,
  - it is subject to an acquisition of control; or
  - it is subject to an ITA 88(2) winding up.

> **Example**   HC Ltd. transfers land with an adjusted cost base of $50,000 and a fair market value of $40,000 to HCSub, a corporation controlled by HC Ltd., i.e., an affiliated person. Two years later, HCSub sells the land for $35,000 to a non-affiliated person.

> **Analysis**   The $10,000 ($40,000 - $50,000) loss on the transfer to HCSub will be disallowed at the time of the transfer. However, when the land is sold by HCSub for $35,000, HC Ltd. will recognize the disallowed loss of $10,000 ($50,000 - $40,000). In addition, HCSub will recognize a $5,000 ($40,000 - $35,000) loss at the time of sale. The result is a total loss for the two companies of $15,000 ($50,000 - $35,000).

Tax Planning

16-59.   To the extent that the asset with the unrealized loss is necessary to the continued operations of the business, for example land on which the enterprise's factory is located, it makes no difference whether it is transferred under the provisions of ITA 85 or outside the election. In either case, the loss will be disallowed at the time of the transfer.

16-60.   If an asset is not essential to the operations of the corporation, a preferable course of action may be to sell it to a non-affiliated person. This will permit the immediate recognition of any loss on its disposition. However, if the asset is an integral part of the operations of the transferor this is not a viable alternative.

16-61.   The other basic point here is, that if the asset in question has an unrealized loss, there is no reason to elect to transfer it under Section 85. The objective that the taxpayer is attempting to achieve in using Section 85 is to defer the taxation of income. When losses are involved on particular assets, including those assets in the Section 85 rollover complicates the election without contributing to the taxpayer's desired goals.

Depreciable Property

General Rules

16-62.   As with other assets, the ceiling for the election is the fair market value of the asset and the general floor is the fair market value of the non-share consideration received by the transferor. However, as was the case with inventories and non-depreciable capital property, a further lower limit is specified in the *Income Tax Act*.

16-63.   ITA 85(1)(e) indicates that for depreciable property, the lower limit is the least of the UCC for the class, the fair market value of each individual property, and the cost of each individual property. This means that the overall lower limit for the election, as specified in ITA 85(1)(e.3), is the greater of:

A. The fair market value of the boot (general floor for all assets), and

B. The least of:

- the balance of the UCC for the class;
- the cost to the taxpayer of each individual property; and
- the fair market value of each individual property.

Examples - Elected Values

16-64.   These rules can be illustrated by the following two examples, each involving the transfer of the only asset in a CCA class:

	Example One	Example Two
Fair Market Value Of The Property	$50,000	$18,000
UCC Of Class (Last Asset In Class)	20,000	20,000
Cost Of The Property	27,000	30,000
Fair Market Value Of The Boot	15,000	15,000

Example One Analysis   In Example One, the range of the election would extend from the UCC of $20,000 as the floor to the fair market value of $50,000. Note that any election in between the UCC of $20,000 and the cost of $27,000 would result in recapture of CCA. The normal election here would be the UCC of $20,000, which results in the transferor not recognizing a capital gain or recapture of CCA. In addition, the transferor would usually take out $20,000 in boot. In Example One, $5,000 more boot could be taken out without creating immediate tax consequences.

Example Two Analysis   In Example Two, using the limits specified in ITA 85(1)(e.3) the ceiling value and the floor value would be the $18,000 fair market value of the property. With the ceiling and floor at the same value, the general rules would indicate that only this $18,000 value could be elected. In Example Two, $3,000 more boot could be taken out without creating immediate tax consequences. Since the transfer of the property removes the last asset in this CCA class, the fact that the elected value is below the UCC suggests a terminal loss. However, as will be discussed beginning in Paragraph 16-70, ITA 85 does not apply to this transfer and this terminal loss will be disallowed.

Example - Order Of Disposition

16-65.   An additional problem arises in the case of depreciable assets in situations where a number of different assets that belong to the same CCA class are being transferred. This problem can be illustrated by the following example:

> **Example**   An individual owns two assets in a particular CCA class and the UCC for that class is $28,000. Data on the two assets is as follows:
>
> | | Asset One | Asset Two |
> |---|---|---|
> | Cost Of Asset | $15,000 | $30,000 |
> | Fair Market Value | 20,000 | 25,000 |

16-66.   The problem here is that the wording of the transfer price rules for depreciable assets requires the floor to be based on the least of the cost of each individual asset, fair market value of each individual asset, but UCC for the class as a whole. This determination has to be made with respect to each asset in the class, with the resulting figures summed for purposes of the election floor.

16-67.   This means that, if the general rules were applied, the floor values would be $15,000 for Asset One, plus $25,000 for Asset Two. This reflects the fact that both of these individual values are less than the $28,000 UCC for the class. However, if these values are elected, a total of $40,000 would be subtracted from the class. Since the UCC balance for the class is only $28,000, this would result in recapture of $12,000.

16-68.   To alleviate this problem, ITA 85(1)(e.1) allows an assumption that the properties are transferred one at a time. This means that for the transfer of Asset One, if the floor value of $15,000 was elected (this assumes that the non-share consideration provided to the transferor does not exceed this amount), this $15,000 would be subtracted from the UCC of $28,000.

16-69.   The resulting UCC balance would be $13,000, and when the depreciable asset rules are applied to Asset Two, this UCC balance of $13,000 would become the floor. If the taxpayer again elected to use the floor value, the $13,000 would be deducted from the UCC and this would reduce the UCC balance to nil without triggering recaptured CCA.

Exercise Sixteen - 2

Subject: Elected Value For Depreciable Property

Eric Li has two depreciable assets - a Class 1 building and a Class 10 vehicle. The assets are to be transferred to a corporation using ITA 85. Relevant information on the assets is as follows:

	Class 1	Class 10
Fair Market Value Of The Property	$475,000	$12,000
UCC Of Class (Last Asset In Class)	150,000	8,000
Cost Of The Property	220,000	28,000
Fair Market Value Of The Boot	250,000	10,000

What is the possible range of values that can be elected for the two properties? Assume he elects the lowest possible value in each case. What are the tax consequences for Mr. Li?

End of Exercise. Solution available in Study Guide.

Depreciable Property - Disallowed Terminal Losses
General Rules
16-70.   In Paragraph 16-64, we noted that the terminal loss resulting from the required election on the asset in Example Two will be disallowed. More specifically, if a depreciable property with a fair market value that is less than its UCC is transferred by a person (individual, trust, or corporation) or a partnership to an affiliated person (see Paragraph 16-54), ITA 13(21.2) indicates that:

- ITA 85 does not apply;

- the proceeds of the disposition are deemed to be the UCC amount, thereby disallowing the terminal loss; and

- the transferee's capital cost for the property is deemed to be the transferor's capital cost, with the excess of that amount over the fair market value of the asset deemed to be CCA deducted in previous periods.

16-71.   In Example Two from Paragraph 16-64, the property had a capital cost of $30,000, a UCC for the class of $20,000, and a fair market value of $18,000. As the $18,000 fair market value was less than the $20,000 UCC of the class, this means that ITA 85 does not apply to this transfer. In addition, ITA 13(21.2) would disallow this loss on any transfer to an affiliated person. However, as you would expect, the loss does not disappear.

16-72.   If the property is simply sold to the corporation for its fair market value, the property will have a deemed capital cost to the transferee of $30,000 and a UCC value of $18,000. The $2,000 disallowed loss will be deemed to be a depreciable property that is owned by the transferor. It will be allocated to the same class as the transferred property for CCA purposes and will be subject to the usual CCA procedures. However, it will be kept in a separate class so that any unamortized amount can be recognized when one of the following events occurs:

- the transferee disposes of the property to a non-affiliated person (includes deemed dispositions);
- the use of the property is changed from income earning to non-income earning;
- if the transferor is a corporation,
  - it is subject to an acquisition of control; or
  - it is subject to an ITA 88(2) winding up.

Tax Planning
16-73.   As was noted in our discussion of capital losses on transfers of non-depreciable capital property, Section 85 is normally used in order to defer the taxation of various types of income. If there is a terminal loss present on a depreciable property, ITA 85 cannot be used. This means that, if the asset is necessary to the continued operations of the business, it will be sold to the corporation at fair market value, with any terminal loss on the transaction being disallowed by ITA 13(21.2). If the asset is not necessary to the continued operations of the business, it would be preferable to sell it to a non-affiliated person.

Eligible Capital Property
General Rules
16-74.   As is the case for all other assets, the general ceiling and floor for making an election under ITA 85(1) is the fair market value of the assets transferred and the fair market value of the non-share consideration received, respectively. As was the case with inventories, non-depreciable property, and depreciable property, a further lower limit is specified in the *Act* for eligible capital property.

16-75.   ITA 85(1)(d) limits the floor to the least of 4/3 of the taxpayer's cumulative eligible capital in respect of the business immediately before the disposition, the cost to the taxpayer of the property, and the fair market value of the property at the time of the disposition. This means that the overall lower limit for the election [see ITA 85(1)(e.3)], is the greater of:

A. The fair market value of the boot (general floor for all assets), and

B. The least of:

  • 4/3 of the cumulative eligible capital balance;
  • the cost to the taxpayer of each individual property; and
  • the fair market value of each individual property.

Examples - Transfers Of Eligible Capital Property

16-76.   Assuming that the corporation has only one eligible capital property, these provisions can be illustrated using the following examples:

	Example One	Example Two
Fair Market Value Of The Property	$60,000	$60,000
Cumulative Eligible Capital Balance	37,500	52,500
4/3 Cumulative Eligible Capital Balance	50,000	70,000
Cost Of The Property	55,000	80,000
Fair Market Value Of The Boot	40,000	40,000

16-77.   In Example One, the range of election values would extend from a floor of $50,000 to a ceiling of $60,000. The floor value would normally be elected because its use would have no immediate tax implications. Note that additional non-share consideration of $10,000 could be taken out in this example without creating immediate tax consequences.

16-78.   In Example Two, $60,000 is both the floor and the ceiling and if this amount is elected, it would result in the reduction of the transferor's cumulative eligible capital account by $45,000 (three-quarters of $60,000). This disposition would normally produce a loss of $7,500 ($52,500 - $45,000). However, such losses may be disallowed. This point will be covered beginning in Paragraph 16-81.

Transfers Of Goodwill

16-79.   As discussed in Chapter 5, the most important component of cumulative eligible capital is usually goodwill. An individual transferring a business to a corporation would generally not have a balance in the cumulative eligible capital account, reflecting the fact that only purchased goodwill is given recognition for either accounting or tax purposes. This means that under the general rules for transfer price elections, the goodwill could be transferred at a value of zero.

16-80.   The danger in doing this is that giving no consideration to goodwill could result in this asset being inadvertently omitted from the election. This would make the transfer a non-arm's length gift and, under ITA 69, the proceeds would be deemed to be fair market value. To avoid this possibility, a value of at least $1 should be assigned to goodwill when assets that constitute a business entity are being transferred to a corporation.

Exercise Sixteen - 3

Subject: Elected Value For CEC

During 2012, Joan's Enterprises acquires an unlimited life franchise at a cost of $135,000. Maximum CEC is deducted for that year. At the beginning of 2013, all of the assets of Joan's Enterprises are transferred to a new corporation. At this time, the fair market value of the franchise is estimated to be $175,000. Joan's consideration for this asset is made up of $135,000 in cash, plus shares in the new corporation with a fair market value of $40,000. What is the possible range of values that can be elected for the franchise? If the minimum value is elected, what would be the tax consequences for Joan's Enterprises?

End of Exercise. Solution available in Study Guide.

Eligible Capital Property - Disallowed Deductions

General Rules

16-81.   When a taxpayer ceases to carry on business, three-quarters of any disposition proceeds allocated to cumulative eligible capital items will be subtracted from the balance in this account. If the result is a negative balance in the cumulative eligible capital account, the result will be an income inclusion under ITA 14(1). Alternatively, if a positive balance remains, it can generally be deducted under ITA 24(1).

16-82.   Note that these amounts are very much like recaptured CCA and terminal losses on depreciable assets. However, these latter items are included or deducted under other Sections of the *Act* and, as a consequence, those terms are not used when the analogous events occur with respect to cumulative eligible capital.

16-83.   With respect to the deduction under ITA 24(1), ITA 14(12) disallows this deduction when the transfer is to an affiliated person (see Paragraph 16-54 for a definition of affiliated person). This is analogous to the disallowance under ITA 13(21.2) of terminal losses on transfers of depreciable assets to affiliated persons (see Paragraph 16-70).

16-84.   There is, however, an important difference. ITA 13(21.2) disallows terminal losses when the transferor is an individual, corporation, trust, or partnership. In contrast ITA 14(12) only disallows the ITA 24(1) deduction when the transferor is a corporation, trust, or partnership. In other words, if the transfer is from an individual to an affiliated person, the deduction is allowed.

16-85.   When ITA 14(12) disallows the deduction, the transferor is deemed to continue to own the cumulative eligible capital. The positive balance in this account will continue to be subject to the usual rules related to writing off cumulative eligible capital until such time as:

- the transferee disposes of the property to a non-affiliated person (includes deemed dispositions);
- the use of the property is changed from income earning to non-income earning;
- if the transferor is a corporation,
    - it is subject to an acquisition of control; or
    - it is subject to an ITA 88(2) winding up.

16-86.   On the occurrence of one of these events, any remaining unamortized balance can be deducted under ITA 24(1).

16-87.   With respect to Example Two from Paragraph 16-76, if the transferor was an individual, the $7,500 [(3/4)($70,000 - $60,000)] loss could be deducted. However, if the transferor was a corporation, trust, or partnership, the $7,500 would be left as a cumulative eligible capital balance in its books. The transferor would continue to write off the balance (he is deemed not to have ceased carrying on business). This would continue until one of the events specified in Paragraph 16-85 occurs. At the occurrence of one of these events, the transferor can deduct the remaining balance in the cumulative eligible capital account under ITA 24(1).

Tax Planning

16-88.   We have previously noted with respect to non-depreciable assets with capital losses or depreciable assets with terminal losses, that they should not be transferred under ITA 85. If such assets are not required in the operations of the business, better tax results can be achieved by simply selling the assets to a non-affiliated person.

16-89.   Implementation of this advice with respect to cumulative eligible capital will, in some circumstances, not be possible. While some balances included in cumulative eligible capital can be sold independently of the related business (e.g., an unlimited life government licence), other components (e.g., goodwill) may have no meaningful value when measured independently of the business. This may require their inclusion in the ITA 85 election, even if it creates a disallowed deduction.

Summary Of Transfer Price Rules

16-90.   Figure 16-1 provides a summary of the transfer price rules that have been discussed in this section.

	Inventory And Non-Depreciable Assets	Depreciable Assets	Cumulative Eligible Capital
Figure 16 - 1			
Summary Of Section 85 Transfer Price Rules			
Ceiling (FMV Of Asset)	X	X	X
Floor - Greater Of:			
A. FMV Of Boot	X	X	X
B. Least Of:			
Tax Cost Of Asset	X	—	—
Cost Of Asset (Not Tax Cost)	—	X	X
FMV Of Asset	X	X	X
UCC Balance	—	X	—
4/3 Of CEC Balance	—	—	X

We suggest you work Self Study Problems Sixteen-1 and 2 at this point.

Allocation Of The Elected Value

Consideration Received By The Transferor (Shareholder)

16-91.   As noted previously, the elected value for the assets transferred is used to establish the adjusted cost base of all consideration received by the transferor. The rules for allocating this total to the various types of consideration that may be used are found in ITA 85(1)(f), (g), and (h). They involve a sequential process that can be outlined as follows:

Elected Value (Total Adjusted Cost Base Of All Consideration)	$xxx
Less: Adjusted Cost Base Of Non-Share Consideration (Fair Market Value)	(xxx)
Adjusted Cost Base Of All Shares Issued (Usually Nil)	$xxx
Less: Adjusted Cost Base Of Preferred Stock Issued	
(Usually Nil, But Limited To Fair Market Value)	(xxx)
Adjusted Cost Base Of Common Stock Issued (A Residual - Usually Nil)	$xxx

Example   In transferring his proprietorship assets to a new corporation, Jason Browning elects a value of $972,000 for the assets transferred. As the fair market value of these assets is $1,650,000, he receives the following consideration:

- Cash of $220,000.
- Preferred shares of the new corporation with a fair market value of $345,000.
- Common shares of the new corporation with a fair market value of $1,085,000.

Analysis   The $972,000 elected value would be allocated as follows:

Elected Value (Total Adjusted Cost Base Of All Consideration)	$972,000
Less: Adjusted Cost Base Of Non-Share Consideration (Fair Market Value)	(220,000)
Adjusted Cost Base Of All Shares Issued (Usually Nil)	$752,000
Less: Adjusted Cost Base Of Preferred Stock Issued (Usually Nil, But Limited To Fair Market Value)	(345,000)
Adjusted Cost Base Of Common Stock Issued (A Residual - Usually Nil)	$407,000

16-92.   The preceding example has been designed to illustrate the allocation of the elected value to all three types of consideration. However, in the usual ITA 85 scenario, minimum asset values will normally be elected in order to avoid the recognition of income on the transfer. Boot will then be taken out in an amount equal to these minimum values. This means that in the usual situation, non-share consideration will be equal to the elected value and, in terms of the preceding allocation process, both preferred and common shares will have an adjusted cost base of nil.

Exercise Sixteen - 4

Subject: Transfers Under Section 85 - ACB Of Consideration

Using ITA 85, Mrs. Jennifer Lee transfers non-depreciable capital property to a corporation at an elected value of $62,000. The property has an adjusted cost base of $62,000 and a fair market value of $176,000. As consideration, she receives a note for $51,000, preferred shares with a fair market value of $53,000, and common shares with a fair market value of $72,000. Indicate the adjusted cost base of the individual items of consideration received by Mrs. Lee.

End of Exercise. Solution available in Study Guide.

Assets Acquired By The Corporation

General Rules

16-93.   With respect to the assets acquired by the transferee corporation, the basic rules are as follows:

Non-Depreciable Property   The elected transfer price becomes the tax cost of these assets to the corporation.

Depreciable Property   Where the transferor's capital cost exceeds the elected value for the property, ITA 85(5) requires that the capital cost to the transferee be equal to the amount that was the capital cost to the transferor. In most cases, the elected value will be equal to the transferor's UCC. ITA 85(5) requires that the difference between these two values be treated as deemed CCA. To illustrate this, consider the following asset:

Cost	$100,000
UCC	67,000
Fair Market Value	105,000
Non-Share Consideration	67,000
Elected Value	67,000

The capital cost of the asset to the transferee will be $100,000, there will be deemed CCA taken of $33,000, and future CCA will be based on the elected value of $67,000. The reason for requiring the transferee to retain the transferor's capital cost is to avoid having the transferor convert potential recaptured CCA into a capital gain, only one-half of which would be taxed.

You should also note that, in the usual situation where the transferor is not dealing at arm's length with the transferee corporation, the first year rules do not apply to the calculation of CCA by the transferee. This is the case as long as the transferor has owned the asset for at least 364 days before the end of the taxation year of the transferee in which the property was acquired, and used it as a capital property to earn business or property income.

16-94.   What these rules mean is that, in cases where the election has been made at an amount equal to the transferor's tax cost, the transferee corporation essentially assumes the tax position of the transferor.

Capital Gains On Transfers Of Depreciable Property

16-95.   The objective of using ITA 85(1) is usually to avoid tax consequences when assets are transferred to a corporation. This means that, in general, the elected values will be equal to the transferor's tax values (adjusted cost base or UCC).

16-96.   There are, however, circumstances in which the transferor may wish to generate a capital gain through the transfer of assets to a corporation. An example of this might be an individual who has large losses in the current year, or who has unused capital or non-capital loss carry forwards that he wishes to claim.

16-97.   This creates a problem with respect to depreciable assets in that, under the general ITA 85 rules, the elected value becomes the basis for calculating future CCA amounts. An election on a depreciable asset at a value in excess of the capital cost would result in a capital gain, only one-half of which would be taxable. Under the usual disposition rules, this same excess would become part of the UCC, the basis for calculating fully deductible amounts of CCA. The following example will illustrate this problem.

Example   Jan Harding plans to transfer a depreciable asset to a Canadian controlled private corporation in which she is the only shareholder. The relevant values are as follows:

Cost	$ 80,000
Fair Market Value	120,000
UCC	75,000
Elected Value	120,000

Analysis   The election at $120,000 would create the following amounts of income:

Recaptured CCA ($80,000 - $75,000)	$ 5,000
Taxable Capital Gain [(1/2)($120,000 - $80,000)]	20,000
Total Income	$25,000

In the absence of a special rule, the cost and UCC of this asset to the corporation would be $120,000. This value would create $45,000 more CCA for the corporation than would have been available to the transferor ($120,000 - $75,000). This has been accomplished through an increase in the transferor's Taxable Income of only $25,000, clearly not an equitable situation from the point of view of the government.

16-98.   ITA 13(7)(e) acts to correct this situation. You may recall that this provision was discussed in some detail in Chapter 9. It is a general provision that applies to all non-arm's length transfers of depreciable assets, including those where ITA 85(1) has been used.

16-99.   When such transfers occur, ITA 13(7)(e) limits the capital cost of the asset for CCA purposes to the transferor's cost, plus one-half of any capital gain that results from the transfer. As applied to the example in Paragraph 16-97, the capital cost to the transferee under ITA 13(7)(e) for CCA, recapture and terminal loss purposes only, would be as follows:

Paid Up Capital Of Shares Issued

Transferor's Cost		$ 80,000
Elected Transfer Price	$120,000	
Transferor's Cost	(80,000)	
Capital Gain	$ 40,000	
Taxable Portion	1/2	20,000
Capital Cost To The Transferee For CCA Purposes		**$100,000**

16-100.   Based on this capital cost, the increase in the CCA base to the corporation is only $25,000 ($100,000 - $75,000), the same amount the transferor recognized as income as a result of the transfer. Note, however, that for future capital gains calculations, the adjusted cost base of the asset to the transferee is the elected value of $120,000.

Paid Up Capital Of Shares Issued

General Rules

16-101.   Establishing the Paid Up Capital (PUC) of the shares received is important as it represents an amount that can be distributed to the shareholders as a tax free return of capital. In general, the amount of PUC for tax purposes is equal to the amount attributed to the shares under the appropriate corporate laws (legal stated capital).

16-102.   While there are some complications in those provinces that still permit the issuance of par value shares, the legal stated capital of a corporation is generally based on the fair market value of the consideration received in return for issued shares. In the case of shares issued in an ITA 85 rollover, this amount would be equal to the fair market value of the assets transferred.

16-103.   From the point of view of the taxpayer receiving the new shares, their adjusted cost base will be determined by the values elected for the transfer of assets. In the normal scenario, the taxpayer will elect minimum values for the assets transferred and these will usually be less than fair market values. With the PUC of the shares initially based on fair market values and adjusted cost base determined using elected values, the initial PUC of the shares will usually be larger than the adjusted cost base of the shares.

Paid Up Capital Reduction

16-104.   As you are now aware, ITA 85 permits assets to be transferred without the recognition of the income that would normally be associated with their disposition.   As the transferor's old tax values are generally flowed through to the transferee corporation, the potential income is deferred until the assets are used or disposed of by that corporation. Consider the following example:

> **Example**   Assets with a fair market value of $200,000, a capital cost of $180,000, and a UCC of $120,000 are transferred under ITA 85 using an elected value of $120,000. The consideration given consists of cash of $120,000 and shares with a fair market value and legal stated capital of $80,000 (total consideration equals the fair market value of $200,000).

16-105.   If these assets had been sold to an arm's length party, the vendor would have had to pay taxes on a total of $70,000, $60,000 ($180,000 - $120,000) in recapture and $10,000 [(1/2)($200,000 - $180,000)] in taxable capital gains. As is the intent of the legislation, these amounts of income are deferred when Section 85 is used properly. The problem is that, if the $80,000 legal stated capital of the shares issued is used as their PUC, this amount can be withdrawn from the corporation on a tax free basis. This would mean the potential recapture and taxable capital gain would permanently escape taxation.

16-106. Given this problem, ITA 85(2.1) requires that the PUC of issued shares be reduced by an amount equal to the total increase in legal stated capital, less any excess of the elected value over non-share consideration given. Continuing with our example, the reduction would be as follows:

Increase In Legal Stated Capital		$80,000
Less Excess, If Any, Of:		
Total Elected Value	($120,000)	
Over The Non-Share Consideration	120,000	Nil
Reduction In Paid Up Capital		**$80,000**

Balance Of Paid Up Capital ($80,000 - $80,000)	**Nil**

16-107. It is easy to see the conceptual basis for this reduction. Unless the non-share consideration is less than the elected value, the PUC reduction will be equal to the full fair market value of the shares, and the resulting PUC will be nil. This process also sets the PUC equal to the adjusted cost base that is allocated to the shares.

16-108. A further tax policy problem, which is not resolved by the PUC reduction, relates to the lifetime capital gains deduction. If the assets in the Paragraph 16-104 example are transferred to a corporation at an elected value of $120,000, this would be their adjusted cost base. If the shares were then sold for their fair market value of $200,000, the result would be an $80,000 capital gain which might be eligible for the lifetime capital gains deduction. In effect, the use of the ITA 85(1) rollover could result in the complete elimination of tax on the $80,000 of income that was present on the assets prior to their transfer.

More Than One Class Of Shares

16-109. In the majority of Section 85 rollovers, the ITA 85(2.1) formula will reduce the PUC of all shares issued to nil. This reflects the fact that the non-share consideration taken will equal the elected value, resulting in the PUC reduction being equal to the increase in legal stated capital. This was the case in the calculation in Paragraph 16-106. If this is the case, having more than one class of shares does not create any difficulties.

16-110. If, however, the non-share consideration is less than the elected value, the PUC reduction must be allocated to the various classes of shares. You will recall that, when we allocated the adjusted cost base, it was a sequential process (see Paragraph 16-91). The total adjusted cost base (i.e., the elected value) was allocated first to non-share consideration, then to preferred shares to the extent of their fair market value, and finally to the common shares.

16-111. This is not the case with the PUC reduction. The formula in ITA 85(2.1) is such that the reduction is allocated to different classes of shares on the basis of their relative fair market values.

> **Example** Joan Creek transfers non-depreciable assets with a fair market value of $1,600,000 to a corporation under the provisions of ITA 85(1). The elected value is equal to the $900,000 cost of the assets and, as consideration, she receives cash of $600,000, redeemable preferred shares with a fair market value of $250,000, and common shares with a fair market value of $750,000.
>
> **Analysis** The total adjusted cost base for the consideration would be allocated as follows:

Elected Value (Total Adjusted Cost Base Of All Consideration)	$900,000
Non-Share Consideration (Fair Market Value)	(600,000)
Adjusted Cost Base Of All Shares Issued	$300,000
Less: Adjusted Cost Base Of Preferred Stock Issued	
(Limited To Fair Market Value)	(250,000)
Adjusted Cost Base Of Common Stock Issued (Residual)	**$ 50,000**

The PUC reduction would be calculated as follows:

Increase In Legal Stated Capital		
($250,000 + $750,000)		$1,000,000
Less Excess, If Any, Of:		
Total Elected Value	($900,000)	
Over The Non-Share Consideration	600,000	(300,000)
Reduction In Paid Up Capital		**$ 700,000**

The PUC of the two classes of shares, reduced by a pro rata allocation of the $700,000 PUC reduction on the basis of relative fair market value, would be as follows:

$$\text{PUC Of Preferred Stock}\left[\$250,000 - \left(\frac{\$250,000}{\$1,000,000}\right)(\$700,000)\right] = \underline{\$75,000}$$

$$\text{PUC Of Common Stock}\left[\$750,000 - \left(\frac{\$750,000}{\$1,000,000}\right)(\$700,000)\right] = \underline{\$225,000}$$

16-112.   Note that the total PUC of the two classes is equal to $300,000 ($75,000 + $225,000). As you would expect, this is equal to the total adjusted cost base of the two classes ($250,000 + $50,000) as well as the difference between the elected value of $900,000 and the non-share consideration of $600,000. The fact that the individual amounts are different reflects the difference between the sequential allocation process for the adjusted cost base amount and the pro rata allocation of the PUC reduction.

Exercise Sixteen - 5

Subject: Transfers Under Section 85 - PUC Reduction

Using ITA 85, Mr. Rob McCleen transfers non-depreciable capital property to a corporation at an elected value of $114,000. The property has an adjusted cost base of $114,000 and a fair market value of $234,000. As consideration he receives a note for $83,000, preferred shares with a fair market value and legal stated capital of $97,000, and common shares with a fair market value and legal stated capital of $54,000. Indicate the adjusted cost base and the PUC of the preferred and common shares that were issued to Mr. McCleen.

End of Exercise. Solution available in Study Guide.

We suggest you work Self Study Problem Sixteen-3 at this point.

Comprehensive Example - Section 85 Rollovers

Basic Information

16-113.   John Martin has been operating an unincorporated business. The tax costs (UCC or adjusted cost base) and fair market values for its assets and liabilities are as follows:

Comprehensive Example - Section 85 Rollovers

	Tax Value	Fair Market Value
Cash	$ 20,000	$ 20,000
Accounts Receivable	50,000	49,000
Inventories	100,000	100,000
Prepaid Expenses	10,000	10,000
Land	50,000	70,000
Building (Capital Cost = $150,000)	110,000	140,000
Equipment (Capital Cost = $70,000)	40,000	35,000
Goodwill	Nil	50,000
Total Assets	$380,000	$474,000

Liabilities	$100,000	$100,000

Excluded Assets

16-114.   The rollover would involve a new corporation, the Martin Company, assuming all of Mr. Martin's liabilities and acquiring all of his business assets except the following:

Excluded Asset	Tax Value	Fair Market Value
Cash	$ 20,000	$ 20,000
Accounts Receivable	50,000	49,000
Prepaid Expenses	10,000	10,000
Equipment	40,000	35,000
Total Values For Excluded Assets	$120,000	$114,000

16-115.   With respect to the Cash and Prepaid Expenses, they are not eligible assets as described under ITA 85(1.1) and cannot be transferred under this rollover provision. However, as their fair market values are equal to their tax values, this is of no consequence.

16-116.   The Accounts Receivable could be transferred under ITA 85. However, the $1,000 ($50,000 - $49,000) loss would have to be treated as a capital loss, which would be disallowed as a superficial loss by ITA 40(2)(g). Further, any additional bad debts incurred by the corporation would also have to be treated as capital losses.

16-117.   The alternative is a joint election under ITA 22. This allows the $1,000 current loss to be treated as a fully deductible business loss. While the corporation will have to include this $1,000 in income, it will then be able to deduct the full amount of any additional bad debts. Taxpayers are not permitted to simultaneously use both the ITA 22 and the ITA 85 elections for their accounts receivable so we have excluded it from the ITA 85 election.

16-118.   With respect to the equipment, its fair market value is less than the UCC for the class, indicating the presence of a terminal loss. If this equipment is transferred to the corporation, with or without the use of ITA 85, this loss will be disallowed. Given this, there is no point in using ITA 85 to make the transfer and the equipment should be excluded from the ITA 85 election. Assuming that it is required in the operation of the business, it should simply be sold to the corporation for its fair market value. Paragraph 16-72 describes the required treatment of the disallowed terminal loss resulting from the sale.

Implementing The Election

16-119.   Mr. Martin is interested in deferring all of the capital gains that are present on his assets and, as a consequence, he elects tax values for most of the assets that are to be transferred under ITA 85. The one exception to this is goodwill, which is transferred at a value of $1 to ensure that it is listed in the election. There would be a $.75 income inclusion under ITA 14(1) with respect to the $1.00 elected value for goodwill.

16-120.   Mr. Martin's total elected value of $260,001 is calculated as follows:

Tax Values Of Total Assets	$380,000
Tax Value Of Excluded Assets (Paragraph 16-114)	(120,000)
Nominal Value To Goodwill	1
Total Elected Value	**$260,001**

16-121.   With respect to the consideration to be given to Mr. Martin, it must equal the fair market value of the assets transferred. This amount would be $360,000 ($474,000 total, less the $114,000 fair market value of the excluded assets listed in Paragraph 16-114).

16-122.   The normal procedure would be to take back non-share consideration, in this example debt, with a fair market value equal to the elected value of $260,001, along with shares with a fair market value equal to the $99,999 excess of the fair market values of the assets transferred over their elected values. The following schedule relates each asset to a particular type of consideration and allocates non-share consideration to each asset only up to the value elected for that particular asset. This allocation has no basis in tax legislation. However, it does provide an analysis that ensures that each asset transferred is supported by an appropriate amount of consideration when measured at fair market value. The table is in a form similar to that used in the T2057 form on which the ITA 85 election is made. Assuming that the non-share consideration is all in the form of debt, the analysis of the rollover would be as follows:

	Elected Value	Consideration At Fair Market Value Non-Share	Consideration At Fair Market Value Share
Inventories	$100,000	$100,000	Nil
Land	50,000	50,000	$20,000
Building (Capital Cost = $150,000)	110,000	110,000	30,000
Goodwill	1	1	49,999
Total Assets	**$260,001**	**$260,001**	**$99,999**

16-123.   The $260,001 in debt consideration is made up of $100,000 in debt of the existing business that has been assumed by the corporation, plus $160,001 in new debt issued by the corporation.

16-124.   From the point of view of the corporation, the elected values would become the tax values to be used in subsequent periods of operation. The adjusted cost base of the shares that were issued to Mr. Martin would be determined as follows:

Total Elected Value	$260,001
Non-Share Consideration	(260,001)
Adjusted Cost Base Of Shares	**Nil**

16-125.   The PUC of these shares would initially be their legal stated capital, an amount equal to their fair market value of $99,999. However, there would be an ITA 85(2.1) reduction in this balance as follows:

Increase In Legal Stated Capital		$99,999
Less Excess, If Any, Of:		
Total Elected Value	($260,001)	
Over The Non-Share Consideration	260,001	Nil
Reduction In Paid Up Capital		**$99,999**

16-126.   At this point, both the adjusted cost base and the PUC of the shares are nil. If they were redeemed at their $99,999 fair market value, Mr. Martin would have to recognize an ITA 84(3) deemed dividend of $99,999. This deemed dividend would reduce the proceeds of disposition for capital gains purposes to nil, resulting in no capital gain on the redemption.

16-127.   Alternatively, if he were to sell the shares at their fair market value, the result would be a capital gain of $99,999. Unlike the redemption scenario which would result in the deferred gain being taxed as a dividend, a sale of shares could completely avoid taxation on the deferred gain. This would happen if the gain resulting from the sale of shares qualified for the lifetime capital gains deduction.

Exercise Sixteen - 6

Subject: Transfers Under Section 85 - Tax Consequences

Jasmine Wiens has operated her alternative medicine pharmacy as an unincorporated business for a number of years. The tangible assets of this business have a fair market value of $850,000 and a tax cost of $275,000. In addition, as the business has been extremely profitable, she estimates that the business has goodwill of $300,000. The total liabilities of the business amount to $83,000. As she no longer needs all of the income that the business is producing, she would like to transfer the business to a new corporation and, in order to defer taxation, she would like to use the provisions of ITA 85(1) for the transfer.

She will make the transfer at an elected value of $275,000. The corporation will assume the $83,000 in business liabilities and, in addition, issue a note payable to Ms. Wiens in the amount of $17,000. Other consideration will be made up of redeemable preferred shares with a fair market value of $125,000 and common shares with a fair market value of $925,000. Any dividends paid by the corporation will be non-eligible. Determine the following:

1.   The adjusted cost base of each type of consideration received by Ms. Wiens.
2.   The paid up capital of each type of share issued by the new corporation.
3.   The tax consequences to Ms. Wiens of the new preferred shares being redeemed at their fair market value immediately.

End of Exercise. Solution available in Study Guide.

We suggest you work Self Study Problems Sixteen-4 to Sixteen-7 at this point.

Gift To Related Party - Section 85

General Rules

16-128.   If the transferor of the assets is the only shareholder of the transferee corporation, the indirect gift rules in ITA 85(1)(e.2) are not applicable. However, Section 85 rollovers are often used for income splitting purposes, and this usually means that other members of the transferor's family will be involved as shareholders in the transferee corporation. The indirect gift rules are designed to ensure that, while other family members will be permitted to share in the future growth and income of the corporation, they are not permitted to receive a portion of the current values of the transferred assets in the form of a gift.

16-129.   ITA 85(1)(e.2) is applicable if the fair market value of the transferred property exceeds the greater of:

1.   the fair market value of all consideration received from the corporation; and
2.   the amount elected for the transfer;

and it is reasonable to regard that excess as a gift made by the taxpayer for the benefit of any related shareholder. In any situation where a party related to the transferor is a shareholder of the transferee corporation, it would be reasonable to regard the excess as a gift.

16-130.   If ITA 85(1)(e.2) is applicable, the tax consequence is that, except for purposes of determining the adjusted cost base of any shares provided to the transferor, the gift amount will be added to the elected value for the transfer to create a deemed elected value. As this deemed elected value becomes the proceeds of disposition for the transferor, this will usually result in a taxable capital gain on the rollover.

16-131.   A less direct consequence is that the fair market value of the transferee's shares will be increased by the amount of the gift. As there will be no corresponding increase in the transferee's adjusted cost base, the sale of these shares will result in a taxable capital gain.

Example

16-132.   The following example will serve to illustrate the application of ITA 85(1)(e.2).

Example   Mr. Pohl owns a non-depreciable capital property with the following values:

Adjusted cost base of property	$ 30,000
Fair market value of property	180,000

A new corporation is formed with all of the common shares being issued to Mr. Pohl's adult son for $1,000 in cash. Using the provisions of ITA 85(1), Mr. Pohl then transfers his non-depreciable property to the corporation at an elected value of $30,000. As consideration for this property, the corporation issues a $30,000 note payable and preferred shares with a fair market value of $100,000. The total consideration received by Mr. Pohl is $130,000 ($30,000 + $100,000).

16-133.   The ITA 85(1)(e.2) excess would be calculated as follows:

Fair Market Value Of Property Transferred	$180,000
Less The Greater Of:	
• FMV Of Consideration Received = $130,000	
• Elected Amount = $30,000	(130,000)
Excess = Gift To Son	$ 50,000

16-134.   As Mr. Pohl's son is the only common shareholder of the new corporation, it would be reasonable to regard this $50,000 as a gift to his son. This would make ITA 85(1)(e.2) applicable to this transaction and Mr. Pohl would have a taxable capital gain determined as follows:

Deemed Elected Value = Deemed Proceeds Of Disposition	
($30,000 + $50,000 Gift)	$80,000
Adjusted Cost Base	(30,000)
Capital Gain	$50,000
Inclusion Rate	1/2
Taxable Capital Gain	$25,000

16-135.   Note that the increase in the elected value resulting from the gift will have to be allocated to specific assets. In our example, we were dealing only with one non-depreciable capital asset. This means that any excess of the elected value over the adjusted cost base of the asset will create a capital gain. However, in a more complex example involving the transfer of a complete business entity, this addition to the elected value could also result in recapture in the case of depreciable assets, or business income in the case of inventories.

16-136.   We noted in Paragraph 16-130 that the ITA 85(1)(e.2) deemed elected value does not apply in determining the adjusted cost base of the shares received by the transferor. Given this, the adjusted cost base of Mr. Pohl's preferred shares would be calculated as follows:

Elected Value (Original)		$30,000
Non-Share Consideration		(30,000)
Adjusted Cost Base - Preferred Shares		**Nil**

16-137.   Note, however, the deemed elected value does apply to the cost figure that is used in the following PUC reduction calculation under ITA 85(2.1). (This would be relevant if there was a share redemption.)

Increase In Legal Stated Capital		$100,000
Less Excess Of:		
Deemed Elected Value	($80,000)	
Over Non-Share Consideration	30,000	(50,000)
PUC Reduction		**$50,000**
PUC After Reduction ($100,000 - $50,000)		**$50,000**

16-138.   The other relevant fact here is that the transferee corporation, in addition to the $1,000 invested by Mr. Pohl's son, has an asset with a fair market value of $180,000. Given this, the fair market value of the son's shares would be $51,000 ($181,000 - $30,000 - $100,000). As there has been no change in the adjusted cost base of the son's shares, a subsequent sale of the shares would result in a capital gain of $50,000 ($51,000 - $1,000).

16-139.   The actual and potential gains resulting from the application of ITA 85(1)(e.2) to this transaction are as follows:

Actual Capital Gain On Transfer	$ 50,000
Potential Gain On Mr. Pohl's Preferred Shares ($100,000 - Nil)	100,000
Potential Gain On Son's Common Shares ($51,000 - $1,000)	50,000
Total Gain	**$200,000**

16-140.   If Mr. Pohl had simply sold his property, the total gain would have been only $150,000 ($180,000 - $30,000), $50,000 less than the total gain in the preceding table. This means that the $50,000 amount of the gift will be subject to double taxation.

16-141.   The way to avoid this problem is fairly obvious. In situations where the rollover is being used for income splitting purposes and other members of the transferor's family will be holding shares, the transferor should always take back an amount of consideration that is equal to the fair market value of the property transferred.

16-142.   This will usually involve the transferor taking back a non-growth security such as preferred shares for the difference between the fair market value of the property and its tax value. Common shares can then be issued to the other family members at a nominal value. While the initial value of these shares will be nominal, it will be these shares that will have growth in value in the future.

Exercise Sixteen - 7

Subject: Gift To Related Party - Section 85

Janice Bellows establishes a new CCPC, arranging to have all of its common shares issued to her adult daughter for cash of $1,000. Ms. Bellows then transfers, using ITA 85, non-depreciable capital property with an adjusted cost base of $50,000 and a fair market value of $110,000. The transfer is made at an elected value of $50,000. As consideration for this property, the corporation gives Ms. Bellows a note for $50,000 and preferred stock with a fair market value and a legal stated capital of $15,000. Ms. Bellows and her daughter immediately sell their shares for their fair market value.

Describe the tax consequences of these transactions for both Ms. Bellows and her daughter. How would these tax consequences differ if Ms. Bellows had simply sold the non-depreciable capital property for its fair market value of $110,000?

End of Exercise. Solution available in Study Guide.

We suggest you work Self Study Problem Sixteen-8 at this point.

Excess Consideration - Section 85

Introduction

16-143.   In the previous section we considered the tax consequences of the transferor receiving consideration that is less than the fair market value of the property transferred. In situations when parties related to the transferor were also shareholders of the transferee corporation, the difference in value could be viewed as a gift to that related party. We also pointed out that the *Income Tax Act* contained provisions which, in effect, penalized the transferor for his behaviour.

16-144.   In this section we are concerned with the opposite case — situations in which the transferor receives consideration with a value in excess of the fair market value of the property being transferred. Such situations may result in the shareholder being assessed a benefit under ITA 15 (see Chapter 15, Corporate Taxation And Management Decisions, for a discussion of shareholder benefits).

16-145.   You may recall from Chapter 14 that, in transactions which result in an increase in PUC that exceeds the related increase in net assets, the excess will be treated as an ITA 84(1) deemed dividend. At first glance, that would appear to be a possibility in an excess consideration situation involving Section 85. However, that is not the case. Even if the total share consideration received by the transferor exceeds the fair market value of the assets transferred, the ITA 85(2.1) PUC reduction will prevent the PUC of the shares from exceeding the value of the transferred assets.

Shareholder Benefit - ITA 15(1)

16-146.   The following example will illustrate a situation in which the use of ITA 85(1) results in a taxable benefit to the transferor.

Example   Ms. Sally Swit transfers non-depreciable capital property with an adjusted cost base of $65,000 and a fair market value of $150,000, to a CCPC in which she is the sole shareholder. She takes back debt with a fair market value of $120,000 and redeemable preferred shares with a fair market value and legal stated capital of $80,000. She elects to make the transfer at $150,000 (she cannot elect above the ceiling of fair market value).

Analysis   The immediate tax effects of the transfer would be a taxable capital gain on the property and an ITA 15(1) shareholder benefit, calculated as follows:

Elected Value Of Property	$150,000
Adjusted Cost Base	(65,000)
Capital Gain	$ 85,000
Inclusion Rate	1/2
Taxable Capital Gain On Property	**$ 42,500**

Fair Market Value Of Consideration	$200,000
Fair Market Value Of The Property	(150,000)
ITA 15(1) Shareholder Benefit	**$ 50,000**

The total effect on Net Income For Tax Purposes is as follows:

Taxable Capital Gain	$ 42,500
Shareholder Benefit	50,000
Total Addition To Net Income For Tax Purposes	**$ 92,500**

Because a $50,000 benefit will be included in Ms. Swit's income as a result of a property acquisition, ITA 52(1) requires that this amount be added to the cost of the property acquired. Given this, the adjusted cost base of the preferred shares would be as follows:

Elected Value	$150,000
Fair Market Value Of Non-Share Consideration	(120,000)
Available For Shares	$ 30,000
ITA 15(1) Shareholder Benefit	50,000
Adjusted Cost Base Of Preferred Stock	**$ 80,000**

The ITA 85(2.1) PUC reduction for the preferred shares would be calculated as follows:

Increase In Legal Stated Capital		$80,000
Less Excess, If Any, Of:		
Elected Value	($150,000)	
Over The Non-Share Consideration	120,000	(30,000)
Reduction In Paid Up Capital		**$50,000**

This would leave a PUC for the preferred shares of $30,000 ($80,000 - $50,000). As this is equal to the increase in net assets ($150,000 - $120,000), there would be no ITA 84(1) deemed dividend.

If the preferred shares were sold for their fair market value, the results would be as follows:

Proceeds Of Disposition	$80,000
Adjusted Cost Base	(80,000)
Capital Gain (Loss)	**Nil**

Alternatively, if the preferred shares were redeemed for their fair market value, the results would be as follows:

Redemption Proceeds	$80,000
PUC	(30,000)
ITA 84(3) Deemed Dividend	**$50,000**

Proceeds Of Disposition	$80,000
Less: ITA 84(3) Deemed Dividend	(50,000)
Adjusted Proceeds Of Disposition	$30,000
Adjusted Cost Base	(80,000)
Capital Loss	($50,000)
Inclusion Rate	1/2
Allowable Capital Loss	($25,000)

Exercise Sixteen - 8

Subject: Benefit To Transferor (Excess Consideration) - Section 85

Mr. Larry Custer uses ITA 85 to transfer non-depreciable capital property to a CCPC in which he owns 100 percent of the shares. The adjusted cost base of the property is $123,000 and he elects the fair market value of $217,000 as the transfer price. In consideration for this property, Mr. Custer receives a note for $195,000 and preferred stock with a fair market value and a legal stated capital of $75,000. Any dividends paid by the corporation will be non-eligible. What are the tax consequences for Mr. Custer if the preferred shares are (1) sold for $75,000 and (2) redeemed for $75,000?

End of Exercise. Solution available in Study Guide.

We suggest you work Self Study Problem Sixteen-9 at this point.

Dividend Stripping — ITA 84.1

Background

The General Concept
16-147.   The term dividend stripping is applied to two types of situations, depending on when the relevant shares were issued by the corporation. In simple terms, both scenarios involve an individual who is attempting to remove assets from a corporation on a tax free basis.

16-148.   Accomplishing this goal would not be a problem if the individual was willing to give up control by selling his shares to an arm's length party. However, when this is not the case and the individual retains control, the dividend stripping rules will often prevent the tax free removal of assets.

16-149.   One approach to removing assets from a corporation while still retaining control would be to pay dividends. However, dividends will be taxed in the hands of the recipient and, being a rational individual, the owner of the corporation would prefer to receive the assets on a tax free basis.

16-150.   The usual approach to accomplishing the goal of removing funds from a controlled corporation on a tax free basis is to convert what is, in effect, a dividend payment into a capital gain that would be eligible for the lifetime capital gains deduction. This is the origin of the term "dividend stripping". ITA 84.1 is a provision that is intended to thwart such efforts.

Pre-1972 Shares
16-151.   At an earlier point in time, the most important application of ITA 84.1 was to prevent the conversion of pre-1972 earnings into a pre-1972 capital gain. As we noted in Chapter 8, prior to 1972, capital gains were not subject to tax in Canada. Given this, such a conversion could have resulted in the tax free receipt of a considerable amount of assets. While such situations still arise, they are not of sufficient importance to cover in a general text

such as this. As a consequence, the application of ITA 84.1 in this type of situation will not receive further attention.

Qualified Small Business Corporation Shares

16-152. The most important current application of the dividend stripping rules from ITA 84.1 involves shares of a qualified small business corporation. The capital gains on dispositions of such shares are eligible for the $750,000 lifetime capital gains deduction (2013 amount). This means that, if an individual can remove the retained earnings of such a corporation in the form of a capital gain, a very large amount of income can be received on a tax free basis. In general, ITA 84.1 serves to make such conversions difficult. The text and problems in this section will focus on this application of the dividend stripping rules that are found in ITA 84.1.

Applicability Of ITA 84.1

16-153. ITA 84.1(1) specifies the conditions under which the dividend stripping rules become applicable. These conditions are as follows:

- there is a disposition by a resident Canadian taxpayer (other than a corporation) of shares of a resident Canadian corporation (the subject corporation);

- the taxpayer held the shares as capital property (i.e., were held to produce income, not for resale at a profit);

- the disposition is made to a corporation with which the taxpayer does not deal at arm's length; and

- the subject corporation must be connected with the purchaser corporation after the disposition of shares (i.e., the purchaser corporation must control the subject corporation or own more than 10 percent of the voting shares and 10 percent of the fair market value of all shares).

16-154. When these conditions are present, the provisions of ITA 84.1 will generally serve to eliminate the individual's ability to achieve their dividend stripping goals.

Dividend Stripping Example

Basic Example

16-155. A simple example will serve to illustrate the application of ITA 84.1 to post-1971 shares. As shown in Figure 16-2 (following page), Ms. Barton is the only shareholder of Barton Industries (BI), a Canadian controlled private corporation. The Company was established in 1986 with an investment of $25,000 on the part of Ms. Barton. There has been no additional investment in the Company and, as a consequence, $25,000 is the adjusted cost base of her shares as well as their PUC. The shares have a fair market value of $850,000 and Ms. Barton has available all of her $750,000 lifetime capital gains deduction. BI is a qualified small business corporation and it has no balance in its GRIP account.

16-156. Ms. Barton could, of course, make use of her lifetime capital gains deduction by selling the BI shares to an arm's length party and realizing a capital gain of $825,000 ($850,000 - $25,000). However, this approach would result in tax payable as the capital gain of $825,000 exceeds the $750,000 deduction that is available for 2013 under the lifetime capital gains provision. In addition, and perhaps more importantly, she would lose control of BI.

16-157. Given these considerations, she chooses to transfer the BI shares to a new company, Barton Holdings Ltd. (BHL), using the provisions of ITA 85(1). Ms. Barton uses an elected value for the transfer of $775,000, in order to limit her capital gain to $750,000 ($775,000 - $25,000). She takes back $775,000 in new debt of BHL, along with the common shares of the new Company. These shares have a fair market value of $75,000 ($850,000 - $775,000) and an adjusted cost base of nil.

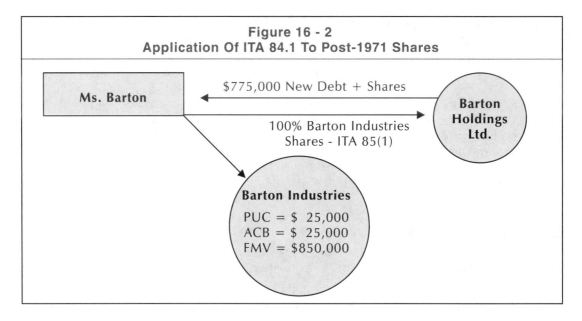

Figure 16 - 2
Application Of ITA 84.1 To Post-1971 Shares

16-158.   Through this procedure, Ms. Barton appears to have realized the required $750,000 of the accrued capital gain on the BI shares and, at the same time, retained control of the Company. However, Ms. Barton:

- is an individual, resident in Canada;
- held the shares as capital property;
- has made a disposition of shares to a corporation with which she does not deal at arm's length; and
- has created connected corporations subsequent to the transaction since BHL owns all of the shares of BI.

16-159.   Given these facts, the dividend stripping provisions of ITA 84.1 would be applicable to this transaction.

ITA 84.1 Procedures

16-160.   The ITA 84.1 procedures begin with a reduction in the PUC of any shares of the subject corporation that are received by Ms. Barton. Note that, when both ITA 85 and ITA 84.1 are involved, the PUC reduction rules specified in ITA 84.1(1)(a) must be used. They would apply as follows in this situation.

Increase In Legal Stated Capital Of BHL Shares		$75,000
Less Excess, If Any, Of:		
PUC Of Barton Industries Shares (Note One)	($ 25,000)	
Over The Non-Share Consideration	775,000	Nil
ITA 84.1(1)(a) PUC Reduction (Note Two)		**$75,000**

Note One   This amount is technically the greater of the PUC of the subject shares and their adjusted cost base. In this example, the two amounts are equal.

Note Two   In those cases where the boot is equal to or exceeds the greater of the PUC and the adjusted cost base of the subject corporation shares, the PUC reduction will be 100 percent of the PUC of the new shares.

16-161.   This would leave the PUC of the new shares at nil ($75,000 - $75,000). Given this, the ITA 84.1(1)(b) deemed dividend would be calculated as follows:

Increase In Legal Stated Capital Of BHL Shares		$ 75,000
Non-Share Consideration		775,000
Total		$850,000
Less The Sum Of:		
PUC And ACB Of Barton Industries (Subject) Shares	($25,000)	
PUC Reduction Under ITA 84.1(1)(a)	(75,000)	(100,000)
ITA 84.1(1)(b) Deemed Dividend (Non-Eligible)		$750,000

16-162.   The results from Ms. Barton's disposition of her BI shares would be as follows:

Elected Proceeds Of Disposition	$775,000
ITA 84.1(1)(b) Deemed Dividend (See Note)	(750,000)
ITA 54 Deemed Proceeds Of Disposition	$ 25,000
Adjusted Cost Base Of Barton Industries Shares	(25,000)
Capital Gain	Nil

Note The definition of proceeds of disposition in ITA 54 indicates that it does not include any amount that is deemed by ITA 84.1(1) to be a dividend. In the absence of this exclusion, the deemed dividend could be taxed a second time as part of a taxable capital gain.

16-163.   As the preceding example makes clear, the effect of ITA 84.1 in this situation is to convert the $750,000 capital gain on the BI shares into an ITA 84.1 deemed dividend. This means that Ms. Barton will not be able to make use of her lifetime capital gains deduction and that she will be subject to taxation on the deemed dividend. ITA 84.1 has clearly served to make this type of transaction unattractive.

16-164.   As a final point, you should note that Ms. Barton could have achieved her goal of triggering a capital gain for purposes of the lifetime capital gains deduction. Her problem was that she also wanted to remove the gain in the form of non-share consideration. If, as an alternative, she had elected the same transfer price of $775,000, but limited the non-share consideration to the $25,000 PUC amount, she would have had her $750,000 capital gain without creating an ITA 84.1 deemed dividend. Note, however, that she does not have the $750,000 in cash. She would be holding shares with a value of $750,000 and an adjusted cost base of nil. In order to have the cash and take advantage of the lifetime capital gains deduction, she would have to sell the shares to an arms' length party and lose control of the corporation.

Exercise Sixteen - 9

Subject: Dividend Strips

Miss Sarah Cole owns 100 percent of the outstanding shares of Cole Inc., a qualified small business corporation. The shares have a PUC and an adjusted cost base of $125,000 and a fair market value of $767,000. The Company has no balance in its GRIP account. Miss Cole uses ITA 85(1) to transfer these shares to Sarah's Holdings Ltd., at an elected value of $767,000. As consideration, she receives a note for $450,000 and preferred shares with a fair market value and a legal stated capital of $317,000. Miss Cole owns all of the shares of Sarah's Holdings Ltd. and has never made use of her lifetime capital gains deduction. What are the tax consequences of this transaction to Miss Cole?

End of Exercise.   Solution available in Study Guide.

We suggest you work Self Study Problem Sixteen-10 at this point.

Capital Gains Stripping — ITA 55(2)

The Problem

16-165.   A problem similar to that involved in dividend stripping arises when a corporation owns shares in a different corporation. If there is an accrued capital gain on these shares, a disposition of the shares will result in the recognition of that income. Further, corporations are not eligible to use the lifetime capital gains deduction. This means that a disposition of the shares will increase both the Taxable Income and Tax Payable of the corporation.

16-166.   While capital gains are subject to corporate income taxes, intercorporate dividends can escape corporate taxes. This means that, if the investor corporation can devise some method of disposing of its investment so that the proceeds of disposition are received in the form of dividends, payment of corporate taxes could be avoided.

16-167.   In the absence of an anti-avoidance provision, this could be accomplished in a variety of ways. If we assume that Investee Company is a wholly owned subsidiary of Investor Company, two ways in which Investor could dispose of Investee are as follows:

- Investee could borrow sufficient funds to pay Investor dividends equal to the accrued capital gain. This could serve to reduce the fair market value of its shares to Investor's adjusted cost base and the disposition could be made with no capital gain being recognized.

- ITA 85(1) could be used to roll the Investee shares into a purchaser corporation in return for redeemable preferred shares. Redemption of the shares would result in an ITA 84(3) deemed dividend as opposed to a capital gain.

16-168.   Such procedures are referred to as capital gains stripping, reflecting the fact that it is an attempt to "strip" out a capital gain in the form of a non-taxable, intercorporate dividend. ITA 55(2) is an anti-avoidance provision designed to prevent such conversions of capital gains to dividends by a corporation disposing of an investment in shares.

Application Of ITA 55(2)

16-169.   The provisions of ITA 55(2) are applicable when:

- A corporation has received dividends that are deductible under ITA 112(1) as part of a transaction, or series of transactions, involving a disposition of shares.

- One of the purposes of the dividend was to effect a significant reduction in any capital gain which, in the absence of the dividend, would have been realized on the disposition of shares.

- The disposition was to an arm's length party, or there has been a significant increase in the interest of an arm's length party, in either corporation.

16-170.   If these conditions are present, the following rules apply to the dividend:

ITA 55(2)(a)   The dividend shall be deemed not to be a dividend received by the corporation.

ITA 55(2)(b)   Where a corporation has disposed of the share, the dividend shall be deemed to be proceeds of disposition of the share except to the extent that it is otherwise included in computing such proceeds.

ITA 55(2)(c)   Where a corporation has not disposed of the share, the dividend shall be deemed to be a gain of the corporation for the year in which the dividend was received from the disposition of a capital property.

16-171.   These rules do not apply if the dividend represents a distribution of what is commonly referred to as "safe income". Safe income is income that has accrued after 1971 or, if the acquisition of the shares was after that date, after the date on which the shares were acquired. To qualify for this exception from the rules, a designation of the safe income is required in the taxpayer's return of income.

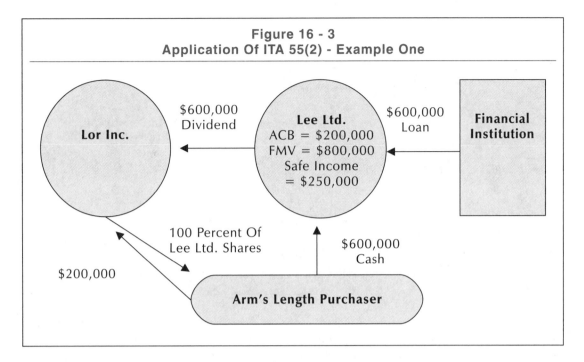

Figure 16 - 3
Application Of ITA 55(2) - Example One

Capital Gains Stripping - Example One

16-172.   The first example is diagramed in Figure 16-3. In this example, Lor Inc. owns 100 percent of the shares of Lee Ltd. The shares have a fair market value of $800,000, an adjusted cost base of $200,000, and a potential capital gain of $600,000. Lee Ltd. has safe income of $250,000. An arm's length purchaser is willing to pay $800,000 for these shares. In order to implement this sale, Lor Inc. arranges the following:

- Lee Ltd. borrows $600,000 from a financial institution.
- The borrowed funds are used to pay a $600,000 tax free dividend to Lor Inc. This reduces the fair market value of Lee Ltd. to $200,000.
- Lor Inc. sells the shares to the arm's length purchaser for $200,000 in cash. As this is the adjusted cost base of the shares, there will be no capital gain.
- The arm's length purchaser invests $600,000 in Lee Ltd., with the funds being used to retire the $600,000 loan.

16-173.   In the absence of ITA 55(2), Lor Inc. would have managed to dispose of its interest in Lee Ltd. in a series of transactions for $800,000 ($200,000 received directly from the purchaser and $600,000 of tax-free dividends financed indirectly by the purchaser), without the recognition of a capital gain. However, ITA 55(2) will prevent this from happening.

16-174.   Under ITA 55(2)(a), the $600,000 dividend will be deemed not to be a dividend. Under ITA 55(2)(b), the dividend will be treated as proceeds of disposition. This results in the following capital gain calculation:

Dividends Received	$600,000
Dividend Attributable To Safe Income (Tax Free)	(250,000)
Deemed Proceeds Of Disposition	$350,000
Actual Proceeds Of Disposition	200,000
Total Proceeds Of Disposition	$550,000
Adjusted Cost Base	(200,000)
Capital Gain	$350,000

Capital Gains Stripping — ITA 55(2)

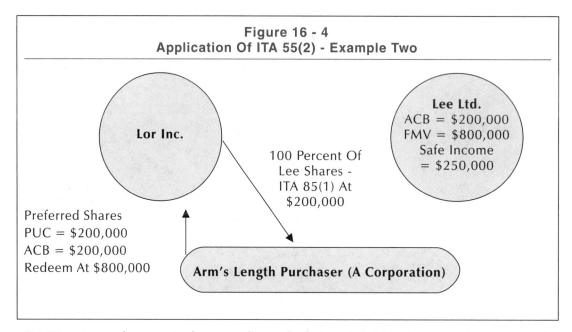

Figure 16 - 4
Application Of ITA 55(2) - Example Two

Lor Inc.

Lee Ltd.
ACB = $200,000
FMV = $800,000
Safe Income
= $250,000

100 Percent Of
Lee Shares -
ITA 85(1) At
$200,000

Preferred Shares
PUC = $200,000
ACB = $200,000
Redeem At $800,000

Arm's Length Purchaser (A Corporation)

16-175.   As can be seen in the preceding calculation, ITA 55(2) has served to convert the portion of the dividend not paid from safe income into a capital gain, which will be taxed. The $250,000 dividend attributable to safe income will be deducted in calculating Taxable Income, resulting in no tax cost.

Capital Gains Stripping - Example Two

16-176.   This example is diagramed in Figure 16-4 and involves the same two Companies that were used in Example One. The only difference is in the approach that they use in attempting to convert the taxable capital gain into a tax free dividend.

16-177.   In this case, ITA 85(1) is used to roll the Lee Ltd. shares into the purchaser corporation at an elected value equal to the $200,000 adjusted cost base of the shares. As consideration for the shares, Lor Inc. takes back $800,000 in redeemable preferred shares. These shares have a PUC and an adjusted cost base of $200,000.

16-178.   The preferred shares are immediately redeemed, resulting in an ITA 84(3) deemed dividend. In the absence of ITA 55(2), the deemed dividend would be calculated as follows:

Redemption Proceeds	$800,000
PUC Of Shares	(200,000)
ITA 84(3) Deemed Dividend [Absence Of ITA 55(2)]	$600,000

16-179.   In this example, ITA 55(2)(a) would deem the portion of the dividend that is not from safe income to not be a dividend. This would reduce the ITA 84(3) dividend as follows:

ITA 84(3) Deemed Dividend	$600,000
Amount Deemed Not To Be A Dividend ($600,000 - $250,000)	(350,000)
ITA 84(3) Deemed Dividend [With ITA 55(2)]	$250,000

16-180.   A comparison of the capital gain on the redemption of the shares assuming the absence of ITA 55(2), and assuming ITA 55(2) is applicable, would be as follows:

	No ITA 55(2)	With ITA 55(2)
Redemption Proceeds	$800,000	$800,000
ITA 84(3) Deemed Dividend	(600,000)	(250,000)
ITA 54 Deemed Proceeds Of Disposition	$200,000	$550,000
Adjusted Cost Base	(200,000)	(200,000)
Capital Gain	Nil	$350,000

16-181.   In this example, ITA 55(2) has served to convert the ITA 84(3) dividend that was not paid from safe income into a capital gain which will be taxed.

Exercise Sixteen - 10

Subject: Capital Gains Strips

Markem Ltd. owns 100 percent of the outstanding common shares of Larkin Ltd. The shares of Larkin have an adjusted cost base of $75,000 and a fair market value of $840,000. Included in its Retained Earnings balance is $225,000 of income that has been earned since its acquisition by Markem Ltd. Markem Ltd. would like to sell its shares in Larkin Ltd. In order to implement this sale, Markem Ltd. has instructed Larkin Ltd. to borrow $750,000 from its bank, and use all of these funds to pay a dividend on the shares held by Markem Ltd. The shares are then sold to Mr. J. Leaner for $90,000. Mr. Leaner is not related to Markem Ltd. or Larkin Ltd. What are the tax consequences to Markem Ltd. of these transactions?

End of Exercise.   Solution available in Study Guide.

We suggest you work Self Study Problem Sixteen-11 at this point

Key Terms Used In This Chapter

16-182.   The following is a list of the key terms used in this Chapter. These terms, and their meanings, are compiled in the Glossary Of Key Terms located at the back of the separate paper Study Guide.

Adjusted Cost Base	Non-Share Consideration
Affiliated Group Of Persons	Paid Up Capital
Affiliated Person - ITA 251.1(1)	PUC
Boot	Recapture Of CCA
Capital Cost	Rollover
Capital Gains Stripping	Safe Income
Controlled - ITA 251.1(3)	Subject Corporation
Corporation	Superficial Loss - ITA 54
Cumulative Eligible Capital (CEC)	Taxpayer
Depreciable Capital Property	Terminal Loss
Dividend Stripping	Transfer
Eligible Capital Property	Transferee
Gift	Transferor
Individual	Undepreciated Capital Cost (UCC)
Non-Depreciable Capital Property	

References

16-183.   For more detailed study of the material in this Chapter, we would refer you to the following:

ITA 13(21.2)	Loss On Certain Transfers
ITA 15(1)	Benefits Conferred On A Shareholder
ITA 40(2)(g)	Superficial Losses
ITA 40(3.4)	Loss On Certain Properties
ITA 54	Definitions (Proceeds Of Disposition And Superficial Loss)
ITA 55(2)	Deemed Proceeds Or Capital Gain
ITA 84.1(1)	Non-Arm's Length Sale Of Shares
ITA 85	Transfer Of Property To Corporation By Shareholders
ITA 89(1)	Definitions
ITA 251.1	Affiliated Persons
IC 76-19R3	Transfer Of Property To A Corporation Under Section 85
IT-188R	Sale of Accounts Receivable
IT-291R3	Transfer Of Property To A Corporation Under Subsection 85(1)
IT-489R	Non-Arm's Length Sale Of Shares To A Corporation

Problems For Self Study

(The solutions for these problems can be found in the separate Study Guide.)

Self Study Problem Sixteen - 1 (Determination Of Transfer Prices)

Ms. Audrey Flack has operated a gift shop for 15 years as a sole proprietorship. After considerable analysis, she has decided that she would experience a number of advantages if she were to incorporate. On December 1, 2013, the assets that she proposes to transfer to the new corporation are as follows:

	Tax Cost	Fair Market Value
Cash	$ 27,000	$ 27,000
Accounts Receivable	51,000	45,000
Inventories	73,000	88,000
Furniture And Fixtures	38,000	45,000
Goodwill	Nil	150,000
Totals	$189,000	$355,000

The capital cost of the Furniture And Fixtures is $62,000.

Ms. Flack will receive no consideration other than shares and, as she has no immediate family, she will be the only shareholder in the new company. She has used all of her lifetime capital gains deduction on other dispositions of capital assets.

Required:

A. If no elections are made by Ms. Flack, and the assets are transferred at fair market values on December 31, 2013, calculate the Taxable Income resulting from the transfer that Ms. Flack would have to report.

B. Indicate the elections that could be used by Ms. Flack to reduce the amount of Taxable Income on the transfer of these assets to the new corporation. Calculate the amount of Taxable Income that would result from the transfer being made using these elections.

Self Study Problem Sixteen - 2 (Determination Of Transfer Prices)

For nearly 20 years, Ms. Monica Speaks has operated a very successful manufacturing business. During much of this period you have constantly reminded her that there would be many advantages associated with incorporation, including the availability of the small business deduction. In the past, she has indicated that she has all of the money that she requires and simply cannot be bothered with the complications associated with incorporation. However, in late 2013, you have finally convinced her that incorporation may be the wisest course of action.

She indicates that she is still concerned with respect to taxes that might arise on the transfer of her business assets to a corporation. In response, you have indicated that Section 85 of the *Income Tax Act* provides a method of transfer that will result in little or no taxation at the time of the transfer. As a consequence, she decides to proceed with incorporation, indicating that all of the shares in the new company (Speaks Inc.) will be issued to her.

On October 1, 2013, the transfer date, the business assets of Ms. Speaks have tax values and fair market values as follows:

	Tax Value	Fair Market Value
Cash	$ 36,300	$ 36,300
Accounts Receivable	78,500	78,500
Inventories	261,000	311,000
Land	196,000	282,000
Building (Cost = $155,500)	103,600	253,000
Equipment (Cost = $222,000)	67,000	32,500
Goodwill	Nil	339,000
Total	$742,400	$1,332,300

Ms. Speaks will only use the ITA 85 provisions to transfer a specific asset if there is a tax advantage in doing so.

Required:

A. Indicate which assets should be transferred under the provisions of ITA 85(1).

B. Given that Ms. Speaks wishes to minimize the tax consequences of the incorporation transaction, calculate the minimum transfer price for each asset.

C. Describe the tax consequences for both Ms. Speaks and Speaks Inc. if she transfers the assets at the values calculated in Part B.

Self Study Problem Sixteen - 3
(Simple Non-Depreciable Asset Transfer - Three Cases)

Ahmed Sindren owns a tract of land that he acquired several years ago for $230,000. An appraiser estimates that the current fair market value of the land is $660,000. He wishes to use ITA 85 to transfer this land to a new corporation, Sindren Inc. in which he is the sole shareholder.

Case A Mr. Sindren elects to transfer the land at $230,000, in return for consideration that consists of shares in the new corporation with a fair market value and legal stated capital of $660,000.

Case B Mr. Sindren elects to transfer the land at $500,000, in return for consideration that consists of shares in the new corporation with a fair market value and legal stated capital of $660,000.

Case C Mr. Sindren elects to transfer the land at $500,000, in return for consideration that consists of a promissory note from the corporation for $500,000, and shares in the new corporation with a fair market value and legal stated capital of $160,000.

Required: For each of the preceding independent cases, determine:

- The immediate tax consequences of the transfer.
- The adjusted cost base of the land to the corporation.
- The adjusted cost base of the shares issued by the corporation.
- The PUC of the shares issued by the corporation.

Self Study Problem Sixteen - 4 (ACB Of Consideration And Sale Of Shares)

During 2012, Mr. Richard Dix acquired a business location consisting of land with a brick store building located on it. The total price was $1,260,000, with $315,000 of this amount allocated to the land and $945,000 allocated to the building.

After operating a grocery store on this property during 2012 and the first six months of 2013 as a proprietorship, Mr. Dix decides to incorporate. In this process, he uses the provisions of ITA 85 to transfer the land and building to the corporation on a tax free basis. He elects a transfer price of $1,241,100. The details of the transfer are as follows:

	Land	Building
Capital Cost Or UCC	$315,000	$ 926,100
Appraised Value	787,500	1,102,500
Elected Amount	315,000	926,100
Consideration:		
Debt*	315,000	926,100
Shares	472,500	176,400

*The debt related to the Land and Building includes the corporation's assumption of an existing mortgage of $519,750. This means that the total new debt issued by the corporation is as follows:

Debt On Land	$ 315,000
Debt On Building	926,100
Total Debt	$1,241,100
Mortgage Assumed	(519,750)
Net Debt Issued	$ 721,350

On December 1, 2013, the corporation pays off the $721,350 of new debt issued at its face value. On December 28, 2013, Mr. Dix sells his shares in the corporation for $894,000.

The corporation is a qualified small business corporation. Mr. Dix has never utilized his lifetime capital gains deduction and he has no Cumulative Net Investment Loss.

Required:

A. Describe the tax consequences of the transfer and compute the adjusted cost base of the consideration received by Mr. Dix.

B. Describe the tax consequences of the debt being paid off and the share sale for Mr. Dix.

Self Study Problem Sixteen - 5 (PUC/ACB And Redemption Of Shares)

Mr. Lardner is the owner of an unincorporated business that is involved in the distribution of various types of paper products. It is his wish that all of the assets of this business be transferred to a new corporation, Lardner Distribution Ltd. Mr. Lardner will be the only shareholder of this new corporation.

The assets of the business have "tax values" (adjusted cost base or UCC, as appropriate) that total $492,000. The liabilities of the business total $122,000. The total fair market value of all of the assets of the business is $746,000. Except in the case of accounts receivable, the fair market values of the individual assets exceed their respective tax values. The accounts receivable have a carrying value of $25,000 and a fair market value of $20,000. A joint election will be made under ITA 22 to transfer them to the corporation and, as a consequence, they will be excluded from the ITA 85 election.

The assets other than the accounts receivable will be transferred under the provisions of Section 85 using a total elected value of $467,000 ($492,000 - $25,000). The new corporation will assume the $122,000 of liabilities owed by the unincorporated business. As consideration for the net assets of the business, Mr. Lardner will receive from the corporation $128,000 in new debt securities, preferred shares with a fair market value of $150,000, and common shares with a fair market value of $326,000. The total value of the consideration, including both the old and the new debt, is equal to the $726,000 fair market value of the assets transferred under ITA 85 ($746,000 - $20,000).

Immediately after the transfer of the assets to Lardner Distribution Ltd., the Company redeems both the preferred shares and the common shares at their respective fair market values. The Company borrows the funds required to make the redemption. Lardner Distribution Ltd. does not have a balance in its General Rate Income Pool (GRIP) account in any of the years under consideration.

Required:

A. Determine the adjusted cost base for both the preferred and common stock issued to Mr. Lardner.

B. Determine the Paid Up Capital for both the preferred and common stock issued to Mr. Lardner.

C. Indicate the tax consequences to Mr. Lardner that would result from the corporation redeeming the preferred and common shares.

Self Study Problem Sixteen - 6
(Transfers To A Corporation And Share Redemption)

Mr. Martin Fleck is the sole owner of an unincorporated retail business. Because he has not been asked to present audited financial statements to any of his creditors, his accounting records are based on the same information as his tax records. As of December 31 of the current year, the Balance Sheet of the business, including additional information on current fair market values, is as follows:

	Tax Values	Fair Market Values
Cash	$ 20,000	$ 20,000
Accounts Receivable	42,000	38,500
Equipment (Cost = $120,000)	62,000	66,000
Land	106,000	185,000
Building (Cost = $246,000)	178,000	323,000
Goodwill	Nil	95,000
Total Assets	$408,000	$727,500
Liabilities	$123,000	$123,000
Owners' Equity	285,000	604,500
Total Equities	$408,000	$727,500

Mr. Fleck has established a new corporation, Fleck Ltd. Unless there is some tax reason not to do so, he would like to transfer all of the assets of the unincorporated business to the new corporation. He is aware that by using the provisions of ITA 85(1) he could avoid any additional taxes at the time of transfer. However, he has a net capital loss carry forward of $20,000 [(1/2)($40,000)]. As he has no other assets with accrued capital gains, he would like to elect

Problems For Self Study

under ITA 85(1) in a manner that will create a $20,000 taxable capital gain. He would like to avoid having any other tax consequences resulting from the transfer.

The corporation will assume all of the liabilities of the unincorporated business. In addition, it will issue new debt to Mr. Fleck in the amount of $77,000 and new common shares with a fair market value equal to the difference between the fair market value of the assets transferred and the fair market value of the non-share consideration received by Mr. Fleck. Fleck Ltd. does not have a balance in its General Rate Income Pool (GRIP) account in any of the years under consideration.

Required:

A. Indicate which assets should be transferred to Fleck Ltd. under the provisions of ITA 85(1). In addition, indicate the values that should be elected for each asset, taking into consideration Mr. Fleck's desire to record a taxable capital gain of $20,000. Explain your conclusions.

B. Determine the fair market value of the common shares issued to Mr. Fleck, as well as their adjusted cost base and their Paid Up Capital.

C. Determine the tax consequences to Mr. Fleck if one-half of the common shares that he received on the rollover were immediately redeemed for their fair market value.

Self Study Problem Sixteen - 7
(Transfers To A Corporation And Share Redemption)

Miss Doreen Brock owns an unincorporated business that operates out of leased premises. Her accounting records are based on the same information that has been used for tax purposes. On December 31 of the current year, the business has the following assets and liabilities:

	Tax Value	Fair Market Value
Accounts Receivable	$ 88,000	$ 85,000
Inventory	174,000	208,000
Equipment (Cost = $420,000)	234,000	317,000
Goodwill	Nil	350,000
Total Assets	$496,000	$960,000
Liabilities	(95,000)	(95,000)
Net Assets	$401,000	$865,000

All of the assets of the unincorporated business will be transferred to the new corporation. The Accounts Receivable will be transferred in return for cash of $85,000. These will be transferred using ITA 22, rather than the provisions of ITA 85(1).

The remaining assets will be transferred under the provisions of ITA 85(1). The total consideration received by Ms. Brock will have a value of $875,000 ($960,000 - $85,000), the fair market value of the assets other than Accounts Receivable.

The consideration is made up of new debt of $75,000, assumption of the old debt of $95,000, preferred stock with a fair market value of $225,000, and common stock with a fair market value of $480,000. The new corporation does not have a balance in its General Rate Income Pool (GRIP) account in any of the years under consideration.

Miss Brock wishes to incorporate her business in a manner that minimizes or eliminates any tax effects resulting from the transaction. She has totally utilized her lifetime capital gains deduction.

Required:

A. Do you agree with the decision to transfer the accounts receivable using ITA 22? Explain your conclusion.

B. Given that Miss Brock wishes to minimize or eliminate current taxes, indicate the values that should be elected for each of the assets to be transferred.

C. Determine the adjusted cost base of the debt, preferred shares, and common shares that would be received by Miss Brock on the rollover.

D. Determine the Paid Up Capital of the common stock and preferred stock that were issued by the new corporation to Miss Brock.

E. Determine the tax consequences to Miss Brock if the preferred and common shares that she received in the rollover were immediately redeemed by the new corporation at fair market values.

Self Study Problem Sixteen - 8 (Gift To Related Party - Section 85)

Mr. Jonathan Cheng is 64 years old and his only family member is his 35 year old daughter Sarah. For over 35 years he has operated an unincorporated retail business in Victoria, British Columbia. His daughter has worked in the business for several years and has gradually assumed greater responsibility for its operations.

Jonathan would like to retire and have his daughter take over the business. To that end, he has arranged for his daughter to establish a new corporation with an investment of $10,000. At the time of incorporation, the cash of $10,000 is the only asset of the corporation and the daughter owns the only common shares issued by the corporation. The new corporation will have a December 31 year end.

Jonathan would like to transfer most of his business assets to his daughter using the provisions of ITA 85. On January 1, 2013, the tax values (UCC or adjusted cost base) and fair market values of these assets are as follows:

	Tax Value	Fair Market Value
Inventories	$ 215,000	$ 232,000
Depreciable Assets - CCA Class 8 (Note One)	85,000	96,000
Land	197,000	430,000
Building (Note Two)	610,000	900,000
Total Assets	$1,107,000	$1,658,000
Liabilities	(160,000)	(160,000)
Net Assets (Owner's Equity)	$ 947,000	$1,498,000

Note One   The capital cost of the assets in Class 8 on January 1, 2013 is $116,000.

Note Two   The capital cost of the Building was $722,000.

The Accounts Receivable of the business will be transferred under ITA 22 rather than ITA 85. Also, a business valuation has indicated that, because of the personal nature of the services Jonathan provides, the business does not have any separable goodwill.

Jonathan will transfer the assets at an elected value of $1,107,000. The new corporation will assume all of the $160,000 of business liabilities. In addition, the corporation issues new debt to Jonathan in the amount of $947,000. He also receives preferred shares with a fair market value of $200,000 and a legal stated capital of $200,000.

Required: Ignore the lifetime capital gains deduction in your solution.

A. Determine the tax consequences to Mr. Cheng that result from the transfer of his business assets to Sarah's corporation. Your answer should include amounts to be included in Mr. Cheng's income as a result of the transfer, as well as the adjusted cost base and PUC of his preferred shares.

B. Determine the tax consequence to Mr. Cheng if Sarah's corporation redeems his preferred shares for $200,000 immediately after they are issued.

C. After a few months of running the business, Sarah finds that having full responsibility for the business is too difficult. On July 1, 2013, she sells all of her common shares for $401,000 to an arms' length party. Determine the tax consequences of this sale.

Self Study Problem Sixteen - 9 (Excess Consideration)

For the last 5 years, Martha Gilmour has operated Gilmour Enterprises as a sole proprietorship. As she no longer needs all of the income that is produced by the business, she would like to transfer the business to Gilmour Ltd., a corporation in which she holds 100 percent of the outstanding common shares. This corporation will have a December 31 year end.

The transfer will take place on January 1, 2013. Ms. Gilmour will use ITA 85(1) to transfer any tangible assets with fair market values in excess of their tax values (adjusted cost base or UCC). These assets, and their relevant values on January 1, 2013 are as follows:

	Tax Value	Fair Market Value
Depreciable Assets - CCA Class 8 (Note One)	$ 48,000	$ 71,000
Land	85,000	165,000
Building (Note Two)	276,000	432,000
Net Assets (Owner's Equity)	$409,000	$668,000

Note One   The capital cost of the assets in Class 8 on January 1, 2013 is $87,000.

Note Two   The capital cost of the Building was $378,000.

The elected value for the Depreciable Assets and the Building will be their tax values, a total of $324,000. However, because Martha has a net capital loss carry forward of $10,000 [(1/2)($20,000)], the Land will be transferred at an elected value of $105,000.

As consideration, Ms. Gilmour will receive non-share consideration of $429,000, plus redeemable preferred shares with a legal stated capital and a fair market value of $439,000.

Required: Ignore the lifetime capital gains deduction in your solution.

A. Determine the immediate tax consequences to Ms. Gilmour that will result from her transfer of the Gilmour Enterprises assets to Gilmour Ltd.

B. Indicate the tax values that will be recorded for the assets that are transferred to Gilmour Ltd. under ITA 85(1).

C. Determine the tax consequence to Ms. Gilmour if, at the beginning of 2014:

1. She sells her shares to an arm's length party for $439,000.

2. Gilmour Ltd. redeems her preferred shares for $439,000.

Self Study Problem Sixteen - 10 (Dividend Stripping)

Ms. Doreen Chisholm owns 75 percent of the outstanding shares of Dor Manufacturing Ltd. (DML). The remaining 25 percent of this Canadian controlled private corporation are held by her daughter, Elaine Lee. DML is a qualified small business corporation.

When the Company was founded ten years ago, all of the shares were issued to Ms. Chisholm in return for $100,000 in cash. This $100,000 amount was the Paid Up Capital of the DML shares, as well as Ms. Chisholm's adjusted cost base.

Five years ago, Ms. Chisholm sold 25 percent of the DML shares to her daughter for cash of $25,000, the fair market value of the shares at that time. There have been no other transactions in the shares since DML was founded. Her daughter continues to hold the remaining 25 percent of the DML shares.

On December 31, 2013, the fair market value of Ms. Chisholm's holding of DML shares is $900,000. At her direction, Ms. Chisholm's lawyer establishes a new company, Dorlaine Inc. Using the provisions of ITA 85(1), Ms. Chisholm's DML shares are transferred to this new Company at an elected value of $825,000. In return for the DML shares, Ms. Chisholm receives debt securities of the new Company with a fair market value of $700,000, along with newly issued Dorlaine Inc. common shares with a fair market value of $200,000.

Also on December 31, 2013, Ms. Chisholm transfers a $500,000 portfolio of investments she is holding personally into Dorlaine Inc. in return for debt securities equal to the investments' fair market values.

Ms. Chisholm has made no use of her lifetime capital gains deduction. Neither of the Companies have a balance in their General Rate Income Pool (GRIP) account in any of the years under consideration.

Required

A. What are the tax consequences to Ms. Chisholm of transferring the DML shares to Dorlaine Inc.? Briefly describe how you would change the transaction to improve Ms. Chisholm's tax position. Do not give consideration to the tax consequences of transferring the portfolio of investments into the corporation.

B. Ms. Chisholm dies on January 1, 2014. The terms of her will leave all of the Dorlaine Inc. shares to her daughter. What are the tax consequences arising as a result of Ms. Chisholm's death?

Self Study Problem Sixteen - 11 (Capital Gains Strips)

Newcastle Inc. is a CCPC. For a number of years, it has owned 100 percent of the outstanding common shares of Oldhouse Ltd. The Oldhouse shares have a PUC and an adjusted cost base of $479,000. At the present time, these shares have a fair market value of $2,397,000.

Oldhouse Ltd. has safe income of $372,000 and has a nil balance in its Refundable Dividend Tax On Hand account. Neither Newcastle Inc. nor Oldhouse Ltd. have a General Rate Income Pool (GRIP) balance.

Varafon Inc., an unrelated corporation, has indicated that it would like to purchase the Oldhouse shares for their fair market value of $2,397,000.

Required: Newcastle is considering two different approaches to selling the Oldhouse shares to Varafon. Indicate the amount and type of income that would accrue to Newcastle under each of these Scenarios.

Scenario One   Using ITA 85, Newcastle transfers the Oldhouse shares to Varafon at an elected value of $479,000. In return for the Oldhouse shares, Newcastle receives Varafon Inc. preferred stock with a PUC of $479,000 and a redemption value of $2,397,000. Immediately after the transfer, Varafon Inc. redeems the preferred stock for $2,397,000.

Scenario Two   Oldhouse Ltd. obtains a bank loan in the amount of $1,918,000 and uses all of the acquired funds to pay a dividend to Newcastle Inc. Subsequent to the receipt of this dividend, Newcastle Inc. sells the Oldhouse shares to Varafon Inc. for $479,000.

Assignment Problems

(The solutions for these problems are only available in
the solutions manual that has been provided to your instructor.)

Assignment Problem Sixteen - 1 (Transfers To A Corporation Vs. Direct Sale)

Several years ago, Ms. Fox acquired a small apartment building for total consideration of $950,000. This total was allocated on the basis of $225,000 for the land and $725,000 for the building.

At present, the property has a fair market value of $1,200,000, with $300,000 of this total attributable to the land. Ms. Fox would like to transfer the property to a corporation using a Section 85 rollover. At the beginning of the current year, the building had a UCC of $582,000. The value elected for the transfer is $807,000 ($225,000 + $582,000). The consideration given to Ms. Fox for the property is 12,000 common shares.

Shortly after the Section 85 rollover is completed, Ms. Fox sells all of the common shares she received as a result of the transfer to Mr. Hound, an arm's length party, for proceeds of $1,200,000.

Required:

A. Describe the tax consequences for Ms. Fox of using Section 85 and selling the common shares.

B. How do these results compare with the tax consequences of simply selling the building directly to Mr. Hound for $1,200,000?

Assignment Problem Sixteen - 2 (Section 85 Rollovers - Short Cases)

The following **independent** cases involve transfers of assets under ITA 85.

Case One   Several years ago an individual acquired an unlimited life franchise at a cost of $160,000. Because of the success of this franchise, it now has a fair market $215,000. The balance in the CEC account is $96,523. The franchise is transferred to a corporation in exchange for preferred shares with a fair market value and legal stated capital of $250,000.

Case Two   Land with a cost of $423,000 and a fair market value of $647,000 is transferred to a corporation in exchange for $47,000 in non-share consideration and $600,000 in preferred stock (fair market value and legal stated capital).

Case Three Merchandise inventories with a fair market value of $87,400 and a cost of $63,200 are transferred in exchange for $70,000 in non-share consideration and $17,400 in common stock (fair market value and legal stated capital).

Case Four   Depreciable assets with a fair market value of $124,000, a capital cost of $115,000, and a UCC of $52,992, are transferred in exchange for non-share consideration of $100,000, preferred shares with a fair market value and a legal stated capital of $10,000, and common shares with a fair market value and a legal stated capital of $14,000. All of the depreciable assets are in the same class.

For each of the four Cases provide the following information:

A. The minimum and maximum transfer prices that could be elected under the provisions of ITA 85.

B. Assuming the minimum value is elected, the amount of capital gain or business income to be included in the income of the transferor.

C. Again assuming that the minimum transfer value is elected, determine the adjusted cost base and PUC of the preferred and common stock consideration. Your answer should include the determination of any shareholder benefit under ITA 15(1) or deemed dividend under ITA 84(1) that will arise on the transfer.

Assignment Problem Sixteen - 3 (ACB Of Consideration And PUC)

Janice Tabor has a depreciable property that she wishes to transfer to a new corporation under the provisions of Section 85(1). The property has a capital cost of $450,000, a UCC of $225,000, and a fair market value of $675,000. The transfer will take place at an elected value of $400,000.

Ms. Tabor is considering the following alternative consideration packages:

| | Alternative | | |
	One	Two	Three
Debt Of The New Corporation	$150,000	$375,000	$300,000
Preferred Shares	150,000	300,000	Nil
Common Shares	375,000	Nil	375,000
Total	$675,000	$675,000	$675,000

All of the amounts in the preceding table are fair market values.

Required:

A. For each of the three alternatives, determine the adjusted cost base of the individual items of consideration received by Ms. Tabor.

B. For each of the three alternatives, determine the legal stated capital and the Paid Up Capital for the preferred and/or common shares issued.

Assignment Problem Sixteen - 4 (ITA 85 Transfer Of Depreciable Asset)

During the current year, Mr. Thomas Nelson transferred a depreciable capital property to a new corporation. Mr. Nelson owns all of the shares in the new corporation. The corporation will have a December 31 year end.

The transferred property was the only asset in its CCA class. It had been purchased several years ago for $225,000. Because of increasing difficulty in acquiring this type of property, it now has a fair market value of $316,000. At the time of the transfer, the balance in the UCC class was $189,600.

In order to absorb a $40,000 capital loss on a stock sale in the current year, he elects to transfer the property at a value of $265,000 ($225,000 + $40,000).

As consideration, Mr. Nelson takes back a note for $150,000, preferred shares with a fair market value of $50,000, and common shares with a fair market value of $116,000.

Required: Describe the income tax implications resulting from this transaction. Your answer should include both current tax implications, and the determination of values that will have future tax implications.

Assignment Problem Sixteen - 5
(Simple Depreciable Asset Transfer - Three Cases)

Paul Kwan owns a rental property that he acquired some years ago for $780,000. Of this total, $280,000 was allocated to the land and $500,000 was allocated to the building.

Assignment Problems

An appraiser has estimated that the current fair market value of the land is $425,000 and the current fair market value of the building is $775,000. The current UCC of the building is $391,000.

Mr. Kwan wishes to use ITA 85 to transfer this property to a new corporation, Kwan Ltd. in which he is the sole shareholder.

Case A   Mr. Kwan elects to transfer the property at an elected value of $280,000 for the land and $391,000 for the building. In return, he receives shares in the new corporation with a fair market value and legal stated capital of $1,200,000 ($425,000 + $775,000).

Case B   Mr. Kwan elects to transfer the property at an elected value of $425,000 for the land and $391,000 for the building. The consideration consists of shares in the new corporation with a fair market value and legal stated capital of $1,200,000.

Case C   Mr. Kwan elects to transfer the property at an elected value of $425,000 for the land and $391,000 for the building. The consideration consists of a promissory note from the corporation for $816,000, along with shares in the new corporation with a fair market value and legal stated capital of $384,000.

Required: For each of the preceding independent cases, determine:

- The immediate tax consequences of the transfer.
- The tax costs of the land and building in the hands of the corporation.
- The adjusted cost base of the shares issued by the corporation.
- The PUC of the shares issued by the corporation.

Assignment Problem Sixteen - 6
(Transfers To A Corporation And Sale/Redemption Of Shares)

In 2010, Karla Manson acquired land with a building situated on it for $920,000. At the acquisition date, It was estimated that the value of the land on which the building was situated was $175,000. The acquisition was financed with a mortgage of $420,000.

She had intended to begin business operations immediately. However, health problems required her to defer beginning operations until 2013. On January 1, 2013, she is ready to being operations and, because she expects the business to be profitable immediately, she decides to transfer the land and building to a new corporation.

The transfer will take place on January 1, 2013 and at that time, relevant facts about the property are as follows:

	Land	Building
Fair Market Value	$300,000	$1,100,000
Adjusted Cost Base/Capital Cost	175,000	745,000
UCC*	N/A	690,000
Mortgage Balance	N/A	375,000

*As the building was used periodically to produce income, Ms. Manson has deducted some CCA.

Ms. Manson will elect a transfer value for the land of $300,000. The corresponding figure for the building will be $700,000.

The corporation will assume the $375,000 mortgage on the building and, in addition, will issue a note to Ms. Manson for $625,000. The corporation will also issue common shares to Ms. Manson with a fair market value of $400,000.

There are no additions to the new corporation's General Rate Income Pool during 2013.

Required:

A. What are the tax consequences of making this transfer at the elected value of $1,000,000? Your answer should include amounts to be included in Ms. Manson's income as a result of the transfer, as well as the corporation's tax values for the assets.

B. Compute the adjusted cost base of each component of the consideration that Ms. Manson has received from the corporation.

C. Compute the PUC of the corporation's newly issued common shares.

D. What amounts would be included in Ms. Manson's Net Income For Tax Purposes if, at a later point in time, she sells her common shares for $400,000?

E. What amounts would be included in Mr. Manson's Net Income For Tax Purposes if, at a later point in time, the corporation redeems her common shares for $400,000?

Assignment Problem Sixteen - 7
(Transfers To A Corporation And Sale Of Shares)

Mike Danforth has, for a number of years, operated a successful proprietorship involved in retail sales of home improvement products. Mr. Danforth has decided to incorporate his business operations under the name of Danforth Inc. on January 2, 2013 using ITA 85. Danforth Inc. will have a December 31 year end.

On January 1, 2013 , the tax values (adjusted cost base or UCC) and fair market values of the assets and liabilities on his Balance Sheet are as follows:

	Tax Value	Fair Market Value
Cash	$ 2,500	$ 2,500
Temporary Investments	27,500	37,500
Accounts Receivable	13,750	12,500
Inventories	17,500	17,500
Prepayments	7,500	7,500
Land	105,000	77,500
Buildings (Cost = $113,000)	70,000	125,000
Equipment (Cost = $48,000)	20,000	7,500
Goodwill	Nil	117,500
Total Assets	$263,750	$405,000
Liabilities	(20,000)	(20,000)
Net Assets (Owner's Equity)	$243,750	$385,000

Other Information:

1. The Temporary Investments contain securities that have been purchased in order to absorb a seasonal excess of cash.

2. With respect to the Accounts Receivable, the $1,250 difference between their tax value and their fair market value reflects Mr. Danforth's estimate of potential bad debts.

3.   The new corporation will assume the outstanding liabilities of the proprietorship.

4. In implementing this rollover, Mr. Danforth will be issued new debt. Additional consideration, in excess of the maximum amount of non-share consideration that can be taken without incurring a tax liability, will be taken in the form of common shares.

5. Mr. Danforth will only use the ITA 85 provisions to transfer a specific asset if there is a tax advantage in doing so.

6. On October 1, 2013, Mr. Danforth sells the shares that he received in this rollover for $208,000. Danforth Inc. is a qualified small business corporation. Mr. Danforth has never utilized his lifetime capital gains deduction and he has no Cumulative Net Investment Loss.

Required:

A. Advise Mr. Danforth with respect to which assets should be transferred under the provisions of ITA 85(1), and the values that should be elected in order to minimize his current Tax Payable. Indicate the appropriate alternative treatment for any assets that you do not recommend transferring with the use of ITA 85(1).

B. Assume that Mr. Danforth only uses ITA 85(1) for those assets which you have indicated should be transferred under this provision. What is the maximum amount of non-share consideration that Mr. Danforth can receive without being subject to additional taxation?

C. Calculate Mr. Danforth's taxable capital gain on the sale of the shares and indicate the effect of the current year sale of shares on his Taxable Income.

Assignment Problem Sixteen - 8
(Transfers To A Corporation And Redemption Of Shares)

Griffeth Enterprises is an unincorporated business owned and operated by Sol Griffeth. As Mr. Griffeth has outstanding management skills, the business has grown very rapidly. Since he no longer needs all of the income that is produced by the business, he would like to transfer the assets of the business to a new corporation. The new corporation would be named Griffeth Ltd. and would have a December 31 year end.

On January 1, 2013, the tax values (adjusted cost base or UCC) and fair market values of the assets and liabilities of Griffeth Enterprises are as follows:

	Tax Value	Fair Market Value
Accounts Receivable	$ 168,000	$ 161,000
Temporary Investments	58,000	49,000
Inventories	310,000	326,000
Furniture And Fixtures	71,000	87,000
Machinery (Cost = $302,000)	275,000	384,000
Land	210,000	432,000
Building (Cost = $656,000)	579,000	713,000
Goodwill	Nil	275,000
Total Assets	$1,671,000	$2,427,000
Liabilities	(104,000)	(104,000)
Net Assets (Owner's Equity)	$1,567,000	$2,323,000

The transfer of the Griffeth Enterprises' assets to Griffeth Ltd. will take place on January 1, 2013, and an election will be made under ITA 85. Griffeth Ltd. will assume the liabilities of Griffeth Enterprises and, in addition, will issue $1,120,000 in new debt to Mr. Griffeth. With respect to share consideration, the new Company will issue preferred stock with a fair market value of $300,000 and common stock with a fair market value of $903,000.

All of the shares issued by Griffeth Ltd. as part of this rollover will be issued to Mr. Griffeth. Griffeth Ltd. does not have a balance in its General Rate Income Pool (GRIP) account in any of the years under consideration.

Required:

A. Determine whether the Accounts Receivable and Temporary Investments should be transferred under the provisions of ITA 85. Explain your conclusion and, if you recommend that ITA 85 should not be used, indicate the appropriate alternative treatment.

B. Without regard to your conclusions in Part A, assume that all of the assets are transferred to the new corporation under the provisions of ITA 85. Indicate the minimum values that can be elected for each of the assets.

C. Assume the transfer of all of the assets of Griffeth Enterprises to Griffeth Ltd. is made using the provisions of ITA 85, and that Mr. Griffeth will elect the values that you have determined in Part B. Determine the adjusted cost base of the non-share consideration, preferred stock and common stock received by Mr. Griffeth. In addition, determine the Paid Up Capital amounts for the preferred stock and the common stock.

D. Indicate the tax consequences to Mr. Griffeth if the preferred stock and common stock that he received in the rollover were:

1. immediately sold for their fair market values; or alternatively
2. immediately redeemed by the new corporation at their fair market values.

Assignment Problem Sixteen - 9 (Gift To Related Party - Section 85)

Ms. Bess Chadwick started an unincorporated business several years ago. The business has been extremely successful and is now worth several million dollars. While she is only 32 years old, she would like to retire. She has developed a taste for luxury travel and would like to spend the next two years pursuing that interest before settling down to a life of leisure in Canada.

Her life and business partner for the last four years has been Biff Bangor. At this stage, she has become somewhat bored with him and does not wish to have him join her in her travels. However, he has been a crucial factor in the success of her business, as well as a wonderful human being so, given this, she would like to transfer the business and its future growth to Biff.

In order to implement these decisions, she has arranged for Biff to establish a new corporation by investing $5,000 in newly issued common shares. At the time of incorporation, the cash of $5,000 is the only asset of the corporation and Biff owns the only common shares issued by the corporation. The new corporation is named Bangor Executive Services and Supplies (BESS) and will have a December 31 year end.

On January 1, 2013, Ms. Chadwick will transfer most of the business assets from her unincorporated business to BESS. On that date, the tax values (UCC or adjusted cost base) and fair market values of these assets is as follows:

	Tax Value	Fair Market Value
Inventories	$1,200,000	$ 1,250,000
Depreciable Assets - CCA Class 8 (Note One)	3,650,000	3,850,000
Land	1,870,000	3,100,000
Building (Note Two)	3,100,000	4,800,000
Total Assets	$9,820,000	$13,000,000
Liabilities	(850,000)	(850,000)
Net Assets (Owner's Equity)	$8,970,000	$12,150,000

Note One   The capital cost of the assets in Class 8 on January 1, 2013 is $4,100,000.

Note Two   The capital cost of the Building was $3,600,000.

The Accounts Receivable of the business will be transferred under ITA 22 rather than ITA 85. Also, a business valuation has indicated that Ms. Chadwick's business does not have any goodwill.

Ms. Chadwick will transfer the assets at an elected value of $9,820,000. The new corporation will assume all of the $850,000 of business liabilities and issue new debt to Ms. Chadwick in the amount of $1,150,000. She will also receive cash of $6,000,000 and redeemable preferred shares with a fair market value and a legal stated capital of $4,500,000.

Required: Ignore the lifetime capital gains deduction in your solution.

A. Determine the tax consequences to Ms. Chadwick that result from the transfer of her business assets to BESS. Your answer should include amounts to be included in Ms. Chadwick's income as a result of the transfer, as well as the adjusted cost base and PUC of her preferred shares.

B. Determine the tax consequence to Ms. Chadwick if BESS redeems her preferred shares for $4,500,000 immediately after they are issued.

C. After a few months of traveling alone, Bess finds, much to her surprise, that she misses Biff and asks him to join her on her travels. Given this much hoped-for invitation, Biff immediately (before she can change her mind) sells his BESS shares to an arm's length party for $550,000 and buys a first class ticket to Paris. Determine the tax consequences of this sale for Biff.

Assignment Problem Sixteen - 10 (Excess Consideration)

For the last 8 years, Mel Gibber has operated Gibber Industries as a sole proprietorship. As his accountant tells him he will save a great deal of income tax if the business is operated through a corporation, he plans to transfer the business to Gibber Inc., a CCPC in which he holds 100 percent of the outstanding shares. This corporation has a December 31 year end.

The transfer will take place on January 1, 2013. Mr. Gibber will use ITA 85(1) to transfer any tangible assets with fair market values in excess of their tax values (adjusted cost base or UCC). These assets, and their relevant values on January 1, 2013 are as follows:

	Tax Value	Fair Market Value
Depreciable Assets - CCA Class 8 (Note One)	$123,000	$ 162,000
Land	220,000	363,000
Building (Note Two)	462,000	587,000
Net Assets (Owner's Equity)	$805,000	$1,112,000

Note One The capital cost of the assets in Class 8 on January 1, 2013 is $167,000.

Note Two The capital cost of the Building was $514,000.

The elected value for the Depreciable Assets and the Building will be their tax values, a total of $585,000. However, because Mel has a net capital loss carry forward of $18,000 [(1/2)($36,000)], the Land will be transferred at an elected value of $256,000.

As consideration, Mr. Gibber will receive non-share consideration of $800,000, plus Gibber Inc. redeemable preferred shares with a legal stated capital and a fair market value of $562,000.

Required: Ignore the lifetime capital gains deduction in your solution.

A. Determine the immediate tax consequences to Mr. Gibber that will result from his transfer of the Gibber Industries assets to Gilmour Ltd.

B. Indicate the tax values that will be recorded for the assets that are transferred to Gibber Inc. under ITA 85(1).

C. Determine the tax consequence to Mr. Gibber if, at the beginning of 2014:

1. He sells his shares to an arm's length party for $562,000.

2. Gibber Inc. redeems his preferred shares for $562,000.

Assignment Problem Sixteen - 11 (Dividend Stripping)

Norton Ltd. is a Canadian controlled private corporation, established six years ago, with an initial investment by Ms. Nora Chadwick of $225,000. In return for her investment, Ms. Chadwick received 22,500 common shares with a paid up capital of $225,000. The corporation has a December 31 year end.

The Company has been very successful and, as a consequence, it is estimated that the current fair market value of the common shares is $2,465,000. Ms. Chadwick has a serious heart condition that has significantly reduced her life expectancy. As a consequence, she would like to transfer any future increase in value of the Norton Ltd. shares to her companion of the last 25 years, Mr. Bobby Borque. Mr. Borque cohabits with Ms. Chadwick in a conjugal relationship.

In order to accomplish this goal, she intends to have Bobby establish a new Company, Borque Inc. All 100 of the common shares of Borque Inc. will be issued to Bobby, in return for a cash investment of $1,000.

Once the new company is established, Ms. Chadwick will transfer all of her common shares in Norton Ltd. to Borque Inc. She will make the transfer under the provisions of ITA 85(1), electing a value of $975,000. It is her intention to take back consideration consisting of a $975,000 interest bearing note (fair market value = $975,000) along with retractable preferred shares with a fair market value and a Paid Up Capital of $1,490,000.

Neither of the Companies have a balance in their General Rate Income Pool (GRIP) account in any of the years under consideration.

Norton Ltd. is a qualified small business corporation and Ms. Chadwick has made no use of her lifetime capital gains deduction. She believes that this rollover transaction has been structured in a manner that will allow her to fully utilize her lifetime capital gains deduction.

Required:

A. Explain the tax consequences of the proposed ITA 85(1) transfer of the Norton Ltd. shares to Borque Inc.

B. Describe how you would change the transaction to improve Ms. Chadwick's tax position, and determine the tax implications that would result from this new approach.

C. As an alternative approach to using her lifetime capital gains deduction, Ms. Chadwick proposes selling 7,534 shares of Norton Ltd. to Borque Inc. for cash. The shares would be sold for their current fair market value and this would produce, in the absence of ITA 84.1, a capital gain of just over $750,000. Explain the tax consequences of this proposed transaction.

Show all calculations to support your answers.

Assignment Problem Sixteen - 12 (Dividend Stripping)

Mr. Doug Johnston is the sole shareholder of Johnston Home Furnishings, a Canadian controlled private corporation involved in the sale of retail products for the home. He has operated this Company for the last 20 years, in most years earning a satisfactory rate of return on the invested assets.

As of December 31, 2013, relevant information as to the values associated with his Company is as follows:

Initial Investment (Paid Up Capital)	$ 478,000
Fair Market Value - December 31, 2013	$3,985,000

Mr. Johnston is nearing retirement and wishes to gradually dispose of his business. In preparation for retirement, he has enrolled in a variety of courses at a local college. One of these courses, Taxation 405, has introduced him to the concept of transferring property to a corporation under Section 85 of the *Income Tax Act*. In reviewing this provision, it has occurred to him that, by transferring the shares of Johnston Home Furnishings to a new company, he could effectively escape taxation on part of the difference between his initial investment of $478,000 and the $3,985,000 fair market value of his business. This reflects the fact that he has made no use of his $750,000 lifetime capital gains deduction.

In view of his analysis of this situation, he has planned to transfer all of the shares of Johnston Home Furnishings to a new company, Johnston Investments. The transfer will be made under the provisions of ITA 85(1) and an elected value of $1,228,000 will be used for the transfer. In return for the shares of Johnston Home Furnishings, Mr. Johnston will receive a non-interest bearing note for $1,228,000 and ten shares of the new company's no par common shares.

The note will be due in one year and Mr. Johnston anticipates that, as a result of dividends received from Johnston Home Furnishings, Johnston Investments will have sufficient cash to pay the entire amount at that time.

Neither of the Companies have a balance in their General Rate Income Pool (GRIP) account in any of the years under consideration.

Required:

A. In the absence of ITA 84.1, indicate the tax consequences of the transfer of the shares of Johnston Home Furnishings to Johnston Investments.

B. Determine whether ITA 84.1 would be applicable in this case. Assuming that ITA 84.1 is applicable, calculate the deemed dividend that would arise on this transfer. In addition, indicate the net economic effect that would result from this transfer combined with a redemption of the Johnston Investments shares at their fair market value of $2,757,000 ($3,985,000 - $1,228,000).

Assignment Problem Sixteen - 13 (Capital Gains Strips)

Lardley Inc., is a Canadian controlled private company. Ten years ago, it acquired 100 percent of the outstanding shares of Domas Ltd. at a cost of $300,000.

The Domas shares have a PUC of $450,000. As the Company has operated very successfully since its acquisition by Lardley, the shares have a current fair market value of $2,300,000. During the period that Lardley Inc. has owned Domas, safe income of $565,000 has accrued. Domas has a nil balance in its Refundable Dividend Tax On Hand account.

Neither company has a General Rate Income Pool (GRIP) balance.

Required: Indicate the amount, and type, of income that would accrue to Lardley Inc. in both of the following **independent** situations:

A. Domas Ltd. obtains a bank loan in the amount of $2,000,000 and uses all of the acquired funds to pay a dividend to Lardley Inc. Subsequent to the receipt of this dividend, Lardley Inc. sells the Domas shares to Ms. Arden, an arm's length party, for $300,000.

B. Using ITA 85(1), Lardley transfers the Domas shares to Arden Ltd., an unrelated corporation. The elected value is $300,000. In return for the Domas shares, Lardley receives Arden Ltd. preferred stock with a PUC of $300,000 and a redemption value of $2,300,000. Immediately after the transfer, Arden Ltd. redeems the preferred stock for $2,300,000.

CHAPTER 17

Other Rollovers And Sale Of An Incorporated Business

Introduction

17-1.   The preceding Chapter gave detailed consideration to the Section 85 rollover provisions, which provide for a tax deferred transfer of property to a corporation. In addition, Chapter 8 dealt with rollovers involving transfers to a spouse and transfers of farm property to children. There are a number of other rollover provisions in the *Act* that will be discussed in this Chapter.

17-2.   These additional rollover provisions cover share for share exchanges among corporations, share exchanges in the process of the reorganization of a corporation, amalgamations of existing corporations, the winding-up of a 90 percent or more owned subsidiary, and conversions of debt to shares. The winding-up of a Canadian corporation that is not a 90 percent owned subsidiary is also covered. This latter transaction does not involve a rollover, but is dealt with in the same Section of the *Income Tax Act* as the winding-up of a 90 percent or more owned subsidiary.

17-3.   In previous editions of this text, we covered business valuations and tax shelters in this Chapter. However, we have found that many users of the text did not have an interest in these subjects. As a result, this material is available as Supplementary Reading No. 6, Business Valuations and No. 7, Tax Shelters, which can be found on the Student CD-ROM that accompanies this text.

Share For Share Exchanges - ITA 85.1

Background

17-4.   ITA 85.1 provides for a rollover in which a shareholder exchanges his shares for shares of an acquiring corporation. When there are many diverse shareholders, a share for share exchange is easier to accomplish than a Section 85 rollover, because there is no need for each shareholder to file an election. Further, the provisions of ITA 85.1 apply automatically, unless the vendor includes any gain or loss on the transaction in his income tax return. Given these features, an ITA 85.1 exchange is an important arrangement in business combination transactions.

Share For Share Exchanges - ITA 85.1

General Rules

17-5.   The general rules for this rollover apply automatically unless the vendor opts to include a gain or loss from the transaction in their income tax return. These general rules are as follows:

ITA 85.1(1)(a)   The vendor is deemed to have:

(i) disposed of the exchanged shares for proceeds of disposition equal to their adjusted cost base.

(ii) acquired the shares of the purchaser at a cost to the vendor equal to the adjusted cost base to the vendor of the exchanged shares immediately before the exchange.

ITA 85.1(1)(b)   The cost to the purchaser of each of the acquired shares is deemed to be the lesser of:

(i) its fair market value immediately before the exchange, and

(ii) its paid-up capital immediately before the exchange.

ITA 85.1(2.1)   The PUC of the purchaser shares that have been issued to the vendor is limited to the PUC of the shares given up by the vendor.

17-6.   You should note that the ITA 85.1(1)(b) provision may be problematical for the purchaser in situations where the adjusted cost base of the vendor's shares exceeds their PUC. If the shares are later sold by the purchaser, that excess of the adjusted cost base over the PUC will be subject to tax as a capital gain since the purchaser's adjusted cost base will be equal to the PUC. This would suggest that, in situations where the adjusted cost base of the shares exceeds their PUC, it might be better to use ITA 85(1) for the transfer.

Conditions For The Application Of ITA 85.1

17-7.   The conditions required for this rollover to be applicable are found in ITA 85.1(1) and (2). To begin, the vendor's shares must be held as capital property. Additional conditions for the applicability of the rollover are as follows:

ITA 85.1(2)(a)   The vendor and purchaser must be dealing with each other at arm's length.

ITA 85.1(2)(b)   The vendor, or persons with whom he does not deal at arm's length, cannot control the purchaser immediately after the exchange. Likewise, they cannot own shares having a fair market value in excess of 50 percent of the total fair market value of the purchasing corporation's outstanding shares.

ITA 85.1(2)(c)   The vendor and purchaser cannot have filed an election under ITA 85 with respect to the exchanged shares.

ITA 85.1(2)(d)   The vendor must not have received any consideration, other than shares of the purchaser, in return for the shares given up in the exchange.

17-8.   You should note that this last condition under ITA 85.1(2)(d) does not prevent the vendor from selling additional shares to the purchaser for non-share consideration.

Example
Application Of ITA 85.1
17-9.   A brief example will serve to illustrate the basic provisions of ITA 85.1:

Example   Ms. Cowper is the sole shareholder of Cowper Inc., owning a total of 1,000 shares with a Paid Up Capital (PUC) and an adjusted cost base of $10,000. The shares of Cowper Inc. have a current fair market value of $125,000.

Mega Holdings Ltd. acquires these shares in return for 5,000 of its common shares. The Mega Holdings shares are currently trading at $25 per share, resulting in a total value for the 5,000 shares of $125,000.

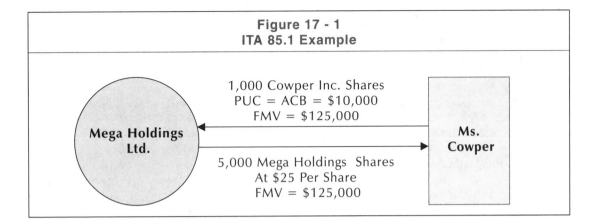

**Figure 17 - 1
ITA 85.1 Example**

Analysis   The information in the example is presented graphically in Figure 17-1.

In the absence of the share for share exchange provisions in ITA 85.1, Ms. Cowper would have a capital gain of $115,000 ($125,000 - $10,000). However, under the rollover provisions of ITA 85.1, the following results apply:

- Ms. Cowper is deemed to have disposed of her shares for an amount equal to the $10,000 adjusted cost base of the Cowper Inc. shares. This means that there is no capital gain on the disposition. [ITA 85.1(1)(a)(i)]

- Ms. Cowper is deemed to have acquired the shares in Mega Holdings Ltd. at a cost equal to the adjusted cost base of the Cowper Inc. shares, or $10,000. [ITA 85.1(1)(a)(ii)]

- The adjusted cost base of the Cowper shares acquired by Mega Holding Ltd. is deemed to be equal to $10,000, the lesser of their fair market value of $125,000, and their PUC of $10,000 [ITA 85.1(1)(b)]. You should note that this limit applies, even in situations where the vendor opted to forego the rollover under ITA 85.1 by including the gain in income (see Paragraph 17-10).

- The PUC of the Mega Holding Ltd. shares that have been issued to Ms. Cowper is limited to the $10,000 PUC of the Cowper shares that have been given up. [ITA 85.1(2.1)]

Opting Out Of ITA 85.1

17-10.   As we have noted, ITA 85.1 applies automatically unless the vendor opts out in their income tax return. In this example, Ms. Cowper could opt out of ITA 85.1 by including the taxable capital gain of $57,500 [(1/2)($125,000 - $10,000)] in her income tax return. Note that, unlike the situation when ITA 85(1) is used in a rollover, there is no flexibility on the transfer value. With respect to the shares that are exchanged, opting out requires that 100 percent of the capital gain on the exchanged shares be included in income. This could be a problem if, for example, Ms. Cowper only wanted to recognize part of the gain on her shares.

17-11.   There are two possible solutions to this problem. The transfer of Ms. Cowper's shares could be made using the provisions of ITA 85(1). This would allow the use of an elected value that would limit the amount of gain that would be recognized.

17-12.   An alternative, perhaps simpler solution, would be to sell a portion of her shares to Mega Holdings for cash. This would allow the recognition of the desired amount of capital gain. The remaining shares could then be exchanged on a tax free basis under ITA 85.1.

Exercise Seventeen - 1

Subject: Share For Share Exchange

Ms. Aly Alee is the sole shareholder of Aayee Ltd., a Canadian controlled private corporation. The corporation was established several years ago by Ms. Alee with an investment of $450,000. It has identifiable net assets with a fair market value of $2,200,000. The shares of her company are acquired by a large publicly traded company, Global Outreach Inc., through the issuance of 50,000 new shares. At the time of this business combination, the Global Outreach Inc. shares are trading at $49 per share. Ms. Alee has fully utilized her lifetime capital gains deduction in the past. Indicate the tax consequences of this transaction to both Ms. Alee and Global Outreach Inc.

End of Exercise. Solution available in Study Guide.

ITA 85.1 In Practice

17-13.   We have illustrated ITA 85.1 using an example that involves a large public company acquiring a corporation with a single shareholder. This is not the usual application of ITA 85.1. ITA 85.1 was designed to be used in situations where a public company acquires a widely held corporation with a large number of shareholders.

17-14.   As noted in Paragraph 17-4, Section 85 can be used as an alternative to Section 85.1. However, in situations where the acquiree has a large number of shareholders, this approach would require the filing of numerous, in some cases hundreds, of separate Section 85 elections. The use of Section 85.1 avoids this by making its application automatic, unless the acquiree includes any gain or loss in income. This is a much more efficient procedure in most business combination situations.

We suggest you work Self Study Problems Seventeen-1 and 2 at this point.

Exchange Of Shares In A Reorganization - ITA 86

Application Of ITA 86(1)

Basic Procedure

17-15.   ITA 86(1) applies when there has been a reorganization involving an exchange of shares within a single corporation. In the usual application, a shareholder of a corporation exchanges shares held in at least one class of existing shares, for authorized shares in the same company, or for authorized shares in the same company combined with non-share consideration. In effect, there is a redemption of the taxpayer's current shareholding, combined with an acquisition of a new shareholding. ITA 86(1) allows this transaction to take place without tax consequences to the taxpayer whose shares are being redeemed.

Use In Estate Freeze

17-16.   One of the most common applications of ITA 86(1) is in an estate freeze, where an owner of a business wishes to pass on the future growth of the business to other family members, or to arrange an orderly succession to another individual or group.

Example   A father holds all of the outstanding common shares of a corporation. These shares have a fair market value in excess of their adjusted cost base and, as a consequence, their sale or redemption would normally result in a deemed dividend and/or a capital gain or capital loss. Further, if the father continues to hold the shares, future growth in the corporation will accrue to him.

Analysis   To avoid this situation, the father will exchange his common shares for newly issued preferred shares of the corporation. The preferred shares will have a fixed redemption value equal to the fair market value of the common shares given up. The fact that their value is fixed will serve to freeze the value of the father's interest in the corporation. If the father wishes to retain control of the corporation, the preferred shares can be structured to provide voting rights sufficient to achieve this objective. Common shares will then be issued to a spouse, a child, or some other related person.

17-17.   As the preferred shares held by the father reflect the full fair market value of the company, the new common shares can be issued to the related person at a fairly nominal value. However, any future growth in the value of the company will accrue to these common shares. ITA 86(1) provides for the father's exchange of shares to take place on a rollover or tax free basis (see Chapter 19 for a more detailed discussion of estate freezes).

Conditions For The Reorganization
General Conditions
17-18.   For the provisions of ITA 86(1) to apply, several conditions must be met.

Shares Must Be Capital Property   First, the original owner's shares must be capital property to the owner. They cannot be part of an inventory of securities that is being held for trading purposes.

All Shares Held By Transferor In A Particular Class   A second condition is that the transaction must result in an exchange of all of the outstanding shares of a particular class that are owned by the transferor. For example, all Class A common shares that are owned by the transferor must be exchanged for some other type of share. Note that there is no requirement that Class A common shares that are held by other shareholders be exchanged as part of the transaction. Further, it is not necessary that other classes of shares owned by the transferor be exchanged for new shares.

Reorganization Of Capital   A third condition is that the share exchange must be integral to a reorganization of the capital of the corporation. This will often require that the articles of incorporation be amended to authorize any new class of shares.

Transferor Must Receive Shares   A final condition is that the transferor must receive shares of the capital stock of the corporation. While this does not preclude the transferor from receiving non-share consideration, such non-share consideration should not exceed the adjusted cost base or the PUC of the shares transferred. If it does, the excess will have to be taken into income, either as a taxable capital gain or loss, a deemed dividend, or some combination of the two income inclusions.

Establishing Market Value For Preferred Shares
17-19.   In the more common applications of ITA 86(1), the new shares received by the transferor will usually be preferred shares. These shares must be designed in such a fashion as to clearly establish their fair market value. If this is not the case, a subsequent dispute with the CRA could result in some of the benefits of using ITA 86(1) being lost. Adding the following characteristics to the preferred shares will serve to establish a defensible fair market value:

- The preferred shares must be redeemable at the option of the shareholder. The CRA rigorously enforces this requirement to protect the fair market value of the preferred shares.

- The preferred shares should be entitled to a dividend at a reasonable rate. Without a reasonable dividend entitlement to the original shareholder, the incoming shareholders could benefit by receiving a disproportionate share of the corporation's future profits. However, there is no requirement for the entitlement to be cumulative.

- The corporation must guarantee that dividends will not be paid on any other class of shares, if the payment would result in the corporation having insufficient net assets to redeem the preferred shares at their specified redemption price.

- The preferred shares must become cumulative if the fair market value of the net assets of the corporation falls below the redemption value of the preferred shares, or if the corporation is unable to redeem the shares on a call for redemption.

- The preferred shares may or may not have normal voting rights. However, they should carry votes on any matter regarding the rights attached to the preferred shares.

- The preferred shares should have preference on liquidation of the corporation. While the very nature of preferred shares tends to guarantee preference, the CRA requires additional assurance that the normal provisions for such shares will not be avoided.

Procedures

General Rules

17-20.   As noted previously, an ITA 86(1) reorganization involves a redemption (disposition) of a given shareholder's holding of a particular class of shares (old shares, hereafter). In return, the shareholder acquires shares of a different class (new shares, hereafter) and, in some reorganizations, non-share consideration. ITA 86(1) specifies a number of rules that apply in such a reorganization of capital. These are as follows:

Non-Share Consideration   ITA 86(1)(a) indicates that the cost to the shareholder of this consideration is deemed to be its fair market value.

Cost Of New Shares   ITA 86(1)(b) indicates that the cost of the new shares to the shareholder is equal to the cost of the old shares, less any non-share consideration received.

Proceeds Of Redemption For Old Shares   Because there is a redemption of shares, there is the possibility of an ITA 84(3) deemed dividend. ITA 84(3)(a) defines such dividends as the excess of the "amount paid" over the PUC of the shares being redeemed. This "amount paid" clearly includes any non-share consideration and, when shares are included in the redemption payment, ITA 84(5)(d) indicates that their value is based on any increase in PUC resulting from the issuance of these shares. Putting this together leads to the conclusion that the total proceeds for the redemption will be equal to the non-share consideration plus the PUC of any new shares issued. Note that, in the usual ITA 86(1) scenario, the PUC of the new shares will often be reduced by a PUC reduction under ITA 86(2.1)(a). (See Paragraph 17-21.)

Proceeds Of Disposition For Old Shares   As the redemption of the old shares is a type of disposition, there is also the possibility of a capital gain or loss. For the purposes of determining the capital gain or loss on this disposition, ITA 86(1)(c) defines the proceeds of disposition for the old shares as being equal to the cost of the new shares (the cost of the old shares, less non-share consideration), plus any non-share consideration received by the taxpayer.

In our general discussion of ITA 84(3) redemptions in Chapter 14, we discuss the possibility that the combination of redemption procedures and disposition procedures could result in the double counting of all or part of any gain on the transaction. As we noted there, this possibility is eliminated by the fact that the ITA 54 definition of proceeds of disposition excludes ITA 84(3) dividends.

PUC Reduction Calculation

17-21.   As noted in the preceding rules, a PUC reduction may be required on the new shares. This is specified in ITA 86(2.1)(a). This reduction is calculated as follows:

Increase In Legal Stated Capital Of New Shares		$xx,xxx
Less The Excess, If Any, Of:		
PUC Of Old Shares	($x,xxx)	
Over The Non-Share Consideration	x,xxx	(x,xxx)
ITA 86(2.1)(a) PUC Reduction		$xx,xxx

17-22.   In reviewing this PUC reduction formula, note that where the non-share consideration is equal to, or greater than the PUC of the old shares, the amount subtracted from the increase in the legal stated capital of the new shares will be nil. This means that the PUC reduction will be equal to the increase in legal stated capital for the new shares. In common sense terms, if the shareholder takes back the full amount of the old PUC in the form of non-share consideration, the PUC of the new shares will be nil.

17-23.   As was the case with rollovers to a corporation under Section 85, if the PUC reduction applies to more than one class of shares, it will generally be allocated to the individual classes on the basis of the relative fair market value of each class.

Example Using ITA 86(1) In An Estate Freeze
Basic Data
17-24.   An example will serve to illustrate the ITA 86(1) procedures. You might note that the example illustrates the manner in which an ITA 86(1) reorganization of capital can be used to freeze the value of an individual's estate. The example is illustrated graphically in Figure 17-2.

> **Example**   Mr. David Jones owns all of the outstanding shares of Jones Inc. These common shares have an adjusted cost base of $50,000 and a paid up capital of $75,000. Because of the successful operations of the Company, the current fair market value of these common shares is $500,000.
>
> Mr. Jones would like to have future growth in the value of the corporation accrue to his daughter, Ms. Veronica Jones. To accomplish this, Mr. Jones exchanges his common shares for a $150,000 note payable from the corporation and preferred shares with a fair market value and a legal stated capital of $350,000. Common shares are purchased by Veronica Jones for $1,000. These are the only Jones Inc. common shares outstanding subsequent to these transactions.

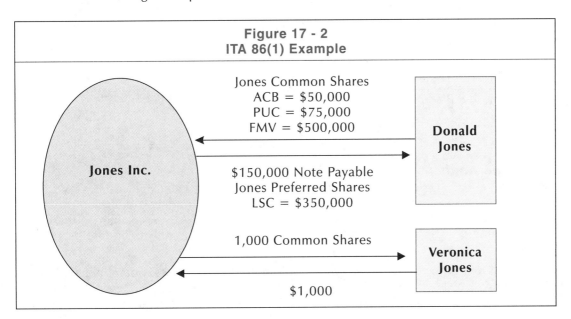

Figure 17 - 2
ITA 86(1) Example

Jones Common Shares
ACB = $50,000
PUC = $75,000
FMV = $500,000

Donald Jones

Jones Inc.

$150,000 Note Payable
Jones Preferred Shares
LSC = $350,000

1,000 Common Shares

Veronica Jones

$1,000

PUC Reduction
17-25.   The first step in applying the ITA 86(1) rules in this situation would be to calculate the required PUC reduction and the resulting PUC value for the preferred shares. As the non-share consideration of $150,000 exceeds the $75,000 PUC of the shares given up, we would expect the PUC reduction formula to reduce the PUC of the preferred shares to nil. The following calculations support this expected result:

Exchange Of Shares In A Reorganization - ITA 86

Cost Of Non-Share Consideration (Note Payable)		$150,000

Legal Stated Capital Of Preferred Shares		$350,000
Less The Excess, If Any, Of:		
PUC Of Shares Given Up	($ 75,000)	
Over The Non-Share Consideration	150,000	Nil
ITA 86(2.1)(a) PUC Reduction		$350,000

Legal Stated Capital Of Preferred Shares	$350,000
ITA 86(2.1)(a) PUC Reduction	(350,000)
PUC Of Preferred Shares	Nil

Other Calculations

17-26.   Other required values can be calculated as follows:

Adjusted Cost Base Of Shares Given Up	$ 50,000
Non-Share Consideration	(150,000)
Adjusted Cost Base Of Preferred Shares	Nil

PUC Of Preferred Shares	Nil
Plus Non-Share Consideration	$150,000
Proceeds Of Redemption - ITA 84(5)(d)	$150,000
PUC Of Shares Given Up	(75,000)
ITA 84(3) Deemed Dividend	$ 75,000

Adjusted Cost Base Of Preferred Shares	Nil
Plus Non-Share Consideration	$150,000
Proceeds Of Disposition - ITA 86(1)(c)	$150,000
ITA 84(3) Deemed Dividend	(75,000)
Adjusted Proceeds Of Disposition	$ 75,000
Adjusted Cost Base Of Shares Given Up	(50,000)
Capital Gain	$ 25,000

Economic Analysis

17-27.   The shares held by his daughter, Veronica, will have an adjusted cost base of $1,000 and this will also be their initial fair market value. However, if the corporation prospers, all future increases in its value will accrue to her. In other words, by exchanging his common shares for non-growth preferred shares, Mr. Jones has frozen the value of his interest in Jones Inc.

17-28.   In reviewing this example, you should note that Mr. Jones' potential gain has not disappeared. If he had simply sold his shares without the reorganization, he would have realized a gain of $450,000 ($500,000 - $50,000). As a result of the reorganization, he has recognized $100,000 ($75,000 dividend + $25,000 capital gain). This gain reflects the excess of the $150,000 non-share consideration received by Mr. Jones, over the $50,000 adjusted cost base of the original shares. Note that Mr. Jones could have avoided having any income as a result of this transaction if he had limited the amount of non-share consideration to $50,000.

17-29.   This reorganization has left an unrecognized gain of $350,000 ($500,000 - $150,000). This gain will remain unrecognized until such time as Mr. Jones' holding of preferred shares is either redeemed or sold for its fair market value of $350,000. As these shares have a PUC of nil, a subsequent redemption would result in an ITA 84(3) deemed dividend of $350,000. As the adjusted cost base of the shares is also nil, a subsequent sale of the shares would result in a capital gain of $350,000, the taxable amount of which would be one-half, or $175,000.

17-30.   A final point here is that this example does not represent a typical ITA 86(1) estate freeze. While it does accomplish the goal of transferring future growth in the corporation to a related party, the approach used has resulted in current Tax Payable for Mr. Jones. This could have been avoided by limiting the non-share consideration to the PUC and adjusted cost base of $50,000. It is this approach that would be used in a typical ITA 86(1) transaction.

Exercise Seventeen - 2

Subject: Exchange Of Shares In Reorganization (ACB = PUC = Boot)

Mr. Sam Samson is the sole shareholder of Samdoo Ltd. It is a Canadian controlled private corporation and its common shares have a fair market value of $2,300,000, an adjusted cost base (ACB) of $1,000,000, and a paid up capital (PUC) of $1,000,000. At this time, Samdoo Ltd. has no balance in its GRIP account. Mr. Samson exchanges all of his Samdoo Ltd. shares for cash of $1,000,000 and preferred shares that are redeemable for $1,300,000. Determine the ACB and the PUC of the redeemable preferred shares. Indicate the amount, and type, of any income that will result from this transaction.

Exercise Seventeen - 3

Subject: Exchange Of Shares In Reorganization (ACB > PUC, PUC = Boot)

Mr. Sam Samson is the sole shareholder of Samdoo Ltd. It is a Canadian controlled private corporation and its common shares have a fair market value of $2,300,000, an adjusted cost base (ACB) of $1,250,000, and a paid up capital (PUC) of $1,000,000. At this time, Samdoo Ltd. has no balance in its GRIP account. Mr. Samson exchanges all of his Samdoo Ltd. shares for cash of $1,000,000 and preferred shares that are redeemable for $1,300,000. Determine the ACB and the PUC of the redeemable preferred shares. Indicate the amount, and type, of any income that will result from this transaction.

Exercise Seventeen - 4

Subject: Exchange Of Shares In Reorganization (ACB > Boot > PUC)

Mr. Sam Samson is the sole shareholder of Samdoo Ltd. It is a Canadian controlled private corporation and its common shares have a fair market value of $2,300,000, an adjusted cost base (ACB) of $1,250,000, and a paid up capital (PUC) of $1,000,000. At this time, Samdoo Ltd. has no balance in its GRIP account. Mr. Samson exchanges all of his Samdoo Ltd. shares for cash of $1,200,000 and preferred shares that are redeemable for $1,100,000. Determine the ACB and the PUC of the redeemable preferred shares. Indicate the amount, and type, of any income that will result from this transaction.

End of Exercises. Solutions available in Study Guide.

We suggest your work Self Study Problem Seventeen-3 at this point.

Gift To Related Person - ITA 86(2)

Background

17-31.   ITA 86(2) contains a rule designed to prevent a taxpayer from using the reorganization of capital rollover provision to confer a benefit on a related person. This rule is applicable whenever the fair market value of the old shares exceeds the sum of the fair market value of the new shares and the fair market value of the non-share consideration received, and it is reasonable to regard all, or part, of this excess as a gift to a related person. You might wish to note that this provision is similar to the provision that is applicable when the use of an ITA 85(1) rollover involves a gift to a related person (see Paragraph 16-128).

17-32.   In situations where ITA 86(2) applies, the rules for the reorganization of share capital are as follows:

Cost Of New Shares   Under ITA 86(2)(e), the cost to the taxpayer of the new shares will be equal to:

- the cost of the old shares; less
- the sum of the non-share consideration, *plus the gift*.

This compares to a cost for the new shares under ITA 86(1)(b) equal to the cost of the old shares, less any non-share consideration.

Proceeds Of Disposition   Under ITA 86(2)(c), the proceeds of the disposition for capital gains purposes on the old shares will be equal to the lesser of:

- the non-share consideration, plus the gift; and
- the fair market value of the old shares.

This compares to the proceeds of disposition under ITA 86(1)(c), which is equal to the cost of the new shares, plus any non-share consideration.

Capital Losses   Under ITA 86(2)(d), any capital loss resulting from the disposition of the old shares will be deemed to be nil.

17-33.   To illustrate these procedures, we will modify the example in Paragraph 17-24 by decreasing the amount of consideration received to create a $100,000 gift. The revised example is as follows:

Example   Mr. David Jones owns all of the outstanding shares of Jones Inc. These common shares have an adjusted cost base of $50,000 and a paid up capital of $75,000. Because of the successful operations of the Company, the current fair market value of these common shares is $500,000.

Mr. Jones would like to have future growth in the value of the corporation accrue to his daughter, Ms. Veronica Jones. To accomplish this, Mr. Jones exchanges his common shares for a $150,000 note payable from the corporation and preferred shares with a fair market value and a legal stated capital of $250,000. Common shares are purchased by Veronica Jones for $1,000. These are the only Jones Inc. common shares outstanding subsequent to these transactions.

Calculation Of Gift

17-34.   The gift involved in this approach is calculated as follows:

Fair Market Value Of Shares Given Up		$500,000
Less Fair Market Value Of Consideration:		
Non-Share Consideration	($150,000)	
Fair Market Value Of Preferred Shares	(250,000)	(400,000)
Gift		$100,000

17-35.   As his daughter is the only holder of common shares, this $100,000 gift would accrue to her. As she is clearly a related person, ITA 86(2) would be applicable.

PUC Reduction

17-36.   The PUC reduction and PUC of the preferred shares is calculated as follows:

Cost Of Non-Share Consideration (Note Payable)		$150,000

Legal Stated Capital Of Preferred Shares		$250,000
Less The Excess, If Any, Of:		
PUC Of Shares Given Up	($ 75,000)	
Over The Non-Share Consideration	150,000	Nil
ITA 86(2.1)(a) PUC Reduction		$250,000

Legal Stated Capital Of Preferred Shares	$250,000
ITA 86(2.1)(a) PUC Reduction	(250,000)
PUC Of Preferred Shares	Nil

Other Calculations

17-37.   The remaining calculations that would be required under ITA 86(2) are as follows:

Adjusted Cost Base Of Shares Given Up		$ 50,000
Less:		
Non-Share Consideration	($150,000)	
Gift (See Paragraph 17-34)	(100,000)	(250,000)
Adjusted Cost Base Of Preferred Shares		Nil

PUC Of Preferred Shares	Nil
Plus Non-Share Consideration	$150,000
Proceeds Of Redemption - ITA 84(5)(d)	$150,000
PUC Of Shares Given Up	(75,000)
ITA 84(3) Deemed Dividend	$ 75,000

Proceeds Of Disposition Under ITA 86(2)(c) - Lesser Of:	
• Fair Market Value Of Shares Given Up = $500,000	
• Non-Share Consideration Plus Gift	
($150,000 + $100,000) = $250,000	$250,000
Less ITA 84(3) Deemed Dividend	(75,000)
Adjusted Proceeds Of Disposition - ITA 54	$175,000
Adjusted Cost Base Of Shares Given Up	(50,000)
Capital Gain	$125,000

17-38.   The final capital gain figure of $125,000 is $100,000 in excess of the gain recorded in the original version of this example in Paragraph 17-26. In effect, the amount of the gift has been added to the capital gain that must be included in the income of Mr. Jones.

17-39.   While there is less deferral of income, the total amount of the gain that will be taxed in Mr. Jones' hands is unchanged. Mr. Jones has preferred shares with a fair market value of $250,000 and a cost of nil, reflecting the initial $450,000 gain that was present, less the $200,000 ($75,000 + $125,000) in income recognized as a result of the reorganization.

17-40.   ITA 86(2) does, however, involve a penalty to Mr. Jones and his daughter, Veronica as a group. The new common shares issued to Veronica will have a fair market value equal to $101,000, the $1,000 she paid plus the $100,000 gift. The $100,000 additional value will not be reflected in the adjusted cost base of her shares and, as a consequence, this amount will be taxed when she disposes of the shares.

17-41.   In effect, the granting of the benefit has increased the amount that will be subject to taxation in the hands of Veronica by the $100,000 amount of the gift, without reducing Mr. Jones' total current and deferred income on the shares. This makes it clear that ITA 86 reorganizations should be structured in a manner that avoids such benefits being granted.

Exercise Seventeen - 5

Subject: Gift To A Related Party - ITA 86(2)

Janrev Inc. is a Canadian controlled private corporation. Its shares have a fair market value of $1,600,000 and a paid up capital (PUC) of $250,000. Ms. Jan Reviser owns 80 percent of the shares. Her shares have an adjusted cost base of $200,000. The remaining 20 percent of the shares are held by her 19 year old daughter and they have an adjusted cost base of $50,000. On May 1, 2013, Ms. Reviser exchanges all of her Janrev Inc. shares for cash of $300,000 and preferred shares that are redeemable for $800,000. At this time, Janrev has no balance in its GRIP account. Indicate the amount, and type, of any income that will result from this transaction.

End of Exercise. Solution available in Study Guide.

Using ITA 86(1) - Tax Planning Considerations
General Usage
17-42.   The major advantages of using ITA 86(1) can be described as follows:

- An ITA 86(1) share reorganization may be simpler to implement than a Section 85 rollover as it does not involve setting up a new corporation.
- The corporate law steps are easier, only requiring shares to be exchanged, and possibly new share classes to be formed.
- The use of ITA 86(1) does not require an election to be filed with the CRA.

17-43.   The disadvantages associated with using ITA 86(1) are as follows:

- When only a single corporation is used, it is difficult to segregate investment income from active business income.
- A single corporation exposes all of the assets to any operating risk, and limited liability protection is reduced.
- In an ITA 86(1) reorganization, all of the taxpayer's shares of a particular class have to be exchanged. This can be a problem if the original shareholder wishes to retain some of the common or growth shares.

17-44.   It usually possible to get around this last disadvantage. This can be accomplished by re-issuing common shares to the original shareholder after the reorganization is completed.

Use In Key Employee Successions
17-45.   In addition to its use in estate freezes, an exchange of shares can be very effective when arranging for gradual succession to a key employee. For example, consider a situation where an employee has little personal equity, but has a good work record with the company and excellent owner-manager potential.

17-46.   An ITA 86(1) reorganization could be used to convert common shares owned by the existing shareholder into preferred shares. The employee could then purchase the common shares over some agreed upon succession period. The annual investments in common shares would likely be modest, as most of the company's value would be reflected in the preferred shares, making the investments feasible for the incoming shareholder. The original owner could continue to be involved in the business throughout the succession years.

17-47.   Eventually, when the original owner is ready to sell the preferred shares, the incoming shareholder will have the benefit of several years of management experience, and should be able to obtain funding to acquire the preferred shares from the original owner.

We suggest you work Self Study Problems Seventeen-4 and 5 at this point.

Amalgamations - ITA 87

The Nature Of An Amalgamation

17-48.   ITA 87 provides for a tax deferred rollover in situations where there is an amalgamation of corporations. This may involve two independent corporations wishing to merge and continue their business affairs on a combined basis. Alternatively, associated or related corporations may amalgamate to pursue common corporate goals.

17-49.   If the two corporations want to transfer their assets to a new corporation on a tax free basis, the rollover provisions of ITA 87 would apply. The following simple example will illustrate this kind of situation (illustrated in Figure 17-3):

Example   The shareholders of Alpha Inc. have shares with an adjusted cost base of $1,000,000 and a fair market value of $5,000,000, while the shareholders of Beta Inc. have shares with an adjusted cost base of $1,700,000 and a fair market value of $5,000,000. All of the assets and liabilities (except intercompany balances) of Alpha Inc. and Beta Inc. are transferred to a new Company, Alpha-Beta Ltd. The shareholders of Alpha Inc. and Beta Inc. exchange their shares for shares in Alpha-Beta Ltd.

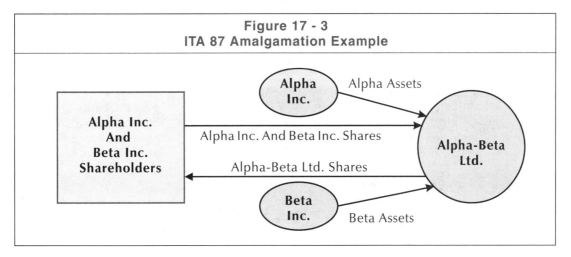

Figure 17 - 3
ITA 87 Amalgamation Example

17-50.   If the assets of Alpha and Beta had simply been sold to a new company, the sales would be viewed as dispositions for proceeds equal to the fair market value of the assets. This would normally result in the realization of significant capital gains and recapture. However, under corporate amalgamation legislation, the combined company is not viewed as a new company. Rather it is viewed as a continuation of the amalgamating companies. ITA 87 does not support this view in that it considers the amalgamated company to be a new company.

17-51.   To facilitate amalgamations of corporations, ITA 87 contains rollover provisions for both the transfer of assets to the amalgamated corporation and for the exchange of shares. ITA 87(1) specifies the conditions necessary for this rollover to apply:

• All of the predecessor corporations must be taxable Canadian corporations.

• All shareholders of the predecessor corporations must receive shares of the amalgamated corporation due to the amalgamation.

- All of the assets and liabilities of the predecessor corporations, other than intercompany balances, must be transferred to the amalgamated corporation in the amalgamation.

- The transfer cannot simply be a normal purchase of property, or involve the distribution of assets on the winding-up of a corporation. It must be supported by corporate legislation which identifies the transaction as an amalgamation.

Position Of The Amalgamated Company

17-52.   The tax values for the amalgamated corporation's assets will simply be the sum of the tax values of the assets that were present in the records of the predecessor corporations. In addition, all types of loss carry forwards (capital, non-capital, and farm) of the predecessor corporations flow through and become available to the amalgamated corporation.

17-53   The predecessor corporations will be deemed to have a taxation year that ends immediately before the amalgamation and, in most situations, this will result in an extra taxation year that will count towards the expiration of losses with a limited carry forward period. The amalgamated corporation is deemed to have been formed on the date of the amalgamation and may choose any year end it wishes.

17-54.   With respect to assets, reserves, loss carry forwards, and other tax accounts of the old companies, ITA 87 provides rollover provisions as follows:

Rollover Provisions In ITA 87 Amalgamations

Item	Rollover Effect
Inventories	At Cost
Depreciable Capital Property	At UCC
Non-Depreciable Capital Property	At ACB
Eligible Capital Property	4/3 Of CEC
Reserves	Flowed Through
Non-Capital Losses	Flowed Through
Net Capital Losses	Flowed Through
Restricted Farm Losses	Flowed Through
General Rate Income Pool (GRIP) (See Note 1)	Flowed Through
Low Rate Income Pool (LRIP) (See Note 2)	Flowed Through
Capital Dividend Account (See Note 3)	Flowed Through
Refundable Dividend Tax On Hand (See Note 3)	Flowed Through

Note 1   If a CCPC is formed as the result of an amalgamation, ITA 89(5) may be applicable. In situations where a predecessor corporation was a CCPC, this subsection provides for the flow through of its GRIP account to the amalgamated company. Where the predecessor was a non-CCPC, a notional GRIP is calculated and flows through.

Note 2   If a non-CCPC is formed as the result of an amalgamation, ITA 89(9) may be applicable. In situations where a predecessor corporation was a non-CCPC, this subsection provides for the flow through of its LRIP account to the amalgamated company. Where the predecessor was a CCPC, a notional LRIP is calculated and flowed through.

Note 3   The capital dividend account and the Refundable Dividend Tax On Hand account are only available to private companies. If either of the predecessor companies is a public company, these accounts would be lost.

17-55.   As can be seen in the preceding table, ITA 87 basically provides for a summing of the relevant tax values of the assets of the two companies that are amalgamating. The amalgamated corporation will be liable for future recapture and capital gains on the same basis as the predecessor corporations.

17-56.   With respect to loss carry forwards, the limitations that were discussed in Chapter 13 are applicable if there is an acquisition of control. As noted, the deemed year end of the predecessor corporations will count as one year in any carry forward period. However, losses carried forward may qualify for deduction in the first taxation year of the amalgamated company.

Position Of The Shareholders

17-57.   The shareholders of the predecessor corporations are deemed to dispose of their shares for proceeds equal to the adjusted cost base of the shares, and they are deemed to acquire the shares of the amalgamated company at the same value. For these general provisions to apply, ITA 87(4) specifies the following conditions:

- The shareholders must not receive any consideration other than shares in the amalgamated company.

- The original shares must be capital property of the shareholders.

- The amalgamation must not result in a deemed gift to a person related to the shareholders.

Vertical Amalgamations (Parent And Subsidiary)

17-58.   In situations where there is a desire to combine a parent and its subsidiary, a choice of rollovers may be available. The alternative to ITA 87, "Amalgamations", is the use of ITA 88(1), "Winding-Up". However, ITA 88(1) is only applicable to situations where the parent company owns 90 percent or more of the shares of each class of capital stock of a subsidiary. In contrast, ITA 87 can be used without regard to the percentage of ownership.

17-59.   You may recall from an advanced financial accounting course that the cost of acquiring a subsidiary will usually exceed both the carrying values and the sum of the fair values of the acquired identifiable assets.

> **Example**   Placor Inc. acquires 100 percent of the outstanding voting shares of Lacee Ltd. at a cost of $1,000,000. At this time the net identifiable assets of Lacee had carrying values of $700,000 and tax values of $650,000. The fair value of these assets totaled $900,000.

17-60.   The excess of the $1,000,000 investment cost over the tax values total of $650,000 creates a problem, without regard to whether ITA 87 or ITA 88(1) is used to amalgamate the subsidiary with the parent. Both of these rollover provisions transfer the subsidiary's assets and liabilities at tax values. This means that, in the absence of a special legislative provision, the $350,000 excess of the investment cost over tax values will be lost.

17-61.   Fortunately, there are provisions that provide a limited amount of relief from this adverse tax consequence. Both ITA 87(11) and ITA 88(1) provide for a "bump-up" in asset values to reflect the parent company's excess of investment cost over tax values. This bump-up provision is only available on certain assets.

17-62.   Further, it is only available under ITA 87(11) if the parent owns 100 percent of the subsidiary's issued shares, or under ITA 88(1) in situations where the parent owns 90 percent or more of the issued shares. No bump-up is available when the parent owns less than 90 percent of the subsidiary's issued shares.

17-63.   The ITA 87 legislation provides for the bump-up by referring to the ITA 88(1) provision. Given this, we will defer our coverage of this until we have completed our discussion of ITA 88(1).

Non-Tax Considerations

17-64.   While a statutory amalgamation does not involve a new company, there are likely to be significant legal complications. Each of the predecessor companies will have contracts with employees, suppliers, and customers. While they are still legally in force, modifications may be required to make the terms more compatible throughout the organization. There may also be problems with creditors. In fact, it is not uncommon for debt covenants to have a provision requiring the approval of debt holders before an amalgamation can take place. These factors may add considerable complexity to the amalgamation process.

Amalgamations - Tax Planning Considerations

17-65.　A Section 87 amalgamation offers a number of opportunities for tax planning. Some of the possibilities include:

- The utilization of loss carry forward amounts that the predecessor corporation(s) might not be able to absorb. Note, however, that if there is an acquisition of control, the usual restrictions on the use of loss carry forwards apply.

- With respect to acquisitions of control in the amalgamation process, we would note that, if the two predecessor corporations are related, an amalgamation will not result in an acquisition of control. However, if they are not related and the shareholders of one of the predecessor corporations have the majority of shares in the amalgamated company, that company will be considered to have acquired the other predecessor company.

- Current year losses of one predecessor corporation can effectively be utilized against Taxable Income of the other.

- Bringing together a profitable and an unprofitable corporation may allow for a faster write-off of capital assets (through CCA) than would otherwise be possible by the unprofitable predecessor corporation.

- The amalgamation may provide for an increase in the amount of the manufacturing and processing profits tax deduction.

17-66.　The timing of an amalgamation can be an important tax planning issue. As the amalgamation transaction results in a deemed year end, the company may have a short fiscal year for purposes of calculating CCA. In addition, outstanding reserves may have to be brought into income sooner, and the short fiscal period will count as a full year in the eligible loss carry forward years.

17-67.　For income tax instalments there is a look through provision. While the amalgamated company does not have a previous tax year on which to base instalment payments of income tax, prepayments continue to be required based on the instalment history of the predecessor corporations.

Exercise Seventeen - 6

Subject:　ITA 87 Amalgamations

During its taxation year ending December 31, 2012, Downer Ltd. incurs a non-capital loss of $93,000 and a net capital loss of $150,000. Neither loss can be carried back. On January 1, 2013, using the provisions of ITA 87, the Company is amalgamated with Upton Inc., an unrelated company that also has a December 31 year end. The combined company is named Amalgo Inc. and it elects to use a December 31 year end. The terms of the amalgamation give 20,000 Amalgo Inc. shares to the Downer Ltd. shareholders and 150,000 Amalgo Inc. shares to the Upton Inc. shareholders. During the year ending December 31, 2013, Amalgo Inc. has Net Income For Tax Purposes of $1,200,000, including over $300,000 in taxable capital gains. During its 2013 taxation year, will Amalgo Inc. be able to deduct the losses incurred by Downer Ltd. prior to the amalgamation? Explain your conclusion.

End of Exercise.　Solution available in Study Guide.

Winding-Up Of A 90 Percent Owned Subsidiary

The Nature Of A Winding-Up

Winding-Up Of Corporations In General

17-68.   IT-126R2 states that a corporation is considered to have been "wound up" where:

(a) it has followed the procedures for winding-up and dissolution provided by the appropriate federal or provincial companies *Act* or winding-up *Act*, or

(b) it has carried out a winding-up, other than by means of the statutory procedures contemplated in (a) above, and has been dissolved under the provisions of its incorporating statute.

17-69.   In general, a winding-up operation requires that all outstanding creditor claims be satisfied and that all corporate property be distributed to the shareholders before the winding-up is undertaken. IT-126R2 also notes that, where there is substantial evidence that dissolution procedures will be completed within a short period of time, Section 88(1) can be used prior to the completion of the wind-up.

17-70.   A winding-up may be undertaken for several reasons. As with amalgamations, a winding-up allows for the losses of a subsidiary to be carried over to the parent corporation. Winding-ups are also undertaken to simplify an organizational structure, or when a subsidiary is ceasing its business operations.

90 Percent Owned Subsidiary

17-71.   The two major Subsections of ITA 88 can be described as follows:

ITA 88(1)   This Subsection is a rollover provision, providing for the tax free combination of the assets of a 90 percent or more owned subsidiary with those of its parent.

ITA 88(2)   This Subsection deals with the general winding-up of corporations, other than those to which ITA 88(1) is applicable. It is not a rollover provision.

17-72.   At this point we are concerned only with the provisions contained in ITA 88(1). The content of ITA 88(2) will be considered beginning in Paragraph 17-95.

17-73   To use the ITA 88(1) rollover, the parent corporation must own at least 90 percent of each class of the subsidiary's shares. Therefore, not all winding-ups of subsidiaries qualify for the treatment described in ITA 88(1). A winding-up involving a subsidiary where a parent corporation has control, but owns less than 90 percent of the issued shares, would be implemented under the provisions of ITA 88(2). This provision would not allow for a tax free transfer of assets.

17-74.   If the parent has the required 90 percent or more ownership, it is permitted to exchange the subsidiary's shares for the assets of the subsidiary on a tax deferred basis. This transaction is very similar to an amalgamation, as it allows the assets of the two companies to be combined without recognizing any accrued capital gains or recaptured CCA on the transfers required to effect the combination.

17-75.   As with other rollovers, there are two components to a winding-up transaction. The first is the acquisition of the subsidiary's assets by the parent, and the second is the deemed disposition of the subsidiary's shares by the parent. We will now turn our attention to these components.

Acquisition Of Assets

General Rules

17-76.   In an ITA 88(1) winding-up, the subsidiary is deemed to have disposed of its assets and the parent is deemed to have acquired the assets on the following basis:

- A cost of nil in the case of Canadian or foreign resource property.

- The "cost amount" to the subsidiary in the case of other property. Cost amount is defined in ITA 248(1) as UCC for depreciable property and adjusted cost base for non-depreciable capital property. For eligible capital property, the cost amount is 4/3 of the subsidiary's cumulative eligible capital.

GRIP Balances

17-77.   ITA 89(6) applies to situations in which a CCPC has wound up a subsidiary under ITA 88(1). If the subsidiary was also a CCPC, this provision provides for a flow through of the subsidiary's GRIP balance to the GRIP balance of the parent company.

17-78.   A second, much more complex provision in ITA 89(6), applies when the subsidiary is a non-CCPC. This provision attempts to measure what the subsidiary's GRIP would have been at the end of its last taxation year had it been a CCPC at that time. This amount will also be included in the parent company's GRIP.

LRIP Balances

17-79.   ITA 89(10) applies when a non-CCPC has wound up a subsidiary under ITA 88(1). If the subsidiary was also a non-CCPC, this provision provides for a flow through of the subsidiary's LRIP balance to the LRIP balance of the parent company.

17-80.   Once again, a second and much more complex provision applies when the subsidiary is a CCPC. This provision attempts to measure what the subsidiary's LRIP would have been at the end of its last taxation year had it been a non-CCPC at that time. This amount will also be transferred to the parent company's LRIP.

Deferral Of Loss Carry Forwards

17-81.   As indicated previously, an ITA 88(1) winding up is very similar to an amalgamation. There is, however, one important difference between an amalgamation under ITA 87 and the winding-up of a subsidiary under ITA 88(1) and this involves loss carry forwards.

17-82.   As is generally the case under ITA 87, non-capital losses and net capital losses of the subsidiary will be available to the parent company when ITA 88(1) is used. However, under ITA 88(1), they will not become available until the first taxation year of the parent that begins after the date that the winding-up period commences.

> **Example** If a parent's fiscal year begins on February 1 and the winding-up commences on February 15, 2013, the losses of the subsidiary will not be available to the parent until its fiscal year beginning February 1, 2014.

17-83.   In those situations where the subsidiary has a different year end than the parent, subsidiary losses are deemed to have occurred in the parent's fiscal year that includes the subsidiary's year end.

> **Example** A parent has a June 30 year end, while its subsidiary has a September 30 year end. A winding-up commences on August 15, 2013 and is completed by August 31, 2013. The subsidiary has a non-capital loss for the period that is terminated on August 31, 2013 by the winding-up.

> **Analysis** The loss will be deemed to have occurred in the parent's year ending June 30, 2014. This would suggest that the loss would not expire until the parent's year ending June 30, 2034. However, ITA 88(1.1)(b) limits the carry forward period to the period that would have been available to the subsidiary if it had not been wound up. This means that, in actual fact, the loss expires on June 30, 2033. The losses of the subsidiary are not available to the parent until its fiscal year beginning on July 1, 2014.

Exercise Seventeen - 7

Subject: Losses In A Winding-Up

Park Inc. has a September 15 year end, while its 100 percent owned subsidiary, Side Ltd., has an October 31 year end.   There is a winding-up of Side Ltd., using the roll-over provision found in ITA 88(1), on June 30, 2013. Side Ltd. has a non-capital loss of $50,000 for the period November 1, 2012 to June 30, 2013. What is the earliest taxation year in which the $50,000 loss can be deducted? If it is not deducted then, in what taxation year will it expire?

End of Exercise. Solution available in Study Guide.

Asset Bump-Up
17-84.   As we pointed out in our discussion of vertical amalgamations, ITA 88(1) provides for a transfer of all or part of the excess of the purchase price of a 90 percent or more owned subsidiary's shares over the tax values of the subsidiary's assets. As noted, this bump-up is also available under ITA 87 when the parent owns 100 percent of the subsidiary. Under either of these provisions, the amount of this bump-up in tax values is limited by two amounts:

1.   The basic amount of the bump-up is found in ITA 88(1)(d)(i) and (i.1). This amount is the excess of the adjusted cost base of the subsidiary shares held by the parent, over the sum of:

    • the tax values of the subsidiary's net assets at the time of the winding-up; and
    • dividends paid by the subsidiary to the parent since the time of the acquisition (including capital dividends).

2.   ITA 88(1)(d)(ii) further limits the amount that can be recognized to the excess of the fair market value of the subsidiary's non-depreciable capital property over their tax values at the time the parent acquired control of the subsidiary.

17-85.   The following example will illustrate these procedures:

Example   On December 31, 2003, ParentCo acquires 100 percent of the outstanding shares of SubCo for $5,000,000. At that time, the only non-depreciable capital property owned by SubCo was land with a fair market value of $2,000,000 and a cost of $1,000,000. Between December 31, 2003 and December 31, 2013, SubCo pays dividends of $150,000 to ParentCo. On December 31, 2013, when the tax values of SubCo's assets total $4,200,000, SubCo is absorbed in a Section 88(1) winding-up.

Analysis The amount of the available asset bump-up will be the lesser of the two amounts described in Paragraph 17-84:

Adjusted Cost Base Of SubCo Shares		$5,000,000
Tax Values Of SubCo Assets At Winding-Up	($4,200,000)	
Dividends Paid By SubCo Since Its Acquisition	(150,000)	(4,350,000)
Excess		$ 650,000

Fair Market Value Of Land At Acquisition	$2,000,000
Cost Of Land At Acquisition	(1,000,000)
Excess	$1,000,000

17-86.   In this situation, the write-up of the land is restricted to the lower figure of $650,000. As a result, the subsidiary is deemed to have disposed of the land for $1,000,000 with no gain or loss. However, the parent is deemed to have acquired the same land for $1,650,000.

Exercise Seventeen - 8

Subject: Winding-Up Of A 90 Percent Or More Owned Subsidiary

On January 1, 2009, Procul Ltd. acquired 100 percent of the outstanding shares of Lorne Inc. at a cost of $1,200,000. At this point in time, the fair market value of Lorne's identifiable net assets was $850,000, including $270,000 for the Land. The tax values of the net assets at that time totalled $410,000.

On December 31, 2013, there is a winding-up of Lorne Inc. under the provisions of ITA 88(1). Lorne Inc. has paid no dividends since its acquisition by Procul Ltd. On December 31, 2013, the condensed Balance Sheet of Lorne Inc. is as follows:

Cash	$120,000
Land - At Cost (Purchased In 2005)	140,000
Depreciable Assets - At UCC (Purchased In 2005)	240,000
Total Assets	**$500,000**
Liabilities	$ 75,000
Shareholders' Equity	425,000
Total Equities	**$500,000**

Determine the tax values that will be recorded for Lorne Inc.'s assets after they have been incorporated into the records of Procul Ltd.

End of Exercise. Solution available in Study Guide.

Disposition Of Shares

17-87.   The disposition of shares component of the winding-up is straightforward. In general, the parent is deemed to have disposed of its shares of the subsidiary for proceeds equal to the adjusted cost base of the shares. As an example, assume the parent had paid $4,000,000 for the subsidiary's shares. This amount would also be the deemed proceeds of the disposition and there would be no capital gain.

17-88.   An exception to this general rule will arise if the tax values of the subsidiary's assets transferred and the paid up capital of the subsidiary's shares is more than the amount paid for the shares by the parent. In this case, the deemed proceeds of disposition will be the lesser of the paid up capital and the tax values of the assets transferred. As a result, a capital gain can arise in these situations.

Example   Prawn Ltd. owns 100 percent of the outstanding shares of Shrimp Inc. The cost of these shares was $4,000,000. This subsidiary is being wound up under the provisions of ITA 88(1). At the time of the winding-up, the tax values of the subsidiary's assets total $4,800,000 and the PUC of the subsidiary's shares is $4,500,000.

Analysis   Given these facts, the exception applies and the deemed proceeds of disposition would be the greater of the $4,000,000 cost of the shares and $4,500,000. This latter figure is the lesser of the $4,800,000 tax value of the subsidiary's assets and the $4,500,000 PUC of the subsidiary's shares. This gives proceeds of disposition of $4,500,000 and a capital gain of $500,000 ($4,500,000 - $4,000,000). It is expected that such gains situations would be fairly rare and, because the proceeds are defined using cost except when it is less than the alternative values, there is no possibility of a capital loss.

Figure 17 - 4
Comparison Of Amalgamation Under ITA 87 And Winding-Up Under ITA 88(1)

Factor	Amalgamation - ITA 87	Winding-Up Of 90% Owned Subsidiary - ITA 88(1)
Valuation of assets	Tax values of assets of predecessor corporations carried forward to amalgamated company.	Tax values of subsidiary's assets carried forward to parent.
Recognition of the excess of investment cost over tax values	Recognition only if 100 percent owned subsidiary. If 100 percent owned, same treatment as ITA 88(1).	Write-up allowed if excess is associated with values of non-depreciable capital property.
Capital cost allowances	Claim in last year of predecessor and first year of amalgamated corporation.	No claim by subsidiary in year of winding-up, but available to parent in year of winding-up.
Loss carry forwards	Carried forward. However, their use may be limited if the amalgamation results in an acquisition of control.	Carried forward, but only available to parent beginning in taxation year after winding-up.
Year end	Deemed year end before amalgamation, counts one year for loss carry forwards.	Year end of parent corporation continued. Subsidiary has a terminal year end that counts as one taxation year.

Tax Planning Considerations - Amalgamation Vs. Winding-Up

17-89.   Figure 17-4 contains a comparison of the features of an amalgamation under ITA 87 and the winding-up of a subsidiary that is at least 90 percent owned under ITA 88(1). A discussion of several of the items follows.

17-90.   A significant consideration in deciding between an amalgamation under ITA 87 and a winding-up under ITA 88(1) is the ability to recognize all or part of the excess of investment cost over tax values. In the case of an ITA 87 amalgamation, recognition is possible only in cases involving a parent and a 100 percent owned subsidiary. Under ITA 88(1), recognition can occur as long as the parent owns 90 percent or more of each class of the subsidiary's issued shares.

17-91.   Under either provision, it is possible that substantial tax values will disappear in the transaction. This would suggest that, when the adjusted cost base of the parent's investment is significantly greater than the tax values of the subsidiary's assets, it may be better to continue to operate the subsidiary as a separate legal entity.

17-92   Under the amalgamation procedures, the predecessor corporations will have a deemed year end, which will count towards the expiry of time limited non-capital loss carry forwards. However, subject to the acquisition of control rules, the amalgamated company will be able to use the losses immediately.

17-93.   In contrast, the parent company that is using ITA 88(1) to absorb a 90 percent owned subsidiary will have its usual year end. However, it will not be able to use subsidiary loss carry forwards until the first taxation year beginning subsequent to the winding-up. In addition, the wind-up will count as an additional year in the expiry of time limited loss carry forwards. The analysis of this situation may be complicated by differing year ends for the two corporations.

17-94.   In considering CCA claims, ITA 87 creates a deemed year end for both predecessor corporations, requiring them to take pro rata CCA claims for what will normally be a short fiscal period. Under the ITA 88(1) procedures, the subsidiary disposes of its assets prior to its year end and, as a consequence, there will be no claim for CCA in the subsidiary's final year. However, CCA may be claimed on these assets by the parent company, subsequent to their being acquired under the winding-up procedures.

17-95.   If the subsidiary is not 100 percent owned, ITA 88(1) cannot be used unless the minority shareholder group is at arm's length with the parent company. If the minority shareholders are at arm's length and ITA 88(1) can be used to transfer the assets belonging to the controlling interest, an application of this Subsection will generally have tax consequences for the non-controlling interest. A winding-up will require reporting of capital gains and recaptured CCA on property distributed by the subsidiary to the minority shareholders. Further, any liquidating dividend paid to the minority shareholders will be a taxable dividend.

We suggest you work Self Study Problem Seventeen-6 at this point.

Winding-Up Of A Canadian Corporation

The Nature Of The Transaction

Wind-Up (Liquidation) Vs. Rollover

17-96.   The winding-up procedures for a Canadian corporation, as described in ITA 88(2), are applicable where a corporation is being liquidated. If, for example, owners of a corporation decide that the business is no longer viable, winding-up procedures can be used in the disposition of the corporation's assets and the distribution of the resulting proceeds to the shareholders.

17-97.   In distinguishing the winding-up of a 90 percent or more owned subsidiary from a liquidating winding-up, you should note that the liquidation of a business has quite different objectives. In the case of the winding-up of a 90 percent or more owned subsidiary, we are usually not disposing of the business but, rather, are transferring its assets to a different legal entity that is controlled by the same investor or group of investors that previously had indirect control of its operations. This explains why a rollover is available on the winding-up of a 90 percent or more owned subsidiary, and no equivalent provision is available for the winding-up when a liquidation is under way.

Distributions To Shareholders

17-98.   While a winding-up can be implemented by distributing corporate assets directly to the shareholders, it is generally simpler for the corporation to liquidate its assets, pay off its creditors, pay any taxes that are applicable at the corporate level, and distribute the after tax proceeds to the shareholders.

17-99.   The distribution to shareholders becomes a fairly complex issue when a corporation is liquidated, as the proceeds available for distribution will consist of a combination of capital being returned, earnings that can be distributed on a tax free basis, and earnings that can only be distributed in the form of taxable dividends. A further complication is that there may be a combination of eligible and non-eligible dividends.

Disposition Of An Incorporated Business

17-100.   Later in this Chapter we will discuss the transfer of an incorporated business to a different group of owners. This can be accomplished through a sale of shares or, alternatively, through a sale of the corporation's assets. If the sale of assets is the more advantageous approach, the provisions of ITA 88(2) apply. That is, the sale of assets will be followed by a winding-up, with the after tax proceeds of the winding-up being distributed to the shareholders. While the business itself will continue to operate, the assets will now be on the books of a different legal entity.

Example
Basic Data
17-101.   The ITA 88(2) procedures will be illustrated in the following example.

Example   The Marker Company, a Canadian controlled private corporation, has been in operation for 20 years. It has a May 31 year end. On June 1, 2013, the following Balance Sheet, based on tax values, has been prepared in contemplation of liquidating the Company:

The Marker Company
Balance Sheet - As At June 1, 2013 (Tax Values)

Accounts Receivable (Net Realizable Value)	$ 12,000
Refundable Dividend Tax On Hand	8,000
Land - At Cost (Note One)	250,000
Building - At UCC (Note Two)	195,000
Total Assets	$465,000
Liabilities	Nil
Common Stock - No Par (Note Three)	$ 10,000
Retained Earnings (Note Three)	455,000
Total Equities	$465,000

Note One   The current fair market value of the Land is $300,000.

Note Two   The cost of the Building was $320,000. Its current fair market value is $350,000.

Note Three   The paid up capital and adjusted cost base of the common shares is $10,000. The Retained Earnings includes $75,000 in the capital dividend account. The Company's GRIP balance is nil.

The assets of the Company are sold for their fair market values which total $662,000 ($12,000 + $300,000 + $350,000). The Company has no other income for the taxation year. The provincial corporate tax rates are 4 percent on income eligible for the small business deduction and 14 percent on other corporate income.

Cash Available For Distribution
17-102.   At the corporate level, the proceeds from the disposition of the individual assets and the related tax effects are as follows:

Asset	Proceeds	Taxable Capital Gain	Active Business Income
Accounts Receivable	$ 12,000	Nil	Nil
Land	300,000	$25,000	Nil
Building	350,000	15,000	$125,000
Totals	$662,000	$40,000	$125,000

The Tax Payable on Marker's Taxable Income of $165,000 ($40,000 + $125,000) would be calculated as follows:

Federal Tax On Active Business Income [(38% - 10% - 17%)($125,000)]	$13,750
Federal Tax On Investment Income [(38% - 10% + 6-2/3%)($40,000)]	13,867
Part I Tax Payable	$27,617
Provincial Tax On Active Business Income [(4%)($125,000)]	5,000
Provincial Tax On Investment Income [(14%)($40,000)]	5,600
Total Tax Payable	$38,217

Winding-Up Of A Canadian Corporation

17-103.   The balance in the Refundable Dividend Tax On Hand account, subsequent to the preceding dispositions, is calculated as follows:

Balance Before Dispositions (From Balance Sheet)	$ 8,000
Addition (See Note)	10,667
Balance Available	$18,667

Note   The addition to the RDTOH would be $10,667, the least of the following figures:

- 26-2/3% Of Investment Income [(26-2/3%)($40,000)] $10,667
- 26-2/3% Of Taxable Income, Less Amount Eligible For Small Business Deduction [(26-2/3%)($165,000 - $125,000)] $10,667
- Federal Part I Tax Payable $27,617

17-104.   The after tax amount of cash that is available for distribution to shareholders is calculated as follows:

Gross Proceeds	$662,000
Tax Payable	(38,217)
Refundable Dividend Tax On Hand*	18,667
Available For Distribution	$642,450

*Given the size of the gross proceeds, the balance in the RDTOH is clearly going to be less than one-third of the dividends that will be declared.

Distribution To Shareholders

17-105.   The balance in the capital dividend account can be distributed to the shareholders as a tax free capital dividend. This balance is calculated as follows:

Balance Before Dispositions (Balance Sheet Note Three)	$ 75,000
Disposition Of Land	25,000
Disposition Of Building	15,000
Capital Dividend Account - Ending Balance	$115,000

17-106.   Prior to the sale of assets, the Company's GRIP balance was nil. As all of the income resulting from the sale of assets was either investment income or eligible for the small business deduction, there would be no addition to the GRIP account resulting from the sale of assets. This means that all dividends paid that are subject to tax would be non-eligible. The non-eligible taxable dividend component of the total distribution to the shareholders is calculated as follows:

Total Distribution	$642,450
Paid Up Capital	(10,000)
ITA 84(2) Deemed Dividend On Winding-Up*	$632,450
Capital Dividend Account	(115,000)
Non-Eligible Dividend Subject To Tax	$517,450

*As explained in Chapter 14, in a winding up, when the total distribution to shareholders exceeds the PUC of the shares being canceled, the excess is an ITA 84(2) deemed dividend. This deemed dividend is treated first as a capital dividend, if the appropriate election is filed. Any excess is treated as an eligible or non-eligible taxable dividend.

17-107.   Treatment of the $115,000 as a capital dividend is conditional on the appropriate election being made under ITA 83(2). The remaining taxable non-eligible dividend will be grossed up to $646,813 [(125%)($517,450)]. The shares will have a federal dividend tax credit of $86,242 [(2/3)(25%)($517,450)].

17-108.   In the ITA 54 definition of "proceeds of disposition", Paragraph j indicates that amounts that are deemed to be a dividend under ITA 84(2) are not included in this amount. As a consequence, in determining the capital gain resulting from the distribution to the shareholders, the ITA 84(2) dividend will be subtracted as follows:

Total Distribution to Shareholders	$642,450
ITA 84(2) Deemed Dividend	(632,450)
Deemed Proceeds Of Disposition	$ 10,000
Adjusted Cost Base Of Shares	(10,000)
Capital Gain	Nil

Exercise Seventeen - 9

Subject: Winding-Up Of A Canadian Corporation

Windown Inc. is a Canadian controlled private company. After disposing of all of its assets and paying all of its liabilities, including Tax Payable resulting from the asset dispositions, the Company is left with cash of $865,000. The PUC of the Company's shares is equal to their adjusted cost base, an amount of $88,000. After the sale of assets, the Company has an RDTOH account balance of $47,000, a capital dividend account balance of $26,000, and a GRIP of nil. Determine the tax consequences to the shareholders associated with making the maximum distribution of cash to shareholders on the winding-up of Windown Inc. on June 1, 2013. Assume that appropriate elections will be made to minimize the taxes that will be paid by the shareholders.

End of Exercise. Solution available in Study Guide.

We suggest you work Self Study Problem Seventeen-7 at this point.

Convertible Properties

Application

17-109.   There is one more rollover that you should be familiar with. ITA 51 contains a provision that permits a holder of shares or debt of a corporation to exchange those securities for shares of that corporation on a tax free basis. For this rollover provision to apply, the following two conditions must be met:

- The exchange must not involve any consideration other than the securities that are being exchanged.

- The exchange must not be part of a reorganization of capital or a rollover of property by shareholders to a corporation under ITA 85 or ITA 86.

17-110.   In practical terms, this provision is designed to accommodate a tax deferred conversion of debt or preferred shares of a corporation into preferred or common shares of the same corporation.

Example   An investor acquires convertible bonds with a par value of $10,000 at a price equal to par value. The bonds are convertible into 50 shares of the issuing company's common stock and, at the time of purchase, this common stock is trading at $18 per share (the conversion value of the bonds is $9,000). The bonds are converted when the common shares are trading at $22 per share.

Analysis   The conversion of the bonds is a disposition and, in the absence of a special provision, the tax consequences would be as follows:

Proceeds Of Disposition [(50)($22)]	$11,000
Adjusted Cost Base	(10,000)
Capital Gain	$1,000

17-111.   The ITA serves to provide relief in this type of situation. ITA 51(1)(c), deems such exchanges not to be a disposition. Given that there is no disposition, no gain will be recognized.

17-112. Going with this provision, ITA 51(1)(d) deems the cost of the acquired shares to be equal to the cost of the shares or debt given up. In effect, ITA 51 allows convertible securities to be converted with no immediate tax consequences. No gain or loss is recorded and the adjusted cost base of investors' securities remains unchanged.

Other Considerations

17-113.   A conversion provision can assist corporations seeking to add an equity kicker to enhance the marketability of their debt or preferred shares. In addition, conversion arrangements can be used to facilitate income splitting within a corporation. Different classes of shares can be used to allow the redistribution of income and, with the ability to convert different classes of shares on a tax deferred basis, an additional element of flexibility is introduced into such arrangements.

17-114.   ITA 51.1 contains a similar provision to cover situations under which bondholders of a particular company are allowed to convert their holdings into a different debt security of that company. Here again, there is a tax deferred rollover with the adjusted cost base of the old bond holding becoming the creditor's adjusted cost base for the new debt security.

17-115.   We would call your attention to the fact that the accounting rules on debt that is convertible into common or preferred shares require that the proceeds from its issuance be divided between the amount paid by investors for the liability component of the financial instrument and the amount paid for the equity option (see IAS 32, *Financial Instruments: Presentation*). This important issue has not, at this point in time, been given recognition in tax legislation. For tax purposes, the full amount received for convertible debt must be allocated to the debt component of the security.

Sale Of An Incorporated Business

Alternatives

17-116.   Assume that you are the sole owner of an incorporated business and that you have decided to dispose of your company. If the business has a value that extends beyond your personal services, it should be possible to arrange a sale of the business. In approaching the problem of selling an incorporated business, you are usually confronted with the following three alternatives:

- Sale of the individual assets of the business, on a piecemeal basis.
- Sale of the total net assets of the business, including any unrecorded intangibles such as goodwill.
- Sale of the shares of the business.

17-117.   In the next section, consideration will be given to the advantages and disadvantages, as well as to the tax effects that are associated with each of these alternatives. However, before turning our attention to these alternatives, some attention must be given to the tax treatment of restrictive covenants.

Restrictive Covenants (a.k.a. Non-Competition Agreements)
General Rules

17-118.   Restrictive covenants are arrangements under which a taxpayer agrees to have his ability to provide goods or services restricted in one or more ways. Such agreements may relate to particular products or services (e.g., the taxpayer will not provide audit services) and may refer to specific geographic areas (e.g., the taxpayer will not provide audit services in the greater Calgary area). They may or may not be limited in terms of time. It is not uncommon, particularly in the case of owner-managed businesses, for the purchaser to require the seller to sign a restrictive covenant.

17-119.   Until recently, the *Income Tax Act* did not contain specific guidance on amounts paid to taxpayers for agreeing to restrictive covenants. In the past, the CRA made repeated efforts to force recipient taxpayers to include such amounts in income. However, the courts foiled such attempts with great regularity, indicating that such receipts could be received by a taxpayer without tax consequences.

17-120.   Ever the sore loser, the CRA concluded that the best way to achieve the desired result would be through new legislation. A proposed ITA 56.4(2) would require that, in general, payments made to a taxpayer for agreeing to a restrictive covenant be included in income as an "other source" under Subdivision d. Under this general treatment, 100 percent of the amount paid would have to be included in the recipient's income when received or receivable.

Exceptions

17-121.   Fortunately for taxpayers, ITA 56.4(3) creates three exceptions to this general rule:

ITA 56.4(3)(a) - Employment Income   In cases where the payment relates to past employment with the payor, the receipt will be treated by the recipient as employment income. While 100 percent of the amount would still be subject to tax, classification as employment income would mean that it does not have to be included in the recipient's income until it is received (employment income is on a cash basis). When this exception is applicable, ITA 56.4(4)(a) allows the payor to treat the payment as wages paid or payable.

ITA 56.4(3)(b) - Cumulative Eligible Capital   When intangible capital property is being sold and the payor and the recipient jointly elect in prescribed form, the payment can be treated by the recipient as a deduction from cumulative eligible capital (CEC). In this case, ITA 56.4(4)(b) requires the purchaser to treat the payment as an eligible capital expenditure.

Without going through the fairly complex details, this treatment can result in none of the payment being currently taxed (if the payment is less than the balance in the recipient's CEC account), three-quarters of the payment being taxed (if the payment is less than the CEC deductions that the recipient has made under ITA 20(1)(b)), one-half of the payment being taxed (the recipient has no CEC balance), or some combination of three-quarters and one-half of the payment being taxed.

Note, however, the requirement that the payor treat the payment as an eligible capital expenditure means that the available deduction will only be three-quarters of the amount paid. Further, it will only be deductible under ITA 20(1)(b) at the rate of 7 percent applied on a declining balance basis.

ITA 56.4(3)(c) - Sale Of An Eligible Interest   An eligible interest is an interest in shares in a corporation that carries on business, or in a partnership that carries on business. In a situation where a restrictive covenant is sold in conjunction with an eligible interest, the amount received can be added to the proceeds of disposition. As was the case with the ITA 56.4(3)(b) exception, the payor and the recipient must file a joint election for this exception to apply. When this exception is applicable, ITA 56.4(4)(c) requires the purchaser to treat the payment as a cost of the purchase.

If this addition creates or increases a capital gain, only one-half of this amount will be subject to tax. Note that the application of this provision is more complex when there is more than one restrictive covenant involved in the sale of a single eligible interest.

17-122.   The first of these exceptions, treatment of the restrictive covenant payment as employment income, is not relevant to the material in this Chapter. However, the other two exceptions are very significant when a business is being sold and will be given further attention in our discussion of the alternative ways in which a business can be sold.

Sale Of Individual Assets
General Procedures
17-123.   Disposing of a business via a piece-by-piece sale of individual assets would only occur in certain situations. These could be described as follows:

- The business has not been successful in producing an adequate rate of return on the assets invested. In such situations, the most reasonable course of action may be the sale of individual assets.

- Some owner-managed businesses have income producing activities that are so closely tied to the skills of the owner/manager that the sale of the business independent of those skills would not be feasible.

17-124   This type of disposition would only be appropriate in limited circumstances. Given that the circumstances associated with the particular business will dictate whether this approach will be used, there is no need to devote any attention to the advantages or disadvantages of this alternative.

Restrictive Covenants - Sale Of Individual Assets
17-125.   In the situations that are involved here, it is unlikely that a restrictive covenant will be used. However, if this was to occur, treatment of the amount involved as cumulative eligible capital would be possible. This treatment will be discussed in the next section dealing with the sale of total assets as a going concern.

Sale Of Assets As A Going Concern
General Procedures
17-126.   In contrast to a liquidation, where the assets are sold on an individual basis, the purchaser in this situation would acquire the corporation's assets as a going concern and, in so doing, would acquire any goodwill or other intangible assets that might be associated with the enterprise.

17-127.   As was the case with the piece by piece sale of individual assets in a liquidation, the sale of all assets as a going concern may result in a combination of business income, capital gains, recapture, and terminal losses.

17-128.   In both types of asset sales, you should note that there are really two transactions involved. The first transaction involves the sale of assets and the payment of liabilities at the corporate level. Included in this process will be the determination of any tax liability resulting from the sale of the assets. At this point, the corporate assets would consist entirely of the after tax proceeds resulting from the disposition of the tangible and other assets of the corporation. In most situations, the owner will choose to distribute these assets and wind up the corporation.

17-129.   This distribution of the after tax proceeds of the sale of corporate assets is the second transaction and, in general, it will involve income tax effects for the recipient shareholders. Given this two transaction process, a complete analysis of the alternatives of selling the assets of the business versus disposing of the shares will require dealing with both taxation on the corporation as a result of disposing of the assets, and personal taxation as a result of distributing the after tax proceeds of this sale.

17-130.   In dealing with the sale of corporate assets, an understanding of the tax effects associated with such dispositions is required. These effects can be outlined as follows:

Cash   In most circumstances, the cash of the business will be retained in the business. If it is "sold", there will be no tax consequences associated with its disposition.

Accounts Receivable   In the absence of any special election, the sale of accounts receivable as a component of the sale of a business will be treated as a capital transaction. This means that any difference between the face value and the consideration received will be treated as a capital loss, only one-half of which will be deductible.

However, ITA 22 provides for a joint election to treat the sale of receivables as an income transaction. This allows the purchaser to treat any difference between the amount paid for the receivables and the amount actually collected as a bad debt expense. A more detailed description of this election is presented in Chapter 6.

Inventories   Even when inventories are sold as part of the sale of a business, any difference between the sales price and the vendor's cost will be treated as ordinary business income. This is provided for in ITA 23 and, unlike the situation with the ITA 22 treatment of receivables, no election is required. For the purchaser, the transfer price becomes the tax cost that will eventually be allocated to cost of goods sold.

Prepayments   There is no specific provision in the *Act* dealing with prepayments. However, in practice, their sale will be treated as an income transaction using the same general procedures that are applied to inventories. However, in most cases, prepayments will have a fair market value equal to their tax value. This means that they can be sold at fair market value without any tax consequences.

Non-Depreciable Capital Assets   The most common non-depreciable capital assets of a business are land and investments. Depending on the amount of consideration received for these assets, the transferor will have a capital gain or loss. With respect to capital losses, they can only be deducted from capital gains.

If some of the consideration being paid for these assets is deferred, the corporation can use capital gains reserves to defer part of the applicable taxation. However, the use of this technique would require continuing the corporation through the deferral period and this may not be in keeping with the objectives of the vendor.

For the purchaser, the adjusted cost base of non-depreciable capital assets will be the purchase price, which presumably is the fair market value.

Depreciable Assets   The disposition of a depreciable asset can result in recapture, a terminal loss, or some combination of recapture and a capital gain. Unlike capital gains, recapture and terminal losses will be subject to 100 percent inclusion in, or deduction from, active business income and will be included in income eligible for the small business deduction.

As was the case with non-depreciable capital assets, if some of the consideration for these assets is not received immediately, reserves can be used to defer the taxation of capital gains.

For the purchaser, the capital cost of depreciable assets will be the purchase price, which presumably is the fair market value.

Goodwill   If goodwill is present, in most cases it will not have a tax value in the records of the transferor. When the goodwill is sold, three-quarters of the consideration received will be subtracted from the cumulative eligible capital (CEC) account. If the existing CEC balance was nil, this will create a negative balance equal to three-quarters of the payment. After being adjusted to reflect the 50 percent capital gains inclusion rate, this negative balance will be included in the corporation's income . However, unlike a taxable capital gain, this inclusion will be included under ITA 14(1) as business income.

If the corporation has a positive CEC balance, the subtraction of three-quarters of the payment may leave a positive balance or, alternatively, a negative balance. In the former case, the positive amount will be deductible in a manner similar to terminal losses on depreciable assets. In the latter case, the negative balance will have to be added to income to the extent that the corporation has made previous CEC deductions. If the negative balance exceeds the previous CEC deductions, the remainder will be adjusted to the 50 percent capital gains inclusion rate and then added to income.

The purchaser will add three-quarters of the amount paid to his CEC balance.

Restrictive Covenants - Sale Of Total Assets

17-131.   Restrictive covenants may take one of two different forms when there is a sale of the total assets of the corporation. If it is anticipated that the corporation will continue in business, the agreement can be between the purchaser of the assets and the corporation. In contrast, if the corporation is to be liquidated, the agreement will likely be between the purchaser and the former owner(s) of the shares. It is also possible that the purchaser will require both the corporation and the former shareholders to sign a restrictive covenant.

17-132.   Whether the agreement is between the purchaser and the corporation or, alternatively, the purchaser and the shareholder(s) of the corporation, treatment of the amount as CEC would be possible (see Paragraph 17-121). If both parties are prepared to sign a joint election requiring the purchaser to add three-quarters of the payment to his CEC balance and the vendor to deduct three-quarters of the payment from his CEC balance, this treatment can be used. You should note that this election is only available when intangible capital property is involved in the sale.

17-133.   From the point of view of the vendor, the result will vary depending on whether there was an existing CEC balance at the time of the deduction. The various alternatives here were covered in our Paragraph 17-130 discussion of the sale of goodwill.

17-134.   If the payment is eligible for the joint election and the election is made, the purchaser will have to treat the payment for the restrictive covenant as an eligible capital expenditure. However, if the payment is not eligible or, if no joint election is filed, ITA 56.4 provides no specific guidance for the purchaser.

17-135.   This means that the purchaser will have to apply basic principles from other Sections of the *Income Tax Act*. Without regard to the fact that the vendor will be taxed on the full amount of the payment under ITA 56.4(2), the purchaser's treatment may involve a deduction of the full amount of the payment, an addition of the payment to one or more assets, or an addition of three-quarters of the payment to his CEC balance. The specific treatment by the purchaser will depend on the nature of the payment as determined under general tax principles.

Sale Of Shares

General Procedures

17-136.   In terms of accounting, legal, and tax considerations, this is the simplest way to sell a business. The calculation of the gain on the sale only requires the adjusted cost base of the shares to be subtracted from the proceeds received from their disposition. Any resulting difference will be a capital gain or loss, and will be subject to the usual treatment accorded to share dispositions.

17-137.   In preparing for the sale of shares, a corporation will declare tax-free capital dividends to the extent of its capital dividend account and taxable dividends for any additional amount which will generate a dividend refund.

Lifetime Capital Gains Deduction

17-138.   If the corporation is a "qualified small business corporation" as defined in ITA 110.6(1), the disposition of shares may qualify for the lifetime capital gains deduction of

$750,000 (2013 figure). The conditions associated with the designation "qualified small business corporation" are discussed in Chapter 11. Note here, however, that this deduction is only available on the sale of shares by an individual. If the corporate assets are sold, either separately or as a group, this valuable deduction is not available.

Restrictive Covenants - Sale Of Shares

17-139.   In cases where a business disposition involves a sale of shares, any restrictive covenant that is required will involve an agreement between the purchaser of the shares and the vendor of the shares. In this situation the exception under ITA 56.4(3)(c) (see Paragraph 17-121) becomes important. The sale of shares would be a disposition of an eligible interest and this would allow the taxpayer receiving payment for the restrictive covenant to include it as part of the proceeds of disposition. As such, it would serve to create or increase a capital gain on the sale, only one-half of which would be taxable.

17-140.   Note that this treatment requires the vendor and purchaser to file a joint election and, if they fail to do so, the vendor will have to include the full amount of the payment in income when it is received or becomes receivable. If the election is filed, the purchaser will include the payment in the cost of his purchase. If the election is not filed, the treatment by the purchaser will require the application of general tax principles.

Evaluation Of Alternatives

Advantages Of Selling Shares

17-141.   Generally speaking, the vendor of a business will favour selling shares over selling assets. Factors favouring this alternative are as follows:

• The sale of shares offers the simplicity of a single transaction. In contrast, in a sale of assets, the vendor must deal with the legal and tax consequences arising at the corporate level. In addition, the vendor must steer the corporation through a winding-up procedure and deal with the personal tax consequences of these procedures. The greater complexity will require additional personal efforts on the part of the vendor. Also, the legal and accounting fees associated with these transactions are likely to be significant.

• Any income produced by the sale of shares will usually be reported as capital gains. At worst, only one-half of such gains are taxable. At best, the taxable gains may be reduced or eliminated through the use of the $750,000 (2013 figure) lifetime capital gains deduction. If assets are sold by the corporation, some of the resulting income could be recaptured CCA, which must be included in income in full. In addition, if capital gains arise on the sale of assets, they will be treated as investment income to the corporation and will not be eligible for the small business deduction.

• If the enterprise has an unused non-capital loss carry forward, it will still be available to the enterprise if shares are sold. Any non-capital loss carry forwards are, of course, subject to the acquisition of control rules, requiring that they be applied against income earned in the same business in which the losses were incurred. However, if the sale of assets alternative is chosen, such loss carry forward balances will be completely unavailable to the purchaser.

• When a payment for a restrictive covenant is a component of the sale of shares, the vendor may be able to treat the amount received as an addition to his proceeds of disposition, rather than an amount that has to be fully included in income. This treatment is conditional on the vendor and purchaser filing a joint election, in which case the purchaser will add the amount paid to his acquisition cost.

• A sale of assets could result in the payment of land transfer taxes that would not be applicable if shares are sold.

Advantages Of Purchasing Assets

17-142.   As just described, there are a number of advantages that can be associated with selling shares, most of them benefitting the vendor. From the point of view of the purchaser, a purchase of assets is generally more desirable than a purchase of shares. Some of the advantages of purchasing assets are as follows:

- In acquiring assets, the purchaser acquires a completely new, and usually higher, set of tax values for the assets transferred. For example, consider a depreciable asset with a capital cost of $100,000, a UCC of $40,000, and a fair market value of $400,000. If shares are acquired, the CCA deductions available to the corporation will continue to be based on $40,000 and, if the assets are subsequently disposed of, capital gains will be determined from the original capital cost of $100,000. In contrast, if the asset was purchased in an arm's length transaction for its fair market value of $400,000, this amount would be the capital cost and UCC to the purchaser. This bump-up in asset values and the availability of higher CCA claims will significantly reduce the tax liabilities of the purchaser from the level that would have prevailed had the shares been purchased.

- Goodwill (cumulative eligible capital) can be recognized when assets are acquired. The CEC deductions related to these amounts are not available if shares are acquired.

- If shares are acquired, all of the assets must be acquired. In a sale of assets, redundant assets can be left out of an acquisition of assets.

- If shares are acquired, the purchaser may become responsible for any future tax reassessments. While this exposure could occur because the purchased corporation continues to operate, it is usually covered in the buy and sell agreement for the transaction. This agreement is normally written to protect the purchaser from future problems in this area.

- A further problem relates to potential non-tax liabilities related to product or environmental liabilities. Again, because the purchased corporation is continuing to operate, it could be responsible for such liabilities. However, this is another issue that may be dealt with in the buy and sell agreement.

- Most of the preceding discussion has implicitly assumed that the corporation's assets have fair market values in excess of their related tax values. If this is not the case and unrealized losses are present, selling assets may be advantageous to the vendor as well as the purchaser. This is based on the fact that the vendor would prefer to have fully deductible terminal or business losses, rather than capital losses that are only one-half deductible against taxable capital gains.

Conclusion

17-143.   While each situation needs to be evaluated on the basis of the specific assets and values involved, in general, a vendor will wish to sell shares while a purchaser will wish to acquire assets. As a result, negotiations will usually involve higher prices being offered for the assets of the business than are offered for the shares of the incorporated business.

17-144.   Because some understanding of business valuations can be helpful in considering the procedures used in the sale of a corporation, we provide very brief coverage of this subject in Supplementary Reading No. 6, Business Valuations, which can be found on the Student CD-ROM that accompanies this text. The following very simplified example illustrates the type of analysis that is required in comparing a sale of assets and a sale of shares.

Example

17-145.   To illustrate the sale of an incorporated business, we will use the following example.

Example   Mr. O'Leary owns all of the outstanding shares of O'Leary Ltd., a Canadian controlled private corporation. Mr. O'Leary has reached retirement age and wishes to dispose of the business. He has received an offer to buy the shares for $180,000 or, alternatively, the assets of the business for $200,000. All of the liabilities of the business have been settled in preparation for the sale.

The cost of Mr. O'Leary's original investment was $50,000. As no additional investment has been made, this is also his adjusted cost base and paid up capital for the outstanding shares. The provincial tax rate on business income eligible for the small business deduction is 4 percent. The provincial rate on all other income is 14 percent. The corporation has no balance in its RDTOH account, its capital dividend account, or its GRIP account. Mr. O'Leary is subject to a combined federal/provincial rate of 46 percent on non-dividend income and 31 percent on non-eligible dividends received.

Relevant information on the assets of the business is as follows:

Asset	Cost	Fair Market Value
Cash	$ 5,000	$ 5,000
Receivables	10,000	10,000
Inventories	55,000	60,000
Land	20,000	40,000
Plant And Equipment (UCC = $45,000)	95,000	60,000
Goodwill	Nil	25,000
Total	$185,000	$200,000

Sale Of Shares For $180,000

17-146.   With respect to the sale of shares, the tax consequences are as follows:

Proceeds Of Disposition	$180,000
Adjusted Cost Base	(50,000)
Capital Gain	$130,000
Inclusion Rate	1/2
Taxable Capital Gain (For Mr. O'Leary)	$ 65,000

17-147.   At a 46 percent rate, the normal Tax Payable on this gain would be $29,900, leaving Mr. O'Leary with after tax funds of $150,100 ($180,000 - $29,900). However, it is likely that O'Leary Ltd. is a qualified small business corporation. If this is the case, the lifetime capital gains deduction could be used to eliminate all of the taxes on this disposition of shares, resulting in Mr. O'Leary retaining the entire $180,000 proceeds. Alternative minimum tax might be applicable if the capital gain is sheltered through the lifetime capital gains deduction.

Sale Of Assets For $200,000

17-148.   The tax consequences resulting from selling the assets are calculated as follows:

Account	Taxable Income
Inventories ($60,000 - $55,000)	$ 5,000
Plant And Equipment - Recaptured CCA ($60,000 - $45,000)	15,000
Goodwill [($25,000)(3/4)(1/2 ÷ 3/4)]	12,500
Active Business Income	$32,500
Taxable Capital Gain On Land [($40,000 - $20,000)(1/2)]	10,000
Corporate Taxable Income	$42,500

17-149.   Except for the $10,000 taxable capital gain on the disposition of Land, all of this income is active business income. The resulting Tax Payable would be calculated as follows:

Sale Of An Incorporated Business

Federal Tax On Active Business Income [(28% - 17%)($32,500)]	$3,575
Federal Tax On Investment Income [(28% + 6-2/3%)($10,000)]	3,467
Federal Part I Tax	$7,042
Provincial Tax On Active Business Income [(4%)($32,500)]	1,300
Provincial Tax On Investment Income [(14%)($10,000)]	1,400
Total Tax Payable	$9,742

17-150   There is no opening balance in the RDTOH. The addition to the account, which will be the balance in the account is $2,667, the least of the following three figures:

• 26-2/3% Of Investment Income [(26-3/2%)($10,000)]	$2,667
• 26-2/3% Of Taxable Income, Less Amount Eligible For Small Business Deduction [(26-2/3%)($42,500 - $32,500)]	$2,667
• Federal Part I Tax Payable	$7,042

17-151.   The allocation to the capital dividend account would be as follows:

Non-Taxable Portion Of Capital Gain On Land [(1/2)($20,000)]	$10,000
Non-Taxable Portion Of Goodwill [($25,000)(1/4)(1/2 ÷ 1/4)]	12,500
Capital Dividend Account	$22,500

17-152.   Given the preceding analysis of the liquidation of the corporate assets, the net cash retained by Mr. O'Leary after the distribution of corporate assets can be calculated as follows:

Proceeds Of Disposition - Sale Of Assets	$200,000
Corporate Tax Payable (Before Dividend Refund)	(9,742)
Dividend Refund (RDTOH balance)	2,667
Available for Distribution	$192,925
Paid Up Capital	(50,000)
ITA 84(2) Deemed Dividend	$142,925
Capital Dividend (Balance In Account - Election Required)	(22,500)
Deemed Taxable Dividend	$120,425
Tax Rate (On Non-Eligible Dividends Received)	31%
Personal Tax Payable On Non-Eligible Dividend	$ 37,332

17-153.   There would be no capital gain on the distribution as shown in the following:

Total Distribution	$192,925
ITA 84(2) Deemed Dividend	(142,925)
Deemed Proceeds Of Disposition	$ 50,000
Adjusted Cost Base Of The Shares	(50,000)
Capital Gain	Nil

17-154.   Based on the preceding calculations, Mr. O'Leary's after tax retention from the sale of assets would be calculated as follows:

Amount Distributed	$192,925
Tax On Deemed Dividend	(37,332)
Cash Retained	$155,593

17-155.   This amount is larger than the $150,100 that would be retained from a sale of shares if the resulting capital gain was subject to tax. However, it is significantly smaller than the $180,000 that would be retained from a sale of shares if the lifetime capital gains deduction could be used to eliminate the entire gain on the sale.

We suggest you work Self Study Problem Seventeen-8 at this point.

Key Terms Used In This Chapter

17-156.   The following is a list of the key terms used in this Chapter. These terms, and their meanings, are compiled in the Glossary Of Key Terms located at the back of the separate paper Study Guide.

Adjusted Cost Base	Parent Company
Amalgamation	Proceeds Of Disposition
Business Combination	PUC
Canadian Corporation	Qualified Small Business Corporation
Control (CICA Handbook)	Recapture Of CCA
Convertible Property	Redemption Of Shares
Corporation	Reorganization Of Capital (ITA 86)
Disposition	Restrictive Covenant
Exchange Of Shares In A	Rollover
Reorganization (ITA 86)	Share For Share Exchange (ITA 85.1)
Gift	Small Business Corporation
Goodwill	Subsidiary
Legal Stated Capital	Taxable Canadian Corporation
Lifetime Capital Gains Deduction	Terminal Loss
Merger	Vertical Amalgamation
Non-Share Consideration	Winding-Up Of A 90% Owned Subsidiary
Paid Up Capital	Winding-Up Of A Canadian Corporation

References

17-157.   For more detailed study of the material in this Chapter, we refer you to the following:

ITA 22	Sale Of Accounts Receivable
ITA 23	Sale Of Inventory
ITA 24	Ceasing To Carry On Business
ITA 51	Convertible Property
ITA 51.1	Conversion Of Debt Obligation
ITA 54	Definitions (Proceeds Of Disposition)
ITA 84(2)	Distribution on Winding-Up, Etc.
ITA 84(3)	Redemption Of shares
ITA 84(5)	Amount Distributed Or Paid Where A Share ...
ITA 85	Transfer Of Property To Corporation By Shareholders
ITA 85.1	Share For Share Exchange
ITA 86	Exchange Of Shares By A Shareholder In Course Of Reorganization Of Capital
ITA 87	Amalgamations
ITA 88(1)	Winding-Up (Of A 90 Percent Owned Subsidiary)

ITA 88(2)	Winding-Up Of A Canadian Corporation
ITA 110.6	Capital Gains Exemption
S4-F3-C1	Price Adjustment Clause
IT-115R2	Fractional Interest In Shares
IT-126R2	Meaning Of "Winding-Up"
IT-140R3	Buy-Sell Agreements
IT-142R3	Settlement Of Debts On The Winding-up Of A Corporation
IT-146R4	Shares Entitling Shareholders To Choose Taxable Or Capital Dividends
IT-149R4	Winding-Up Dividend
IT-188R	Sale Of Accounts Receivable
IT-243R4	Dividend Refund To Private Corporations
IT-287R2	Sale Of Inventory
IT-302R3	Losses Of A Corporation - The Effect That Acquisitions Of Control, Amalgamations, And Windings-Up Have On Their Deductibility - After January 15, 1987
IT-444R	Corporations — Involuntary Dissolutions
IT-450R	Share For Share Exchange
IT-474R2	Amalgamations Of Canadian Corporations

Problems For Self Study

(The solutions for these problems can be found in the separate Study Guide.)

Self Study Problem Seventeen - 1 (Section 85.1 Share For Share Exchange)

Jenny Jerome is the only shareholder of Jenny's Cupcakes Inc. This business is based on her mother's recipes for gourmet cupcakes. It has been very successful and, as a consequence, Jenny has been approached by a large public corporation, London Speciality Bakeries Ltd., with a view to acquire the shares in her corporation.

The shares of Jenny's Cupcakes Inc. have a PUC and an adjusted cost base of $125,000, and a current fair market value of $725,000. London Speciality Bakeries Ltd. has offered Jenny 100,000 of its shares in return for all of her shares in Jenny's Cupcakes Inc. The London Speciality Bakeries shares are currently selling for $7.25 per share.

Required: Advise Jenny with respect to the tax consequences that would arise from accepting the London Speciality Bakeries offer. In addition, indicate the adjusted cost base of the Jenny's Cupcakes shares in the hands of London Speciality Bakeries Ltd.

Self Study Problem Seventeen - 2 (Section 85.1 Share For Share Exchange)

At the beginning 2004, Sarah Hartman opened a retail business in rented facilities near her home. As she anticipated losses in the first couple of years of operation, she did not incorporate. She planned to use these losses to offset her employment income.

By January 1, 2008, the business had established itself as a profitable entity, at which point Sarah decided to incorporate. The new corporation will be called Hartman Inc. and will have a December 31 year end.

On January 1, 2008, the following values are relevant:

Tax Values Of Business Assets	$ 842,000
Fair Market Value Of Business Assets	1,560,000

On this date, these assets are transferred to the corporation under the provisions of ITA 85(1) at a total elected value of $842,000. As consideration, she receives a note for $360,000, along with 6,000 Hartman Inc. shares with a fair market value of $1,200,000. No other shares of Hartman Inc. have been issued.

On January 1, 2013, she receives an offer from Grande Ltd. to acquire all 6,000 of the shares of Hartman Inc. in return for 150,000 Grande Ltd. shares with a fair market value of $2,700,000. Subsequent to this transaction, Sarah will remain at arm's length with Grande Ltd.

Sarah has used all of her lifetime capital gains deduction on the disposition of another successful corporation that she owned. However, not all of her efforts have been so fortunate. She has a $625,000 net capital loss carry forward resulting from bad decisions in her trading of Canadian public company shares.

Required:

A. Advise Sarah with respect to the tax consequences that would arise for her from accepting the Grande Ltd. offer. Your answer should consider both the application of ITA 85.1 and opting out of this provision.

B. Indicate the adjusted cost base of the Hartman Inc. shares in the hands of Grande Ltd.

C. Advise Sarah as to the alternative approaches that might simultaneously make use of her net capital loss carry forward and minimize her current payment of taxes.

Self Study Problem Seventeen - 3 (ITA 86(1) Reorganization)

John Farnsworth owns 75 percent of the outstanding common shares of Farnsworth Inc. His original investment was $99,000 on December 31, 2010. On this same date, his only daughter acquires the remaining 25 percent of the common shares of Farnsworth Inc. for $33,000.

Mr. Farnsworth's original investment of $99,000 is also the paid up capital and the adjusted cost base of his shares. On December 31, 2013, the fair market value of Mr. Farnworth's shares is $450,000.

As Mr. Farnsworth is nearing retirement, he would like to freeze the value of his estate. To this end, he exchanges his common shares in Farnsworth Inc. for cash of $69,000 and preferred shares that are redeemable at his discretion for $381,000 in cash (this totals $450,000, the fair market value of Mr. Farnsworth's shares). The new preferred shares have a legal stated capital of $99,000 and a fair market value of $381,000. The Company has a nil balance in its General Rate Income Pool (GRIP) account.

The exchange takes place on December 31, 2013.

Required: Determine the following:

A. The paid up capital of the newly issued redeemable preferred shares.

B. The adjusted cost base of the newly issued redeemable preferred shares.

C. The proceeds of redemption that would be used to calculated any ITA 84(3) deemed disposition resulting from the reorganization, as well as the proceeds of disposition that Mr. Farnsworth would use to calculate any capital gain resulting from the reorganization.

D. The tax consequences for Mr. Farnsworth of this reorganization of the capital of Farnsworth Inc.

E. The tax consequences for Mr. Farnsworth if the new Farnsworth Inc. preferred shares are redeemed for $381,000.

F. The tax consequence for Mr. Farnsworth if the new Farnsworth Inc. preferred shares are sold for $381,000.

Self Study Problem Seventeen - 4 (Section 86 Reorganization With Gift)

Mr. Mark and his son, Jack, own, respectively, 80 percent and 20 percent of the 1,000 common shares of Markit Ltd. They acquired their shares four years ago, when the Company was incorporated, for $8,000 and $2,000, respectively. The current fair market value of the Markit shares is $2,400,000. Markit Ltd. is not a qualified small business corporation.

The Company has a nil balance in its General Rate Income Pool (GRIP) account for all years under consideration.

Mr. Mark wishes to freeze the value of his shares at their current value. To accomplish this goal, he will exchange these shares for preferred shares of Markit Ltd. with legal stated capital of $8,000 and a fair market value of $1,600,000. Subsequent to this reorganization of capital, his son, Jack, will own all of the outstanding common shares.

Required:

A. Describe the immediate tax consequences of this transaction to Mr. Mark, including the following:

   • the amount of any gift that Mr. Mark has made to Jack;
   • the PUC of the new preferred shares;
   • the adjusted cost base for the new preferred shares;
   • the amount of any deemed dividends arising on the exchange; and
   • any capital gain or loss resulting from the exchange of the common shares.

B. Describe the tax consequences of this transaction to Jack.

C. Describe the tax consequences of this transaction to Mr. Mark, if the new preferred shares in Markit Ltd. were redeemed at their fair market value of $1,600,000.

Self Study Problem Seventeen - 5 (Section 86 Reorganization With Gift)

Mr. Jerry Long owns 90 percent of the outstanding common shares of Long Industries Ltd., while his 35 year old daughter, Ms. Gerri Long, owns the remaining 10 percent. The Company was established in 2000 by Mr. Ian Seto, an unrelated party, with an initial investment of $100,000. No further investment was made by Mr. Seto and, during 2003, Mr. Long purchased 100 percent of the shares for their fair market value of $360,000.

During 2007, he gave 10 percent of the shares to his daughter. The fair market value of 100 percent of the shares at that time was $450,000.

It is now December 1, 2013, and the fair market value of 100 percent of the Long Industries Ltd. shares is $900,000. In order to freeze his estate, Mr. Long would like to use the provisions of ITA 86 to reorganize the capital of the corporation. He is considering two alternative approaches to structuring this reorganization as follows:

Approach One   Mr. Long would exchange all of his common shares in return for a note with a fair market value of $90,000, and retractable preferred shares with a legal stated capital of $234,000 and a fair market value of $720,000.

Approach Two   Mr. Long would exchange all of his common shares in return for a note with a fair market value of $50,000, and retractable preferred shares with a legal stated capital of $40,000 and a fair market value of $660,000.

The Company has a nil balance in its General Rate Income Pool (GRIP) account for all years under consideration.

Required:

A. For each of the two suggested approaches determine:

i.   the amount of any gift that Mr. Long has made to his daughter.
ii. the PUC of the new preferred shares.
iii. the adjusted cost base for the new preferred shares.
iv. the amount of any deemed dividends arising on the exchange of shares.
v.   any capital gain or loss resulting from the exchange of the common shares.

B.   Using your Part A results, compare the tax consequences of Mr. Long selling the preferred shares at their fair market value as of the date of the reorganization for the two approaches.

C.   Using your Part A results, compare the tax consequences of the corporation redeeming Mr. Long's shares at their fair market value as of the date of the reorganization for the two approaches.

D.   For each of the two approaches, provide a brief description of the net economic effect of the reorganization transaction that includes whether or not he has succeeded in freezing his estate.

Self Study Problem Seventeen - 6 (Section 87 Vs. Section 88)

Ricon Ltd. owns 100 percent of the outstanding shares of Lynn Inc. Ricon acquired the Lynn shares in 2011 at a cost of $390,000. Their current fair market value is $425,000. Lynn Inc. has no debt and deals at arm's length with Ricon Ltd.

The only asset owned by Lynn Inc. is a parcel of land. Lynn had paid $175,000 for this land in 2006 and, at the time Ricon Ltd. acquired the shares of Lynn Inc., the fair market value of the land was $390,000. The land now has a fair market value of $425,000. Lynn has paid no dividends since its shares were acquired by Ricon.

The two Companies wish to combine using either ITA 87 or ITA 88(1).

Required: Which provision should be used in this situation? Explain your conclusion.

Self Study Problem Seventeen - 7 (Winding-Up Of A Corporation)

Intertel Inc., a Canadian controlled private corporation, has been in operation for a number of years, and in the beginning was a profitable enterprise. However, in recent years it has become apparent that its competitive position has been badly eroded and it is not likely to earn a satisfactory return on its invested capital. As a consequence, the shareholders have agreed to a liquidation of the Company. The Company's year end is December 31.

In contemplation of the liquidation, a Balance Sheet has been prepared based on the tax values of its assets and liabilities as at January 1, 2013. This Balance Sheet, after all closing entries, is as follows:

Intertel Inc.
Balance Sheet (Tax Values)
As At January 1, 2013

Inventories (Net Realizable Value And Tax Cost)	$ 43,750
Refundable Dividend Tax On Hand	33,750
Land - Adjusted Cost Base	778,750
Building - Undepreciated Capital Cost	732,500
Total Assets	**$1,588,750**
Liabilities	$ Nil
Paid Up Capital	68,750
Retained Earnings	1,520,000
Total Equities	**$1,588,750**

Other Information:

1. The Land has a current fair market value of $1,553,750. The Building had an capital cost of $1,093,750. The building's fair market value on January 1, 2013 is $1,591,250.

2. On January 1, 2013, the Company has a balance in its Capital Dividend account of $268,750. It has a nil balance in its General Rate Income Pool (GRIP) account.

3. The adjusted cost base of the shares is equal to $68,750, the original capital investment by the shareholders.

4. The provincial tax rate on income eligible for the small business deduction is 4 percent. The provincial rate on other income is 12 percent.

5. No dividends were paid in the previous year ending December 31, 2012.

6. All of the assets are disposed of at their fair market values on January 1, 2013. The after tax proceeds from the sale are distributed to shareholders on January 15, 2013.

Required:

A. Calculate the amount that will be available for distribution to the shareholders after the liquidation.

B. Determine the components of the distribution to the shareholders, and the amount of taxable capital gains that will accrue to them once the proceeds of the liquidation are distributed. Assume that appropriate elections or designations will be made to minimize the taxes that will be paid by the shareholders.

Self Study Problem Seventeen - 8 (Sale Of Assets vs. Shares)

Mr. Donald Brock is the sole shareholder of Brock Enterprises, a Canadian controlled private corporation. The company was incorporated by Mr. Brock with an investment of $52,500. No additional shares have been issued since that time.

While the business has, for the most part, operated successfully, Mr. Brock wishes to devote his attention to other matters and is planning to sell the company. The corporation has a December 31 year end.

To date, he has received two different offers for the business. An individual has offered to pay $455,000 cash for all of the shares of Brock Enterprises. Alternatively, a company has offered to pay $477,000 cash for all of the non-cash assets of the business, along with assuming all current liabilities. The sale of the business will take place early in January, 2013.

In order to be in a better position to analyze the offers that he has received for the business, Mr. Brock has had a statement of assets prepared as at January 1, 2013. This statement, which provides the values included in his accounting records, values that are relevant for tax purposes and the estimated fair market values, is as follows:

	Accounting Book Value	Tax Value	Fair Market Value
Cash	$ 14,000	$ 14,000	$ 14,000
Accounts Receivable	24,500	24,500	24,500
Inventories	105,000	105,000	109,500
Land	35,000	35,000	70,000
Building (Note)	122,500	35,000	136,500
Equipment (Note)	87,500	63,000	42,000
Goodwill	Nil	Nil	164,500
Totals	$388,500	$276,500	$561,000

Note   The accounting value in the assets schedule equals its capital cost (the accumulated amortization is shown with the equities).

The related accounting and tax figures on the equity side of the Balance Sheet, on this same date, were as follows:

	Accounting Book Value	Tax Value
Current Liabilities	$ 70,000	$ 70,000
Future Income Tax Liability	10,500	N/A
Accumulated Amortization On Buildings And Equipment	77,000	N/A
Common Stock - No Par	52,500	52,500
Capital Dividend Account	N/A	70,000
Other Income Retained	N/A	84,000
Retained Earnings	178,500	N/A
Totals	$388,500	$276,500

On January 1, 2013, Brock Enterprises has no balance in its RDTOH account or its General Rate Income Pool (GRIP) account.

On income that is eligible for the federal small business deduction, the provincial rate is 4 percent. On all other corporate income, the provincial rate is 13 percent.

Mr. Brock will be in the maximum tax bracket and will be taxed at an overall combined rate of 47 percent on regular income. The provincial dividend tax credit is equal to one-third of the gross up for all dividends.

Required: Determine which of the two offers Mr. Brock should accept. Ignore the lifetime capital gains deduction. Assume that appropriate elections or designations will be made to minimize the taxes that will be paid by Mr. Brock.

Assignment Problems

(The solutions for these problems are only available in the solutions manual that has been provided to your instructor.)

Assignment Problem Seventeen - 1 (Section 85.1 Share For Share Exchange)

In 2005, Jerry Boseman opened a retail business in rented facilities that were near his residence. He chose not to incorporate the business because he anticipated that there would be losses for at least two or three years. As he was employed at this time, he planned to use the losses to offset his employment income.

As the business had become profitable by the end of 2008, he decides to incorporate. The new corporation will be called Jerry's Flowers Ltd. and will have a December 31 year end.

On January 1, 2009, the following values were established for the assets of the business:

Tax Values Of The Business Assets	$ 986,000
Fair Market Value Of The Business Assets	$2,340,000

On this date, these assets are transferred to the corporation under the provisions of ITA 85(1) at a total elected value of $986,000. As consideration, Jerry receives a note for $500,000, along with 1,000 Jerry's Flowers Ltd. shares with a market value of $1,840 each. No other shares were issued by the corporation.

On January 1, 2013, he receives an offer from Large Flowers Inc. to acquire all of his Jerry's Flowers Ltd. shares. As consideration, he would receive 50,000 Large Flowers Inc. shares. These shares are currently trading at $75 per share. Jerry is at arm's length with Large Flowers Inc. and will remain so subsequent to the exchange of shares.

Jerry has used all of his lifetime capital gains deduction on the disposition of another successful corporation that he owned. Unfortunately for Jerry, his investment track record has had its ups and downs. He has an $800,000 net capital loss carry forward resulting from a "hot" stock tip from his wife at that time (now ex-wife).

Required:

A. Advise Jerry with respect to the tax consequences that would arise for him from accepting the Large Flowers Ltd. offer. Your answer should consider both the application of ITA 85.1 and opting out of this provision.

B. Indicate the adjusted cost base of the Jerry's Flowers shares in the hands of Large Flowers Inc.

C. Advise Jerry as to the alternative approaches that might simultaneously make use of his net capital loss carry forward and minimize his current payment of taxes.

Assignment Problem Seventeen - 2 (ITA 86(1) Share Exchange)

Mimi Farrow is the founder and sole shareholder of Farrow Ltd. Her initial and only investment was $600,000 in return for all 6,000 of the Company's common shares. This figure represents both the PUC and the adjusted cost base of these shares. The Company has a December 31 year end and has enjoyed a high level of profits since its first year of operations.

On August 1, 2013, the condensed Balance Sheet of the business is as follows:

Farrow Ltd.
Balance Sheet
As At August 1, 2013

Tangible Assets (Tax Values)	$11,625,000
Bank Loan	$ 1,112,000
Common Stock (No Par - 6,000 Shares)	600,000
Retained Earnings	9,913,000
Total Debt And Shareholders' Equity	$11,625,000

An independent appraiser has indicated that the fair market value of the tangible assets of the business are equal to their tax values. In addition to tangible assets, the appraiser indicates that the business has $1,500,000 of goodwill.

Ms. Farrow has contacted you with respect to transferring future growth in Farrow Ltd. to her 23 year old son, Woody. However, for at least a few years, she would like to retain control of the operations of the business. She has also indicated that, while she thinks Woody has great future potential as a director of movies based on his intense feelings of anxiety and dread, he has not enjoyed any financial success to date. Given this, he would only be able to invest $5,000 in the corporation at this time.

She has heard of a procedure called an exchange of shares in a reorganization that would allow her to transfer future growth in Farrow Ltd. to Woody without any immediate tax consequences. She has asked for your advice in this matter.

Required: Advise Ms. Farrow. Include in your solution the August 1, 2013 Balance Sheet after your proposed share transactions.

Assignment Problem Seventeen - 3 (Section 86 Reorganization With Gift)

Nome Industries was founded in 2005 with the issuance of 15,000 common shares for $60 per share in cash to Gnancy Gnome. No additional shares have been issued since the inception of the Company.

In 2007, Derek Blume and his son, James acquired all of the shares at a price of $85 per share from Ms. Gnome. Derek acquired 12,000 of the shares, while James acquired the remaining 3,000.

On January 1, 2013, the fair market value of the Nome shares is $1,500,000 ($100 per share). The Company is not a qualified small business corporation and it has a nil balance in its General Rate Income Pool (GRIP) account for all years under consideration.

Derek has been diagnosed with lung cancer. Given the high probability of a limited life expectancy, he would like to freeze the value of his shares at their January 1, 2013 fair market value. To accomplish this, he intends to exchange his 12,000 common shares for cash of $200,000 and 8,000 preferred shares with a legal stated capital and a redemption value of $800,000. Subsequent to this transaction, his son James will own all of the outstanding common shares of Nome Industries.

Required:

A. Describe the immediate tax consequences of this transaction to Derek Blume, including the following:

- the amount of any gift that Derek has made to James;
- the PUC of the new preferred shares;
- the adjusted cost base for the new preferred shares;
- the amount of any deemed dividends arising on the exchange; and
- any capital gain or loss resulting from the exchange of the common shares.

B. Describe the tax consequences of this transaction to James.

C. Describe the tax consequences of this transaction to Derek Blume, if the new preferred shares in Nome Ltd. were redeemed at their fair market value of $800,000 during 2013.

Assignment Problem Seventeen - 4 (Section 86 Reorganization With Gift)

Ms. Suzanne Platt founded the corporation Platt Industries Ltd. (PIL) with an initial investment of $120,000 in cash. At that time, she was issued common shares with a fair market value and paid up capital equal to her investment of $120,000.

Thanks to Ms. Platt's expertise in managing the enterprise, after 10 years, the fair market value of her common shares increased from their original value of $120,000, to a fair market value of $960,000 on December 31, 2009. On this date, she sells 25 percent of the common shares of PIL to her 22 year old son for $240,000. The son uses funds that he won in a lottery to pay for the shares.

In December, 2013, Ms. Platt decides to retire. She would like to transfer control of PIL to her son and, if possible, freeze the value of her interest in the Company. As at December 31, 2013, her holding of PIL common shares has a fair market value of $1,350,000. It is her understanding that she can exchange her common shares in PIL for a combination of non-voting preferred shares and non-share consideration without incurring any immediate tax consequences. With this in mind, she has proposed two alternative approaches to transferring control of PIL to her son:

Approach One She exchanges her common shares in PIL for cash of $50,000 and preferred shares that are redeemable at her discretion for $1,300,000. The preferred shares have a legal stated capital of $90,000 and a fair market value of $1,300,000.

Approach Two She exchanges her common shares in PIL for cash of $50,000 and preferred shares that are redeemable at her discretion for $1,270,000. The preferred shares have a legal stated capital of $1,270,000 and a fair market value of $1,270,000.

PIL is not a qualified small business corporation. The Company has a nil balance in its General Rate Income Pool (GRIP) account for all years under consideration.

Required: For each of the two suggested approaches determine:

A. The amount of the gift to a related party, if any, resulting from the exchange of shares.

B. The paid up capital of the newly issued preferred shares.

C. The adjusted cost base of the newly issued preferred shares.

D. The proceeds of redemption/disposition that Ms. Platt received for the old common shares of PIL.

E. The immediate tax consequences for Ms. Platt of the reorganization of the capital of PIL.

F. The tax consequences for Ms. Platt if the new PIL preferred shares are immediately redeemed for their fair market value.

Assignment Problem Seventeen - 5 (Section 87 vs. Section 88)

Limbo Company currently has the following assets:

Asset	Capital Cost	Tax Value	FMV
Equipment	$ 1,000	$ 300	$ 700
Land	14,000	14,000	16,500
Goodwill	Nil	Nil	2,000

There are no liabilities and no tax loss carry forwards. Limbo is 100 percent owned by Dunbar Holdings Ltd., who purchased the shares of Limbo Company for $21,000 five years ago. At that time, the Equipment was valued at its capital cost of $1,000 and the Land was valued at $19,000, for a total of $20,000. At that time, goodwill was estimated to be $1,000

Limbo has paid no dividends since its acquisition by Dunbar.

Dunbar does not wish to have Limbo continue as a separate legal entity. As a consequence, it will use either ITA 87 or ITA 88(1) to absorb Limbo into its operations.

Required: Outline what the tax consequences would be if:

A. Limbo was amalgamated into Dunbar Holdings using Section 87.

B. Limbo was rolled into Dunbar Holdings using a Section 88(1) winding-up.

Assignment Problem Seventeen - 6 (Section 88(1) Winding-Up)

In 2009, Acme Ltd. purchased all of the outstanding shares of Cross Industries for cash of $1,400,000. The assets of Cross Industries at the time of the acquisition had tax values of $1,250,000, and included a piece of land that was being held as a location for a possible second manufacturing facility. This land had been acquired in 2004 for $640,000 and, at the time Acme acquired the Cross shares, it had a fair market value of $705,000.

Acme believes that the operations of Cross Industries have become so integrated with its own, that it no longer makes sense to operate Cross as a separate entity. As a consequence, they are considering the possibility of absorbing Cross using an ITA 88(1) winding-up. At this time, the tax values of the assets of Cross Industries total $1,270,000. The Company is still holding the land for the additional manufacturing facility and it now has a fair market value of $790,000. Cross Industries has paid Acme Ltd. dividends totaling $20,000 since its acquisition.

Required: Explain the tax implications of the proposed winding-up from the point of view of both Acme Ltd. and Cross Industries.

Assignment Problem Seventeen - 7 (Winding-Up Of A Corporation)

Due to his advanced age, Gordon Korngold, the only shareholder of Korngold Ltd., has decided to retire. As the Company activities are largely based on Gordon's effort, he intends to sell the assets of the company, followed by a wind-up and distribution of the resulting cash.

Korngold Ltd. is a CCPC with a December 31 taxation year end. In contemplation of this liquidation, a Balance Sheet has been prepared based on the tax values of its assets and liabilities as at January 1, 2013, the end of the Company's taxation year. This Balance Sheet, after all closing entries, is as follows:

Korngold Ltd.
Balance Sheet
As At January 1, 2013

Inventories (Net Realizable Value And Tax Cost)	$ 48,650
Refundable Dividend Tax On Hand	32,345
Land - Adjusted Cost Base	942,450
Building - Undepreciated Capital Cost	723,640
Total Assets	$1,747,085
Liabilities	$ 313,260
Paid Up Capital	625,000
Capital Dividend Account	326,470
Other Income Retained	482,355
Total Equities	$1,747,085

Other Information:

1. The current fair market value of the Land is $2,600,000.

2. The Building had an capital cost of $1,160,000. Its fair market value on January 1, 2013 is $1,846,000.

3. The adjusted cost base of the common shares is equal to $625,000, their paid up capital.

4. On January 1, 2013, the Company has a nil balance in its General Rate Income Pool (GRIP) account.

5. All of the assets are disposed of on January 1, 2013 at their fair market values. The corporation's liabilities are also paid on this date. The after tax proceeds from the sale are distributed to shareholders on January 15, 2013.

6. The provincial tax rate for the corporation on income that qualifies for the small business deduction is 3 percent. On all other income, the provincial rate is 14 percent.

7. No dividends have been paid in the previous two years.

Required:

A. Calculate the amount that will be available for distribution to Mr. Korngold after the liquidation.

B. Determine the components of the distribution to Mr. Korngold, and the amount of taxable capital gains that will accrue to him as a result of the winding-up of Korngold Ltd. Assume that appropriate elections or designations will be made to minimize the taxes that will be paid by Mr. Korngold.

Assignment Problem Seventeen - 8 *(Sale Of Assets vs. Shares)*

Mr. Carl Lange is 78 years old and has no living relatives. For many years, he has been the sole shareholder of Alcove Ltd., a Canadian controlled private corporation with a December 31 year end. The company was incorporated by Mr. Lange with an investment of $135,000. No additional shares have been issued since that time.

As he has no associates or relatives in a position to take over the operation of the business, he would like to sell the business and devote his attention to his interest in 19th century poetry.

He has received two offers for the corporation. The first is an offer to buy all of the shares for $2,380,000. He has received an alternative offer to acquire the business by purchasing the corporate assets. The specific assets that would be bought, and the prices that would be paid, are as follows:

Accounts Receivable	$ 91,000
Inventories	298,000
Land	656,000
Building	652,000
Goodwill	719,000
Total	$2,416,000

Both offers would require the purchase to take place on January 2, 2013.

On January 1, 2013, the Balance Sheet of Alcove Ltd. is as follows:

Term Deposits	$ 529,000
Accounts Receivable (Face Amount = $98,000)	83,000
Inventories At Cost	237,000
Land At Cost	167,000
Building At Net Book Value*	215,000
Total Assets	$1,231,000
Liabilities	$355,000
Paid Up Capital	135,000
Retained Earnings	741,000
Total Equities	$1,231,000

*The capital cost of the Building was $582,000, it is the only asset in its CCA class, and the UCC balance for the class is $176,000.

At January 1, 2013, there is no balance in the Company's Capital Dividend Account (CDA), Refundable Dividend Tax On Hand account (RDTOH), or General Rate Income Pool (GRIP) account.

The Term Deposits have been on the Company's books for over five years. They represent an investment of excess funds. Mr. Lange had no personal need for these funds and he wished to defer personal taxation on the earnings they were generating. All of the Company's non-current assets have been acquired in the last ten years.

On income that is eligible for the federal small business deduction, the provincial rate is 3 percent. On all other corporate income, the provincial rate is 14 percent.

Mr. Lange will have other sources of income in excess of $200,000 and, as a consequence, his tax rate on all additional income is 29 percent at the federal level, plus an additional 14 percent at the provincial level. He lives in a province where the provincial dividend tax credit on both eligible and non-eligible dividends is equal to one-third of the gross up. Mr. Lange has not used any of his lifetime capital gains deduction.

If Mr. Lange accepts the offer to purchase the business' assets, Mr. Lange will sell the Term Deposits at their carrying values. The fair market values for these assets are equal to their carrying values. With respect to the sale of the Accounts Receivable, a joint election under ITA 22 will be made for the transfer. There would be a winding-up of the corporation subsequent to the sale of its assets.

Required: Determine which of the two offers will provide Mr. Lange with the largest amount of personal, after tax funds. Ignore the possibility that Mr. Lange might be subject to the alternative minimum tax. Assume that appropriate elections or designations will be made to minimize the taxes that will be paid by Mr. Lange.

Assignment Problem Seventeen - 9 (Sale Of Assets vs. Shares)

Mr. David Carson is the president and only shareholder of Carson Enterprises Ltd., a Canadian controlled private corporation. The Company's fiscal year ends on December 31. Mr. Carson established the Company by investing $265,000 in cash. There have been no other shares issued since then.

Mr. Carson is considering selling the corporation and, in order to better evaluate this possibility, he has prepared a special Statement Of Assets. In this special statement, comparative disclosure is provided for the values included in his accounting records, values that are relevant for tax purposes, and fair market values. This statement is as follows:

Carson Enterprises Ltd.
Statement Of Assets
As At January 1, 2013

	Accounting Net Book Value	Tax Value	Fair Market Value
Cash	$ 54,500	$ 54,500	$ 54,500
Accounts Receivable	406,000	406,000	372,250
Inventories	869,750	869,750	976,000
Land	201,500	201,500	405,000
Building (Note One)	538,000	469,250	2,061,000
Equipment (Note Two)	434,000	294,000	171,250
Goodwill	Nil	Nil	811,000
Totals	$2,503,750	$2,295,000	$4,851,000

Note One   Mr. Carson built this Building on the Land for a total cost of $1,281,000.

Note Two   The Equipment had a cost of $807,500.

At the same time that this Statement Of Assets was prepared, a similar Statement Of Equities was drawn up. This latter statement contained the following accounting and tax values:

	Accounting Book Value	Tax Value
Current Liabilities	$ 697,000	$ 697,000
Loan From Shareholder	137,500	137,500
Future Income Tax Liability	542,000	N/A
Common Stock - No Par	265,000	265,000
Capital Dividend Account	N/A	164,500
Other Income Retained	N/A	1,031,000
Retained Earnings	862,250	N/A
Totals	$2,503,750	$2,295,000

In addition to the information included in the preceding statements, the following other information about the Company is available:

- The Company has available non-capital loss carry forwards of $83,000.

- The Company has available a net capital loss carry forward of $129,650 [(1/2)($259,300)].

- Carson Enterprises Ltd. is subject to a provincial tax rate of 3 percent on income that qualifies for the federal small business deduction and 14 percent on income that does not qualify for this deduction.

- On December 31, 2012, the Company has no balance in either its RDTOH account or its General Rate Income Pool (GRIP) account.

Mr. Carson has received two offers for his Company, and he plans to accept one of them on January 2, 2013. The first offer involves a cash payment of $3,508,000 in return for all of the shares of the Company. Alternatively, another investor has expressed a willingness to acquire all of the assets, including goodwill, at a price equal to their fair market values. This investor would assume all of the liabilities of the corporation and has agreed to file an ITA 22 election with respect to the Accounts Receivable. If the assets are sold, it is Mr. Carson's intention to wind up the corporation.

Mr. Carson will have over $300,000 in income from other sources and, as a consequence, any income that arises on the disposition of this business will be taxed at the maximum federal rate of 29 percent, combined with a provincial rate of 14 percent. He lives in a province where the provincial dividend tax credit on both eligible and non-eligible dividends is equal to one-third of the gross up. He has used all of his lifetime capital gains deduction in prior years.

Required: Determine which of the two offers Mr. Carson should accept. Ignore the possibility that Mr. Carson might be subject to the alternative minimum tax. Assume that appropriate elections or designations will be made to minimize the taxes that will be paid by Mr. Carson.

CHAPTER 18

Partnerships

Introduction

Taxable Entities In Canada

18-1.   As is noted in Chapter 1, the *Income Tax Act* (ITA) is applicable to individuals (human beings), corporations, and trusts. In the case of individuals and corporations, these taxable entities have a separate legal existence. In contrast, trusts are simply arrangements for transferring property and, as such, are not separate legal entities. Partnerships are similar to trusts in that they do not have a legal existence separate from the participating partners. More to the point here is the fact that, under the provisions of the *Income Tax Act*, partnerships are generally not defined taxable entities. An exception to this is "SIFT Partnerships" which are taxable under Part IX.1 of the *Act* (see discussion later in this Chapter).

18-2.   The *Income Tax Act* deals with the fact that partnerships are generally not taxable entities through the use of a deeming rule. A deeming rule is a statutory fiction that requires an item or event be given a treatment for tax purposes that is not consistent with the actual nature of the item or event. We have encountered a number of such rules in previous chapters:

- A member of the Canadian armed forces is deemed to be a resident of Canada, even if he does not set foot in the country during the year.

- A change in use is deemed to be a disposition of an asset combined with its immediate re-acquisition.

- The death of an individual results in a deemed disposition of all of his capital property.

18-3.   The deeming rule that is applicable to partnerships is that, for purposes of determining the income or loss of its members, such organizations are considered to be a person resident in Canada. Note that this rule applies only for the purpose of calculating the income or loss of members. It does not make a partnership a taxable entity and there is no requirement that these organizations file a separate income tax return.

18-4.   In general terms, a partnership is treated as a flow-through entity. The preceding deeming rule requires that an income figure be determined at the partnership level using the usual rules for various types of income (e.g., business income, property income, capital gains). Then the income or loss of the partnership is allocated to the taxable entities (i.e., individuals, trusts, or corporations) based on the amounts agreed to in the partnership agreement, or in equal proportions in the absence of a partnership agreement. This process is illustrated in Figure 18-1.

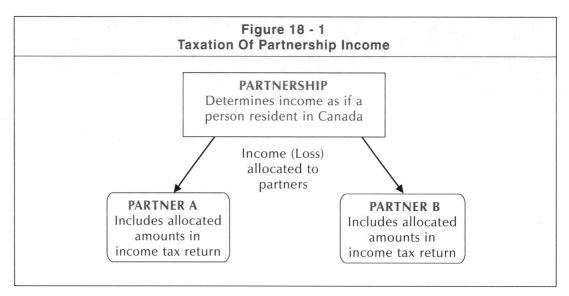

Figure 18 - 1
Taxation Of Partnership Income

PARTNERSHIP
Determines income as if a
person resident in Canada

Income (Loss)
allocated to
partners

PARTNER A
Includes allocated
amounts in
income tax return

PARTNER B
Includes allocated
amounts in
income tax return

18-5.   We would note that, while partnerships are not taxable entities under the *Income Tax Act*, they are considered taxable entities for GST purposes (see Chapter 21).

Chapter Coverage

18-6.   In this Chapter we will examine the income taxation rules that are applicable to partnerships. We will begin by defining partnerships. This will be followed by an examination of the various types of partnerships, as well as other arrangements that resemble partnerships. These other arrangements include co-ownerships, joint ventures, and syndicates. Our focus will then shift to looking at the rules for calculating income for a partnership and the process of allocating this income and other amounts to partners.

18-7.   Other issues that will be covered include:

- the determination of the adjusted cost base of a partnership interest;
- admitting and retiring partners;
- limited partnerships, limited partnership losses and the at-risk rules;
- the transfer of property between the partners and the partnership; and
- reorganizing a partnership as a new partnership, as a corporation, and as a sole proprietorship.

Partnerships Defined

The Importance Of Defining A Partnership

18-8.   The general rules for determining the income tax consequences for partnerships and their members are found in Subdivision j of Division B of Part I of the *Income Tax Act*, ITA 96 through 103. However, since these rules apply specifically to partnerships, we must first determine if we are, in fact, looking at a partnership. To do this requires a definition of a partnership.

18-9.   The importance of this definition is that it allows us to distinguish a partnership from other similar types of organizations such as syndicates, joint ventures, and co-ownership arrangements. This is necessary in that, unlike the situation for these other types of organizations, there is a separate calculation of the income of a partnership.

18-10.   As we have noted, this calculation must be carried out using the assumption that the partnership is a separate person resident in Canada. Further, as the calculation must be used for allocating income to all of the members of the partnership, partners have no flexibility with respect to the amounts to be included in their required tax returns. For example, a partner does not have the discretion to take an alternative amount of CCA.

18-11. In contrast, if the organization is considered to be a co-ownership, syndicate, or joint venture (see Paragraph 18-24), there is no requirement for a separate calculation of income. This provides the participants with much greater flexibility in determining the tax procedures to be used. In this case, one participant could take maximum CCA, while others take a lower amount, or even none at all.

Basic Partnership Elements

18-12. Unfortunately, there is no specific definition of a "partnership" in the *Income Tax Act*. There are several definitions of certain types of partnerships. For example ITA 102(1) defines a "Canadian Partnership" and ITA 197(1) defines a "SIFT Partnership". However, all of these specialized definitions presume that a partnership already exists. This leaves the question of defining a partnership unanswered.

18-13. While the *Income Tax Act* does not provide a definition of a partnership, IT-90, *What Is A Partnership?*, provides the following guidance:

Paragraph 2 Generally speaking, a partnership is the relation that subsists between persons carrying on business in common with a view to profit. However, co-ownership of one or more properties not associated with a business, (which under Common Law might be a joint tenancy or a tenancy in common), does not of itself create a partnership, and this is so regardless of an arrangement to share profits and losses. For guidance on whether a particular arrangement at a particular time constitutes a partnership, reference should be made to the relevant provincial law on the subject, and such law will be viewed as persuasive by the CRA.

18-14. While additional guidance from provincial legislation may be required in particular situations, this Paragraph 2 establishes the three basic elements that are required for an organization to be considered a partnership:

1. There must be two or more persons (taxable entities) involved.
2. These persons must be carrying on a business.
3. The business must be carried on with a view to making a profit.

18-15. While it is not listed as a basic element of such arrangements, the presence of a valid partnership agreement would serve to support the view that a partnership exists. Such agreements will usually include provisions that deal with many issues, including the following:

- the initial and ongoing partner contributions and ownership percentage of each partner,
- the responsibilities of each partner and the division of work between the partners,
- how income and drawings will be allocated and how much compensation is to be paid,
- signing authority on the partnership bank accounts and required approval for purchases,
- procedures for bringing in new partners, and
- procedures to deal with the withdrawal or death of a partner, or the sale of the business.

Types Of Partnerships

General Partnerships

18-16. A general partnership is one in which all of the partners are general partners. As defined in the *Guide For The T5013 Partnership Information Return* (T4068):

A **general partner** is a partner whose personal liability for the debts and obligations of the partnership are not limited.

18-17. Provincial partnership law provides additional guidance on the rights, duties and obligations of general partners. These include:

- Each partner is considered to act on behalf of the partnership, which means that the actions of each partner are generally binding on the other partners.

- Partners are jointly and severally liable for partnership debt and wrongful acts of other partners. This means that a partner can be liable, together with all other partners, for unpaid partnership debt and wrongful acts of other partners.

- Property contributed to the partnership or acquired with partnership funds is considered partnership property and is to be held exclusively for partnership use.

- Partners are entitled to share equally in profits and losses, unless there is an agreement to the contrary.

- Partners are not entitled to remuneration or to interest on capital contributions. As is explained later in this Chapter, any remuneration or interest on capital is treated as an income allocation and is not deductible to the partnership.

18-18.   When the term partnership is used without a qualifying adjective, the reference is normally to a general partnership.

Limited Partnerships

18-19.   A limited partnership is a partnership with at least one general partner (i.e., a partner whose liability is unrestricted) and one or more limited partners. To be considered a limited partnership, the partnership has to be registered as such under the appropriate provincial registry. In the absence of such registration, the partnership will be considered a general partnership.

18-20.   A limited partner has the same rights, duties, and obligations as a general partner with one important difference, a limited partner is only liable for partnership debt and wrongful or negligent actions of other partners to the extent of the partner's actual and promised contributions to the partnership.

Example   A limited partner contributes $1,000 and agrees to contribute a further $2,000 within a certain period of time. That partner will be potentially liable for up to $3,000 of claims against the partnership.

18-21.   It should be noted, however, that a limited partner will lose his limited liability protection, and therefore become a general partner, if he participates in the management of the partnership.

Limited Liability Partnerships (LLP)

18-22.   This form of partnership is only available to certain types of professionals as specified in provincial legislation. For example, in Ontario, only lawyers, chartered accountants, and certified general accountants are currently permitted to form such partnerships. In contrast, Alberta extends this legislation to include several other professional groups.

18-23.   Unlike members of limited partnerships, members of limited liability partnerships are personally liable for most types of partnership debt. There is, however, an important exception. Members of limited liability partnerships are not personally liable for obligations arising from the wrongful or negligent action of:

- their professional partners; or
- the employees, agents or representatives of the partnership who are conducting partnership business.

We suggest you work Self Study Problem Eighteen-1 at this point.

Co-Ownership, Joint Ventures And Syndicates

Introduction

18-24.   Our major concern in this Chapter is the taxation of partnerships. However, as we have noted, there are other types of organizations that have structures similar to partnership arrangements. Co-ownership, joint ventures, and syndicates are specific types of arrangements that contain features common to partnerships. For example, each of these organizational structures requires two or more persons. This common feature is but one of several that may make it difficult to determine whether a specific arrangement is, in fact, a partnership or, alternatively, a different type of arrangement.

18-25.   As was discussed in the preceding material, the ability to distinguish these arrangements from partnerships is a critical factor in determining how a given organization will be taxed. To facilitate this process, the following material will provide additional clarification as to the nature of these other types of organizations.

Co-Ownership

18-26.   Two or more persons co-own property when they share a right of ownership in the property. For income tax purposes, the most important consideration is that profits and losses are shared in partnerships, but are typically accounted for individually by joint or co-owners.

18-27.   Two common forms of co-ownership are joint tenancy and tenancy in common. A joint tenancy is a form of property ownership where two or more joint tenants have ownership and possession of the same property. Individual interests are identical and the property cannot be sold or mortgaged without the consent of the other joint tenant(s). Spouses commonly own their principal residence and other properties in joint tenancy.

18-28.   In a tenancy in common arrangement, tenants can sell or mortgage their interests without the consent of other tenants in common. An example of a situation where a tenancy in common might be used would be the ownership of a vacation property by three brothers.

Joint Ventures

Defined

18-29.   Those of you familiar with financial reporting will recognize that some corporations are referred to as joint ventures. They are distinguished by the fact that control of the corporation is shared by two or more of the shareholders. This type of joint venture does not present any special problems in terms of tax procedures. They are subject to the same rules that are applicable to other corporate taxpayers.

18-30.   Our concern here is with unincorporated joint ventures. Like partnerships, joint ventures are not defined taxable entities under the *Income Tax Act*. Further, such arrangements are not governed by provincial legislation. However, both the *Income Tax Act* and the *Excise Tax Act* refer to joint ventures, implicitly giving recognition to this form of organization.

18-31.   The similarity of partnerships and joint ventures has led the CRA to make the following statement in 1988:

> Unlike partnerships, the concept of joint venture is not recognized by statute (i.e. provincial legislation). Although the Canadian courts have, in certain cases, recognized joint venture as being a business relationship that is distinct from partnership, in our experience, many so-called joint ventures are in fact partnerships... The CRA would rely on provincial partnership law in making such a determination.

18-32.   This would suggest that, even if participants in a joint venture call the arrangement a joint venture, if it contains the three basic partnership elements, it will be considered a partnership for tax purposes and treated accordingly.

18-33.   Despite this lack of clarity, joint ventures do appear to exist for tax purposes. Factors that have been used to distinguish this type of organization include:

- co-venturers contractually do not have the power to bind other co-venturers;
- co-venturers retain ownership of property contributed to the undertaking;
- co-venturers are not jointly and severally liable for debt of the undertaking;
- co-venturers share gross revenues, not profits; and
- while partnerships may be formed for the same purpose as a joint venture, they are usually of longer duration and involve more than a single undertaking.

Tax Procedures

18-34.   If an arrangement is considered to be a joint venture rather than a partnership, there will be no separate calculation of income at the organization level. The participants will be subject to the usual rules applicable to individuals or corporations. As we have noted, this will provide these taxable entities with greater flexibility on such issues as how much CCA can be taken for the current year.

Syndicates

18-35.   A syndicate is generally defined as a group of persons who have agreed to pool their money or assets for some common purpose. Because a syndicate is not a legal entity, a reference to an interest in a syndicate usually means an interest in the combined assets of the syndicate members. The Canadian courts have traditionally reserved the name "syndicate" for specialized projects that are financial in nature. An example of a syndicate would be an association of insurance companies who combine forces to underwrite substantial high-risk insurance policies.

18-36.   There are no specific income tax rules that apply to syndicates. This means that, if there are any activities of the syndicate that result in assessable amounts of income, the relevant amounts will have to be allocated to the members of the syndicate.

We suggest you work Self Study Problem Eighteen-2 at this point.

Partnership Income, Losses, And Tax Credits

Introduction

18-37.   The goal of partnership taxation is to apply the income tax consequences of partnership income, losses, and tax credits to the persons who are its partners. To implement this, a two stage process is involved:

Stage 1   Determine, at the partnership level, the various components of partnership income. While the partnership may have property income and/or capital gains, for most partnerships, the most important component will be net business income.

Stage 2   Allocate the amounts that were determined in Stage 1 to the members of the partnership on the basis of the provisions of the partnership agreement.

18-38.   As we have noted, Stage 1 requires the assumption that the partnership is a person resident in Canada. In implementing this assumption, we generally begin with the partnership's accounting figure for business income. The normal procedure is to convert this figure to Net Business Income for tax purposes. This conversion is based on a reconciliation process which is very similar to the reconciliation process that is used to determine Net Business Income For Tax Purposes. There are, however, some items that are specific to the calculation of business income for partnerships.

18-39.   Following the determination of the amount of business income to be allocated to partners, separate calculations are carried out for amounts of capital gains and the amounts of property income that will be allocated to the members of the partnership.

18-40.   While it would be possible to calculate a Net Income For Tax Purposes for the partnership, this usually is not done. Such a figure has no real meaning for a non-taxable entity such as a partnership. Further, the calculation would serve no real purpose as the allocations to the partners are on a source-by-source basis. We would also note that there is no calculation of Taxable Income for a partnership. Again, as partnerships are not taxable entities, such a figure would have no real meaning.

Applicable Concepts

Taxation Year

18-41.   ITA 96(1)(a) indicates that partnership income must be calculated as if the partnership was a separate person resident in Canada. ITA 96(1)(b) follows this by indicating that this calculation should be made as if the taxation year of the partnership were its "fiscal period". The ITA 249.1(1) definition of "fiscal period" indicates that, if any member of a partnership is an individual or a professional corporation, the partnership must have a December 31 year end. Otherwise, the only restriction is that the fiscal period cannot end more than 12 months after it begins. In effect, this means that, if all of the members of a partnership are corporations (other than professional corporations), the partnership can use any year end.

18-42.   ITA 249.1(4) provides an exception to the general taxation year end rules that are described in the preceding paragraph. This exception applies if:

- all of the members of the partnership are individuals; and
- an election is filed with the CRA using a prescribed form (T1139) prior to the end of the partnership's first fiscal year.

18-43.   If these conditions are met, the partnership can elect to use a non-calendar year as its fiscal period. The complications associated with making this election are discussed in Chapter 6, Business Income. The proposed amendment discussed below would require income adjustments similar to those required for "additional business income". Additional business income is also covered in Chapter 6.

> **Example**   ABC Partnership has five corporate partners, two of which are professional corporations, and one partner who is an individual. The new partnership wants to choose a March 31 fiscal year end.
>
> **Analysis**   The partnership must use a December 31 fiscal year end. The presence of both an individual and professional corporations as partners prevents the use of a non-calendar fiscal period under the ITA 249.1(1) definition. Similarly, the presence of corporations prevents the election of a non-calendar fiscal period under ITA 249.1(4).
>
> **Proposed Amendment**   The CRA has been concerned with the ability of a corporate member of a partnership to defer taxes because it has a different year end from the partnership. Consider a partnership that has a year ending January 31, 2013 and a corporate member with a December 31, 2013 year end. The corporation would not have to include the partnership income earned during the year ending January 31, 2013 until it files its return for the corporate year ending December 31, 2013. In effect, this provides an 11 month deferral of income recognition.
>
> To deal with this problem, the proposed amendments would require the corporation to include 334/365 of the partnership income for its year ending January 31, 2013 in its corporate tax return for the year ending December 31, 2012. This accrual would be deducted in the corporate taxation return for the year ending December 31, 2013, with a new accrual added for 334/365 of the partnership income for the year ending January 31, 2014.

Partnership Property

18-44.   In general, partners legally own a percentage interest in partnership property in co-ownership. The partnership cannot own property since it is not a legal entity. This creates a problem for income tax purposes because the partnership income tax rules require that the partnership determine its income or loss as if it were a separate person.

18-45.   If the partnership does not own partnership property, then gains and losses from the disposition of such property would not be considered those of the partnership. In addition, the partnership would not be able to claim CCA or write off Cumulative Eligible Capital. The *Income Tax Act* resolves this problem with an assumption that the partnership, for income tax purposes, is considered to own partnership property.

Retention Of Income Characteristics

18-46.   Partnerships are treated as a conduit for transferring income from an originating source into the hands of the partners. Further, it is an unfiltered conduit in that the character of various types of income is not altered as it flows through to the partners. If a partnership earns dividend income, taxable capital gains, or realizes a business loss, these sources would be received as dividend income, taxable capital gains, or business losses in the hands of the partners.

> **Example** Partnership Deux has two equal general partners. It earns $50,000 of interest income and realizes a $20,000 capital gain.   None of this amount is withdrawn by the two partners. Corporation Dos has two equal shareholders. It also earns $50,000 of interest income and realizes a $20,000 capital gain. The corporation does not pay out any of this amount as dividends.

> **Analysis - Partnership** For Partnership Deux, each partner is considered to have received $25,000 [(1/2)($50,000)] of interest income and to have realized a $5,000 taxable capital gain [($20,000)(1/2)(1/2)]. Note that the income is subject to taxation, despite the fact that none of it has been withdrawn from the partnership (see next section on Accrual Basis).

> **Analysis - Corporation**   In the case of Corporation Dos, the shareholders will not be taxed until the income is withdrawn from the corporation. The income will, however, be taxed at the corporate level on the basis of its nature (e.g., capital gains, business, or property income). When it is distributed to the shareholders, it will not retain its characteristics as capital gains, business, or property income. Rather, the entire distribution will be taxed in the hands of the shareholders as dividends.

18-47.   In addition to retaining its basic character, the originating location of each source of income is retained. If, for example, a partnership earns dividends on shares of U.S. corporations, this income would be received by the partners as foreign source dividends. Not surprisingly, the related foreign tax credits would also be flowed through to the partners.

Accrual Basis

18-48.   The partnership must calculate its net business income on an accrual basis unless its partners are professionals who can elect under ITA 34 to use the billed basis of income recognition (see Chapter 6, Business Income). On its determination, this income is then allocated to the partners. The partners include their share of this income at the time of allocation, without regard to when the funds are withdrawn from the partnership. It is the allocation, not the receipt of the funds, which creates income for the partners that is subject to tax.

18-49.   In effect, this places the partners on an accrual basis for the determination of their individual business income amounts. As the income is taxed when it is accrued at the partnership level and allocated to the individual partners, it will not be taxed again when it is withdrawn from the partnership.

Exercise Eighteen - 1

Subject: Partnership Income - Accrual Basis

During the year ending December 31, 2013, PQR Partnership has business income of $55,000, capital gains of $40,000, and receives eligible dividends of $10,000. Norm Peters has a 50 percent interest in the income of this partnership. During 2013, Norm withdraws $30,000 from the partnership. Determine the tax consequences for Mr. Peters for the 2013 taxation year.

End of Exercise. Solution available in Study Guide.

Calculating The Amounts To Be Allocated

Net Business Income

18-50.   For most partnerships, the major income source to be allocated is the partnership's Net Business Income. As we have noted, this is a reconciliation process which starts with accounting Net Income. Various items are then added or subtracted to arrive at the partnership's Net Business Income. A discussion of the major items in this reconciliation process follows.

Salaries Or Wages To Partners (Add Back)   Partnership agreements often provide that partners be paid salaries or wages to recognize the time they devote to partnership business. As the determination of these amounts are usually carried out on a non-arm's length basis, the CRA takes the position that these amounts cannot be deducted as expenses in the determination of the partnership's Net Business Income.

The required adjustment here is to add back any deducted amounts of salaries and wages to partners to arrive at the partnership's Net Business Income. This means that, in effect, amounts designated in the partnership agreement as salaries become part of the Net Business Income that will be allocated to partners. The salary allocation called for in the partnership agreement becomes, from a tax point of view, a priority allocation of Net Business Income. After this allocation has been made, any residual amount of Net Business Income will be shared as per the partnership agreement (e.g., equally, or otherwise).

Interest On Partner Capital Contributions (Add Back)   Partnership agreements may provide that partners receive interest on capital contributions. Here again, the CRA's view is that such amounts cannot be deducted as expenses in the determination of partnership income.

As was the case with salaries and wages paid to partners, any amounts of interest on partner capital contributions that have been deducted in the determination of accounting Net Income will be added back to arrive at the partnership's Net Business Income. As was the case with salaries to partners, this addition means that, from a tax point of view, interest on partner capital contributions becomes a priority allocation of Net Business Income.

Example - Salaries And Interest On Capital Contributions   Bob and Ray are partners who share income equally after a provision has been made for their salaries and interest on capital contributions. For the year ending December 31, 2013, the Income Statement of the partnership, prepared in accordance with GAAP, is as follows:

Revenues		$135,000
Expenses:		
Cost Of Sales	($45,000)	
Salary To Bob	(30,000)	
Salary To Ray	(10,000)	
Interest On Ray's Capital Contributions	(11,000)	
Other Expenses	(10,000)	(106,000)
Accounting Income		$ 29,000

Analysis   For tax purposes, the Net Business Income of the Bob And Ray Partnership would be calculated as follows:

Accounting Income		$29,000
Add:		
Salaries To Bob and Ray	$40,000	
Interest On Capital Contributions	11,000	51,000
Net Business Income		$80,000

This amount would be allocated to the two partners as follows:

	Bob	Ray
Priority Allocation For Salaries	$30,000	$10,000
Priority Allocation For Interest	N/A	11,000
Allocation Of Residual On Equal Basis		
[(50%)($80,000 - $40,000 - $11,000)]	14,500	14,500
Total Business Income Allocation	$44,500	$35,500

Note that, even though the accounting statements referred to Bob and Ray's salaries, these amounts are allocated as Net Business Income to the two partners. While practice varies in this area, in most cases the amounts referred to in the partnership agreement as salaries will not be subject to the usual payroll procedures (e.g., employment insurance, CPP contributions, and payroll taxes). This is because they will be taxed as business income, not as employment income.

Drawings (Add Back)   Drawings by partners cannot be deducted in the determination of partnership income.

As GAAP for partnerships is not clearly laid out, partnership drawings may or may not be deducted in the determination of accounting Net Income. To the extent they have been deducted in determining accounting income, they will have to be added back in the determination of the partnership's Net Business Income.

Dividend Income (Deduct)   Dividends received will be included in the partnership's accounting Net Income figure. These amounts will be allocated to partners as a separate source of income. This is discussed in more detail starting at Paragraph 18-54.

Given this, dividends must be deducted in converting the partnership's accounting Net Income to the partnership's Net Business Income.

Charitable Donations (Add Back)   These amounts are normally deducted in the determination of a partnership's accounting Net Income. In converting this figure to Net Business Income, these amounts will have to be added back.

Donations made by a partnership that otherwise qualify as charitable donations are flowed to the partners based on their partnership agreement. Corporations are entitled to a deduction in arriving at Taxable Income, whereas individuals are entitled to a credit against Tax Payable. Donations, and the related credit or deduction, are only allocated to those partners who are partners on the last day of the partnership's year end.

Political Contributions (Add Back)   As political contributions are normally subtracted in the determination of accounting Net Income, these amounts will have to be added back to arrive at the partnership's Net Business Income.

A proposed ITA 127(4.2) provides that qualifying political contributions are allocated to each partner as per the partnership agreement. Similar to charitable donations, the allocation of the contributions and the related credit is dependent on being a partner on the last day of the partnership's year in which the political contribution was made.

Personal Expenditures (Add Back)   In some situations, a partnership may pay personal expenses of one or more partners. While these amounts may be deducted as an expense for accounting purposes, they are not deductible to the partnership in determining Net Business Income. To the extent that these amounts have been deducted in the determination of accounting Net Income, they will have to be added back in the determination of the partnership's Net Business Income.

Business Transactions With Partners (No Adjustment) There are no legal restrictions on the ability of partners to enter into legitimate business transactions with their partnerships. Examples include loans made by partners to the partnership and the renting of a partner's property to the partnership. As long as the transactions are on regular commercial terms, such transactions will be treated for tax purposes in the same manner as transactions with persons who are not partners.

In general, such transactions will not require any adjustment of the accounting Net Income to arrive at the partnership's Net Business Income.

Capital Cost Allowance Any CCA that is deducted on partnership property must be deducted at the partnership level. As you would expect, the half-year rule, the available for use rules, the rental property restrictions, and other depreciable property rules are all applicable when determining the amount of CCA that a partnership may claim.

You should note that this requirement removes the possibility of individual partners taking different amounts of CCA. If maximum CCA is deducted at the partnership level, all partners must, in effect, deduct maximum CCA.

It is not uncommon in partnership financial statements for the amortization figures to be based on the CCA amounts used for tax purposes. If this is the case, no net adjustment is required in converting accounting Net Income to the partnership's Net Business Income. However, the normal procedure, even when the amounts involved are the same, would be to add back the amortization figures used in the accounting statements, and deduct the appropriate CCA figure.

Amounts Related To Dispositions Of Capital Assets Accounting Net Income will include 100 percent of the accounting gains and losses on dispositions of depreciable and non-depreciable capital assets. These amounts must be added back (losses) or deducted (gains) in the determination of the partnership's Net Business Income.

As net taxable capital gains will be allocated to the partners as a separate source of income, these amounts are not included in the calculation of the partnership's Net Business Income. This is discussed in more detail starting at Paragraph 18-52.

As you will recall from Chapter 5, a disposition of a depreciable capital asset can also result in recapture of CCA or terminal losses. If recapture occurs, it will be added to accounting Net Income in order to arrive at the partnership's Net Business Income. Similarly, terminal losses will be deducted.

Reserves The use of reserves is discussed in both Chapter 6 (e.g., reserve for bad debts) and Chapter 8 (e.g., capital gains reserve). These reserves are claimed by the partnership in exactly the same manner as individuals, corporations, and trusts.

In general, the amounts involved in the application of reserve procedures are the same as the related amounts for accounting purposes. For example, the amount deducted for bad debts in the accounting statements is usually the same net amount that results from the application of reserve procedures in tax returns. However, the normal procedure here in determining the partnership's Net Business Income is to remove the accounting amounts and replace these amounts with the tax figures, even when the amounts are the same.

18-51. Figure 18-2 (following page) provides a list of the more common additions and deductions that arise in the process of converting the accounting income of a partnership into Net Business Income. You will note that many of the items presented here are the same as those presented in Figure 6-3 in Chapter 6 which covers business income.

Figure 18 - 2
Conversion - Partnership Accounting Income
To Partnership Net Business Income

Additions To Accounting Income:
- Specific To Partnerships
- Salaries of partners
- Interest on capital accounts
- Drawings of partners (if deducted)
- Personal expenditures of partners (if deducted)

- General Business (Additions)
- Amortization, depreciation, and depletion of tangible and intangible assets (Accounting amounts)
- Recapture of CCA
- Tax reserves deducted in the prior year
- Losses on the disposition of capital assets (Accounting amounts)
- Charitable donations
- Political contributions
- Interest and penalties on income tax assessments
- Non-deductible automobile costs
- Fifty percent of business meals and entertainment expenses
- Club dues and cost of recreational facilities
- Non-deductible reserves (accounting amounts)
- Fines, penalties, and illegal payments

Deductions From Accounting Income:
- Specific To Partnerships
- None

- General Business (Deductions)

- Capital cost allowances (CCA)
- Terminal losses
- Tax reserves claimed for the current year
- Gains on the disposition of capital assets (Accounting amounts)
- Deductible warranty expenditures
- Landscaping costs
- Dividends included in accounting income
- Other property income included in accounting income

Exercise Eighteen - 2

Subject: Partnership Net Business Income

The JL Partnership has two partners. Partner J, because he is actively managing the partnership, receives an annual salary of $45,000. Because Partner L has contributed most of the capital for the business, he receives an interest allocation of $22,000. The partnership agreement calls for the remaining profits, and all other allocations, to be split 60 percent to J and 40 percent to L. The salary and interest amounts are deducted in the determination of accounting Net Income.

During the taxation year ending December 31, 2013, the partnership's accounting Net Income is $262,000. Other relevant information is as follows:

- The accountant deducted amortization charges of $26,000. Maximum CCA is $42,000.
- Accounting Net Income includes a deduction for charitable donations of $2,500.
- Accounting Net Income includes a gain on the sale of land of $24,000.

Determine the amounts of Net Business Income that will be allocated to Partner J and Partner L for the year ending December 31, 2013.

End of Exercise. Solution available in Study Guide.

Capital Gains And Losses

18-52.   In the preceding section, we noted the need to remove any accounting gains and losses on capital asset dispositions in the determination of Net Business Income. If dispositions created recapture of CCA or terminal losses, these amounts were added or deducted in the determination of Net Business Income. However, capital gains and losses were not included.

18-53.   As you would expect, capital gain and losses are allocated to the members of the partnership to be included in their tax returns. Without going into great detail, once these amounts are allocated they are subject to the same rules that would apply if the gains and losses had resulted from dispositions by the individual partners. One-half of the net gains will be included in Net Income For Tax Purposes. On some gains the lifetime capital gains deduction may be available and some losses may qualify as Business Investment Losses. If the partner is a private corporation, there will be an addition to the capital dividend account.

Dividend Income

18-54.   As we have noted in the preceding section, dividends received by a partnership are removed in the determination of the partnership's Net Business Income. When they are allocated to the members of the partnership to be included in their tax returns, they retain their character as eligible, non-eligible or capital dividends. Their treatment subsequent to allocation will depend on the type of taxpayer involved and/or the type of dividend received:

- Partners who are individuals must gross up the dividends by either 38 percent (for eligible dividends) or 25 percent (for non-eligible dividends). The dividends are then eligible for the usual dividend tax credits.

- Dividends allocated to corporate partners will not be grossed up. One hundred percent of the amount allocated will be included in Net Income For Tax Purposes. To the extent the dividends are from taxable Canadian corporations, they can be deducted in the determination of the corporation's Taxable Income.

- Capital dividends received by the partnership are allocated as capital dividends to the partners, generally retaining their tax-free nature.

Foreign Source Income

18-55.   Foreign source income received by a partnership will be allocated to the partners as either business or property income. As you would expect, the amounts that will be allocated to the partners will be the pre-withholding amounts that accrued to the partnership. That is, to the extent that foreign taxes were withheld, they will be added to the amount received for purposes of allocating this income to the members of the partnership. As the pre-withholding amounts of foreign source income are allocated to the partners, tax legislation allows the partners to use the available credits that result from their allocation of this withholding. The calculation of these amounts would be as discussed in Chapters 7 and 11.

Exercise Eighteen - 3

Subject: Partnership Income Allocations

The ST Partnership has two partners who share all types of income on an equal basis. Partner S and T are both individuals. The Partnership's accounting Net Income for the year ending December 31, 2013 is $146,000. No salaries or interest payments to partners have been included in this calculation. However, the $146,000 includes $12,000 in eligible dividends, as well as a $31,000 gain on the sale of unused land. Amortization Expense deducted is equal to maximum CCA. Determine the amounts that will be included in the Net Income For Tax Purposes of Partner S and Partner T for the year ending December 31, 2013.

End of Exercise. Solution available in Study Guide.

Allocations Of Related Tax Credits

18-56.   In the preceding sections, we have covered the various types of income that will be allocated to partners and the related tax credits. The type of income and expenditures that could give rise to tax credits can be summarized as follows:

* Dividend Income - tax credit is available if the partner is an individual.
* Charitable Donations - tax credit is available if the partner is an individual.
* Foreign Source Income - tax credit is available to all partners if foreign tax is withheld.
* Political Contributions - tax credit is available to all partners, but as covered in Chapter 4, the *Federal Accountability Act* bans political contributions by corporations.

Exercise Eighteen - 4

Subject: Allocations To Partners - Related Tax Credits

For the year ending December 31, 2013, the MN Partnership has correctly computed its Net Business Income to be $141,000. The partnership agreement calls for all allocations to Partner M and Partner N to be on a 50:50 basis. Partner M and N are both individuals. In determining the Net Business Income amount, the partnership's accountant added back $3,500 in charitable donations and $1,200 in contributions to a registered political party. In addition, $4,200 in eligible dividends received were deducted. The partners have made no charitable donations or political contributions as individuals. Determine the amount of any tax credits that will be available to Partner M and Partner N for the year ending December 31, 2013.

End of Exercise. Solution available in Study Guide.

Methods Of Allocation

18-57.   As we have seen in the preceding sections, income amounts must be allocated on a source-by-source basis. While a partnership agreement might simply state that all types of income will be allocated on the same basis, there is nothing to prevent different allocations for different sources. For example, business income could be allocated on an equal basis, with capital gains being allocated to one individual partner.

18-58.   There are many ways in which the members of a partnership may agree to allocate income or loss. These allocations may be fixed, variable, or a combination of fixed and variable elements. Factors such as the value of services provided to the partnership (a salary component), capital contributions (an interest component), and amounts of risk assumed (personal assets at risk) may be taken into consideration. Alternatively, allocations may be based upon fixed ratios determined by the partners or, in the absence of some other agreement, the equal fixed ratios that automatically apply under partnership law.

18-59.   In general, the CRA will accept any income allocation agreement that is reasonable. It is possible, however, that the agreement could be constructed in a manner that would reduce or postpone taxes (e.g., an example of this would be the allocation of all partnership losses to partners with high levels of current income). In addition, an allocation could be used for income splitting purposes (e.g., allocation of large amounts of partnership income to a low-income spouse on a basis that is not consistent with his contribution of services or capital). In either of these circumstances, the CRA can apply ITA 103(1) or (1.1) to re-allocate the income on the basis that is reasonable in the circumstances.

We suggest you work Problems Eighteen-3 and 4 at this point.

The Partnership Interest

The Concept

18-60.   A person who is a member of a partnership has the right to participate in profits and losses of the partnership and the right to an interest in partnership property, usually on the dissolution of the partnership. Such rights, collectively referred to as a partnership interest, constitute property for income tax purposes much in the same manner as a share of capital stock of a corporation.

18-61.   A partnership interest is generally considered a non-depreciable capital property and, as a consequence, a disposition of a partnership interest will usually result in a capital gain or loss.

18-62.   In many cases, a partnership interest is acquired when a partnership is formed. Each designated member of the new organization will acquire an interest, usually through the contribution of an amount of capital that is specified in the partnership agreement.

18-63.   Alternatively, a partnership interest can be acquired from an existing partnership. This type of transaction can take two forms:

- The interest can be acquired directly from a current partner or partners by purchasing their interest.

- The interest can be acquired directly from the partnership by transferring assets to this organization.

Acquiring A Partnership Interest

New Partnership

18-64.   For founding members of a new partnership, establishment of the adjusted cost base (ACB) of the partnership interest is very straightforward. For each of the partners, the ACB of their interest will simply be the fair value of the assets contributed to the partnership. If the contributions involve non-monetary assets, appraisals may be required. This, however, is a practical complication that does not alter the basic concept that is involved.

Admission To Existing Partnership

18-65.   From a technical point of view, partnership law provides that a partnership terminates on a change in the composition of the members (e.g., admissions or withdrawals of partners). However, this problem can be overridden by the partnership agreement. In the discussion that follows, we assume that a partnership is not dissolved because of a change in its members. This assumption is consistent with the tax treatment of the partnership accounts. That is, tax law does not require the admission or withdrawal of a partner to be treated as a termination of the partnership, followed by the formation of a new partnership.

18-66.   In those cases where a partnership interest is purchased directly from an existing partner, the procedures are very straightforward. If a person becomes a partner by acquiring another partner's interest, then cost will equal the purchase price. For example, if Mr. Davis acquires the one-third interest of Mr. Allan for $90,000, then both the cost to Mr. Davis and the proceeds of disposition to Mr. Allan would be $90,000.

18-67.   The situation becomes more complex when the partnership interest is acquired through direct payments to more than one partner.

> **Example**   An existing partnership has three equal partners, each of whom has made a capital contribution of $16,000. They would like to bring in a new equal partner, with each partner then having a 25 percent interest in the organization. The new partner, Mr. Zheng agrees to pay $30,000 to each of the existing partners for one-quarter of their one-third interest. Note that by selling one-quarter of their one-third interest, each partner retains a 25 percent interest [(75%)(1/3) = 25%].

Analysis   Mr. Zheng would have an ACB of $90,000, the consideration given up for the 25 percent interest.

Each of the original partners would have a capital gain calculated as follows:

Proceeds Of Disposition To Each Partner	$30,000
ACB of Part Interest [(25%)($16,000)]	(4,000)
Capital Gain For Each Partner	$26,000

18-68.   The capital accounts in the accounting records of the partnership and the partners' ACB will be as follows:

	Partner 1	Partner 2	Partner 3	Mr. Zheng
Capital Before Admitting Zheng	$16,000	$16,000	$16,000	Nil
Adjustment For Admission Of Zheng	(4,000)	(4,000)	(4,000)	$12,000
Ending Capital Accounts	$12,000	$12,000	$12,000	$12,000
ACB Of Partnership Interest	$12,000	$12,000	$12,000	$90,000

18-69.   Note that, while the accounting values for the interests of the original three partners are equal to their ACBs, this is not the case for Mr. Zheng. In contrast to his accounting value of $12,000, his ACB would be his cost of $90,000 [(3)($30,000)].

18-70.   To this point, we have only considered situations where assets were given to individual partners in return for the new partner's acquired interest. There are also situations in which the new partner makes a payment directly to the partnership in return for his interest.

18-71.   Returning to the example in Paragraph 18-67, if Mr. Zheng had paid the $90,000 directly to the partnership, there would be no tax consequences for the existing partners. No disposition of any part of their interest would have occurred and, as a consequence, no capital gain would be recorded and the ACBs of their interests would remain at $16,000. Mr. Zheng's interest would be recorded at $90,000 for both tax and accounting purposes.

Exercise Eighteen - 5

Subject: Admission Of A Partner

Alan and Balan are equal partners in the Alban Partnership. On September 1, 2013, Alan and Balan's partnership capital account balances are $48,000 each. This is also equal to the adjusted cost base of their interests. As the result of paying $40,000 to each of Alan and Balan, Caitlan is admitted as an equal partner (1/3 interest) on September 1, 2013. Calculate the tax effects of the partner admission for Alan and Balan. In addition, determine the accounting balances for each of the partner's capital accounts after the admission of Caitlan, as well as the adjusted cost base for each partner after the admission of Caitlan.

End of Exercise. Solution available in Study Guide.

Adjusted Cost Base Of The Partnership Interest
Basic Concept

18-72.   As we have noted, a partnership interest is viewed in tax legislation as a non-depreciable capital asset. A discussed in Chapter 8, the adjusted cost base (ACB) of a capital property is defined in ITA 54 as its cost, plus or minus the adjustments in ITA 53.

18-73.   In the preceding section, we illustrated how the ACB of a partnership interest would be determined at the time a partnership interest is acquired.

18-74.   Subsequent to its acquisition, the partnership interest is determined by starting with the ACB of the preceding year and adjusting it for various items. The most common adjustments are for:

- current year income allocations;
- current year Drawings; and
- current year capital contributions.

18-75.   There are, however, many other possible adjustments and most of these will be covered in this section. It is important to note the importance of making these adjustments. If the ACB of a partnership interest was not adjusted for these items, any amount in excess of cost paid for such an interest would be treated as a gain resulting from a disposition. This inequitable result is prevented through adjustments to the ACB of the partnership interest.

Timing Of Adjustments

18-76.   Before proceeding to a discussion of the more common adjustments to the cost base of a partnership interest, some attention must be given to the timing of these adjustments. With respect to capital contributions and drawings, the timing is very straightforward. These adjustments are made at the time of the contribution or drawing.

18-77.   In contrast, those adjustments related to allocations of income or tax credits are not made during the period in which the income or tax credit arises. Rather, these adjustments to the ACB of a partnership interest are made on the first day of the following fiscal period, which is normally a year. These procedures will be illustrated in the material that follows.

Adjustments For Partnership Income Components

18-78.   It would be unusual, in any given year, for the adjusted cost base of a partnership interest not to be adjusted for partnership income allocations. As this must be added on a source-by-source basis, specific sources are given separate consideration here:

Net Business Income   As discussed in our section on partnership income determination, accounting Net Income must be converted to the partnership's Net Business Income. This amount is allocated to each partner on the basis of the partnership agreement. The amounts so determined will be added (Net Business Income) or subtracted (Net Business Loss) to the adjusted cost base of each partner. As noted, this increase or decrease does not occur until the first day of the following fiscal period.

> **Example**   Tom and Theresa begin the Double T partnership in January, 2013 and select December 31 as their year end. They each contribute $1,000 to Double T. During 2013, the partnership earns $21,000 in gross service revenue. The only expenses incurred are $6,000 in business meals and entertainment.

> **Analysis**   Accounting Net Income for the partnership would be $15,000 ($21,000 - $6,000). However, Net Business Income would be $18,000, the $15,000 of accounting Net Income, plus $3,000, the non-deductible one-half of the expenses for business meals and entertainment. This means that each partner would be allocated $9,000 [(1/2)($18,000)] in business income, and each partnership interest would be increased by the same amount. While the income amounts would be included in the partners' 2013 tax return, the addition to the adjusted cost base would not be made until January 1, 2014.

Capital Gains And Losses   As discussed previously, these amounts will be allocated to the partners on the basis of the partnership agreement. Once these amounts are allocated, the taxable or allowable amounts (one-half) will be included in the partner's tax returns.

Despite the fact that only one-half of these amounts will be taxable or deductible, the adjustment to the ACB of the partnership interest is for the full amount and occurs on the first day of the following fiscal period. This inclusion of the full amount provides for the non-taxable one-half of the gain to be recovered on a tax free basis if the partnership interest is sold.

Example   Weekday Partnership has four equal partners and a December 31 year end. Each partner contributed $1,950 when the partnership began on May 1, 2013. Weekday used the initial contributions of $7,800 to acquire two parcels of land. Both parcels were capital property and were sold in December, 2013. The sale of parcel A resulted in a capital gain of $5,300 and the sale of parcel B resulted in a capital loss of $700. There were no other transactions during the fiscal year.

Analysis   The net capital gain that would be allocated to each partner is $1,150 [(1/4)($5,300 – $700)]. One-half of this amount would be included in each partner's tax return.

The ACB of each partnership interest is calculated as follows:

ACB - May 1, 2013 to December 31, 2013	$1,950
Capital Gain Allocated [(1/4)($5,300)]	1,325
Capital Loss Allocated [(1/4)($700)]	(175)
ACB Of Partnership Interest – January 1, 2014	$3,100

Dividends   As previously discussed, taxable dividends earned by a partnership retain their character (i.e., eligible, non-eligible or capital) when they are allocated to the partners. In calculating the ACB of a partnership interest, a partner's share of both capital and taxable dividends is added to the ACB of his partnership interest on the first day of the following fiscal period.

Example   Fred and Barney are equal partners in Stone-Works Partnership that began operations January 1, 2013. A December 31 year end was selected. Each partner initially contributed $5,000. The only income received by the partnership was $13,000 of eligible dividends, and $4,200 of capital dividends. No amounts were withdrawn from the partnership in 2013.

Analysis   Each partner is required to include one-half of the taxable dividends of $13,000, plus an additional 38 percent gross-up, in his 2013 Net Income For Tax Purposes. This amounts to income of $8,970 [(50%)($13,000)(138%)]. In conjunction with this allocation, each partner would be eligible for a federal dividend tax credit of $1,347 [(50%)($13,000)(38%)(6/11)]. The capital dividends are not included in each partner's income as they are tax free. The ACB of Fred and Barney's interest would be as follows:

ACB - January 1, 2013 to December 31, 2013	$ 5,000
Allocation Of Dividends Subject To Tax [(50%)($13,000)]	6,500
Allocation Of Capital Dividends [(50%)($4,200)]	2,100
ACB Of Partnership Interest - January 1, 2014	$13,600

Two things should be noted in this calculation. First, for purposes of calculating the ACB of the partnership interests, no gross up is added to the dividends subject to tax. Second, the dividends are not added to the ACB until the first day of the year following their allocation to the partners.

Adjustments For Capital Contributions And Drawings
18-79.   These adjustments require little in the way of explanation:

• Net capital contributions are added to the adjusted cost base of the partner's interest.
• Drawings reduce the adjusted cost base of the partnership interest.

Note that bona fide loans by a partner to the partnership are not considered capital contributions. Similarly, loans from the partnership to a partner are not considered to be drawings.

Example The ACB of Mr. Allan's partnership interest is $20,450 at January 1, 2013. In March, 2013, he contributes $8,200 to the partnership as a capital contribution and makes withdrawals of $2,000 in each of May, August, and November, 2013.

Analysis The ACB of Mr. Allan's partnership interest is calculated as follows:

ACB – January 1, 2013	$20,450
Capital Contributions – March 2013	8,200
Drawings – May, August And November 2013 [($2,000)(3)]	(6,000)
ACB – December 31, 2013	$22,650

Charitable Donations and Political Contributions

18-80. Amounts donated or political contributions made by a partnership in a particular year are considered donated or contributed by each partner in proportion to that partner's profit sharing ratio. As it is the individual partners who enjoy the benefits of making the contributions (i.e., the deductions or tax credits), such amounts reduce the ACB of a partnership interest. Note, however, this adjustment does not occur until the first day of the following fiscal period.

Example During the taxation year ending December 31, 2013, a partnership donated $7,500 to charitable organizations. The three partners, who are all individuals, each have a one-third interest in profits. All donations are eligible for the charitable donations tax credit.

Analysis Each of the three partners would be entitled to allocations of $2,500 towards the calculation of their individual charitable donations tax credit for 2013. As a consequence of this allocation, the ACB of each of their partnership interests would be reduced by $2,500. As we have noted, this reduction does not occur until January 1, 2014.

Negative ACB

18-81. In general, if negative adjustments to the ACB of a capital asset exceed its cost plus any positive adjustments to the ACB, the excess must be taken into income under ITA 40(3) as a capital gain. While technically an ACB can only be positive or nil, it is common to refer to assets that have experienced such adjustments as having a negative adjusted cost base.

18-82. This creates a problem for partnership interests in that withdrawals are deducted from the ACB of the partnership interest in the year they occur, while income allocations are only recorded on the first day of the following year. As partners usually withdraw their anticipated income allocations during the year in which they accrue, negative ACBs for partnership interests would not be unusual.

18-83. Because of this problem, the *Income Tax Act* allows general partners to carry forward a negative ACB, without taking the capital gain into income. This deferral is applicable until the partner disposes of his interest, either through a sale or as the result of a deemed disposition at death.

Example During 2013, in anticipation of the 2013 allocation of partnership income, a partner draws $42,000 from the partnership. For 2013, his share of partnership income is $45,000. On January 1, 2013, his partnership interest has an ACB of $25,000.

Analysis On December 31, 2013, the ACB of this partnership interest would be nil and there would be an excess of drawings over the January 1, 2013 ACB of $17,000 ($25,000 - $42,000). In the absence of a special provision for partnership interests, $8,500 [(1/2)($17,000)] would have to be taken into the partner's income as a taxable capital gain. However, because of the special provision applicable to partnership interests, this will not be the case. Note that, on January 1, 2014, the ACB of this interest would be $28,000 ($25,000 - $42,000 + $45,000).

18-84.   When the disposition results from a deemed disposition at death, there are rollover provisions that allow a continued carry forward of the negative ACB when the partnership interest is bequeathed to a spouse or common-law partner, or a trust in favour of a spouse or common-law partner.

18-85.   Note that the preceding rules only apply to active general partners. In the case of limited partners (see Paragraph 18-88) or general partners who are not active in the partnership, the deferral of the gain that is implicit in carrying forward a negative ACB is not available. Such amounts must be taken into income in the year in which they occur.

Exercise Eighteen - 6

Subject: ACB Of Partnership Interest

On January 1, 2013 Raymond and Robert form the RR Partnership. The partnership has a December 31 year end. The partnership agreement provides Robert with a 40 percent share of profits and losses. Robert initially contributes $12,500 and makes a further contribution of $7,200 on June 10, 2013. He withdraws $4,000 on October 31, 2013. RR Partnership has the following sources of income for 2013:

Capital Gain On Corporate Shares	$11,600
Eligible Dividends Received From Canadian Corporations	3,100
Net Business Income	46,700

Determine the ACB of Robert's partnership interest on December 31, 2013, and at January 1, 2014. In addition, determine the amount that would be included in Robert's 2013 Net Income For Tax Purposes as a consequence of his interest in the RR Partnership.

End of Exercise. Solution available in Study Guide.

Disposition Of A Partnership Interest

Sale To An Arm's Length Party

18-86.   If a partnership interest is sold to an arm's length party, the tax effects are very straightforward. The adjusted cost base of the partnership interest is subtracted from the proceeds resulting from its sale. If the result is positive, it is a capital gain, one-half of which will be taxed in the hands of the partner. Alternatively, if the result is negative, one-half of this amount will be an allowable capital loss which can be deducted by the partner to the extent of his current year taxable capital gains. Any unused amount can be carried over to previous and subsequent years.

Withdrawal From Partnership

18-87.   When a partner withdraws from a partnership, he is essentially disposing of his interest in that partnership. While this could involve using partnership assets to buy out the partner, the more normal procedure is to have one or more of the other partners purchase the interest of the withdrawing partner.

Example   The QST Partnership has three partners who share all income amounts on an equal basis. The ACB of their partnership interests are as follows:

Partner Q	$250,000
Partner S	250,000
Partner T	250,000

Partner T has decided to retire and will withdraw from the partnership. In return for his interest, each of the remaining partners will pay him $175,000.

Analysis Partner T will have a taxable capital gain of $50,000 [(1/2)($175,000 + $175,000 - $250,000)]. There will no immediate tax consequences to partners Q and S. However, the ACB of each of their interests will be increased to $425,000, the original $250,000, plus the additional investment of $175,000.

You might wish to note that, assuming the assets of the partnership are not revalued, the accounting values for the interests of each of the remaining partners will be $375,000 [$250,000 + (1/2)($250,000)].

> **We suggest your work Self Study Problems Eighteen-5 and 6 at this point.**

Limited Partnerships And Limited Partners

Definitions

Limited Partner

18-88.   A limited partnership is one that has at least one limited partner and one general partner. As defined in most provincial legislation, a limited partner is one whose liability for the debts of the Partnership is limited to the amount of his contribution to the Partnership, and who is not permitted to participate in the management of the Partnership. A partner whose liability is limited under partnership law is considered a limited partner for income tax purposes.

18-89.   While the term "limited partner" generally refers to a partner who is relieved of general responsibility for amounts in excess of his capital contribution, the definition also includes partners whose liability is limited by the presence of specific contractual arrangements. Examples of this type of situation include:

- guarantees that someone will acquire their partnership interest regardless of its value;
- provisions indicating that amounts a partner has agreed to contribute to the partnership may never have to be paid; and
- provisions that guarantee the partner that he will be reimbursed for any partnership losses, usually by the general partner.

18-90.   Note that members of a limited liability partnership (see Paragraph 18-22) do not fall within the definition of a limited partner. They have limited responsibility for certain types of liabilities (e.g., liabilities arising as the result of negligent action by their professional partners). However, they continue to have unlimited liability for other partnership obligations.

At-Risk Rules

Basic Concept

18-91.   Historically, limited partnership structures have been used to fund high-risk ventures that benefit from generous income tax incentives. These structures have been used with Canadian films, Canadian mining and exploration operations, scientific research and experimental development, real estate, and construction.

18-92.   General partners entice investors with limited liability protection, combined with the advantages of significant flow through of deductible losses and other tax incentives. The general partners usually do not share in the deductions, receiving their compensation through fees that are charged to the limited partners for managing the partnership.

18-93.   The at-risk rules were introduced in order to restrict the ability of certain investors in partnerships, typically limited partners, to receive tax deductions or tax credits in excess of the amount that they stand to lose on their investment. In simplified terms, the at-risk rules work to ensure that $30,000 of tax deductions are not available to a limited partner who has less than $30,000 at risk.

Limited Partnerships And Limited Partners

The At-Risk Amount

18-94. The at-risk amount sets the annual limit on the amount of tax preferences and incentives that may flow through to limited partners. Specifically, the *Income Tax Act* provides restrictions on the allocation to limited partners of scientific research and experimental development credits, resource expenditures, investment tax credits, non-farming business losses, and property losses. Under ITA 96(2.2), the at-risk amount is calculated at the end of a partnership's fiscal period as follows:

ACB Of The Partnership Interest		$xxx
Share Of Partnership Income (But Not Losses) For The Current Period		
(Current Year Income Allocation For ACB Purposes - See Paragraph 18-95)		xxx
Subtotal		$xxx
Less:		
Amounts Owed To The Partnership	($xxx)	
Other Amounts Intended To Reduce The Investment Risk	(xxx)	(xxx)
At-Risk Amount		$xxx

18-95. The addition of the share of partnership income (not losses) is intended to ensure that current year income allocations, which will not be added to the ACB of the partnership interest until the following fiscal year, are taken into consideration at the end of the current year. The amount that is added here is the same income allocation that will be added to the ACB. That is, it does not include the dividend gross up, nor is it adjusted downwards for the non-taxable portion of capital gains.

18-96. The at-risk amount is reduced by two amounts. The first represents the outstanding balance of any amount owing by the partner to the partnership for the acquisition of the partnership interest. This amount is subtracted as it is included in the partnership interest but, prior to its actual payment, it is not really at risk.

18-97. The second amount relates to financial incentives designed to reduce the investment risk or exposure to the limited partner. An example of this would be a promise by the general partner to acquire the partnership interest at an amount in excess of the value of the partnership interest at the option of the limited partner.

Limited Partnership Losses

18-98. The at-risk rules limit the ability of a limited partner to utilize certain types of losses. The rules do not directly affect farm losses and capital losses since these losses carry their own restrictions. Farm losses during the current year may be limited by the restricted farm loss rules and, in addition, any carry over of such restricted farm losses can only be applied against farming income (see Chapter 6). Similarly, current year allowable capital losses are only deductible to the extent of current year taxable capital gains.

18-99. ITA 96(2.1) indicates that a partner's share of losses, other than those associated with farming or the disposition of capital assets, can be deducted to the extent of the at-risk amount. The excess is referred to as the "limited partnership loss". It is a carry forward balance that can be carried forward indefinitely and can only be claimed against future income from the partnership or increases of the at-risk amount from that same partnership. There is no carry back of limited partnership losses.

> **Example**　On January 1, 2013, Jenny Johnson acquires a 10 percent limited partnership interest in Tax-Time, a partnership that provides tax preparation services. This interest cost her $15,000, with $6,000 paid in cash and the balance of $9,000 payable in 36 months, without interest. At December 31, 2013, Tax-Time determines that it has a $22,000 capital gain and an $111,000 business loss. Jenny is allocated 10 percent of these amounts.

> **Analysis**　As a 10 percent limited partner, Jenny is allocated a portion of the business loss equal to $11,100. However, her at-risk amount restricts the business loss that

Jenny may be able to use. The at-risk amount is calculated as follows:

ACB Of The Partnership Interest		$15,000
Share Of Partnership Income [(10%)($22,000 Capital Gain)]		2,200
Subtotal		$17,200
Less:		
Amounts Owed To The Partnership	($9,000)	
Other Amounts Intended To Reduce		
The Investment Risk	Nil	(9,000)
At-Risk Amount – December 31, 2013		$ 8,200

For 2013, Jenny will be able to deduct her share of the total partnership loss to the extent of her $8,200 at-risk amount. This will leave a non-deductible limited partnership loss for 2013 of $2,900 ($11,100 - $8,200). In general, Jenny will be able to use the limited partnership loss in 2014 or subsequent years if her at-risk amount increases. This may occur if she makes additional contributions, is allocated additional income from the partnership in 2014, or pays the amount owed to the partnership. It should also be noted that there are special adjustments to the ACB of a limited partner's partnership interest that are beyond the scope of this material.

Note There are a number of tax shelters that are based on the use of losses generated in limited partnership arrangements. Given this, you might be interested in Supplementary Reading No. 7, which provides a general overview of tax shelter arrangements. This additional reading can be found on the Student CD-ROM which is included with your text.

Exercise Eighteen - 7

Subject: Limited Partnership Loss

During 2013, Stuart Jones acquires an interest in a mining limited partnership for $200,000. An initial $50,000 is paid immediately, with the $150,000 balance payable in eight years. The general partner has agreed to acquire Stuart's interest at any subsequent date, returning his $50,000 payment and assuming responsibility for the $150,000 payable. For 2013, the limited partnership has allocated losses of $75,000 to Stuart. How much of this loss is Stuart entitled to claim as a deduction on his 2013 tax return? What is the amount of his limited partnership loss at the end of 2013?

End of Exercise. Solution available in Study Guide.

We suggest you work Self Study Problem Eighteen-7 at this point.

Transfer Of Property To And From A Partnership
Definition Of Canadian Partnership

18-100. Since the ITA treats partners as distinct from the partnership, transferring property between the partners and the partnership may have income tax consequences. Such consequences are generally dependent on the purpose of the property transfer and whether the underlying partnership meets the ITA 102 definition of a "Canadian partnership":

ITA 102 In this subdivision, "Canadian partnership" means a partnership all of the members of which were, at any time in respect of which the expression is relevant, resident in Canada.

18-101.   Whether the partnership is a general, limited, or limited liability partnership is irrelevant to the determination of its status as a Canadian partnership. In addition, the definition does not require that the partnership be formed in Canada. For example, a U.S. based partnership with all Canadian resident members would qualify.

18-102.   If the required conditions are met, the *Income Tax Act* contains rollover provisions that provide for tax deferral on such transactions. However, where the conditions are not met, the transfers will be taxed as a disposition/acquisition at fair market value.

18-103.   In covering this material on property transfers, we will first look at the rules applicable to transfers of property to and from a partnership when a rollover provision is not used. This will be followed by a discussion of some of the more commonly used partnership rollover provisions.

Transfers With No Rollover Provision
Transfers From Partners To The Partnership
18-104.   If a person transfers property to a partnership of which he is member, or to a partnership of which he becomes a member as a result of the transfer, ITA 97(1) deems the person to have disposed of the property at fair market value and the partnership to have acquired the property at the same amount.

18-105.   In general, the fair market value of the transferred asset is added to the ACB of the transferor's partnership interest. However, this addition would be reduced by any consideration given to the contributor because of his contribution. This rule is applicable without regard to whether the partnership qualifies as a Canadian partnership.

> **Example**   Diane Jefferson is a member of CG Partnership. She is required to make an additional 2013 capital contribution to the partnership and decides to make the contribution by transferring investments that she had purchased for $10,000. At the time of the transfer, they have a fair market value of $24,000.
>
> **Analysis**   Diane will be considered to have disposed of the investments for $24,000. This will result in a $7,000 [(1/2)($24,000 - $10,000)] taxable capital gain for 2013. Diane will also be considered to have made a $24,000 capital contribution that will increase the ACB of her partnership interest by the same amount. The partnership will be considered to have acquired the investments from Diane for $24,000.

Exercise Eighteen - 8

Subject: Transfers From Partner To Partnership (No Rollover)

Charles Woodward is one of four equal partners in LIU Partnership (LIU). During the current year, Charles contributes a tract of land to the partnership. Charles does not use a rollover provision to make the transfer. Charles acquired the land for $33,000 and, at the time of transfer, it is valued at $100,000. Describe the tax consequences to Charles and LIU in the following three situations:

A. No consideration is received from LIU.
B. Charles receives $25,000 in cash from LIU on the transfer.
C. Charles receives $112,000 in cash from LIU on the transfer.

End of Exercise. Solution available in Study Guide.

Transfers From The Partnership To Partners
18-106.   If a partnership transfers property to a partner, ITA 98(2) deems the partnership to have disposed of the property at fair market value and the partner to have acquired the property at the same amount. There is no requirement that the partner remains a partner after the transfer and the rule is applicable without regard to whether the partnership qualifies as a

Canadian partnership. This provision is typically used when a partnership is dissolved, or when partial distributions of partnership property are made in an ongoing partnership.

Example   Bill Davis is a 40 percent partner in the FV Partnership. The partnership owns a piece of land that has an ACB of $2,900 and transfers it to Bill in June, 2013 for no consideration. The land has a fair market value of $10,000 at this time.

Analysis   The partnership is considered to have disposed of the land for its fair market value of $10,000, resulting in a capital gain of $7,100 ($10,000 - $2,900). Bill's share of this gain is $2,840 [(40%)($7,100)]. This amount will be allocated to Bill and, as a consequence, he will report a taxable capital gain of $1,420 [(1/2)($2,840)] in his 2013 tax return. Bill will also be considered to have acquired the land for $10,000 and to have made a withdrawal from the partnership of $10,000. The ACB of his partnership interest will be reduced by the $10,000 withdrawal and increased by the $2,840 allocation of the capital gain.

Exercise Eighteen - 9

Subject: Transfers From Partnership To Partners

Darlene is one of five equal partners in the DG Partnership. During the taxation year ending December 31, 2013, DG distributes some of its investments to each of the partners. The distributed investments have an adjusted cost base of $39,000 and, at the time of transfer, they have a fair market value of $94,000. Darlene receives one-fifth of these investments. At the time of this transfer, the adjusted cost base of Darlene's partnership interest is $30,000. What are the tax consequences to DG and Darlene with respect to this distribution? Your answer should include Darlene's adjusted cost base for the investments and the amount of her partnership interest on both December 31, 2013, and on January 1, 2014.

End of Exercise. Solution available in Study Guide.

Common Partnership Rollovers
Transfers From Partners To The Partnership
18-107.   If a person transfers property to a Canadian partnership and all members of that partnership jointly elect, then property transferred to the partnership may be transferred on a rollover basis. This means that the property can be transferred at elected values (usually tax values), rather than at the fair market values that must be used in the absence of a rollover provision. This rule applies both to persons who are existing partners, as well as to persons who become partners by contributing property to the partnership.

18-108.   ITA 97(2) indicates that, for this type of transfer, the ITA 85(1) rules apply. The ITA 85(1) rules are generally applicable to transfers of property to a corporation and are discussed in detail in Chapter 16. There are, however, some differences in the application of these rules when the transfer is to a partnership. The more notable of these differences are as follows:

• Real property inventory can be transferred to a partnership, but not to a corporation.

• When a transferor takes back consideration with a value less than that of the property transferred to a corporation, it may involve a gift to a related party. In the case of transfers to a partnership, the gift portion is added to the ACB of the partnership interest. As discussed in Chapter 16, if such a transfer was made to a corporation, it would usually result in double taxation of the gifted amount.

• When a transferor receives consideration in excess of the value of the property transferred to a corporation, the excess is subject to taxation. When this happens in conjunction with a transfer of property to a partnership, the excess is generally viewed as a drawing and is not subject to taxation.

18-109.   Differences between the elected amounts and consideration other than a partnership interest affect the ACB of the partnership interest.

Example   Janice Donovan will join the On-Off Partnership that provides interior lighting products. She plans to make an initial capital contribution of a parcel of land with an ACB of $100,000 and a fair market value of $250,000. She wishes to transfer the land at an elected value of $160,000. The existing members agree and file a joint election authorizing the transaction for $160,000. Janice has a choice between three different packages of consideration:

A. No cash.
B. Cash of $100,000.
C. Cash of $160,000.

Analysis   ITA 97(2) uses the transfer limits described within ITA 85. The basic acceptable transfer range is from the land's ACB of $100,000 to its fair market value of $250,000. While not applicable in this case, the elected value is also limited to the amount of non-partnership interest consideration received. The relevant values for the three Cases are as follows:

Case	ACB Of Partnership Interest	Capital Gain
No Cash	$160,000	$60,000
Cash Of $100,000	$ 60,000	60,000
Cash Of $160,000	Nil	60,000

Exercise Eighteen - 10

Subject: Transfers From Partner To Partnership (With Rollover)

Samantha Floren is one of three equal partners in the SFL Partnership. During the current year, Samantha transfers land to the partnership as a capital contribution. She had acquired the land several years ago for $156,000. At the time of transfer, it is valued at $263,000. She would like to use any available rollover provision in order to minimize her current taxes. Assuming the appropriate rollover provision is used, what are the tax consequences of this transfer?

End of Exercise. Solution available in Study Guide.

Partnership Property Transferred To A New Partnership

18-110.   A partnership may be dissolved in a number of situations. Included would be the addition or retirement of partners in cases where the partnership agreement does not provide for the continuation of the partnership. The dissolution of a partnership is considered to be a disposition of partnership property and, in the absence of a rollover provision, would result in tax consequences to the partners. However, this treatment can be avoided if the partnership property is transferred to a new partnership.

18-111.   ITA 98(6) provides automatic (i.e., no election is required) rollover treatment where all of the property of a Canadian partnership that has ceased to exist is transferred to a new Canadian partnership. A further condition is that all of the members of the new partnership must have been members of the old partnership.

18-112.   While many rollover provisions provide tax free treatment by providing for a deemed disposition at the tax cost of the property, ITA 98(6) takes a different approach. This Subsection deems the old and new partnerships to be the same entity, with the result being that there is no disposition of the property and no tax consequences to the transferor. This means that the ITA 98(6) rollover involves fewer complications than would be found in most rollover applications.

18-113.   It is important to note that, while all of the members of the new partnership have to have been members of the old partnership, not all of the members of the old partnership have to become members of the new partnership. This rollover is typically used when there is no continuity provision in place, and an existing partner retires.

18-114.   The retirement of a partner usually involves distributing some of the partnership property to the retiring partner. This makes it impossible to fully comply with the requirement of ITA 98(6) that all of the property of the old partnership be transferred. This problem was resolved by IT-338R2, "Partnership Interests - Effects On Adjusted Cost Base Resulting From The Admission Or Retirement Of A Partner", which states that all of the property of the old partnership is considered to mean all the property after the settlement of a retired partner's interest. While IT-338R2 has been archived, it would appear that this guidance is still applicable.

Partnership Property Transferred To A Sole Proprietorship

18-115.   This rollover applies automatically where a Canadian partnership ceases to exist and, within three months of the cessation date, one of the partners continues to carry on the partnership business as a sole proprietor. This rollover treatment is provided for partnership property distributed to the proprietor and, in general, ensures that there are no tax consequences associated with the disposition of that proprietor's partnership interest.

18-116.   There is an exception in situations where the tax cost of partnership property received by the proprietor exceeds the ACB of his or her partnership interest. In this case, there will be a capital gain.   Alternatively, if the ACB of the proprietor's partnership interest exceeds the tax cost of partnership property received by the proprietor, the rules allow the tax cost of non-depreciable partnership property to be increased to reflect this difference.

18-117.   This rollover typically applies where one of the partners in a two-person partnership retires or dies, leaving the remaining person to continue the business. As a partnership must have at least two partners, there is no possibility of the partnership continuing. Note, however, that the rollover only applies to the partner who continues the business. A retiring partner will have a disposition at fair market value with the usual tax consequences associated with such a disposition.

Partnership Property Transferred To A Corporation

18-118.   The decision to convert a partnership to a corporation, or to incorporate a partnership, generally arises when a partnership that has realized losses in its initial years becomes profitable. Prior to that time, the partnership form is useful as it allows the partners to use the partnership losses to offset their income from other sources.   Once the partnership has become profitable, corporate status may be preferred because of the availability of the small business deduction, the possibility of deferring taxes on income retained within the corporation, or the desire to split income with other related persons.

18-119.   The process of incorporating a partnership on a tax deferred basis generally requires two rollovers, ITA 85(2) and ITA 85(3). Under ITA 85(2), eligible partnership property is transferred to a taxable Canadian corporation for either shares or a combination of shares and other consideration. The transfer takes place at elected values which can include the tax cost of the property, thereby avoiding tax consequences to the partnership. This rollover treatment is only available if the corporation and all the partners jointly elect rollover treatment.

18-120.   At this point, the partnership is holding shares in the corporation and the partners are continuing to hold their partnership interests. ITA 85(3) then provides for a transfer at tax values of the partnership's holding of the corporation's shares to the partners in return for their partnership interests. This is accompanied by a wind-up of the partnership.

18-121.   If the following conditions are met, the ITA 85(3) rollover treatment is automatic, with no election required:

- The partnership must have disposed of property to a taxable Canadian corporation under ITA 85(2).
- The partnership must be wound up within 60 days of the disposition of its property to the corporation.
- Immediately before the partnership is wound up, the only property it holds is money or property received from the corporation as a result of the application of ITA 85(2).

18-122.   The winding-up of a partnership usually requires the distribution of all partnership property, the settlement of partnership obligations, as well as certain provincial formalities such as de-registration.

18-123.   These rules are designed to provide a tax free means of incorporating a partnership. However, tax consequences may arise in two particular instances. First, ITA 85(2) only applies to "eligible property" as defined in ITA 85(1.1). The major item that would not be included in this definition would be an inventory of real property (i.e., real property held for sale rather than use). If such non-eligible property is transferred from a partnership to a corporation, the transfer will be at fair market value, resulting in the usual tax consequences.

18-124.   A second situation in which the incorporation of a partnership may result in tax consequences would arise when a partner receives consideration in excess of the ACB of his partnership interest. While this may result in a capital gain, it can be avoided with the proper use of the ITA 85(3) rollover provision.

Example   Danielle and Christine are equal partners in the Flag Partnership. The recent success of the business has led to a decision to incorporate. The only asset Flag owns is an inventory of flags that cost $50,000, but is currently worth $200,000. The ACB of each partner's partnership interest is $34,000. The corporation will issue only common shares as consideration for the acquisition of the flag inventory.

Analysis   Danielle, Christine, and the corporation will jointly elect to transfer the inventory from the Flag Partnership at its tax cost of $50,000. Flag will be deemed to have disposed of the inventory for $50,000 and the corporation will be considered to have acquired the inventory for $50,000. No tax consequences will arise on the disposition. Flag Partnership will receive common shares of the corporation that will have an ACB and PUC of $50,000. At this point, Flag Partnership owns shares of the corporation and the corporation owns the inventory.

When the Flag Partnership distributes the shares to Danielle and Christine, the following tax consequences will arise:

- The Flag Partnership will be considered to have disposed of the shares for their tax cost of $50,000, resulting in no tax consequences.
- Each partner will be considered to have acquired the shares for an amount equal to the ACB of her partnership interest ($34,000).
- Each partner will be considered to have disposed of her partnership interest for the cost of the shares acquired from the partnership ($34,000). As a result, there is no capital gain or loss.

We suggest you work Self Study Problem Eighteen-8 at this point.

Specified Investment Flow Through Partnerships

18-125.   Because partnerships are not taxable entities, income is flowed through such structures without income taxes being assessed at the partnership level. As we shall see in Chapter 19, trusts are also "flow-through" entities. That is, even though trusts are taxable entities for income tax purposes, if all of their income is distributed to beneficiaries, no taxes will be paid at the trust level.

18-126. Until 2011, this flow-through feature of partnerships and trusts resulted in the conversion of a large number of business entities into publicly traded partnerships and trusts. As the government viewed this development as a significant form of tax avoidance, legislation was introduced which designated most of these publicly traded entities as specified invest-ment flow through partnerships and trusts (SIFTs). The legislation was such that it made SIFTs sufficiently unattractive that they have largely disappeared (as noted in Chapter 7, real estate partnerships and trusts were exempted from these rules). Given that SIFTs are now fairly rare, we will not continue to provide coverage of these entities in *Canadian Tax Principles*.

Key Terms Used In This Chapter

18-127. The following is a list of the key terms used in this Chapter. These terms, and their meanings, are compiled in the Glossary Of Key Terms located at the back of the separate paper Study Guide.

At-Risk Amount	Limited Liability Partnership
At-Risk Rules	Limited Partner
Canadian Partnership	Limited Partnership
Co-Ownership	Limited Partnership Loss
Deeming Rule	"Negative" Adjusted Cost Base
General Partner	Partner
General Partnership	Partnership
Joint Tenancy	Partnership Interest
Joint Venture	Syndicates
Limited Liability	Tenancy In Common

References

18-128. For more detailed study of the material in this Chapter, we refer you to the following:

ITA 40(3)	Negative ACB
ITA 53(1)(e)	Addition To Cost Base Of An Interest In A Partnership
ITA 53(2)(c)	Deduction From Cost Base Of An Interest In A Partnership
ITA 85(2)	Transfer Of Property To Corporation From Partnership
ITA 85(3)	Where Partnership Wound Up
ITA 96	General Rules (Partnerships And Their Members)
ITA 97	Contribution Of Property To Partnership
ITA 98	Disposition Of Partnership Property
ITA 99	Fiscal Period Of Terminated Partnership
ITA 100	Disposition Of An Interest in a Partnership
ITA 102	Definition Of "Canadian Partnership"
ITA 103	Agreement To Share Income
IT-81R	Partnerships - Income Of Non-Resident Partners
IT-90	What Is A Partnership?
IT-231R2	Partnerships - Partners Not Dealing At Arm's Length
IT-242R	Retired Partners
IT-278R2	Death Of A Partner Or Of A Retired Partner
IT-378R	Winding Up Of A Partnership
IT-413R	Election By Members Of A Partnership Under Subsection 97(2)
IT-457R	Election By Professionals To Exclude Work In Progress From Income
IT-471R	Merger Of Partnerships
T4068	Guide for the T5013 Partnership Information Return

Problems For Self Study

(The solutions for these problems can be found in the separate Study Guide.)

Self Study Problem Eighteen - 1 (Existence Of Partnership)

Wayout Ltd. is a company that has operated a vinyl record business for years. Wayout owns three buildings in Toronto and operates a store in each building. The management always believed that records would make a comeback and refused to introduce CD's. As a result, Wayout Ltd. is expected to declare bankruptcy within the next few months. If Wayout Ltd. sold all of its property, significant tax losses would result. As Wayout has had no profits for years, the losses cannot be used as a carry back. Wayout's accountant recommends the following plan to stave off bankruptcy:

1. A general partnership will be formed and a partnership agreement written up with Wayout Ltd. as the managing partner.

2. The partnership agreement will provide the following:

    * the required capital contributions by each partner;
    * the profit/loss sharing ratios (1 percent to Wayout and 99 percent split equally among the other investors);
    * the appointing of accountants to file necessary partnership tax returns;
    * that each partner will have a say in the management;
    * that the property contributed by Wayout Ltd. is partnership property; and
    * that the partnership will be dissolved upon the final sale of partnership property.

3. Wayout Ltd. will contribute all of the property from two of its locations, including the land and buildings. The property will be transferred on a rollover basis.

4. Ninety-nine individual Canadian investors will each contribute $10,000 to the partnership.

If this plan is put into place, Wayout Ltd. will have access to almost $1 million of new capital to deal with creditors and invest in the remaining store. In addition, it is anticipated that each investor will be allocated $50,000 in losses. The estimated tax savings, assuming a marginal tax rate of 40 percent, will be $20,000.

Required: Will a valid partnership be created? Analyze the facts using the three elements of a partnership. Ignore other income tax implications.

Self Study Problem Eighteen - 2 (Partnership Vs. Joint Venture)

Mr. Marrazzo owns an undeveloped parcel of land in Suburbia. He purchased the land four years ago with the intention of developing residential lots. The land cost $400,000 and has a fair market value of $1,300,000 on December 1, 2013.

Banks are reluctant to lend for real estate development, so Mr. Marrazzo has been unsuccessful in obtaining the $1,200,000 financing that is required for site servicing costs. Digger Inc., a heavy equipment supplier, agrees to provide the required financing on an interest-free basis for 50 percent of the profits from the sale of the lots.

Mr. Marrazzo proceeds with his plan in 2013. Site servicing costs during 2014 total $1,200,000. All the lots are sold before December 31, 2014 for proceeds of $4,400,000.

The preceding events could have been organized under several different scenarios. Two possibilities are as follows:

> **Case A**   A partnership is created with Digger Inc. on December 1, 2013. Mr. Marrazzo transfers the land to the partnership under the provisions of ITA 97(2) in order to defer the accrued gain on the land. The partnership agreement specifies that Mr. Marrazzo is entitled to 100 percent of the gain that has accrued on the property up to December 1, 2013 and 50 percent of any subsequent gains.

Case B   He enters into a joint venture agreement with Digger Inc. on December 1, 2013. He transfers the property to Digger Inc. on December 1, 2013. Digger Inc. will provide Mr. Marrazzo with 50 percent of the profits resulting from the sale of the land.

Required:

A. Calculate the amount that will be added to Mr. Marrazzo's Net Income For Tax Purposes in 2013 and 2014 for Case A and Case B and compare the results.

B. Calculate the adjusted cost base of the partnership interest for both Mr. Marrazzo and Digger Inc. on December 31, 2014 and January 1, 2015.

Self Study Problem Eighteen - 3 (Partnership Income Allocation)

Mr. Baker and Mr. Caldwell are members of a partnership that provides accounting services. The Partnership's Income Statement for the year ending December 31, 2013 is as follows:

Baker And Caldwell
Partnership Income Statement
Year Ending December 31, 2013

Fees Received In Cash		$403,000
Capital Gains On Temporary Holdings Of Canadian Securities		14,000
Eligible Dividends Received From Canadian Corporations		48,000
Total Revenues		$465,000
Less Expenses:		
Salaries And Wages	($197,000)	
Rent On Office Space	(19,200)	
Interest On Bank Loans	(5,800)	
Amortization - Office Furniture And Equipment	(12,500)	
General Office Expenses	(28,400)	
Charitable Donations	(7,200)	
Costs Of Attending Convention	(2,800)	(272,900)
Net Income (Accounting Values)		$192,100

Other Information:

1. The partnership agreement calls for all income and losses to be allocated equally to the two partners.

2. The Salaries And Wages in the preceding Income Statement include a payment of $44,000 to each of the two partners.

3. The convention costs were for the two partners to attend the annual conference of the Canadian Institute Of Certified General Management Accountants.

4. Both partners use their personal vehicles for business purposes and pay their own operating expenses. Mr. Caldwell's car cost $24,000 and, at the beginning of the current year, it had a UCC of $13,500. His operating expenses for the year were $4,000, for a total of 48,000 kilometers driven. Only 25 percent of these kilometers were for personal use.

5. At the beginning of the current fiscal year, the partnership had fees receivable from clients of $27,000. At the end of the year, the corresponding balance was $56,000. The partners have not elected under ITA 34 to use the billed basis of accounting.

6. At the beginning of the year, the UCC of the office furniture was $26,000. During 2013, computer equipment was purchased for $8,500. Prior to this time, all computer equipment was leased.

Required: Calculate the minimum Net Income For Tax Purposes for Mr. Caldwell for 2013. Include in the calculation Mr. Caldwell's share of Net Business Income from the partnership. Also indicate other amounts that would be allocated to Mr. Caldwell by the partnership, as well as any credits against federal Tax Payable that would result from these allocations. Ignore GST and PST considerations.

Self Study Problem Eighteen - 4 (Partnership Income Allocation)

Jennifer, Christine, and Danny recently graduated from college and began a coffee bean roasting business called the Canadian Coffee Club ("CCC") that they operate as a partnership. They share profits and losses equally.

Their accountant has prepared the following statement for the year ending December 31, 2013.

Canadian Coffee Club
Partnership Income Statement
Year Ending December 31, 2013

Gross Business Revenues		$86,000
Operating Expenses	($31,500)	
Administrative Expenses	(17,300)	(48,800)
Net Income From Coffee Roasting Business		$ 37,200

Other Information:

1. Included in operating and administrative expenses are the following:

    - $2,400 of salaries to each of the three partners.

    - $3,300 of interest to Christine ($1,300 relates to a bona fide loan she made to CCC and the remaining $2,000 relates to her capital contribution).

    - $1,100 paid to Danny for personal expenses.

    - $1,700 to Jennifer as a reimbursement of CCC expenses.

    - $1,000 of charitable donations

    - $1,450 of accounting amortization.

2. The partnership is entitled to maximum CCA of $2,000.

3. In addition to the business results recorded in the accounting income statement, the partnership had the following additional amounts of 2013 income:

• Eligible Dividends Received	$3,440
• Gain On Sale Of Common Shares	6,000

    The shares that were sold during 2013 had an adjusted cost base of $11,000. They were sold for $17,000.

Required:

A. Calculate the amounts of income from the partnership that would be included in the Net Income For Tax Purposes of each of the partners.

B. Indicate the amount of any federal tax credits that would be available to the partners as a result of their interest in the partnership.

Self Study Problem Eighteen - 5
(Partnership Income And Sale Of Partnership Interest)

Mark and Matt Doan are brothers and professional engineers. In early 2012 they formed a partnership in order to provide professional engineering services. When the partnership was formed each of the brothers made a capital contribution of $280,000 in cash. They have agreed to share all profits and losses equally.

During the partnership taxation year ending December 31, 2012, the partnership had Net Income For Tax Purposes of $180,000, all of which was business income. The partnership made no charitable donations in 2012. During 2012, Mark withdrew $75,000 in partnership funds, while Matt's drawings were only $23,000.

The partnership's 2013 Income Statement, prepared in accordance with generally accepted accounting principles, is as follows:

Income Statement
Mark And Matt Doan Partnership
Year Ending December 31, 2013

Revenues		$708,000
Operating Expenses:		
Rent	($48,000)	
Amortization Expense (Note 1)	(12,000)	
Office Salaries	(41,000)	
General Office Costs	(18,000)	
Meals And Entertainment	(23,000)	
Charitable Donations	(17,000)	(159,000)
Operating Income		$549,000
Other Income:		
Gain On Sale Of Investments (Note 2)	$14,000	
Eligible Dividends Received From Canadian Corporations	8,000	22,000
Net Income		$571,000

Note 1 Maximum 2013 CCA, which the partners intend to deduct, is $19,000.

Note 2 The gain resulted from the sale of temporary investments. The investments had an adjusted cost base of $60,000 and were sold for $74,000.

Other Information

1. During 2013, Mark had drawings of $190,000 while Matt had drawings of $290,000.

2. During 2013 Matt's only income other than amounts related to owning the partnership, was eligible dividends received from Canadian companies of $34,000. Assume that other than credits related to partnership allocations and the eligible dividends he received personally, Matt's only tax credit was his basic personal credit.

3. On January 1, 2014, Matt sells his interest in the partnership to an arm's length individual for $535,000.

Required: Calculate Matt's federal Tax Payable for the year ending December 31, 2013. In addition, determine the taxable capital gain or allowable capital loss that would result from Matt's sale of his partnership interest. Ignore any CPP implications with respect to self-employment income.

Self Study Problem Eighteen - 6 (Withdrawal Of A Partner)

On March 1, 2011, John Olson, his son Fred Olson, and Eric Beam form a partnership to provide accounting and tax services. The partners each contribute $225,000 and agree that all income and losses are to be shared equally. The fiscal year for the partnership is established to end on December 31.

For the period March 1, 2011 to December 31, 2013, the following information is available:

1. The partnership earned net business income of $195,000.

2. The partnership realized a capital gain of $66,000 (this amount is not included in the net business income figure).

3. The partnership made a number of charitable donations during the period. The total amount involved was $12,000, and this total was allocated equally to each of the three partners (this amount is not included in the net business income figure).

4. During this period, Eric Beam made withdrawals from the partnership totaling $43,000.

5. Additional capital was required to expand the operations of the office and, as a consequence, each partner contributed an additional $54,000 in cash.

Eric Beam decided to withdraw from the partnership effective January 1, 2014. After some negotiations, each of the other partners agreed to pay him $177,500 in cash for one-half of his interest in the partnership, a total of $355,000. John's payments are made on February 1, 2014, and Fred pays one month later, on March 1. The partnership has net business income of $15,000 in both January and February.

Eric Beam incurred legal and accounting fees in conjunction with this transaction totaling $1,800.

Required:

A. Calculate the adjusted cost base of Eric Beam's partnership interest as of January 1, 2014.

B. Determine the amount of Eric Beam's gain or loss on the disposition of his partnership interest. Explain how this amount, and any other amounts related to the partnership, will be taxed in his hands during 2014.

C. Indicate how the adjusted cost base of each partner's interest will be affected by the withdrawal of Eric Beam from the partnership.

Self Study Problem Eighteen - 7 (Limited Partnership)

Yoho Airways became a limited partner in the new Frontier Holidays Partnership on January 1, 2013. The partnership agreement required a payment of $50,000 for a 10 percent interest in the Partnership. Of this amount, $30,000 was paid in cash in 2013, with the remainder paid in January, 2014. Yoho's share of all income and losses of the Frontier Holidays Partnership is 10 percent.

Frontier experienced a $400,000 loss in 2013, a $70,000 loss in 2014, followed by no income or loss in 2015. In each of the years under consideration, Yoho Airways has sufficient income from other sources to be able to use any Frontier Holidays Partnership losses that are deductible.

Required: For each of 2013, 2014 and 2015, calculate the following for Yoho Airways:

- The adjusted cost base at the end of the year.
- The at-risk amount.
- The limited partnership income (loss) for the year.
- The deductible income (loss) for the year.
- The limited partnership loss carry forward at the end of the year.

Self Study Problem Eighteen - 8
(Partnership Winding-Up & Transfer To Corporation)

A number of years ago, Jack Porter, Cid Quinn, and Norman Roberts established the Porter, Quinn, and Roberts Partnership. At the time the partnership was formed, each of the partners invested $350,000 in cash. The partnership agreement calls for all income and losses to be shared equally. The fiscal year of the partnership ends on December 31.

On January 1 of the current year, the adjusted cost base of the interests of the three partners is as follows:

Jack Porter	$ 382,000
Cid Quinn	526,000
Norman Roberts	726,000
Total	$1,634,000

The total tax cost of the net assets of the partnership is equal to the $1,634,000 adjusted cost base of the partnership interests. On January 2 of the current year, the net assets of the partnership are transferred to a corporation under the provisions of ITA 85(2). The elected values are equal to the tax costs of the individual assets and liabilities. In return, the corporation provides the following consideration to the partnership:

Cash	$ 722,000
Preferred Shares (At Fair Market Value)	540,000
Common Shares (At Fair Market Value)	1,080,000
Total Consideration	$2,342,000

On February 20 of the current year, the partners decide to wind up the partnership. Reflecting this decision, the consideration provided by the corporation is transferred to the individual partners. Under the terms of the partnership agreement, they receive the following amounts:

	Porter	Quinn	Roberts	Total
Cash	$ 78,000	$222,000	$422,000	$ 722,000
Preferred Shares	180,000	180,000	180,000	540,000
Common Shares	360,000	360,000	360,000	1,080,000
Total	$618,000	$762,000	$962,000	$2,342,000

Required:

A. Determine the adjusted cost base of each of the assets received by the partners as a result of the transfer of partnership assets to the corporation.

B. Calculate the capital gain or loss for each partner resulting from the transfer of the consideration received by the partnership to the partners in return for the partnership interest.

Assignment Problems

(The solutions for these problems are only available in the solutions manual that has been provided to your instructor.)

Assignment Problem Eighteen - 1 (Existence Of Partnership)

Barry and Lance Booker are brothers who live in the same New Brunswick community. Barry is an accountant who specializes in advising small businesses. Lance has held various jobs in restaurants over the last few years. However, he is currently between jobs.

Assignment Problems

As a result of information he has accumulated while working with his accounting clients, Barry has started a new business involving catering services. To this end, he has acquired a building, furniture, and equipment. He has also registered the business and opened up a bank account under his own name. Barry spends a few hours each day managing the business.

As he is aware of Lance's financial difficulties, he has decided to treat his brother as a partner in this business, sharing profits on a 50:50 basis when filing their annual income tax returns. There is no formal partnership agreement.

Required: In the following two **independent** Cases, determine whether a partnership exists.

A.   Lance's involvement with the business consists of helping Barry pick out furniture and equipment and occasionally taking messages when Barry is out of town. It appears that the business will be consistently profitable.

B.   Lance does all the accounting, payroll and invoicing for the business. He also does most of the ordering and is responsible for paying the suppliers. It is unlikely that the business will be profitable in its first year of operation.

Assignment Problem Eighteen - 2 (Existence Of Partnership)

Mr. Poliacik joined Mr. Ewing's practice by entering into a business association with Mr. Ewing. They operated under the name " Ewing/Poliacik". Mr. Poliacik made no capital contribution on joining.

Both individuals were lawyers. Mr. Poliacik's specialty was litigation. Mr. Ewing was involved in non-litigation matters.

An agreement was signed, but it never referred to the individuals as partners or the association as a partnership. When asked why they did not refer to themselves as partners, Mr. Poliacik stated that they did not know each other well enough to accept the risks of partnership. The agreement stated that all fees billed by each individual belonged to that individual.

Both parties agreed to open a combined general and trust bank account. Both parties had signing authority on the general account, although Mr. Poliacik's authority was limited to client disbursements only. Mr. Ewing had sole signing authority on the trust account. The accounts did not indicate that they were registered to a partnership.

Mr. Poliacik's fees were to be split based on a graduated scale. The first $100,000 was to be split 50:50, then 60:40 on the next $25,000, 80:20 on the next $25,000 and 90:10 thereafter. The larger percentage went to Mr. Poliacik. In addition, Mr. Poliacik was entitled to 10 percent of fees billed by Mr. Ewing to clients introduced by Mr. Poliacik.

Mr. Ewing agreed to be 100 percent liable for office expenses and bookkeeping services. Mr. Poliacik's share of the office operating expenses was $62,500 in the first year. This amount would be adjusted in the future as the expenses increased. Mr. Poliacik was not entitled to the 10 percent finder's fee from Mr. Ewing until his share of the annual expenses had been paid.

Mr. Poliacik was required to pay his own income taxes, CPP, employer health tax and professional insurance.

There were no income tax filings as partners. The combined business was not registered for GST purposes. There were no filings with the law society indicating that Mr. Poliacik and Mr. Ewing were partners.

Required: Determine whether the business association is a partnership. [Adapted from Poliacik (TCC) 1999 DTC 3482]

Assignment Problem Eighteen - 3 (Partnership Vs. Joint Venture)

Chantale Bergeron is a real estate agent who had dreamed of becoming a real estate developer for a long time. In 2010, she received a substantial inheritance and purchased a tract of land with the intention of developing a group of residential lots. She paid $1,200,000 for the land which she had secretly learned from contacts would soon be adjacent to a new highway exit.

As Chantale had spent her inheritance purchasing the land and had no track record in the development business, she had difficulty in finding financing for the required $700,000 in site servicing costs. She finally located a developer, Elise Ltd. who was willing to provide the required $700,000 on an interest free basis in return for 40 percent of the profit resulting from the sale of the lots.

By December 31, 2013, it was estimated that the land's fair market value had increased to $2,000,000 because of the opening of the highway exit. During 2014, the sites are developed, with the servicing costs coming in at the estimated $700,000. All of the lots are sold prior to December 31, 2014 for total proceeds of $3,700,000.

> **Case A**   On December 31, 2013, Chantale and Elise Ltd. enter into a joint venture agreement. Chantale transfers the land to Elise Ltd. At the end of 2014, Elise Ltd. provides Chantale with 60 percent of the profits resulting from the development and the sale of the lots.

> **Case B**   On December 31, 2013, Chantale and Elise Ltd. form a partnership to develop the lots. Chantale transfers the land to the partnership using the ITA 97(2) rollover provision to defer the gain on the transfer. The partnership agreement specifies that Chantale is entitled to all of the deferred gain on the land transfer at December 31, 2013, as well as 60 percent of the profits resulting from the sale of the lots.

Required:

A. Calculate the amount that will be added to Chantale's Net Income For Tax Purposes in 2013 and 2014 for Case A and Case B and compare the results.

B. Calculate the adjusted cost base of the partnership interest for both Chantale and Elise Ltd. on December 31, 2014 and January 1, 2015.

Assignment Problem Eighteen - 4 (Partnership Income Allocation)

Sam and Allen Foster are both Certified General Management Accountants. Since acquiring their professional designations, they have both worked for a large firm of Certified General Management Accountants. However, at the beginning of 2013, they have decided to leave this firm and form a two man partnership specializing in tax and accounting work for owner-managed corporations.

The agreement for the new partnership calls for business income to be shared equally. In addition, charitable contributions will be allocated equally to the two brothers. However, as Allen has contributed most of the capital for the new partnership, he will receive 80 percent of any capital gains or dividends received by the partnership.

Other Information:

1. The brothers plan to deduct the maximum CCA for tax purposes which is $41,000.

2. The brothers have decided to use the ITA 34 election to report Taxable Income on a billed basis. The revenues in the Accounting Net Income include $56,000 in unbilled work-in-process. As this is their first year of operation, there was no unbilled work-in-process balance on January 1.

For the year ending December 31, 2013, their results, prepared on a GAAP basis, are as follows:

Sam And Allen Foster
Partnership Income Statement
Year Ending December 31, 2013

Revenues		$965,000
Expenses:		
Salaries To Staff	($114,000)	
Office Rent	(82,000)	
Office Supplies	(30,000)	
Amortization	(32,000)	
Business Meals And Entertainment	(14,000)	
Charitable Donations	(13,000)	
Salary To Sam	(150,000)	
Salary To Allen	(150,000)	(585,000)
Net Business Income		$380,000
Other Income:		
Capital Gains	$ 8,000	
Eligible Dividends Received	16,000	24,000
Accounting Net Income		$404,000

Required:

A. Calculate the amounts of income from the partnership that would be included in the Net Income For Tax Purposes of each of the two brothers.

B. Indicate the amount of any federal tax credits that would be available to the two brothers as a result of their interest in the partnership.

Assignment Problem Eighteen - 5 (Partnership Income And ACB)

Two of your university friends, who became lawyers, left the firms where they were employed, and set up their own practice on January 1, 2013. They started the practice by contributing $10,000 working capital each and decided to split the profits equally. They pay themselves equal salaries that they withdraw throughout the year. Their bookkeeper has prepared the following financial statements:

Friends Forever Law Practice
Balance Sheet
As At December 31, 2013

Cash	$ 2,000
Accounts Receivable	30,000
Work In Progress	25,000
Computer Hardware (At Cost)	10,000
Computer Applications Software (At Cost)	8,000
Total Assets	$75,000
Accounts Payable	$15,000
Initial Partner Capital	20,000
Income For The Period	40,000
Total Equities	$75,000

Friends Forever Law Practice
Income Statement
For The Year Ending December 31, 2013

Revenues	$230,000
Meals And Entertainment	$ 6,000
Office Supplies	4,000
Partners' Salaries	130,000
Rent	24,000
Secretary's Salary	26,000
Total Expenses	$190,000
Income For The Period (Accounting Values)	$ 40,000

The work in progress represents work done by the lawyers at their standard charge rate that has not been billed to clients at the year end.

Required:

A. Your friends have come to you to determine the minimum amount that they must include in their 2013 tax returns as business income from the partnership.

B. They would also like to know if there are any partnership related expenses that they may have incurred personally that they can deduct on their 2013 tax return.

C. Compute the ACB of each partner's partnership interest at December 31, 2013 and January 1, 2014.

Your answers should ignore GST and PST considerations.

Assignment Problem Eighteen - 6
(Partnership Income And Sale Of Partnership Interest)

Don and Derek Duffy are brothers and lawyers. While they have worked independently for several years, on January 1, 2012, they have decided to form a partnership. On January 1, 2012, they each make a capital contribution of $350,000 in cash. Because Don's experience is in a more lucrative area of law, he is to receive 60 percent of all partnership income, with Derek receiving the remaining 40 percent. Capital gains realized by the partnership, dividends received by the partnership and charitable donations will be shared equally.

During the partnership taxation year ending December 31, 2012, the partnership has net business income for tax purposes of $335,000. The partnership had no capital gains or losses or dividend income during 2012. The partnership made no charitable donations in 2012. During this taxation year, Don withdrew $130,000, while Derek withdrew $102,000.

Other Information

1. The revenues in the accounting based Income Statement include $105,000 in unbilled work in progress. There was no unbilled work in progress at the end of the previous year. The brothers will use the ITA 34 election to record the partnership income on a billed basis.

2. During 2013, Don had drawings of $310,000 while Derek had drawings of $242,000.

3. During 2013, Don's only income was from the partnership. Assume that other than credits related to partnership allocations, Don's only tax credit was his basic personal credit.

4. On January 1, 2014, Don sells his interest in the partnership to an arm's length individual for $643,000.

5. The partnership's 2013 Income Statement, prepared in accordance with generally accepted accounting principles, is as follows:

Income Statement
Derek And Don Duffy Partnership
Year Ending December 31, 2013

Revenues		$823,000
Operating Expenses:		
Rent	($95,000)	
Amortization Expense (Note 1)	(22,000)	
Office Salaries	(46,000)	
General Office Costs	(42,000)	
Meals And Entertainment	(16,000)	
Charitable Donations	(12,000)	(233,000)
Operating Income		$590,000
Other Income:		
Gain On Sale Of Investments (Note 2)	$26,000	
Eligible Dividends Received From		
Canadian Corporations	22,000	48,000
Net Income		$638,000

Note 1 Maximum 2013 CCA, which the partners intend to deduct, is $35,000.

Note 2 The gain resulted from the sale of temporary investments. The investments had an adjusted cost base of $57,000 and were sold for $83,000.

Required: Calculate Don's federal Tax Payable for the year ending December 31, 2013. In addition, determine the taxable capital gain or allowable capital loss that would result from Don's sale of his partnership interest. Ignore any CPP implications with respect to self-employment income.

Assignment Problem Eighteen - 7 (Withdrawal Of A Partner)

On May 1, 2011, Susan Field, Christine Black, and John Henderson form a partnership to provide management consulting services. The partners each contribute $350,000 and agree that all income and losses are to be shared equally. The fiscal year for the partnership is established to end on December 31.

For the period May 1, 2011 to December 31, 2013, the following information is available:

• The partnership earned net business income of $273,000.

• The partnership realized a $42,000 capital gain (this amount is not included in the net business income figure).

• During 2013, the partnership made a number of charitable donations. The total amount involved was $9,000, and this total was allocated equally to each of the three partners (this amount is not included in the net business income figure).

• During this period, John Henderson made withdrawals from the partnership totaling $81,000.

• Additional capital was required to expand the operations of the office and, as a consequence, each partner contributed an additional $100,000 in cash.

John Henderson decided to withdraw from the partnership effective January 1, 2014. After some negotiations, each of the other partners agreed to pay him $275,000 in cash for one-half of his interest in the partnership, a total of $550,000. The payments are made on January 31, 2014. The partnership has net business income of $21,000 in January, 2014.

John incurred legal and accounting fees in conjunction with this transaction totaling $2,500.

Required:

A. Calculate the adjusted cost base of John Henderson's partnership interest as of January 1, 2014.

B. Determine the amount of John Henderson's gain or loss on the disposition of his partnership interest. Explain how this amount, and any other amounts related to the partnership, will be taxed in his hands during 2014.

C. Indicate how the adjusted cost base of each partner's interest will be affected by the withdrawal of John Henderson from the partnership.

Assignment Problem Eighteen - 8 (Limited Partnership)

On January 1, 2013, Bob Billions acquires a 12 percent limited partner interest in the Who-Do-You-Trust Partnership. The total cost of the interest is $65,000, with $5,000 being paid in cash. A $60,000 interest-free promissory note is signed for the balance. The note is to be paid in 6 payments of $10,000 each. Payments are due on December 1 of each year, commencing in 2013.

As part of the agreement, the general partner is obligated to acquire Bob's interest on December 31, 2018 for $5,000 more than its fair market value at that time.

Bob's share of all of the income and losses of the Who-Do-You-Trust Partnership is 12 percent.

For the year ending December 31, 2013, the Partnership had the following sources of income and loss:

Business Loss	($510,000)
Interest Income	63,000
Eligible Dividends Received From Canadian Corporations	31,000
Capital Gains	53,000

Required: Calculate the following amounts for Bob's investment in the Who-Do-You-Trust Partnership for 2013:

- The at-risk amount on December 31, 2013.
- The limited partnership income (loss) for the year.
- The deductible loss for the year.
- The limited partnership loss carry forward at the end of the year.
- The adjusted cost base on December 31, 2013 and January 1, 2014.
- The at-risk amount on January 1, 2014.

Assignment Problem Eighteen - 9
(Partnership Winding-Up & Transfer To Corporation)

A number of years ago, Jack Howard, Bud Jones, and Dwight Delaney established the Howard, Jones, and Delaney Partnership. At the time the partnership was formed, each of the partners invested $600,000 in cash. The partnership agreement calls for all income and losses to be shared equally. The fiscal year of the partnership ends on December 31.

On January 1 of the current year, the adjusted cost base of the partnership interests that are applicable to the three partners are as follows:

Jack Howard	$1,173,000
Bud Jones	930,000
Dwight Delaney	756,000
Total	$2,859,000

The total tax cost of the net assets of the partnership is equal to the $2,859,000 adjusted cost base of the partnership interests. On January 2 of the current year, the net assets of the partnership are transferred to a corporation under the provisions of ITA 85(2). The elected values are equal to the tax costs of the individual assets and liabilities. In return, the corporation provides the following consideration to the partnership:

Cash	$1,200,000
Preferred Shares (At Fair Market Value)	900,000
Common Shares (At Fair Market Value)	1,800,000
Total Consideration	$3,900,000

The partnership will be liquidated within 60 days of the ITA 85(2) rollover and property received from the corporation by the partnership will be transferred to the three partners in accordance with ITA 85(3). Under the terms of the partnership agreement, they receive the following amounts:

	Howard	Jones	Delaney	Total
Cash	$ 620,000	$ 377,000	$ 203,000	$1,200,000
Preferred Shares	300,000	300,000	300,000	900,000
Common Shares	600,000	600,000	600,000	1,800,000
Total	$1,520,000	$1,277,000	$1,103,000	$3,900,000

Required:

A. Determine the adjusted cost base of each of the assets received by the partners as a result of the transfer of partnership assets to the corporation.

B. Calculate the capital gain or loss for each partner resulting from the transfer of the consideration received by the partnership to the partners in return for the partnership interest.

Assignment Problem Eighteen - 10 (Additional Business Income)

Note This problem involves knowledge of "additional business income" when the election of a non-calendar fiscal period is made. This material is covered in Chapter 6 of the text.

On April 1, 2010, Craig Cardinal and Don Kvill formed a partnership to teach small craft flying lessons. They elected to use a March 31 fiscal year end, to coincide with the end of the winter aircraft maintenance program and the beginning of the summer training schedule. The two partners share equally in the profits of the partnership.

In the partnership income calculation for their 2011 tax returns, the "additional business income" was calculated to be $42,200. During the year ending March 31, 2012, the partnership earned Taxable Income of $64,000 and the partners withdrew $26,000 each.

From April 1, 2012 to March 31, 2013, the partnership earned Taxable Income of $58,000 and the partners withdrew $20,000 each.

Required: Determine the minimum amount of partnership income that Craig Cardinal and Don Kvill will have to include in their personal tax returns for the years 2012 and 2013.

CHAPTER 19

Trusts And Estate Planning

Introduction

19-1.   As is noted in Chapter 1, the *Income Tax Act* recognizes three groups of taxpayers: individuals, corporations, and trusts. In previous Chapters we have given detailed consideration to the determination of Taxable Income and Tax Payable for both individuals and corporations. In this Chapter, we will turn our attention to how this process works in the case of trusts.

19-2.   Also in Chapter 1, we provide a brief introduction to tax planning, providing general descriptions of tax avoidance, tax deferral, and income splitting. In this Chapter we will find that trusts are one of the most powerful weapons in the tax planner's arsenal. They can provide a convenient and cost effective mechanism for splitting large amounts of property income among family members. Trusts can also be used to access the deferral and income splitting opportunities that are present in estate freeze transactions. In addition, they can play a significant role in many other tax and business planning arrangements.

19-3.   While trusts remain a very powerful tax planning tool, you should note that over the years, the Government has introduced various legislative changes which have made trusts more difficult to use for this purpose. This includes the introduction of the tax on split income (a.k.a., the kiddie tax), the elimination of the general preferred beneficiary election, trust migration rules, and various changes that affect offshore trusts.

19-4.   A further problem is that many tax professionals do not have a very complete understanding of how to use trusts. This probably reflects the fact that the implementation and maintenance of effective trust structures requires both legal and accounting training. In some cases, particularly those involving estates, some degree of knowledge of sociology, philosophy, conflict resolution, and religion could also be helpful.

19-5.   We have previously encountered trusts in this text. In Chapter 7, which deals with property income, we indicated that most mutual funds are organized as trusts. Also in that Chapter, we noted the use of real estate investment trusts (REITs). In Chapter 10, when we considered various types of retirement savings arrangements, we noted that most of these arrangements involve the use of trusts. Registered Pension Plans, Registered Retirement Savings Plans, Registered Retirement Income Funds, and Deferred Profit Sharing Plans, all involve assets being contributed to a trust.

19-6.   In this Chapter, we will not revisit the types of trusts that were considered in earlier Chapters. Rather, our focus in this Chapter will be on personal trusts that have been established by individuals as a part of a tax or estate planning scenario. This will include both trusts established during the lifetime of an individual, as well as trusts that arise as a consequence of the death of an individual. While trusts can be very important in tax planning arrangements that involve private corporations, we will not deal with this subject. In our view, the complexities involved in such arrangements go beyond the scope of this text.

19-7.   In our material in this Chapter on estate planning we will give specific attention to the use of trusts, but due to the importance of this subject, we will expand our coverage of estate planning to issues that go beyond the use of trusts. Particular attention will be given to general coverage of estate freeze transactions.

Basic Concepts

What Is A Personal Trust?

Legal Perspective

19-8.   From a legal perspective, a personal trust is a relationship that arises when a settlor transfers property to a trustee to hold and administer for the exclusive benefit of the beneficiaries. This relationship is depicted in Figure 19-1.

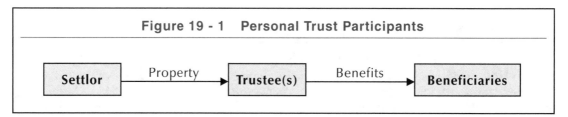

Figure 19 - 1   Personal Trust Participants

Settlor → Property → Trustee(s) → Benefits → Beneficiaries

19-9.   The settlor is the person who sets up the trust and makes the initial transfer of property to the trustee. The trustee is the individual or institution that holds formal legal title to that property, while the beneficiaries are persons who will benefit from the property that is held by the trustee. The beneficiaries can have an interest in the income from the property, the capital value of the property, or both.

19-10.   While each of these roles is separate in terms of its function in the trust arrangement, it is possible for more than one of the roles to be played by a single individual. A common example of this would be a father who is the settlor of a trust in favour of his children, but also serves as one of the trustees who holds the trust assets.

19-11.   A basic feature of trust arrangements is the separation of the legal and beneficial ownership of the transferred property. Outside of trust arrangements, the legal owner of a property is normally entitled to any benefits associated with owning the property. This is not the case here. While the trustee holds legal title to the property, all of the benefits will accrue to the persons who are specified as the beneficiaries of the trust.

19-12.   Note that the trust is not a separate entity, from a legal perspective. A trust cannot own property, cannot enter into contracts, and cannot be a defendant or plaintiff in a legal action. With respect to the transferred property, these rights and obligations belong to the trustee(s).

19-13.   Trusts are subject to provincial legislation and, as a consequence, the detailed rules will vary from province to province. One point to note, however, is that it is generally difficult to vary or revoke a trust. This is of particular importance in the case of deceased individuals. While the content of a will can be challenged by a disgruntled beneficiary and its intentions altered by a surviving spouse, this is a much more difficult process when assets are placed in a trust.

Tax Perspective

19-14.   While a trust is not a separate entity from a legal perspective, the *Income Tax Act* takes a different view. With respect to this issue, the *Act* states the following:

> **ITA 104(2)**   A trust shall, for the purposes of this Act, and without affecting the liability of the trustee or legal representative for that person's own income tax, be deemed to be in respect of the trust property an individual, ...

19-15.   By indicating that, with respect to trust property, a trust is deemed to be an individual, the *Act* gives trusts separate entity tax status. This means that there must be a determination of Taxable Income and Tax Payable for a trust, and that a trust will have to file a separate income tax return.

Trusts And Estates

19-16.   The dictionary contains several definitions of the term estate, the most general of which indicates that an estate consists of the property and possessions of any individual. However, as the term is used in the *Income Tax Act*, the meaning is more restrictive. In this context, the term estate refers to the property of a deceased person. Further, the *Act* uses the terms trust and estate as having the same meaning. This approach is indicated as follows:

> **ITA 104(1)**   In this Act, a reference to a trust or estate (in this subdivision referred to as a "trust") shall, ...

19-17.   This is a somewhat peculiar approach to terminology in that a trust is not the same as an estate, from a legal perspective. When an individual dies and bequeaths his property through a will, his estate will be administered by an executor. This executor will have responsibilities similar to those of a trustee. However, the beneficiary of a trust holds an equitable title to the trust property, while the trustee holds legal title. In contrast, the beneficiary of an estate does not have any interest in the estate assets while they are under the administration of an executor.

19-18.   Given these differences, why does the *Act* treat the terms trust and estate in an identical manner? The answer is procedural in nature. When an individual dies and bequeaths his property through a will, immediate distribution of all of his property may not be possible. For example, if there is real estate that must be sold, this process may require a significant period of time.

19-19.   During the period between an individual's death and the time that all of his property is distributed to his beneficiaries, it is possible that some income will accrue on the estate property held by the executor. The deceased person's income to the date of death will be included in his final tax return. However, the income earned by the estate during the period that it is administered by the executor cannot be allocated to either the deceased person or to his beneficiaries. To solve this problem, the *Act* requires that the income of the estate be included in a trust return (T3). As the rules for filing a return for this "estate" are the same as those applicable to a trust, the *Act* treats these two terms as synonyms.

Establishing A Trust

Three Certainties

19-20.   The trusts that we are dealing with in this Chapter are established by words that are set out in a trust agreement. While some provinces allow, under limited circumstances, the use of oral trust agreements, this is rarely a wise course of action. Even if such agreements are accepted for legal purposes, the CRA tends to be skeptical of such agreements and may take the position that no trust exists.

19-21.   In deciding whether or not a trust has, in fact, been created, it is important to look at what the courts have referred to as the three certainties. These can be described as follows:

> **Certainty Of Intention**   The person creating the trust must intend to create the trust and that intention must be clear to outside observers. This is usually accomplished by preparing a written document establishing the trust.

Certainty Of Property   The property that is to be held in the trust must be known with certainty at the time the trust is created. This is usually accomplished by specifying the property in the trust document.

Certainty Of Beneficiaries   The persons who will benefit from the trust property must be known with certainty at the time the trust is created. This is usually accomplished by specifying these persons in the trust document. Note that these persons must either be named as persons (e.g., Ms. Sally Phar) or be part of an identifiable class (e.g., my children). When a class designation is used, it must refer to a clearly identifiable group of persons. For example, designating "friends" as beneficiaries would not create an identifiable group.

19-22.   In addition to establishing the facts required by the three certainties criteria, there must be an actual transfer of the trust property to the trustee. Until this transfer is completed, the trust does not exist.

Importance Of Proper Documentation

19-23.   Care must be taken to ensure that all of the necessary actions to create a trust have been carried out effectively. If one or more of the required elements is missing, the tax consequences can be significant. For example, if an individual attempted to establish a trust to split income with his adult children, a failure to complete all of the requirements necessary to that process could result in his being taxed on the property income, rather than having it taxed in the hands of his adult children. This could result in the payment of a significant amount of additional tax.

Exercise Nineteen - 1

Subject: Establishing A Trust

In each of the following Cases, an individual is attempting to establish a trust. For each of these Cases, indicate whether the attempt has been successful. Explain your conclusion.

Case A   Jack Black sends a cheque to his sister to be used for the education of her two children.

Case B   Jane Folsem transfers property to a trustee, specifying that the income from the property should be distributed to her friends.

Case C   Robert Jones transfers property to a trustee, specifying that the income from the property should be distributed to his children.

Case D   Suzanne Bush has signed an agreement that specifies that she will transfer her securities portfolio to a trustee, with the income to be distributed to her spouse.

End of Exercise. Solution available in Study Guide.

Returns And Payments - Trusts

19-24.   Because they are considered by the government to be taxable entities, trusts must file tax returns. As discussed in Chapter 2, Procedures and Administration, the trust tax return (T3 return) must be filed within 90 days of a trust's year end. With respect to the payment of taxes, the tax payable on trust income is due no later than 90 days after a trust's year end. Note that trusts are not generally required to make instalment payments.

19-25.   With respect to penalties and interest related to late filing or late payment of taxes, the rules for trusts are the same as those that are applicable to individuals.

Non-Tax Reasons For Using Trusts

19-26.   In this Chapter we are largely concerned with the tax planning uses of trusts. However, it is important to note that trusts have non-tax uses which, in some situations, may be more important than the tax features of the particular arrangement. Some of these non-tax uses are as follows:

Administration Of Assets   A trust can be used to separate the administration of assets from the receipt of benefits. For example, an individual with extensive investment knowledge might have assets transferred to a trust for his spouse at the time of his death. The goal here could be to provide professional management of the assets for the benefit of a spouse with only limited knowledge of investments.

Protection From Creditors   An individual proprietor of a business might place some of his personal assets in a trust in order to protect them from claims by the creditors of the business. However, if this transfer is made when the individual is experiencing financial difficulties with his business, there are provisions in bankruptcy and other legislation which may undo the transfer.

Privacy   If assets are bequeathed in a will, they will be subject to probate, the results of which are available to the public. This is not the case with assets that are in a trust when an individual dies.

Avoiding Changes In Beneficiaries   If a father places assets in a trust for the benefit of his minor children, it ensures that these children will be the ultimate beneficiaries of the property. In contrast, if, as is common, his will bequeaths his assets to his wife with the intention that his children will be the ultimate beneficiaries of his property, his wife has no legal obligation to carry out this intention. This can be a particularly important issue if the surviving spouse remarries and other children become part of her family.

19-27.   While there are additional examples of non-tax uses of trusts, the preceding should serve to give you some idea of the versatility of trust arrangements.

Classification Of Trusts

Introduction

19-28.   The CRA's *Trust Guide* lists 18 different types of trusts, largely based on definitions that are included in the *Income Tax Act*. Understanding the meaning of the terms on this CRA list is complicated by the fact that some of the listed items are, in fact, a sub-classification of other items included on the list (e.g., an alter ego trust is a type of personal trust). A further roadblock to understanding the classification of trusts is that trusts are also classified in popular usage in terms of their goals or objectives. Such terms as "family trusts" and "spend-thrift trusts" are commonly used, despite the fact that they have no real meaning in terms of tax legislation.

19-29.   In this material, we will not provide a comprehensive classification of trusts, nor will we attempt to provide definitions for all of the terms that are applied to trusts in tax legislation and general practice. As indicated in the introduction to this Chapter, our coverage is limited to trusts that have been established by individuals as part of a tax or estate planning scenario. As all of these trusts fall within the classification of personal trusts, we will begin by considering this category.

Personal Trusts
General Definition

19-30.   The *Income Tax Act* contains the following definition of a personal trust:

ITA 248(1)   Personal Trust means
(a) a testamentary trust, or

(b) an inter vivos trust, no beneficial interest in which was acquired for consideration payable directly or indirectly to
    (i)   the trust, or
    (ii) any person who has made a contribution to the trust by way of transfer, assignment or other disposition of property.

Testamentary Trust

19-31.   As is often the case in tax legislation, an understanding of the Personal Trust definition requires definitions of some of the included terms. The first of these definitions is:

ITA 108(1)   Testamentary Trust in a taxation year means a trust that arose on and as a consequence of the death of an individual, other than ...

19-32.   You will recall that, as used in the *Income Tax Act*, the term trust means trust or estate. This means that a testamentary trust can either be specifically established through an individual's will or, alternatively, if no trust is explicitly established in the will, the deceased individual's estate becomes a trust for tax purposes.

19-33.   If a testamentary trust is established for an individual's spouse or common-law partner, it is referred to as a spousal or common-law partner trust and special tax rules apply. There is no special designation for testamentary trusts with beneficiaries other than a spouse.

Inter Vivos Trust

19-34.   The *Income Tax Act* also contains a definition of inter vivos trust:

ITA 108(1)   Inter Vivos Trust means a trust other than a testamentary trust.

19-35.   As a testamentary trust is one that is established by the death of an individual, for our purposes, an alternative way of defining an inter vivos trust is that it is a trust that is established by a living individual.

19-36.   In this material, we will give consideration to four categories of inter vivos trusts. Two of these categories, alter ego trusts and joint spousal or common-law partner trusts, are defined in the *Income Tax Act*. The remaining two, family trusts and spousal or common-law partner trusts are defined only through common usage in practice.

Testamentary Vs. Inter Vivos Trusts

Types Of Testamentary And Inter Vivos Trusts

19-37.   As defined in the previous section, the basic classification of personal trusts is between testamentary and inter vivos trusts. In this Chapter, we will deal with two types of testamentary trusts and four types of inter vivos trusts. This sub-classification is outlined in Figure 19-2:

Figure 19 - 2 Classification Of Personal Trusts	
Testamentary	**Inter Vivos**
Spousal Or Common-Law Partner Other Beneficiaries	Spousal Or Common-Law Partner Alter Ego Joint Spousal Or Common-Law Partner Family

19-38.   The individual types of trusts identified in Figure 19-2 can be described as follows:

Spousal Or Common-Law Partner Trust This category of trust is not defined in the *Income Tax Act*. Rather, it is a term that is used when a trust is established for a spouse or common-law partner. Such trusts can either be an inter vivos trust established by a living person or, alternatively, a testamentary trust that is established when an individual dies.

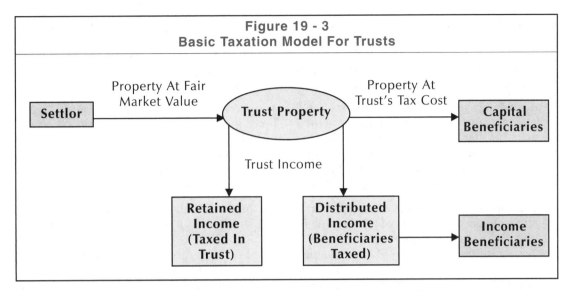

Figure 19 - 3
Basic Taxation Model For Trusts

As will be discussed when we present material on the taxation of trusts, if such trusts meet certain conditions, the *Income Tax Act* contains rollover provisions (ITA 73(1.01) for inter vivos trusts and ITA 70(6) for testamentary trusts) which allow property to be transferred to the trustee on a tax free basis. When these conditions are met, the trust is usually referred to as a qualifying spousal or common-law partner trust.

Alter Ego Trust An alter ego trust is an inter vivos trust created by an individual who is 65 years of age or older with himself as the sole beneficiary during his lifetime. As was the case with spousal or common-law partner trusts, if certain conditions are met, the *Income Tax Act* contains a rollover provision that allows property to be transferred into or out of the trust on a tax free basis.

Joint Spousal Or Common-Law Partner Trust A joint spousal or joint common-law partner trust is an inter vivos trust created by an individual who is 65 years of age or older. Similar to the alter ego trust, this type of trust is created with the individual and his spouse or common-law partner as the sole beneficiaries during their lifetimes. Also similar to the alter ego trust scenario, if certain conditions are met, there is a roll-over provision in the *Income Tax Act* that allows property to be transferred into the trust on a tax free basis.

Family Trust While the term family trust is not always used in a consistent manner, it generally refers to a trust that has been established by an individual for the benefit of family members. While a family trust could be a testamentary trust, the term is usually used in reference to an inter vivos trust. The most common goal of this type of trust is income splitting.

Taxation Of Trusts

The Basic Model

19-39. While there are many variations that depend on the particular type of trust we are dealing with, as well as complications associated with the measurement of trust Taxable Income and Tax Payable, the basic model for the taxation of trusts is as shown in Figure 19-3. There are three features of this basic model that should be noted:

> **Settlor's Transfer Of Property To The Trust** When property is transferred to a trust by a settlor, it generally results in a disposition for tax purposes. In the usual situation, these dispositions are deemed to occur at fair market value, triggering various tax consequences (e.g., capital gains, recapture, or terminal losses). There are, however, some important rollover provisions for property transferred into a trust. These are discussed beginning in Paragraph 19-41.

Transfers Of Trust Property To Beneficiaries   If trust property is transferred to a capital beneficiary, ITA 107(2) provides a rollover provision that allows the property to be transferred at the tax cost to the trust. The proceeds of disposition to the trust and the cost to the beneficiary will be equal to the tax cost that is recorded in the trust. For exceptions to this general provision, see Rollovers To Beneficiaries beginning in Paragraph 19-54.

Income From The Trust Property   Once property has been transferred to the trust, income will begin to accrue to the trust. It is fundamental to most of the tax planning uses of trusts that income earned in the trust can be deducted by the trust from Net Income For Tax Purposes of the trust to the extent that it is either distributed to beneficiaries or they are entitled to enforce payment. We will find that in many situations, trusts will distribute all of their income, resulting in no Tax Payable at the trust level.

Any income that a trust does not distribute to beneficiaries will be taxed in the trust. Subsequent distribution of this income is on a tax free basis. At this point you should note that there is a very important difference in the calculation of Tax Payable for an inter vivos trust and the calculation of Tax Payable for a testamentary trust. In the case of an inter vivos trust, all of the income that is retained in the trust is taxed at the maximum federal rate of 29 percent. In contrast, Tax Payable for a testamentary trust is calculated using the graduated rate schedule that is applicable to individuals.

19-40.   While it is not illustrated in Figure 19-3, there is a special anti-avoidance rule that is designed to prevent extended deferral of the potential tax on capital gains. This rule requires a deemed disposition of capital assets after they have been held in the trust for 21 years and will be discussed in detail beginning in Paragraph 19-60.

Exercise Nineteen - 2

Subject: Basic Taxation Of Trusts

On January 1, 2013, Joanne March transfers debt securities with a fair market value of $220,000 to a newly established inter vivos trust for which her 28 year old daughter, Jocelyn, is the only beneficiary. The cost of these securities to Joanne March was $200,000. During 2013, the securities earn and receive interest of $15,000, all of which is distributed to Jocelyn. On January 1, 2014, the securities are transferred to Jocelyn in satisfaction of her capital interest in the trust. At this time, the fair market value of the securities has increased to $230,000. Jocelyn sells all of the securities for $230,000 on January 5, 2014.

Indicate the tax consequences for Joanne, Jocelyn, and the trust, in each of the years 2013 and 2014.

End of Exercise. Solution available in Study Guide.

Rollovers To A Trust

Introduction

19-41.   The general taxation model for trusts requires that contributions to the trust be recorded at fair market value, often resulting in a significant tax cost for the contributor. However, as we noted in our material on the classification of trusts, spousal or common-law partner trusts, alter ego trusts, and joint spousal or common-law partner trusts can make such transfers on a rollover basis, provided certain specific conditions are met.

19-42.   In this section we are concerned with the conditions that qualify these three special types of trusts for the tax free rollover of contributions. When the trust qualifies, the rollover is accomplished by deeming the property to have been disposed of by the settlor at either its adjusted cost base (non-depreciable property) or its UCC (depreciable property), resulting in no tax consequences for the settlor at the time of transfer. The trust is deemed to have acquired the property at a value equal to the proceeds of disposition to the settlor. In the case of depreciable property, the trust retains the settlor's original capital cost for purposes of determining recapture of CCA.

19-43.   We will revisit these three types of trusts in our later section on tax planning. At that point we will discuss how these trusts can be used to reduce or defer taxes.

Qualifying Spousal Or Qualifying Common-Law Partner Trust

19-44.   You may recall from Chapter 9 that ITA 73(1.01) contains a rollover provision that allows a living individual to transfer capital property to a spouse or common-law partner without tax consequences. ITA 70(6) provides for a similar rollover for the capital property of a deceased individual.

19-45.   While we did not discuss this in Chapter 9, these rollovers apply whether the transfer is directly to the spouse or common-law partner or, alternatively, to a trust in favour of a spouse or common-law partner. However, in the case of a transfer to a trust, the trust arrangement must meet certain conditions in order to qualify for the rollover. When it meets these conditions, it is commonly referred to as a qualifying spousal or common-law partner trust.

19-46.   With respect to inter vivos spousal or common-law partner trusts, the conditions for qualifying for the rollover are as follows:

ITA 73(1.01)(c)(i)   The individual's spouse or common-law partner is entitled to receive all of the income of the trust that arises before the spouse's or common-law partner's death and no person except the spouse or common-law partner may, before the spouse's or common-law partner's death, receive or otherwise obtain the use of any of the income or capital of the trust.

19-47.   A similar provision provides the rollover conditions for testamentary spousal or common-law partner trusts:

ITA 70(6)(b)   A trust, created by the taxpayer's will, that was resident in Canada immediately after the time the property vested indefeasibly in the trust and under which
(i)   the taxpayer's spouse or common-law partner is entitled to receive all of the income of the trust that arises before the spouse's or common-law partner's death, and
(ii) no person except the spouse or common-law partner may, before the spouse's or common-law partner's death, receive or otherwise obtain the use of any of the income or capital of the trust.

19-48.   When these conditions are met, any property that is contributed to the trust, either by a living person or as the result of the individual's death, will be transferred at the individual's tax cost. For non-depreciable property, this value is the transferor's adjusted cost base. For depreciable property, the transfer is at the transferor's UCC amount. However, for purposes of determining recaptured CCA, the transferor's original capital cost is deemed to be the transferee's capital cost.

19-49.   While these rollover provisions are, in general, a desirable way to avoid paying taxes on transfers to a spousal or common-law partner trust, there may be circumstances where the taxpayer would prefer a transfer at fair market value. For example, if the settlor of the trust has unused capital loss carry forwards or property that is eligible for the lifetime capital gains deduction, he might wish to trigger capital gains in order to absorb these amounts. Fortunately, the settlor has the choice of electing out of the rollover provisions. For inter vivos transfers, the election is under ITA 73(1). For testamentary transfers the election that can be made by the settlor's legal representative is under ITA 70(6.2).

Exercise Nineteen - 3

Subject: Transfer To Spousal Trust

Louise died late this year, and bequeathed a parcel of land to a qualifying spousal trust created in her will. Louise is survived by her husband who is to receive the land from the trust three years after her death if it has not been sold. The land has an adjusted cost base of $60,000 and was valued at $90,000 on the date of her death. Determine the tax consequences of the transfer, including the adjusted cost base for the land in the trust and in her husband's hands if it is transferred.

End of Exercise. Solution available in Study Guide.

Alter Ego Trust

19-50.   An alter ego trust is an inter vivos trust established by a settlor who is 65 years of age or older at the time the trust is settled. To qualify for a tax free rollover of assets to the trust, the *Income Tax Act* specifies the following conditions:

ITA 73(1.01)(c)(ii)   The individual is entitled to receive all of the income of the trust that arises before the individual's death and no person except the individual may, before the individual's death, receive or otherwise obtain the use of any of the income or capital of the trust.

19-51.   As was the case with the spousal or common-law partner trust, an individual can elect out of this rollover, choosing to have the transfer to the trust take place at fair market value.

Joint Spousal Or Joint Common-Law Partner Trust

19-52.   Like an alter ego trust, a joint spousal or common-law partner trust is an inter vivos trust established by a settlor who is 65 years of age or older at the time the trust is settled. The difference in this case is that both the settlor and his spouse or common-law partner are beneficiaries of the trust. More specifically, to qualify for the tax free rollover of assets to the trust, the *Income Tax Act* specifies the following conditions:

ITA 73(1.01)(c)(iii) either

(A) the individual or the individual's spouse is, in combination with the other, entitled to receive all of the income of the trust that arises before the later of the death of the individual and the death of the spouse and no other person may, before the later of those deaths, receive or otherwise obtain the use of any of the income or capital of the trust, or

(B) the individual or the individual's common-law partner is, in combination with the other, entitled to receive all of the income of the trust that arises before the later of the death of the individual and the death of the common-law partner and no other person may, before the later of those deaths, receive or otherwise obtain the use of any of the income or capital of the trust.

19-53.   As was the case with the alter ego trust, an individual can elect out of this rollover, choosing to have the transfer to the trust take place at fair market value.

Exercise Nineteen - 4

Subject: Transfers To Trusts

An individual has common shares with a cost of $1,000 and a current fair market value of $1,600. Seven Scenarios are presented for the transfer of these shares by the settlor to a trust. For each Scenario, indicate the tax consequences to the settlor at the time of transfer, as well as the adjusted cost base of the property within the trust.

Scenario 1:   Transfer to inter vivos trust for adult child.
Scenario 2:   Transfer to inter vivos trust for minor child.
Scenario 3:   Transfer to testamentary trust for friend.
Scenario 4:   Transfer to inter vivos qualifying spousal trust.
Scenario 5:   Transfer to testamentary qualifying spousal trust.
Scenario 6:   Transfer to joint spousal trust.
Scenario 7:   Transfer to alter ego trust.

End of Exercise. Solution available in Study Guide.

Rollovers To Capital Beneficiaries

General Rule

19-54.   As is the case with transfers by a settlor into a trust, the transfer of assets to a capital beneficiary is a disposition. However, for many trusts ITA 107(2) provides a tax free rollover for these transfers. The rollover is accomplished by deeming the property to have been disposed of by the trust at either its adjusted cost base (non-depreciable property) or its UCC (depreciable property).

19-55.   The beneficiary is deemed to have acquired the property at a value equal to the cost amount to the trust, resulting in no tax consequences at the time of transfer to the beneficiary. In the case of depreciable property, the beneficiary retains the capital cost of the property to the trust for purposes of determining subsequent recapture of CCA.

Exceptions

19-56.   The logic of the preceding rule is based on the fact that the transfer of assets into the trust was, in terms of the beneficial interest in the assets, a transfer of the assets to the beneficiaries. Provided that tax was assessed on the transfer into the trust, it would not be equitable to assess tax again when the asset is legally transferred to the beneficiaries.

19-57.   We have noted, however, that with certain types of trusts, the transfer from the settlor to the trust is not a taxable transaction. Specifically, qualifying spousal or common-law partner trusts, alter ego trusts, and joint spousal or common-law partner trusts can use a rollover provision to transfer assets into a trust. Since no tax was assessed on the transfer into these trusts, it would not seem equitable to allow the assets to be transferred to all beneficiaries on a rollover basis.

19-58.   Tax legislation agrees with this view.   The ITA 107(2) rollover does not apply in the following cases:

- if property is transferred out of an **alter ego** trust to anyone other than the settlor,

- if property is transferred out of a **joint spousal** or common-law partner trust to anyone other than the settlor or the spouse or common-law partner, and

- if property is transferred out of a **qualifying spousal** or common-law partner trust to anyone other than a spouse or common-law partner.

19-59.   When the ITA 107(2) rollover provision does not apply, the transfer of assets from the trust to a capital beneficiary will be recorded at the fair market value of the transferred assets. This will generally result in tax consequences for the trust.

21 Year Deemed Disposition Rule

19-60.   Trust arrangements ordinarily allow capital gains on trust assets to accumulate without tax consequences for extended periods of time. Unless the capital assets are sold or distributed by the trust, accrued gains will not attract any taxes and the assets can be left in a trust for periods that exceed the life of the individual establishing the trust.

19-61.   In order to place limits on this deferral process, ITA 104(4)(b) requires that there be a deemed disposition and reacquisition of trust capital property every 21 years. The disposition is deemed to be at fair market value, resulting in the recognition of any accrued gains on the assets. In the case of depreciable assets, if the deemed proceeds are less than the original capital cost, the original value is retained for purposes of determining recapture.

19-62.   This rule is generally applicable only to personal trusts and does not apply to trusts such as employee benefit plans or registered education savings plans. Further, the rules are modified in the case of qualifying spousal or common-law partner trusts, alter ego trusts, and joint spousal or common-law partner trusts.

19-63.   For qualifying spousal or common-law partner trusts, the deemed disposition occurs with the death of the spouse or common-law partner. In the case of alter ego trusts, the death of the settlor is the event that triggers the deemed disposition. Finally, with joint spousal or common-law partner trusts, the deemed disposition occurs only at the later of the death of the settlor or the death of the spouse or common-law partner.

Net Income For Tax Purposes Of A Trust

Basic Rules

19-64.   The overriding principle in determining the Net Income For Tax Purposes of a trust results from the statement in ITA 104(2) that a trust should be treated as an individual. This means that the general rules used by individuals, as modified by trust legislation, are applicable in computing a trust's Net Income For Tax Purposes.

19-65.   Capital gains and losses are realized on the disposition of capital assets. Also, in the calculation of Net Income For Tax Purposes, any taxable dividends that are not allocated to beneficiaries are grossed up as they would be for individuals. Finally, deductions are allowed for non-capital, net capital, and certain other types of loss carry overs.

19-66.   There are, however, additional items that must be added or deducted in calculating the Net Income For Tax Purposes of a trust. These items can be described as follows:

Amounts Paid Or Payable To Beneficiaries   As was noted in our description of the basic trust taxation model, a trust can deduct amounts that are paid or payable to one or more beneficiaries. This is usually the most important of the adjustments to the trust's income in that, in many cases, all of the trust's income will be allocated to beneficiaries. Because of the importance of this deduction, it will be the subject of a separate section of this Chapter beginning in Paragraph 19-76.

Trustee's Or Executor's Fees   Any amounts paid that are related to earning trust income, or that are paid to an executor or trustee whose principal business includes the provision of such services, are deductible to the trust.

Amounts Paid By The Trust And Allocated To The Income Of A Beneficiary   A trust can make payments to third parties to provide goods or services to beneficiaries. The CRA considers such amounts to be another way of paying income to beneficiaries and, as a consequence, such amounts are deductible to the trust and included in the income of the beneficiaries.

Income Allocated To A Preferred Beneficiary   As will be discussed beginning in Paragraph 19-68, trusts can allocate income to a preferred beneficiary while retaining the income in the trust. While such retained income would normally be taxed in the trust, because it is being taxed in the hands of a beneficiary, it can be deducted from the income of the trust.

Amounts Deemed Not Paid   A trust can designate amounts to be deemed not paid when they are, in fact, paid or payable to beneficiaries. This means that the trust will include these amounts in its own Net Income For Tax Purposes and the beneficiaries will be able to receive these amounts on a tax free basis. The reasons for doing this are discussed beginning in Paragraph 19-71.

Amounts Retained For Beneficiary Under 21 Years Of Age Provided the eventual payment is not subject to any future condition, amounts that are held in trust for a beneficiary who is under 21 at the end of the year can be deducted by the trust and taxed in the hands of the beneficiary. (See Paragraph 19-73.)

19-67. While positive amounts of all types of income can be allocated to beneficiaries, losses cannot be. If a trust has a disposition that results in a capital loss, or other activities that result in a non-capital loss, such losses must be used within the trust, either as a carry back to a previous year, or as a carry forward to a subsequent year. Note, however, that if the trust distributes capital assets with accrued losses, the fact that the transfer to a beneficiary is usually at the trust's tax cost means that such accrued losses can, in effect, be transferred to a beneficiary.

Preferred Beneficiary Election

19-68. Normally a trust can only deduct amounts that are paid or payable to a beneficiary. An exception to this can arise if a joint election is made by a trust and a beneficiary. Under this preferred beneficiary election, the beneficiary will be taxed on amounts that remain in the trust [ITA 104(14)], and the trust can deduct these amounts [ITA 104(12)].

19-69. The preferred beneficiary election is only available for certain disabled beneficiaries. The beneficiary must either be eligible for the disability tax credit, or be eligible to be claimed by another individual as an infirm dependant 18 years or older.

19-70. This election is normally used in situations where it is desirable to have income taxed in the hands of a low income individual without actually giving that individual full access to the funds. An example of this would be a mentally disabled child with no other source of income, but lacking in the ability to deal responsibly with financial matters.

Amounts Deemed Not Paid

19-71. Amounts paid or payable to a beneficiary are normally deducted by the trust and included in the income of the beneficiary. However, ITA 104(13.1) permits a trust to designate all or part of its income as "not to have been paid" or "not to have become payable in the year". As we have noted, the amounts so designated are not included in the beneficiaries' Net Income and are not deductible in computing the Net Income of the trust. This designation is only available to trusts that are resident in Canada throughout the taxation year and are subject to Part I tax.

19-72. The reasons for using this designation include the following:

Lower Rates In the case of a testamentary trust that pays taxes at graduated rates, the trust may have a lower marginal tax rate than the beneficiary.

Instalment Avoidance Trusts are generally not required to make instalment payments. In contrast, if the income is taxed in the hands of a beneficiary, that individual may be required to make instalment payments on the trust income.

Use Of Trust Losses As previously noted, a trust cannot allocate losses to beneficiaries. This means that the only way that an unused current year trust loss can be used is through a carry over to another year. With many trusts, this cannot happen under normal circumstances because they are legally required to distribute all of their income to beneficiaries, resulting in a nil Net Income For Tax Purposes. A solution to this problem is to designate sufficient income as having not been paid to absorb the loss carry forward. This can satisfy the legal requirement to distribute the income, while simultaneously creating sufficient Net Income For Tax Purposes to absorb the loss carry forward.

Amounts Retained For A Beneficiary Under 21 Years Of Age

19-73. If benefits are actually paid to a minor beneficiary, the amounts can clearly be deducted by the trust. However, an adult settlor may decide that it would be better for the income to be held in trust until the beneficiary reaches some specified age. Provided the beneficiary has not reached 21 years of age prior to the end of the year, ITA 104(18) deems amounts that are retained to have become payable during the year. This means that the trust will be able to deduct the amount retained and the beneficiary will be subject to taxes on it.

19-74.   To qualify for this treatment, the amounts must be vested with the beneficiary and there cannot be any future condition that would prevent payment. When these amounts are eventually distributed, they will be received by the beneficiary on a tax free basis.

Taxable Income Of A Trust

19-75.   Once the Net Income For Tax Purposes of a trust is determined, calculation of Taxable Income involves the same deductions that would be available to individuals. Provided there is a positive Net Income For Tax Purposes, the trust can deduct non-capital losses of other years, net capital losses of other years, and farming and fishing losses of other years. The carry over periods for these losses that are applicable to individuals are equally applicable to trusts. Note that the ability to deduct net capital losses and restricted farm losses is dependent on having taxable capital gains or farm income included in the trust's Net Income For Tax Purposes for the current year.

Exercise Nineteen - 5

Subject: Trust Net And Taxable Income

During the current year, the Jordan family trust, an inter vivos trust, has business income of $220,000. Of this amount, $50,000 is retained in the trust, with a joint election being made to have this amount taxed in the hands of a disabled beneficiary with no other income. The remaining $170,000 is distributed to the other beneficiaries of the trust.

At the beginning of the current year, the trust had a business loss carry forward of $35,000. In order to make use of this loss, the trust designates an amount of $35,000 under ITA 104(13.1) as not having been paid during the year.

Determine the trust's Net Income For Tax Purposes and Taxable Income for the current year. Briefly explain why the trust would make the preferred beneficiary election and designate amounts not paid that were paid.

End of Exercise. Solution available in Study Guide.

Income Allocations To Beneficiaries

General Rules

19-76.   Since a trust is a separate taxable entity, any income that is earned by trust assets will initially accrue to the trust. As we have noted, however, any income that is allocated to a beneficiary can be deducted in the calculation of the trust's Net Income For Tax Purposes. Correspondingly, the amount deducted by the trust must generally be included in the Net Income For Tax Purposes of the relevant beneficiary. In effect, when trust income is allocated to a beneficiary, the obligation to pay taxes on that income is transferred from the trust to the beneficiary.

19-77.   We have also noted that a trust can make payments to third parties for goods or services that will be provided to a beneficiary. These can include such expenses as day care, tuition, and medical fees. These amounts are deductible by the trust as allocations to beneficiaries, but will be considered income paid or payable to the beneficiaries.

19-78.   For a trust to be able to deduct amounts that will be distributed to beneficiaries, the amounts must be paid or payable. While it is easy to determine whether an amount has been paid, questions often arise in determining whether or not an amount is payable to a beneficiary. ITA 104(24) provides that:

> ... an amount is deemed not to have become payable to a beneficiary in a taxation year unless it was paid in the year to the beneficiary or the beneficiary was entitled in the year to enforce payment of it.

19-79.   Issuing a promissory note or a cheque payable to the beneficiary for the share of the trust income will usually fulfill the payable requirement. The CRA expands the definition of payable in IT-286R2 by stating that an amount is not considered to be payable in any of the following circumstances:

- A beneficiary can only enforce payment of an amount of income by forcing the trustee to wind up the trust.
- The beneficiary's right to income is subject to the approval of a third party.
- Payment of income is at the trustee's discretion.
- The beneficiary has the power to amend the trust deed and must do so to cause the income to be payable.

Discretionary And Non-Discretionary Distributions

19-80.   Both testamentary and inter vivos trusts can be set up as either discretionary or non-discretionary trusts. A discretionary trust is one in which the trustees are given the power to decide the amounts that will be allocated to each of the beneficiaries, usually on an annual basis.

19-81.   In many cases, this discretionary power will apply only to annual income distributions. However, the trust could be structured to provide discretion on both income and capital distributions, or to capital distributions only. The trustees may also be given the power to control the timing of distributions to beneficiaries.

19-82.   When discretionary trusts are used, it is important that only the amounts allocated to beneficiaries are considered to be paid or payable. If, for example, a trustee's exercise of discretion requires the approval of a third party, IT-286R2 would indicate that the amounts are not payable. This would result in the trust not being able to deduct the allocated amounts.

19-83.   A non-discretionary trust is one in which the amounts and timing of allocations to income and capital beneficiaries are specified in the trust agreement. In many cases, a given trust agreement may have a combination of discretionary and non-discretionary provisions.

Flow Through Provisions
General Applicability
19-84.   Income that is paid out to beneficiaries through a trust is deemed to be property income unless there is a rule that says otherwise. Fortunately, there is a flow through rule that allows certain types of income paid out of a trust to retain the same tax characteristics as when it was earned in the personal trust. The most significant types of income covered by this flow through rule are capital gains, taxable dividends and capital dividends.

19-85.   This is a very important feature of personal trusts in that capital gains and dividends, especially capital dividends, are taxed much more favourably than other types of income. Since property income is fully taxed at an individual's regular rates, in the absence of such a flow through rule, in many instances the use of trusts would be much less attractive.

Dividends
19-86.   If either eligible or non-eligible dividends from taxable Canadian corporations are received by a trust and distributed to beneficiaries of the trust, the beneficiaries will use the same gross up and tax credit procedures that would be applicable had they received the dividends directly. At the trust level, these amounts will not be grossed up and the amount received and distributed will be deducted in the determination of the trust's Net Income.

19-87.   In contrast, if either eligible or non-eligible dividends from taxable Canadian corporations are retained in the trust, the grossed up amount of these dividends will be included in the trust's Net Income For Tax Purposes. Consistent with this, the trust will be able to deduct the appropriate dividend tax credit when it determines its Tax Payable for the year. Since capital dividends are tax free, they would have no effect on the trust's Tax Payable.

Capital Gains
19-88.   Under trust law, capital gains that are realized in the trusts are considered to be an addition to capital and, in the absence of a special provision in the trust agreement, would not be payable to income beneficiaries. However, tax legislation views one-half of capital gains as a taxable amount. As a consequence, if this amount is not paid out to beneficiaries, it will be taxed in the hands of the trust. The remaining one-half of the capital gain will become part of the trust's capital and can be paid to beneficiaries on a tax free basis at any point in time.

19-89.   If the trust pays out the full amount of the capital gain, the flow through rule means that one-half of this amount will be included in the recipient's income as a taxable capital gain. The remaining one-half is received as a tax free distribution of capital.

19-90.   It is important to note that the capital gains that we are discussing here are those that result from dispositions within the trust. As covered in Paragraph 19-54, if the trust distributes capital assets on which there are accrued capital gains, ITA 107(2) deems the transfer to be at the trust's tax cost resulting in no tax consequences to the trust. The accrued gains will not be subject to tax until the recipient beneficiary chooses to dispose of the assets received.

Tax On Split Income
19-91.   As discussed in Chapter 11, an individual who is under 17 years of age before the beginning of the year (i.e., who has not reached 18 years of age by the end of the year) is subject to a tax on split income (a.k.a., kiddie tax). This tax is applicable to specified types of income including dividends from private companies, benefits or loans received from private companies, and partnership income if the partnership is providing property or services to a business owned by a related individual. The tax is assessed at the maximum federal rate of 29 percent on all eligible amounts, with the only available tax credits being the dividend tax credit and credits for foreign taxes assessed on foreign source income.

19-92.   If any of the specified types of income are earned by a trust and allocated to a beneficiary who is under 17 years of age before the beginning of the year, they will retain their tax characteristics in the hands of the beneficiary. Because of this, the income will be subject to the tax on split income.

Exercise Nineteen - 6

Subject: Flow Through To Beneficiaries

During 2013, the Ho family trust received eligible dividends from publicly traded Canadian corporations in the amount of $100,000. In addition, it received non-eligible dividends from the family owned Canadian controlled private corporation in the amount of $30,000. Its only other source of income was a capital gain of $20,000 on a disposition of investments in publicly traded equity securities.

The only beneficiary of the trust is the family's 19 year old son, Bryan Ho. During the current year, $60,000 of the eligible dividends from public companies, all of the non-eligible dividends from the family's private company, and all of the $20,000 capital gain were paid to Bryan.

Indicate the tax effects of these transactions on the Net Income For Tax Purposes for both the trust and for Bryan.

End of Exercise. Solution available in Study Guide.

Business Income, CCA, Recapture, And Terminal Losses

19-93. Under trust law, the amount of income that may be distributed to beneficiaries should be determined after providing for amortization expense calculated using methods similar to those specified under generally accepted accounting principles. While this could create a difference between a trust's accounting Net Income and its Net Income For Tax Purposes, this problem is resolved by most trustees by setting accounting amortization expense equal to maximum CCA.

19-94. Business income must be calculated at the trust level, prior to allocation to the beneficiaries. This calculation would include the CCA deduction, as well as any recapture or terminal losses that might arise during the year. Since the flow through rule for trusts does not cover business income, any business income allocated to beneficiaries is distributed as property income. If this was not the case, business income flowed through a trust could create a liability for CPP and GST/HST which would complicate matters for many beneficiaries.

Exercise Nineteen - 7

Subject: CCA And Recapture On Trust Assets

The Husak family trust has only one beneficiary, Martin Husak, the 32 year old son of the settlor, Dimitri Husak. It is an inter vivos trust and its only asset is a rental property with a fair market value equal to its capital cost. The trust is required to distribute all of its income to Martin. During the year ending December 31, 2013 the property will have net rental income, before the deduction of CCA, of $32,000. Maximum CCA for the year will be $26,000. Dimitri is considering having the trust sell the rental property at the end of 2013. If that is done, there will be recapture of CCA of $65,000. He has asked you to compare the tax consequences for both Martin and the trust if (1) the sale takes place in December, 2013 and (2) the trust continues to hold the property.

End Of Exercise. Solution Available In Study Guide

Principal Residence Exemption

19-95. This exemption is usually considered to be available only to individuals. However, personal trusts can also benefit from the principal residence capital gain exemption. A residence held in a trust will qualify for the exemption if the residence was ordinarily inhabited in the year by a beneficiary of the trust, or by a spouse or common-law partner, former spouse or common-law partner, or child of a beneficiary. As well, the full gain on a principal residence will qualify for the exemption where the trust has more than one beneficiary, but only one of the beneficiaries occupies the residence.

Tax Payable Of Personal Trusts

Testamentary vs. Inter Vivos Trusts

General Approach

19-96. In keeping with the previously expressed idea that trusts are to be taxed in the same manner as individuals, the Tax Payable for a trust is calculated using the same rates that are applicable to individuals. However, how these rates will be applied differs, depending on whether the trust is an inter vivos trust or, alternatively, a testamentary trust. These differences will be discussed in the material that follows.

Rates For Testamentary Trusts

19-97. Testamentary trusts are taxed using the same schedule of progressive rates that apply to individuals. For 2013, the rates range from a low of 15 percent on the first $43,561 of Taxable Income to a maximum of 29 percent on taxable amounts in excess of $135,054. These rates are applied to Taxable Income, generally determined after the amounts allocated to beneficiaries have been deducted.

Rates For Inter Vivos Trusts

19-98.   Under ITA 122(1), inter vivos trusts are generally subject to a flat federal tax rate of 29 percent on all trust income that is not distributed to beneficiaries, allocated to a preferred beneficiary, or held in trust for a beneficiary under 21 years of age. Since the top federal marginal rate for individuals is also 29 percent, the flat federal tax levy on trusts is equal to, or greater than, the tax that would be paid by a beneficiary receiving the income. Given this, there is little income tax incentive to allow income to accumulate in an inter vivos trust.

Multiple Testamentary Trusts

19-99.   The fact that the full range of progressive rates is available to each testamentary trust suggests that when an individual wishes to have several beneficiaries of his estate, a separate testamentary trust should be established for each one. In contrast to the use of a single trust for all beneficiaries, this arrangement would provide for multiple applications of the low rates in the progressive rate schedule that is applicable to individuals.

19-100.   While there is no general prohibition against an individual establishing a separate trust for each of his beneficiaries, there is concern that this type of arrangement might be used for the purpose of creating multiple applications of the low tax brackets.

19-101.   To prevent multiple trusts from being created solely for this purpose, ITA 104(2) notes that where substantially all of the property of two or more trusts has been received from a single individual and the income from the trusts will ultimately accrue to the same beneficiary, group or class of beneficiaries, the CRA may designate the multiple trusts as a single trust. The CRA has indicated that members of one family could be viewed as a class of beneficiaries.

19-102.   To avoid this result, a will should include a clear direction as to whether distinct trusts are to be established for each beneficiary. Further, guidance should be provided stating that trust administrators can seek independent investment objectives suitable to the needs of the respective beneficiaries. Ideally, each trust should be created with separate terms.

Tainted Testamentary Trusts

19-103.   Contributions by living persons to an existing testamentary trust can cause that trust to become tainted and lose its testamentary status. If this happens, the trust will no longer benefit from the use of graduated rates and will be taxed as an inter vivos trust with all of its income taxed at the maximum federal rate of 29 percent.

Other Tax Payable Considerations

Availability Of Tax Credits

19-104.   While, in principle, trusts are to be taxed in the same manner as individuals, there are obvious differences between a legally constructed entity and a living, breathing human being. These differences are reflected in the fact that trusts are not eligible for many of the tax credits that are available to individuals.

19-105.   To begin, ITA 122(1.1) specifically prohibits a trust from taking any of the credits listed under ITA 118 (personal tax credits). Further, most of the other credits listed in ITA 118.1 through 118.9 are clearly directed at individuals (e.g., a trust is not likely to have medical expenses). However, some tax credits are available to trusts, generally on the same basis as they are available to individuals. These include:

- donations and gifts (As is the case with individuals, there is a credit of 15 percent on the first $200 of donations and 29 percent on additional amounts.)
- eligible and non-eligible dividend tax credits
- foreign tax credits
- investment tax credits

Alternative Minimum Tax

19-106.   As is the case with individuals, trusts are subject to the alternative minimum tax legislation. However, there is one important difference. The exemption with respect to the first $40,000 of income is only available to testamentary trusts. For inter vivos trusts, the alternative minimum tax calculation is based on all income amounts.

Tax Free Dividends

19-107.   As discussed in Chapter 15 (see Paragraph 15-88), an individual with no other source of income and with no tax credits other than the basic personal credit can receive up to $43,438 in non-eligible dividends without incurring a liability for federal tax. The corresponding tax free figure for eligible dividends is $49,740 (there would be no alternative minimum tax at this level - see Paragraph 19-129). This reflects the fact that, because of the dividend tax credit, dividends absorb other tax credits at a much slower rate than other types of income.

19-108.   The point here is that, while every Canadian resident individual will have, as a minimum, their basic personal credit, a trust that receives dividends may not have any tax credits other than those related to dividends that are left to be taxed in the trust.

19-109.   In the case of an inter vivos trust that has all of its income taxed at the maximum rate of 29 percent, there will be no tax free dividends. Tax will be assessed on all dividends that are left in the trust, starting with the first dollar retained.

19-110.   The situation is somewhat better with testamentary trusts that are subject to graduated rates. In the 15 percent tax bracket, the effective rate on non-eligible dividends received is 18.75 percent [(15%)(125%)], while the dividend tax credit is at a rate of 16-2/3 percent [(25%)(2/3)] of dividends received. Here again, there will be no tax free dividends. However, as long as the grossed up dividends do not exceed the 15 percent federal tax bracket, the effective rate on non-eligible dividends is 2.08 percent (18.75% - 16-2/3%).

19-111.   Eligible dividends fare better. In the lowest federal tax bracket, these dividends are taxed at an effective rate of 20.7% [(15%)(138%)]. The dividend tax credit rate on these dividends is 20.72 percent [(38%)(6/11)]. As the credit rate exceeds the tax payable rate, tax free dividends can be paid to a testamentary trust. Without going through the detailed calculations, a testamentary trust with no tax credits other than those resulting from dividends can receive eligible dividends of $31,657 without paying federal taxes.

Exercise Nineteen - 8

Subject: Tax Payable On Trust Dividends

A trust's only income for 2013 is $100,000 in eligible dividends. The only beneficiary of the trust is the settlor's 32 year old son. The son has no income other than that provided by the trust and no tax credits other than his basic personal credit and credits related to any trust income. Ignoring any alternative minimum tax implications, determine the Taxable Income and federal Tax Payable for both the trust and beneficiary under the following alternative assumptions:

A.   The trust is a testamentary trust and distributes all of the 2013 dividends to the beneficiary.

B.   The trust is a testamentary trust and does not distribute any of the 2013 dividends to the beneficiary.

C.   The trust is an inter vivos trust and does not distribute any of the 2013 dividends to the beneficiary.

End of Exercise. Solution available in Study Guide.

We suggest you work Self Study Problems Nineteen-1, 2, and 3 at this point.

Income Attribution - Trusts

General Rules

19-112.   We introduced the income attribution rules, as they apply to individuals, in Chapter 9. Briefly summarized, they are as follows:

Transfer To A Spouse Or Common-Law Partner   Under ITA 74.1(1), if property is transferred to a spouse or common-law partner for consideration that is less than fair market value, income earned by this property while it is held by that person, as well as any capital gain resulting from a disposition of the property by the transferee, will be attributed back to the transferor. These rules also apply, without regard to the value of the consideration, when the transferor does not elect out of the ITA 73 rollover provision.

Transfer To A Related Minor   Under ITA 74.1(2), if property is transferred to a related individual under the age of 18 for consideration that is less than fair market value, income earned by this property while it is held by the minor will be attributed back to the transferor until the year the individual is 18 or older. Capital gains on a subsequent sale of the property will not be attributed back to the transferor.

19-113.   While we did not discuss this point in Chapter 9, these rules are equally applicable when there is a transfer to a trust where a spouse, common-law partner, or a related minor is a beneficiary. As was the case with individuals, these rules apply to any transfer where the consideration is less than the fair market value of the property transferred.

19-114.   You should note that attribution does not occur at the time the assets are transferred to a trust in which a spouse, common-law partner, or related minor is a beneficiary. Rather, attribution occurs when income from those assets is allocated to one of these individuals. If the trust chooses to be taxed on the income before allocation, or if the income is allocated to individuals other than a spouse, common-law partner, or related minor, income will generally not be attributed to the transferor.

Exercise Nineteen - 9

Subject: Income Attribution - Trusts

Last year, Trevor Carlisle transferred to a family trust, for no consideration, bonds that pay interest of $27,000 per annum. The beneficiaries of the trust are Trevor's spouse, Carmen, and their two children, Mitch (16 years old) and Rhonda (22 years old). The beneficiaries have no income other than that from the trust. The trust income and capital gains are allocated equally, and are payable to each beneficiary during the year. Total interest income earned by the trust during the year was $27,000. As well, a capital gain of $6,000 was realized on the trust's disposition of one of the bonds that Trevor transferred into the trust. Determine the Taxable Income of each beneficiary and calculate any effect the trust income will have on the Taxable Income of Trevor.

End of Exercise. Solution available in Study Guide.

We suggest you work Self Study Problems Nineteen-4 and 5 at this point.

Attribution To Settlor (Reversionary Trust)

19-115.   There is a further form of income attribution that is unique to trust situations. Both income from holding the transferred property and capital gains from the disposition of the transferred property will be attributed back to the settlor if a trust meets the conditions specified in ITA 75(2).

19-116.   ITA 75(2) is applicable, without regard to the identity of the beneficiaries of the trust, if any one of the following conditions is satisfied:

1. The transferred property can revert to the settlor at a later point in time. In this situation, the trust is commonly referred to as a reversionary trust.

2. The transferred property will pass to persons to be determined by the settlor at a later point in time. This requirement prevents the settlor from adding additional beneficiaries, or classes of beneficiaries, subsequent to the creation of the trust.

3. The transferred property cannot be disposed of except with the settlor's consent or in accordance with the settlor's direction.

19-117.   The safest way to deal with the second condition is to not have the settlor act as a trustee. If that is not a practical alternative, it would be prudent to have at least three trustees and have majority approval of decisions. If the settlor is one of two trustees or, if decisions require unanimous approval by all trustees including the settlor, ITA 75(2) may apply. However, the CRA has indicated that the evaluation of condition 2 must be made on a case-by-case basis, considering all relevant circumstances.

Purchase Or Sale Of An Interest In A Trust

Income Interest
19-118.   An income interest in a trust is the right of a beneficiary under the trust to receive all or part of the income from the trust. The purchaser of an income interest in a trust will have a cost equal to the fair market value of the consideration given for that interest. This cost can be deducted against amounts of trust income that would otherwise be included in the individual's Taxable Income. Any portion of the cost that is not deducted against income from the trust in the current year can be carried forward for deduction against allocated trust income in subsequent years. When income allocations have reduced the cost of the interest to nil, subsequent receipts of income will be fully taxable.

19-119.   From the point of view of the vendor of an income interest, the proceeds of disposition will be equal to the fair market value of the consideration received. If the cost of the income interest (often nil) is different than the proceeds received, there will be a gain or loss on the disposition. As an income interest is not a capital asset, the gain or loss on its disposition will be treated as a fully taxable or deductible property income or loss.

Capital Interest
19-120.   As defined in ITA 108(1), a capital interest is all of the rights of a beneficiary of a trust, other than an income interest. As the name implies, a capital interest is a capital asset and any gain or loss on its disposition will be treated as a capital gain or loss.

19-121.   When a capital interest in a trust is purchased, the adjusted cost base is equal to the fair market value of the consideration given. This amount will be reduced by future distributions of assets from the trust. As we have noted, ITA 107(2) generally provides for a tax free rollover of assets from a trust to a beneficiary.

19-122.   If a beneficiary sells a capital interest in a trust, the proceeds of disposition will equal the fair market value of the consideration received. Unless the taxpayer has purchased the capital interest, its adjusted cost base will be nil. This means that the entire proceeds of disposition could be a capital gain. However, to determine the gain on a disposition of a capital interest in a trust resident in Canada, ITA 107(1)(a) defines the adjusted cost base to be the greater of:

• the adjusted cost base as usually determined, and
• the "cost amount" to the beneficiary.

19-123.   ITA 108(1) defines this cost amount as the beneficiary's proportionate interest in the net assets of the trust at their carrying value to the trust. This prevents the beneficiary from being taxed on the cost amount of the trust's assets, an amount that could be received on a tax free basis as a distribution from the trust. Capital losses on capital interest dispositions are determined in the usual manner. Since ACB is usually nil, such losses are uncommon.

Exercise Nineteen - 10

Subject: Sale Of A Capital Interest

The Jardhu family trust was established when the father transferred publicly traded securities with a cost of $120,000 and a fair market value of $250,000 into the trust. The beneficiaries of the trust are the father's two sons, Sam, aged 25 and Mehrdad, aged 27. They have an equal interest in the income and capital of the trust.

At the beginning of the current year, Mehrdad sells his capital interest in the trust to Sam. There have been no capital distributions from the trust. At the time of the sale, the fair market value of the securities in the trust is $380,000. Based on this, the transfer price for the capital interest is $190,000 [(1/2)($380,000)]. Determine the tax consequences of this transaction to each of the two brothers.

End of Exercise. Solution available in Study Guide.

Tax Planning

Family Trusts

Defined

19-124.   As we have noted, the term family trust is not defined in the *Income Tax Act*. Rather, it is a term that is used in practice to refer to a personal trust that has been established with members of the settlor's family as beneficiaries. These trusts can either be inter vivos trusts established during the settlor's lifetime or, alternatively, testamentary trusts created when the settlor dies. The provisions of these trusts often contain a fixed arrangement for the payments to beneficiaries. However, in some cases they are established with the payments to the beneficiaries left to the discretion of the trustees.

19-125.   While family trusts can be used for a variety of purposes, the most common objective of these trusts is income splitting. This process was introduced in Chapter 1, with further elaboration on the role of corporate structures in income splitting discussed in Chapter 15. In this Chapter we will give attention to income splitting in the context of family trusts.

Discretionary Trusts

19-126.   As we have noted, a family trust is usually established for income splitting purposes, typically by a wealthy individual with children or other family members who are in low tax brackets. Such individuals commonly have difficulty deciding which of their family members are, and will continue to be, the most deserving. A solution to this problem is the use of a discretionary trust.

19-127.   The provisions of discretionary trusts leave the amount and/or timing of payments to beneficiaries at the discretion of the trustees. This means that, if a particular beneficiary neglects his family duties on a regular basis, or appears to be profligate in his spending habits, his share of the income can be reduced, eliminated, or delayed to a later date. Tax planners like to point out that this provides the settlor with great flexibility. A less charitable view of the settlor's objectives is that this type of arrangement provides for continued control over the behaviour of family members (e.g., if a child fails to show up for family dinners, he can be reminded that his receipts from the family trust are discretionary).

19-128.   It is important to note that the settlor of the trust cannot be in a position of unilateral control over the amount and timing of the discretionary distributions, particularly if he is also one of the beneficiaries. If the settlor is in a position of control, the provisions of ITA 75(2) (see Paragraph 19-115) may be applicable, resulting in all of the income being attributed back to him. The usual way to avoid this problem is to have at least three trustees, with the amount of the discretionary distributions determined by majority rule. The CRA has indicated that, for this approach to be effective, the settlor cannot be a required part of the majority.

Income Splitting

19-129.   If a family trust is set up properly, the potential tax savings from income splitting can be significant. As alternative minimum tax (AMT) can be applicable if a large enough sum of eligible dividends are received, included in the following table is the AMT calculation for the daughter which shows that there will be no AMT in this case. The following table compares the federal Tax Payable on eligible dividends of $49,740 received by:

- a father who is subject to the maximum federal tax rate of 29 percent, and
- his adult daughter with no other source of income.

	Father	Daughter	AMT (Daughter)
Eligible Dividends Received	$49,740	$49,740	$49,740
Gross Up At 38 Percent	18,901	18,901	N/A For AMT
Taxable Dividends/Income	$68,641	$68,641	$49,740
Federal Tax			
[(29%)($68,641)]	$19,906		
[(15%)($43,561) + (22%)($25,080)]		$12,052	
[(15%)($49,740 - $40,000)]			$ 1,461
Federal Dividend Tax Credit			
[(55%)($18,901)] (Note 1)	(10,396)	(10,396)	N/A For AMT
Basic Personal Credit (Note 2)	N/A	(1,656)	(1,656)
Federal Tax Payable/AMT	$ 9,510	Nil	Nil

Note 1   We have rounded 6/11 to 55 percent in order to avoid rounding problems in making the calculations provide the desired result.

Note 2   Since the father would have other income against which he could apply his basic personal credit, it has not been taken into consideration in the preceding calculations.

19-130.   This example illustrates that if an individual in the top federal tax bracket transfers investments that pay annual eligible dividends of $49,740 to a trust and the trust distributes this income to a beneficiary with no other source of income and who is not subject to the income attribution rules, there is a federal tax savings of $9,510. The corresponding savings in provincial taxes would increase this amount significantly. This tax savings would be available per beneficiary if there were multiple beneficiaries. Of equal importance is the fact that this is not a one-time event. These tax savings can be accomplished on an annual basis as long as the beneficiaries have no other source of income.

19-131.   In the preceding example, up to $1,300 [($1,461 - $1,656) ÷ 15%] more of eligible dividends could be paid to the daughter before AMT would be payable. If personal tax credits were available that applied against the AMT, such as education related credits, considerably more eligible dividends could be received tax free. Note, however, in situations where the beneficiary will be subject to the tax on split income on private company dividends at the maximum rate of 29 percent (see Chapter 11), it would be much more difficult to use a family trust to provide tax savings.

Exercise Nineteen - 11

Subject: Family Trusts

Sarah Block is holding debt securities which produce interest income of $110,000 per year. She has other sources of income in excess of $200,000. She has two children. Her daughter, Jerri, is 22 years old and currently has no income that is subject to tax. Jerri's only tax credit is the basic personal credit. Sarah's son, Mark, is 26 years old. He is married and his wife has no income of her own. Mark has annual net rental income of $45,000. Assume that Mark's only tax credits are the basic personal credit and the spousal credit.

Determine the savings in federal taxes that could be achieved by transferring the debt securities to a family trust with her two children as equal income beneficiaries. The trust will be required to distribute all of its income on an annual basis.

End of Exercise. Solution available in Study Guide.

Qualifying Spousal Or Common-Law Partner Trusts

19-132.   As is discussed in Chapter 9, a rollover of assets to a spouse can be accomplished without the use of a trust. In the case of a living individual, the rollover is provided for under ITA 73(1) and (1.01), while for a deceased individual, the enabling provision is ITA 70(6). This makes it clear that a trust is not required to implement a tax free transfer of property for the benefit of a spouse. Why then are we concerned with qualifying spousal or common-law partner trusts? There are essentially two important reasons:

1. A trust can provide for the appropriate management of the transferred assets, particularly when these assets include an active business. In many cases, the spouse or common-law partner of a settlor may have no experience in the management of assets and, in such situations, the trust document can ensure that professional management is used. If the assets were simply transferred to the spouse or common-law partner, the use of such management would be left to the discretion and control of the transferee.

2. Also of importance is that the use of a trust can ensure that the assets are distributed in the manner desired by the settlor. While qualification requires that the transferred assets must "vest indefeasibly" with the spouse or common-law partner, the trust document can specify who the assets should be distributed to after the spouse or common-law partner dies. This could ensure, for example, that the assets are ultimately distributed only to the settlor's children if the spouse or common-law partner was to remarry.

Alter Ego Trusts

19-133.   The most commonly cited reason for using an alter ego trust is that the trust property will not be included in the settlor's estate and, as a consequence, will not be subject to probate procedures (probate is a court process that proves the authenticity and validity of a will). There are a number of advantages associated with avoiding probate:

• The probate fees can be high. In Ontario, for example, they are equal to 0.5 percent on the first $50,000 of the fair market value of the estate, plus 1.5 percent of the excess, with no upper limit.   On a $10 million estate these fees would total almost $150,000, a payment that can be completely eliminated with the use of an alter ego trust.

• The probate process can be time consuming. This can create difficulties for the management of an active business, as well as liquidity problems for the estate.

- When assets such as real estate are held in more than one jurisdiction (e.g., Canada and the U.S.), the probate procedures must be undertaken in multiple jurisdictions.

- Once probated, a will is in the public domain. For a nominal fee, any interested individual can obtain a copy, with the possibility that this will invade the privacy of surviving family members.

19-134. While this point has not been widely discussed in the literature that we have seen on this subject, an additional tax feature involved in establishing an alter ego trust is the possibility of establishing the trust in a low tax rate province. When there is a deemed disposition at death or on emigration, the taxation will occur in the province where the trust is resident. Given that, for 2013, there was an 11 percentage point difference between the maximum combined federal/provincial tax rate in Alberta (39%) and the corresponding maximum rate in Nova Scotia and Quebec (50%), this could result in a substantial tax savings.

19-135. We would also note that there is a significant non-tax reason for using an alter ego trust. From a legal point of view, it is much easier to challenge the validity of a will than it is to challenge the validity of a trust. Courts can be asked to consider moral obligations to family members in distributing the assets of an estate. With a trust, there is no will to challenge.

Joint Spousal Or Joint Common-Law Partner Trusts

19-136. A joint spousal or joint common-law partner trust has the same tax characteristics as an alter ego trust. The basic difference is that these trusts are established to hold the combined assets of both an individual and his spouse or common-law partner. Given this, their tax planning features are largely the same as those discussed for alter ego trusts in the preceding Paragraphs.

Estate Planning

Non-Tax Considerations

19-137. The subject of estate planning is complex and involves considerations that go well beyond the scope of this text. In fact, appropriate planning for a large estate will often involve lawyers, investment advisors, accountants, and tax advisors. Indeed, it may even be necessary to have religious advisors or psychological counselors participate in order to deal with some of the moral or emotional issues that are involved.

19-138. The following points are among the more important non-tax considerations in planning an estate:

Intent Of The Testator The foremost goal of estate planning is to ensure that the wishes of the testator (a person who has died and left a will) are carried out. This will involve ensuring that the assets left by the testator are distributed at the appropriate times and to the specified beneficiaries. The primary document for ensuring that the intent of the testator is fulfilled is, of course, the will.

Preparation Of A Final Will The major document in the estate planning process is the final will. It should be carefully prepared to provide detailed instructions for the disposition of assets, investment decisions to be made, and the extent to which trusts will be used. An executor should be named to administer the estate, and the will should be reviewed periodically to ensure that it reflects the testator's current wishes and family status.

Preparation Of A Living Will Equally important to the preparation of a final will, a living will provides detailed instructions regarding investments and other personal decisions in the event of physical or mental incapacity at any point in a person's lifetime. A power of attorney is similar, except that it does not require the individual to be mentally or physically incapacitated in order to be used.

Ensuring Liquidity A plan should be established to provide for liquidity at the time of death. Major expenses, often including funeral expenses and income taxes, will arise at this time. Funds needed for these payments should be available, or adequate life insurance should be arranged in advance, to avoid the need for emergency sales of capital assets to raise the necessary cash.

Simplicity   While the disposition of a large estate will rarely be simple, effective estate planning should ensure that the plan can be understood by the testator and all beneficiaries of legal age. In addition, any actions that can reduce the cost and complexity of administering the estate should be considered. This might involve disposing of investments in non-public shares, or repatriating assets that are located in foreign countries that might become subject to foreign taxation.

Avoidance Of Family Disputes   Unfortunately, disputes among beneficiaries are a common part of estate settlement procedures. If equitable treatment of beneficiaries is a goal of the testator, efforts should be made to ensure that all beneficiaries believe that they have been treated in an equitable manner. If the testator wants to distribute assets in a fashion that could be viewed as inequitable by any of the interested parties, care should be taken to make this intention unequivocal.

Expediting The Transition   The procedures required in the settlement of an estate should be designed to expedite the process. A long settlement period can increase uncertainties related to the value of assets, add to the complications associated with the required distribution of the assets, and prolong the frustration of the beneficiaries.

Tax Considerations

19-139.   In addition to the preceding non-tax considerations, estate planning must also consider various tax factors. Fundamental tax planning goals for all taxpayers apply equally to estate planning. Briefly, these goals involve the legal and orderly arrangement of one's affairs, before the time of a transaction or event, to reduce and defer income taxes.

19-140.   In effective estate planning, the overriding income tax goals are to defer and minimize tax payments. Several important issues should be considered in dealing with this objective. These can be described as follows:

Prior To Death   Planning should attempt to minimize taxes for the individual in the years prior to death. If the individual earns income that is not required in these years, attempts should be made to defer the payment of tax and transfer the before-tax income to the ultimate beneficiaries. The use of a discretionary trust can assist in achieving this goal.

Year Of Death   Planning should attempt to minimize income taxes payable in the year of death. Deemed dispositions will occur at death and, in addition, amounts in certain types of deferred income plans usually must be included in the taxpayer's final return. Relief can be achieved through tax deferred rollovers to a spouse and transfers of certain types of property (e.g., farm property) to children or grandchildren. The will can also contain instructions to ensure that the maximum RRSP contribution is made to the spouse's RRSP within the deadline.

Income Splitting   Effective planning should allow income splitting among family members who are in lower tax brackets. This can be accomplished by the appropriate splitting of income (e.g., paying salaries and wages for services rendered) and distributing property among beneficiaries throughout a taxpayer's lifetime, recognizing the limitations imposed by the tax on split income.

Foreign Jurisdictions   Planning should normally attempt to minimize taxes that will be incurred in foreign jurisdictions. This is especially true for jurisdictions with significant estate taxes as such taxes are generally not eligible for foreign tax credits or deduction in Canada. To the extent that it is consistent with the individual's investment plans and the residence of intended beneficiaries, holdings of foreign assets at death, or distributions to beneficiaries in foreign locations, should usually be avoided by residents of Canada. Minimizing foreign investments will also simplify the administration of an estate.

Administration Period   Planning should minimize taxes payable while the estate is being administered. Discretion provided to trustees in distributing the income of an inter vivos trust may assist in achieving this goal.

19-141.   Most of the tax procedures related to these issues have already been introduced. We have discussed spouse and common-law partner rollovers in previous Chapters and the use of trusts was covered earlier in this Chapter. An important aspect of estate planning that requires additional consideration is the estate freeze. Procedures to be used in these arrangements are outlined in the material that follows.

Estate Freeze

Objectives Of An Estate Freeze

19-142.   The objective of an estate freeze is, as the name implies, to freeze the value of the estate for tax purposes at a particular point in time. Typically, arrangements are made for all future appreciation to accrue to related parties such as a spouse, children, or grandchildren. Transfers of income generating private company shares to minor children may be deferred to avoid the tax on split income.

Example   Mr. Chisholm is a wealthy and successful entrepreneur who has a wife and two young children. He owns a variety of capital assets that are producing Taxable Income and appreciating in value. He has several objectives in creating his estate plan:

- During the remainder of his life, Mr. Chisholm would like to transfer all or part of his Taxable Income to a group of individuals and charities who will ultimately be the beneficiaries of his estate.

- Mr. Chisholm would like to freeze the tax values of his assets and allow future growth to accrue to the intended beneficiaries.

- Since the current fair market value of his assets exceeds their tax cost, Mr. Chisholm would like to avoid any immediate taxation resulting from a disposition of these assets with accrued gains.

- Mr. Chisholm would like the transfer of future growth in asset values to accrue so that his beneficiaries will not be subject to taxation in the year of the estate freeze, in any intervening years, or in the year of his death.

- Mr. Chisholm wants to retain the right to the current value of the property at the time of the estate freeze. In addition, he wishes to retain control of the use of the property until his death.

19-143.   This example will be used as a basis for discussing a variety of techniques that can be used to freeze an estate's value. Some of these techniques will achieve all of Mr. Chisholm's goals, while others will only succeed in achieving one or two of them.

Techniques Not Involving Rollovers

Gifts

19-144.   Mr. Chisholm can freeze the value of his estate without using rollover provisions. The most straightforward technique is to simply give property to his prospective beneficiaries. While this would accomplish the goal of transferring future growth in the estate to the beneficiaries, unless the transfer was to a spouse or common-law partner, this approach would have the serious drawback of attracting immediate taxation on any difference between the fair market value of the assets and Mr. Chisholm's tax cost.

19-145.   In addition, if the person receiving the gift is a spouse or minor child, income attribution rules could apply after the gift is made. Further drawbacks are the fact that Mr. Chisholm would lose control over the assets and that certain income received by minor children may be subject to the tax on split income.

19-146.   While gifts result in a loss of control, Mr. Chisholm may want to accelerate his donations to registered charities. The value of the tax credit associated with such gifts can more
than offset any income arising as the result of such distributions. In particular, if a gift is made
of shares listed on a designated stock exchange, the capital gains inclusion rate is reduced to
nil (See Chapter 11).

Instalment Sales

19-147.   Mr. Chisholm could freeze the value of the estate by selling the assets to the
intended beneficiaries on an instalment basis. Capital gains could be deferred until payment
is received, but the gains would need to be reported over the next five years based on the
capital gains reserve calculations.

19-148.   To avoid income attribution and inadequate consideration problems, the sale
should be made at fair market value. However, if the intended beneficiaries do not have sufficient assets to make the purchase, this may not be a feasible solution. A further problem is that
Mr. Chisholm would lose control over the property.

Establishing A Trust

19-149.   An estate freeze can also be accomplished by setting up a trust in favour of one or
more beneficiaries. Here again, this will transfer income and future growth from Mr. Chisholm's hands to the trust. The trust can be structured so that he retains some control over the
assets in the trust.

19-150.   The problem with this arrangement is that, except in the case of a qualifying spouse
or common-law partner trust, a joint spousal or common-law partner trust, or an alter ego
trust, there is no rollover provision that provides for tax deferred transfers of assets to a trust.
As a result, if the trust is set up for beneficiaries other than Mr. Chisholm or his spouse, Mr.
Chisholm will incur taxation on any capital gains accrued at the time of the transfer. As well,
any dividends received from a private corporation by minor beneficiaries will be subject to
the tax on split income, whether the shares are held directly or through a trust.

Use Of A Holding Company

19-151.   Mr. Chisholm could transfer assets to a holding company in which intended beneficiaries have a substantial equity interest, without using a rollover provision. This will freeze
the value of his estate and, if the assets transferred have fair market values that are equal to or
less than their adjusted cost base, it can be an effective vehicle for realizing losses. However,
without the use of a rollover provision, such as that found in ITA 85, any capital gains or recapture amounts that have accrued to the time of the transfer will become subject to immediate
taxation.

Section 86 Share Exchange

Nature Of The Exchange

19-152.   Chapter 17 provided an overview of ITA 86 which applies to the exchange of shares
by a shareholder in the course of a reorganization of capital. In certain situations, a share
exchange constitutes the best solution to the estate freeze problem. Specifically, this rollover
is most appropriate in a situation that involves an individual who is the sole owner of a
successful private corporation.

19-153.   By exchanging common shares for preferred shares that have equal value, the
owner will, in effect, eliminate his participation in the future growth of the company. At the
same time, common shares can be issued to intended beneficiaries at a nominal value, and
these shareholders can participate in the company's future income and any growth in the
value of its assets.

Example

19-154.   While detailed consideration was given to ITA 86 rollovers in Chapter 17, the
following simple example will serve to review these procedures.

Example   Over her lifetime, Mrs. Hadley has been the sole owner and driving force behind Hadley Inc., a manufacturing business located in Alberta. At the end of the current year, the condensed Balance Sheet of this Company was as follows:

Hadley Inc.
Balance Sheet

Net Identifiable Assets	$10,000,000
Common Stock (No Par - 1,000 Shares)	$ 2,000,000
Retained Earnings	8,000,000
Total Shareholders' Equity	$10,000,000

On the basis of an independent appraisal, the fair market value of this business was established at $15,000,000. Mrs. Hadley has a husband and three adult children and would like them to share equally in her estate. The $2,000,000 Common Stock account is both the adjusted cost base and the PUC of her shares.

19-155.   Under ITA 86, Mrs. Hadley can exchange, on a tax deferred basis, her common shares that have an adjusted cost base of $2 million (also the amount of contributed capital and PUC) for preferred shares with a redemption value of $15 million (the fair market value of the business). These preferred shares would have no participation in the future growth of the Company and, as a result, Mrs. Hadley has effectively frozen the value of her estate.

19-156.   If Mrs. Hadley wishes to retain control of the Company, the preferred shares can be established as the only outstanding voting shares. While this share exchange will be free of any capital gains taxation, Mrs. Hadley's adjusted cost base and PUC for the new preferred shares remains at the former common share value of $2 million. If the preferred shares are sold for their market value of $15 million, a $13 million capital gain will result ($15 million - $2 million). Alternatively, if the shares are redeemed for $15 million by the Company, there will be a $13 million taxable dividend under ITA 84(3).

19-157.   The tax cost basis for the identifiable assets owned by the Company has not been altered by the share exchange transaction.

19-158.   At this point, the redemption value of Mrs. Hadley's preferred shares represents the entire fair market value of the business and, as a consequence, the value of any common shares issued will not exceed the amount contributed by the investors. This means that such shares can be issued for a nominal value, without any appearance that the purchasers are indirectly receiving a gift from Mrs. Hadley. Thus, 1,000 common shares could be issued to Mrs. Hadley's intended beneficiaries at $10 per share as follows:

Spouse (250 Shares At $10)	$ 2,500
Child One (250 Shares At $10)	2,500
Child Two (250 Shares At $10)	2,500
Child Three (250 Shares At $10)	2,500
Total Common Stock Contributed	$10,000

19-159.   These common shares would benefit from the future income and growth in asset values that may be experienced by Hadley Inc.

19-160.   As illustrated in this example, a Section 86 rollover can provide an ideal solution to the estate freeze problem. It can be used to transfer all future growth in the estate into the hands of intended beneficiaries with no immediate tax effects on the individual making the transfer. The beneficiaries will be taxed on income earned subsequent to the estate freeze (if any beneficiary is a minor, they will have to pay the tax on split income on any dividends received). Further, by issuing non-voting shares to the beneficiaries, the individual undertaking the freeze can retain control of the business. In addition, a Section 86 rollover is fairly straightforward to administer and does not require the formation of a separate holding corporation.

Rollover Provisions - Section 85 vs. Section 86

19-161 A Section 85 rollover of property to a holding corporation can also be used to implement an estate freeze. The rollover provisions of ITA 85 were given full consideration in Chapter 16, and will not be repeated here.

19-162. In comparing the use of ITA 85 and ITA 86, you should note that Section 85 can be used in a broader variety of circumstances than is the case with Section 86. More specifically, Section 86 deals only with exchanges of shares in the course of the reorganization of an existing corporation. This means that Section 86 can only be used in situations where the assets involved in the estate freeze are shares of a corporation. Section 85 would have to be used if the estate consists of other types of property.

19-163. When Section 86 can be used, it is an easier procedure to implement. Unlike Section 85, which requires a formal election to be made and either an existing corporation or the formation of a new corporation, Section 86 applies automatically once the required conditions are met. By using a Section 86 reorganization, the savings in legal and accounting fees can be significant. The many complexities involved in effecting an estate freeze using rollovers make it difficult to comment on the relative desirability of Sections 85 and 86 for estate freezes in general terms.

SIFT Partnerships And Trusts

19-164. As was noted in Chapter 18, legislation which became fully effective in 2011 has served to largely eliminate SIFT partnerships and trusts. Given this, we no longer provide coverage of this subject in *Canadian Tax Principles*.

Key Terms Used In This Chapter

19-165. The following is a list of the key terms used in this Chapter. These terms, and their meanings, are compiled in the Glossary Of Key Terms located at the back of the separate paper Study Guide.

Alter Ego Trust	Preferred Beneficiary Election
Beneficiary	Qualifying Spousal or
Capital Interest (In A Trust)	Common-Law Partner Trust
Discretionary Trust	Reorganization Of Capital (ITA 86)
Estate	Reversionary Trust
Estate Freeze	Rollover
Executor	Settlor
Family Trust	Split Income
Income Attribution	Spousal Or Common-Law Partner Trust
Income Interest (In A Trust)	Tax Planning
Income Splitting	Testamentary Trust
Inter Vivos Trust	Trust
Joint Spousal Or Common-Law	Trustee
Partner Trust	Twenty-One (21) Year
Non-Discretionary Trust	Deemed Disposition Rule
Personal Trust	Will
Preferred Beneficiary	

References

19-166.   For more detailed study of the material in this Chapter, we would refer you to the following:

ITA 70(6)	Transfers To Spousal Trusts On Death
ITA 73(1)	Inter-Vivos Transfers To Spousal Trusts
ITA 74.1 to 74.5	Attribution Rules
ITA 75(2)	Trust (Attribution To Settlor)
ITA 85(1)	Transfer Of Property To Corporation By Shareholders
ITA 86(1)	Exchange Of Shares By A Shareholder In Course Of Reorganization Of Capital
ITA 104 to 108	Trusts And Their Beneficiaries
ITA 122	Tax Payable By Inter Vivos Trust
ITA 122.1	Definitions (SIFT Trusts)
ITA 197	Tax On SIFT Partnership
IC-76-19R3	Transfer Of Property To A Corporation Under Section 85
IT-209R	Inter-Vivos Gifts Of Capital Property To Individuals Directly Or Through Trusts
IT-286R2	Trusts - Amount Payable
IT-291R3	Transfer Of Property To A Corporation Under Subsection 85(1)
IT-305R4	Testamentary Spouse Trusts
IT-342R	Trusts - Income Payable To Beneficiaries
IT-369R	Attribution Of Trust Income To Settlor
IT-381R3	Trusts - Capital Gains And Losses And The Flow-Through Of Taxable Capital Gains To Beneficiaries
IT-385R2	Disposition Of An Income Interest In A Trust
IT-394R2	Preferred Beneficiary Election
IT-406R2	Tax Payable By An Inter Vivos Trust
IT-447	Residence Of A Trust Or Estate
IT-465R	Non-Resident Beneficiaries Of Trusts
IT-510	Transfers and Loans of Property Made After May 22, 1985 to a Related Minor
IT-511R	Interspousal And Certain Other Transfers And Loans Of Property
IT-524	Trusts - Flow Through Of Taxable Dividends To A Beneficiary After 1987
T4013	Trust Guide

Problems For Self Study

(The solutions for these problems can be found in the separate Study Guide.)

Self Study Problem Nineteen - 1 (Testamentary Trusts - Tax Payable)

On June 6, 2013, Mr. Fred Masters died at his home in Corner Brook, Newfoundland. Under the terms of his will, all of his property was transferred to a testamentary trust. The trust document establishes December 31 as the year end for the trust and contains the following additional provisions:

1. Thirty percent of the income is to be paid to Mr. Masters' daughter, Mrs. Joan Nelson.

2. Fifty percent of the income is to be paid to Mr. Masters' son, Charles Masters.

3. The remaining income is to be retained by the trust, to be distributed at the discretion of the trustees. No discretionary distributions were made prior to December 31, 2013.

Neither of his children have any income other than income from the trust.

Between June 6 and December 31, 2013, the trust had the following income and expenses:

Eligible Dividends Received From Canadian Companies		$ 87,000
Interest On British Bonds (Net Of 15 Percent Withholding Tax)		93,500
Net Rental Income:		
Rental Revenues	$128,000	
Rental Expenses Other Than CCA	(74,000)	
CCA Claimed	(33,000)	21,000
Total Income		$201,500

Required:

A. Determine the Taxable Income for the trust and each beneficiary for 2013.

B. Calculate the total federal Tax Payable for the trust for 2013.

Self Study Problem Nineteen - 2 (Testamentary Trusts - Tax Payable)

A testamentary trust was created when Mr. Rowand died four years ago. The beneficiaries are his wife, Mrs. Rowand and Roger Rowand, Mr. Rowand's adult son. For the year ended December 31, 2013, the following amounts are reported for the trust:

Business Income	$20,000
Interest	3,000
Non-Eligible Dividends Received From CCPC	50,000
Rent Receipts	12,000
Rental Operating Expenses	6,000
CCA On Rental Property	2,000

Mrs. Rowand and Roger have no other sources of income. They have no personal tax credits under ITA 118 other than their basic personal credit.

Case One The trust provides for one-half of any dividend income to be retained in the trust. The remaining one-half of the dividend income, as well as all of the other net income is to be paid 60 percent to Mrs. Rowand and 40 percent to Roger Rowand.

Case Two All of the trust's income will be allocated to Mrs. Rowand and Roger on a 60 percent and 40 percent basis.

Required:

A. For both Cases, calculate Taxable Income and federal Tax Payable for 2013 for each person, including the trust.

B. Compare the total federal Tax Payable by all persons in Case One with the total Tax Payable by all persons in Case Two. Explain any difference.

Self Study Problem Nineteen - 3 (Inter Vivos Trusts - Tax Payable)

Ms. Tanya Robinson is a very successful businessperson. She wishes to have most of her property ultimately transferred to her son, Malcolm and daughter, Maisy. Both of Ms. Robinson's children are over 30 years old. To achieve her goal, she transferred a substantial amount of property to a trust in their favour 10 years ago. The trust has a December 31 year end, and Ms. Robinson assists with its management. However, she has no beneficial interest in either its income or its capital.

The terms of the trust call for Malcolm to receive 30 percent of the income, while Maisy receives 50 percent. The remaining income is to accumulate within the trust, to be paid to Ms. Robinson's two children at the time of her death. For the purpose of distributions to beneficiaries, trust income includes any capital gains earned in the trust. The 2013 income figures for the trust are as follows:

Interest On Government Bonds	$ 65,000
Eligible Dividends From Canadian Corporations	250,000
Revenues From Rental Property	492,000
Cash Expenses On Rental Property	342,000

In previous years, CCA was deducted from the rental income in order to determine net rental income. However, in November, 2013, the rental property was sold. The property consisted of an apartment building and the land on which it was located. It was transferred into the trust when the trust was first established. The relevant information related to the disposition is as follows:

	Building	Land
Proceeds Of Disposition	$4,560,000	$2,300,000
Undepreciated Capital Cost	3,380,000	N/A
Capital Cost/Adjusted Cost Base	3,840,000	1,430,000

This is the first disposition of capital property by the trust since its establishment.

Required:

A. Calculate the Taxable Income of the trust, Malcolm, and Maisy for 2013.

B. Calculate the federal Tax Payable for the trust, for the year ending December 31, 2013.

C. Will the 21 year deemed disposition rule affect the trust or beneficiaries in 2013? What actions should be taken to mitigate the effect of the rule and when?

Self Study Problem Nineteen - 4 (Inter Vivos Trusts - Income Attribution)

In planning an estate freeze, Mrs. Dion plans to settle cash and portfolio investments in a trust. The terms of the trust will provide that:

• Sixty percent of the annual income will be paid to her husband, Mr. Dion.

• Forty percent of the annual income will be allocated to the Dion twins, who are 20 years old and in university. The income will be split equally, and the timing of payments is at the discretion of the trustee.

• The trust capital will be distributed on December 31, 2024, following the same allocation as for income.

The trust's income will consist of interest, dividends, and capital gains.

Required:

A. Identify the type of trust that is being used.

B. Indicate what the trust's year end date will be.

C. Indicate the persons that will have to include the trust's income in their Net Income For Tax Purposes.

D. Explain how your answer to Part C would change if Mrs. Dion forms the trust by the settlement of a nominal amount of cash. Mrs. Dion then lends money to the trust to purchase the portfolio investments from her at fair market value.

E. Explain how the taxation of the trust income will change if Mr. and Mrs. Dion were living separately because of a marriage breakdown.

Self Study Problem Nineteen - 5 (Testamentary Trusts - Transfers Of Assets)

Mrs. Turner died on October 1, 2012. The capital cost and the fair market value of the assets she owned at the time of her death were as follows:

Asset	Capital Cost	Fair Market Value
Principal Residence - Land	$ 20,000	$ 120,000
Principal Residence - Building	80,000	145,000
Cottage - Land	40,000	200,000
Cottage - Building	112,000	122,000
Warehouse - Land	55,000	75,000
Warehouse - Building (UCC = $45,000)	85,000	85,000
Stock Market Portfolio	220,000	280,000

According to her will, the principal residence and the warehouse were transferred to a trust for the benefit of her 32 year old daughter, Melanie. After Mrs. Turner's death, Melanie moved into the principal residence and intends to live there indefinitely. The trust is to pay for the maintenance of the principal residence.

The cottage and stock market portfolio were transferred into another trust for the exclusive benefit of Mr. West, Mrs. Turner's second husband.

Mr. West died of grief on January 10, 2013. The fair market values of all of the assets did not change between October 1, 2012 and January 10, 2013.

Required: Describe the income tax consequences for Mrs. Turner, her daughter Melanie, and Mr. West, resulting from:

A. the transfers of property to the two trusts; and

B. the death of Mr. West.

Assignment Problems

(The solutions for these problems are only available in
the solutions manual that has been provided to your instructor.)

Assignment Problem Nineteen - 1 (Transfer Of Property To And From Trusts)

Each of the following independent Cases involve transfers of property to trusts by a settlor for no consideration. Two of the Cases also involve capital distributions from trusts to capital beneficiaries.

A. A gift of depreciable capital property is made to an inter vivos trust in favour of the settlor's adult children. The capital cost of the property to the settlor was $23,300. On the date of the gift, the UCC was $15,400 and the fair market value was $26,400.

B. A gift of depreciable capital property is made to an inter vivos trust in favour of the settlor's adult children. The capital cost of the property to the settlor was $19,500. On the date of the gift, the property had a UCC of $12,400, and a fair market value of $15,200. At a later time, when the property is distributed to a capital beneficiary, the property has a UCC of $13,600 and a fair market value of $17,600.

C. A transfer of non-depreciable capital property is made to a qualifying spousal testamentary trust. The cost of the capital property to the deceased spouse was $18,200, and the fair market value on the date of the transfer to the trust is $76,400. At the time of his death, the decedent had net capital loss carry forwards in excess of $91,500.

D. A gift of non-depreciable capital property is made to an inter vivos trust in favour of the settlor's adult children. The adjusted cost base of the property to the settlor was $85,400. Its fair market value on the date of the gift is $123,200.

E. A gift of non-depreciable capital property is made to an inter vivos trust in favour of the settlor's adult children. The adjusted cost base of the property to the settlor was $43,200. On the date of the gift, the property had a fair market value of $51,600. At a later time, when the value of the property has increased to $61,400, this property is distributed to a capital beneficiary of the trust.

F. Capital property is transferred to an alter ego trust. The cost of the capital property to the settlor was $14,200 and the fair market value on the date of the transfer is $23,100.

Required: For each Case indicate:

1. The tax consequences to the settlor that result from the transfer of property to the trust assuming the transfer price is chosen to optimize the tax position of the settlor.

2. The tax value(s) for the transferred property that will be recorded by the trust.

3. In those cases where property is transferred to a beneficiary, the tax consequences to the trust and the tax value(s) that will be recorded by the beneficiary.

Assignment Problem Nineteen - 2 (Inter Vivos Trusts - Income Attribution)

In the process of planning an estate freeze, Gerald Butler intends to transfer a large group of investments to a trust. The terms of this trust will require that, on an annual basis, 50 percent of the income of the trust be distributed to his wife, Inara Dickson, with the remaining 50 percent going to their son, Barry. Barry is 25 years old and has employment income of about $35,000 per year.

The trust's income will consist of interest, dividends, and capital gains.

The terms of the trust require that all of the trust's assets be distributed on December 3, 2024, using the same allocation that is used for annual distributions.

Required:

A. Identify the type of trust that is being used.

B. Indicate what the trust's year end date will be.

C. Indicate the persons that will have to include the trust's income in their Net Income For Tax Purposes.

D. Explain how your answer to Part C would change if Mr. Butler forms the trust by the settlement of a nominal amount of cash. Mr. Butler then lends money to the trust to purchase the portfolio investments from him at fair market value.

E. Explain how the taxation of the trust income will change if Mr. Butler and Ms. Dickson were living separately because of a marriage breakdown.

Assignment Problem Nineteen - 3 (Trusts And Income Splitting)

Genevieve Marcoux is a biochemist who annually earns a $175,000 salary. In addition, she has $40,000 in investment income from an $800,000 term deposit she inherited.

Genevieve is a single mother with two children. Her daughter, Lisa, is 21 years old and attends university in the U.S. Lisa plans to become a medical doctor and expects to attend university for another seven years. Lisa's tuition and books cost $30,000 (Canadian) each year. Genevieve's son, Philip, is one year old, and is cared for by a nanny who is paid $14,500 a year.

When Philip is five years old, Genevieve intends to send him to a private school, and the fees will be comparable to the cost of a nanny. In addition, Genevieve incurs $500 each month in direct expenses for each child, totaling $12,000 a year. Genevieve does not expect either Lisa or Philip to earn any Taxable Income until they complete university.

Genevieve would like to transfer the term deposit to a trust for her children, so the family can benefit from income splitting currently, and in the future. While she supports her children fully, she does not want them to receive any cash directly from the trust until they are each 35 years old. Until then, she wants the trust to pay for their care, education, and other direct expenses.

Required: Outline how a trust might be used to split income among Genevieve's family members.

Assignment Problem Nineteen - 4 (Testamentary Trusts - Tax Minimization)

Mr. Hyde died early in 2013, and a testamentary trust was established under his will. The trust will have a December 31 year end. The beneficiaries of the trust are Mrs. Hyde, an architect earning more than $200,000 per year, and her son, Ross, an unemployed actor with no reliable source of income in the foreseeable future.

The trust agreement required annual payments of $25,000 and $15,000 to be made to Mrs. Hyde and Ross, respectively. While the payments to Mrs. Hyde are fixed, the trustee may pay Ross additional amounts from the trust as he considers appropriate for Ross's personal needs. The trustee can make discretionary capital distributions to either beneficiary in any year. After 10 years, the remaining capital and any retained income of the trust will be distributed to Ross.

For the years ended December 31, 2013 and 2014, the trustee projects the following trust income receipts:

Trust Income	2013	2014
Interest	$23,000	$24,000
Eligible Dividends Received From		
Canadian Corporations	22,000	24,000
Total Income	$45,000	$48,000

The 2013 and 2014 payments to Mrs. Hyde and Ross will be as follows:

Trust Payments	2013	2014
Mrs. Hyde	$25,000	$25,000
Ross Hyde	15,000	20,000

Required: With a view to minimizing total Tax Payable by the trust and the beneficiaries, determine the amount and type of income that should be distributed to each beneficiary. In addition, calculate the total minimum 2013 federal tax payable on the trust's income in the hands of the trust and the beneficiaries after the distributions. What tax advice do you have for the trustee for 2014?

Assignment Problem Nineteen - 5 *(Inter Vivos Trusts - Tax Payable)*

Ms. Sally Jurgens is a very successful advertising executive. About 10 years ago, she transferred a large group of investments into a trust in favour of her two children. The fiscal year of the trust ends on December 31, and Ms. Jurgens has no beneficial interest in either the income or capital of the trust.

Under the terms of the trust, her daughter Jessica is to receive 45 percent of all of the income of the trust, while her son Joseph is to receive 40 percent of this income. Jessica is aged 32 while Joseph is 28. Both children are single and have no current sources of income other than the trust.

The undistributed income is to accumulate within the trust, to be paid out to the children at the time of Ms. Jurgen's death.

The income figures for the year ending on December 31, 2013, are as follows:

Interest Income On GICs	$126,000
Eligible Dividends Received From Canadian Corporations	462,000
Revenues From Rental Property	125,000
Cash Expenses On Rental Property	83,000

On October 1, 2013, the rental property was sold. The property consisted of an apartment building and the land on which it was located, all of which was transferred into the trust when it was established. The relevant information related to the disposition is as follows:

	Building	Land
Proceeds Of Disposition	$962,000	$250,000
Undepreciated Capital Cost	627,000	N/A
Capital Cost/Adjusted Cost Base	725,000	85,000

This is the first disposition of capital property by the trust since its establishment.

Required:

A. Calculate the Taxable Income of the trust, Jessica Jurgens, and Joseph Jurgens for the year ending December 31, 2013.

B. Calculate the federal Tax Payable for the trust, for the year ending December 31, 2013.

Assignment Problem Nineteen - 6
(Testamentary Trusts - Transfer and Tax Payable)

At the occurrence of Mary Staple's death on March 31, 2013, all of her property was transferred to a testamentary trust with a December 31 year end.

The terms of the trust require that 30 percent of the trust's income be distributed to her 27 year old son, Mac Staple, with 40 percent going to her 22 year old daughter, Muff Staple. The remaining 30 percent will be retained by the trust to be used for discretionary distributions to either child.

In October, 2013, a discretionary distribution of $25,000 was made to Muff. The trust will designate this distribution to be a combination of rental income and interest income.

Information on the transferred property is as follows:

	Tax Cost	Fair Market Value March 31, 2013
Public Company Shares	$1,420,000	$2,156,000
Government Of Canada Bonds	562,000	562,000
Rental Property		
Land	622,000	787,000
Building (Cost = $850,000)	684,000	1,230,000

Assignment Problems

Between March 31 and December 31, 2013, the following income and expense amounts were recorded by the trust:

Eligible Dividends Received		$ 85,000
Interest On Bonds		17,000
Net Rental Income:		
Rental Revenues	$132,450	
Rental Expenses Other Than CCA	(31,500)	
CCA Claimed	(23,400)	77,550
Total Income		$179,550

Required:

A. Determine the tax consequences in Mary's final return resulting from her death and the transfer of property to the trust on March 31, 2013.

B. Determine the Taxable Income for the trust and each beneficiary for 2013.

C. Calculate the total federal Tax Payable for the trust for 2013.

Assignment Problem Nineteen - 7 (Estate Freeze)

Mr. John Spencer is a wealthy friend of yours who is nearing retirement age. He has a wife, two married children, and several grandchildren. He has heard the term "estate freeze" and he understands that implementing one would help organize his affairs.

Required: Provide Mr. Spencer with an explanation of an estate freeze and briefly describe some of the ways in which this process can be carried out.

Assignment Problem Nineteen - 8 (Estate Freeze)

Mr. and Mrs. Zahar own a very lucrative company, Zeus Goose Ltd. The fair market value of the common shares is $5,000,000 and they have a nominal cost base and paid up capital.

The Zahar's want to set up an estate freeze to pass on future growth of the Company to their three children, all of whom are in their twenties. Mr. and Mrs. Zahar are in their early fifties and want to continue to control the Company for many years. While they have obtained information on how a corporate reorganization can be used to effect an estate freeze, they would also like to investigate the use of trusts in their estate planning.

Required: Outline important issues that should be considered by Mr. and Mrs. Zahar if they are to use trusts in an estate freeze.

Assignment Problem Nineteen - 9 (Estate Planning)

One of your clients, Daniel Loh has read several articles describing the tax advantages of charitable donations. Mr. Loh is 73 years old and has had a very successful career in business in Canada. As a consequence, he owns a wide variety of investments in publicly traded securities and private company shares, as well as real estate in Canada and Singapore. You estimate that his assets have a current value in excess of $15 million.

Due to a car accident in Singapore that disfigured him horribly and made him a recluse, he has never married and has no friends or living relatives. When he dies, he intends to leave all of his assets to a group of his favourite charities.

As he has never spent any time on estate planning, he has asked you to help him understand the issues and give him suggestions of what he should consider.

Required: Write a brief report providing the advice requested by your client.

CHAPTER 20

International Issues In Taxation

Introduction

Subjects Covered

20-1. This Chapter 20 is something of a potpourri of issues that are loosely related by their association with transactions and events that extend beyond Canada's borders. In some cases, we are dealing with the application of Canadian tax law to transactions and events that occur outside of Canada. In other cases, we are concerned only with the fact that individual taxable entities are moving between Canada and other jurisdictions. Some of these transactions and events relate to taxation that is associated with the laws that exist in jurisdictions outside of Canada.

20-2. In dealing with the diverse nature of the material covered, we have organized this Chapter as follows:

Residence As noted in Chapter 1, the Canadian income tax is largely based on the assessment of residents of Canada. Issues associated with the determination of a taxable entity's residence will be given detailed consideration in this Chapter.

Taxation Of Canadian Source Income Earned By Non-Residents While the basic approach to the assessment of income tax in Canada is to assess tax on Canadian residents, under certain circumstances, non-residents can be required to pay Canadian income taxes. Depending on the type of income, the tax may be assessed under Part I or, alternatively, Part XIII of the *Income Tax Act*. Detailed consideration will be given to both of these provisions.

Immigration And Emigration We touched on this subject in Chapter 8 when we covered the deemed disposition of most capital assets when an individual emigrates from Canada. In this Chapter, we will consider some of the other complications associated with leaving Canada, as well as tax considerations related to immigration.

Taxation Of Foreign Source Income Earned By Residents This material begins by discussing the reporting requirements applicable to Canadian residents who have foreign investments. This is followed by material dealing with non-resident taxpayers who have the following types of income:

- foreign source employment income;

- foreign source income from unincorporated businesses;

- foreign source interest income; and

- capital gains resulting from the disposition of foreign assets.

The remainder of the chapter provides limited coverage of dividend income received by Canadian residents from non-resident entities. This would include material on foreign affiliates, controlled foreign affiliates, and foreign accrual property income (FAPI). Some of this material is extremely difficult to understand and because of this, some instructors may choose not to include it in their courses.

The Role of International Tax Treaties

20-3.   Tax treaties are entered into between countries for the purpose of facilitating cross-border trade and investment by removing income tax obstacles. For example, a Canadian resident employed in the U.S. is potentially subject to Canadian tax under the residence approach. In the absence of a treaty, he could also be subject to U.S. tax on the same income under the source approach. This would, of course, create a significant impediment to cross-border employment.

20-4.   In addition to dealing with double taxation problems such as this, treaties also provide income tax certainty, prevent discrimination, ensure a proper division of cross-border revenues, and provide an information-sharing mechanism for the purposes of administration and enforcement of each country's tax laws.

20-5.   In cases where there are conflicts, Canada's tax treaties generally override the *Income Tax Act*. This override occurs through legislation that implements the tax treaty, as well as specific provisions of the *Income Tax Act* that recognize the priority given to the tax treaty. For example, ITA 2(3) requires a U.S. resident to pay Canadian tax on employment income earned in Canada. The tax treaty, on the other hand, may, in specific circumstances, state that such income is only taxable in the U.S. In such cases, the inconsistency is resolved in favour of the tax treaty with the result that no Canadian tax is payable by the U.S. resident.

Residence

Importance

20-6.   Residence is the cornerstone of Canadian income taxation. If a person is considered a resident of Canada in a given year, that person will be subject to Canadian income tax for that year on all sources of income, regardless of where that income is earned. Alternatively, if the person is a non-resident, Canadian Part I tax will only apply to Canadian employment income, Canadian business income, and gains on the disposition of Taxable Canadian Property.

20-7.   Residency status is determined by applying certain rules and guidelines that originate from jurisprudence, common law, the *Income Tax Act*, and tax treaties. These rules vary depending on whether the person is an individual, corporation, or trust. In the material that follows, we will give detailed consideration to the rules applicable to each of these categories of taxpayers.

Residence Of Individuals

General Concept

20-8.   For the average Canadian individual whose job, family, dwelling place, and other personal property are all located in Canada, the concept of residence is not at all ambiguous. Such individuals would clearly be Canadian residents and, as a result, they would be liable for Canadian taxation on their worldwide income. Short departures from the country for holidays or business activities would not have any effect on this conclusion.

20-9. However, for a growing number of individuals, the question of residence is more complex. It is also an important question. As tax rates and tax rules in different countries vary tremendously, the location of a person's residence can have a significant impact on the amount of taxes that will have to be paid.

20-10. While the term resident is not specifically defined in the *Income Tax Act*, Income Tax Folio, S5-F1-C1, *Determining An Individual's Residence*, provides extensive guidance in this area. The most generally applicable statement in this Folio is as follows:

> **Paragraph 1.10** The most important factor to be considered in determining whether an individual leaving Canada remains resident in Canada for tax purposes is whether the individual maintains residential ties with Canada while abroad. While the residence status of an individual can only be determined on a case by case basis after taking into consideration all of the relevant facts, generally, unless an individual severs all significant residential ties with Canada upon leaving Canada, the individual will continue to be a factual resident of Canada and subject to Canadian tax on his or her worldwide income.

20-11. Paragraph 1.11 of S5-F1-C1 goes on to point out that the ties that will almost always be considered significant are:

> **Dwelling** If an individual maintains a dwelling place in Canada, it will generally result in the individual being considered a resident. One possible exception to this rule would be when an individual who leaves Canada rents out a former dwelling place to an arm's length party. In this type of situation, owning a Canadian residence may not be considered a residential tie.

> **Spouse Or Common-Law Partner** If an individual has a spouse or common-law partner who remains in Canada, it will generally result in the individual being considered a Canadian resident. An exception here would be when the individual was living separate or apart from the spouse or common-law partner prior to their departure from Canada.

> **Dependants** If an individual has dependants, such as minor children, who remain in Canada, it will generally result in the individual being considered a Canadian resident.

20-12. S5-F1-C1 also implies that, even in the absence of one of the preceding ties, an individual may still be considered to be a resident of Canada on the basis of secondary residential ties. Paragraph 1.14 contains the following examples of residential ties:

- Personal property in Canada (such as furniture, clothing, automobiles, and recreational vehicles);
- social ties with Canada (such as memberships in Canadian recreational or religious organizations);
- economic ties with Canada (such as employment with a Canadian employer and active involvement in a Canadian business, and Canadian bank accounts, retirement savings plans, credit cards, and securities accounts);
- landed immigrant status or appropriate work permits in Canada;
- hospitalization and medical insurance coverage from a province or territory of Canada;
- a driver's license from a province or territory of Canada;
- a vehicle registered in a province or territory of Canada;
- a seasonal dwelling place in Canada or a leased dwelling place referred to in ¶1.12;
- a Canadian passport; and
- memberships in Canadian unions or professional organizations.

20-13. S5-F1-C1 notes that these secondary ties must be looked at collectively and that it would be unusual for a single secondary tie to be sufficient for an individual to be classified as a Canadian resident.

Exercise Twenty - 1

Subject: Residential Ties

At the end of the current year, Simon Farr departed from Canada in order to take a permanent position in Ireland. He was accompanied by his wife and children, as well as all of his personal property. Due to depressed real estate prices in his region, he was unable to sell his residence at a satisfactory price. However, he was able to rent it for a period of two years. He also retained his membership in the Ontario Institute Of Chartered Accountants. After his departure, would he still be considered a Canadian resident for tax purposes? Explain your conclusion.

End of Exercise. Solution available in Study Guide.

Temporary Absences

20-14.   Many of the problems associated with establishing residency involve situations where an individual leaves Canada for a temporary period of time. The issue here is, under what circumstances should an individual be viewed as having retained their Canadian residency status during the period of their absence from Canada?

20-15.   It is an important issue in that, if they are viewed as having retained their Canadian residency status, they will be subject to Canadian taxation on their worldwide income during the period of absence from Canada. While credits against Canadian income tax payable would usually be available for any income taxes paid in the foreign jurisdiction, the foreign taxes paid may be insufficient to cover the full Canadian tax liability.

20-16.   S5-F1-C1 makes it clear that the length of the period of time during which the individual is absent from Canada is not a determining factor with respect to residency. If an individual severs all primary and secondary residential ties, it appears that he will cease to be a Canadian resident without regard to the period of his absence.

20-17.   If some residential ties are retained during a temporary absence, other factors will be considered. As described in S5-F1-C1, these are as follows:

Intent   The issue here is whether the individual intended to permanently sever residential ties with Canada. If, for example, the individual has a contract for employment, if and when he returns to Canada, this could be viewed as evidence that he did not intend to permanently depart. Another factor would be whether the individual complied with the rules related to permanent departures (i.e., as noted in Chapter 8, there is a deemed disposition of an individual's property at the time of departure from Canada, resulting in the need to pay taxes on any gains).

Frequency Of Visits   If the individual continues to visit Canada on a regular and continuing basis, particularly if other secondary residential ties are present, this would suggest that he did not intend to permanently depart from Canada.

Residential Ties Outside Of Canada   A further consideration is whether or not the individual establishes residential ties in another country. If someone leaves Canada and travels for an extensive period of time without settling in any one location, it will be considered as evidence that he has not permanently departed from Canada.

20-18.   It is clear that there is considerable room for differences of opinion as to whether an individual has ceased to be a Canadian resident during a temporary absence from Canada. It is equally clear that the issue should be given careful attention by taxpayers who find themselves in this situation. The potential tax consequences of failing to deal properly with residency issues can be significant.

Exercise Twenty - 2

Subject: Temporary Absences

Jane is a Canadian citizen who is employed by a multi-national corporation. While she has worked for many years in the Canadian office of this organization, she agreed to transfer to the corporation's office in Florida. Before leaving, she disposed of her residence and other personal property that she did not wish to move. She canceled her Alberta driver's licence and health care card, and closed all of her Canadian banking and brokerage accounts.

Because her boyfriend remained in Edmonton, she flew back to Canada at least once a month. After 26 months, she decided that between the excessive heat and humidity in Florida and the travel required to maintain the relationship with her boyfriend, she would return to Canada. At this point, her boyfriend is not her common-law partner. Would Jane be considered a Canadian resident during the 26 months that she was absent from Canada? Explain your conclusion.

End of Exercise. Solution available in Study Guide.

Part Year Residence

20-19.   In a year in which a person clearly commences or terminates residency in Canada, they will be taxed in Canada on their worldwide income for the part of the year in which they are resident in Canada. While the courts have indicated that establishing residence is a complex matter that involves many considerations, the date of entry will often be based on the immigration rules. However, for departures from Canada, Paragraph 1.22 of S5-F1-C1 indicates that the date on which an individual becomes a non-resident is the latest of:

- the date the individual leaves Canada,
- the date the spouse or common-law partner and/or other dependants of the individual leave Canada, and
- the date the individual becomes a resident of the country to which they are immigrating.

20-20.   Situations involving part year residency require a fairly complex prorating of income, deductions, and personal tax credits. For example, an individual who is a resident of Canada for only part of the year will not be entitled to a full personal tax credit (see Chapter 4). The process for prorating such deductions and credits is specified in ITA 114 and ITA 118.91.

Exercise Twenty - 3

Subject: Part Year Residence

Mark is a Canadian citizen and, since graduating from university, has been employed in Vancouver. He has accepted a new position in the United States and, as of February 1 of the current year flies to Los Angeles to assume his responsibilities. (He has been granted a green card to enable him to work in the U.S.) His wife remains behind with their children until June 15, the end of their school year. On that date, they fly to Los Angeles to join Mark. Their residence is sold on August 1 of the current year, at which time a moving company picks up their furniture and other personal possessions. The moving company delivers these possessions to their new house in Los Angeles on August 15. Explain how Mark will be taxed in Canada during the current year.

End of Exercise. Solution available in Study Guide.

Exercise Twenty - 4

Subject: Part Year Residence

Mr. Jonathan Kirsh was born in Kansas and, until the current year, had lived in various parts of the United States. On September 1 of the current year he moves to Lethbridge, Alberta to begin work at a new job. He brings his family and all of his personal property with him. However, he continues to have both a chequing and a savings account in a U. S. financial institution. Explain how Mr. Kirsh will be taxed in Canada during the current taxation year.

End of Exercise. Solution available in Study Guide.

Sojourners And Other Deemed Residents

20-21. Individuals who are considered Canadian residents on the basis of the residential ties that we have discussed are generally referred to as factual residents. ITA 250(1) extends the meaning of resident to include certain other individuals who are considered deemed residents. As we shall see, an individual can be a deemed resident even if they do not set foot in Canada in the relevant taxation years.

20-22. There are two important tax consequences associated with deemed residents:

- Deemed residents are taxed on their worldwide income for the entire taxation year. This is in contrast to part year residents who are only subject to Canadian taxation during that portion of the taxation year that they are present in Canada.

- Deemed residents are not deemed to reside in a specific province and, as a consequence, they are not subject to provincial taxes. In order to maintain fairness with other Canadian taxpayers, deemed residents are required to pay an additional federal tax equal to 48 percent of the basic federal tax that is otherwise payable. This will result in an overall tax liability that is either lower or higher than that of a factual resident, depending on the province that is being compared.

20-23. Included on the list of deemed residents of Canada are the following:

1. Sojourners in Canada for 183 days or more.

2. Members, at any time during the year, of the Canadian armed forces when stationed outside of Canada.

3. Ambassadors, ministers, high commissioners, officers or servants of Canada, as well as agents general, officers, or servants of a province, provided they were Canadian residents immediately prior to their appointment.

4. An individual performing services, at any time in the year, in a country other than Canada under a prescribed international development assistance program of the Government of Canada, provided they were resident in Canada at any time in the 3 month period preceding the day on which those services commenced.

5. A child of a deemed resident, provided they are also a dependant whose net income for the year was less than the base for the basic personal tax credit ($11,038 for 2013).

6. An individual who was at any time in the year, under an agreement or a convention with one or more other countries, entitled to an exemption from an income tax otherwise payable in any of those countries, because at that time the person was related to, or a member of the family of, an individual who was resident in Canada.

20-24. Of these items, numbers 1 and 6 require further explanation. With respect to item 1, a sojourner is an individual who is temporarily present in Canada for a period of 183 days or more during any one calendar year. Because of ITA 250(1), this person is deemed to be a Canadian resident for the entire year.

20-25.   For this sojourner rule to apply, the individual must be a resident of another country during the 183 days in question. This means that an individual who gives up his residence in another country and moves to Canada early in a taxation year will be considered a part year resident, not a sojourner. Correspondingly, a Canadian resident who leaves Canada to take up residence in another country on September 1 will not be a sojourner, despite the fact that he is in Canada for more than 183 days in the year. As noted, this is an important distinction because the sojourner is liable for Canadian tax on his worldwide income for the entire year.

20-26.   S5-F1-C1 indicates that sojourning means establishing a temporary residence and would include days spent in Canada on vacation trips. However, the Bulletin makes it clear that individuals who, for employment purposes, commute to Canada on a daily basis, are not considered to be sojourning.

20-27.   Item 6 refers to situations where someone is exempt from tax in a foreign country because they are related to an individual who is a Canadian resident. For example, the spouse of a Canadian diplomat working in the U.S. would be exempt from U.S. income taxes under the governing international tax treaty because she is the spouse of the diplomat. As the diplomat would be a deemed resident of Canada under item 3, the spouse would be a deemed resident of Canada under item 6.

Exercise Twenty - 5

Subject: Individual Residency

Ms. Suzanne Blakey was born 24 years ago in Paris, France. She is the daughter of a Canadian High Commissioner serving in that country. Her father still holds this position. However, Ms. Blakey is now working in London. The only income that she earns in the year is from her London marketing job and is subject to taxes in England. She has never visited Canada. Determine the residency status of Suzanne Blakey.

End of Exercise. Solution available in Study Guide.

Individuals With Dual Residency

20-28.   There are situations in which the application of the normal residency rules would result in an individual being considered a resident of more than one country. For example, a member of the Canadian armed forces is deemed to be a resident of Canada, but might also be considered a resident by the country in which he is stationed.

20-29.   In the absence of some mechanism for dealing with the problem, such an individual could be subject to double taxation, with each country of residence assessing taxes on the basis of their domestic legislation. In such situations, the presence of an international tax treaty becomes crucial. These bilateral treaties contain provisions, generally referred to as tie-breaker rules, which are designed to provide relief from the potential double taxation that is inherent in dual residence situations.

20-30.   While there is a general presumption that the provisions of international treaties override domestic tax legislation, these tie-breaker rules are of such importance that they are formally acknowledged in Canada's *Income Tax Act*. Specifically, ITA 250(5) indicates that a person is deemed not to be a resident of Canada if the terms of a particular tax treaty make him a resident of another country and not a resident of Canada.

20-31.   As an example of a typical set of tie-breaker rules, the Canada/U.S. tax treaty resolves the dual residency problem for individuals by examining a list of factors. These factors are applied in the following order:

Permanent Home   If the individual has a permanent home available in only one country, the individual will be considered a resident of that country. A permanent home means a dwelling, rented or purchased, that is continuously available at all times. For this purpose, a home that would only be used for a short duration would not be considered a permanent home.

Centre of Vital Interests   If the individual has permanent homes in both countries, or in neither, then this test looks to the country in which the individual's personal and economic relations are greatest. Such relations are virtually identical to the ties that are examined when determining factual residence for individuals.

Habitual Abode   If the first two tests do not yield a determination, then the country where the individual spends more time will be considered the country of residence.

Citizenship   If the tie-breaker rules still fail to resolve the issue, then the individual will be considered a resident of the country where the individual is a citizen.

Competent Authority   If none of the preceding tests resolve the question of residency then, as a last resort, the so-called "competent authority procedures" are used. Without describing them in detail, these procedures are aimed at opening a dialogue between the two countries for the purpose of resolving the conflict.

Exercise Twenty - 6

Subject: Dual Residency - Individuals

Using the tie breaker rules, determine the resident status of Dizzy and Donna for 2013 in the following two Cases:

Case 1   Dizzy Jones is an unmarried saxophone player from Los Angeles who has always lived in the U.S. He decides to spend some time in Canada and arrives in Vancouver on May 5, 2013, looking for work in various nightclubs. A friend watches his home in Los Angeles while he is gone. He lives in boarding rooms and hotels throughout his time in Canada and returns to Los Angeles on February 14, 2014.

Case 2   Donna, a U.S. citizen, lives in the state of New York. In the fall of 2012, while attending a business convention in Toronto, she met Donald. They decided to get married the following year and live permanently in the U.S. as soon as Donald could arrange his business affairs in Canada. In December, 2012, Donna took an eight month leave of absence from her job and gave notice to her landlord. On January 1, 2013, they moved in together, sharing an apartment in Toronto which was leased on a monthly basis while Donald finalized his business affairs. In August, 2013, they terminated the lease and returned to New York where they were married and purchased a house.

End Of Exercise. Solution Available In Study Guide

Residence Vs. Citizenship

20-32.   While Canada assesses taxes on the basis of residence, some other countries base the liability for tax on citizenship. Of particular importance in this regard is the United States. There are a significant number of Canadian resident individuals who are also citizens of the U.S. In the absence of mitigating legislation, such individuals would be taxed twice on most types of income.

20-33.   Fortunately, the Canada/U.S. tax treaty provides for this situation. In very simplified terms, such individuals are allowed to credit Canadian taxes paid against their U.S. tax liability. As, in general, Canadian taxes on individuals are higher than U.S. taxes on a given amount of income, the U.S. tax liability is usually eliminated.

20-34.   Despite the fact that the balance owing to the U.S. is usually nil, U.S. citizens who are Canadian residents must file a U.S. tax return each year. If this important requirement is overlooked, it can lead to significant difficulties with U.S. tax authorities.

We suggest you work Self Study Problems Twenty-1, 2, and 3 at this point.

Residence Of Corporations

20-35. Being an artificial legal entity, a corporation does not reside anywhere in the same physical sense that the term applies to an individual. To some extent, the jurisdiction of incorporation can assist in finding an answer to the residency question. More specifically, ITA 250(4)(a) indicates that corporations which are incorporated in Canada after April 26, 1965 are deemed to be resident in Canada.

20-36. For corporations incorporated in Canada prior to April 27, 1965, ITA 250(4)(c) indicates that these corporations would also be treated as residents if at any time, in any taxation year ending after April 26, 1965:

- they were resident in Canada (under the mind and management concept discussed in the following Paragraphs), or
- carried on business in Canada.

20-37. What jurisdiction a company was incorporated in is not, however, the end of the story. If this were the case, it would be possible to escape Canadian taxation by the simple act of incorporating outside of the country. Beyond the rules described in the preceding Paragraph, a well established common law principle applies.

20-38. This is the idea that a corporation is resident in the jurisdiction in which the mind and management of the company are located. Such factors as the location of the board of directors meetings and where day-to-day decisions are made are used to determine the location of the mind and management of the corporation. If the conclusion is that the mind and management is in Canada, then a corporation that is not incorporated in Canada will be considered a resident for Canadian tax purposes.

20-39. This "mind and management" criteria would also apply to a corporation that was incorporated in Canada prior to April 27, 1965. Such a corporation would become a resident if, at any time after April 26, 1965, its mind and management was located within Canada. Unlike the foreign jurisdiction corporation, which would be considered to be a Canadian resident only as long as the mind and management remained in Canada, a pre-April 27, 1965 Canadian corporation that became a resident because of the mind and management criteria would remain a Canadian resident, even if the mind and management were moved to a different jurisdiction.

Corporations - Dual Residency

20-40. As was the case with individuals, a corporation may be considered to be resident in more than one country. For example, a corporation that was incorporated in Canada after April 26, 1965 might have its mind and management located in the U.S. This would make this company a deemed resident of Canada and a factual resident of the U.S.

20-41. In situations such as this, tax treaties again become very important. In the absence of such treaties, companies could be subject to taxation in both the countries where they are considered to be resident. As an example of such treaty provisions, the Canada/U.S. tax treaty indicates that, in situations where a company is considered to be a resident of both countries, the corporation will be deemed to be a resident only in the country in which it is incorporated.

Exercise Twenty - 7

Subject: Corporate Residency

Roswell Ltd. was incorporated in the state of New York in 2008. It carries on business in both the United States and Canada. However, all of the directors of the Company live in Kemptville, Ontario and, as a consequence, all of the directors meetings are held in Kemptville. Determine the residency status of Roswell Ltd.

End of Exercise. Solution available in Study Guide.

Exercise Twenty - 8

Subject: Corporate Residency

Sateen Inc. was incorporated in Manitoba in 2007. However, since 2010, all of the Company's business has been carried on outside of Canada. Determine the residency status of Sateen Inc.

Exercise Twenty - 9

Subject: Dual Residency - Corporations

Using the tie breaker rules, determine the resident status of the corporations in the following two Cases:

Case 1   Taxco is a company incorporated in Nova Scotia in 2010 to hold investments in other Canadian companies. Taxco never carried on business in Canada. All the shareholders and members of the board of directors are residents of the U.S. All board of directors meetings are held in the U.S.

Case 2   Junkco is a company incorporated in Delaware in 2011. The majority of the members of the board of directors, however, reside in Montreal, where all board of directors meetings take place. Junkco does not carry on any business in Canada.

End of Exercises. Solutions available in Study Guide.

We suggest you work Self Study Problems Twenty-4 and 5 at this point.

Residence Of Trusts

20-42.   The residence of a trust can only be determined by examining the circumstances involved in each case. In general, however, IT-447 indicates that a trust is considered to reside where the trustee, executor, administrator, heir, or other legal representative who manages the trust or controls the trust assets resides. If this location is not clear, the same IT Bulletin indicates that the authorities will look at the location where the legal rights with respect to the trust assets are enforceable, and the location of the trust assets.

20-43.   IT-447 was issued in 1980 and has not been modified since its issuance. However, a recent court case (*Garron Vs. The Queen*, 2009 DTC 1287) appears to take a somewhat different approach. In this Tax Court of Canada case, the judge made the following statement:

> "I conclude, then, that the judge-made test of residence that has been established for corporations should also apply to trusts, with such modifications as are appropriate. That test is 'where the central management and control actually abides'."

20-44.   This Tax Court Of Canada decision was appealed, first to the Federal Court Of Appeal, and finally to the Supreme Court Of Canada. In both cases the appeal was dismissed.

Part I Tax On Non-Residents

Introduction

Applicability

20-45.   As we noted previously, ITA 2(1) states that Canadian taxes are payable by residents of Canada on their taxable income for a taxation year. While this statement makes it clear that residents are responsible for paying Canadian income taxes, it does not address the question of whether non-residents are responsible for such taxes.

20-46.   With respect to Part I taxes (taxes assessed on Taxable Income), ITA 2(3) specifies that non-residents are, in fact, responsible for Canadian taxes on certain types of income. As listed in that subsection, non-residents are responsible for:

- income earned while carrying on a business in Canada;
- employment income earned in Canada; and
- gains and losses resulting from dispositions of Taxable Canadian Property.

20-47.   In this section we will give attention to the assessment of Canadian Part I tax on non-residents in situations where they have any of these three types of income. As part of this discussion, we will provide coverage of the provisions of the U.S./Canada tax treaty that relate to such situations. Coverage of other international tax treaties goes beyond the scope of this text.

20-48.   You will note that ITA 2(3) covers business income, employment income, and capital gains on Taxable Canadian Property. However, this subsection does not refer to property income. Further there is no reference to pension income, management fees, or capital gains on Canadian property other than those items that are classified as Taxable Canadian Property. This means that, in general, non-residents are not responsible for paying Part I tax on these types of income.

20-49.   However, this is not the end of the story. When these other types of income are from a Canadian source and are allocated to non-residents, a separate Part XIII tax is applicable. The application of this tax will be covered beginning in Paragraph 20-70.

Filing Requirements
20-50.   In those situations where a non-resident has Tax Payable under Part I, a Canadian income tax return is required. The normal filing dates for individuals and corporations are applicable in such situations. No Canadian income tax return is required if there is no Part I Tax Payable.

Taxable Income
20-51.   As some of the items that must be included in a Canadian income tax return by non-residents are exempted by various international tax treaties, such amounts can be deducted in determining Taxable Income. In addition, under ITA 115(1), non-residents will also be able to deduct Canadian employment losses, Canadian business losses, various types of loss carry overs, Canadian stock option benefits, Canadian dividends received (corporations only), and charitable donations (corporations only).

20-52.   If 90 percent or more (substantially all) of the taxpayer's income is included in their Part I tax return, the other deductions that are available to residents, such as the home relocation load interest deduction, become available to non-residents.

Tax Payable
20-53.   Unless the non-resident's Part I return includes 90 percent or more of their total income, ITA 118.94 prohibits the use of the majority of non-refundable tax credits. However, the following credits will be available to non-residents filers who are individuals, without regard to the amount and type of their income:

- charitable donations tax credit
- disability tax credit
- tuition tax credit
- EI and CPP tax credits
- interest on student loan tax credit

Carrying on Business in Canada
General Rules
20-54.   As we have noted, non-residents are subject to Part I tax in Canada on income from businesses carried on in Canada. The rules for calculating business income discussed in

Chapter 6 are generally applicable to non-residents. However, for non-residents, ITA 253 expands the concept of a business by deeming non-residents to be carrying on a business with respect to certain activities such as:

- Producing, growing, mining, creating, manufacturing, fabricating, improving, packing, preserving, or constructing, in whole or in part, anything in Canada.

- Soliciting orders or offering anything for sale in Canada through an agent or servant, whether the contract or transaction is to be completed inside or outside Canada.

- Disposing of certain property, such as real property inventory situated in Canada, including an interest in, or option on, such real property.

20-55.   These rules are intended to ensure that certain Canadian activities that are connected to the non-resident's foreign business, are potentially taxable in Canada as business income. Without these rules, it could be questionable whether the non-resident person would be considered to be carrying on a business in Canada.

> **Example**   A U.S. business sends sales representatives to Canada to solicit orders. If the sales contracts can only be finalized in the U.S., under the general rules applicable to business income, it could be argued that no business was carried on in Canada. However, ITA 253 makes it clear that the soliciting of orders in Canada is carrying on business in Canada, without regard to where the contracts are finalized.

Canada/U.S. Tax Treaty On Business Income

20-56.   The treaty allows Canada to tax the business income of U.S. residents, provided that business is operated in Canada through what is referred to as a permanent establishment.

20-57.   Article V of the Canada/U.S. tax treaty defines a "permanent establishment" as a fixed place of business through which the business of a non-resident is wholly or partly carried on. The treaty provides additional clarification by adding that fixed places of business include a place of management, a branch, an office, a factory, a workshop, a mine, an oil or gas well, a quarry or other place of extraction of natural resources. Additional rules provide permanent establishment status only if certain conditions are met (e.g., most construction projects are only considered permanent establishments if they last for more than twelve months).

20-58.   The treaty specifically excludes facilities from being considered a fixed place of business if they are used exclusively for certain activities. These activities include:

- use of facilities solely for storage, display, or delivery of goods;
- maintenance of a stock of goods or merchandise for storage, display, or delivery;
- maintenance of a fixed place of business solely for purchasing goods or merchandise, or for collecting information; or
- maintenance of a fixed place of business solely for the purpose of carrying on any other activity of a preparatory or auxiliary character.

20-59.   The tax treaty also deems certain persons to be permanent establishments of a non-resident. Two examples of this are as follows:

- An agent who acts on behalf of a non-resident enterprise and who is authorized to conclude contracts in the name of that enterprise, is considered a permanent establishment.

- An individual who acts on behalf of a business and meets both a physical presence test (183 days or more in any 12 month period beginning or ending in the year) and a gross revenue test (that more than 50% of the gross active business revenues of the U.S. business are from services performed by that individual during the period the individual is in Canada), is considered a permanent establishment.

Exercise Twenty - 10

Subject: Carrying On Business In Canada

In each of the following Cases, determine whether Jazzco, a U.S. corporation, is taxable in Canada:

Case 1 Jazzco, a U.S. corporation, is the parent company of Bluesco, a company incorporated in Ontario. Jazzco produces and sells Jazz CDs, while Bluesco produces and sells Blues CDs. Jazzco sells CDs to Bluesco, who in turn sells them in Canada.

Case 2 Jazzco sets up a factory in Toronto where they produce CDs for the Canadian market. The CDs are sold exclusively to an independent Canadian franchise retail outlet at a 50 percent mark-up.

Case 3 Jazzco manufactures Jazz CDs in the U.S. Jazzco ships CDs to a warehouse located in Calgary that they have rented on a five year lease. Jazzco has employed an individual in Calgary to sell the CDs throughout western Canada. The employee, however, is not allowed to conclude contracts without approval by the U.S. office.

Case 4 Assume the same facts as in Case 3, except that the employee has the authority to conclude contracts on behalf of the employer.

Case 5 Assume the same facts as in Case 3, except that the employee has an office in the warehouse premises where he solicits orders.

End of Exercise. Solution available in Study Guide.

Canadian Source Employment Income
General Rules

20-60. As noted, under ITA 2(3), non-resident individuals are subject to Part I tax on Canadian source employment income. For this purpose, net employment is calculated using the same rules that are applicable to residents earning Canadian source employment income. These rules were covered in Chapter 3.

20-61. In addition to this provision, ITA 115(2) deems certain non-resident individuals to be employed in Canada, even when the work is not carried on in this country. Such individuals include:

- Individuals who have become residents of another country and continue to receive employment remuneration from a resident Canadian source, provided a tax treaty exempts that remuneration from taxation in the foreign country.

- Non-resident individuals who have received signing bonuses and other similar amounts that relate to services to be performed in Canada, in situations where the resident Canadian employer is entitled to deduct the amounts in computing Canadian Taxable Income.

20-62. The basic idea behind these provisions is that, if payments are made to a non-resident that are deductible to a Canadian resident, the payments will be taxed in Canada if they are not taxed in the other country. Note, however, that employee remuneration is generally exempted from Canadian taxation if it is subject to tax by the foreign country.

Canada/U.S. Tax Treaty On Employment Income

20-63. In general, a source country has the right to tax the employment income of non-residents when it is earned within its borders. This view is reflected in ITA 2(3) which assesses Part I tax on Canadian source employment income earned by non-residents. However, the Canada/U.S. tax treaty contains two special rules which create exceptions to this general approach.

$10,000 Rule   Under this rule if, during a calendar year, a U.S. resident earns employment income in Canada that is $10,000 or less in Canadian dollars, then the income is taxable only in the U.S.

183 Day Rule   This rule exempts Canadian source employment income from Canadian taxation, provided it is earned by a U.S. resident who was physically present in Canada for no more than 183 days during any twelve month period commencing or ending in the calendar year.   This exemption is conditional on employment income not being paid by an employer with a permanent establishment in Canada who would be able to deduct the amount paid from their Canadian Taxable Income. Stated alternatively, if the employment income exceeds $10,000 and is deductible in Canada, it will be taxed in Canada, even if the employee is present in Canada for less than 183 days during the year.

20-64.   It is important not to confuse the 183 day period in the treaty with the 183 day sojourner rule for determining residence. While the treaty rule applies to any physical presence in Canada, the sojourner rule applies to temporary visits or stays. Daily commutes to Canada from the U.S. for employment purposes would count towards the 183 days in the treaty rule, but not towards the 183 days in the sojourner rule.

Exercise Twenty - 11

Subject: Non-Resident Employment In Canada

Dawn Johnson is employed by Alberta Oil Ltd. as an oil well technician in Edmonton. She has accepted a transfer to the Egyptian offices of the Company for three years beginning January 1, 2013. Dawn severs her residential ties to Canada on December 31, 2012 and takes up residence in Egypt. Alberta Oil continues to pay her salary. Although the government of Egypt would normally tax such salary, the tax treaty between Canada and Egypt exempts the salary from tax in Egypt. Is Dawn required to pay Canadian tax on the salary paid to her by Alberta Oil? Justify your conclusion.

Exercise Twenty - 12

Subject: Non-Resident Employment In Canada - Canada/U.S. Tax Treaty

In each of the following Cases, determine whether the employment income is taxable in Canada:

Case 1   David resides in the state of Washington. He accepted temporary employment as a technician with a Canadian company to do service calls in the Vancouver area for four months beginning September 1, 2013. The Canadian employer agreed to pay him $2,800 Canadian per month. David remained a non-resident of Canada throughout his Canadian employment.

Case 2   Assume the same facts as in Case 1, except the employer was resident in Washington and did not have a permanent establishment in Canada.

Case 3   Sandra resides in Detroit, Michigan and has commuted daily to a full-time job in Windsor, Ontario for the last three years. In 2013, she spent 238 days at her job in Canada. She works for the municipality of Windsor and earned $50,000 Canadian in employment income. Sandra is a U.S. resident throughout the year.

End of Exercises. Solutions available in Study Guide.

Dispositions of Taxable Canadian Property
General Rules
20-65.   As we have previously noted, under ITA 2(3), non-residents are taxable on gains resulting from dispositions of Taxable Canadian Property. The general rules for dealing with capital gains and losses were covered in detail in Chapter 8. While we only considered their application to Canadian residents in that Chapter, these rules are equally applicable to non-residents.

20-66.   As defined in ITA 248(1), the main categories of Taxable Canadian Property are as follows:

• Real property situated in Canada.

• Eligible capital property or inventories of a business carried on in Canada.

• A share of an unlisted corporation, an interest in a partnership, or an interest in a trust if, at any time within the preceding 60 months, more than 50 percent of its FMV of the share or interest was derived from certain properties including Canadian real property, Canadian resource properties and timber resource properties.

• A share of a listed corporation only if, at any time within the preceding 60 months, at least 25 percent of the issued shares of any class were owned by the non-resident taxpayer and/or non-arm's length persons, and more than 50 percent of the shares' FMV was derived from certain properties including Canadian real property, Canadian resource properties and timber resource properties.

Clearance Certificates
20-67.   There are, of course, problems related to having a non-resident comply with Canadian tax rules related to dispositions of Taxable Canadian Property. To deal with this, ITA 116 requires a non-resident, who anticipates a disposal of Taxable Canadian Property, to file Form T2062, "Request by a Non-Resident of Canada for a Certificate of Compliance Related to the Disposition of Taxable Canadian Property". This form, which must be filed within 10 days of the planned disposition, must be accompanied by a payment of 25 percent of the anticipated capital gain on the disposition (some types of security are acceptable). When these conditions are met, a certificate of compliance will be issued. There is a penalty for disposing of a Taxable Canadian Property without obtaining a compliance certificate.

20-68.   As Canadian tax authorities are still dealing with a non-resident, this procedure does not ensure compliance. What serves to ensure that Canadian taxes will be paid is a requirement that, if the non-resident seller does not acquire a compliance certificate, the purchaser (usually a Canadian resident) is responsible for the 25 percent payment on behalf of the non-resident. Further, if the actual price exceeds the price specified in the certificate, the purchaser becomes responsible for paying 25 percent of the excess.

Canada/U.S. Tax Treaty On Taxable Canadian Property Dispositions
20-69.   While the general rule in ITA 2(3) indicates that non-residents are taxable on gains resulting from dispositions of Taxable Canadian Property, it is necessary to examine the Canada/U.S. tax treaty to see if any of its provisions override this general rule. The treaty acts to limit Canadian taxation on U.S. residents to gains arising from only the following specific types of Taxable Canadian Property:

• real property situated in Canada;
• property forming part of a permanent establishment of the non-resident in Canada; and
• investments such as shares of Canadian corporations and interests in Canadian partnerships and trusts where the value of those investments is primarily attributable to real property situated in Canada.

Exercise Twenty - 13

Subject: Dispositions Of Taxable Canadian Property

In each of the following Cases the individual is a U.S. resident who is disposing of a property. Determine whether any gain on the disposition is taxable under Part I in Canada.

Case 1   In 2013, Nancy Gordon disposed of shares of a widely held Canadian public company that she acquired in 2010. Nancy never owned more than one-quarter of one percent of the outstanding shares of this company. The company's assets consist entirely of real estate situated in Canada.

Case 2   In 2008, Joe Nesbitt acquired a condo in Whistler that he rented to Canadian residents. He sold the condo in 2013 at a considerable gain. Joe never occupied the condo.

Case 3   Assume the same facts as in Case 2, except that Joe incorporates a private corporation under British Columbia legislation solely to acquire the condo. At a later point in time, Joe sells the shares at a considerable gain.

Case 4   Assume the same facts as in Case 3, except the corporation is created under Washington state legislation.

End of Exercise. Solution available in Study Guide.

We suggest you work Self Study Problem Twenty-6 at this point.

Part XIII Tax On Non-Residents

Introduction
Applicability
20-70.   In the preceding section of this Chapter, we dealt with the application of Part I tax to certain specific types of income. As noted in Paragraph 20-49, this leaves many other types of Canadian source income that are not subject to Part I tax in the hands of non-residents.

20-71.   The Part XIII tax is designed to correct this situation. ITA 212 provides a long list of income types to which this tax is applicable. While most of the items on the list fall into the property income category, there are other items such as pension benefits. Notably absent, however, are taxable capital gains on assets other than Taxable Canadian Property. Capital gains on dispositions of other Canadian assets are not taxed in the hands of non-residents, either under Part I or Part XIII.

20-72.   Three other points are relevant here:

- Part XIII tax is an alternative to Part I tax. There are no situations in which both taxes would be applied to a single income source.

- Non-residents are not required to file a Canadian tax return for income that is subject to Part XIII tax.

- In general, it is the resident payer who is responsible for withholding the Part XIII tax from payment(s) being made to the non-resident, as well as remitting the withheld amounts to the CRA. The payer is also responsible for filing an information return (NR4) indicating the amounts withheld.

20-73.   As indicated, Part XIII tax applies to a long list of income types. However, in the following material, we will limit our coverage to interest, royalties, rents, dividends, and pension benefits earned or accruing to non-residents.

The Nature Of Part XIII Tax

20-74.   This is a very different type of tax than that which is assessed under Part I. Under Part I, the relevant tax rate is applied to Taxable Income, a figure that is made up of components which are calculated on a net basis. For example, interest revenues are only included after any related expenses are deducted. In contrast, the Part XIII tax is assessed on the gross amount of income received.

> **Example**   Ms. Johnson borrows $100,000 to invest in high yield bonds. During the current year, they produce interest income of $9,000, while the interest costs for the borrowing amount to $4,000.

> **Analysis**   If Ms. Johnson was a Canadian resident being taxed under Part I of the *Income Tax Act*, the applicable tax rate would be applied to $5,000 ($9,000 - $4,000). In contrast, if Ms. Johnson was a non-resident being taxed under Part XIII, the Part XIII withholding rate would be applied to the $9,000 in interest received.

Rates

20-75.   The Part XIII rate that is specified in ITA 212(1) is 25 percent for all types of income listed in ITA 212. However, this rate is rarely applied when the recipient of the income is resident in a country with which Canada has a tax treaty. All of these treaties have provisions which, while allowing the applicability of the Part XIII tax, modify the rate. This is further complicated by the fact that the rate modifications vary between the various types of income subject to the Part XIII tax.

20-76.   Comprehensive treatment of the various rates that are applicable under Canada's many international tax treaties would not be appropriate in a general text such as this. However, because it would appear to be the most important of these treaties, attention will be given to the rates that are applicable under the Canada/U.S. tax treaty.

Interest Payments

Part XIII Rules

20-77.   ITA 212(1)(b) assesses Part XIII tax on only two types of interest. These are as follows:

> **Participating Debt Interest**   Participating debt interest is defined in ITA 212(3) as interest that is dependent on the use of property (e.g., royalties), or that is calculated by reference to revenue, cash flow, or profit. What is being described here is amounts that, while they may be called interest, are more like business income. They are not based on a principal sum and the passage of time.

> **Interest Paid To Non-Arm's Length Non-Residents**, unless the interest is **Fully Exempt Interest**. Fully exempt interest is defined in ITA 212(3) as interest paid or payable on certain types of government issued or guaranteed debt (e.g., debt issued by the government of Canada or a province).

20-78.   Another way of stating this would be to note that Part XIII only applies (1) to arm's length arrangements when the interest payments are related to "participating debt", and (2) to non-arm's length arrangements if the interest is not fully exempt.

Canada/U.S. Tax Treaty On Interest Payments

20-79.   When it is established that Part XIII tax is applicable, it is then necessary to consult the relevant international tax treaty to determine whether Canada has the right to tax such amounts. For U.S. residents, the Canada/U.S. tax treaty states the following:

> **Article XI**   Interest arising in a Contracting State and beneficially owned by a resident of the other Contracting State may be taxed only in that other State.

20-80.   This means that, with respect to interest paid to U.S. residents, Canada does not have the right to withhold taxes under Part XIII. Residents of the U.S. are exempt from the Part XIII tax, even in the situations described in Paragraph 20-77.

Exercise Twenty - 14

Subject: Interest Payments To Non-Residents

In each of the following Cases, determine whether the interest payments made to non-residents are subject to Part XIII withholding tax, and if so, at what rate.

Case 1   Jason, a resident of a country that does not have a tax treaty with Canada, earned $3,000 in interest from a term deposit in a Canadian bank during 2013.

Case 2   Janice, a resident of a country that does not have a tax treaty with Canada, earned interest of $1,800 on Canada Savings Bonds during 2013.

Case 3   Julian, a resident of Ottawa, acquired a vacation property in a country that does not have a tax treaty with Canada. The property is mortgaged with a bank in the foreign country. Julian paid $12,000 in interest to the foreign bank in 2013.

Case 4   Jasmine, a resident of Manitoba, paid $5,000 in interest on a loan from her brother, a resident of Ohio during 2013.

End of Exercise.   Solution available in Study Guide.

Dividend Payments
Part XIII Rules
20-81.   Most types of dividends are subject to the 25 percent Part XIII tax. This includes capital dividends, despite the fact that they are not subject to tax when received by Canadian residents.

Canada/U.S. Tax Treaty On Dividend Payments
20-82.   While there is nothing in the Canada/U.S. tax treaty to prevent the application of this tax to U.S. residents, the treaty serves to reduce the applicable rate. In this case, there are two different reduced rates, depending on the percentage of the dividend paying corporation that is owned by the non-resident recipient.

5 Percent Rate   If the U.S. resident recipient is a corporation and owns 10 percent or more of the voting shares of the resident Canadian company that is paying the dividend, the applicable rate is only 5 percent. This 5 percent rate for inter-corporate dividends reflects a view that dividend payments between parent companies and their subsidiaries should be less heavily taxed to encourage international trade and investment.

15 Percent Rate   Other dividends paid by resident Canadian companies to U.S. residents are subject to the Part XIII withholding tax at a reduced rate of 15 percent.

Royalty Payments
Part XIII Rules
20-83.   Royalties paid or credited to non-residents by a person resident in Canada are generally subject to a 25 percent Part XIII withholding tax under ITA 212(1)(d). Specifically excluded under Canadian legislation are payments for copyright use, payments made under cost-sharing arrangements where the costs are shared with non-residents, and payments made that are deductible under Part I against income earned outside Canada.

Canada/U.S. Tax Treaty On Royalty Payments
20-84.   The Canada/U.S. tax treaty, in general, allows the imposition of Part XIII tax on royalties. However, it is at a reduced rate of 10 percent. The treaty further provides that copyright and computer software royalties are not taxable by the source country.

Rental Income
Part XIII Rules
20-85.   The situation with rent payments is more complex. While ITA 212(1)(d) lists rents as one of the items subject to Part XIII tax, the *Income Tax Act* is designed to give priority to Part I tax over Part XIII tax. However, as we have noted in our discussion of the small business deduction, a taxpayer's rental activities may be so extensive that they can be considered a business. If this is the case, the non-resident taxpayer will be earning business income which will be subject to Part I tax in Canada. If this is the case, the taxpayer will have to file an income tax return including these amounts. However, there will then be no requirement to pay Part XIII tax on the rental revenues.

An Important Election For Rental Income Of Non-Residents
20-86.   If the non-resident is not carrying on a rental business in Canada, Part XIII tax is applicable. This creates a significant problem in that the Part XIII tax is applied to gross rental revenues, a figure that will usually be much larger than net rental income.

> **Example**   Marcia Dorne, a resident of a non-treaty country, owns a rental property in Canada. The gross rent on this property is $120,000 for the year and is paid monthly at a rate of $10,000. The property is so heavily financed that net rental income, as determined by the Part I rules, is $12,000 for the year before CCA of $11,000.

> **Analysis**   In the absence of an alternative approach, Marcia would be subject to Part XIII tax of $30,000 [(25%)($120,000)] for the year.

20-87.   Fortunately, there is an alternative approach. Under ITA 216, Marcia can elect to pay taxes under Part I, rather than under Part XIII. In the preceding example, this election would result in Part I taxes being paid on the net rental income of $12,000. If Marcia had no other source of Canadian income, this $12,000 would be taxed at the lowest federal rate of 15 percent and, when combined with the 48 percent federal surtax on income not earned in a province, the total Part I tax would be $222 [(15%)($11,000)(148%)]. This is well below the $30,000 that would be assessed under Part XIII.

20-88.   With respect to this election, two other points are worth noting:

- In general, this election can only be made in situations where the rental property is real property located in Canada.

- If a non-resident taxpayer makes this election, they will file a separate return including only the revenues and expenses related to their rental property. They cannot make any deductions from Net Income in the determination of Taxable Income and they cannot deduct any of the personal tax credits available under ITA 118.

Solution To The Cash Flow Problem
20-89.   Unfortunately, use of the ITA 216 election to pay under Part I tax does not relieve the payer from the requirement to withhold Part XIII tax. This will, in many cases, create a significant tax flow problem for the non-resident landlord. Consider the example from Paragraph 20-86.   The person paying the rent would have to withhold a total of $30,000 from the payments made to Marcia Dorne. As a result, she would have a negative cash flow of $18,000 [(75%)($120,000) - ($120,000 - $12,000)]. While the withheld Part XIII tax would eventually be refunded, there is a significant outflow of cash during the rental period.

20-90.   Fortunately, there is a solution to this problem. A non-resident taxpayer can file Form NR6, "Undertaking to File an Income Tax Return by a Non-Resident Receiving Rent from Real Property or Receiving a Timber Royalty". If this undertaking is filed, the payer can base the required withholding on 25 percent of the estimated net rental income before the deduction of CCA. In our Paragraph 20-86 example, the Part XIII withholding would be reduced from $2,500 per month [(25%)($10,000)] to $250 per month [(25%)(1/12)($12,000)]. Any difference between this amount and the actual net rental income, including any available deduction for CCA, would be claimed when Marcia Dorne's Part I tax return is filed.

Canada/U.S. Tax Treaty On Rental Income

20-91.   The Canada/U.S. tax treaty allows the imposition of Part XIII tax to rental income. When the rental property is real property, the statutory Part XIII rate of 25 percent is applicable. However, where the rental property is something other than real property in Canada (e.g. equipment or machinery), the Canada/U.S. tax treaty reduces the Part XIII withholding rate from 25 to 10 percent.

Exercise Twenty - 15

Subject: Rental Payments To Non-Residents

In each of the following Cases, determine how the rental payments made to non-residents will be taxed by Canada.

Case 1   Rentco is a U.S. corporation with worldwide rental facilities dedicated to various equipment rentals. Rentco has offices in Saskatchewan, where it rents out farming equipment.

Case 2   In 2010, Jack Foster, a U.S. resident, acquired a hunting and fishing lodge in northern Ontario that he rents out. In 2013, he rented the lodge to Canadian residents exclusively. Jack received $42,000 in gross rents and estimates that expenses, including CCA, totaled $14,000.

Case 3   Assume the same facts as in Case 2, with one additional consideration. Jack acquired three motor boats in 2011, which he rented to guests of the lodge. In 2013, he received $8,000 in gross boat rents and estimates boat related expenses of $7,000.

End of Exercise.   Solution available in Study Guide.

Pension Payments And Other Retirement Related Benefits

Part XIII Rules

20-92.   Amounts received by non-residents as pension or other retirement related benefits are generally subject to tax under Part XIII. This would include OAS payments, CPP payments, death benefits, certain retiring allowances, as well as payments from RRSPs, RRIFs, and DPSPs.

20-93.   There are some exceptions under Canadian legislation that are designed to ensure that a non-resident will only be taxed on amounts that would have been taxable had the non-resident been resident in Canada at the time the benefits were earned. For example, a non-resident may receive a pension from a former Canadian employer, most of which relates to years in which the person was non-resident and worked outside Canada. Part XIII may exempt the part of the pension that relates to employment outside Canada.

An Important Election For Pension Income Of Non-Residents

20-94.   In a manner similar to the ITA 216 election available for rental income paid to non-residents, ITA 217 allows the non-resident recipient of pension income to be taxed under Part I of the *Income Tax Act*, rather than under Part XIII. As was the case with the ITA 216 election, the use of the alternative may result in some loss of credits against Tax Payable.

20-95.   For a low income individual, using the ITA 217 election can provide a significant advantage in that it can allow the individual to make use of some of the tax credits that are available under Part I. However, for high income individuals, the Part XIII rate is likely to be lower than the rate that would be applicable under Part I of the *Act*. In most cases, this will more than offset the loss of tax credits.

Canada/U.S. Tax Treaty On Pension Payments And Benefits

20-96. The Canada/U.S. tax treaty permits the application of Part XIII tax to pension or other related benefits paid to U.S. residents. As usual, the treaty acts to reduce the applicable Part XIII rate, in this case to 15 percent. However, this rate is only available on benefits that are periodic payments. If the benefit is a lump-sum payment (e.g., a retiring allowance), the statutory Part XIII rate of 25 percent must be used.

20-97. Payments from OAS, CPP and QPP are generally subject to Part XIII tax and eligible for the optional Part I treatment discussed in Paragraph 20-94. However, with respect to OAS and CPP payments made to a resident of the U.S., the treaty specifies that these will only be taxed in the U.S. There will be no withholding or filing requirements on these amounts.

20-98. Two other important provisions under the U.S./Canada treaty can be described as follows:

Contributions To Local Plans By Non-Residents   The treaty allows deductions for contributions by non-residents to "qualifying retirement plans" that are located in the other country. This means that U.S. residents who contribute to a qualifying Canadian plan can deduct their contributions from Canadian income and, alternatively, Canadian residents who contribute to a U.S. plan can deduct their contributions from U.S. income. Two points are relevant here:

- For U.S. residents working in Canada, qualifying retirement plans include RPPs, DPSPs, and group RRSPs. Individual RRSPs do not qualify.

- Deductions for contributions to Canadian plans are limited by the available RRSP contribution room.

Contributions and Accruing Benefits By Residents   The second provision relates to ongoing contributions and benefits accruing under a pension plan in the country in which the individual is resident. Contributions to such plans are deductible in the other country, but benefits accruing would not be taxable. For example, if a U.S. resident employed in Canada continued to make contributions to a U.S. plan, the U.S. contributions would be deductible against Canadian employment income. However, any pension benefits that accrued would not be taxable in Canada.

Shareholder Loans To Non-Residents

20-99. In Chapter 15, we gave attention to the rules associated with shareholder loans. It was noted that, in general, the principal of such loans had to be included in a taxpayer's Net Income For Tax Purposes. There are a number of exceptions to this rule. However, in situations where the principal is not included, there is still a taxable benefit to the shareholder if the interest rate on the loan was less than the prescribed rate.

20-100. As non-residents are generally not required to file a Part I tax return, corporate loans to non-resident shareholders would be exempt from these rules in terms of the application of Part I tax. However, ITA 214(3)(a) indicates that if ITA 15 of the *Income Tax Act* (Benefit Conferred On Shareholder) would require an amount to be included in income, that amount will be viewed as a dividend paid to the non-resident shareholder, resulting in the application of Part XIII tax. A refund of the Part XIII tax will become available when the loan is repaid.

20-101. Such loans to non-resident shareholders escape this treatment if they are repaid within one year of the end of the taxation year in which the loan is provided. If the principal is not included in income and the interest rate on the loan is less than the prescribed rate, a benefit will be calculated in the same manner as the interest benefit on such loans when they are made to a resident shareholder. However, when a non-resident is involved, this benefit will be treated as a dividend subject to Part XIII tax.

We suggest you work Self Study Problem Twenty-7 at this point.

Immigration And Emigration

Entering Canada - Immigration
Deemed Disposition/Reacquisition

20-102.   The rules related to entering Canada are found in ITA 128.1(1). Paragraph (b) of this subsection indicates that, with certain exceptions, a taxpayer is deemed to have disposed of all of their property immediately before entering Canada for proceeds equal to fair market value. Paragraph (c) calls for a deemed reacquisition of the property at the same fair market value figure.

20-103.   This process establishes a new cost basis for the taxpayer's property, as at the time of entering Canada. The goal here is to avoid having Canadian taxation apply to gains that accrued prior to the individual's immigration.

> **Example** An individual enters Canada with securities that cost $100,000 and have a current fair market value of $150,000.

> **Analysis** In the absence of the ITA 128.1(1)(b) and (c) deeming provisions, a subsequent sale of these securities for $150,000 would result in the $50,000 accrued gain being taxed in Canada, despite the fact that it accrued prior to the individual becoming a Canadian resident.

20-104.   The properties that are excluded from the deemed disposition/reacquisition are listed in ITA 128.1(1)(b). In general, these are items that would already have been subject to tax in Canada if the taxpayer was a non-resident. They include:

- Taxable Canadian Property.
- Inventories and eligible capital property of a business carried on in Canada.
- **"Excluded Right or Interest"**   This concept is defined in ITA 128.1(10). The definition includes RPP balances, RRSP balances, DPSP balances, stock options, death benefits, retiring allowances, as well as other rights of individuals in trusts or other similar arrangements.

Departures From Canada - Emigration
Deemed Disposition On Leaving Canada

20-105.   As was noted in Chapter 8, when a taxpayer leaves Canada, ITA 128.1(4)(b) calls for a deemed disposition of all property owned at the time of departure. The disposition is deemed to occur at fair market value (see Paragraph 20-108 for treatment under the Canada/U.S. tax treaty). If the taxpayer is an individual, certain types of property are exempted from this deemed disposition rule. The major categories of exempted property are:

- Real property situated in Canada, Canadian resource properties, and timber resource properties.
- Property of a business carried on in Canada through a permanent establishment. This would include capital property, eligible capital property, and inventories.
- Excluded rights or interests of the taxpayer as described in Paragraph 20-104.

Exercise Twenty - 16

Subject: Emigration

Ms. Gloria Martell owns publicly traded securities with an adjusted cost base of $28,000 and a fair market value of $49,000.   During the current year, she permanently departs from Canada still owning the shares.   What would be the tax consequences of her departure, if any, with respect to these securities?

End of Exercise. Solution available in Study Guide.

Exercise Twenty - 17

Subject: Emigration

Mr. Harrison Chrysler owns a rental property in Nanaimo, B.C. with a capital cost of $190,000 and a fair market value of $295,000. The land values included in these figures are $45,000 and $62,000, respectively. The UCC of the building is $82,600. During the current year, Mr. Chrysler permanently departs from Canada. What are the current and possible future tax consequences of his departure with respect to this rental property?

End of Exercise.   Solution available in Study Guide.

Problems With The Current System

20-106.   Taxpayer emigration is a problem area for those in charge of Canadian tax policy. To begin, Canada is significantly out of line with all of its trading partners in the manner in which it deals with the accrued capital gains of emigrants.

20-107.   As an illustration of this problem, consider Mr. Poutine, who departs from Canada at a time when he owns capital assets with an adjusted cost base of $80,000 and a fair market value of $120,000. On his departure from Canada, Mr. Poutine will be deemed to have disposed of these assets at their fair market value of $120,000, resulting in an assessment for a capital gain of $40,000. In many other countries, this would not occur. Mr. Poutine would be able to remove his assets without taxation and retain an unchanged adjusted cost base.

20-108.   The deemed disposition can result in double taxation as Mr. Poutine's new country of residence may consider his adjusted cost base to be the original value of $80,000. Fortunately the Canada/U.S. tax treaty provides a fix for this situation. Under Article XIII(7), Mr. Poutine can elect to have a deemed disposition at fair market value for U.S. tax purposes as well as for Canadian tax assessment, but this fix is not available for all countries.

20-109.   A further problem in this area is the ability of some taxpayers to avoid the Canadian emigration tax rules, resulting in large sums of money being removed from Canada on a tax free basis. Some types of assets can be removed tax free on the assumption that they will be subject to Canadian taxation at a later point in time. This might not happen if one of Canada's bilateral tax treaties prohibits Canadian taxation after an individual has been a non-resident for a specified period of time.

20-110.   Other leakages can occur when assets are bumped up in value for foreign tax purposes, with no corresponding change in the Canadian tax base. This is essentially what happened in the Bronfman trust case, in which several billion dollars in assets were removed from Canada without being subject to Canadian income taxes on accrued gains.

Elective Dispositions

20-111.   As noted in the preceding Paragraphs, certain types of property are exempted from the deemed disposition rules. There may, however, be circumstances in which an individual wishes to override these exemptions and trigger capital gains at the time of departure. An important example of this would be farm property that qualifies for the lifetime capital gains deduction. (See Chapter 11 for details of this deduction.)

20-112.   An individual may wish to trigger income or losses on the exempted property at the time of departure for other reasons. An example of this would be an emigrant who wants to realize a loss on exempt property in order to offset a gain on non-exempt property.

20-113.   Such situations are provided for in ITA 128.1(4)(d), which allows an individual to elect to have a deemed disposition on certain types of properties that are exempt from the general deemed disposition rule. The properties on which the election can be made include real property situated in Canada, Canadian resource and timber resource properties, as well as property of a business carried on in Canada through a permanent establishment. Note that, if this election results in losses (capital or terminal), they can only be used to offset income resulting from other deemed dispositions. They cannot be applied against other sources of income, including capital gains from actual dispositions, for the taxation year.

Exercise Twenty - 18

Subject: Emigration

Ms. Gloria Lopez owns shares in a Canadian private company with an adjusted cost base of $120,000 and a fair market value of $235,000. In addition, she owns a rental property with a fair market value of $130,000 ($30,000 of this can be attributed to the land) and a cost of $220,000 ($60,000 of this can be attributed to the land). The UCC of the building is $142,000. During the current year, Ms. Lopez permanently departs from Canada. Calculate the minimum Net Income For Tax Purposes that will result from her departure with respect to the shares and the rental property.

End of Exercise. Solution available in Study Guide.

Security For Departure Tax

20-114.   The preceding deemed disposition rules can be very burdensome for an emigrating individual. If the individual has substantial amounts of property on which gains have accrued, the deemed disposition rules can result in a hefty tax bill. This is further complicated by the fact that there are no proceeds of disposition to provide funds for paying this liability.

20-115.   In recognition of this problem, ITA 220(4.5) through (4.54) allow the taxpayer to provide security in lieu of paying the tax that results from the deemed dispositions. Similar provisions have been added such as ITA 220(4.6) through (4.63) for dealing with trusts distributing Taxable Canadian Property to non-residents.

20-116.   ITA 220(4.5) requires the CRA to accept "adequate security". Guidance on what constitutes adequate security is found in the CRA's guide "Emigrants And Income Tax" (T4056) as follows:

> Bank letters of guarantee, bank letters of credit, and bonds from the Government of Canada or a province or territory of Canada are considered acceptable forms of security. Other types of security may also be acceptable, such as shares in private or publicly traded corporations, certificates in precious metals, various other marketable securities, a charge or mortgage on real property, or valuable personal property.

20-117.   If the taxpayer elects under ITA 220(4.5), interest does not accrue on the tax that has been deferred until the amount becomes unsecured. This will usually be at the time when there is an actual disposition of the property that was subject to the deemed disposition.

20-118.   A final point here is that ITA 220(4.51) creates deemed security on an amount that is the total amount of taxes under Part I that would be payable, at the highest tax rate that applies to individuals, on Taxable Income of $50,000. This amount is one-half of a $100,000 capital gain, and the effect of this provision is to exempt emigrants from the requirement to provide security on the first $100,000 in capital gains resulting from their departure.

We suggest you work Self Study Problem Twenty-8 at this point.

Unwinding A Deemed Disposition
The Problem
20-119.   A potential problem can arise when an individual departs from Canada and, at a later point in time, returns. A simple example will serve to illustrate this difficulty:

Example   John Fuller emigrates from Canada on June 1, 2013. At that time, he owns shares of a private company with a fair market value of $200,000 and an adjusted cost base of $125,000. As a result of the deemed disposition/reacquisition of these shares, he has a taxable capital gain of $37,500 [(1/2)($200,000 - $125,000)]. In 2014, he returns to Canada. At the time of immigration, he still owns the shares and their fair market value has increased to $260,000.

20-120.   In the absence of any special provision (and ignoring the deemed security rules discussed in Paragraph 20-114), Mr. Fuller's departure from Canada would cost him the taxes paid on the $37,500 taxable capital gain arising on the deemed disposition at emigration. On his return, the adjusted cost base of his property would be increased to $260,000 (deemed disposition/re-acquisition on immigration). However, the fact remains that his temporary absence has resulted in an out-of-pocket tax cost on the $37,500 taxable capital gain.

The Solution

20-121.   ITA 128.1(6) provides relief in this type of situation. With respect to Taxable Canadian Property such as Mr. Fuller's, ITA 128.1(6)(a) allows a returning individual to make an election with respect to property that was Taxable Canadian Property at the time of emigration. The effect of making this election is that the deemed disposition that was required under ITA 128.1(1)(b) at the time of departure, is reversed when the individual returns to Canada. As there is no real basis for establishing whether an emigrant will eventually return as an immigrant, ITA 128.1(6) has no influence on the tax consequences arising at the time of emigration.

20-122.   Returning to our example from Paragraph 20-119, if this election is made, the addition to Taxable Income that was assessed when Mr. Fuller left Canada would be reversed through an amended return, resulting in a refund of the taxes paid.

20-123.   As the deemed disposition at departure has been reversed, there would be no need for a disposition/reacquisition when he returns to Canada. This means that after the appropriate election and amended return are filed, Mr. Fuller would wind up in the same tax position as he was in before he departed from Canada. That is, he would own securities with an adjusted cost base of $125,000 with no net taxes paid as a result of his departure and return.

20-124.   ITA 128.1 contains additional provisions for specialized situations. Coverage of the following topics goes beyond the scope of this text, but they have been listed here for your information:

- ITA 128.1(6)(b) contains a fairly complex provision related to situations in which dividends are paid on shares while the individual is absent from Canada.

- ITA 128.1(6)(c) contains a further provision dealing with property other than Taxable Canadian Property. This includes an election that allows the emigrant to partially reverse the tax effects resulting from his deemed disposition on departure.

- ITA 128.1(7) contains a provision that deals with situations where there is a loss on the property while a trust beneficiary is absent from Canada. This provision only applies to beneficiaries who are individuals and who have received distributions from the trust while they were a non-resident.

Short-Term Residents

20-125.   With the increasing presence of multi-national firms in the Canadian business environment, it has become common for executives and other employees to find themselves resident in Canada for only a small portion of their total working lives. In the absence of some special provision, the deemed disposition rules could be a significant hardship to employees who are in this position.

20-126.   For example, if Ms. Eng was transferred from Hong Kong to work in Canada for three years, she could become liable on departure for capital gains taxation on all of her capital property owned at the time that she ceases to be a resident of Canada. The liability could put a severe drain on her available liquid assets and could result in taxation on personal items such as paintings and furniture. This would not be an equitable situation and could discourage the free movement of employees to and from Canada.

20-127.   In recognition of the preceding problem, ITA 128.1(4)(b)(iv) provides an exception to the deemed disposition rules that applies to taxpayers who, during the ten years preceding departure, have been resident in Canada for a total of 60 months or less. For such taxpayers, the deemed disposition rules do not apply to any property that was owned immediately before the taxpayer last became resident in Canada, or was acquired by inheritance or bequest during the period after he last became resident in Canada. However, the rules still apply to property acquired other than by inheritance or bequest during the period of residency.

Exercise Twenty - 19

Subject: Short Term Residents

During 2010, Charles Brookings moves to Canada from the U.K. He has not previously lived in Canada. At this time his capital assets consist of shares in a U.K. company and a tract of vacant land in Canada which he had inherited. The shares have a fair market value of $250,000 and an adjusted cost base of $175,000. The land has a cost of $95,000 and a fair market value of $120,000. During 2011, he acquires shares of a Canadian public company for $75,000. During 2013, after finding Canada a tad uncivilized for his tastes, he moves back to the U.K. At this time, the shares in the U.K. company have a fair market value of $280,000, the shares of the Canadian company have a fair market value of $92,000 and the land has a fair market value of $130,000. What are the tax consequences of his emigration from Canada?

End of Exercise. Solution available in Study Guide.

Foreign Source Income Of Residents

Introduction

20-128.   It would be a fairly easy task to write an entire book on the tax issues associated with the foreign source income of Canadian residents. As an example, draft legislation on non-resident trusts and foreign investment entities ran to nearly 900 pages in its print edition. In addition to being extensive, much of this material is extremely complex, in some cases almost beyond the understanding of mere mortals.

20-129.   Despite this complexity, the importance of this subject mandates that we give some attention to the issues, even in an introductory text such as this. Although some aspects of foreign source income of Canadian residents are relatively straightforward, you should be aware that this material is not an adequate resource for making important decisions in this potentially complicated area.

20-130.   We will begin this section on foreign source income of residents by discussing the reporting requirements applicable to Canadian residents who have foreign investments. This will be followed by sections dealing with resident taxpayers who have the following types of income:

- foreign source employment income;
- foreign source income from unincorporated businesses;
- foreign source interest income; and
- capital gains resulting from the disposition of foreign assets.

20-131.   The issues involved for taxpayers having these types of income sources are not overly complex. However, a completely different situation arises when Canadian resident taxpayers receive income from what tax legislation refers to as non-resident entities. These entities are defined as corporations, trusts, or any other type of entity that was formed, organized, last continued under, or governed under the laws of a country, or a political subdivision of a country, other than Canada. In order to simplify our presentation of this material, we will limit our coverage of this material to non-resident corporations paying dividends to Canadian resident taxpayers.

Foreign Investment Reporting Requirements

20-132.   As you are aware, residents of Canada are liable for income taxes on their world-wide income. This means, for example, that if a Canadian resident has a bank account in the United Kingdom, any interest earned on that account should be reported in the appropriate Canadian tax return.

20-133.   In an attempt to ensure that all foreign income is reported by Canadian residents, an information return for foreign income must be filed by certain taxpayers. The filing requirement for the form T1135 is as follows:

> Canadian resident individuals, corporations, and trusts, as well as partnerships, who held certain property outside Canada with a total cost amount of more than $100,000 at any time in the tax year, have to file Form T1135, Foreign Income Verification Statement.

20-134.   The reporting requirement is for specified foreign property that includes the following:

- Funds in foreign bank accounts.
- Shares of non-resident corporations, even if held by a Canadian stockbroker. However, shares held in a self-directed RRSP are not included.
- Land and buildings located outside Canada (other than personal use property).
- Interests in mutual funds that are organized in a foreign jurisdiction.
- Debts owed to residents by non-residents.
- An interest in a partnership where non-resident members are entitled to 90 percent or more of the share of partnership income, and the partnership holds specified foreign property.
- Patents, copyrights, or trademarks held outside Canada.

20-135.   The following items are not included in the definition of specified foreign property:

- Property used exclusively to carry on an active business.
- Personal use property, such as a cottage.
- Shares or debt of a non-resident corporation or trust that is a foreign affiliate.
- An interest in a U.S. Individual Retirement Account (IRA).
- An interest in a non-resident trust that provides pension or other employee benefits, but that does not pay income tax in the jurisdiction where it is resident.

20-136.   In addition to reporting the presence of these properties, the person must report the total income that they have produced. This would include any capital gains resulting from dispositions.

20-137.   Substantial penalties will result from failure to comply with these reporting requirements. In general, there are two types of penalties. The first is for failure to file the prescribed form on time. This penalty is $500 for each month late if the return is filed within 24 months of the filing date. If the late filing exceeds 24 months, additional penalties may be charged, generally based on the value of the foreign investment. The second penalty is for purposefully making false statements on a filed return. Such penalties are generally equal to a minimum of $24,000 and can be as much as 5 percent of the value of the investment property.

Exercise Twenty - 20

Subject: Foreign Investment Reporting

During 2013, Simon Taylor, a Canadian resident, has a U.K. bank account with a balance of £40,000. In 2012, he made a two year interest free loan of £45,000 to his brother-in-law in Scotland. No formal loan agreement was involved. Assume 1£ = $1.55 for 2013.   Describe any foreign investment reporting obligations that Simon has for 2013.

End of Exercise. Solution available in Study Guide.

We suggest you work Self Study Problem Twenty-9 at this point.

Foreign Source Employment Income
The Problem
20-138.   Individuals who are residents of Canada are taxable on employment income regardless of where the employment duties are performed. This creates a potential problem in that an individual earning employment income in a foreign country could be subject to Canadian taxes because they have retained their status as a Canadian resident and, at the same time, be subject to taxes in the foreign country because it is the source of the employment income. Tax treaties would normally be used to resolve this potential conflict.

Canada/U.S. Tax Treaty - Foreign Source Employment Income
20-139.   This problem is, of course, the mirror image of the problem that arises when a U.S. resident is earning employment income while working in Canada. In our discussion of that situation (see Paragraph 20-60), we noted that, in general, the source country has the right to tax employment income. We also noted that, under the Canada/U.S. tax treaty, there were two exceptions to this rule. As applied to a situation where a Canadian resident is earning U.S. employment income, these exceptions are as follows:

$10,000 Rule   Under this rule if, during a calendar year, a Canadian resident earns employment income in the U.S. that is $10,000 or less in U.S. dollars, then the income is taxable only in Canada.

183 Day Rule   This rule exempts U.S. source employment income from U.S. taxation, provided it is earned by a Canadian resident who was physically present in the U.S. for no more than 183 days during any twelve month period commencing or ending in the calendar year.   This exemption is conditional on employment income not being paid by an employer with a permanent establishment in the U.S. who would be able to deduct the amount paid from their U.S. Taxable Income. Stated alternatively, if the employment income exceeds $10,000 and is deductible in the U.S., it will be taxed in the U.S., even if the employee is present in the U.S. for less than 183 days during the year.

We suggest you work Self Study Problem Twenty-10 at this point.

Foreign Source Business Income (Unincorporated Sources)
The Problem
20-140.   The general rule that Canadian residents are taxable on their worldwide income would suggest that Canadian residents are taxable on foreign source business income. As was the case with foreign source employment income, this creates a potential problem in that a person earning business income in a foreign country could be subject to Canadian taxes because they have retained their status as a Canadian resident and, at the same time, be

subject to taxes in the foreign country because it is the source of the business income.

20-141.   In many cases, the potential for double taxation is dealt with through international tax treaties. If this is not the case, a Canadian resident may have some amount of taxes withheld in the foreign jurisdiction. In these circumstances, Canada uses foreign tax credits to deal with the problem. While these credits were covered in detail in Chapter 11 for individuals and Chapter 12 for corporations, a simple example where the detailed calculations would have resulted in a foreign tax credit equal to the foreign tax withheld will serve to review the general approach used:

Example   Ms. Johnson, a Canadian resident, is subject to a Canadian marginal tax rate of 45 percent on all of her worldwide income. During the current year, she earns foreign source business income of $1,000, from which the source country assesses and withholds taxes at a rate of 15 percent.

Analysis   The pretax amount of foreign income would be included in Taxable Income, with the foreign taxes paid by Ms. Johnson, a Canadian resident, generating a credit against Canadian Tax Payable. Applying this to the preceding example results in the following calculations:

Foreign Business Income Received	$ 850
Foreign Tax Withheld	150
Gross Income = Taxable Income Addition	$1,000
Canadian Tax Payable [(45%)($1,000)]	$ 450
Foreign Tax Credit = Foreign Tax Withheld	(150)
Net Canadian Tax Payable	$ 300
Foreign Tax Withheld	150
Total Taxes Payable	$ 450
After Tax Retention ($1,000 - $450)	$ 550
Overall Tax Rate ($450 ÷ $1,000)	45%

As this simple example makes clear, this represents a very equitable solution to situations where foreign taxes are withheld on income that will be taxed again in Canada. The combined foreign and Canadian taxes total $450, exactly the same amount that would have been paid if Ms. Johnson had received the $1,000 in business income from a Canadian source.

Canada/U.S. Tax Treaty - Foreign Source Business Income

20-142.   As was discussed when we considered the Canadian business income of non-residents, the Canada/U.S. tax treaty indicates that business income will be taxed in the source country in those situations where the business is operated through a permanent establishment. Applying this here would mean that if a Canadian resident earns business income in the U.S. without having a permanent establishment in that country, it will be taxed in Canada, rather than in the U.S. Alternatively, if the business income is earned through a permanent establishment in the U.S., it will be taxed in that country. Any taxes withheld by the U.S. would be eligible for treatment as a foreign business tax credit. (See Chapters 11 and 12 for detailed coverage of this credit.)

Foreign Source Interest Income

The Problem

20-143.   Resident Canadian taxpayers are taxable on interest income, generally without regard to the source. As was the case with employment income, this raises the possibility of double taxation. In most cases this issue will be resolved by an international tax treaty. If the issue is not resolved by treaty, the Canadian resident would have tax deductions and/or credits based on any foreign taxes withheld.

Canada/U.S. Tax Treaty - Foreign Source Interest Income

20-144. As noted in Paragraph 20-79, Article XI of the Canada/U.S. tax treaty indicates that interest paid to the other jurisdiction will be taxed in that jurisdiction. This means that U.S. residents receiving interest from a Canadian source are not subject to the Canadian Part XIII tax. Correspondingly, Canadian residents receiving interest income from a U.S. source will be subject to Part I taxes in Canada on that interest income.

Exercise Twenty - 21

Subject: Foreign Tax Credits

Jason Abernathy is a Canadian resident. Although he has no permanent establishment in the U.S., in 2013, he earns $18,000 of U.S. source business income. Income taxes of $1,800 were assessed and withheld at the source on that income. In calculating his foreign tax credit, his Adjusted Division B Income is equal to $100,000 and his Tax Otherwise Payable is equal to $21,000. All amounts are in Canadian dollars. Jason's marginal combined federal/provincial tax rate is 44 percent. Determine his after tax retention and overall tax rate on his foreign source business income.

End of Exercise. Solution available in Study Guide.

Foreign Source Capital Gains

The Problem

20-145. The rules of the *Income Tax Act* relating to the calculation of capital gains and losses are generally applicable to residents of Canada on dispositions of property regardless of the location of that property. As was the case with foreign source employment and business income, dispositions of foreign property may result in potential taxation in both Canada and the foreign country. Again, the tax treaties would normally offer a way to resolve any conflicts.

Canada/U.S. Tax Treaty - Foreign Source Capital Gains

20-146. In general, the Canada/U.S. tax treaty gives priority to tax to the vendor's country of residence. However, the treaty allows the U.S. to tax gains from the disposition of real property interests situated in the U.S., as well as gains on most types of property that are used in a permanent establishment through which a Canadian resident has carried on business in the U.S.

Problems With Foreign Source Dividend Income

20-147. Most foreign source investment income is taxed under the rules that are applicable to similar sources of income earned in Canada. An exception to this is dividends received from non-resident corporations.

20-148. As you are aware, dividends paid to Canadian residents by taxable Canadian corporations receive very favourable tax treatment. When such dividends are received by individuals, they are subject to the gross up and tax credit procedures, a process that significantly reduces the effective tax rate on this type of income. When the recipient shareholder is a corporation, the dividends generally escape all taxation in that they can be deducted under ITA 112(1) in the calculation of Taxable Income. Both of these provisions are designed to make up for the fact that the dividends represent an income stream that has already been subject to Canadian tax at the corporate level.

20-149.   The basic problem with dividends received from a non-resident corporation is that the corporation that paid the dividends has not paid taxes in Canada. In fact, in some jurisdictions (e.g., tax havens), the corporation may not have paid any taxes whatsoever. This means that the usual reason for providing favourable treatment of dividend income is not relevant when dividends are received from a non-resident corporation.

20-150.   A further problem is that the foreign source dividends do not reflect the type of income that provided for the payment of dividends by the foreign corporation. Again, as you are aware, Canadian taxes are generally assessed differently on alternative types of income. For example, a CCPC will be taxed much more heavily on property income as compared to the taxes that would be paid on active business income. To maintain fairness in the system, provisions had to be created that reflect the different sources of income that enabled the non-resident corporation to pay dividends.

20-151.   In general, foreign source dividends must be included in a resident taxpayer's Net Income For Tax Purposes under ITA 90(1). When foreign source dividends are received by individuals, they do not get the benefit of the gross up and tax credit procedures. When they are received by corporations, they are not generally deductible under ITA 112(1).

20-152.   While the elimination of favourable tax treatment for dividends from a foreign source provides a partial solution to the problem of dividends being paid out of corporate income that has not been taxed in Canada, two significant problems remain:

1. This procedure can result in double taxation. For example, income earned by a foreign subsidiary of a Canadian corporation could be fully taxed in the foreign jurisdiction and, in the absence of the ITA 112(1) dividend deduction, it would be taxed again in Canada.

2. Under the general rules applicable to corporations, income from a non-resident corporation will not be taxed in Canada until such time as it is distributed to Canadian residents. This means that a Canadian resident can achieve significant tax deferral by placing investments in a foreign corporation, in situations where the income from the investments is not currently needed. This is particularly attractive when the non-resident corporation is located in a jurisdiction where there is little or no taxation of investment income.

20-153.   The first of these problems has been dealt with by developing the concept of a "foreign affiliate". As will be discussed in a subsequent section of this Chapter, dividends received from this type of non-resident corporation may be deductible, in whole or in part, to a recipient Canadian corporation. A partial solution to the second problem is contained in what are referred to as the Foreign Accrual Property Income (FAPI) rules. These rules apply to a subset of foreign affiliates referred to as controlled foreign affiliates.

20-154.   In the following material, we will give consideration to dividends from foreign corporations that are received by:

• individuals resident in Canada;
• Canadian corporations that are not affiliated with the foreign corporation;
• Canadian corporations that are affiliated with the foreign corporation but do not control it; and
• Canadian corporations that control the foreign corporation.

20-155.   We would remind you that our presentation of this material is at a very basic level and should be considered only as an overview of the topic and not as a guide for making real world decisions in this complex area.

Foreign Source Dividends Received By Individuals

20-156.   If a resident Canadian individual receives a dividend from a foreign corporation and there is no withholding of tax by the foreign jurisdiction, the amount received will be included in that individual's Net Income For Tax Purposes. It will not be grossed up and it will not generate a dividend tax credit.

20-157.   Alternatively, if there is withholding by the foreign jurisdiction, the pre-withholding amount of the dividend will be included in the individual's Net Income For Tax Purposes. To the extent that the withholding is 15 percent or less, the individual is entitled to a foreign tax credit. Any withholding in excess of 15 percent is eligible for a deduction from Net Income For Tax Purposes.

20-158.   While it would rarely be an appropriate choice, the individual would have the alternative of deducting the entire amount withheld, rather than using the eligible portion as a tax credit.

Example   Martin Fingle is entitled to $25,000 in dividends from a foreign corporation in which he owns shares. The foreign jurisdiction withholds $5,000 (20%), providing a net receipt of $20,000. In addition to the dividend, Martin has Canadian source interest income of $65,000. He has no tax credits other than his basic personal credit and any credits related to foreign taxes withheld. He has no deductions from Net Income For Tax Purposes in determining Taxable Income.

Analysis   Martin's Taxable Income would be calculated as follows:

Interest Income	$65,000
Foreign Dividends (100%)	25,000
Excess Withholding [(20% - 15%)($25,000)]	(1,250)
Net Income For Tax Purposes And Taxable Income	$88,750

His Tax Payable would be calculated as follows:

First $87,123	$16,118
Tax On Next $1,627 ($88,750 - $87,123) At 26%	423
Tax Before Credits	$16,541
Personal Tax Credit	(1,656)
Part I Tax Payable Before Foreign Tax Credit	$14,885
Foreign Tax Credit (See Note)	(3,750)
Federal Tax Payable	$11,135

Note   The foreign tax credit would be the lesser of:

- Amount Withheld (Limited To 15% Of $25,000) = $3,750

- $\left[\dfrac{\text{Foreign Non-Business Income}}{\text{Division B Income}}\right](\text{Tax Payable}) = \left[\dfrac{\$25,000}{\$88,750}\right](\$14,885) = \$4,193$

20-159.   While Martin could have deducted all of the withheld amount, his tax savings from this deduction would only be $1,300 [(26%)($5,000)]. This is clearly not as desirable as the $3,750 (15 percent foreign tax credit) alternative.

We suggest you work Self Study Problem Twenty-11 at this point.

Foreign Dividends Received From Non-Affiliated Corporations

20-160.   The pre-withholding amount of a dividend received by a Canadian corporation from a foreign corporation that is not an affiliate, would be included in the corporation's Net Income For Tax Purposes. As a foreign affiliate is not involved, there would be no deduction in the determination of the corporation's Taxable Income.

Example Martin Fingle Inc., a Canadian public corporation, is entitled to $25,000 in dividends from a foreign corporation in which it owns less than 1 percent of the shares. The foreign jurisdiction withholds $5,000 (20%), providing a net receipt of $20,000. The corporate tax rate on this income, after the general rate reduction, will be 25 percent (38% - 13%). Assume that Martin Fingle Inc. has no other source of income during the year.

Analysis The Corporation's Taxable Income will be $25,000, the pre-withholding amount of the dividend. Tax Payable, before the application of the foreign tax credit will be $6,250 [(25%)($25,000)]. As a corporation's use of foreign non-business tax credits is not limited to 15 percent, the tax credit will be $5,000, the lesser of:

- Amount Withheld (no 15% limit) = $5,000

- $\left[\dfrac{\text{Foreign Non-Business Income}}{\text{Division B Income}} \right] (\text{Tax Payable}) = \left[\dfrac{\$25,000}{\$25,000} \right] (\$6,250) = \$6,250$

Dividends Received From Non-Controlled Foreign Affiliates

Foreign Affiliate Defined

20-161. A foreign affiliate of a Canadian taxpayer is defined in ITA 95(1) as a non-resident corporation in which that taxpayer has an equity percentage of at least 1 percent. As well, the aggregate equity percentages of the taxpayer and each person related to the taxpayer must be at least 10 percent. The ownership percentage can be established on either a direct or indirect basis, and is defined as the greatest percentage holding in any class of the non-resident corporation's capital stock.

20-162. As an example of both the direct and indirect application of this rule, consider the following example:

Example Candoo, a resident Canadian corporation, owns 70 percent of the only class of shares of Forco One, a non-resident corporation. In turn, Forco One owns 20 percent of the only class of shares of Forco Two, a second non-resident corporation.

Analysis Forco One is a foreign affiliate of Candoo because of Candoo's 70 percent direct ownership. Forco Two is also a foreign affiliate of Candoo because the indirect ownership percentage is 14 percent [(70%)(20%)].

20-163. We would also note that the ownership thresholds are applied on a shareholder by shareholder basis. A non-resident company will be a foreign affiliate of a Canadian resident, only if that resident owns directly or indirectly at least 1 percent of the shares of that non-resident company and, in addition, that resident, together with related persons, owns at least 10 percent of the shares of that non-resident company.

Example Carson Ltd. and Dawson Inc., two resident Canadian companies, each own 8 percent of Belgique, a non-resident corporation. While Carson Ltd. is part of a related group that controls Belgique, Dawson Inc. is not related to any of the other shareholders of Belgique.

Analysis Belgique would be a foreign affiliate of Carson Ltd. as Carson Ltd. owns more than 1 percent of the shares and, in addition, is part of a related group that owns more than 10 percent of the shares. Belgique would not be a foreign affiliate of Dawson Inc.

20-164. A foreign affiliate may or may not be a controlled foreign affiliate. In this section we are limiting our discussion to situations where control is not present. In the next section of this chapter, we will provide limited coverage of controlled foreign affiliates. Note that the rules discussed in this section apply to all foreign affiliates, whether or not control exists.

Exercise Twenty - 22

Subject   Identifying Foreign Affiliates

Canvest is a resident Canadian corporation that has three investments in the shares of non-resident corporations. For each of the investments in non-resident corporations described below, determine whether the investee is a foreign affiliate.

Forco 1   Canvest owns 3 percent of Forco 1. A Canadian subsidiary of Canvest owns 8 percent of Forco 1.

Forco 2   Canvest owns 9 percent of Forco 2. Canvest is not related to any of the other shareholders of Forco 2.

Forco 3   Canvest owns 5 percent of Forco 3. The spouse of the shareholder who has a controlling interest in Canvest owns the other 95 percent of the shares of Forco 3.

End of Exercise. Solution available in Study Guide.

Dividends Received From Foreign Affiliates - Basic Concepts

20-165.   We have previously noted that, in general, only dividends received from a taxable Canadian corporation can be deducted under ITA 112(1) in the determination of the Taxable Income of a resident Canadian corporation. However, ITA 113(1) provides a similar deduction for dividends received by a resident corporate shareholder from a foreign affiliate.

20-166.   Unlike the fairly straightforward application of ITA 112(1), the application of ITA 113(1) is very complex in that it is applied differently depending on the country where the foreign affiliate is located and income source from which the dividend is being paid. The ITA 113(1) rules are implemented by a process in which the foreign affiliate's Surplus balances are tracked by type of income and source country. We would remind you that the term Surplus in tax work is the equivalent of the term Retained Earnings in accounting work.

20-167.   While there are other types of surplus that determine the tax status of dividends from foreign affiliates, in this text we will only provide coverage of Exempt Surplus and Taxable Surplus. Coverage of other surplus balances goes beyond the scope of this introductory text.

20-168.   When a dividend is paid by a foreign affiliate it is assumed to come first from any Exempt Surplus balance that is available. If there is no Exempt Surplus balance, or if the dividend is larger than the Exempt Surplus balance, the required amount will then be removed from the Taxable Surplus balance.

Exempt Vs. Taxable Surplus

20-169.   The content of these surplus balances requires the allocation of income from four different sources. They are as follows:

- active business income
- investment income (e.g., interest and rents)
- capital gains on dispositions of assets used to produce active business income
- capital gains on dispositions of assets not used to produce active business income

20-170.   The situation is further complicated in that the classification of a particular type of income will depend on whether the foreign affiliate is located in country with which Canada has a tax treaty or a Tax Information Exchange Agreement (TIEA). For example, active business income is allocated to Exempt Surplus in a country where a tax treaty or TIEA is in effect. Alternatively, this type of income is allocated to Taxable Surplus in other countries.

20-171.   Based on this two-way allocation, the items included in Exempt Surplus are as follows:

- For a foreign affiliate that is located in a country with which Canada has a tax treaty or a tax information exchange agreement (TIEA):
    - Active business income
    - The taxable one-half of capital gains on dispositions of property used in producing active business income.

- For all foreign affiliates, without regard to the location of the foreign affiliate:
    - The non-taxable one-half of capital gains on dispositions of all types of capital property.

20-172.   Using a similar approach, the items included in Taxable Surplus are as follows:

- For a foreign affiliate that is located in a country with which Canada does not have a tax treaty or a TIEA:
    - Active business income
    - The taxable one-half of capital gains on dispositions of property used in producing active business income.

- For all foreign affiliates, without regard to the location of the foreign affiliate:
    - The taxable one-half of capital gains on dispositions of capital property other than that used in producing active business income.
    - Investment income, which includes income from property and from non-active businesses.

Dividends Paid From Exempt Surplus

20-173.   When a dividend is paid from a foreign affiliate's Exempt Surplus, Canadian tax legislation, in effect, cedes all of the taxation of this income stream to the foreign jurisdiction. This is without regard to the level of local taxation in the foreign jurisdiction or amounts of tax withheld by that jurisdiction.

20-174.   In order to apply this approach, ITA 113(1)(a) allows the full amount of the foreign affiliate dividend to be deducted in the determination of the resident corporation's Taxable Income.

Example   A Canadian company receives a $90,000 dividend from a foreign affiliate. The affiliate had paid a $100,000 dividend from its exempt surplus (an after foreign taxes balance), with the foreign jurisdiction withholding $10,000 from the distribution to Canada.

Analysis   The Canadian corporation will include the pre-withholding $100,000 dividend in its Net Income For Tax Purposes, and will deduct the $100,000 included amount under ITA 113(1)(a) in the determination of Taxable Income under ITA 113(1)(a). No Canadian taxes will be paid on the dividend and, consistent with this result, no foreign tax credit will be available for the $10,000 that was withheld by the foreign jurisdiction.

Dividends Paid From Taxable Surplus

20-175.   With respect to foreign affiliate dividends paid from Taxable Surplus, the goal here is to apply ITA 113(1) in a manner that attempts to have the overall level of taxation, both domestic and foreign, be the equivalent of the amount of taxes that would be paid in Canada on the same stream of income. Currently this rate is equal to 25 percent.

Basic Rate	38%
General Rate Reduction	(13%)
Overall Federal Rate	25%

20-176.   While this could have been accomplished using credits against Tax Payable, the government chose to do the required adjustments through deductions under ITA 113(1). Given the desire to apply an overall tax rate of 25 percent, tax amounts will have to be converted to income using a factor of 4 (1 ÷ 25%). Stated alternatively, every $1 of tax paid must be converted to Taxable Income of $4.

20-177. To achieve the desired overall tax rate of 25 percent, two adjustments are required:

ITA 113(1)(b) adjusts Taxable Income to reflect the income taxes paid in the foreign jurisdiction.

ITA 113(1)(c) adjusts Taxable Income to reflect taxes withheld by the foreign jurisdiction on payments to non-residents of that jurisdiction.

20-178.   An example will serve to illustrate these provisions.

Example   Cancor, a taxable Canadian corporation, owns 50 percent of the outstanding shares of Forco, a corporation located in a country that does not have a tax treaty or a TIEA with Canada. All of Forco's income is from active business activities. During 2013, Forco pays dividends of $90,000. Of this total, $42,750 is received by Cancor, with $2,250 being withheld by the foreign jurisdiction. Forco is subject to a tax rate of 10 percent in the foreign jurisdiction.

Analysis   Dividends paid are an after tax amount. This means that the original income stream that formed the basis for the current dividend was $100,000 [$90,000 ÷ (1 - 10%)], with taxes of $10,000 being paid prior to the dividend declaration.

Given this, Cancor's share of these taxes would be $5,000 [(1/2)($10,000)]. Taking this and the $2,250 in withholding into account, to achieve an overall tax rate of 25 percent on the original $50,000 income stream would require additional Canadian taxes as follows:

Required Total Tax [(25%)($50,000)]	$12,500
Foreign Taxes Paid By Foreign Affiliate	(5,000)
Foreign Taxes Withheld From Dividend	(2,250)
Required Additional Canadian Tax	$ 5,250

As we have noted, ITA 113(1) accomplishes this result with two adjustments. The first is related to the $5,000 in foreign tax paid. The $5,000 in taxes paid reflects, at a 25 percent rate, $20,000 ($5,000 ÷ 25%) in Taxable Income. This would suggest multiplying the foreign tax paid by 4. However, this does not take into consideration the fact that income has already been reduced by $5,000 from $50,000 to $45,000 by these taxes. Given this, ITA 113(1)(b) requires that the $5,000 in foreign taxes be multiplied by a relevant factor of 3 [(1 ÷ 25%) - 1]. This deduction equals $15,000.

In applying ITA 113(1)(c), we need to adjust for the $2,250 in taxes withheld from the dividend payment. Given this, ITA 113(1)(c) requires that this amount be multiplied by 4 (1 ÷ 25%). This results in a deduction of $9,000, reflecting the amount of income that would result in the payment of $2,250 in taxes.

Putting all of this together results in the following calculation of Tax Payable:

Net Income For Tax Purposes	$45,000
ITA 113(1)(b) Deduction For Foreign Tax Paid	(15,000)
ITA 113(1)(c) Deduction For Foreign Tax Withheld	(9,000)
Taxable Income	$21,000
Required Rate	25%
Canadian Tax Payable	$ 5,250

This, as expected, is the same amount that we calculated in the preceding table using a more intuitive approach that is not based on the ITA 113 legislation.

Dividends Received From Controlled Foreign Affiliates
Controlled Foreign Affiliate Defined
20-179.   While establishing the concept of a foreign affiliate alleviated the problem of excessive taxation on dividends received by Canadian corporations from non-resident corporations, it did not deal with the problem of using a non-resident corporation to defer Canadian taxation on property income. In order to deal with this issue, the government developed the concept of a "controlled foreign affiliate".

20-180.   In somewhat simplified terms, ITA 95(1) defines a controlled foreign affiliate of a Canadian taxpayer as a foreign affiliate of that taxpayer that is:

1.   controlled by the Canadian resident on the basis of his own shareholdings; or

2.   controlled by the Canadian resident, together with:

   • persons (residents or non-residents) who are not at arm's length with the Canadian resident;
   • up to four Canadian residents who are not related to the taxpayer (referred to as "relevant" shareholders; and
   • any other persons (residents or non-residents) who are related to the "relevant" Canadian shareholders.

Example   Cantext, a Canadian public company, owns 11 percent of the voting shares of Fortext, a company located in Germany. Two other resident Canadian corporations, who are not related to Cantext, each own an additional 15 percent of the voting shares of Fortext. A French subsidiary of one of these other Canadian companies owns 20 percent of the voting shares of Fortext.

Analysis   Fortext is a foreign affiliate of Cantext since Cantext holds more than 10 percent of the voting shares of Fortext. It is a controlled foreign affiliate in that:

   • Cantext owns 11 percent;
   • two unrelated Canadian companies (relevant shareholders) own an additional 30 percent; and
   • a company related to one of the relevant shareholders owns another 20 percent.

This gives a total holding of 61 percent, enough to provide control of Fortext. Note that Fortext is also a controlled foreign affiliate of both the other Canadian corporations.

20-181.   The significance of the controlled foreign affiliate concept is that, if an investment in a non-resident corporation falls within this definition, the Canadian shareholder must recognize its foreign accrual property income (FAPI, hereafter) prior to its actual distribution. That is, the FAPI of controlled foreign affiliates must be recorded as it is earned, rather than when it is distributed in the form of dividends.

20-182.   This provision is somewhat mitigated by the fact that Canadian residents are not required to report the FAPI of controlled foreign affiliates unless it exceeds $5,000. The $5,000 exemption figure recognizes that the calculation of FAPI is quite complex and should not be required when the amount of income is small. As FAPI income is taxed as it accrues, dividends subsequently paid out of such income are not taxable.

Foreign Accrual Property Income (FAPI)
General Rules
20-183.   In simplified terms, FAPI is the passive income of a controlled foreign affiliate. FAPI includes income from property (e.g. interest, portfolio dividends), income from non-active businesses (e.g. rental income), as well as the taxable one-half of capital gains resulting from the disposition of properties that are not used in an active business. An important distinguishing feature of this type of income is that, with the exception of rental income, its source can be easily moved from one tax jurisdiction to another.

20-184.   The property income definition for FAPI also includes income from a foreign investment business. This type of business is analogous to the specified investment business that is used in determining income eligible for the small business deduction (see Chapter 12).

20-185.   As is the case with the specified investment business rules, a foreign affiliate would be considered to be earning active business income if it either employs more than five full time employees or the equivalent of more than five full time employees, to earn income that would normally be considered property income. This "five-employee" exception is especially important in deciding whether foreign rental income is active (exempt from the FAPI rules) or passive (subject to the FAPI rules).

Taxation Of FAPI

20-186.   As noted in Paragraph 20-177, if a taxpayer has an investment in a controlled foreign affiliate, FAPI must be accrued as it is earned by that affiliate. Note that this is a separate issue from the taxation of dividends from either controlled or other foreign affiliates. We will deal with this latter issue in the next section. Not surprisingly, we will find that if dividends are paid out of FAPI income that has been accrued by a taxpayer, the dividends will not be taxed a second time when received by that investor.

> **Example**   Paul Peterson, a Canadian resident, owns 80 percent of the shares of Tabasco Ltd., a company that is incorporated in Trinidad. During 2013, the Company has income of $100,000, all of which is earned by passive investments. No income taxes are paid on this income in Trinidad, and no dividends are paid out of this income to Mr. Peterson.
>
> **Analysis**   Tabasco Ltd. is clearly a controlled foreign affiliate. Further, all of its income is from passive sources. Given this, under ITA 91(1), Mr. Peterson will have to include $80,000 [(80%)($100,000)] in his Canadian Net Income For Tax Purposes for the current year.

20-187.   The preceding example was simplified by the fact that Tabasco Ltd. was not subject to taxes in the foreign country. If it had been, the income of this controlled foreign affiliate would have been subject to double taxation. Fortunately, the *Income Tax Act* provides relief in the form of a deduction under ITA 91(4) that is designed to compensate for foreign taxes that have been paid on FAPI.

20-188.   Note that this is a deduction against income, rather than a tax credit. As you will recall from discussions in other Chapters (e.g., the value of investment tax credits), a deduction against income will only reduce Tax Payable by the amount of the deduction multiplied by the tax rate. This means that its value to the taxpayer is less than the amount of foreign taxes paid and, given this, it would not be equitable to set the deduction equal to those taxes.

20-189.   The ITA 91(4) deduction recognizes this difference by multiplying the foreign taxes paid on FAPI by what is referred to as a relevant tax factor (RTF, hereafter). As defined in ITA 95(1), the RTF for individuals is different than it is for corporations.

> **Canadian Resident Individual**   If the investor in the controlled foreign affiliate is an individual, the RTF is 2.2. This is based on the notional assumption that the Canadian tax rate on this income would have been about 45.45 percent if the individual had received it from a Canadian source (1 ÷ 45.45% = 2.2).
>
> **Canadian Resident Corporation**   If the investor in the controlled foreign affiliate is a corporation, the RTF for 2013 is 4. This RTF is based on 1, divided by a notional tax rate that would have applied if the income had been received from a Canadian source (1 ÷ 25% = 4). For 2013, that rate of 25 percent is 38 percent, less the 2013 General Rate Reduction of 13 percent.

20-190.   If the controlled foreign affiliate's income is taxed in the foreign jurisdiction at the notional rate applicable to the investor, the ITA 91(4) deduction will completely eliminate the FAPI. In most cases, the foreign tax rate will be below the notional rates, resulting in some FAPI being included in income. Note, however, that the ITA 91(4) deduction cannot exceed the FAPI.

Example Continued (Foreign Taxes Paid)   Paul Peterson, a Canadian resident, owns 80 percent of the shares of Tabasco Ltd., a company that is incorporated in Trinidad. During 2013, the Company has income of $100,000, all of which is earned by passive investments. The Company pays Trinidadian taxes at a rate of 20 percent. No dividends are paid out of this income to Mr. Peterson.

Analysis   The tax consequences to Mr. Peterson would be as follows:

FAPI [(80%)($100,000)]	$80,000
Lesser Of:	
• FAPI = $80,000	
• ITA 91(4) Deduction [(2.2)(80%)(20%)($100,000)] = $35,200	(35,200)
Net Addition To Net Income For Tax Purposes	$44,800

Exercise Twenty - 23

Subject: FAPI

Forco is a wholly owned foreign subsidiary of Canco, a resident Canadian company. Forco earns $100,000 of investment income in 2013 and pays 18 percent in tax in the foreign jurisdiction. None of the after tax income is paid out as dividends. What is the effect of this information on Canco's 2013 Net Income For Tax Purposes?

End of Exercise. Solution available in Study Guide.

Dividends From FAPI

20-191.   A final problem remains when the controlled foreign affiliate subsequently distributes the FAPI to the Canadian resident shareholders as a dividend. While these dividends must be included in income, the *Income Tax Act* provides a deduction to reflect the fact that all or a part of the dividend may have already been taxed in an earlier year as FAPI.

20-192.   The deduction is provided solely through ITA 91(5) in the case of individuals and a combination of ITA 91(5) and ITA 113(1)(b) in the case of corporations. The deductions are designed to eliminate taxation on previously taxed FAPI. It is equal to the lesser of the dividends received and the FAPI previously taxed to that shareholder after the ITA 91(4) deduction. Any withholding taxes on dividends paid to corporate shareholders of foreign affiliates are eligible for a deduction under ITA 113(1)(c).

Example Continued (Dividend Paid)   Paul Peterson, a Canadian resident, owns 80 percent of the shares of Tabasco Ltd., a company that is incorporated in Trinidad. During 2013, the Company has income of $100,000, all of which is earned by passive investments. The Company pays Trinidadian taxes at a rate of 20 percent. Tabasco Ltd. declares and pays dividends of $40,000 in January, 2014. There is no withholding tax on this dividend.

Analysis   As shown in Paragraph 20-190, Mr. Peterson's addition to Net Income For Tax Purposes in 2013 was $44,800. The consequences of receiving the dividend in 2014 would be nil as shown in the following calculation.

Foreign Source Dividend [(80%)($40,000)]	$32,000
Deduct Lesser Of:	
• Previous FAPI After ITA 91(4) Deduction = $44,800	
• Dividend Received = $32,000	(32,000)
Addition To Net Income For Tax Purposes	Nil

Exercise Twenty - 24

Subject: Dividends From FAPI (An Extension Of Exercise Twenty - 23)

Forco is a wholly owned foreign subsidiary of Canco, a resident Canadian company. Forco earns $100,000 of investment income in 2013 and pays 18 percent in tax in the foreign jurisdiction. In 2014, Forco distributes its net after-tax FAPI of $82,000 to Canco as a dividend. Assume that there are no withholding taxes on the dividend payment. What is the effect of this information on Canco's 2014 Net Income For Tax Purposes?

End of Exercise. Solution available in Study Guide.

We suggest you work Self Study Problem Twenty-12 at this point.

Transfer Pricing

20-193.   For those of you who are interested in our material on transfer pricing, please refer to Supplementary Reading No. 8.

Key Terms Used In This Chapter

20-194.   The following is a list of the key terms used in this Chapter. These terms, and their meanings, are compiled in the Glossary Of Key Terms located at the back of the separate paper Study Guide.

Business Income	International Taxation
Capital Gain	Non-Resident
Competent Authority	Part Year Resident
Controlled Foreign Affiliate	Permanent Establishment
Deemed Resident	Person
Dividends	Pre-Acquisition Surplus
Double Taxation	Resident
Dual Resident	Residential Ties
Employment Income	Revenue Jurisdiction Approach
Exempt Surplus	Sojourner
Foreign Accrual Property Income (FAPI)	Source Jurisdiction Approach
Foreign Affiliate	Tax Haven
Interest Income	Taxable Canadian Property
International Tax Treaty	Taxable Surplus
(a.k.a., International Tax Convention)	Tie-Breaker Rules

References

20-195.   For more detailed study of the material in this Chapter, we would refer you to the following:

ITA 2(3)	Tax Payable By Non-Resident Persons
ITA 20(11)	Foreign Taxes On Income From Property Exceeding 15 Percent
ITA 90	Dividends Received From Non-Resident Corporation

ITA 91	Amounts To Be Included In Respect Of Share Of Foreign Affiliate
ITA 94	Application Of Certain Provisions To Trusts Not Resident In Canada
ITA 95	Definitions [Foreign Accrual Property Income]
ITA 113	Deduction In Respect Of Dividend Received From Foreign Affiliate
ITA 114	Individual Resident In Canada For Only Part Of Year
ITA 115	Non-Resident's Taxable Income In Canada
ITA 116	Disposition By Non-Resident Person Of Certain Property
ITA 118.91	Part-Year Residents
ITA 118.94	Tax Payable By Non-Resident (Tax Credits)
ITA 126	Foreign Tax Credits
ITA 212	Tax On Income From Canada Of Non-Resident Persons (This is the principal section in ITA Part XIII which deals with Canadian property income of non-resident persons.)
ITA 216	Alternatives Re Rents And Timber Royalties
ITA 217	Alternative Re Canadian Benefits
ITA 247	Transfer Pricing
ITA 248(1)	Definitions (Taxable Canadian Property)
ITA 249	Definition Of "Taxation Year"
ITA 250(1)	Person Deemed Resident
ITA 253	Extended Meaning Of "Carrying On Business"
IC 72-17R6	Procedures Concerning The Disposition Of Taxable Canadian Property By Non-Residents Of Canada - Section 116
IC 75-6R2	Required Withholding from Amounts Paid to Non-Resident Persons Performing Services in Canada
IC 76-12R6	Applicable Rate of Part XIII Tax on Amounts Paid or Credited to Persons in Countries With Which Canada Has a Tax Convention
IC 77-16R4	Non-Resident Income Tax
IC 87-2R	International Transfer Pricing
IC 94-4R	International Transfer Pricing: Advance Pricing Agreements (APA)
IC 06-1	Income Tax Transfer Pricing And Customs Valuation
S5-F1-C1	Determining An Individual's Residency Status
S5-F2-C1	Foreign Tax Credit
IT-137R3	Additional Tax On Certain Corporations Carrying On Business In Canada
IT-168R3	Athletes And Players Employed By Football, Hockey And Similar Clubs
IT-173R2	Capital Gains Derived In Canada By Residents Of The United States
IT-176R2	Taxable Canadian Property - Interests In And Options On Real Property And Shares
IT-262R2	Losses Of Non-Residents And Part-Year Residents
IT-270R3	Foreign Tax Credit
IT-303	Know-How And Similar Payments To Non-Residents
IT-420R3	Non-Residents - Income Earned In Canada
IT-447	Residence Of A Trust Or Estate
IT-451R	Deemed Disposition And Acquisition On Ceasing To Be Or Becoming Resident In Canada
IT-465R	Non-Resident Beneficiaries Of Trusts
IT-468R	Management Or Administration Fees Paid To Non-Residents
IT-497R4	Overseas Employment Tax Credit
RC4445	Payments To Non-Residents For Services Provided In Canada
T4056	Emigrants And Income Tax
T4058	Non-Residents And Income Tax
T4061	Non-Resident Tax Withholding, Remitting, And Reporting
T4131	Canadian Residents Abroad

Problems For Self Study

(The solutions for these problems can be found in the separate Study Guide.)

Self Study Problem Twenty - 1 (Residential Ties)

Paul Brossard accepts an offer to move to the U.S. from Canada to become a manager for a revitalized Black Hills Gold Savings and Loan branch in South Dakota. Paul has resigned from his Canadian federal government position, and severed his professional association ties. Further, he purchased a home in South Dakota. However, his daughter is nearing completion of an elite French immersion secondary school program in Ottawa, so Paul's wife and daughter intend to remain in Canada for two years. They continue to live in the family home in Ottawa.

After six months in South Dakota, the Savings and Loan branch closed. Paul then sold the U.S. home and moved back to Canada.

Required: Assess whether or not Paul became a non-resident of Canada, and if Paul will be taxed in Canada for the period during which he was living and working in the U.S.

Self Study Problem Twenty - 2 (Part Year Residency Of Individuals)

The following facts relate to three individuals who spent a part of the current year in Canada:

Mr. Aiken   Mr. Aiken is a businessman and a U.S. citizen who moved to Canada and established residence in the middle of June. After the move, he spent the remaining 192 days of the year in Canada.

Mr. Baker   Mr. Baker is a businessman and a Canadian citizen who moved out of Canada in the middle of July and established residence in the U.S. Prior to his move, he spent the preceding 192 days of the year in Canada.

Mr. Chase   Mr. Chase is a professional athlete and a U.S. citizen. His residence is located in Nashville, Tennessee, and during most of the year his wife and children live in that city. Mr. Chase plays for a Canadian team and, during the current year, his work required him to be in Canada for a total of 192 days.

Required: All of the preceding individuals were in Canada for a total of 192 days. Explain their residence status for income tax purposes in the current year and their liability for Canadian income taxes.

Self Study Problem Twenty - 3 (Residency Of Individuals)

Determine whether the following persons are Canadian residents for the current year. Explain the basis for your conclusion. Ignore any possible implications related to tax treaties.

A.   Jane Smith was born in Washington, D.C., where her father has been a Canadian ambassador for 15 years. She is 12 years old, has no income of own, and has never been to Canada.

B.   Marvin Black lives in Detroit, Michigan. He works on a full time basis throughout the year in Windsor, Ontario.

C.   John Leather was born in Canada and, until September 12 of the current year, he has never been outside of the country. On this date, he departed from Canada and established a home in Savannah, Georgia.

D.   Francine Donaire is a citizen of France and is married to a member of the Canadian armed forces stationed in France. She has been in Canada only on brief visits since she and her husband have been married, and had never visited the country prior to that time. She is exempt from French taxation because she is the spouse of a member of the Canadian armed forces.

E. Robert Green lived most of his life in Texas. Early in the current year, he moved to Edmonton to take a job with a local oil exploration company. As he found the weather to be too cold in Edmonton, he resigned during the fall and returned to Texas.

F. Susan Allen is a Canadian citizen who has lived in New York City for the past 7 years.

Self Study Problem Twenty - 4 (Residency Of Corporations)

Determine whether the following corporations are Canadian residents for the current year. Explain the basis for your conclusion.

A. AMT Ltd. was incorporated in New Brunswick in 1964. Until 1988, all of the directors' meetings were held in that province. However, since that time, the directors have met on a regular basis in Portland, Maine.

B. UIF Inc. was incorporated in the state of Montana in 1968. However, until four years ago all of the directors' meetings were held in Vancouver, British Columbia. Four years ago, the president of the Company moved to Helena, Montana and since that time all of the directors' meetings have been held in that city.

C. BDT Ltd. was incorporated in Alberta in 1990. However, it is managed in Mexico, where all directors' and shareholders' meetings have been held since incorporation.

D. QRS Inc. was incorporated in New York state. However, all of the directors are residents of Ontario and all meetings of the Board of Directors have been held in that province since incorporation.

Self Study Problem Twenty - 5 (Residency Of Individuals And Corporations)

For each of the following persons, indicate how they would be taxed in Canada for the current year. Your answer should explain whether the person is a Canadian resident, what parts of their income would be subject to Canadian taxation, and the basis for your conclusions.

A. Molly London was born in Salmon Arm, British Columbia. On October 31, after a very serious dispute with her fiancé, she quit her job, left Salmon Arm and moved all her belongings to San Diego, California. She has vowed to never set foot in Canada again.

B. Daryl Bennett is a Canadian citizen living and working in Sault Ste. Marie, Michigan. He has a summer cottage in Sault Ste. Marie, Ontario, where he spent July and August. As his only sister lives in Sault Ste. Marie, Ontario, he spent a total of 27 days during the year staying with her in her home.

C. Tweeks Inc. was incorporated in Vermont in 1980 by two U.S. citizens who were residents of Quebec. All of the directors are residents of Quebec and all meetings of the Board of Directors have been held in Montreal since incorporation.

D. Bordot Industries Ltd. was incorporated in British Columbia on September 29, 1973. However, the directors of the corporation have always lived in Blaine, Washington. All of their meetings have been held at a large waterfront property just south of Blaine.

Self Study Problem Twenty - 6 (Part I Tax On Non-Residents)

In each of the following independent cases, determine the applicability of Part I tax on the described income or entity. In each case, explain your conclusion.

Case A   Marion is a U.S. citizen who accepts temporary employment in Toronto. She works for four months in that city, earning a total of $12,800. Her employer is a taxable Canadian company.

Case B Marion is a U.S. citizen who is asked by her U.S. employer to spend four months temporarily working in Toronto. During this four month period, her earnings total $12,800.

Case C Delcar Inc. is a U.S. manufacturing company. For its Canadian sales, it ships product to a Halifax warehouse that is rented under a 3 year lease. The Company has employed Andrew, a Halifax resident, to sell the product throughout the eastern Provinces. Andrew does not have the authority to conclude individual contracts without approval from the U.S. head office. He works out of an office in his home.

Case D Delcar Inc. is a U.S. manufacturing company. For its Canadian sales, it ships product to a Halifax warehouse that is rented under a 3 year lease. The Company has employed Andrew, a Halifax resident, to sell the product throughout the eastern Provinces. A significant portion of the warehouse space is used as an office by Andrew. He does not have the authority to conclude individual contracts without approval from the U.S. head office.

Case E Michael is a U.S. citizen who lives in Buffalo, New York. Several years ago he established an Ontario corporation in order to acquire a rental property in Toronto. The corporation has no other assets and its shares are not publicly traded. During the current year, the shares of this corporation are sold, resulting in a capital gain.

Case F Michael is a U.S. citizen who lives in Buffalo, New York. Several years ago he established a New York corporation in order to acquire a rental property in Toronto. The corporation has no other assets and its shares are not publicly traded. During the current year, the shares of this corporation are sold, resulting in a capital gain.

Self Study Problem Twenty - 7 (Part XIII Tax On Non-Residents)

Provide the information required in each of the following cases. Each of your answers should include an explanation for your conclusion.

Case A Marilyn is a resident of a country that does not have a tax treaty with Canada. During the current year she receives $4,100 in interest from a savings account at a Canadian bank. Would this amount be subject to Part XIII tax?

Case B Mark is a resident of a country that does not have a tax treaty with Canada. He holds a security issued by a Canadian corporation that pays interest on the basis of the amount of revenue earned by the corporation. During the current year, he receives interest of $2,200 from this corporation. Would this amount be subject to Part XIII tax?

Case C Mark is a resident of the U.S. He holds a security issued by a Canadian corporation that pays interest on the basis of the amount of revenue earned by the corporation. During the current year, he receives interest of $2,200 from this corporation. Would this amount be subject to Part XIII tax?

Case D Darlene is a resident of a country that does not have a tax treaty with Canada. She owns a Canadian real property that produces gross rents from Canadian residents during the current year of $35,000. Expenses, including maximum CCA, totaled $27,000 during the current year. She has no other source of Canadian income. Determine her tax payable (1) under Part XIII assuming she does not elect out of Part XIII tax, (2) under Part I if she does elect out of Part XIII tax.

Case E Darlene is a resident of the U.S. She owns a Canadian real property that produces gross rents from Canadian residents during the current year of $35,000. Expenses, including maximum CCA, totaled $27,000 during the current year. She has no other source of Canadian income. Determine her tax payable (1) under Part XIII assuming she does not elect out of Part XIII tax, (2) under Part I if she does elect out of Part XIII tax.

Case F   Brian is a resident of the U.S. During the current year, he receives $22,000 in dividends from a Canadian corporation. He owns 15 percent of the voting shares of this company. Determine Brian's Part XIII tax payable for the current year.

Self Study Problem Twenty - 8 (Emigration - Tax Planning)

Holly Rancher, a Canadian resident, has been asked by the Brazilian government to start a strip farming operation in the Brazilian rain forest. Holly's two teenage sons are very reluctant to leave Canada, while her husband is quite enthusiastic about the opportunity.

Holly and her husband own equal shares in the following assets:

	Fair Market Value	Capital Cost Or Adjusted Cost Base
Home in Cochrane, Alberta	$500,000	$200,000
Land Rover truck (personal use only)	15,000	20,000
Cash	10,000	

In addition, Holly owns the following assets personally:

	Fair Market Value	Capital Cost Or Adjusted Cost Base
Cottage on Lake Manitou	$165,000	$145,000
RRSP	55,000	Nil
Shares in IOU Ranch Ltd, CCPC	40,000	25,000
Shares in public companies	40,000	30,000

Both the home and cottage were purchased 3 years ago. Assume that the value of the land of both properties has not changed since their purchase. The cottage has never been rented and is very rarely used since Holly's sons refuse to go there.

Holly is seriously considering the Brazilian government's offer, and would like to know what the tax effect of a move would be. Holly has fully utilized her lifetime capital gains deduction.

Required:

A. Analyze the Canadian income tax effect if Holly becomes a non-resident of Canada. As part of your answer, calculate any amounts of income that will be deferred at time of departure. Assume that she does not make any elections at the time of her move.

B. Identify important factors that could influence Holly's residence status.

C. If Holly decides to move to Brazil, and in so doing becomes a non-resident of Canada, identify effective tax planning opportunities to be considered.

Self Study Problem Twenty - 9 (Foreign Investment Reporting Rules)

The following assets are owned by different Canadian taxpayers who hold no other foreign investments at any time during the year. All amounts are in Canadian dollars. For each asset, determine whether the foreign investment reporting rules apply. Explain your conclusions.

A. Term deposits totaling $23,000, located in a bank in Missoula, Montana.

B. A cottage in Michigan purchased for $127,000 with a current fair market value of $86,000. The cottage is used by the taxpayer and his family throughout the year.

C. Shares in a U.S. public company with a cost of $112,000 and a current fair market value of $220,000. One-half of these shares are held in the taxpayer's Canadian brokerage trading account and the other half are held in the taxpayer's self-directed RRSP.

D. A small manufacturing plant and related machinery with a total cost of $490,000. The plant is located in Boise, Idaho and was purchased by a Canadian public corporation.

Self Study Problem Twenty - 10 *(Foreign Source Employment Income)*

For both of the following Cases, determine whether the individual will be taxed in the U.S. Explain your conclusion.

A. A Canadian resident hockey player is recruited during the off-season to lead one hockey school in Florida and another in Ontario. The hockey schools are run by a Florida promoter, and the hockey player is paid US$1,000 per day. Each of the schools lasts for seven days, resulting in total earnings of US$14,000 for 14 days. He has no other U.S. source income.

B. A Montreal theater production firm employs a Winnipeg expert animator to prepare special three-dimensional animation effects. During the current year, the animator works in California for three periods, each of which is for two months (60 days). In California, the work involves using special animation equipment that is unavailable in Canada. The animator is paid a total of $150,000 for his work.

Self Study Problem Twenty - 11
(Foreign Source Dividends Received By An Individual)

Mona Lister is a resident of Canada. During 2013, she has the following amounts included in her Net Income For Tax Purposes:

Net Employment Income	$87,000
Dividends From Foreign Companies Before Foreign Tax Withheld:	
Foreign Country 1 - Hispanic Ltd. (Before $5,750 Withholding)	23,000
Foreign Country 2 - Deutsch Inc. (Before $1,400 Withholding)	14,000

Mona has no deductions in converting Net Income For Tax Purposes to Taxable Income. Her only tax credits are the basic personal credit, employment related credits, and any credits related to the dividends received.

Required: Determine Mona's Federal Tax Payable for the year ending December 31, 2013.

Self Study Problem Twenty - 12 *(Taxation Of Foreign Affiliate Dividends)*

BK Inc. is a Canadian resident corporation with a taxation year that ends on December 31.

BK has a 40 percent interest in two foreign corporations. The first, Alta Inc. is located in a country with which Canada has an international tax treaty. It also has a December 31 year end and, during the year ending December 31, 2013, all of the Company's income was from active business activities. This income was subject to a tax rate of 15 percent in its local jurisdiction.

During 2013, the Company paid a dividend of $85,000 of which $30,600 was received by BK Inc. This amount reflects a payment of $34,000 [(40%)($85,000)] to BK Inc., less withholding of taxes in the foreign jurisdiction of $3,400 [(10%)($34,000)]. On December 31, 2012, Alta Inc. had an Exempt Surplus balance of $221,000.

The second corporate interest, Bolt Ltd., is located in a country with which Canada does not have a tax treaty or a Tax Information Exchange Agreement (TIEA). It also has a December 31 year end and, during the year ending December 31, 2013, all of the Company's income was from active business activities. It was subject to a tax rate of 5 percent in its local jurisdiction.

During 2013, Bolt Ltd. paid a dividend of $190,000. BK Inc.'s share of this dividend was $76,000. However, the foreign jurisdiction withheld $11,400 [(15%)($76,000)], providing BK Inc. with a net receipt of $64,600. On December 31, 2012, Bolt Ltd. had a Taxable Surplus balance of $950,000.

Both of the foreign corporations have earned nothing other than active business income since their incorporation. Further, the tax rate for both corporations on this type of income has remained unchanged since their incorporation.

All of the shares of the two corporations that are not owned by BK Ltd. are owned by non-resi-dent persons that are not related to BK Ltd.

Required: Determine the amount of Taxable Income and Canadian Tax Payable that would result from the receipt of these dividends by BK Inc.

Assignment Problems

(The solutions for these problems are only available in
the solutions manual that has been provided to your instructor.)

Assignment Problem Twenty - 1 (Residency After Departure From Canada)

Mr. Leduc is a U.S. citizen who has spent most of his working life in the employ of a Canadian subsidiary of a U.S. company. While he has been located in several Canadian cities where the subsidiary has offices, he has spent the last several years working in Vancouver.

Early in the current year, Mr. Leduc is offered an opportunity for advancement within the orga-nization of the U.S. parent company. However, the opportunity is conditional on his moving to Chicago by no later than February 15. While moving on such short notice presents a consid-erable inconvenience to him, he concludes that the opportunity is too good to pass up and, as a consequence, he completes his move to Chicago by February 12.

Because of the short notice involved, Mr. Leduc's wife and children decide to remain in Vancouver until the end of the school term. Mr. Leduc also feels that this will provide a greater opportunity to sell the family residence at a reasonable price.

The family residence is not sold until June 20, at which time Mr. Leduc's wife and children depart from Canada and establish residency in Chicago.

Required   For purposes of assessing Canadian income taxes, determine when Mr. Leduc ceased to be a Canadian resident and the portion of his annual income which would be assessed for Canadian taxes. Explain your conclusions.

Assignment Problem Twenty - 2 (Residency After Departure From Canada)

Mr. David Hamilton was a long-time resident of Canada. On January 13, 2012, he departed from Canada to work in Qatar. The work was done under a contract of employment with an American company that was operating in Qatar.

1. Mr. Hamilton did not obtain resident status in Qatar or in any other country. He did not have a postal address in Qatar.

2. Mr. Hamilton obtained a work permit in Qatar that was valid until August 13, 2015.

3. After the work permit expired, Mr. Hamilton had to leave Qatar. He subsequently returned several times to meet with friends and business associates there.

4. Mr. Hamilton's Canadian driver's licence expired in August, 2011 and was not renewed.

5. After taking intensive driving courses, Mr. Hamilton acquired a driver's licence in Qatar in December, 2012 that was valid for 5 years.

6. Mr. Hamilton gave up his Canadian health card in 2013.

7. Mr. Hamilton had two sons who remained in Canada. One of the sons, Harold, had signif-icant health issues.

8. Mr. Hamilton kept a credit card, bank account, an RRSP and investments in Canada when he began work in Qatar.

9. Mr. Hamilton continued to hold a Canadian passport.

10. He visited Canada four times in 2012 and three times during 2013 Each visit was for 2 weeks. His visits were largely to see his sons and mother. The relationship with his wife was strained before he left for Qatar and deteriorated significantly afterwards. This led to their divorce in 2013. After Harold advised him to follow his dream of leaving Canada, he began the process of permanently leaving Canada. To this end, on July 1, 2013, he gave his share of the family home to his wife and closed all of his Canadian financial accounts. He paid regular support payments after the divorce occurred.

11. During his visits to Canada, he stayed in hotels and used rented vehicles.

12. In 2012, Mr. Hamilton's accountant filed a tax return for him as a resident of Canada.

13. Mr. Hamilton is well respected in his profession and considered to be a very responsible employee.

Despite filing a tax return in 2012 as a resident of Canada, Mr. Hamilton believes that he gave up his Canadian residency on January 13, 2012 and wishes to revise his 2012 tax return to reflect this.

Required: Determine whether Mr. Hamilton is a resident of Canada. If you conclude he is not, provide the date that he ceased to be a Canadian resident. Provide reasons for your conclusion.

Assignment Problem Twenty - 3 (Residency Of Individuals - 5 Cases)

For each of the following persons, indicate how they would be taxed in Canada for the year ending December 31, 2013. Your answer should explain whether the person is a Canadian resident, what parts of their income would be subject to Canadian taxation, and the basis for your conclusions.

Case A   John is a citizen of the U.K. who has landed immigrant status in Canada. He has been employed in Canada for over 15 years. In 2012, he won $1.5 million in a lottery. He has decided to use these funds to spend two years touring Europe and Asia. His wife and children will remain at the family home in New Brunswick. He was not present in Canada during any part of 2013.

Case B   In 2012, Jane's Canadian employer asked her to spend three years working in their Hong Kong office. Her employment contract requires her to return to Canada in 2015. Jane severs all of her residential ties with Canada and moves to Hong Kong in November, 2012. She is not present in Canada during any part of 2013.

Case C   Laura is married to a member of the Canadian armed forces who is serving in Ghana. She is a citizen of Ghana and has never visited Canada. During 2013, because her husband is a member of the Canadian armed forces, she is not subject to taxation in Ghana.

Case D   Martha Mendoza is a U.S. citizen who lives in Buffalo, New York. During 2013 she is employed 5 days per week in Fort Erie, Ontario. Her 2013 salary is $52,000. In addition, she has $2,000 (Canadian) of interest on a savings account with a Buffalo bank.

Case E   Barry Long is a Canadian citizen who has lived and worked in Canada all of his life. When he is offered a significant increase in salary if he accepts a position in Spain, he accepts this position and on March 1, 2013, he moves to Spain. While he immediately establishes residency in Spain, he is not joined by his wife and children until July 1, 2013. As they are unable to sell their Canadian home at an acceptable price, the property is rented under a long-term residential lease.

Assignment Problem Twenty - 4 *(Residency Of Corporations - 4 Cases)*

Indicate which of the corporations described in the following Cases would be considered residents of Canada for the current year. Explain the basis for your conclusion. 65

Case A   Bonix Ltd. was incorporated in Canada in 1961. While it operated in Canada for a number of years, all of its operations and management relocated to the United States in 2008.

Case B   Dorad Inc. was incorporated in Ohio in 2003. For several years, all of its directors were residents of Canada, with board meetings being held in Windsor, Ontario. However, in 2008, all of the directors moved to Toledo, Ohio. All board of director meetings are now held in that city.

Case C   Upton Inc. was incorporated in Delaware in 2008. However, the head office of the corporation is in Halifax, Nova Scotia. All of the directors of the corporation are Canadian residents and all meetings of the board of directors are held in Halifax.

Case D   Carlin Inc. was incorporated in Canada in 2005. However, its directors have always been residents of the U.K., with all of the company's board of directors meetings held in that country.

Assignment Problem Twenty - 5 *(Residency/Dual Residency - Individuals)*

Determine the residency status of the three individuals in the following Cases. Use the tie-breaker rules found in the Canada/U.S. tax treaty where appropriate.

Case A   Brad is a U.S. citizen who has been living in Seattle, Washington. Through an online dating service, he meets Sarah in 2012. She is a Canadian citizen who lives and works in Vancouver. After several face-to-face meetings they conclude that they should marry and, after much discussion, they decide that they will live in Seattle after the marriage. Since Sarah is committed to remaining in her position in Vancouver until September, 2013, in December, 2012, Brad takes a 10 month leave of absence from his job and gives up his apartment in Seattle. On January 1, 2013, they move in together sharing an apartment in Vancouver which is leased on a month-to-month basis. On September 15, 2013, they get married, terminate the Vancouver lease, and move to a newly purchased house in Seattle.

Case B   Helen is a single individual who makes her living painting portraits of wealthy individuals. She is a U.S. citizen and has, in recent years, worked in Burlington, Vermont. Of late, business has dropped off and, as a consequence, she decided to try working in Montreal. Because of the uncertainty involved in her line of work, she does not sell her Burlington residence, asking a friend to watch it while she is absent. On April 15, 2013, she moves to Montreal. She lives in various Montreal hotels until January 15, 2014. At this time she concludes that the work situation is no better in Montreal than it was in Burlington. Given this, she returns to Burlington.

Assignment Problem Twenty - 6 *(Part I Tax On Non-Residents)*

The following material describes several independent cases which involve U.S. citizens or companies that have some type of Canadian source income.

Case 1   Marlene is a U.S. citizen and also a resident of that country. Several years ago, she established an Alberta private company in order to acquire rental properties in Calgary and Edmonton. Other than necessary cash balances used for operations, all of the assets of the corporation are rental properties in these two cities. During the current year, she sells all of the shares of the Alberta corporation, resulting in a capital gain of $275,000.

Case 2   Maria is a U.S. citizen and is also a resident of that country. She is the sole share-holder of a U.S. private company that owns a block of rental properties located in Canada's maritime provinces. During the current year, she sells all of the shares in this company, realizing a capital gain of $410,000.

Case 3   Manuflex, a U.S. manufacturing company ships its products to a Lethbridge, Alberta warehouse. The warehouse is rented on a month-to-month lease that can be cancelled by either party with 60 days notice. They have hired Mark Bridges, a Lethbridge resident, to sell their product throughout western Canada. Mark works out of an office in his home. He does not have authority to conclude individual sales contracts without approval from the U.S. head office.

Case 4   Manuflex, a U.S. manufacturing company ships its products to a Lethbridge, Alberta warehouse. The warehouse is rented on a month-to-month lease that can be cancelled by either party with 60 days notice. They have hired Mark Bridges, a Lethbridge resident, to sell their product throughout western Canada. Mark uses a significant part of the warehouse space as an office. He does not have authority to conclude individual sales contracts without approval from the U.S. head office.

Case 5   Saul Bekham is a U.S. citizen who accepts temporary employment in Regina. This work requires him to live in Canada for 4 months. During this period, his employment income is $63,000, all of which is paid by a resident Canadian corporation.

Case 6   Sarah Block is a U.S. citizen who is asked by her U.S. employer to work in Canada for a period of 3 months. During this period, her earnings total $36,000, all of which is paid by her U.S. employer.

Required: For each of the preceding cases, determine the applicability of Part I tax on the Canadian source income.

Assignment Problem Twenty - 7 (Permanent Establishments)

A U.S. gun cabinet manufacturer is considering entering the Canadian market. The company will use one of the following approaches to expand its market in Canada:

    A. Advertising in gun magazines.

    B. Selling cabinets to Canadian distributors. The distributors pay the shipping costs on the cabinets from the U.S. port or border crossing closest to them.

    C. Direct sales to wholesalers by non-exclusive agents. The agents will represent other suppliers.

    D. Direct sales to wholesalers by full-time salespeople in each of three regions of Canada. No sales offices will be opened, and the cabinets will be shipped from a warehouse in the U.S. Shipment will be made only after a customer's credit and contract are approved by the U.S. head office.

    E. Direct sales to wholesalers by full-time salespeople who report to a sales office in each of three regions of Canada. The sales offices will co-ordinate marketing and shipping of products from two warehouses located in Canada. However, formal approval of contracts will be administered in the U.S. head office.

    F. The sales offices described in Part E would be independent profit centres, with regional credit managers. The four warehouses from which orders are filled will be near the sales offices.

Required: For each market expansion approach, assess whether or not the U.S. manufacturer will be deemed to have a permanent establishment in Canada. Justify your assessment, and identify any other information required to support your position.

Assignment Problem Twenty - 8 (Part XIII Tax On Non-Residents)

Each of the following independent situations involves a non-resident individual who has Canadian source income during the current year.

1. Felix is a resident of a country that does not have a tax treaty with Canada. He is the owner of a Canadian rental property that has gross rents of $48,000 from Canadian residents. During the current year, expenses related to this property, including maximum CCA, totaled $18,000.

2. Saul is a resident of the U.S. He owns Canadian machinery which is leased throughout the current year to Canadian residents. Gross rents are $123,000, while related expenses, including maximum CCA total $23,000.

3. Olaf is a resident of a country that does not have a tax treaty with Canada. During the current year, he earns $2,220 of interest on a savings account provided by a Canadian bank.

4. Karl is a resident of a country that does not have a tax treaty with Canada. He owns debt securities issued by a Canadian company that pay interest at a rate that is determined by the profits earned by the company. During the current year, he receives interest of $565 from this investment.

5. Clark is a resident of the U.S. He owns debt securities in a Canadian company that pay interest at a rate that is determined by the profits earned by the company. During the current year, he receives interest of $722 from this investment.

6. Betty is a resident of a country that does not have a tax treaty with Canada. During the current year, she receives dividends of $2,400 from a private Canadian company. Betty owns 20 percent of the shares of this company.

Required: For each of these situations, indicate how the Canadian source income would be taxed under Canadian tax legislation.

Assignment Problem Twenty - 9 (Emigration - Tax Planning)

Horace Richards, a resident of Nova Scotia, plans to emigrate from Canada on December 31, 2013. On that date, he will own the following assets:

Savings Account   The balance in this account is $85,600.

Residence   This property was purchased in 2002 for $130,000, including $45,000 for the land. Its fair market value on December 31, 2013 is $240,000, including $60,000 for the land.

Cottage   This property was purchased in 2001 for $345,000, including $95,000 for the land. Because a large nearby development has flooded the market with low price units, it has a fair market value on December 31, 2013 of $300,000, including a value for the land of $50,000. Horace has rented out this property since its purchase and reported a small rental income every year. He has never taken CCA on the property.

SUV   Horace owns a Honda SUV that cost $35,000. Its fair market value on December 31, 2013 is $18,000.

RRSP   The December 31 balance in Horace's RRSP is $186,000.

Shares In A CCPC   Horace is the only shareholder of Richard's Rock, a CCPC. The adjusted cost base of these shares is $87,000 and they have a December 31, 2013, fair market value of $123,000.

Shares In Public Companies   Horace owns a portfolio of publicly traded shares which have an adjusted cost base of $120,000. Their fair market value on December 31, 2013, is $135,000.

Assignment Problems

Required:

A. For each of the listed assets, indicate the tax consequences, including any amounts of deferred income, that would result from Horace's emigration from Canada. Assume that he does not make any elections at the time of his move.

B. Under ITA 128.1(4)(d), taxpayers can elect to have a deemed disposition on certain assets where a deemed disposition is not automatic. Determine if Horace could use this election to minimize his tax obligation at the time of his departure. If he can, calculate the amount of the reduction in Net Income For Tax Purposes that would result from the use of this election.

Assignment Problem Twenty - 10
(Comprehensive Review Problem - Residency Of Individuals)

Note   This problem covers material from several other Chapters of the text.

Debbie Maari is the vice-president of communications for an international advertising agency. Having risen to the pinnacle of success in Canada, she is en route to Hong Kong to rebuild the firm's base in the Pacific Rim. The transfer will be for an indefinite duration, and Debbie has already obtained approval for immigration that does not restrict the length of her family's stay in Hong Kong. Debbie's family includes her husband and the family pets.

Debbie's husband is a sales representative for a pharmaceuticals firm, and he plans to develop a client base in Asia over the next six months. Meanwhile, he plans to service his North American clients from Toronto, and will commute monthly to Hong Kong.

On November 1, 2013, Debbie owned the following assets:

Description	Date Acquired	Original Cost	Fair Market Value
Shares in CCPC Inc., a private company	2005	$ 90,000	$ 140,000
Shares in Sorrento Co., a Canadian public company	2003	180,000	110,000
House	2004	300,000	450,000
Whistler ski chalet	2011	125,000	185,000
Sports car	2008	18,000	15,000
Paintings	1999	50,000	175,000
RRSP	Various	66,000	86,000

Debbie owns 100 percent of the house and ski chalet. She plans to sell all of the assets within a year, except for the house and ski chalet, which she plans to rent out. She has used all of her lifetime capital gains deduction in previous years.

Debbie's firm is prepared to pay her a $50,000 allowance to cover moving costs, with no requirement that Debbie provide supporting receipts. The allowance will be paid by the Hong Kong office after her arrival there.

Debbie has enquired about the Hong Kong tax system and has been informed that the personal tax rates are lower than the rates in Canada. Further, the Hong Kong tax system is expected to continue as a "source" system rather than a "residence" system, meaning that only income arising in, or derived from, Hong Kong will be taxable there. Any additional income that Debbie earns in 2013 while a resident of Canada will be taxed in Canada at a combined federal/provincial rate of 45 percent.

Required: Debbie would like to know the Canadian tax implications of moving to Hong Kong, and whether there are any tax planning opportunities to minimize her Canadian Tax Payable for the current and future years.

Assignment Problem Twenty - 11 *(Foreign Investment Reporting Rules)*

Amy Borody works and resides in Winnipeg, Manitoba. Amy has diversified her investment portfolio by investing in Germany. During 2013, she earned the following amounts of investment income. The dividends and interest are net of any German withholding taxes. The withholding rate on the interest was 10 percent and the withholding rate on the dividends was 15 percent.

Dividends From German Public Corporation (Amount Received)	€ 5,100
Interest on German Term Deposits (Amount Received)	€19,800
Net rental income from Munich apartment	€18,000

Ms. Borody uses the election to have her net rental income taxed in Canada under Part I, rather than under Part XIII. As she does not take CCA on the rental property, all of the rents and related expenses can be translated using the 2013 exchange rate.

Assume that the exchange rate throughout 2013 was €1 = $1.35.

Required: Indicate the amounts of investment income that would be included in Ms. Borody's 2013 Net Income For Tax Purposes, as well as any tax credits that would be available to Ms. Borody to offset this income. In addition, indicate whether Ms. Borody would be required to file the foreign investment reporting form.

Assignment Problem Twenty - 12 *(Foreign Investment Reporting Rules)*

The following assets are owned by different Canadian taxpayers who hold no other foreign investments at any time during the year. All amounts are in Canadian dollars. For each asset, determine whether the foreign investment reporting rules apply. Explain your conclusions.

A. A warehouse in Miami with a cost of $568,000, owned by a Canadian corporation, and used to store its products for distribution.

B. A cottage in Cape Cod, Massachusetts, purchased for $56,000 cash down, and assumption of a $200,000 mortgage. The cottage is used by the taxpayer and his extended family throughout the year.

C. A condo in Clearwater, Florida, purchased for $215,000. The condo is rented to Canadians for 8 months of the year and used by the taxpayer the remaining 4 months.

D. A U.S. bank account and a mortgage resulting from the sale of a farm in Montana to a U.S. resident three years ago. The original amount of the mortgage was $150,000. However, the amount owing at the beginning of the current year is $67,000. The taxpayer's bank account in a U.S. bank has a balance of between $10,000 and $15,000 throughout the year.

E. A yacht with a cost of $450,000 which was purchased and is docked at Marina del Rey, California. The yacht is used by the Vancouver taxpayer for his legendary monthly parties.

F. Shares in a U.S. public company with a cost of $286,000 and a current fair market value of $84,000. One-half of these shares are held in the taxpayer's Canadian brokerage trading account and the other half are held in the taxpayer's self-directed RRSP.

Assignment Problem Twenty - 13
(Foreign Source Dividends Received By An Individual)

Mark Lender lives and is employed on a full time basis in Canada. His net employment income is $57,500. In addition he has the following other sources of income:

Taxable Capital Gains	$ 4,500
Eligible Dividends From A Canadian Company	12,000
Dividends From Foreign Companies Before Foreign Tax Withheld:	
Foreign Country 1 - SP Ltd. (Before $4,250 Of Withholding)	$17,000
Foreign Country 2 - FR Ltd. (Before $800 Of Withholding)	8,000

He has the following deductions available in determining his Taxable Income:

Net Capital Loss Carry Forward	$8,000
Business Loss Carry Forward	$6,200

His only tax credits are the basic personal credit, employment related credits, and any credits related to the dividends received.

Required: Determine Mark's Federal Tax Payable for the year ending December 31, 2013.

Assignment Problem Twenty - 14 (Taxation Of Foreign Affiliate Dividends)

CTP is a Canadian public corporation that has acquired 15 percent of the shares of FTP, a corporation that is established in a foreign country. During the year ending December 31, 2012, FTP earns $20,000 in investment income, $70,000 from an active business and $20,000 of capital gains from the sale of investment assets.

In early 2013, FTP distributes all of its 2012 after tax income as a dividend to its shareholders. FTP has no additional income in 2013.

In both 2012 and 2013, CTP is subject to a federal tax rate of 25 percent.

The following Cases make use of the preceding information. However, the individual Cases make various additional or alternative assumptions.

Required: Provide the information that is requested in each of the following Cases.

Case 1   FTP is a non-controlled foreign affiliate of CTP. Assume that it is located in a country that does not have a tax treaty or a TIEA with Canada, that this country does not assess income taxes on corporations and does not assess withholding taxes on dividend payments to non-residents. What are the tax consequences for CTP resulting from its investment in FTP during 2012 and 2013? Include the increase in Net Income For Tax Purposes and total Taxes Payable for both years in your solution.

Case 2   Assume the same facts as in Case 1, except that FTP is a controlled foreign affiliate of CTP. How would the tax consequences for CTP differ from the tax consequences described in Case 1, for 2012 and 2013?

Case 3   Assume the same facts as in Case 1, except that FTP is not a foreign affiliate of CTP. How would the tax consequences for CTP differ from the tax consequences described in Case 1, for 2012 and 2013?

Case 4   Assume the same facts as in Case 1, except that FTP is located in a country that has a tax treaty with Canada. How would the tax consequences for CTP differ from the tax consequences described in Case 1, for 2012 and 2013?

Case 5   FTP is a non-controlled foreign affiliate of CTP. Assume that FTP is located in a country that has a tax treaty with Canada, that this country assesses income taxes on active business income at a rate of 10 percent and does not assess withholding taxes on dividend payments to non-residents. The income taxes paid by FTP in the foreign country total $7,000 [(10%)($70,000)]. What are the tax consequences for CTP resulting from its investment in FTP during 2012 and 2013?

Case 6   Assume the same facts as in Case 5, except that the foreign country levies the 10 percent income tax on all of FTP's 2012 income. This income tax would total $11,000 [(10%)($110,000)]. In addition, a further 8 percent withholding tax of $7,920 [(8%)($110,000 - $11,000)] was assessed on the dividend paid in 2013. The resulting dividend payment was $91,080 ($110,000 - $11,000 - $7,920). What are the tax consequences for CTP resulting from its investment in FTP during 2012 and 2013?

Assignment Problem Twenty - 15 (Canadian Source Income - Short Cases)
Case A
Mr. Jack Holt is an employee of Stillwell Industries, an American manufacturing Company. During the period June 15 through December 6 of the current year, Mr. Holt worked in Canada providing technical assistance to a Canadian subsidiary of Stillwell Industries. His salary was U.S. $5,500 per month. During the period that Mr. Holt was in Canada, Stillwell Industries continued to deposit his salary into his normal U.S. bank account. Both his salary for this period and all of his related travelling expenses were billed to the Canadian subsidiary.

Required: Explain Mr. Holt's tax position, including the question of whether any withholdings should have been made with respect to Canadian taxes owing.

Case B
Mr. John McQueen was for many years a resident of Ontario. On his retirement ten years ago, he returned to his native Scotland and has not since returned to Canada. However, he has retained considerable investments in Canada, as follows:

- **Common Stocks**   He has a large portfolio of common stocks that are registered in the name of his Toronto broker. The broker receives all dividends and periodically sends a cheque to Mr. McQueen in Scotland.

- **Mortgage Portfolio**   He has a large portfolio of second mortgages. All collections on these mortgages are made by a Toronto law firm and are deposited into a Toronto bank account in the name of Mr. McQueen.

Required: Who is responsible for tax withholdings under Part XIII of the *Income Tax Act,* and on which amounts must withholdings be made?

Case C
Hotels International is a U.S. corporation with hotel properties throughout the world. It has recently developed a property in Nova Scotia that will open during the current year. A long-term management lease has been signed with Hotel Operators Ltd., a Canadian company specializing in the management of hotels. Under the terms of the lease, Hotel Operators Ltd. will pay all of the operating expenses of the hotel and, in addition, make an annual lease payment of $1,250,000 to the American owners of the new hotel.

Required: Will the U.S. corporation, Hotels International, be subject to Canadian income taxes on the annual lease payment, and, if so, to what extent?

Case D
The Maple Company, a public company resident in Canada, has 2,400,000 shares of its no par common stock outstanding. Sixty percent of these shares are owned by its American parent, the Condor Company. The remaining shares are owned by Canadian residents. In addition to the common shares, the Condor Company holds all of an outstanding issue of Maple Company debenture bonds. Two of the five directors of the Maple Company are Canadian residents, while the remaining three are residents of the United States. During the current year, the Maple Company paid a dividend of $1 per share on its common stock and interest of $900,000 on its outstanding debenture bonds.

Required: Calculate the amount of Part XIII taxes to be withheld by the Maple Company with respect to the interest and dividend payments to its American parent.

CHAPTER 21

GST/HST

Introduction

Background

Introduction Of The GST

21-1.   After significant controversy, a goods and services tax (GST, hereafter) was introduced in Canada on January 1, 1991. This broadly based, multi-stage transaction tax replaced the more narrowly focused federal sales tax on manufactured goods. The GST was originally introduced at a rate of 7 percent. However, this rate was reduced to 6 percent in 2006, with a further reduction to 5 percent on January 1, 2008. There have been no other GST rate changes implemented or proposed since that date.

21-2.   The concept underlying this tax was that it would be applied in an even-handed manner to all goods and service transactions. However, tax policy is often more influenced by political considerations than it is by economic logic. As a result, by the time the tax was actually introduced, it was burdened by a complex web of exemptions and modifications that significantly increased the cost of compliance.

21-3.   The developers of this tax also hoped that the provinces would be willing to amalgamate their provincial sales taxes with the federal GST in order to provide taxpayers with a uniform national approach to the taxation of goods and service transactions. This could have resulted in very substantial savings in both compliance costs and administrative costs. This, however, did not happen.

21-4.   Only the Province of Quebec showed any early signs of cooperation in this area (the Provinces of Alberta, British Columbia, and Ontario initially took legal action against the federal government, claiming that the GST was unconstitutional). In 1992, Quebec introduced a similar, but not identical, transaction tax. This was, and continues to be, referred to as the Quebec Sales Tax (QST). As part of this process, there was an agreement that both the QST and GST collected in Quebec would be administered by the Province of Quebec.

Harmonized Sales Tax (HST)

21-5.   This situation continued until 1997, when three of the Atlantic provinces, New Brunswick, Nova Scotia, and Newfoundland implemented a harmonized sales tax (HST, hereafter) that contained both a federal and a provincial tax component. In the harmonization process, these provinces eliminated their separate provincial sales taxes.

21-6.   This tax was fully harmonized in that it applied to various transactions on the same basis as was the case with the GST and was administered by the federal government. The elimination of the provincial sales tax administrative structures, along with resulting consistent application of this harmonized tax, both reduced costs and simplified taxpayer compliance.

21-7.   There has been further progress in this area. On July 1, 2010 both Ontario and British Columbia implemented an HST and Prince Edward Island implemented an HST on April 1, 2013.

21-8.   Some of this progress was reversed when, after a bitterly fought referendum, the residents of British Columbia voted to repeal the HST and return to a Provincial Sales Tax (PST, hereafter) system. This change was implemented as of April 1, 2013.

21-9.   The harmonized sales tax is, in effect, a combination of the 5 percent GST rate and provincial rate that varies from 8 percent to 10 percent (as of April 1, 2013). This gives overall rates of 13 percent to 15 percent.

21-10.   A major advantage of this HST system is that the task of administering these taxes has been assumed by the federal government. This does not, however, eliminate flexibility at the provincial level. This is evidenced by the differences in the provincial tax component rate, as well as by different exemptions on the provincial portion of the HST for a number of items.

The Current Situation

21-11.   These developments have left Canada with a somewhat cluttered transaction tax landscape. The various arrangements are summarized in the following table:

Figure 21 - 1 2013 Transaction Taxes In Canada			
Type Of Tax	**Province**	**Rates**	**Tax Administration**
GST Only	Alberta	5% + 0%	Federal
GST and PST	British Columbia		
	From April 1, 2013	5% + 7%	Federal and Provincial
	Manitoba	5% + 7%	Federal and Provincial
	Saskatchewan	5% + 5%	Federal and Provincial
	Prince Edward Island		
	To March 31, 2013	5% + 10%	Federal And Provincial
HST	British Columbia		
	To March 31, 2013	12%	Federal
	New Brunswick	13%	Federal
	Newfoundland	13%	Federal
	Nova Scotia	15%	Federal
	Ontario	13%	Federal
	Prince Edward Island		
	From April 1, 2013	14%	Federal
GST and QST	Quebec	5% + 9.975%	Provincial

21-12.   This table illustrates some of the complexity of the current situation due to the different rates and regimes that are in use. This is further complicated by the fact that in the HST provinces, some items are exempted from the provincial component of the tax in some provinces.

21-13.   It is obvious that the transaction tax situation in Canada is extremely complex due to the fact that the provinces control the rates and special exemptions for these taxes. While there may be benefits that result from maintaining this level of flexibility at the provincial level, there is some question as to whether these benefits justify the resulting administrative and compliance costs.

How This Text Deals With This Complexity

21-14.   It is clearly not appropriate in a general textbook on taxation to attempt detailed coverage of the GST and HST procedures applicable in each province. It is likely that an attempt to do this would require a completely separate third volume.

21-15.   The GST is applicable to all provinces either as a separate sales tax or as a component of HST. Fortunately, many of the provisions for the HST are identical to those for the GST. This means that, in general, the concepts and procedures involved are the same for both the GST and the HST.

21-16.   Given this situation, our discussion and examples will focus on one of two scenarios:

- Situations where only the GST is applicable. Alberta is the only province where this situation applies.

- Situations where the HST is applicable.

21-17.   We will not use examples involving those provinces where both GST and PST are in effect, nor will attention be given to the unique situation in Quebec.

21-18.   With the exception of a brief Chapter 3 discussion of the GST component of employee benefits, all of our material on GST is included in this Chapter. This includes consideration of the Employee And Partner GST Rebate, as well as the application of GST to the purchase and sale of capital assets. We have also included GST procedures and administration in this chapter.

21-19.   We view this as an extremely important subject. The great majority of businesses in Canada file GST returns. In addition, many organizations, such as charities and unincorporated businesses must file GST returns, even though they are not required to file income tax returns. Given the pervasiveness of this tax and the amounts that can be involved, it is our view that some understanding of its application is an essential component of the knowledge base of every professional accountant and businessperson.

Transaction Tax Concepts

General Description

21-20.   While taxes like the GST and HST are often referred to as commodity taxes, the title is not appropriate as the term commodity does not include services. When both goods and services are subject to a tax, what we are really concerned with is the taxation of transactions as opposed to the taxation of income.

21-21.   In both Canada and the U.S., the bulk of federal tax revenues has traditionally been generated by taxes on personal and corporate income. However, transaction taxes have been widely used in both countries at the provincial or state level. In addition, there has been a worldwide trend towards increased use of transaction taxes, with many industrialized countries now relying heavily on this type of taxation.

21-22.   Some of the factors that support the increased use of transaction taxes are as follows:

- **Simplicity**   Transaction taxes are easy to administer and collect. No forms are required from individuals paying the tax and, if the individual wishes to acquire a particular good or service, it is difficult to evade payment.

- **Incentives To Work**   An often cited disadvantage of income taxes is that they can discourage individual initiative to work and invest. Transaction taxes do not have this characteristic.

- **Consistency**   Transaction taxes avoid the fluctuating income and family unit problems that are associated with progressive income tax systems.

- **Keeping The Tax Revenues In Canada**   While some types of income can be moved out of Canada, resulting in the related taxes being paid in a different jurisdiction, taxes on Canadian transactions remain in Canadian hands.

21-23.   Given these advantages for transaction taxes, why is income taxation still used? The answer to this question largely involves the question of fairness. In general, transaction taxes relate to consumption. When this is combined with the fact that lower income individuals usually spend a larger portion of their total income on consumption, transaction taxes are assessed at higher effective rates on individuals with lower incomes. Using more technical terminology, transaction taxes are usually regressive.

21-24.   This is in conflict with the widely held belief that fairness requires that individuals with higher incomes should have their income taxed at higher average rates. This goal is best accomplished through the continued use of a progressive income tax system.

21-25.   The federal government has compensated for the regressive nature of the GST by providing a GST tax credit that is available to low income individuals who file income tax returns. Similar provisions are being added at the provincial level in those venues where the HST is used.

21-26.   There are a number of different ways in which transaction taxes can be applied. These alternatives will be given consideration in the material that follows.

Example

21-27.   In discussing the various approaches that can be used in the application of transaction taxes, a simple example is useful. Such an example is diagramed in Figure 21-2. As can be seen in Figure 21-2, our example involves a manufacturer who produces 1,000 units of product at a cost of $4 of raw materials per unit, a total cost of $4,000. All of the 1,000 units are sold to a wholesaler for $10 per unit. The wholesaler then sells 800 of the units to a retailer for $25 per unit. The retailer, in turn, sells 500 of the units to a consumer for $50 per unit.

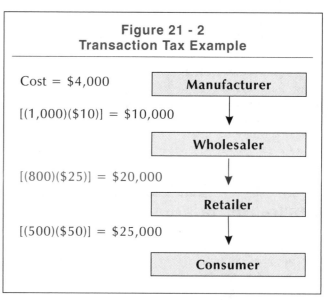

Figure 21 - 2
Transaction Tax Example

Cost = $4,000 → Manufacturer

[(1,000)($10)] = $10,000 → Wholesaler

[(800)($25)] = $20,000 → Retailer

[(500)($50)] = $25,000 → Consumer

Single Stage
Transaction Taxes - Retail Sales Tax

21-28.   A single stage transaction tax could be applied at any level in this example. The most common type of single stage tax is applied at the consumer level. This would be the familiar retail sales tax that is collected in several Canadian provinces. For example, if the transactions depicted in Figure 21-2 took place in Manitoba, a 7 percent retail sales tax would be assessed on the $25,000 price that the retailer charged the consumer, resulting in a provincial sales tax of $1,750 being paid by the consumer.

21-29.   The consumer level is probably the most appropriate level to apply a single stage transaction tax. The tax is visible and its incidence is relatively clear. In contrast, when a wholesale or manufacturer's tax is used, complications can arise when business relationships are formed that blur the lines between the manufacturing, wholesale, and retail levels. This can occur with vertical integration, and necessitates estimates or notional values for transfers between the manufacturing, wholesale, or retail levels of an organization.

Multi-Stage Transaction Taxes - Turnover Tax

21-30.   Again referring to Figure 21-2, it would be possible to impose a multi-stage transaction tax at any combination of the various levels depicted. For example, the tax could be applied at the wholesale and retail levels, without application at the manufacturing level. Alternatively, the manufacturing and wholesale levels could be taxed without application at the retail level. An extension of this taxation to all levels is sometimes referred to as a turnover tax, with transactions being taxed at all levels in the distribution chain.

21-31.   The problem with such a turnover tax is that it involves the pyramiding of taxes when there is no credit for taxes paid earlier in the chain. For example, if there was a 5 percent turnover tax in place, the manufacturer in Figure 21-2 would charge the wholesaler $10.50 per unit. When the wholesaler applies his normal markup of 250 percent of cost ($25 ÷ $10), the price would be $26.25 per unit [($10.50)(2.5)]. Of this $26.25, $0.025 [($0.50)(5%)] would represent a tax on the tax that was charged to the wholesaler by the manufacturer. If the 5 percent tax was also applied to the transfers to the retailer and to the ultimate consumer, there would be further applications of tax on previously assessed amounts of tax. Given this pyramiding problem, turnover taxes are not widely used.

Value Added Tax (VAT)

Types

21-32.   VATs are multi-stage transaction taxes that can be assessed in two basic ways:

Accounts-Based Method   In this approach, the tax is assessed on the basis of the value added at each level of the business process. It is usually based on some type of accounting based determination of income.

Invoice-Credit Method   In this approach, tax is assessed on gross sales. The taxpayer is then provided with a credit based on purchases made. No accounting based determination of income is required.

21-33.   These two approaches will be illustrated in the material which follows.

Accounts-Based VAT

21-34.   Internationally, the most common type of VAT uses the accounts-based method. Using this method, transactions are taxed at each level in the distribution chain. Using whatever rate is established, the VAT is applied to the value added by the business to goods and services, rather than to the gross sales of the business.

21-35.   If we assume a 5 percent rate of tax in the example presented in Figure 21-2, this method would require the raw materials supplier to charge tax on his sale price of $4 per unit. The manufacturer would then charge tax on the difference between the sales price of $10 per unit sold and the related input costs of $4 per unit sold. In corresponding fashion, the wholesaler would charge the 5 percent on the difference between the manufacturer's invoice of $10 per unit sold and the wholesale price of $25 per unit sold (i.e., the value added by the wholesaler). Finally, the retailer would charge the VAT on the difference between the retail price of $50 per unit sold and the wholesaler's price of $25 per unit sold. The total tax calculation is as follows:

Raw Materials [(5%)(1,000)($4)]	$ 200
Manufacturer To Wholesaler [(5%)(1,000)($10 - $4)]	300
Wholesaler To Retailer [(5%)(800)($25 - $10)]	600
Retailer To Consumer [(5%)(500)($50 - $25)]	625
Total Value Added Tax	$1,725

Invoice-Credit VAT

21-36.   This is the approach that is used in Canada for GST/HST calculations. Under this approach, each vendor charges tax on the full selling price. This tax is then offset by a credit for the tax that was paid on the costs incurred by the business (these are referred to as input tax credits).

21-37.   Continuing to assume a 5 percent rate of tax is applied to our basic example from Figure 21-2, the invoice-credit VAT calculations would be as follows:

Raw Materials Supplier

GST Collected [(5%)(1,000)($4))] (No Input Tax Credits)	$200
Net GST Payable	$200

Manufacturer

GST Collected [(5%)(1,000)($10)]	$500
Input Tax Credits [(5%)(1,000)($4)]	(200)
Net GST Payable	$300

Wholesaler

GST Collected [(5%)(800)($25)]	$1,000
Input Tax Credits [(5%)(1,000)($10)]	(500)
Net GST Payable	$ 500

Retailer

GST Collected [(5%)(500)($50)]	$1,250
Input Tax Credits [(5%)(800)($25)]	(1,000)
Net GST Payable	$ 250

Comparison

21-38.   Under the invoice-credit approach, the total tax that was paid at all levels is $1,250 ($200 + $300 + $500 + $250), significantly less than the $1,725 that was paid using the account-based approach. The reason for this is that, when the invoice-credit approach is used, the enterprise receives tax credits for all purchases, without regard to whether or not the goods are sold. In this example, at both the wholesale and retail levels, purchases exceed sales. The tax credits are claimed from the government on units purchased, while the taxes collected are paid to the government on units sold. This means that enterprises benefit from having their purchases exceed their sales. In contrast, under an accounts-based VAT system, the tax to be paid is based on units sold and no benefit is received for taxes paid on units that are still on hand.

21-39.   In general, if purchases and sales are equal, the tax that is assessed under an invoice-credit VAT system is similar to that assessed under an accounts-based VAT system. This can be seen at the manufacturer level in our example. In the case of the manufacturer, the units purchased and sold were equal. For this enterprise, the two VAT approaches resulted in exactly the same net tax ($300).

21-40.   Given that the accounts-based VAT approach is more commonly used on a world-wide basis, there is some question as to why Canada chose to use the alternative invoice-credit approach. While background documents on the GST legislation do not provide a direct answer to this question, it would appear that the major advantage of the invoice-credit approach is that it does not rely on an accounting determination of value added. The tax is charged on all taxable goods sold, with input tax credits available for taxes paid on all expenditures for inputs used in commercial activities. The fact that there is no matching requirement avoids the controversies that can arise when various types of cost matching and allocation procedures are required.

21-41.   It can also be argued that the invoice-credit approach is more equitable as it is more closely associated with actual cash flows than would be the case with an accounts-based system. The cash required to pay transaction taxes is based on purchases, without regard to when these inputs result in sales. As the invoice-credit approach provides for credits based on purchases, it can be argued that this approach is fairer to the enterprises that are involved in the production/distribution chain.

21-42.   There is a further question of why the government chose to use a multi-stage tax, rather than implementing a less complex, single stage, federal sales tax at the retail level. An often cited reason is related to tighter administration and control. With the multi-stage approach, a vendor does not have to determine whether or not customers of particular goods and services are exempt because they are one or more steps away from the retail or final consumption level.

21-43.   An additional reason for using a multi-stage tax is that it is applied further up the distribution chain. This, of course, means that the tax revenues accrue to the government at an earlier point in time.

Exercise Twenty-One - 1

Subject: Alternative VAT Approaches

During a taxation period, Darvin Wholesalers purchased merchandise for $233,000. Merchandise sales during this period totalled $416,000 and the cost of the merchandise sold was $264,000. Ignoring all other costs incurred by Darvin and assuming a rate of 5 percent, how much tax would be paid by Darvin under an account-based VAT system and, alternatively, under an invoice-credit VAT system?

End of Exercise. Solution available in Study Guide.

We suggest you work Self Study Problem Twenty-One-1 at this point.

Liability For GST/HST

Basic Charging Provision

21-44.   The basic charging provision for GST is found in the *Excise Tax Act* (ETA). It is as follows:

> **ETA 165(1)   Imposition of goods and services tax** — Subject to this Part, every recipient of a taxable supply made in Canada shall pay to Her Majesty in right of Canada tax in respect of the supply calculated at the rate of 5% on the value of the consideration for the supply. [**Byrd/Chen Note** Additional legislation changes this rate to the appropriate rate in those provinces where the HST has been adopted.]

21-45.   In order to understand this charging provision, it will be necessary to give attention to the concept of supply. We will cover this in the next section of this chapter.

21-46.   Note that the tax is assessed on the recipient of, rather than the provider of, taxable supplies. As we shall find in a later section of this Chapter, responsibility for collection of the tax is with the provider of the taxable supplies (the GST/HST registrant).

The Concept Of Supply

21-47.   The term "goods and services tax" implies that it is a tax that is applied to goods and services or, more specifically, transactions that involve the provision of goods and services. The term that is used by the *Excise Tax Act* in referring to such transactions is "supply". This term is defined in the *Act* as follows:

ETA 123   **Supply** means the provision of property or a service in any manner, including sale, transfer, barter, exchange, licence, rental, lease, gift or disposition.

21-48.   While this definition includes most of the items that we would consider to be revenues under GAAP, it is actually a much broader term. It would include all of the following:

- the sale, rental, or transfer of goods,
- the rendering of services,
- licensing arrangements for copyrights or patents,
- the lease, sale, or other transfer of real property, and
- barter transactions or gifts.

Supply Categories

NOTE ON GST/HST DIFFERENCES   While the HST provinces use the same categories of supply that are used in the federal GST legislation, some fully taxable items are given point-of-sale rebates for the provincial component of the HST (e.g., Ontario provides a point-of- sale rebate for children's clothing). In effect, purchasers pay only the federal GST rate of 5 percent on these items.

A full description of these differences for all of the HST provinces goes beyond the scope of this text. Given this, the examples that are described in the following discussion include items that fall into the fully taxable category under the federal GST legislation. Because of provincial rebates in the HST provinces, purchasers of some of these items will not pay the full HST rate.

Taxable Supplies
General Rules
21-49.   The *Excise Tax Act* defines taxable supplies as follows:

ETA 123(1)   **Taxable supply** means a supply that is made in the course of a commercial activity.

21-50.   Expanding on this definition, commercial activity is defined in the *Excise Tax Act* as follows:

ETA 123(1)   **Commercial Activity** of a person means

(a) a business carried on by the person (other than a business carried on without a reasonable expectation of profit by an individual, a personal trust or a partnership, all of the members of which are individuals), except to the extent to which the business involves the making of exempt supplies by the person,

(b) an adventure or concern of the person in the nature of trade (other than an adventure or concern engaged in without a reasonable expectation of profit by an individual, a personal trust or a partnership, all of the members of which are individuals), except to the extent to which the adventure or concern involves the making of exempt supplies by the person, [**Byrd/Chen Note** In somewhat simplified terms, an adventure or concern in the nature of trade is a one-shot business venture, as opposed to an ongoing activity.] and

(c) the making of a supply (other than an exempt supply) by the person of real property of the person, including anything done by the person in the course of or in connection with the making of the supply

21-51.   As used here, the term business has the following meaning:

ETA 123(1)   **Business** includes a profession, calling, trade, manufacture or undertaking of any kind whatever, whether the activity or undertaking is engaged in for profit, and any activity engaged in on a regular or continuous basis that involves the supply of property by way of lease, licence or similar arrangement, but does not include an office or employment;

21-52.   Stated in practical, every-day language, this says that if you are providing goods or services in the course of business activity, or if you selling or leasing real property, you are providing taxable supplies unless:

- the business does not have a reasonable expectation of profit (this criteria only applies to businesses run by individuals, certain partnerships, or certain trusts);
- the supplies are exempt supplies; or
- the services are employment services.

21-53.   Taxable supplies fall into two categories. The first category is supplies that we will refer to as fully taxable supplies. The second category is supplies that are zero-rated.

Fully Taxable Supplies

21-54.   Fully taxable supplies are those that are taxed at the 5 percent federal GST rate or the appropriate HST rate (13, 14, or 15 percent). Examples of fully taxable supplies include:

- transportation in Canada,
- restaurant meals and beverages,
- clothing and footwear,
- furniture,
- admissions to concerts, athletic and other events
- contractors' services,
- legal and accounting fees,
- haircuts, and
- cleaning services.

Zero-Rated Supplies

21-55.   The *Excise Tax Act* provides a list of taxable supplies that are designated as zero-rated. While these supplies are said to be taxable, they are taxed at zero percent, rather than the regular GST or HST rate.

21-56.   At first glance, this concept seems a bit senseless in that there is no tax charged on either zero-rated supplies or exempt supplies. However, an important difference exists. Because zero-rated supplies are considered to be taxable supplies, the providers of such supplies can recover the GST/HST paid on business purchases as input tax credits. In contrast, providers of exempt supplies are not eligible for input tax credits (see Paragraph 21-106).

21-57.   In addition, as zero-rated supplies are considered taxable at a rate of zero percent, they are included in the threshold amounts for determining the filing frequency of a registrant's GST or HST returns. This is covered beginning in Paragraph 21-136.

21-58.   Common items included in the category of zero-rated supplies are as follows:

- prescription drugs,
- medical devices such as wheelchairs, eye glasses, canes, hospital beds, and artificial limbs,
- basic groceries,
- most agricultural and fishing products,
- goods and services exported from Canada, and
- foreign travel and transportation services (see following Paragraph).

21-59.   Some elaboration is required for the meaning of foreign travel. Surface travel by ship, bus, or train is zero-rated when the origin or termination point is outside Canada (e.g., a train trip to the U.S. is zero-rated). Domestic surface travel is fully taxable at the GST or HST rate.

21-60.   In the case of air travel, the GST/HST rules can be complicated. International air travel is zero-rated only when flights are deemed to be outside of continental North America, not just outside of Canada. For example, this broader definition makes Canadian air travel to and from the United States fully taxable at the 5 percent GST rate or the appropriate HST rate.

Exempt Supplies

21-61.   As was the case with zero-rated supplies, the *Excise Tax Act* provides a list of supplies that are exempt from GST. Persons supplying exempt items do not collect GST/HST and are not eligible for input tax credits for GST/HST paid on the related purchases. As we shall see when we discuss input tax credits, this means that suppliers of exempt supplies pay GST/HST that is not refundable to them on goods and services required to operate their business. As a consequence, the non-recoverable GST/HST paid is a cost of doing business that is likely to be passed on to customers in the form of higher prices.

21-62.   Some common items that are included in the category of exempt supplies are as follows:

- basic health care and dental services (which does not include cosmetic surgery),
- financial services provided to Canadian residents,
- sales of used residential housing and long-term residential rents (e.g., rentals for more than 30 days),
- most land sold by individuals where the land was not used in a business,
- educational courses leading to certificates or diplomas, tutoring for credit courses, and music lessons,
- child or personal care services, and
- a wide variety of services provided by charities, not-for-profit, and government organizations (see discussion under Specific Applications at Paragraph 21-190).

Applying the GST/HST Rate

Place Of Supply

The Problem

21-63.   The rate at which GST or HST will be applied varies from a low of 5 percent in provinces where only the GST is applicable (e.g., Alberta), to a high of 15 percent under Nova Scotia's HST regime. The size of this range makes the question of which rate should be applied to a particular supply of goods and services a significant issue.

21-64.   A further question relates to whether the tax should be assessed on the basis of the location of the registrant providing the supply or, alternatively, the location of the recipient of the supply. Prior to 2010, the place of supply rules were mostly based on the location of the supplier. The current rules rely more heavily on where the recipient is located. This means that a supplier must be able to deal with the transaction taxes in any province his goods and services are delivered to, as well as the transaction taxes in the province where he is located.

21-65.   There are, of course, many complications in the application of these rules. What follows provides only a basic overview of how these rules work.

Tangible Goods

21-66.   The rules for tangible goods are relatively straightforward. A GST/HST registrant will calculate taxes on the basis of the rules that are in effect in the province where the goods are delivered. The following examples will illustrate the application of this approach.

Ontario To Ontario   If an Ontario registrant sells a shirt to a recipient in Ontario, HST will be charged at a 13 percent rate.

Ontario To Alberta   If an Ontario registrant sells a shirt that is to be shipped to a recipient in Alberta, only GST at a 5 percent rate will be charged.

Ontario To Newfoundland   If an Ontario registrant sells a shirt that is to be shipped to a recipient in Newfoundland, HST will be charged at 13 percent.

Ontario To Quebec   If an Ontario registrant sells a shirt that is to be shipped to a recipient in Quebec, only GST at a 5 percent rate will be charged. This example makes the point that Quebec is using a separate transaction tax (QST), rather than harmonizing with the federal GST.

Real Property

21-67.   As real property cannot be moved across provincial boundaries, there are few complications in this area. The GST or HST will be assessed on the basis of the rules in effect in the province where the real property is located. For example, on the sale of real property in Ontario, HST will be applicable at a rate of 13 percent.

Services

21-68.   This area has the most complications in terms of the place of supply rules. The basic idea is that the place of supply is the province where the services are used.

Example A professor at a Manitoba university is also a freelance editor of a widely used accounting text. He does his editing in his office in Winnipeg. His editing fees are consistently in excess of $50,000 per year. Because of this, he is a GST registrant (Manitoba does not participate in the HST program). His work is sent to the Toronto office of the publisher and cheques for his fees are issued from that office.

Analysis   As the services are "used" in Ontario, the editor would bill HST at 13 percent.

Applying The Rate
Consideration Received

21-69.   To determine the amount of GST or HST to be charged, the appropriate rate is applied to the amount of consideration received in return for the delivery of taxable supplies. In most cases, the consideration will be monetary and the amount to be recorded is obvious. If the consideration is non-monetary (e.g., a barter transaction), GST/HST is still applicable. In this case, however, an estimate will have to be made of the fair market value of the consideration received.

21-70.   The amount of consideration to be used for purposes of calculating the GST/HST includes all non-refundable federal taxes, provincial taxes other than retail sales taxes, and duties and fees that are imposed on either the supplier or recipient in respect of the property or services supplied.

Effect Of Trade-Ins

21-71.   Where a good owned by an entity that is not registered for GST/HST is traded in towards the supply of a new good, GST/HST is only required to be levied on the net amount after the trade-in. These types of transactions are most often seen in the automotive business, where used cars are traded in when purchasing a newer automobile.

Example   John Bailey, a resident of Alberta, is acquiring a new Volvo at a cost of $52,000. He is given a trade-in allowance of $21,000 on his old vehicle.

Analysis   The applicable GST would be $1,550 [(5%)($52,000 - $21,000)].

Collection And Remittance Of GST/HST

21-72.   As you are aware, income taxes are collected from the same person on whom the tax is assessed. An individual will calculate his Tax Payable by applying the appropriate rates to his Taxable Income. This same individual is also responsible for the payment of this tax.

21-73.   The situation is different with GST/HST. We noted previously that the basic GST/HST charging provision assesses the tax on the recipient of the taxable supply. However, the basic responsibility for the collection and remittance of the GST/HST falls on the provider of the taxable supply. This approach is implemented by requiring providers of taxable supplies to become GST registrants. Registration is discussed in the section which follows.

21-74.   As an example of this process, consider a situation where a retailer is featuring a GST holiday.

> **Example**   An Alberta store advertises a GST holiday, indicating that merchandise can be purchased without paying the GST. A customer pays the marked price of $2,500 for a new freezer and no additional amount is added for GST.
>
> **Analysis**   From the customer's point of view, he has not paid the GST. However, the store will have to treat the $2,500 as a GST inclusive amount. For GST purposes, the $2,500 received was made up of $2,380.95 ($2,500 ÷ 105%) for the freezer and GST of $119.05 [(5%)($2,380.95)]. The store must include the GST received of $119.05 in its GST return.

21-75.   You should note that, while the vendor is responsible for the collection of GST/HST, this does not relieve the purchaser of the responsibility for payment. If a vendor fails to collect the tax, the CRA can assess the purchaser for the unremitted amount. This, however, would be a fairly rare procedure.

Registration

Meaning Of Person For GST/HST

21-76.   For GST/HST purposes, the *Excise Tax Act* defines a person as follows:

> **ETA 123(1)   Person** means an individual, a partnership, a corporation, the estate of a deceased individual, a trust, or a body that is a society, union, club, association, commission or other organization of any kind;

21-77.   Note that this definition is broader than the one that is included in the *Income Tax Act*. For income tax purposes, the term "person" includes only individuals, corporations, and trusts. Of importance here is the fact that the GST definition includes unincorporated businesses, partnerships, and not-for profit organizations.

Who Must Register

Basic Requirement

21-78.   As we have previously indicated, the collection of GST/HST is administered through a registration requirement for providers of taxable supplies. This requirement is as follows:

> **ETA 240(1)**   Every person who makes a taxable supply in Canada in the course of a commercial activity engaged in by the person in Canada is required to be registered for the purposes of this Part, except where
>
> (a) the person is a small supplier;
> (b) the only commercial activity of the person is the making of supplies of real property by way of sale otherwise than in the course of a business; or
> (c) the person is a non-resident person who does not carry on any business in Canada.

21-79.   This requirement contains several terms and concepts that require further elaboration. We will deal with these items in the section which follows.

Commercial Activity - Inclusions

21-80.   ETA 240(1) requires registration only when "taxable supplies" are delivered in the course of "commercial activity". We have previously covered both of these definitions in our discussion of taxable supplies beginning in Paragraph 21-49.

21-81.   In simple terms, any person who provides non-exempt goods or services, in the course of a business activity, is required to register for the GST/HST unless that person is covered by one of the exceptions listed in ETA 240(1).

Commercial Activity - Exclusions

21-82.   There are several items that might be considered commercial activity that are excluded in the preceding definitions:

No Reasonable Expectation Of Profit   Business activity that is carried on by an individual without a reasonable expectation of profit is not considered to be commercial activity.

Provision Of Exempt Supplies   When a person is providing exempt supplies (e.g., financial services), there is no requirement to register.

Employment Services   The provision of employment services is not considered to be commercial activity.

21-83.   When a person is involved in one of these excluded activities, there is no requirement to register for the GST for that activity.

Exemption For Non-Residents

21-84.   The ETA 240(1) requirement to register, in general excludes non-residents. The major exception to this would be when a non-resident person carries on business in Canada. This exception would apply, without regard to whether the business is carried on through a permanent establishment. An additional exception could arise in situations where a non-resident has registered for GST/HST on a voluntary basis.

21-85.   In general, resident is defined for GST/HST purposes in the same manner that it is defined for income tax purposes. We would refer you to Chapter 20 for a discussion of the issues associated with residence determination.

Exemption For Small Suppliers

Last Four Calendar Quarters Test

21-86.   The ETA 240(1) registration requirement indicates that it is not applicable to "small suppliers". The idea here is that a small supplier is a person whose delivery of taxable supplies, including those of associated businesses, is less than $30,000 per year. This provision is intended to provide compliance relief for the operators of small businesses.

21-87.   The basic test for qualification as a small supplier is based on calendar year quarters (i.e., January to March, April to June, July to September, and October to December). Under this test, an entity qualifies as a small supplier in the current quarter and the month following the current quarter if, during the calendar four quarters preceding the current quarter, the entity and its associated entities did not have cumulative taxable supplies exceeding $30,000.

21-88.   If taxable supplies accumulate to $30,000 in any period consisting of two to four quarters (they do not have to be in the same calendar year), the entity will have to begin collecting GST/HST on the first day of the second month following the end of the quarter in which the $30,000 level is reached. Note that there is a 30 day grace period for registration, subsequent to the date on which the supplier begins to collect GST/HST.

Example   Supplier A opened for business on January 1, 2013, and earned the following revenues from taxable supplies during the year:

Quarter	Months	Taxable Supplies
One	January to March	$ 7,000
Two	April to June	8,000
Three	July to September	20,000
Four	October to December	9,000
Total		$44,000

Analysis   Supplier A's revenues accumulate to more than $30,000 in the third quarter of 2013 ($7,000 + $8,000 + $20,000 = $35,000). This means that Supplier A is required to collect the GST/HST starting on November 1, 2013, which is the first day of the second month after the end of the July to September quarter. Formal registration will be required within 30 days of November 1, 2013.

Calendar Quarter Test

21-89.   An exception to the last four calendar quarters test exists where a person's total revenues from taxable supplies exceed $30,000 in a single calendar quarter. When the $30,000 threshold is exceeded in a single quarter, the person ceases to qualify as a small supplier and must register for, and collect, GST/HST. The person is deemed to be a registrant beginning with the supply (sale) that caused the threshold to be exceeded. This test is referred to as the "calendar quarter test".

Example   Supplier B started in business on January 1, 2013. The business is an art gallery and Supplier B had only two sales in 2013, one for $39,000 on May 15 and the other for $5,000 on August 28.

Quarter	Months	Taxable Supplies
One	January to March	Nil
Two	April to June (May 15)	$39,000
Three	July to September (August 28)	5,000
Four	October to December	Nil
Total		$44,000

Analysis   Supplier B would become a registrant as of the May 15 sale, reflecting the fact that this single sale pushes the sales for that quarter past the $30,000 threshold amount. From that point, GST/HST should have been collected on all taxable supplies made. While collection of tax revenue is required starting on the deemed registration day, Supplier B has 30 days in which to formally register.

21-90.   In reviewing the two preceding examples, note that Supplier A and Supplier B each earned taxable revenue of $44,000 in the four calendar quarters for 2013. Supplier B, however, exceeded the $30,000 threshold in Quarter Two. This results in Supplier B being deemed to be registered starting with the May 15 transaction. In contrast, Supplier A will not have to start collecting GST/HST until November 1, 2013 using the last four calendar quarters test.

Exercise Twenty-One - 2

Subject: Requirement To Register

Ms. Sharon Salome and Mr. Rock Laughton begin separate businesses on April 1, 2013. The quarterly sales of taxable items for both businesses are as follows:

Calendar Quarter	Sharon Salome	Rock Laughton
April To June, 2013	$10,000	$ 8,000
July To September, 2013	4,000	13,000
October To December, 2013	35,000	4,000
January To March, 2014	40,000	17,000

At what point in time will Ms. Salome and Mr. Laughton have to begin collecting GST? At what point will they be required to register?

End of Exercise. Solution available in Study Guide.

Voluntary Registration

21-91.   The small supplier exemption can represent an advantage to persons with limited commercial activity whose clients are consumers and not businesses that can claim input tax credits. With some advance planning, the exemption can be extended within a family group, provided members are not considered associated. For example, it may be desirable for family members to undertake commercial activities on an individual basis rather than on a group basis to maximize any potential benefit from the small supplier exemption. In this scenario, however, the entities cannot be controlled by the same individual or group of individuals.

21-92.   There is, however, a disadvantage to this exemption. If a person does not register, they cannot receive input tax credits for GST/HST paid. They are effectively treated as the final consumer. This means that the business must either absorb the GST/HST paid on its costs or, alternatively, pass the GST/HST paid on purchases and expenses on to its customers in the form of higher prices.

21-93. . Given this problem, voluntary registration is an alternative. Any person engaged in commercial activity in Canada can apply to be registered, even if taxable sales are less than the $30,000 small supplier threshold. It is likely that the main reason for voluntary registrations is to claim input tax credits for the GST/HST paid on purchases.

Registrants Ineligible For The Small Supplier Exemption
21-94.   ETA 240 contains two other subsections which effectively prohibit the use of the small supplier exemption for certain type of suppliers. ETA 240(1.1) indicates that suppliers of taxi and limousine services must register, even if their revenues are less than $30,000 per year. In a similar fashion, ETA 240(2) requires registration of non-residents who enter Canada for the purpose of making taxable supplies of admissions in respect of a place of amusement, a seminar, an activity or an event.

We suggest working Self Study Problem Twenty-One-2 at this point.

Input Tax Credits

Vendors Of Fully Taxable And Zero-Rated Supplies
General Rules
21-95.   A GST/HST registrant must collect and remit GST/HST on supplies of fully taxable goods and services. In the process of supplying these goods and services, the registrant will incur costs, some of which are likely to include GST/HST. To the extent that these costs have been incurred in commercial activity (i.e., supplying either fully taxable or zero-rated goods and services), the registrant can claim a refund of the GST/HST that has been included in these costs.

21-96.   The refunds that are available to the registrant are referred to as input tax credits. As was the case with some credits against income tax payable, input tax credits can be thought of as refundable. That is, if the available input tax credits for the period exceed the GST/HST collections for the period, the registrant can claim a GST/HST refund.

21-97.   As will be discussed in the sections which follow, the rules for claiming input tax credits vary, depending on whether the GST/HST was paid on current expenditures (e.g., purchases of merchandise inventories) or, alternatively, capital expenditures (e.g., buildings or equipment). The rules also vary with the type of capital expenditure on which the GST/HST was paid.

21-98.   It is important to note that, in claiming input tax credits there is no matching of costs and revenues. Input tax credits on inventory purchases become available at the time of purchase, not when the goods are sold and charged to income for accounting purposes. Input tax credits on capital expenditures become available when the asset is acquired, not over the useful life of the asset.

Current Expenditures
21-99.   With respect to current expenditures, if all, or substantially all (generally understood in tax work to mean 90 percent or more), of a current expenditure is related to commercial activity, then all of the GST/HST that was paid can be claimed as an input tax credit. In contrast, if 10 percent or less of an expenditure is related to commercial activity, no input tax credit can be claimed. If the percentage of the current expenditure used for commercial

activity is between 10 and 90 percent, the input tax credit available is calculated by multi-plying the total GST/HST paid by the percentage of commercial activity usage.

Capital Expenditures

21-100.   In line with the basic idea that input tax credits are not matched against amounts of GST/HST collected on sales, the GST/HST paid on purchases of capital assets used in commercial activities is eligible for treatment as an input tax credit at the time of purchase, regardless of when the purchases are paid for, or how they are amortized.

21-101.   In situations where a capital asset is used only partially for commercial activity, the approach used to calculate the available input tax credits will depend on the type of capital asset involved:

Real Property (Land And Buildings)   For this type of property, the input tax credit available is in proportion to the extent to which the property is used in commercial activities. That is, if the building is used 35 percent for commercial activities, the input tax credit will be equal to 35 percent of the GST/HST paid on its acquisition. In other words, input tax credits on real property are available on a pro rata basis, with the available portion based on usage in commercial activities.

As is the case with current expenditures, if commercial usage is 10 percent or less, the purchaser cannot claim any input tax credit. Alternatively, if the usage is 90 percent or more, 100 percent of the GST/HST paid can be claimed as an input tax credit.

Personal Capital Property (Capital Property Other Than Real Property)   In order for the input tax credits to be available on personal capital property, the assets must be used "primarily" in commercial activities. In tax work, "primarily" is generally understood to be more than 50 percent. If commercial usage is 50 percent or less, none of the GST/HST paid on the personal capital property's acquisition can be claimed as an input tax credit. If commercial usage is more than 50 percent, the registrant is eligible for an input tax credit equal to 100 percent of the GST/HST paid.

Restrictions On Claiming Input Tax Credits

21-102.   As noted in previous Chapters of this text, income tax legislation restricts the deductibility of certain types of business costs. For many of these items, there is a corresponding restriction on the ability of the business to claim input tax credits for GST/HST purposes. Some of the more common restrictions are as follows:

Passenger Vehicles   No input tax credits are available for GST/HST paid on the portion of the cost or lease payment of a passenger vehicle that is in excess of the deduction limits (for 2013, these limits are $30,000 cost and $800 monthly lease payments, excluding GST/HST and PST). Also, if the vehicle is owned by a registrant who is an individual or a partnership and the vehicle is used partly for business (less than 90 percent) and partly for personal use, the input tax credit is prorated based on the annual CCA claimed.

Club Memberships   No input tax credit is allowed for GST/HST paid on membership fees or dues in any club whose main purpose is to provide dining, recreational, or sporting facilities.

Provision Of Recreational Facilities   No input tax credits are available for the GST/HST costs of providing certain types of recreational facilities to employees, owners, or related parties.

Business Meals And Entertainment   The recovery of GST/HST on meals and entertainment expenses is limited to 50 percent of the amounts paid.

Personal Or Living Expenses   Input tax credits cannot be claimed on costs associated with the personal or living expenses of any employee, owner, or related individual. An exception is available when GST/HST is collected on the provision of the item to the employee, owner, or related individual.

| | **Figure 21 - 3** | |
| | **Maximum Input Tax Credits** | |
Taxable Purchase	**Percentage Used In Commercial Activities = X%**	**Input Tax Credit**
Current Expenditures	X% ≤ 10%	Nil
and Real Property	10% < X% < 90%	X%
	X% ≥ 90%	100%
Personal Capital Property	X% ≤ 50%	Nil
(Excluding Passenger Vehicles*)	X% > 50%	100%
*Special rules apply to certain items. See Paragraph 21-102.		

Reasonableness   Both the nature and value of a purchase must be reasonable in relation to the commercial activities of the registrant before an input tax credit can be claimed. This is similar to the test of reasonableness that is found in the *Income Tax Act*.

21-103.   Restrictions also apply to the time allowed for claiming input tax credits. For large businesses, whose sales are less than 90 percent taxable but in excess of $6 million, and listed financial institutions, the time limit is generally two years from the date the input tax credit was first available. For all other registrants the time limit is four years.

Summary Of Rules
21-104.   The rules for apportioning the maximum available input tax credits on purchases are summarized in Figure 21-3.

Vendors Of Exempt Supplies
21-105.   Vendors of exempt supplies cannot claim any GST/HST paid on purchases that relate to exempt supplies. In some situations, vendors are involved in making fully taxable or zero-rated supplies, as well as exempt supplies. Since these businesses can only recover GST/HST paid on their fully taxable or zero-rated activities, they must apportion their input tax credits on a "reasonable" basis. This applies to both current and capital expenditures that cannot be directly identified with particular exempt or taxable activities.

Accounting vs. Income Tax vs. GST/HST
Differences
21-106.   The concept of matching is integral to the determination of business income for both accounting and income tax purposes. For GST/HST purposes, the matching concept is not relevant. GST/HST is collected when taxable supplies are provided and input tax credits are refunded when the inputs for such provisions are purchased. No attempt is made to match credits on inputs used to make these provisions with the point in time when the provisions are made.

21-107.   Other significant differences between accounting, income tax and GST/HST procedures are as follows:

- Most accounting and income tax allocations, for example amortization or CCA, are irrelevant for GST/HST purposes. GST/HST paid on capital expenditures that are eligible for input tax credits can generally be claimed in the period in which the expenditure is made.

- Many deductible expenses for income tax purposes do not affect the GST/HST payable or receivable. For example, GST/HST does not apply to employee wages, interest, property taxes, and educational services. While such costs are usually fully deductible in the calculation of Net Income For Tax Purposes, they do not require the payment of GST/HST and, as a consequence, do not generate input tax credits.

Similarities
21-108. In contrast to these differences, there are some features that are common to GST/HST and income tax calculations. For example, GST/HST is normally collected and revenue is recognized for income tax purposes when an invoice is issued for the provision of goods or services. When the invoice is paid is not a relevant consideration for either income tax or GST/HST purposes.

21-109. Similarly, if an account receivable becomes uncollectible, an adjustment is required for both income tax and GST/HST purposes. Also, as we have noted, some of the restrictions that apply in the deductibility of certain expenses for income tax purposes (e.g., 50 percent of business meals and entertainment and certain costs of owning or leasing automobiles) are also contained in the GST/HST legislation.

Financial Statement Presentation
21-110. This issue is covered in IAS No. 18, *Revenue*. This international accounting standard indicates that taxes that are to be refunded should not be included in reported revenues. There is no corresponding statement with respect to expenses. However, it would be logical to assume that any GST/HST paid that is eligible for an input tax credit would not be included in the reported expense. Note, however, that even though the revenues and expenses are reported net of GST/HST, the amounts due to and recoverable from the government must be included in the receivables and payables of the enterprise.

Example One - Fully Taxable And Zero-Rated Supplies
21-111. In this example, we will assume that the company sells only fully taxable and zero-rated supplies.

Example Marson Ltd. is located in the province of Alberta which does not have a provincial sales tax and does not participate in the HST system. In the following Income Statement of Marson Ltd. for the year ending December 31, 2013, all of the items are recorded net of any GST collected or paid.

Sales	$9,500,000
Expenses:	
Cost Of Goods Sold	$6,500,000
Amortization Expense	900,000
Salaries And Wages	1,500,000
Other Expenses	200,000
Total Expenses Excluding GST And Income Taxes	$9,100,000
Net Income Before GST And Income Taxes	$ 400,000

Other Information:
1. Of the total Sales, $6,800,000 were fully taxable supplies. The remaining $2,700,000 ($9,500,000 - $6,800,000) were zero-rated.

2. Purchases of merchandise exceeded the Cost Of Goods Sold by $2,200,000, net of GST. All of the merchandise sold and purchased involved fully taxable supplies.

3. Of the Other Expenses, 80 percent related to fully taxable supplies, while the remaining 20 percent related to zero-rated supplies.

4. During 2013, capital expenditures totaled $7,500,000, net of GST, and the amounts have not been paid. These consisted of $5,000,000 for an office building and $2,500,000 for furniture and fixtures. The office building was used

60 percent for fully taxable supplies and 40 percent for zero-rated supplies. The furniture and fixtures were used 55 percent for fully taxable supplies and 45 percent for zero-rated supplies.

Analysis   Based on this information Marson Ltd. is eligible for a GST refund calculated as follows:

GST Collected [(5%)($6,800,000)]	$340,000
Input Tax Credits:	
Purchases [(5%)($6,500,000 + $2,200,000)]	(435,000)
Amortization Expense	Nil
Salaries And Wages	Nil
Other Expenses [(5%)(80% + 20%)($200,000)]	(10,000)
Building [(5%)(60% + 40%)($5,000,000)]	(250,000)
Furniture And Fixtures [(5%)(55% + 45%)($2,500,000)]	(125,000)
GST Payable (Refund) - With Zero-Rated Supplies	($480,000)

21-112.   You will note that, while Marson Ltd. is showing a positive Net Income for accounting purposes, the Company is eligible for a GST refund. This example clearly illustrates the fact that GST reporting is not based on the matching principle. The input tax credits are available on the entire amount of capital expenditures, without regard to whether they have been paid for or amortized for accounting purposes. In addition, input tax credits are available on all of the inventory purchases, without regard to whether the merchandise has been sold.

Example Two - Fully Taxable And GST Exempt Supplies

21-113.   In this example, we have revised the Marson Ltd. example so that the Company sells fully taxable and GST exempt supplies. The revised information is repeated here for your convenience.

Example   Marson Ltd. is located in the province of Alberta which does not have a provincial sales tax and does not participate in the HST system. In the following Income Statement of Marson Ltd. for the year ending December 31, 2013, all of the items are recorded net of any GST collected or paid.

Sales	$9,500,000
Expenses:	
Cost Of Goods Sold	$6,500,000
Amortization Expense	900,000
Salaries And Wages	1,500,000
Other Expenses	200,000
Total Expenses Excluding GST And Income Taxes	$9,100,000
Net Income Before GST And Income Taxes	$ 400,000

Other Information:

1. Of the total Sales, $6,800,000 were fully taxable supplies. The remaining $2,700,000 ($9,500,000 - $6,800,000) were GST exempt supplies.

2. Purchases of merchandise exceeded the Cost Of Goods Sold by $2,200,000, net of GST. All of the merchandise sold and purchased involved fully taxable supplies.

3. Of the Other Expenses, 80 percent related to fully taxable supplies, while the remaining 20 percent related to GST exempt supplies.

4. During 2013, capital expenditures totaled $7,500,000, net of GST, and the amounts have not been paid. These consisted of $5,000,000 for an office

building and $2,500,000 for furniture and fixtures. The office building was used 60 percent for fully taxable supplies and 40 percent for GST exempt supplies. The furniture and fixtures were used 55 percent for fully taxable supplies and 45 percent for GST exempt supplies.

Analysis   Based on this revised information, the GST refund for Marson Ltd. would be calculated as follows:

GST Collected [(5%)($6,800,000)]	$340,000
Input Tax Credits:	
Purchases [(5%)($6,500,000 + $2,200,000)]	(435,000)
Amortization Expense	Nil
Salaries And Wages	Nil
Other Expenses [(5%)(80%)($200,000)]	(8,000)
Building [(5%)(60%)($5,000,000)]	(150,000)
Furniture And Fixtures [(5%)(100%)($2,500,000)]	(125,000)
GST Payable (Refund) - With GST Exempt Supplies	($378,000)

21-114.   In this example, where some of the costs relate to the provision of exempt supplies, only 80 percent of the GST on Other Expenses is eligible for an input tax credit. Similarly, only 60 percent of the GST paid on the Building is eligible. However, because the Furniture And Fixtures were personal capital property and used primarily (more than 50 percent) for commercial activity, the full amount of the GST paid is eligible for an input tax credit, even though 45 percent of their usage was for the provision of GST exempt supplies.

Exercise Twenty-One - 3

Subject: HST Calculation

All of the operations of March Ltd. are located in New Brunswick where the relevant HST rate is 13 percent. During the current quarter, March Ltd. has taxable sales of $1,223,000 before HST. Its cost of sales for the period was $843,000 before HST and its merchandise inventories increased by $126,000, again before HST. Salaries and wages for the period totalled $87,000, interest expense was $16,000, and amortization expense was $93,000. No capital expenditures were made during the period. Determine the net HST payable or refund for the quarter.

Exercise Twenty-One - 4

Subject: HST Calculation

Ms. Marsha Stone lives and works in Newfoundland where the relevant HST rate is 13 percent. During the current year she delivers accounting services that are billed at $224,000. Rent for this period on her office premises totals $25,800 and she pays a clerical assistant an annual salary of $18,500. Her capital expenditures during the period are for new office furniture with a cost of $36,000 and computer hardware and software for $20,000. All amounts are before the addition of HST and the assets are used 100 percent for the provision of taxable supplies. She files her HST return on an annual basis. Determine the net HST payable or refund for the year.

End of Exercises. Solutions available in Study Guide.

Exercise Twenty-One - 5

Subject: Input Tax Credits On Capital Expenditures

Modam Ltd. is located in Alberta and all of its operations are in that province. During its current quarter, Modam Ltd. purchases an office building and land for a total of $1,200,000 before GST. The Company spends an additional $226,000 (before GST) on office equipment. The building will be used 40 percent for taxable supplies and 60 percent for exempt supplies. The office equipment is to be allocated in the same ratio. For accounting purposes, the building will be amortized over 40 years, while the office equipment will be written off over 4 years. Determine the input tax credits that Modam Ltd. can claim as a result of these capital expenditures.

End of Exercise. Solution available in Study Guide.

We suggest working Self Study Problems Twenty-One-3 and 4 at this point.

Relief For Small Businesses

Quick Method Of Accounting

General Rules

21-115.   Eligible businesses, defined as businesses with annual GST/HST included taxable sales, including those of associated businesses, of $400,000 or less during the year, can elect to use the Quick Method of determining the net GST/HST remittance. Both fully taxable and zero-rated supplies are included in calculating the $400,000 threshold, while exempt supplies, supplies made outside of Canada, sales of real and personal capital property, and provincial sales taxes are excluded. In addition, businesses involved in legal, accounting and financial consulting services are not eligible for the Quick Method.

21-116.   If the Quick Method election is filed, the registrant charges GST or HST at the normal rate on taxable sales. The major advantage of this method is that the business is not required to keep detailed records of current expenditures that are eligible for input tax credits. Note, however, that when this method is used for current expenditures, the registrant can still claim input tax credits on capital expenditures. This means that there will continue to be a need to track the input tax credits on specific capital expenditures.

21-117.   In the absence of detailed records on current expenditures eligible for input tax credits, a specified percentage, the remittance rate, is applied to the GST/HST inclusive total of fully taxable sales to determine the amount of GST/HST to be remitted.

21-118.   Note that the remittance rate is not an alternative GST/HST rate. It is based on an assumed relationship between revenues subject to GST/HST and costs on which input tax credits are available. For example, the Quick Method remittance rate for service providers in Alberta is 3.6 percent. The following example illustrates (without going into the algebra that is involved) that this rate is based on the assumption that, for service providers subject only to GST, eligible costs are equal to 24.4 percent of fully taxable sales.

> **Example**   An Alberta GST registrant who is providing fully taxable services has taxable revenues of $50,000 in its second, third and fourth quarters. Its eligible current expenditures for these quarters are $5,000, $12,200 (24.4%) and $30,000 respectively.

Analysis   The GST Payable under the Quick Method is $1,890 [(3.6%)(105%)($50,000)]. The Quick Method results are the same for each quarter as the calculation is based on revenues and is not affected by the amount of current expenditures. GST Payable under the regular and Quick Method would be as follows:

	Quarter 2	Quarter 3	Quarter 4
GST On Revenues [(5%)($50,000)]	$2,500	$2,500	$2,500
Input Tax Credits On Costs At 5%	(250)	(610)	(1,500)
GST Payable - Regular Method	$2,250	$1,890	$1,000
GST Payable - Quick Method*	(1,890)	(1,890)	(1,890)
Increase (Decrease) In GST Payable	$ 360	Nil	($ 890)

*The 1 percent credit described in Paragraph 21-123 would be claimed in the first quarter. Note that, in Quarter 3, when current expenditures are equal to the assumed 24.4 percent of fully taxable sales, the regular method and the Quick Method produce identical results. In Quarter 2, when current expenditures are below 24.4 percent, the Quick Method results in a lower amount payable. In contrast, in Quarter 4, when current expenditures exceed 24.4 percent, the Quick Method results in a higher amount payable.

More generally, when current expenditures, as a percent of fully taxable sales, are normally less than the percentage assumed in the Quick Method rate, use of the Quick Method is a desirable alternative. In contrast, when such expenditures normally exceed the assumed rate, the use of the Quick Method will result a higher amount payable.

Quick Method Categories

21-119.   Conceptually, an equitable application of the Quick Method would require a large number of different rates in order to reflect the various cost structures that are present in different lines of business. However, this was clearly not a practical alternative, particularly since the goal of the Quick Method was simplification. Given this, the government decided to have rates for only two broad categories.

21-120.   The categories to which the two rates are applied can be described as follows:

Businesses That Resell Goods   These businesses are given a lower rate to reflect a higher percentage of eligible costs. In order to use these rates, the cost of goods purchased for resale (GST/HST inclusive) in the previous year must be equal to 40 percent or more of the revenue from sales of taxable supplies for that year (GST/HST inclusive). Examples of types of businesses eligible for this low rate include grocery and convenience stores, computer game stores, gas service stations, antique dealers, and boutiques.

Service Providers   These higher rates (double the resellers') apply to service businesses such as consultants (other than financial), hair salons, restaurants, dry cleaners, travel agents, and taxi drivers. Since legal, accounting, and financial consulting businesses are not eligible for the Quick Method, they cannot use these rates.

Specific Quick Method Remittance Rates

21-121.   As noted in the introduction to this Chapter, in addition to the GST rate of 5 percent that is used in provinces that do not participate in the HST program, there are three different HST rates as of April 1, 2013:

- 13 percent in New Brunswick, Newfoundland, and Ontario
- 14 percent in Prince Edward Island
- 15 percent in Nova Scotia

21-122.   As the Quick Method is designed to approximate the results under the regular method of calculating GST or HST, different Quick Method remittance rates are required in each of these situations. The relevant rates are as shown in Figure 21-4 (following page).

	Figure 21 - 4	
Quick Method Remittance Rates As At April 1, 2013 (Excluding Quebec)		
GST/HST Rate	**Businesses That Purchase Goods For Resale**	**Service Providers**
GST Only At 5 Percent (B.C., Alberta, Manitoba, and Saskatchewan)	1.8%	3.6%
HST At 13 Percent (New Brunswick, Newfoundland, And Ontario)	4.4%	8.8%
HST At 14 Percent (Prince Edward Island)	4.7%	9.4%
HST At 15 Percent (Nova Scotia)	5.0%	10.0%

21-123.   Two things should be noted about these rates:

1. In the application of all of the rates in Figure 21-4, there is a credit equal to 1 percent of the first $30,000 of GST/HST inclusive sales in the year ($300 maximum).

2. These are the rates that are used by a business in the specified province that has all of its activities in that province. For businesses that deliver supplies in provinces other than their province of residence, calculations can be quite a bit more complicated. The CRA provides detailed information in its guide, "Quick Method Of Accounting For GST/HST" (RC4058).

Example Of Quick Method

21-124.   As an example of the Quick Method, consider a quarterly filing office supply store, located and operating only in Alberta, with annual taxable sales of less than $400,000. Its first quarter taxable sales were $40,000, resulting in GST included sales of $42,000 [(105%)($40,000)]. Purchases of inventory totaled $26,600 before GST. Qualifying capital expenditures during the first quarter were $3,000 before GST. Under the regular method, the first quarter GST payable would be calculated as follows:

Sales [(5%)($40,000)]	$2,000
Purchases [(5%)($26,600)]	(1,330)
Capital Expenditures [(5%)($3,000)]	(150)
First Quarter GST Payable - Regular Method	$ 520

21-125.   Alternatively, the required first quarter GST payable, as determined by the Quick Method, is calculated as follows:

Basic Tax [(1.8%)(105%)($40,000)]	$756
Credit On First $30,000 [(1%)($30,000)]	(300)
Subtotal	$456
Input Tax Credit On Current Expenditures	Nil
Input Tax Credits On Capital Expenditures [(5%)($3,000)]	(150)
First Quarter GST Payable - Quick Method	$306

21-126.   The Quick Method can be preferable, even if adequate data is available to make the calculations under the regular method. For example, a freelance writer, operating out of his principal residence, is not likely to have significant expenditures that qualify for input tax credits. In this case, the Quick Method may result in a smaller net GST payment than the regular calculation of actual GST collected, less input tax credits. It will certainly be less time consuming to file his GST return since input tax credit information on non-capital expenditures will not be needed.

Exercise Twenty-One - 6

Subject: Quick Method

Robbins Hardware sells only fully taxable supplies to customers in Alberta which does not participate in the HST program and has no provincial sales tax. During the first quarter of the year, the business has sales of $42,500, before the inclusion of GST. They have taxable purchases totaling $21,000 before GST. They do not make any capital expenditures during the quarter. Using the Quick Method, determine the GST that is payable for the quarter.

Exercise Twenty-One - 7

Subject: Quick Method

Guy's Boots sells only fully taxable shoes and boots to customers in New Brunswick where the HST rate is 13 percent. During the first quarter of the year, Guy's Boots has sales of $56,100, before HST. Current expenses, all of which were subject to HST, total $23,400 (before HST). Due to a major renovation of the store, Guy's Boots has capital expenditures of $42,000 (before HST). Compare the use of the Quick Method and the regular method for this quarter.

End of Exercises. Solutions available in Study Guide.

We suggest working Self Study Problems Twenty-One-5 and 6 at this point.

Small Suppliers Exemption

21-127. This is covered beginning at Paragraph 21-86 and will not be repeated here.

Streamlined Input Tax Credit Method

21-128. A method for claiming input tax credits and rebates is available to registrants with annual GST/HST taxable sales, including those of associated businesses, of $1,000,000 or less in the preceding year. An additional requirement is that annual GST/HST taxable purchases total no more than $4,000,000. Note that this method is also referred to as the "simplified" input tax credit method.

21-129. Rather than tracking GST/HST paid on each purchase, the streamlined method bases input tax credits on the total GST/HST inclusive amounts of fully taxable purchases. This amount would also include any non-refundable provincial sales taxes paid on taxable supplies. Once this total is established, it is multiplied by the following factor:

Applicable GST/HST Rate ÷ (100 Plus The Applicable GST/HST Rate)

Examples The factor in Alberta would be 5/105. The factor in New Brunswick or Ontario would be 13/113.

21-130. The following items are excluded from the base to which the factor is applied:

- Capital expenditures for real property (these are tracked separately for input tax credit purposes).
- Purchases of zero-rated supplies, such as groceries and prescription drugs.
- Purchases of exempt supplies, such as interest payments.
- Purchases made outside Canada, which are not subject to GST/HST.
- Purchases from non-registrants.
- Refundable provincial sales taxes (only in Quebec).
- Expenses not eligible for input tax credits (e.g., 50 percent of the cost of meals and entertainment).

21-131.   There is no election required to use this method and it does not affect the calculation of the GST/HST on sales that must be remitted. The following example illustrates this method as applied in the province of New Brunswick.

Example Garth Steel Ltd. operates solely in the province of New Brunswick. Its only activities involve the provision of fully taxable supplies. During the current year, it has current expenditures of $75,000, real property expenditures of $145,000 and expenditures for capital property other than real property of $25,000. All of these figures are before HST which was charged on all of these expenditures. In addition, the Company paid salaries of $200,000.

Analysis The Company's input tax credit for the current year would be as follows:

HST Included Amounts For Taxable Expenditures Other Than	
Real Property [(113%)($75,000 + $25,000 + Nil)]	$113,000
Factor	13/113
Input Tax Credit On Taxable Expenditures	$ 13,000
Input Tax Credit On Real Property Expenditure	
[(13%)($145,000)]	18,850
Input Tax Credit For The Current Year	$ 31,850

21-132.   As noted, the streamlined method base only includes purchases of fully taxable goods. A further restriction on the amounts claimed is that credits can be claimed only to the extent that the purchases included in the streamlined method base are used to provide fully taxable or zero-rated goods and services. Where a supply is used to provide both taxable and exempt goods and services, the input tax credit claim must be pro-rated so that only the portion that applies to taxable goods and services is claimed.

Exercise Twenty-One - 8

Subject: Streamlined Input Tax Credit Method

Simplicity Inc. operates in Alberta where there is no provincial sales tax and no participation in the HST program. For the current year, the Company has GST inclusive sales of $315,000. It has GST inclusive purchases of merchandise and other current expenditures of $189,000. Capital expenditures consist of real property (land and a building) costing $150,000 and personal capital property totaling $50,000. These amounts are before the inclusion of GST. Using the streamlined method of accounting for input tax credits, determine Simplicity's GST payable or refund for the current year.

End of Exercise. Solution available in Study Guide.

GST/HST Procedures And Administration

GST/HST Returns And Payments

Timing Of Liability

21-133.   In general, the supplier becomes responsible for the tax at the earliest of when the invoice for goods or services is issued, when payment is received, and when payment is due under a written agreement. Following this rule, a registrant usually becomes responsible for remitting GST/HST in the reporting period in which a customer is invoiced, even if this is not the same period in which the cash is actually received.

21-134.   Similarly, input tax credits for GST/HST payable to suppliers can be claimed in the reporting period invoices are issued, even if the supplier is paid in a later period.

Figure 21 - 5 Assigned And Optional Reporting Periods		
Threshold Amount Of Annual Taxable Supplies	**Assigned Reporting Period**	**Optional Reporting Period**
$1,500,000 Or Less	Annual	Monthly Or Quarterly
More Than $1,500,000 Up To $6,000,000	Quarterly	Monthly
More Than $6,000,000	Monthly	None

Taxation Year For GST/HST Registrants

21-135.   Every registrant is required to have a "fiscal year" for GST/HST purposes. Normally, this fiscal year corresponds to the taxation year for income tax purposes. However, if registrants are using a non-calendar year for income tax purposes they have the option of using the calendar year or, alternatively, using their fiscal year for income tax purposes. For example, a company with a fiscal year ending on January 31, 2013 and subject to quarterly filing requirements could choose a three month reporting period ending on January 31, 2013, or a three month reporting period ending on March 31, 2013. The GST/HST fiscal year determines the reporting periods and filing deadlines for GST/HST returns.

Filing Due Date

21-136.   All businesses and organizations that are registered to collect GST/HST are required to file a GST/HST return on a periodic basis, even if there is no activity during the relevant period. Filing frequencies for the remittance of GST/HST are determined by the total annual worldwide taxable supplies made by the registrant and its associated entities. The normal periods, along with the options that are available on an elective basis, are shown in Figure 21-5.

21-137.   A registrant may elect to have a shorter filing period than the one that is assigned for their amount of taxable supplies. This may be advantageous for registrants who normally receive a GST/HST refund, such as businesses with significant exports or zero-rated sales (e.g., pharmacies and grocery stores).

21-138.   For monthly and quarterly filers, GST/HST returns are due one month after the end of the filing period. In general, for annual filers, GST/HST returns are due three months after the end of the reporting period.

Payments And Instalments

21-139.   In general, payment of amounts owing are due when the GST/HST returns are due. This is one month after the end of the reporting period for monthly and quarterly filers, and three months after the year end for annual filers.

21-140.   Instalment payments are not required for monthly or quarterly filers. However, annual filers are required to make quarterly instalments if the GST/HST remitted for the previous fiscal year was $3,000 or more. Each instalment will be one-quarter of the net tax owing from the previous year. These instalments are due one month after the end of each quarter. For example, calendar year filers are required to make instalments by April 30, July 31, October 31, and January 31. For annual filers below the $3,000 threshold, the net tax is due on the GST/HST return filing due date which is three months after the end of their fiscal year.

Interest

21-141.   If the GST/HST return shows an amount owing and it is not paid by the due date, interest is assessed. Interest is also assessed on late or deficient instalments. The applicable rates are the same as those used for income tax purposes:

- on taxes owed to the government, the rate is the prescribed rate plus 4 percent; and
- on amounts owed to the taxpayer, the rate is the prescribed rate plus 2 percent.

21-142.   As is the case with interest on late income tax instalments, interest on late GST/HST payments is not deductible.

Late Filing Penalty

21-143.   The GST/HST late filing penalty is equal to one percent of the unpaid amount, plus one-quarter of one percent per month for a maximum of 12 months. Unlike the income tax situation, there is no doubling of this penalty for a second offense.

Associated Persons

21-144.   You may have noticed that there are a number of GST/HST rules that are related to the amount of supplies delivered during the period. In order to prevent the avoidance of these rules (e.g., splitting a business into two parts so that each would qualify for the Quick Method), GST/HST legislation has rules for associated persons.

21-145.   Two or more persons are associated for GST/HST purposes where there is substantial common ownership. For example, where one corporation controls another, the two corporations are associated. An association may exist between two or more corporations, between an individual and a corporation, and among an individual, partnership, trust and corporation.

21-146.   While associated persons file separate GST/HST returns, they must combine their total taxable sales of goods and services in certain situations, such as when determining:

- whether they qualify for the small supplier's exemption,
- whether they are eligible for the Quick Method of accounting,
- whether they are eligible for the simplified method of calculating input tax credits,
- the required filing frequency of their returns (i.e., monthly, quarterly or annual).

Refunds And Rebates

21-147.   In a period during which input tax credits exceed GST/HST collections, a refund may be claimed in the GST/HST return for that period. Provided all required returns have been filed and are up to date, interest on unpaid refunds starts accruing 30 days after the later of the last day of the reporting period and the day after the registrant's return is filed.

21-148.   The *Excise Tax Act* also provides for a number of rebates of the GST/HST paid by consumers under certain circumstances. For example, if a GST/HST amount is paid in error, or by a foreign diplomat, a rebate of the GST/HST may be claimed on a General Rebate Application Form. Our coverage of the GST/HST rebate for new housing begins in Paragraph 21-169.

Books And Records

21-149.   For GST/HST purposes, every registrant must keep adequate books and records. This requirement is found in ETA 286(1). Such records must be maintained at the registrant's place of business or at the individual's residence in Canada.

21-150.   All books and records, along with the accounts and vouchers necessary to verify them, must be kept for a period of six years from the end of the last taxation year to which they relate. This is the same record retention limit that is applicable for income tax purposes.

Appeals

Informal Procedures

21-151.   As is the case with income tax disputes, the usual first step in disputing an assessment or reassessment is to contact the CRA. In many cases the proposed change or error can be corrected or resolved through telephone contact or by letter. In order to authorize a person or firm to represent a GST/HST registrant in such disputes, a consent form must be signed and filed with the CRA.

Notice Of Objection

21-152.   If the informal contact with the CRA does not resolve the issue in question, the taxpayer should file a notice of objection. For GST/HST purposes, a formal notice of objection procedure is required.

21-153.   In GST/HST disputes, the notice of objection must be filed within 90 days of the date on the notice of assessment. Unlike the situation with income tax objections, there is no general extension of this time period for GST/HST registrants who are individuals, nor is there any extension for individual GST/HST registrants in the year of their death. Failure to meet the 90 day deadline may result in the taxpayer losing all rights to pursue the matter in question.

21-154.   On receiving the notice of objection, the Minister is required to reply to the GST/HST registrant:

- vacating the assessment;
- confirming the assessment (refusing to change);
- varying the amount of the assessment; or
- reassessing.

21-155.   Unresolved objections will be subject to review by the Assistant Director of Appeals in each Tax Services Office. These reviewers are instructed to operate independently of the assessing divisions and should provide an unbiased second opinion. If the matter remains unresolved after this review, the taxpayer must either accept the Minister's assessment or, alternatively, continue to pursue the matter to a higher level of appeal. The taxpayer has the right to bypass this notice of objection procedure and appeal directly to a higher level.

21-156.   As noted in Chapter 2, in income tax disputes, the Minister cannot institute collection procedures until after the notice of objection period has expired. When dealing with GST/HST disputes, collection procedures are not delayed by the objection process. This more aggressive approach is allowed by GST/HST legislation and probably reflects the fact that the government considers GST/HST balances assessed as amounts collected in trust by the registrant on behalf of the government.

Tax Court Of Canada, Federal Court Of Appeal, And The Supreme Court Of Canada

21-157.   Procedures for handling GST/HST disputes in these courts are basically the same as the procedures for handling income tax disputes. These procedures are described in Chapter 2 and the description will not be repeated here.

General Anti-Avoidance Rule

21-158.   The GST/HST legislation includes a general anti-avoidance rule (GAAR). This rule is found under Section 274 of the *Excise Tax Act* and is very similar to the GAAR found in the *Income Tax Act*.

21-159.   While the GST/HST GAAR is intended to prevent abusive tax avoidance transactions, it is not intended to interfere with legitimate commercial transactions. If a transaction is considered by the CRA to be an avoidance transaction, the tax consequences of the transaction may be adjusted. This could involve denying an input tax credit, allocating an input tax credit to another person, or recharacterizing a payment. But, as with the application of the income tax GAAR, it does not apply if a transaction is undertaken primarily for bona fide purposes other than to obtain a GST/HST benefit.

Employee And Partner GST/HST Rebate

General Concept

21-160.   Many of the expenses employees can deduct against employment income include a GST/HST component. If the individual was a GST/HST registrant earning business income, these GST/HST payments would generate input tax credits. However, employment is not considered to be a commercial activity and, as a consequence, employees who have no separate commercial activity cannot be registrants. This means that they will not be able to use the usual input tax credit procedure to obtain a refund of GST/HST amounts paid with respect to their employment expenses. A similar analysis applies to partners who have partnership related expenses that are not included in partnership net income or loss.

21-161. The Employee and Partner GST/HST Rebate allows employees and partners to recover the GST/HST paid on their employment or partnership related expenditures, including vehicles and musical instruments, in a way that is similar to the input tax credits that they would have received if they were GST/HST registrants. Form GST370 is used to claim the GST/HST rebate and is filed with the employee or partner's tax return.

21-162. To qualify for this rebate, the individual must be either an employee of a GST/HST registrant, or a member of a partnership that is a GST/HST registrant. Employees of financial institutions are not eligible for the rebate. However, employees of charities, not-for-profit organizations, universities, school boards, and municipalities are eligible as long as the organizations that they work for are registered. In addition, employees of provincial governments, Crown corporations, and the federal government qualify for the rebate. To claim the rebate, the individual must have unreimbursed expenses that are eligible for income tax deductions against employment or partnership income.

Calculating The GST/HST Rebate Amount

21-163. As explained in the preceding section, the rebate is based on the GST/HST amounts included in those costs that can be deducted in the determination of employment income. In terms of calculations, this is accomplished by multiplying the GST/HST and non-refundable PST included in the cost by a fraction in which the GST/HST rate is the numerator and one hundred plus the GST/HST rate is the denominator.

> **Example** Marcia Valentino is employed in Manitoba. She has deductible cell phone expenses during 2013 of $2,000. She paid $100 in GST (5%) and $140 in non-refundable PST (7%). She deducted $2,240 in her calculation of 2013 employment income.
>
> **Analysis** Ms. Valentino's rebate would be $107 [($2,240)(5/105)]. This is more than the $100 in GST she paid as the rebate base includes the non-refundable PST.

21-164. Eligible expenses exclude expenses for which a non-taxable allowance was received, zero-rated and exempt supplies, supplies acquired outside of Canada, supplies acquired from non-registrants, and expenses incurred when the employer was a non-registrant.

Example

21-165. The following simple example illustrates the calculation of the GST/HST rebate for an employee:

> **Example** Tanya Kucharik is employed in Newfoundland. She is a very successful sales manager and used her car 93 percent for employment related purposes during 2013. She claimed the following expenses on Form T777, Statement of Employment Expenses, for 2013 (all HST taxable amounts include applicable HST at 13 percent):
>
> | | |
> |---|---:|
> | Cellular phone charges | $ 1,200 |
> | Gas, maintenance and car repairs (93%) | 17,500 |
> | Insurance on car (93%) | 1,023 |
> | Capital cost allowance (CCA) on car (93%) | 3,100 |

The car on which the CCA was deducted was purchased during 2013. Note that car insurance is a financial service on which no HST is charged as it is an exempt supply.

> **Analysis** On Form GST370, her GST/HST rebate would be as follows:

	Eligible Expenses	HST Rebate (13/113)
Eligible Expenses Other Than CCA		
($1,200 + $17,500)	$18,700	$2,151
Eligible CCA On Which HST Was Paid	3,100	357
Totals	$21,800	$2,508

21-166.   The employment related expenses that are listed in this calculation will be deducted in Ms. Kucharik's income tax return for 2013.   Under normal circumstances, the HST rebate for 2013 expenses will be claimed in Ms. Kucharik's 2013 tax return. As a result, this amount will be received in 2014, either as part of the 2013 refund or as a decrease in the amount owed for 2013.

21-167.   As the rebate constitutes a reduction in the incurred costs that were deducted by the employee, an adjustment of the deduction is required for amounts that are received. This is accomplished by including the $2,151 HST rebate on expenses other than capital cost allowance in Net Income For Tax Purposes in the year in which it is received (2014 in Ms. Kucharik's case). In similar fashion, the amount of any rebates received that related to capital cost allowance ($357) will be deducted from the capital cost of the relevant asset in the year in which it is received (again 2014, in the case of Ms. Kucharik).

21-168.   While the rebate is normally claimed in the return in which the expenses are deducted, it can be claimed in any income tax return submitted within four years of the year in which the expenses are claimed.

We suggest working Self Study Problem Twenty-One-7 at this point.

Residential Property And New Housing Rebate

General Rules For Residential Property

21-169.   Residential real estate is an area of considerable importance to most Canadians. Given this, it is not surprising that residential real estate is provided special treatment under the GST/HST legislation.

21-170.   In somewhat simplified terms, GST/HST applies to residential property only on the first sale of a new home. If a new home is resold in substantially unaltered condition, no GST/HST will apply on this later transaction. If the homeowner undertakes renovations, such as a kitchen GST/HST will be charged on the materials and other costs going into the renovation. By contrast, if a used home is acquired and substantially renovated before the home is lived in by the purchaser, the acquisition will be treated as a new home purchase and the transaction will be taxable for GST/HST purposes. The CRA defines a substantial renovation as one in which 90 percent or more of the interior of an existing house is removed or replaced.

New Housing Rebate

Calculating The Rebate

21-171.   While sales of new homes attract both GST and HST at the applicable rates, rebates of the amount paid are available. In provinces that do not participate in the HST program, the rebate is equal to 36 percent of the GST paid. However, the situation with participating HST provinces is much more complex, including provincial variations in the HST rebate percentage, as well as the price thresholds. Because of this additional complexity, we will deal only with non-participating provinces in this section. The CRA has a detailed guide covering the many complexities in this area, "GST/HST New Housing Rebate" (RC4028).

21-172.   With its traditional aversion to providing tax incentives related to luxury expenditures, the government has limited this rebate to a maximum value of $6,300, the amount of the GST rebate on a $350,000 home [(36%)(5%)($350,000) = $6,300]. In addition, the rebate is phased out for houses costing more than $350,000 and completely eliminated for homes costing more than $450,000. All of these amounts are before the inclusion of GST.

21-173.   The government's policy goals are accomplished by calculating the rebate as follows:

$$[A][(\$450,000 - B) \div \$100,000],\text{ where}$$

A = The lesser of 36 percent of the GST paid and $6,300; and

B = The greater of $350,000 and the cost of the home.

21-174.   A simple example will illustrate the application of this formula.

Example On November 1, 2013, Gilles and Marie Gagnon acquire a new home with a cost of $420,000, paying an additional amount in GST of $21,000 [(5%)($420,000)].

Analysis As 36 percent of the GST paid is $7,560, an amount in excess of the limit of $6,300, the rebate available to Gilles and Marie will be $1,890 {[$6,300][($450,000 - $420,000) ÷ $100,000]}.

Implementing The Rebate

21-175.   While the GST could be included in the price paid by the home purchaser, with that individual claiming the rebate, this is not the usual industry practice. The usual practice is for the builder to charge the purchaser an amount that is net of the rebate, with the purchaser assigning rights to the GST rebate to the builder.   In the case of our example, the builder would charge Gilles and Marie $439,110 ($420,000 + $21,000 - $1,890). From the point of view of convenience for the purchaser, this appears to be an appropriate practice.

> **We suggest working Self Study Problems Twenty-One-8 and 9 at this point.**

Sale Of A Business

Sale Of Assets

21-176.   The sale of the taxable assets of a business is a taxable supply under the GST/HST. This applies regardless of the legal form in which the business is carried on. However, where "all or substantially all" of the assets that the purchaser needs to carry on a business are being acquired by the purchaser, the GST/HST legislation allows the vendor and purchaser to elect to treat the supply as if it were zero-rated.

21-177.   This applies to businesses that provide exempt supplies, as well as to businesses that provide fully taxable or zero-rated supplies. The use of the election is not permitted when the vendor is a registrant and the purchaser is a non-registrant. However, without regard to the type of business, the election can be used when both the vendor and the purchaser are not GST/HST registrants.

21-178.   If the election is made, the vendor does not collect GST/HST on the sale of taxable supplies, and the purchaser cannot claim an input tax credit. As a result, a transfer of the assets of a business can be made without payment of GST/HST. If the election is not made, GST/HST will be collected on the sale. Offsetting input tax credits may be available to the purchaser through the normal input tax credit procedures.

21-179.   In determining whether "all or substantially all" of the assets necessary to carry on the business are transferred, the CRA relies on a 90 percent or more test. The CRA has several policy papers on this election in order to provide registrants with guidance in determining compliance with the 90 percent or more test.

Sale Of Shares

21-180.   As a general rule, the sale of shares in a corporation is not a taxable supply because, under the GST/HST legislation, the sale of a financial instrument such as a share is an exempt supply. As a result, share for share exchanges are not taxable for GST/HST purposes.

Other Situations

Section 85 Rollovers

21-181.   When property used in a commercial activity is rolled into a corporation under Section 85 of the *Income Tax Act*, the rollover is a taxable transaction for GST/HST purposes. For example, if a sole proprietorship or partnership transfers property when a business is incorporated, the rollover of property will be deemed to be a taxable supply for consideration equal to the fair market value of the property. This amount will then be subject to GST/HST.

21-182.   A joint election may be available to avoid any related GST/HST liability, providing the vendor sells or transfers all, or substantially all (i.e., 90 percent or more) of the assets that can reasonably be regarded as being necessary for the purchaser to carry on the business. A further requirement is that, if the vendor is a GST/HST registrant, the purchaser must also be a GST/HST registrant.

21-183.   If the transfer of property is a taxable supply, GST/HST will be payable on the total fair market value of the share and non-share consideration exchanged for the property, with the elected amount under Section 85 of the *Income Tax Act* being irrelevant. If the transferred property is subsequently used in commercial activities, an input tax credit may be claimed by the transferee for any GST/HST paid on the transfer of the property.

Amalgamations, Mergers, Winding-Up Of A Business

21-184.   Where two corporations are merged or amalgamated into a single corporation, or the activities of one corporation are wound up through a merger with another corporation, the new corporation is generally treated for GST/HST purposes as a person separate from each of the predecessor corporations.

21-185.   If the transfer of assets involves an amalgamation under ITA 87 or a winding-up under ITA 88(1), the transfer of assets is deemed not to be a taxable supply for GST/HST purposes and no election is required. The asset or property transferred on the merger or amalgamation is not a taxable supply under the legislation. As a result, there are no GST/HST consequences.

Transfers Within Corporate Groups

21-186.   Transfers of goods and services between members of corporate groups will normally attract GST/HST. However, an election can be made to have such transfers deemed to be made for nil consideration (only for GST/HST purposes), resulting in no required payment of GST/HST.

21-187.   The conditions for this election are quite strict and require either the ownership of at least 90 percent of the voting shares of one corporation by the other, or that the companies be sister corporations owned by a parent corporation. In addition, the electing corporations must be Canadian residents and the supplies involved must be used exclusively (more than 90 percent) in a commercial activity.

Holding Companies

21-188.   Although many holding companies only hold shares or debt and do not carry on a "commercial activity" in the usual sense, GST/HST legislation allows holding companies to register for the GST/HST and claim input tax credits if they hold shares or debt in another company that owns property that is used at least 90 percent for commercial activities. These provisions allow holding companies to obtain refunds of GST/HST paid on the purchase of property or services solely related to the holding of the shares or debt.

Ceasing To Carry On Business

21-189.   When a person ceases to carry on a commercial activity, or becomes a small supplier and, as a result, ceases to be a registrant, the person is deemed to have sold all assets at fair market value upon deregistration. If the assets were used for commercial purposes, GST/HST will be payable on the deemed dispositions.

Specific Applications

21-190.   There are many GST/HST procedures that are specific to certain types of transactions or organizations (e.g., import transactions or charitable organizations). Detailed coverage of such procedures clearly goes beyond the scope of a text which focuses on income taxation. However, we do believe that it is useful to provide you with some general information on some of these specific areas:

- **Imports**   In general, imports are subject to GST/HST.

- **Exports**   In general, exports of goods and services from Canada are zero-rated. This means that while no GST/HST is charged on exports, input tax credits can be claimed by the exporter.

- **Charities**   In general, the revenues of registered charities are exempt from GST/HST. However, revenues from commercial activities (e.g., museum gift shop revenues) are fully taxable subject to the small supplier threshold of $50,000 (a special rule for charities expands the small supplier threshold from $30,000 to $50,000). A special provision provides for a 50 percent rebate of the federal GST paid on purchases related to exempt activities. In the HST provinces, there is a 50 percent rebate of the federal portion of the HST on such purchases, as well as an additional rebate of the provincial portion of the HST. The provincial rebate varies from province to province.

- **Not-For-Profit Organizations**   In general, the revenues of not-for-profit organizations are fully taxable (in contrast to the situation with registered charities). However, exemptions are provided for such services as subsidized home care and meals on wheels. As was the case with registered charities, qualifying not-for-profit organizations receive a 50 percent rebate of the federal GST paid on purchases related to exempt activities. In the HST provinces, there is a 50 percent rebate of the federal portion of the HST on such purchases, as well as an additional rebate of the provincial portion of the HST. The provincial rebate varies from province to province.

  To be classified as a qualifying not-for-profit organization, the organization must receive significant government funding. Such funding is regarded as significant when at least 40 percent of total revenues come from this source.

- **Government Bodies**   All federal government departments receive a full rebate of the GST/HST paid on purchases by means of a tax remission order. Each provincial and territorial government is registered as a separate entity for the GST/HST, and uses "certificates" to receive point of purchase relief from the GST/HST.

- **Crown Corporations**   Crown corporations are not GST/HST exempt and are registered as separate persons for purposes of the GST/HST.

- **Municipalities, Universities, Schools And Hospitals (MUSH)**   These organizations are classified as "Public Institutions" in the GST/HST legislation and, except where there are specific exemptions, their revenues are fully taxable. Examples of exemptions include property taxes for municipalities, course fees for universities, and medical services for hospitals. Rebates for the federal GST paid on purchases related to exempt activities are available, with the rates varying from 67 percent for universities to 83 percent for hospitals to 100 percent for municipalities. In the HST provinces, the same rebates are available for the federal portion of the HST, as well as an additional rebate of the provincial portion of the HST. The provincial rebate varies from province to province.

- **Financial Institutions**   The GST/HST legislation defines financial institutions to include "listed" financial institutions, such as banks and insurance companies, as well as deemed financial institutions (e.g., businesses with financial revenues exceeding specified threshold levels). Revenues from providing financial services are designated as exempt. This means that, for an institution where the bulk of its revenues is from the provision of financial services, only limited input tax credits will be available.

21-191.   These brief comments serve only to give a very general view of the approach taken to these specific types of transactions and organizations. If you are dealing with any of these applications you will, of course, have to consult a more specialized source of information.

Partnerships And GST/HST

General Rules

21-192.   The ITA treats a partnership as a person only for the purpose of computing income or loss to its partners. The *Excise Tax Act* considers partnerships to be persons that are generally required to register for the GST/HST with respect to commercial activities. In addition, anything a partner does with respect to partnership activities is considered done by the partnership and not by the partners themselves.

21-193.   The result is that it is the partnership, and not the partners, who is required to register for the GST/HST with respect to partnership business. Given this, partnerships are required to collect and remit GST/HST on taxable supplies and are eligible for input tax credits. Partners are jointly and severally liable however with respect to GST/HST that relates to the partnership business.

Partner Expenses

21-194.   Non-reimbursed expenditures for property or services incurred personally by individual partners, which relate to the partnership business and that are deductible for income tax purposes by the partners, are generally eligible for the Employee And Partner GST/HST Rebate. Such property and services include office expenses, travel expenses, meals and entertainment, parking, lodging and CCA on certain capital assets such as motor vehicles. This rebate was discussed beginning in Paragraph 21-160.

21-195.   A partner can only claim a rebate to the extent that the partnership could have otherwise claimed an ITC if it had incurred the expense directly. This means that, if a partnership provides only exempt goods or services, the partners would not be eligible to claim a GST/HST partner rebate for expenses that they deduct from their share of partnership income.

Disposition Of A Partnership Interest

21-196.   A partnership interest may be disposed of or acquired in many situations. These include the admission of a new partner or retirement of an existing partner. A partnership interest is considered a "financial instrument" and is exempt from the GST/HST. In addition, any legal and accounting fees related to the acquisition or disposition of a partnership interest are not eligible for an input tax credit since they relate to a financial instrument and not to the partnership's business. Finally, drawings and capital contributions that specifically relate to a partnership interest are considered "financial services" and are also exempt from the GST/HST.

Transfers Between Partners And Partnerships

21-197.   In general, there is no GST/HST counterpart to the rollover rule that allows property to be transferred by a partner to a partnership on a tax deferred basis. An exception to this is the case where a business is being transferred and 90 percent or more of the property that is necessary to carry on that business is also transferred. In such cases, the transfer is not subject to GST/HST as long as both transferor and transferee are registrants.

21-198.   Transfers of property between partnerships and partners may be subject to GST/HST, generally depending on the status of the transferor and transferee as registrants and whether they are engaged in commercial activities. GST/HST is not applicable to transfers of cash, accounts receivable, or debt however, since these are either not considered property for GST/HST purposes or are considered exempt financial services.

Reorganization Of The Partnership

21-199.   The admission of new partners or retirement of existing partners that terminate the old partnership and result in the creation of a new partnership will not cause the new partnership to register for GST/HST as a new person. As a result, there are no GST/HST implications on the transfer of the old partnership property to the new partnership.

21-200.   There are no GST/HST implications to the new partnership where a partnership has ceased to exist, more than half of its members form a new partnership, and transfer 90 percent or more of the property they receive on the cessation of the old partnership to the new partnership. The new partnership is considered to be a continuation of the old partnership for GST/HST purposes.

Trusts And GST/HST

21-201.   A trust is included in the definition of person under the *Excise Tax Act* and, as a consequence, a trust that is engaged in commercial activities is required to register and collect GST/HST on taxable supplies. However, an interest in a trust is considered to be a financial instrument, so the sale of an interest in a trust is an exempt financial service and is not subject to GST/HST.

21-202.   A distribution of trust property by a trustee to a beneficiary of a trust is treated as a supply by the trust. The consideration is the same as proceeds of disposition for purposes of the *Income Tax Act*. Distributions of non-commercial property by a trust in the process of the settlement of an estate are generally not considered to be in the course of commercial activities of the trust and are GST/HST exempt. Similarly, a distribution of financial securities is GST/HST exempt as a financial service. The GST/HST only applies to properties acquired by the trust that are used in a commercial activity.

21-203.   Where property is settled through the use of an inter vivos trust, including an alter ego or joint spousal or common-law partner trust, the consideration for the property transferred is deemed to equal the amount determined under the *Income Tax Act*. The supply is considered to be made at fair market value and GST/HST is payable on all taxable supplies. However, when an estate is settled, an election can be filed to distribute any property of a deceased registrant without the payment of GST/HST. In this situation, the beneficiary of the deceased's estate must be a registrant, and the beneficiary is deemed to have acquired the property for use exclusively in a commercial activity.

Key Terms Used In This Chapter

21-204.   The following is a list of the key terms used in this Chapter. These terms, and their meanings, are compiled in the Glossary Of Key Terms located at the back of the separate paper Study Guide.

Commercial Activity	Partner And Employee GST/HST Rebate
Commodity Tax	Personal Capital Property
Employee And Partner GST/HST Rebate	Quick Method
Exempt Goods And Services	Registrant
Fully Taxable Goods And Services	Streamlined ITC Accounting
Goods And Services Tax (GST/HST)	Small Suppliers Exemption
Harmonized Sales Tax (HST)	Supply
Input Tax Credit (ITC)	Transaction Tax
MUSH	Value Added Tax (VAT)
New Housing GST/HST Rebate	Zero-Rated Goods And Services

Problems For Self Study

(The solutions for these problems can be found in the separate Study Guide.)

Self Study Problem Twenty-One - 1 (Turnover Tax vs. GST)

Assume a provincial government is considering the replacement of its retail sales tax with either:

- a provincial GST that is harmonized with the federal GST, or
- a pure turnover tax, so that businesses will have to account for and remit tax collected on transactions at all levels in the distribution chain.

Assume widgets normally move from the raw materials supplier, to the manufacturer, to the wholesaler, to the retailer, and ultimately to the consumer.

Assume a sale price of $200, plus tax, by the raw materials supplier to the manufacturer. There is a mark-up of 40 percent of the before tax cost at each subsequent turnover. The relevant tax applies to the selling price at each turnover.

Required: Calculate the provincial transaction tax rate required to raise the same amount of tax revenue as a provincial GST of 8 percent at each turnover.

Self Study Problem Twenty-One - 2 (Registration Requirements)

Chantelle Chance is a hairdresser who started in business on October 1, 2012 and has not registered to collect the GST. Revenues from her business for her first year of operation were as follows:

First Quarter (October To December, 2012)	$ 4,000
Second Quarter (January To March, 2013)	6,500
Third Quarter (April To June, 2013)	9,000
Fourth Quarter (July To September, 2013)	9,500
Total Ending September 30, 2013	$29,000

For the quarter ending December 31, 2013, business revenues were $11,500.

Required: Advise Chantelle if she needs to register her business for the GST, and if so, state when GST collection should start, and by what date she must be registered.

Self Study Problem Twenty-One - 3 (Regular GST Return

Lassen Ltd., an Alberta corporation, is an annual filer for GST purposes. Alberta does not participate in the HST program and does not have a provincial sales tax.

The Income Statement for the current year is as follows (all amounts are before the addition of applicable GST):

Sales		$5,700,000
Less Expenses:		
Cost Of Goods Sold	$2,600,000	
Amortization Expense	720,000	
Salaries And Wages	640,000	
Interest Expense	120,000	
Other Expenses	370,000	4,450,000
Income Before Taxes		$1,250,000
Less: Federal And Provincial Income Taxes		(340,000)
Net Income		$ 910,000

Other Information:

1. Sales included $1,200,000 in exempt supplies and $2,400,000 in zero-rated supplies. The remaining sales were fully taxable for GST purposes.

2. All of the goods sold involved the provision of either fully taxable or zero-rated supplies. During the year, inventories of these goods decreased by $200,000. GST was paid on all goods that were purchased for resale during the year.

3. Capital expenditures for the year amounted to $4,000,000, with GST being paid on all amounts. Of this total, $3,000,000 was for an office building that will be used 40 percent for the provision of fully taxable or zero-rated supplies. The remaining $1,000,000 was for equipment that will be used 70 percent in the provision of exempt supplies. GST was paid on the acquisition of all assets on which amortization is being taken during the year.

4. All of the Other Expenses involved the acquisition of fully taxable supplies and were acquired to assist in the provision of fully taxable supplies. Included is $40,000 reimbursed to sales employees for meals while travelling for business.

5. Of the Salaries And Wages, 40 percent were paid to employees involved in providing exempt supplies.

Required: Calculate the net GST payable or refund that Lassen will remit or receive for the current year.

Self Study Problem Twenty-One - 4 (HST Payable - Exempt vs. Zero-Rated)

Kapit Ltd. is a corporation with all of its operations located in New Brunswick. New Brunswick participates in the HST program. The HST rate in the province is 13 percent.

The Company's Income Statement for the current fiscal year ending December 31 is as follows:

Sales		$2,300,000
Less Expenses:		
Cost Of Goods Sold	($1,356,000)	
Amortization Expense	(248,000)	
Salaries And Wages	(362,000)	
Interest Expense	(47,000)	
Other Expenses	(162,000)	(2,175,000)
Income Before Taxes		$ 125,000
Less: Income Taxes		(46,000)
Net Income		$ 79,000

The above amounts do not include any applicable HST amounts. Kapit is an annual filer for HST purposes.

Other Information:

1. Of the total Sales, $1,955,000 were for supplies that are fully taxable for HST purposes.

2. HST was paid on all merchandise purchased. During the year, inventories of these goods decreased by $212,000, net of HST. All of the goods sold involved the provision of fully taxable supplies.

3. Capital expenditures for the year amounted to $2,175,000 before HST. Of this total, $725,000 was for equipment that will be used 48 percent in the provision of fully taxable supplies. The remaining $1,450,000 was for a building that will be used 73 percent for providing fully taxable supplies. HST was paid on all amounts.

4. HST was paid on all of the Other Expenses. These expenses related to the provision of fully taxable supplies. Included was $5,000 in club memberships for senior management.

5. Of the Salaries And Wages, 61 percent were paid to employees involved in providing fully taxable supplies.

Required: Calculate the net HST payable or refund that Kapit will remit or receive for the current year assuming that Kapit's sales, other than the $1,955,000 in fully taxable supplies, were of:

  A. zero-rated supplies.
  B. exempt supplies.

Self Study Problem Twenty-One - 5 (Quick Method)

Bombardeaux provides commuter train plumbing services in Canada and France. The firm's offices are located in Alberta and all of its Canadian sales, operating expenses, and capital expenditures are in that province. Bombardeaux is registered for GST purposes and files annually. The firm has elected to use the Quick Method for its GST remittances.

Alberta does not participate in the HST program and does not have a provincial sales tax. When the Quick Method is used in the province, the quick method remittance rate is 1.8 percent for a retail business and 3.6 percent for a service provider.

Bombardeaux paid no GST installments for the current year as none were required. The following transactions occurred in the current year:

	Amount	GST	Total
Operating Revenue			
Canada	$70,000	$3,500	$73,500
France	43,000	Nil	43,000
Operating Expenses			
Canada - Taxable	22,000	1,100	23,100
Canada - Exempt	15,000	Nil	15,000
France	21,000	Nil	21,000
Capital Expenditures			
Canada	20,000	1,000	21,000
France	88,000	Nil	88,000

Required: Calculate the GST payable (refund) for the current year.

Self Study Problem Twenty-One - 6 (Regular And Quick Method HST Returns)

Konzak Inc. is a business that is located in Ontario. The HST rate in Ontario is 13 percent. When the Quick Method is used in the province, the remittance rate is 4.4 percent for a retail business and 8.8 percent for a service provider.

All of the Company's revenues and expenses are incurred in Ontario and it files its HST return on an annual basis. It has one associated business which had sales of taxable goods totalling $160,000 (before HST) for the year ending December 31, 2013.

Konzak Inc.'s Income Statement for the year ending December 31, 2013 is as follows (all amounts are without the inclusion of applicable HST):

Revenues:		
Fully Taxable Goods	$226,700	
Exempt Services	62,300	$289,000
Less Expenses:		
Cost Of Goods Sold	($104,300)	
Amortization Expense	(21,600)	
Salaries And Wages	(18,300)	
Interest Expense	(11,400)	
Other Operating Expenses	(41,800)	(197,400)
Income Before Taxes		$ 91,600
Less: Federal And Provincial Income Taxes		(32,400)
Net Income		$ 59,200

For the previous year ending December 31, 2012, Konzak's cost of goods purchased for resale totalled $92,500 and the revenue from sales of taxable supplies totalled $190,000. Both amounts are before HST.

Other Information:

1. Inventories of taxable goods increased by $14,600 (before HST) during the year.

2. A capital expenditure was made during the year at an HST inclusive cost of $98,310. The expenditure was for equipment that will be used 52 percent for the provision of fully taxable goods. HST was paid on the acquisition of all assets on which amortization is being taken during this period.

3. All of the Other Operating Expenses involved the acquisition of fully taxable supplies and were acquired to assist in the provision of fully taxable supplies.

4. Of the Salaries And Wages, 55 percent were paid to employees involved in providing exempt services.

Required:

A. Calculate the net HST payable or refund that Konzak Inc. will remit or receive for the current year using regular HST calculations.

B. Determine if Konzak Inc. is eligible to use the Quick Method.

C. Assume that Konzak Inc. is eligible to use the Quick Method. Calculate the net HST payable or refund that Konzak Inc. will remit or receive for the current year using the Quick Method.

Self Study Problem Twenty-One - 7 (Employee GST/HST Rebate Including CCA)

Bryan Lord is employed in New Brunswick by XNB Ltd., an HST registrant. New Brunswick participates in the HST program. The HST rate in the province is 13 percent.

Mr. Lord is required to travel for his employer throughout the province. He uses his own car for this travel and pays all other costs out of his own funds. He does not receive an allowance for this travel and receives no reimbursements.

The car is used 100 percent for employment related purposes. It was purchased in November 2012 at a total cost of $27,120, which includes HST at 13 percent of $3,120. On his 2012 tax return he claimed $4,068 [(1/2)(30%)($27,120)] of CCA on this car and claimed an HST rebate of $468 [($4,068)(13/113). His Notice of Assessment, received in June, 2013, indicated that his 2012 return was accepted as filed.

In his 2013 tax return, he deducts the following amounts in the calculation of employment income:

Accommodation (Includes HST Of $585)	$ 5,085
Deductible Portion Of Meals And Entertainment (Includes HST Of $455)	3,955
Automobile Costs:	
Gas And Maintenance (Includes HST Of $780)	6,780
Interest On Automobile Loan	2,100
Insurance	1,100
Total Deductions Excluding CCA	$19,020

Mr. Lord intends to claim the maximum CCA on his car.

Required: Calculate the maximum CCA that Mr. Lord can claim on his car for 2013. In addition, calculate the 2013 GST/HST rebate that Mr. Lord will claim as a result of his deductible expenses.

Self Study Problem Twenty-One - 8 (New Housing GST Rebate)

All of the following independent Cases involve an individual purchasing a new house in Alberta for a total payment of $200,000. Note that, Alberta does not participate in the HST program and does not have a provincial sales tax.

Varying assumptions are made with respect to what is included in the $200,000 payment.

Case A   The price includes GST.

Case B   The price does not include any GST.

Case C   The price includes GST, net of the new housing rebate.

Required: For each Case, determine:

- the pre-rebate amount of GST;
- the amount of the GST rebate that can be claimed;
- who would claim the GST rebate; and
- the net amount of GST that will be paid.

Self Study Problem Twenty-One - 9 (GST On Real Property Sale)

A home renovator, operating in Alberta, purchases a flood damaged house from a private individual for upgrading and resale. The purchase price of the house is $85,000. The renovator, a GST registrant, completely guts and remodels 100 percent of the interior and creates an addition to the house that includes a country kitchen, jacuzzi room, and art studio. The electrical wiring is replaced and a new roof is installed. As a result of the renovations, the renovator sells the house for $200,000 before consideration of commissions and transfer fees.

The costs associated with the house and its renovation are as follows:

Purchase Price		$ 85,000
Renovation Costs:		
Subcontractors - No GST Included	$10,700	
Subcontractors - GST Included	21,000	
Materials - GST Included	31,500	
Employee Wages	6,000	69,200
Total Costs		$154,200

Alberta does not participate in the HST program and does not have a provincial sales tax.

Required: What are the GST consequences of this undertaking for the renovator and the purchaser of the renovated house? Calculate the cost of the house to the purchaser and the net profit on the sale for the renovator, ignoring the effect of commissions and transfer fees. Include a calculation of the GST remittance of the renovator in your solution.

Assignment Problems

(The solutions for these problems are only available in
the solutions manual that has been provided to your instructor.)

Assignment Problem Twenty-One - 1
(Turnover Tax vs. Single Stage Consumer Tax)

The government is considering introducing a pure turnover tax, so that businesses will only have to account for and remit tax collected on transactions.

Assume goods normally move from the raw materials supplier, to the manufacturer, to the wholesaler, to the distributor, to the retailer, and finally to the consumer. Assume a sale price of $500, plus tax, by the raw materials supplier to the manufacturer. There is a mark-up of 50 percent of the before tax cost at each subsequent turnover and the tax applies to the selling price at each turnover.

Required: Calculate the transaction tax rate required to raise the same amount of tax revenue as a 7 percent single stage tax at the consumer level.

Assignment Problem Twenty-One - 2 (Registration Requirements)

Name-Your-Income is a new unincorporated business which offers accounting services emphasizing the flexibility of accounting standards. During its first six calendar quarters, the following fees were recorded:

January Through March, 2013	$8,500
April Through June, 2013	6,200
July Through September, 2013	7,400
October Through December, 2013	7,600
January Through March, 2014	8,400
April Through June, 2014	9,200

Required: Name-Your-Income would like to know if, and when, the business needs to register for, and start collecting, GST.

Assignment Problem Twenty-One - 3 (Registration Requirements)

Quarterhorse Saddles started operations on April 1, 2013, and has selected a September 30th year end. Quarterhorse Saddles has elected to file GST on a quarterly basis. The business specializes in the custom manufacture of saddles for quarter horses. All billings for a given month are billed on the last day of the month.

During the first year of operations, Quarterhorse Saddles provided the following services:

Month	Value Of Services
April, 2013	$12,000
May	16,000
June	9,000
July	9,000
October	5,000
November	7,000

Month	Value Of Services
February, 2014	4,000
March	10,000
April	in progress

Required:

A. Identify when Quarterhorse Saddles was required to register for and collect the GST.

B. Assume the GST is only applied to services after the $30,000 threshold is passed. Calculate the GST collectible for each quarter and specify the due date.

Assignment Problem Twenty-One - 4 *(Regular GST Return)*

Bestomer's Best Balloons is a proprietorship, operating only in Alberta, that is registered to file GST tax returns on a monthly basis. Alberta does not participate in the HST program and does not have a provincial sales tax.

The following is a summary of the financial statement information for December. All amounts are presented without the inclusion of applicable GST.

Sales	$69,000
Expenses:	
Cost Of Balloons Sold (Note)	$12,000
Salaries And Wages	19,000
Operating Costs	14,500
Amortization Expense	10,000
Total Expenses	$55,500
Income Before Income Taxes	$13,500
Less: Federal And Provincial Income Taxes	(4,500)
Net Income	$ 9,000

GST was paid on purchases of balloons and all operating costs. The inventory of balloons at the end of the month was $4,000. The corresponding figure at the beginning of the month was $3,000.

Required: Outline the GST treatment of each of the items presented and calculate the GST remittance for December.

Assignment Problem Twenty-One - 5 *(Regular HST Return)*

Master's Maps is an unincorporated business owned by George Masters. All of its operations are located in Ontario. The HST rate in the province is 13 percent.

The business is an HST registrant that sells both fully taxable and zero-rated goods. In addition, Master's Maps provides exempt services. Master's is an annual filer for HST purposes.

The Income Statement for the current year is as follows (all amounts are before the addition of applicable HST):

Revenues:		
Fully Taxable Goods	$326,000	
Zero-Rated Goods	153,000	
Exempt Services	211,000	$690,000
Less Expenses:		
Cost Of Fully Taxable Goods Sold	($243,000)	
Cost Of Zero-Rated Goods Sold	(101,000)	
Amortization	(56,000)	
Salaries And Wages	(29,000)	
Interest Expense	(8,000)	
Other Operating Expenses	(14,000)	(451,000)
Income Before Taxes		$239,000
Less: Federal And Provincial Income Taxes		(101,000)
Net Income		**$138,000**

Other Information:

1. Inventories of fully taxable goods decreased by $12,000 during this period, while inventories of zero-rated goods increased by $9,000. The zero-rated sales were generated by purchasing and selling zero-rated supplies.

2. Capital expenditures for this period amounted to $950,000, with HST being paid on all amounts. Of this total, $680,000 was for a building that will be used 25 percent for the provision of fully taxable supplies and 20 percent for the provision of zero-rated supplies. The remaining $270,000 was for equipment that will be used 70 percent in the provision of zero-rated supplies. HST was paid on the acquisition of all assets on which amortization is being taken during this period.

3. Of the Other Operating Expenses, 73 percent were related to the provision of fully taxable and 20 percent to the provision of zero-rated supplies.

4. Of the Salaries And Wages, 55 percent were paid to employees involved in providing exempt supplies.

Required: Calculate the net HST payable or refund that Master's Maps will remit or receive for the current year.

Assignment Problem Twenty-One - 6 *(Quick Method)*

Billy Bob, Bubba, Nancy Sue and Sally Ann Cody are siblings. Each of them runs a separate unincorporated business. All of the businesses operate in Ontario where the HST rate is 13 percent. If the Quick Method is used in that province, the Ontario quick method remittance rate is 4.4 percent for a retail business and 8.8 percent for a service provider.

The siblings provide you with the following annual information for their businesses. All amounts are reported inclusive of HST. None of the sales or purchases were zero-rated or exempt, and none of the businesses made any capital expenditures during the year.

	Type Of Business	Sales	Purchases
Billy Bob	Guided Fishing Trips	$ 90,400	$ 24,860
Bubba	Fishing Equipment Sales	197,750	135,600
Nancy Sue	Cooking Equipment Sales	158,200	45,200
Sally Ann	Individualized Cooking Courses	107,350	67,800

Required: Recommend whether any of the businesses should use the Quick Method to calculate net HST remittances. Show your calculations.

Assignment Problem Twenty-One - 7 (Regular And Quick Method GST Returns)

Brown Retail is an unincorporated business located in Alberta. Alberta does not have a provincial sales tax and does not participate in the HST program. During the years ending December 31, 2012 and December 31, 2013, the enterprise had the following sales (all figures are before GST):

Sales	2012	2013
Exempt Educational Courses	$ 65,000	$ 80,000
Fully Taxable Goods	275,000	350,000
Services Exported From Canada	28,000	20,000
Total Sales	$368,000	$450,000

The fully taxable purchases for the same period (all figures are before GST) were as follows:

Purchases	2012	2013
Books Included In Course Fees	$ 32,000	$ 15,000
Goods For Resale	160,000	200,000
Capital Expenditure (Related To Delivery OF Fully Taxable Goods)	37,000	20,000
Totals Purchases	$229,000	$235,000

Required:

A. Determine Brown Retail's GST payable (refund) for the year ending December 31, 2013 using:

i. the regular GST method.

ii. the quick method. Include your calculations to determine the quick method remittance rate.

B. Assume that the sales of GST exempt educational courses were instead zero-rated basic groceries and the related purchases were zero-rated purchases. How would this change your answer to Part A(ii)?

Assignment Problem Twenty-One - 8 (Regular And Quick Method GST Returns)

Larkin Ltd. is a retail business located in Ontario. The HST rate in this Province is 13 percent. When the Quick Method is used in Ontario, the remittance rate is 4.4 percent for a retail business and 8.8 percent for a service provider.

All of the Company's revenues and expenses are incurred in Ontario. The Company has no associated business and files its HST return on an annual basis.

For the year ending December 31, 2013, its Income Statement is as follows (all amounts are without the inclusion of applicable HST):

Revenues:		
Fully Taxable Goods	$103,000	
Exempt Services	38,000	$141,000
Less Expenses:		
Cost Of Goods Sold	($ 63,000)	
Amortization Expense	(9,000)	
Salaries And Wages	(8,000)	
Rent	(24,000)	
Interest Expense	(4,000)	
Other Operating Expenses	(12,000)	(120,000)
Income Before Taxes		$ 21,000
Less: Federal And Provincial Income Taxes		(7,000)
Net Income		$ 14,000

Other Information:

1. Inventories of taxable goods increased by $6,000 during the year.

2. All of the Other Operating Expenses involved the acquisition of fully taxable supplies and were acquired to assist in the provision of fully taxable supplies.

4. Of the Salaries And Wages, 22 percent were paid to employees involved in providing exempt services.

5. A capital expenditure was made during the year at a HST inclusive cost of $36,160. The expenditure was for equipment that will be used 60 percent for the provision of fully taxable goods. HST was paid on the acquisition of all assets on which amortization is being taken during this period.

Required:

A. Calculate the net HST payable or refund that Larkin Ltd. will remit or receive for the current year using regular HST calculations.

B. Determine if Larkin is eligible to use the Quick Method.

C. Assume that Larkin is eligible to use the Quick Method. Calculate the net HST payable or refund that Larkin Ltd. will remit or receive for the current year using the Quick Method.

Assignment Problem Twenty-One - 9 (Employee GST Rebate Including CCA)

Mr. George Christmas is a resident of Saskatchewan, a province that does not participate in the HST program. Residents are subject to the 5 percent GST, plus a non-refundable provincial sales tax of 5 percent.

He is employed by a large public company with all of its operations in Saskatchewan. The Company is a GST registrant.

George is required to travel as part of his job. For this travel, he uses his own car and pays for all costs out of his own funds. He does not receive any reimbursement or allowance from his employer.

The car that he uses was purchased in July, 2012 for $27,500. On top of the list price of $25,000, this amount includes $1,250 (5%) of GST and $1,250 (5%) of non-refundable provincial sales tax. The vehicle is used 100 percent for employment related purposes.

During 2012, George claimed $4,125 of CCA [(30%)(1/2)($27,500)] and a GST rebate on the CCA of $196 [($4,125)(5/105)]. His 2012 return was accepted as filed.

In his 2013 tax return, George deducts the following amounts in the calculation of his net employment income:

Accommodation (Includes Provincial Sales Tax Of $400 And GST Of $400)	$ 8,800
Deductible Portion Of Meals And Entertainment	
(Includes Provincial Sales Tax Of $250 And GST Of $250)	5,500
Automobile Costs:	
Gas And Maintenance	
(Includes Provincial Sales Tax Of $450 And GST Of $450)	9,900
Interest On Automobile Loan	2,600
Insurance	1,200
Total Deductions Excluding CCA	$28,000

For 2013, George intends to claim the maximum CCA on his car.

Required: Calculate the maximum CCA that George can claim on his car for 2013. In addition, calculate the 2013 GST rebate that George will claim as a result of his deductible expenses.

Assignment Problem Twenty-One - 10 (Regular And Streamlined HST Returns)

Nikkee Sports is a retail business situated in Ontario. All of its revenues occur and expenses are incurred in that province. It has no associated business and files its GST return on an annual basis. Ontario has a 13 percent HST.

Nikkee's Income Statement for the current year is as follows (all amounts are shown before applicable HST amounts):

Revenues:		
Fully Taxable Goods	$265,000	
Exempt Services	73,000	$338,000
Less Expenses:		
Cost Of Goods Sold (All Taxable)	($140,000)	
Amortization Expense	(23,000)	
Salaries And Wages	(17,000)	
Rent	(18,000)	
Interest Expense	(50,000)	
Other Operating Expenses	(21,000)	(269,000)
Income Before Taxes		$ 69,000
Less: Federal And Provincial Income Taxes		(14,000)
Net Income		$ 55,000

Other Information:

1. Inventories of taxable goods increased by $13,000 during the year.

2. A capital expenditure was made during the year at an HST inclusive cost of $62,150. The expenditure was for equipment that will be used 60 percent for the provision of fully taxable goods. HST was paid on the acquisition of all assets on which amortization is being taken during this period.

3. All of the Other Operating Expenses involved the acquisition of fully taxable supplies and were acquired to assist in the provision of fully taxable supplies.

4. The rent was not subject to HST as it was paid to a non-registrant. The proportion of the leased property that is used for the provision of exempt services is 20 percent.

5. Of the Salaries And Wages, 40 percent were paid to employees involved in providing exempt services.

Required:

A. Calculate the net HST payable or refund that Nikkee Sports will remit or receive for the current year using regular GST calculations.

B. Calculate the net HST payable or refund that Nikkee Sports will remit or receive for the current year using the Streamlined Input Tax Credit Method.

Assignment Problem Twenty-One - 11 (New Housing GST Rebate)

Martin Walker lives in Alberta, a Province that does not participate in the HST program and does not have a provincial sales tax.

He is planning to purchase a home in Edmonton and, at this point, he has narrowed down his choice to one of three properties:

	Purchase Price	Planned Improvements
Property A - Used (Note 1)	$240,000	$110,000
Property B - Used	387,000	None
Property C - New (Note 2)	323,000	22,000

Note 1   Property A would require major improvements. More than 90 percent of the interior will have to be replaced. The improvements will be done by the vendor and will be added to the purchase price, resulting in a total price of $350,000 ($240,000 + $110,000).

Note 2   Property C is under construction. Of the planned improvements, $10,000 will be completed by the builder at the same time that the house is being finished. These costs will be added to the purchase price, resulting in a total payable to the builder of $333,000. After the house is finished and transferred to Martin, he would finish the remaining improvements using materials with a cost of $12,000.

Required: Before making any offer to purchase, Martin has asked you to determine what the GST and total out-of-pocket costs of each purchase would be.

INDEX

This index includes the entries for both Volume I and II. Volume II begins on page 541.

This index includes the entries for both Volume I and II. Volume II begins on page 541.

This index includes the entries for both Volume I and II. Volume II begins on page 541.

Deductions From Income, continued

This index includes the entries for both Volume I and II. Volume II begins on page 541.

This index includes the entries for both Volume I and II. Volume II begins on page 541.

This index includes the entries for both Volume I and II. Volume II begins on page 541.

This index includes the entries for both Volume I and II. Volume II begins on page 541.

This index includes the entries for both Volume I and II. Volume II begins on page 541.

This index includes the entries for both Volume I and II. Volume II begins on page 541.

This index includes the entries for both Volume I and II. Volume II begins on page 541.

This index includes the entries for both Volume I and II. Volume II begins on page 541.

This index includes the entries for both Volume I and II. Volume II begins on page 541.

This index includes the entries for both Volume I and II. Volume II begins on page 541.

This index includes the entries for both Volume I and II.   Volume II begins on page 541.

This index includes the entries for both Volume I and II. Volume II begins on page 541.

0 1341 1416107 5

This index includes the entries for both Volume I and II. Volume II begins on page 541.